THE SECRET DOCTRINE.

HELENA PETROVNA BLAVATSKY
1831 — 1891

THE SECRET DOCTRINE:

THE SYNTHESIS

OF

SCIENCE, RELIGION, AND PHILOSOPHY.

BY

H. P. BLAVATSKY,

AUTHOR OF "ISIS UNVEILED."

सत्यात् नास्ति परो धर्मः ।

"There is no Religion higher than Truth."

VOL. I.—COSMOGENESIS.

London :
THE THEOSOPHICAL PUBLISHING COMPANY, LIMITED,
7, Duke Street, Adelphi, W.C.
WILLIAM Q. JUDGE,
117, Nassau Street, New York.
THE MANAGER OF THE *THEOSOPHIST*,
Adyar, Madras.

——

1888.

THEOSOPHICAL UNIVERSITY PRESS
PASADENA, CALIFORNIA 91109
1988

CENTENNIAL EDITION
A photographic facsimile of the original edition of 1888
Frontispiece photo by Sarony, c. 1877, New York

∞

The paper in this book meets the standards for permanence
and durability of the Council on Library Resources.

Library of Congress Catalog Card Number 74-76603
Hardcover ISBN 1-55700-001-8
Softcover ISBN 1-55700-002-6

Manufactured in the United States of America

This Work

I Dedicate to all True Theosophists,

In every Country,

And of every Race,

For they called it forth, and for them it was recorded.

PREFACE.

The Author—the writer, rather—feels it necessary to apologise for the long delay which has occurred in the appearance of this work. It has been occasioned by ill-health and the magnitude of the undertaking. Even the two volumes now issued do not complete the scheme, and these do not treat exhaustively of the subjects dealt with in them. A large quantity of material has already been prepared, dealing with the history of occultism as contained in the lives of the great Adepts of the Aryan Race, and showing the bearing of occult philosophy upon the conduct of life, as it is and as it ought to be. Should the present volumes meet with a favourable reception, no effort will be spared to carry out the scheme of the work in its entirety. The third volume is entirely ready; the fourth almost so.

This scheme, it must be added, was not in contemplation when the preparation of the work was first announced. As originally announced, it was intended that the " Secret Doctrine " should be an amended and enlarged version of " Isis Unveiled." It was, however, soon found that the explanations which could be added to those already put before the world in the last-named and other works dealing with esoteric science, were such as to require a different method of treatment: and consequently the present volumes do not contain, in all, twenty pages extracted from " Isis Unveiled."

The author does not feel it necessary to ask the indulgence of her readers and critics for the many defects of literary style, and the imperfect English which may be found in these pages. She is a foreigner, and her knowledge of the language was acquired late in life. The English tongue is employed because it offers the most widely-diffused medium for conveying the truths which it had become her duty to place before the world.

These truths are in no sense put forward as a *revelation* ; nor does the author claim the position of a revealer of mystic lore, now made public for the first time in the world's history. For what is contained in this work is to be found scattered throughout thousands of volumes embodying the scriptures of the great Asiatic and early European religions, hidden under glyph and symbol, and hitherto left unnoticed because of this veil. What is now attempted is to gather the oldest tenets together and to make of them one harmonious and unbroken whole. The sole advantage which the writer has over her predecessors, is that she need not resort to personal speculations and theories. For this work is a partial statement of what she herself has been taught by more advanced students, supplemented, in a few details only, by the results of her

own study and observation.   The publication of many of the facts herein stated
has been rendered necessary by the wild and fanciful speculations in which
many Theosophists and students of mysticism have indulged, during the last
few years, in their endeavour to, as they imagined, work out a complete system
of thought from the few facts previously communicated to them.

It is needless to explain that this book is not the Secret Doctrine in its
entirety, but a select number of fragments of its fundamental tenets, special
attention being paid to some facts which have been seized upon by various
writers, and distorted out of all resemblance to the truth.

But it is perhaps desirable to state unequivocally that the teachings, however
fragmentary and incomplete, contained in these volumes, belong neither to the
Hindu, the Zoroastrian, the Chaldean, nor the Egyptian religion, neither to
Buddhism, Islam, Judaism nor Christianity exclusively. The Secret Doctrine is
the essence of all these.   Sprung from it in their origins, the various religious
schemes are now made to merge back into their original element, out of which
every mystery and dogma has grown, developed, and become materialised.

It is more than probable that the book will be regarded by a large section of
the public as a romance of the wildest kind; for who has ever even heard of
the book of Dzyan ?

The writer, therefore, is fully prepared to take all the responsibility for what
is contained in this work, and even to face the charge of having invented the
whole of it.   That it has many shortcomings she is fully aware ; all that she
claims for it is that, romantic as it may seem to many, its logical coherence and
consistency entitle this new Genesis to rank, at any rate, on a level with the
" working hypotheses " so freely accepted by modern science.   Further, it
claims consideration, not by reason of any appeal to dogmatic authority, but
because it closely adheres to Nature, and follows the laws of uniformity and
analogy.

The aim of this work may be thus stated : to show that Nature is not " a
fortuitous concurrence of atoms," and to assign to man his rightful place in the
scheme of the Universe ; to rescue from degradation the archaic truths which
are the basis of all religions ; and to uncover, to some extent, the fundamental
unity from which they all spring ; finally, to show that the occult side of Nature
has never been approached by the Science of modern civilization.

If this is in any degree accomplished, the writer is content.   It is written in
the service of humanity, and by humanity and the future generations it must be
judged.   Its author recognises no inferior court of appeal.   Abuse she is
accustomed to ; calumny she is daily acquainted with ; at slander she smiles in
silent contempt.

De minimis non curat lex.

H. P. B.

London, October, 1888.

TABLE OF CONTENTS.

VOLUME FIRST.

COSMOGENESIS.

BOOK I.—PART I.

COSMIC EVOLUTION.

BOOK I.—PART II.

THE EVOLUTION OF SYMBOLISM IN ITS APPROXIMATE ORDER.

BOOK I.—PART III.

SCIENCE AND THE SECRET DOCTRINE CONTRASTED.

CONTENTS. XV

N.B.—The Index and Glossary will be found at the close of Volume II.

INTRODUCTORY.

"Gently to hear, kindly to judge."
—SHAKESPEARE.

SINCE the appearance of Theosophical literature in England, it has become customary to call its teachings " Esoteric Buddhism." And, having become a habit—as an old proverb based on daily experience has it—" Error runs down an inclined plane, while Truth has to laboriously climb its way up hill."

Old truisms are often the wisest. The human mind can hardly remain entirely free from bias, and decisive opinions are often formed before a thorough examination of a subject from all its aspects has been made. This is said with reference to the prevailing double mistake (*a*) of limiting Theosophy to Buddhism: and (*b*) of confounding the tenets of the religious philosophy preached by Gautama, the Buddha, with the doctrines broadly outlined in " Esoteric Buddhism." Any thing more erroneous than this could be hardly imagined. It has enabled our enemies to find an effective weapon against theosophy; because, as an eminent Pali scholar very pointedly expressed it, there was in the volume named " neither esotericism nor Buddhism." Th esoteric truths, presented in Mr. Sinnett's work, had ceased to be esoteric from the moment they were made public ; nor did it contain the religion of Buddha, but simply a few tenets from a hitherto hidden teaching which are now supplemented by many more, enlarged and explained in the present volumes. But even the latter, though giving out many fundamental tenets *from the* SECRET DOCTRINE *of the East*, raise but a small corner of the dark veil. For no one, not even the greatest living adept, would be permitted to, or could—even if he would—give out promiscuously, to a mocking, unbelieving world, that which has been so effectually concealed from it for long æons and ages.

" Esoteric Buddhism " was an excellent work with a very unfortunate title, though it meant no more than does the title of this work, the " SECRET DOCTRINE." It proved unfortunate, because people are always in the habit of judging things by their appearance, rather than their meaning ; and because the error has now become so universal, that even most of the Fellows of the Theosophical Society have fallen victims to the same misconception. From the first, however, protests were raised by Brahmins and others against the title ; and, in justice to myself, I must add that " Esoteric Buddhism " was presented to me as a completed volume, and that I was entirely unaware of the manner in which the author intended to spell the word " Budh-ism."

This has to be laid directly at the door of those who, having been the first to bring the subject under public notice, neglected to point out the difference between " Buddhism "—the religious system of ethics preached by the Lord Gautama, and named after his title of Buddha, " the Enlightened "—and *Budha*, " Wisdom," or knowledge (*Vidya*), the faculty of cognizing, from the Sanskrit root " Budh," *to know*. We theosophists of India are ourselves the real culprits, although, at the time, we did our best to correct the mistake. (See *Theosophist*, June, 1883.) To avoid this deplorable misnomer was easy ; the spelling of the word had only to be altered, and by common consent both pronounced and written "Budhism," instead of " Buddhism." Nor is the latter term correctly spelt and pronounced, as it ought to be called, in English, Buddhaïsm, and its votaries " Buddhaïsts."

This explanation is absolutely necessary at the beginning of a work like this one. The " Wisdom Religion " is the inheritance of all the nations, the world over, though the statement was made in " Esoteric Buddhism " (*Preface* to the original Edition) that " two years ago (*i.e.* 1883), neither I *nor any other European living*, knew the alphabet of the Science, here for the first time put into a scientific shape," etc. This error must have crept in through inadvertence. For the present writer knew all that which is " divulged " in " Esoteric Buddhism "— and much more—*many years* before it became her duty (in 1880) to impart a small portion of the Secret Doctrine to two *European* gentlemen, one of whom was the author of " Esoteric Buddhism " ; and surely the present writer has the undoubted, though to her, rather equivocal, privilege of being a European, by birth and education. Moreover, a considerable part of the philosophy expounded by Mr. Sinnett was taught in America, even before *Isis Unveiled* was published, to two Europeans and to my colleague, Colonel H. S. Olcott. Of the three teachers the latter gentleman has had, the first was a Hungarian Initiate, the second an Egyptian, the third a Hindu. As permitted, Colonel Olcott has given out some of this teaching in various ways; if the other two have not, it has been simply because they were not allowed: their time for public work having not yet come. But for others it has, and the appearance of Mr. Sinnett's several interesting books is a visible proof of the fact. It is above everything important to keep in mind that no theosophical book acquires the least additional value from pretended authority.

In etymology *Adi*, and *Adhi* Budha, the *one* (or the First) and "Supreme Wisdom" is a term used by Aryâsanga in his Secret treatises, and now by all the mystic Northern Buddhists. It is a Sanskrit term, and an appellation given by the earliest Aryans to the Unknown deity; the word "Brahmâ" not being found in the Vedas and the early works. It means the absolute Wisdom, and "Adi-bhûta" is translated "the primeval uncreated cause of all" by Fitzedward Hall. Æons of untold duration must have elapsed, before the epithet of Buddha was so humanized, so to speak, as to allow of the term being applied to mortals and finally appropriated to one whose unparalleled virtues and knowledge caused him to receive the title of the "Buddha of Wisdom unmoved." *Bodha* means the innate possession of divine intellect or "understanding"; "Buddha," the acquirement of it by personal efforts and merit; while *Buddhi* is the faculty of cognizing the channel through which divine knowledge reaches the "Ego," the discernment of good and evil, "divine conscience" also; and "Spiritual Soul," which is the vehicle of *Atma*. "When *Buddhi* absorbs our Egotism (destroys it) with all its *Vikaras*, Avalôkitêshvara becomes manifested to us, and Nirvana, or *Mukti*, is reached," "Mukti" being the same as Nirvana, *i.e.*, freedom from the trammels of "Maya" or *illusion*. "Bodhi" is likewise the name of a particular state of trance condition, called *Samadhi*, during which the subject reaches the culmination of spiritual knowledge.

Unwise are those who, in their blind and, in our age, untimely hatred of Buddhism, and, by re-action, of "Budhism," deny its esoteric teachings (which are those also of the Brahmins), simply because the name suggests what to them, as Monotheists, are noxious doctrines. *Unwise* is the correct term to use in their case. For the Esoteric philosophy is alone calculated to withstand, in this age of crass and illogical materialism, the repeated attacks on all and everything man holds most dear and sacred, in his inner spiritual life. The true philosopher, the student of the Esoteric Wisdom, entirely loses sight of personalities, dogmatic beliefs and special religions. Moreover, Esoteric philosophy reconciles all religions, strips every one of its outward, human garments, and shows the root of each to be identical with that of every other great religion. It proves the necessity of an absolute Divine Principle in nature. It denies Deity no more than it does the Sun. Esoteric philosophy has never rejected God in Nature, nor Deity as the absolute and abstract *Ens*. It only refuses to accept any of the gods of the so-called monotheistic religions, gods created by man in his own image and likeness, a blasphemous and sorry caricature of the Ever Unknowable. Furthermore, the records we mean to place before the reader embrace the esoteric tenets of the whole world since the beginning of our humanity, and Buddhistic occultism occupies therein only its legitimate place, and no more. Indeed, the secret portions of the "*Dan*" or "*Jan-na*"* ("*Dhyan*") of Gautama's metaphysics—grand as they appear to one unacquainted with the tenets of the Wisdom Religion of antiquity—are but a very small portion of the whole. The Hindu Reformer limited his public teachings to the purely moral and physiological aspect of the Wisdom-Religion, to Ethics and MAN alone. Things "unseen and incorporeal," the mystery of Being outside our terrestrial sphere, the great Teacher left entirely untouched in his public lectures, reserving the hidden Truths for a select circle of his Arhats. The latter received their Initiation at the famous Saptaparna cave (the *Sattapanni* of Mahavansa) near Mount Baibhâr (the Webhâra of the Pali MSS.). This cave was in Rajagriha, the ancient capital of Mogadha, and was the *Cheta* cave of Fa-hian, as rightly suspected by some archæologists.†

Time and human imagination made short work of the purity and philo-

---

* *Dan*, now become in modern Chinese and Tibetan phonetics *ch'an*, is the general term for the esoteric schools, and their literature. In the old books, the word *Janna* is defined as "to reform one's self by meditation and knowledge," a second *inner* birth. Hence Dzan, *Djan* phonetically, the "Book of *Dzyan*."

† Mr. Beglor, the chief engineer at Buddhagaya, and a distinguished archæologist, was the first, we believe, to discover it.

sophy of these teachings, once that they were transplanted from the secret and sacred circle of the Arhats, during the course of their work of prose-lytism, into a soil less prepared for metaphysical conceptions than India ; *i.e.*, once they were transferred into China, Japan, Siam, and Burmah. How the pristine purity of these grand revelations was dealt with may be seen in studying some of the so-called "esoteric" Buddhist schools of antiquity in their modern garb, not only in China and other Buddhist countries in general, but even in not a few schools in Thibet, left to the care of uninitiated Lamas and Mongolian innovators.

Thus the reader is asked to bear in mind the very important differ-ence between *orthodox* Buddhism—*i.e.*, the public teachings of Gautama the Buddha, and his esoteric *Budhism*. His Secret Doctrine, however, differed in no wise from that of the initiated Brahmins of his day. The Buddha was a child of the Aryan soil, a born Hindu, a Kshatrya and a disciple of the "twice born" (the initiated Brahmins) or Dwijas. His teachings, therefore, could not be different from their doctrines, for the whole Buddhist reform merely consisted in giving out a portion of that which had been kept secret from every man outside of the "enchanted" circle of Temple-Initiates and ascetics. Unable to teach *all* that had been imparted to him—owing to his pledges—though he taught a philosophy built upon the ground-work of the true esoteric knowledge, the Buddha gave to the world only its *outward* material body and kept its *soul* for his Elect. (See also Volume II.) Many Chinese scholars among Orientalists have heard of the "Soul Doctrine." None seem to have understood its real meaning and importance.

That doctrine was preserved secretly—too secretly, perhaps—within the sanctuary. The mystery that shrouded its chief dogma and aspira-tions—Nirvana—has so tried and irritated the curiosity of those scholars who have studied it, that, unable to solve it logically and satisfactorily by untying the Gordian knot, they cut it through, by declaring that Nirvana meant *absolute annihilation.*

Toward the end of the first quarter of this century, a distinct class of literature appeared in the world, which became with every year more defined in its tendency. Being based, *soi-disant*, on the scholarly researches of Sanskritists and Orientalists in general, it was held scientific. Hindu, Egyptian, and other ancient religions, myths, and emblems were made to yield anything the symbologist wanted them to yield, thus often giving out the rude *outward* form in place of the *inner* meaning. Works, most remarkable for their ingenious deductions and speculations, in *circulo vicioso*, foregone conclusions generally changing places with premises as in the syllogisms of more than one Sanskrit and Pali scholar, appeared rapidly in succession, over-flooding the libraries with dissertations rather on phallic and sexual worship than on real symbology, and each contradicting the other.

This is the true reason, perhaps, why the outline of a few fundamental truths from the Secret Doctrine of the Archaic ages is now permitted to see the light, after long millenniums of the most profound silence and secrecy. I say "a *few* truths," advisedly, because that which must remain unsaid could not be contained in a hundred such volumes, nor could it be imparted to the present generation of Sadducees. But, even the little that is now given is better than complete silence upon those vital truths. The world of to-day, in its mad career towards the unknown—which it is too ready to confound with the unknowable, whenever the problem eludes the grasp of the physicist— is rapidly progressing on the reverse, material plane of spirituality. It has now become a vast arena—a true valley of discord and of eternal strife—a necropolis, wherein lie buried the highest and the most holy aspirations of our Spirit-Soul. That soul becomes with every new generation more paralyzed and atrophied. The "amiable infidels and accomplished profligates" of Society, spoken of by Greeley, care little for the revival of the *dead* sciences of the past; but there is a fair minority of earnest students who are entitled to learn the few truths that may be given to them now; and *now* much more than ten years ago, when " Isis Unveiled," or even the later attempts to explain the mysteries of esoteric science, were published.

One of the greatest, and, withal, the most serious objection to the correctness and reliability of the whole work will be the preliminary STANZAS: " How can the statements contained in them be verified?" True, if a great portion of the Sanskrit, Chinese, and Mongolian works quoted in the present volumes are known to some Orientalists, the chief work—that one from which the Stanzas are given—is not in the possession of European Libraries. The Book of Dzyan (or "Dzan") is utterly unknown to our Philologists, or at any rate was never heard of by them under its present name. This is, of course, a great drawback to those who follow the methods of research prescribed by official Science; but to the students of Occultism, and to every genuine Occultist, this will be of little moment. The main body of the Doctrines given is found scattered throughout hundreds and thousands of Sanskrit MSS., some already translated—disfigured in their interpretations, as usual,—others still awaiting their turn. Every scholar, therefore, has an opportunity of verifying the statements herein made, and of checking most of the quotations. A few new facts (*new* to the profane Orientalist, only) and passages quoted from the Commentaries will be found difficult to trace. Several of the teachings, also, have hitherto been transmitted orally: yet even those are in every instance hinted at in the almost countless volumes of Brahminical, Chinese and Tibetan temple-literature.

However it may be, and whatsoever is in store for the writer through malevolent criticism, one fact is quite certain. The members of several esoteric schools—the seat of which is beyond the Himalayas, and whose ramifications may be found in China, Japan, India, Tibet, and even in Syria, besides South America—claim to have in their possession the *sum total* of sacred and philosophical works in MSS. and type: all the works, in fact, that have ever been written, in whatever language or characters, since the art of writing began; from the ideographic hieroglyphs down to the alphabet of Cadmus and the Devanagari.

It has been claimed in all ages that ever since the destruction of the Alexandrian Library (see *Isis Unveiled*, Vol. II., p. 27), every work of a character that might have led the profane to the ultimate discovery and comprehension of some of the mysteries of the Secret Science, was, owing to the combined efforts of the members of the Brotherhoods, diligently searched for. It is added, moreover, by those who know, that once found, save three copies left and stored safely away, such works were all destroyed. In India, the last of the precious manuscripts were secured and hidden during the reign of the Emperor Akbar.*

It is maintained, furthermore, that every sacred book of that kind, whose text was not sufficiently veiled in symbolism, or which had any

---

* Prof. Max Müller shows that no bribes or threats of Akbar could extort from the Brahmans the original text of the Veda; and boasts that European Orientalists have it (*Lecture on the " Science of Religion,"* p. 23). Whether Europe has the *complete text* is very doubtful, and the future may have very disagreeable surprises in store for the Orientalists.

direct references to the ancient mysteries, after having been carefully
copied in cryptographic characters, such as to defy the art of the best
and cleverest palæographer, was also destroyed to the last copy.
During Akbar's reign, some fanatical courtiers, displeased at the
Emperor's sinful prying into the religions of the infidels, themselves
helped the Brahmans to conceal their MSS. Such was Badáoní, who
had an *undisguised horror* for Akbar's mania for idolatrous religions.*

Moreover in all the large and wealthy lamasaries, there are subterranean crypts and *cave-libraries*, cut in the rock, whenever the *gonpa* and
the *lhakhang* are situated in the mountains. Beyond the Western Tsay-
dam, in the solitary passes of *Kuen-lun*† there are several such hiding-
places. Along the ridge of Altyn-Toga, whose soil no European foot
has ever trodden so far, there exists a certain hamlet, lost in a deep
gorge. It is a small cluster of houses, a hamlet rather than a monastery,
with a poor-looking temple in it, with one old lama, a hermit, living
near by to watch it. Pilgrims say that the subterranean galleries and
halls under it contain a collection of books, the number of which,
according to the accounts given, is too large to find room even in the
British Museum.‡

All this is very likely to provoke a smile of doubt. But then, before

---

* Badáoní wrote in his *Muntakhab at Tawarikh* : " His Majesty relished inquiries
into the sects of these infidels (who cannot be counted, so numerous they are, and who
have no end of *revealed books*) . . . As they (the Sramana and Brahmins) surpass other
learned men in their treatises on morals, on physical and religious sciences, and reach a
high degree *in their knowledge of the future*, in spiritual power, and human perfection,
they brought proofs based on reason and testimony, and inculcated their doctrines so
firmly that no man could now raise a doubt in his Majesty even if mountains were to
crumble to dust, or the heavens were to tear asunder." This work " was kept secret,
and was not published till the reign of Jahângir." (Ain i Akbari, translated by Dr.
Blochmann, p. 104, note.)

† Karakorum mountains, Western Tibet.

‡ According to the same tradition the now desolate regions of the waterless land
of Tarim—a true wilderness in the heart of Turkestan—were in the days of old
covered with flourishing and wealthy cities. At present, hardly a few verdant oases
relieve its dead solitude. One such, sprung on the sepulchre of a vast city swallowed
by and buried under the sandy soil of the desert, belongs to no one, but is often visited
by Mongolians and Buddhists. The same tradition speaks of immense subterranean
abodes, of large corridors filled with tiles and cylinders. It may be an idle rumour,
and it may be an actual fact.

the reader rejects the truthfulness of the reports, let him pause and reflect over the following well known facts. The collective researches of the Orientalists, and especially the labours of late years of the students of comparative Philology and the Science of Religions have led them to ascertain as follows: An immense, incalculable number of MSS., and even printed works *known to have existed, are now to be found no more.* They have disappeared without leaving the slightest trace behind them. Were they works of no importance they might, in the natural course of time, have been left to perish, and their very names would have been obliterated from human memory. But it is not so ; for, as now ascertained, most of them contained the true keys to works still extant, and *entirely incomprehensible,* for the greater portion of their readers, *without those additional volumes of Commentaries and explanations.* Such are, for instance, the works of Lao-tse, the predecessor of Confucius.*

He is said to have written 930 books on Ethics and religions, and *seventy* on magic, *one thousand in all.* His great work, however, the *heart* of his doctrine, the " Tao-te-King," or the sacred scriptures of the *Taosse,* has in it, as Stanislas Julien shows, only " about 5,000 words " (*Tao-te-King,* p. xxvii.), hardly a dozen of pages, yet Professor Max Müller finds that " the text is unintelligible without commentaries, so that Mr. Julien had to consult more than sixty commentators for the purpose of his translation," the earliest going back as far as the year 163 B.C., *not earlier,* as we see. During the four centuries and a half that preceded this *earliest* of the commentators there was ample time to veil the true Lao-tse doctrine from all but his initiated priests. The Japanese, among whom are now to be found the most learned of the priests and followers of Lao-tse, simply laugh at the blunders and hypotheses of the European Chinese scholars ; and tradition affirms that the commentaries to which our Western Sinologues have access are not the *real occult* records, but intentional veils, and that the true commentaries, as well as almost all the texts, have long since *disappeared* from the eyes of the profane.

---

* " If we turn to China, we find that the religion of Confucius is founded on the Five *King* and the Four *Shu*-books, in themselves of considerable extent and surrounded by voluminous Commentaries, without which even the most learned scholars would not venture to fathom *the depth of their sacred canon.*" (*Lectures on the " Science of Religion."* p. 185. Max Müller.) But they have not fathomed it—and this is the complaint of the Confucianists, as a very learned member of that body, in Paris, complained in 1881.

If one turns to the ancient literature of the Semitic religions, to the Chaldean Scriptures, the elder sister and instructress, if not the fountain-head of the Mosaic Bible, the basis and starting-point of Christianity, what do the scholars find? To perpetuate the memory of the ancient religions of Babylon ; to record the vast cycle of astronomical observations of the Chaldean Magi ; to justify the tradition of their splendid and eminently occult literature, what now remains ?—only a few fragments, *said to be by* Berosus.

These, however, are almost valueless, even as a clue to the character of what has disappeared. For they passed through the hands of his Reverence the Bishop of Cæsarea—that self-constituted censor and editor of the sacred records of other men's religions—and they doubtless bear to this day the mark of his eminently veracious and trustworthy hand. For what is the history of this treatise on the once grand religion of Babylon?

Written in Greek by Berosus, a priest of the temple of Belus, for Alexander the Great, from the astronomical and chronological records preserved by the priests of that temple, and covering a period of 200,000 years, it is now lost. In the first century B.C. Alexander Polyhistor made a series of extracts from it—*also lost.* Eusebius used these extracts in writing his *Chronicon* (270—340 A.D.). The points of resemblance— almost of identity—between the Jewish and the Chaldean Scriptures,* made the latter most dangerous to Eusebius, in his *rôle* of defender and champion of the new faith which had adopted the Jewish Scriptures, and with them an absurd chronology. It is pretty certain that Eusebius did not spare the Egyptian Synchronistic tables of Manetho—so much so that Bunsen† charges him with mutilating history most unscrupulously. And Socrates, a historian of the fifth century, and Syncellus, vice-patriarch of Constantinople (eighth century), both denounce him as the most daring and desperate forger.

Is it likely, then, that he dealt more tenderly with the Chaldean records, which were already menacing the new religion, so rashly accepted?

---

* Found out and proven only *now*, through the discoveries made by George Smith (*vide* his " Chaldean account of Genesis "), and which, thanks to this Armenian forger, have misled all the *civilized nations* for over 1,500 years into accepting Jewish derivations *for direct Divine Revelation !*

† Bunsen's "*Egypt's Place in History*," vol. i. p. 200

So that, with the exception of these more than doubtful fragments, the entire Chaldean sacred literature has disappeared from the eyes of the profane as completely as the lost Atlantis. A few facts that were contained in the Berosian History are given in Part II. of Vol. II., and may throw a great light on the true origin of the Fallen Angels, personified by Bel and the Dragon.

Turning now to the oldest Aryan literature, the Rig-Veda, the student will find, following strictly in this the data furnished by the said Orientalists themselves, that, although the Rig-Veda contains only "about 10,580 verses, or 1,028 hymns," in spite of the Brâhmanas and the mass of glosses and commentaries, it is not understood correctly to this day. Why is this so? Evidently because the Brâhmanas, "the scholastic and oldest treatises on the primitive hymns," *themselves require a key*, which the Orientalists have failed to secure.

What do the scholars say of Buddhist literature? Have they got it in its completeness? Assuredly not. Notwithstanding the 325 volumes of the *Kanjur* and the *Tanjur* of the Northern Buddhists, each volume we are told, "weighing from four to five pounds," nothing, in truth, is known of Lamaism. Yet, the sacred canon of the Southern Church is said to contain 29,368,000 letters in the Saddharma alankâra,* or, exclusive of treatises and commentaries, "five or six times the amount of the matter contained in the Bible," the latter, in the words of Professor Max Müller, rejoicing only in 3,567,180 letters. Not-withstanding, then, these "325 volumes" (*in reality* there are 333, *Kanjur* comprising 108, and *Tanjur* 225 volumes), "the translators, instead of supplying us with correct versions, have interwoven them *with their own commentaries*, for the purpose of justifying the dogmas of their several schools."† Moreover, "according to a tradition preserved by the Buddhist schools, both of the South and of the North, the sacred Buddhist Canon comprised originally 80,000 or 84,000 tracts, *but most of them were lost*, so that there remained but 6,000," the professor tells his audiences. "Lost" as usual for Europeans. But who can be quite sure that they are likewise lost for Buddhists and Brahmins?

Considering the sacredness for the Buddhists of every line written

---

* Spence Hardy, "*The Legends and Theories of the Buddhists*," p. 66.
† "*Buddhism in Tibet*," p. 78.

upon Buddha or his " Good Law," the loss of nearly 76,000 *tracts* does seem miraculous. Had it been *vice versâ*, every one acquainted with the natural course of events would subscribe to the statement that, of these 76,000, five or six thousand treatises *might have been* destroyed during the persecutions in, and emigrations from, India. But as it is well ascertained that Buddhist Arhats began their religious exodus, for the purpose of propagating the new faith beyond Kashmir and the Himalayas, as early as the year 300 before our era,* and reached China in the year 61 A.D.† when Kashyapa, at the invitation of the Emperor Ming-ti, went there to acquaint the " Son of Heaven" with the tenets of Buddhism, it does seem strange to hear the Orientalists speaking of such a loss as though it were really possible. They do not seem to allow for one moment the possibility that the texts may be *lost* only for West and *for themselves*; or, that the Asiatic people should have the unparalleled boldness to keep their most sacred records out of the reach of foreigners, thus refusing to deliver them to the profanation and misuse of races even so " vastly superior " to themselves.

Owing to the expressed regrets and numerous confessions of almost every one of the Orientalists (See Max Müller's *Lectures* for example) the public may feel sufficiently sure (*a*) that the students of ancient religions have indeed very few data upon which to build such final conclusions as they generally do about the old religions, and (*b*) that such lack of data does not prevent them in the least from dogmatising. One would imagine that, thanks to the numerous records of the Egyptian theogony and mysteries preserved in the classics, and in a number of ancient writers, the rites and dogmas of Pharaonic Egypt ought to be well understood at least; better, at any rate, than the too abstruse philosophies and Pantheism of India, of whose religion and language Europe had hardly any idea before the beginning of the present century. Along the Nile and on the face of the whole country, there stand to this hour, exhumed yearly and daily, fresh relics which eloquently tell their own history. Still it is not so. The learned Oxford philologist himself confesses the truth by saying that " Though . . . we see still standing the Pyramids, and the ruins of temples and labyrinths, their walls

---

* Lassen, (" Ind. Althersumkunde " Vol. II, p. 1,072) shows a Buddhist monastery erected in the Kailas range in 137 B.C.; and General Cunningham, earlier than that.

† Reverend T. Edkins, "*Chinese Buddhism.*"

the gods of many nations. Thus, though the Mother of Mercury (Budha, Thot-Hermes, etc.), was Maïa, the mother of Buddha (Gautama), also Mâyâ, and the mother of Jesus, likewise Maya (illusion, for Mary is *Mare*, the Sea, the great illusion symbolically)—yet these three characters have no connection, nor can they have any, since Bopp has "laid down his code of phonetic laws."

In their efforts to collect together the many skeins of unwritten history, it is a bold step for our Orientalists to take, to deny, *a priori*, everything that does not dovetail with their special conclusions. Thus, while new discoveries are daily made of great arts and sciences having existed far back in the night of time, even the knowledge of writing is refused to some of the most ancient nations, and they are credited with barbarism instead of culture. Yet the traces of an immense civilization, even in Central Asia, are still to be found. This civilization is undeniably *prehistoric*. And how can there be civilization without a literature, in some form, without annals or chronicles? Common sense alone ought to supplement the broken links in the history of departed nations. The gigantic, unbroken wall of the mountains that hem in the whole table-land of Tibet, from the upper course of the river Khuan-Khé down to the Kara-Korum hills, witnessed a civilization during milleniums of years, and would have strange secrets to tell mankind. The Eastern and Central portions of those regions—the Nan-Schayn and the Altyne-taga—were once upon a time covered with cities that could well vie with Babylon. A whole geological period has swept over the land, since those cities breathed their last, as the mounds of shifting sand, and the sterile and now dead soil of the immense central plains of the basin of Tarim testify. The borderlands alone are superficially known to the traveller. Within those table-lands of sand there is water, and fresh oases are found blooming there, wherein no European foot has ever yet ventured, or trodden the now treacherous soil. Among these verdant oases there are some which are entirely inaccessible even to the native profane traveller. Hurricanes may "tear up the sands and sweep whole plains away," they are powerless to destroy that which is beyond their reach. Built deep in the bowels of the earth, the subterranean stores are secure; and as their entrances are concealed in such oases, there is little fear that anyone should discover them, even should several armies invade the sandy wastes where—

covered with hieroglyphic inscriptions, and with the strange pictures of gods and goddesses. . . . . On rolls of papyrus, which seem to defy the ravages of time, we have even fragments of what may be called the sacred books of the Egyptians; yet, though much has been deciphered in the ancient records of that mysterious race, the main-spring of the religion of Egypt and the original intention of its ceremonial worship *are far from being fully* disclosed to us."[*] Here again the mysterious hieroglyphic documents remain, but the keys by which alone they become intelligible have disappeared.

Nevertheless, having found that "there is a natural connection between language and religion"; and, secondly, that there was a *common* Aryan religion before the separation of the Aryan race; a *common* Semitic religion before the separation of the Semitic race; and a *common* Turanian religion before the separation of the Chinese and the other tribes belonging to the Turanian class; having, in fact, only discovered "three ancient centres of religion" and "three centres of language," and though as entirely ignorant of those primitive religions and languages, as of their origin, the professor does not hesitate to declare "that a truly *historical basis* for a scientific treatment of those principal religions of the world has been gained!"

A "scientific treatment" of a subject is no guarantee for its "historical basis"; and with such scarcity of data on hand, no philologist, even among the most eminent, is justified in giving out his own conclusions for *historical* facts. No doubt, the eminent Orientalist has proved thoroughly to the world's satisfaction, that according to Grimm's law of phonetic rules, Odin and Buddha are two different personages, quite distinct from each other, and he has shown it *scientifically*. When, however he takes the opportunity of saying in the same breath that Odin "was worshipped as the supreme deity *during a period long anterior to the age of the Veda* and of Homer" (*Compar. Theol.*, p. 318), he has not the slightest " *historical* basis" for it. He makes *history* and *fact* subservient to his

---

[*] So little acquainted are our greatest Egyptologists with the funerary rites of the Egyptians and the outward marks of the difference of sexes made on the mummies, that it has led to the most ludicrous mistakes. Only a year or two since, one of that kind was discovered at Boulaq, Cairo. The mummy of what had been considered the wife of an unimportant Pharaoh, has turned out, thanks to an inscription found on an amulet hung on his neck, to be that of Sesostris—the greatest King of Egypt!

own conclusions, which may be very "scientific," in the sight of Oriental scholars, but yet very wide of the mark of actual truth. The conflicting views on the subject of chronology, in the case of the Vedas, of the various eminent philologists and Orientalists, from Martin Haug down to Mr. Max Müller himself, are an evident proof that the statement has no *historical* basis to stand upon, "internal evidence" being very often a Jack-o'-lantern, instead of a safe beacon to follow. Nor has the Science of modern Comparative Mythology any better proof to show, that those learned writers, who have insisted for the last century or so that there must have been "fragments of a primeval revelation, granted to the ancestors of the whole race of mankind . . . . preserved in the temples of Greece and Italy," were entirely wrong. For this is what all the Eastern Initiates and Pundits have been proclaiming to the world from time to time. While a prominent Cinghalese priest assured the writer that it was well known that the most important Buddhist tracts belonging to the sacred canon were stored away in *countries and places inaccessible to the European pundits*, the late Swami Dayanand Sarasvati, the greatest Sanskritist of his day in India, assured some members of the Theosophical Society of the same fact with regard to ancient Brahmanical works. When told that Professor Max Müller had declared to the audiences of his "Lectures" that the theory . . . . "that *there was a primeval preternatural revelation* granted to the fathers of the human race, finds but few supporters at present,"—the holy and learned man laughed. His answer was suggestive. "If Mr. *Moksh Mooller*, as he pronounced the name, were a Brahmin, and came with me, I might take him to a *gupta* cave (a secret crypt) near Okhee Math, in the Himalayas, where he would soon find out that what crossed the *Kalapani* (the black waters of the ocean) from India to Europe were only the *bits of rejected copies of some passages from our sacred books*. There *was* a "primeval revelation," and it still exists; nor will it ever be lost to the world, but will reappear; though the Mlechchhas will of course have to wait."

Questioned further on this point, he would say no more. This was at Meerut, in 1880.

No doubt the mystification played, in the last century at Calcutta, by the Brahmins upon Colonel Wilford and Sir William Jones was a cruel one. But it had been well deserved, and no one was more to be blamed

---

in that affair than the Missionaries and Colonel Wilford th
The former, on the testimony of Sir William Jones himself (
Res., Vol. 1., p. 272), were silly enough to maintain that "th
were even now almost Christians, because their Brahmâ, Vi
Mahesa were no other than the Christian trinity."* It w
lesson. It made the Oriental scholars doubly cautious; but
it has also made some of them too shy, and caused, in its rea
pendulum of foregone conclusions to swing too much the ot
For "that first supply on the Brahmanical market,"
Colonel Wilford, has now created an evident necessity and des
Orientalists to declare nearly every archaic Sanskrit manu
modern as to give to the missionaries full justification for
themselves of the opportunity. That they do so and
full extent of their mental powers, is shown by the absurd att
late to prove that the whole Purânic story about Chrishna was *p*
by the Brahmins from the Bible ! But the facts cited by the
Professor in his Lectures on the "*Science of Religion*," concer
now famous interpolations, for the benefit, and later on to the
of Col. Wilford, do not at all interfere with the conclusions to w
who studies the Secret Doctrine must unavoidably come. Fo
results show that neither the *New* nor even the *Old* Testament b
anything from the more ancient religion of the Brahmans and Bu
it does not follow that the Jews have not borrowed all they kne
the Chaldean records, the latter being mutilated later on by Eu
As to the Chaldeans, they assuredly got their primitive learning fi
Brahmans, for Rawlinson shows an undeniably Vedic influence
early mythology of Babylon; and Col. Vans Kennedy has long
justly declared that Babylonia was, from her origin, the seat of S
and Brahman learning. But all such proofs must lose their va
the presence of the latest theory worked out by Prof. Max M
What it is everyone knows. The code of phonetic laws has now b
a universal solvent for every identification and "connection" be

---

* See Max Müller's "Introduction to the Science of Religion." Lecture O
Analogies in comparative Theology, pp. 288 and 296 *et seq.* This relates to the
forgery (on leaves inserted in old Purânic MSS.), in correct and archaic Sansk
all that the Pundits of Col. Wilford had heard from him about Adam and Ab
Noah and his three sons, etc., etc

> " Not a pool, not a bush, not a house is seen,
>   And the mountain-range forms a rugged screen
>   Round the parch'd flats of the dry, dry desert. . . . ."

But there is no need to send the reader across the desert, when the same proofs of ancient civilization are found even in comparatively populated regions of the same country. The oasis of Tchertchen, for instance, situated about 4,000 feet above the level of the river Tchertchen-D'arya, is surrounded with the ruins of archaic towns and cities in every direction. There, some 3,000 human beings represent the relics of about a hundred extinct nations and races—the very names of which are now unknown to our ethnologists. An anthropologist would feel more than embarrassed to class, divide and subdivide them ; the more so, as the respective descendants of all these *antediluvian* races and tribes know as little of their own forefathers themselves, as if they had fallen from the moon. When questioned about their origin, they reply that they know not whence their fathers had come, but had heard that their *first* (or earliest) men were ruled by the great genii of these deserts. This may be put down to ignorance and superstition, yet in view of the teachings of the Secret Doctrine, the answer may be based upon primeval tradition. Alone, the tribe of Khoorassan claims to have come from what is now known as Afghanistan, long before the days of Alexander, and brings legendary lore to that effect as corroboration. The Russian traveller, Colonel (now General) Prjevalsky, found quite close to the oasis of Tchertchen, the ruins of two enormous cities, the oldest of which was, according to local tradition, ruined 3,000 years ago by a hero and giant ; and the other by the Mongolians in the tenth century of our era. " The emplacement of the two cities is now covered, owing to shifting sands and the desert wind, with strange and heterogeneous relics ; with broken china and kitchen utensils and human bones. The natives often find copper and gold coins, melted silver, ingots, diamonds, and turquoises, and what is the most remarkable—broken glass. . . . ." " Coffins of some undecaying wood, or material, also, within which beautifully preserved embalmed bodies are found. . . . . The male mummies are all extremely tall powerfully built men with long waving hair. . . . . A vault was found with twelve dead men *sitting* in it. Another time, in a separate coffin, a young girl was discovered by us. Her eyes were closed with golden discs, and the jaws held firm by a golden circlet running from under the chin across the top of the head. Clad in a narrow woollen garment, her bosom was covered with golden stars, the feet being left naked." (From a lecture by N. M. Prjevalsky.) To this, the famous traveller adds that all along their way on the river Tchertchen they heard legends about twenty-three towns buried ages ago by the shifting sands of the deserts. The same tradition exists on the Lob-nor and in the oasis of Kerya.

The traces of such civilization, and these and like traditions, give us the right to credit other legendary lore warranted by well educated and learned natives of India and Mongolia, when they speak of immense libraries reclaimed from the sand, together with various reliques of ancient MAGIC lore, which have all been safely stowed away.

To recapitulate. The Secret Doctrine was the universally diffused religion of the ancient and prehistoric world. Proofs of its diffusion, authentic records of its history, a complete chain of documents, show-ing its character and presence in every land, together with the teaching of all its great adepts, exist to this day in the secret crypts of libraries belonging to the Occult Fraternity.

This statement is rendered more credible by a consideration of the fol-lowing facts : the tradition of the thousands of ancient parchments saved when the Alexandrian library was destroyed ; the thousands of Sanskrit works which disappeared in India in the reign of Akbar ; the universal tradition in China and Japan that the true old texts with the com-mentaries, which alone make them comprehensible—amounting to many thousands of volumes—have long passed out of the reach of profane hands; the disappearance of the vast sacred and occult literature of Babylon ; the loss of those keys which alone could solve the thousand riddles of the Egyptian hieroglyphic records ; the tradition in India that the real secret commentaries which alone make the Veda intelligible, though no longer visible to profane eyes, still remain for the initiate, hidden in secret caves and crypts; and an identical belief among the Buddhists, with regard to their secret books.

The Occultists assert that all these exist, safe from Western spoliating hands, to re-appear in some more enlightened age, for which in the words of the late Swami Dayanand Sarasvati, " the Mlechchhas (outcasts, savages, those beyond the pale of Aryan civilization) will have to wait."

For it is not the fault of the initiates that these documents are now " lost " to the profane ; nor was their policy dictated by selfishness, or any desire to monopolise the life-giving sacred lore. There were portions of the Secret Science that for incalculable ages had to remain concealed from the profane gaze. But this was because to impart to the unprepared multitude secrets of such tremendous importance, was equivalent to giving a child a lighted candle in a powder magazine.

The answer to a question which has frequently arisen in the minds of students, when meeting with statements such as this, may be outlined here.

"We can understand," they say, "the necessity for concealing from the herd such secrets as the Vril, or the rock-destroying force, discovered by J. W. Keely, of Philadelphia, but we cannot understand how any danger could arise from the revelation of such a purely philosophic doctrine, as, *e.g.*, the evolution of the planetary chains."

The danger was this: Doctrines such as the planetary chain, or the seven races, at once give a clue to the seven-fold nature of man, for each principle is correlated to a plane, a planet, and a race; and the human principles are, on every plane, correlated to seven-fold occult forces—those of the higher planes being of tremendous power. So that any septenary division at once gives a clue to tremendous occult powers, the abuse of which would cause incalculable evil to humanity. A clue, which is, perhaps, no clue to the present generation—especially the Westerns—protected as they are by their very blindness and ignorant materialistic disbelief in the occult; but a clue which would, nevertheless, have been very real in the early centuries of the Christian era, to people fully convinced of the reality of occultism, and entering a cycle of degradation, which made them rife for abuse of occult powers and sorcery of the worst description.

The documents were concealed, it is true, but the knowledge itself and its actual existence had never been made a secret of by the Hierophants of the Temple, wherein MYSTERIES have ever been made a discipline and stimulus to virtue. This is very old news, and was repeatedly made known by the great adepts, from Pythagoras and Plato down to the Neoplatonists. It was the new religion of the Nazarenes that wrought a change for the worse—in the policy of centuries.

Moreover, there is a well-known fact, a very curious one, corroborated to the writer by a reverend gentleman attached for years to a Russian Embassy—namely, that there are several documents in the St. Petersburg Imperial Libraries to show that, even so late as during the days when Freemasonry, and Secret Societies of Mystics flourished unimpeded in Russia, *i.e.*, at the end of the last and the beginning of the present century, more than one Russian Mystic travelled to Tibet *via* the Ural mountains in search of knowledge and initiation *in the unknown crypts of Central Asia.* And more than one returned years later, with a rich store of such information as could never have been given him anywhere in Europe. Several cases could be cited, and well-known names brought forward, but for the fact that such publicity might annoy the surviving relatives of the said late Initiates. Let any one look over the Annals and History of Freemasonry in the archives of the Russian metropolis, and he will assure himself of the fact stated.

This is a corroboration of that which has been stated many times before, and, unfortunately, too indiscreetly. Instead of benefiting humanity, the virulent charges of deliberate invention and imposture with a purpose thrown at those who asserted but a truthful, if even a little known fact, have only generated bad Karma for the slanderers. But now the mischief is done, and truth should no longer be denied, whatever the consequences. Is it a new religion, we are asked? By no means; it is not a *religion*, nor is its philosophy *new*; for, as already stated, it is as old as thinking man. Its tenets are not now published for the first time, but have been cautiously given out to, and taught by, more than one European Initiate—especially by the late Ragon.

More than one great scholar has stated that there never was a religious founder, whether Aryan, Semitic or Turanian, who had *invented* a new religion, or revealed a new truth. These founders were all *transmitters*, not original teachers. They were the authors of new forms and inter-pretations, while the truths upon which the latter were based were as old as mankind. Selecting one or more of those grand verities— actualities visible only to the eye of the real Sage and Seer—out of the many orally revealed to man in the beginning, preserved and perpetuated in the *adyta* of the temples through initiation, during the MYSTERIES and by personal transmission—they revealed these truths to the masses. Thus every nation received in its turn some of the said truths, under the veil of its own local and special symbolism; which, as time went on, developed into a more or less philosophical cultus, a Pantheon in mythical disguise. Therefore is Confucius, a very ancient legislator in historical chronology, though a very modern Sage in the World's History, shown by Dr. Legge*—who calls him "emphatically a *transmitter*, not a maker"—as saying: "I only hand on: I cannot create new things. I believe in the ancients and therefore I love them."† (Quoted in "Science of Religions" by Max Müller.)

The writer loves them too, and therefore believes in the ancients, and the modern heirs to their Wisdom. And believing in both, she now transmits that which she has received and learnt herself to all those who will accept it. As to those who may reject her testimony,—*i.e.*, the great majority—she will bear them no malice, for they will be as right in their way in denying, as she is right in hers in affirming, since they look at TRUTH from two entirely different stand-points. Agreeably with the rules of critical scholarship, the Orientalist has to reject *a priori* whatever evidence he cannot fully verify for himself. And how can a Western scholar accept on hearsay that which he knows nothing about? Indeed, that which is given in these volumes is selected from *oral*, as much as from written teachings. This first instalment of the esoteric doctrines is based upon Stanzas, which are the records of a people unknown to ethnology; it is claimed that they are written in a tongue absent from the nomenclature of languages and dialects with which philology is acquainted; they are said to emanate from a source (Occultism) repudiated by science; and, finally, they are offered through an agency, incessantly discredited before the world by all those who hate unwelcome truths, or have some special hobby of their own to defend. Therefore, the rejection of these teachings may be expected, and must be accepted beforehand. No one styling himself a "scholar," in whatever department of exact science, will be permitted to regard these teachings seriously. They will be derided and rejected *a priori* in this century; but only in this one. For in the twentieth century of our era scholars will begin to recognize that the *Secret Doctrine* has neither been invented nor exaggerated, but, on the contrary, simply outlined; and finally, that its teachings antedate the Vedas.‡ Have not the latter been derided, rejected, and

---

* Lǔn-Yü (§ 1 a) Schott. "Chinesische Literatur," p. 7.

† "Life of Confucius," p. 96.

‡ This is no pretension to *prophecy*, but simply a statement based on the knowledge of facts. Every century an attempt is being made to show the world that Occultism

called " a modern forgery " even so recently as fifty years ago ? Was not Sanskrit proclaimed at one time the progeny of, and a dialect derived from, the Greek, according to Lemprière and other scholars ? About 1820, Prof. Max Müller tells us, the sacred books of the Brahmans, of the Magians, and of the Buddhists, " were all but unknown, their very existence was doubted, and there was not a single scholar who could have translated a line of the Veda . . . of the Zend Avesta, or . . . of the Buddhist Tripitaka, and now the Vedas are proved to be the work of the highest antiquity whose ' preservation amounts almost to a marvel' (Lecture on the Vedas).

The same will be said of the Secret Archaic Doctrine, when proofs are given of its undeniable existence and records. But it will take centuries before much more is given from it. Speaking of the keys to the Zodiacal mysteries as being almost lost to the world, it was remarked by the writer in " Isis Unveiled " some ten years ago that : " The said key must be turned *seven* times before the whole system is divulged. We will give it but *one* turn, and thereby allow the profane one glimpse into the mystery. Happy he, who understands the whole ! "

The same may be said of the whole Esoteric system. One turn of the key, and no more, was given in " Isis." Much more is explained in these volumes. In those days the writer hardly knew the language in which the work was written, and the disclosure of many things, freely spoken about now, was forbidden. In Century the Twentieth some disciple more informed, and far better fitted, may be sent by the Masters of Wisdom to give final and irrefutable proofs that there exists a Science called *Gupta-Vidya ;* and that, like the once-mysterious sources of the Nile, the source of all religions and philosophies now known to the world has been for many ages forgotten and lost to men, but is at last found.

Such a work as this has to be introduced with no simple *Preface*, but with a volume rather ; one that would give *facts*, not mere disquisitions, since the SECRET DOCTRINE is not a treatise, or a series of vague theories, but contains all that can be given out to the world in this century.

It would be worse than useless to publish in these pages even those

is no vain superstition. Once the door permitted to be kept a little ajar, it will be opened wider with every new century. The times are ripe for a more serious knowledge than hitherto permitted, though still very limited, so far.

portions of the esoteric teachings that have now escaped from confinement, unless the genuineness and authenticity—at any rate, the *probability*—of the existence of such teachings was first established. Such
statements as will now be made, have to be shown warranted by various
authorities: those of ancient philosophers, classics and even certain
learned Church Fathers, some of whom knew these doctrines because
they had studied them, had seen and read works written upon them ;
and some of whom had even been personally initiated into the ancient
Mysteries, during the performance of which the arcane doctrines were
allegorically enacted. The writer will have to give historical and
trustworthy names, and to cite well-known authors, ancient and modern,
of recognized ability, good judgment, and truthfulness, as also to name
some of the famous proficients in the secret arts and science, along
with the mysteries of the latter, as they are divulged, or, rather,
partially presented before the public in their strange archaic form.

How is this to be done? What is the best way for achieving such
an object? was the ever-recurring question. To make our plan clearer,
an illustration may be attempted. When a tourist coming from a well-
explored country, suddenly reaches the borderland of a *terra incognita*,
hedged in, and shut out from view by a formidable barrier of impassable rocks, he may still refuse to acknowledge himself baffled in his
exploratory plans. Ingress beyond is forbidden. But, if he cannot
visit the mysterious region personally, he may still find a means of
examining it from as short a distance as can be arrived at. Helped
by his knowledge of landscapes left behind him, he can get a general
and pretty correct idea of the transmural view, if he will only
climb to the loftiest summit of the altitudes in front of him. Once
there, he can gaze at it, at his leisure, comparing that which he
dimly perceives with that which he has just left below, now that he
is, thanks to his efforts, beyond the line of the mists and the cloud-
capped cliffs.

Such a point of preliminary observation, for those who would like
to get a more correct understanding of the mysteries of the pre-
archaic periods given in the texts, cannot be offered to them in these
two volumes. But if the reader has patience, and would glance at the
present state of beliefs and creeds in Europe, compare and check it
with what is known to history of the ages directly preceding and

following the Christian era, then he will find all this in Volume III. of this work.

In that volume a brief recapitulation will be made of all the principal adepts known to history, and the downfall of the mysteries will be described; after which began the disappearance and final and systematic elimination from the memory of men of the real nature of initiation and the Sacred Science. From that time its teachings became Occult, and Magic sailed but too often under the venerable but frequently misleading name of Hermetic philosophy. As real Occultism had been prevalent among the Mystics during the centuries that preceded our era, so Magic, or rather Sorcery, with its Occult Arts, followed the beginning of Christianity.

However great and zealous the fanatical efforts, during those early centuries, to obliterate every trace of the mental and intellectual labour of the Pagans, it was a failure; but the same spirit of the dark demon of bigotry and intolerance has perverted systematically and ever since, every bright page written in the pre-Christian periods. Even in her uncertain records, history has preserved enough of that which has survived to throw an impartial light upon the whole. Let, then, the reader tarry a little while with the writer, on the spot of observation selected. He is asked to give all his attention to that millennium which divided the pre-Christian and the *post*-Christian periods, by the year ONE of the Nativity. This event—whether historically correct or not—has nevertheless been made to serve as a first signal for the erection of manifold bulwarks against any possible return of, or even a glimpse into, the hated religions of the Past; hated and *dreaded*—because throwing such a vivid light on the new and intentionally veiled interpretation of what is now known as the "New Dispensation."

However superhuman the efforts of the early Christian fathers to obliterate the Secret Doctrine from the very memory of man, they all failed. Truth can never be killed; hence the failure to sweep away entirely from the face of the earth every vestige of that ancient Wisdom, and to shackle and gag every witness who testified to it. Let one only think of the thousands, and perhaps millions, of MSS. burnt; of monuments, with their too indiscreet inscriptions and pictorial symbols, pulverised to dust; of the bands of early hermits and ascetics roaming about among the ruined cities of Upper and Lower Egypt, in desert and mountain, valleys and highlands, seeking for and eager to destroy every obelisk and pillar, scroll or parchment they could lay their hands on, if it only bore the symbol of the *tau,* or any other sign borrowed and appropriated by the new faith; and he will then see plainly how it is that so little has remained of the records of the Past. Verily, the fiendish spirits of fanaticism, of early and mediæval Christianity and of Islam, have from the first loved to dwell in darkness and ignorance; and both have made

> "———— the sun like blood, the earth a tomb,
> The tomb a hell, and hell itself a murkier gloom!"

Both creeds have won their proselytes at the point of the sword; both have built their churches on *heaven-kissing hecatombs of human victims.* Over the gateway of Century I. of our era, the ominous words " the KARMA OF ISRAEL," fatally glowed. Over the portals of our own, the future seer may discern other words, that will point to the Karma for cunningly made-up HISTORY, for events purposely perverted, and for great characters slandered by posterity, mangled out of recognition, between the two cars of Jagannâtha—Bigotry and Materialism; one accepting too much, the other denying all. Wise is he who holds to the golden mid-point, who believes in the eternal justice of things. Says Faigi Diwan, the " witness to the wonderful speeches of a free-thinker who belongs to a thousand sects ": " In the assembly of the day of resurrection, when past things shall be forgiven, the sins of the Ka'bah will be forgiven for the sake of the dust of Christian churches." To this, Professor Max Müller replies: " The sins of Islam are *as worthless as the dust of Christianity. On the day of resurrection both Muhammadans and Christians will see the vanity of their religious doctrines.* Men fight about religion on earth; in heaven they shall find out that there is only one true religion—the worship of God's SPIRIT."*

In other words—" THERE IS NO RELIGION (OR LAW) HIGHER THAN TRUTH "—" SATYÂT NÂSTI PARO DHARMAH "—the motto of the Maharajah of Benares, adopted by the Theosophical Society.

As already said in the *Preface,* the Secret Doctrine is not a version of " Isis Unveiled "—as originally intended. It is a volume explanatory of

---

* " Lectures on the Science of Religion," by F. Max Müller, p. 257.

it rather, and, though entirely independent of the earlier work, an indispensable corollary to it. Much of what was in Isis could hardly be understood by theosophists in those days. The Secret Doctrine will now throw light on many a problem left unsolved in the first work, especially on the opening pages, which have never been understood.

Concerned simply with the philosophies within our historical times and the respective symbolism of the fallen nations, only a hurried glance could be thrown at the panorama of Occultism in the two volumes of Isis. In the present work, detailed Cosmogony and the evolution of the four races that preceded our Fifth race Humanity are given, and now two large volumes explain that which was stated on the first page of Isis Unveiled alone, and in a few allusions scattered hither and thither throughout that work. Nor could the vast catalogue of the Archaic Sciences be attempted in the present volumes, before we have disposed of such tremendous problems as Cosmic and Planetary Evolution, and the gradual development of the mysterious Humanities and races that preceded our "Adamic" Humanity. Therefore, the present attempt to elucidate some mysteries of the Esoteric philosophy has, in truth, nothing to do with the earlier work. As an instance, the writer must be allowed to illustrate what is said.

Volume I. of "Isis" begins with a reference to "an old book"—

"So very old that our modern antiquarians might ponder over its pages an indefinite time, and still not quite agree as to the nature of the fabric upon which it is written. It is the only original copy now in existence. The most ancient Hebrew document on occult learning—the *Siphrah Dzeniouta*—was compiled from it, and that at a time when the former was already considered in the light of a literary relic. One of its illustrations represents the Divine Essence emanating from Adam* like a luminous arc proceeding to form a circle; and then, having attained the highest point of its circumference, the ineffable glory bends back again, and returns to earth, bringing a higher type of humanity in its vortex. As it approaches nearer and nearer to our planet, the Emanation becomes more and more shadowy, until upon touching the ground it is as black as night."

---

* The name is used in the sense of the Greek word ἄνθρωπος.

The "very old Book" is the original work from which the many
volumes of *Kiu-ti* were compiled. Not only this latter and the *Siphrah
Dzeniouta* but even the *Sepher Jezirah*,* the work attributed by the
Hebrew Kabalists to their Patriarch Abraham (!), the book of *Shu-king*,
China's primitive Bible, the sacred volumes of the Egyptian Thoth-
Hermes, the Purânas in India, and the Chaldean *Book of Numbers* and
the *Pentateuch* itself, are all derived from that one small parent volume.
Tradition says, that it was taken down in *Senzar*, the secret sacerdotal
tongue, from the words of the Divine Beings, who dictated it to the sons
of Light, in Central Asia, at the very beginning of the 5th (our) race;
for there was a time when its language (the *Sen-zar*) was known to the
Initiates of every nation, when the forefathers of the Toltec understood
it as easily as the inhabitants of the lost Atlantis, who inherited
it, in their turn, from the sages of the 3rd Race, the *Manushis*, who learnt
it direct from the *Devas* of the 2nd and 1st Races. The "illustration"
spoken of in "Isis" relates to the evolution of these Races and of our
4th and 5th Race Humanity in the Vaivasvata Manvantara or "Round;"
each Round being composed of the Yugas of the seven periods of
Humanity; four of which are now passed in *our* life cycle, the middle
point of the 5th being nearly reached. The illustration is symbolical,
as every one can well understand, and covers the ground from the
beginning. The old book, having described Cosmic Evolution and explained the origin of everything on earth, including physical man, after
giving the true history of the races from the *First* down to the Fifth (our)
race, goes no further. It stops short at the beginning of the *Kali Yuga*
just 4989 years ago at the death of Krishna, the bright "Sun-god," the
once living hero and reformer.

But there exists another book. None of its possessors regard it as
very ancient, as it was born with, and is only as old as the Black Age,

---

* Rabbi Jehoshua Ben Chananea, who died about A.D. 72, openly declared that he
had performed "miracles" by means of the *Book of Sepher Jezireh*, and challenged
every sceptic. Franck, quoting from the Babylonian *Talmud*, names two other thau-
maturgists, Rabbis Chanina and Oshoi. (See "*Jerusalem Talmud, Sanhedrin*," c. 7, etc.;
and "*Franck*," pp. 55, 56.) Many of the Mediæval Occultists, Alchemists, and Kabalists
claimed the same; and even the late modern *Magus*, Eliphas Lévi, publicly asserts it
in print in his books on Magic.

namely, about 5,000 years. In about nine years hence, the first cycle of the first five millenniums, that began with the great cycle of the Kali-Yuga, will end. And then the last prophecy contained in that book (the first volume of the prophetic record for the Black Age) will be accomplished. We have not long to wait, and many of us will witness the Dawn of the New Cycle, at the end of which not a few accounts will be settled and squared between the races. Volume II. of the Prophecies is nearly ready, having been in preparation since the time of Buddha's grand successor, Sankarâchârya.

One more important point must be noticed, one that stands foremost in the series of proofs given of the existence of one primeval, universal Wisdom—at any rate for the Christian Kabalists and students. The teachings were, at least, partially known to severa of the Fathers of the Church. It is maintained, on purely historical grounds, that Origen, Synesius, and even Clemens Alexandrinus, had been themselves initiated into the mysteries before adding to the Neo-Platonism of the Alexandrian school, that of the Gnostics, under the Christian veil. More than this, some of the doctrines of the Secret schools—though by no means all—were preserved in the Vatican, and have since become part and parcel of the mysteries, in the shape of disfigured additions made to the original Christian programme by the Latin Church. Such is the now materialised dogma of the Immaculate Conception. This accounts for the great persecutions set on foot by the Roman Catholic Church against Occultism, Masonry, and *heterodox* mysticism generally.

The days of Constantine were the last turning-point in history, the period of the Supreme struggle that ended in the Western world throttling the old religions in favour of the new one, built on their bodies. From thence the vista into the far distant Past, beyond the " Deluge " and the Garden of Eden, began to be forcibly and relentlessly closed by every fair and unfair means against the indiscreet gaze of posterity. Every issue was blocked up, every record that hands could be laid upon, destroyed. Yet there remains enough, even among such mutilated records, to warrant us in saying that there is in them every possible evidence of the actual existence of a Parent Doctrine. Fragments have survived geological and political cataclysms to tell the story ; and every survival shows evidence that the now *Secret* Wisdom was once the one fountain head, the ever-flowing perennial source, at which were fed all its streamlets—the later religions of all nations—from the first down to the last. This period, beginning with Buddha and Pythagoras at the one end and the Neo-Platonists and Gnostics at the other, is the only focus left in History wherein converge for the last time the bright rays of light streaming from the æons of time gone by, unobscured by the hand of bigotry and fanaticism.

This accounts for the necessity under which the writer has laboured to be ever explaining the facts given from the hoariest Past by evidence gathered from the historical period. No other means was at hand, at the risk even of being once more charged with a lack of method and system. The public must be made acquainted with the efforts of many World-adepts, of initiated poets, writers, and classics of every age, to preserve in the records of Humanity the Knowledge of the existence, at least, of such a philosophy, if not actually of its tenets. The Initiates of 1888 would indeed remain incomprehensible and ever a seemingly impossible myth, were not like Initiates shown to have lived in every other age of history. This could be done only by naming Chapter and Verse where may be found mention of these great characters, who were preceded and followed by a long and interminable line of other famous Antediluvian and Postdiluvian Masters in the arts. Thus only could be shown, on semi-traditional and semi-historical authority, that knowledge of the Occult and the powers it confers on man, are not altogether fictions, but that they are as old as the world itself.

To my judges, past and future, therefore—whether they are serious literary critics, or those howling dervishes in literature who judge a book according to the popularity or unpopularity of the author's name, who, hardly glancing at its contents, fasten like lethal *bacilli* on the weakest points of the body—I have nothing to say. Nor shall I condescend to notice those crack-brained slanderers—fortunately very few in number—who, hoping to attract public attention by throwing discredit on every writer whose name is better known than their own, foam and bark at their very shadows. These, having first maintained for years that the doctrines taught in the *Theosophist*, and which culminated in "Esoteric Buddhism," *had been all invented by the present writer*, have finally turned round, and denounced "Isis Unveiled" and the rest as a plagiarism from Eliphas Lévi (!), Paracelsus (! !), and, *mirabile dictu*, Buddhism and Brahmanism (! ! !) As well charge Renan with having stolen his *Vie de Jésus* from the Gospels, and Max Müller his " Sacred Books of the East" or his "Chips" from the philosophies of the the Brahmins and Gautama, the Buddha. But to the public in general and the readers of the "Secret Doctrine" I may repeat what I have stated all along, and which I now clothe in the words of Montaigne : Gentlemen, " I HAVE HERE MADE ONLY A NOSEGAY OF CULLED FLOWERS, AND HAVE BROUGHT NOTHING OF MY OWN BUT THE STRING THAT TIES THEM."

Pull the "string" to pieces and cut it up in shreds, if you will. As for the nosegay of FACTS—you will never be able to make away with these. You can only ignore them, and no more.

We may close with a parting word concerning this Volume I. In an INTRODUCTION prefacing a Part dealing chiefly with Cosmogony, certain subjects brought forward might be deemed out of place, but one more consideration added to those already given have led me to touch upon them. Every reader will inevitably judge the statements made from the stand-point of his own knowledge, experience, and consciousness, based on what he has already learnt. This fact the writer is constantly obliged to bear in mind : hence, also the frequent references in this first Book to matters which, properly speaking, belong to a later part of the work, but which could not be passed by in silence, lest the reader should look down on this work as a fairy tale indeed—a fiction of some modern brain.

Thus, the *Past* shall help to realise the PRESENT, and the latter to better appreciate the PAST. The errors of the day must be explained and swept away, yet it is more than probable—and in the present case it amounts to certitude—that once more the testimony of long ages and of history will fail to impress anyone but the very intuitional—which is equal to saying the very few. But in this as in all like cases, the *true* and the *faithful* may console themselves by presenting the sceptical modern Sadducee with the mathematical proof and memorial of his obdurate obstinacy and bigotry. There still exists somewhere in the archives of the French Academy, the famous law of probabilities worked out by an algebraical process for the benefit of sceptics by certain mathematicians. It runs thus : If two persons give their evidence to a fact, and thus impart to it each of them $\frac{5}{6}$ of certitude; that fact will have then $\frac{35}{36}$ of certitude; *i.e.*, its probability will bear to its improbability the ratio of 35 to 1. If three such evidences are joined together the certitude will become $\frac{215}{216}$. The agreement of ten persons giving each $\frac{1}{2}$ of certitude will produce $\frac{1023}{1024}$, etc., etc. The Occultist may remain satisfied, and care for no more.

PROEM.

PAGES FROM A PRE-HISTORIC PERIOD.

An Archaic Manuscript—a collection of palm leaves made impermeable to water, fire, and air, by some specific unknown process—is before the writer's eye. On the first page is an immaculate white disk within a dull black ground. On the following page, the same disk, but with a central point. The first, the student knows to represent Kosmos in Eternity, before the re-awakening of still slumbering Energy, the emanation of the Word in later systems. The point in the hitherto immaculate Disk, Space and Eternity in Pralaya, denotes the dawn of differentiation. It is the Point in the Mundane Egg (see Part II., "The Mundane Egg"), the germ within the latter which will become the Universe, the ALL, the boundless, periodical Kosmos, this germ being latent and active, periodically and by turns. The one circle is divine Unity, from which all proceeds, whither all returns. Its circumference— a forcibly limited symbol, in view of the limitation of the human mind —indicates the abstract, ever incognisable PRESENCE, and its plane, the Universal Soul, although the two are one. Only the face of the Disk being white and the ground all around black, shows clearly that its plane is the only knowledge, dim and hazy though it still is, that is attainable by man. It is on this plane that the Manvantaric manifestations begin; for it is in this SOUL that slumbers, during the Pralaya, the Divine Thought,* wherein lies concealed the plan of every future Cosmogony and Theogony.

---

* It is hardly necessary to remind the reader once more that the term "Divine Thought," like that of "Universal Mind," must not be regarded as even vaguely shadowing forth an intellectual process akin to that exhibited by man. The "Unconscious," according to von Hartmann, arrived at the vast creative, or rather Evolutionary Plan, "by a clairvoyant wisdom superior to all consciousness," which in the Vedantic language would mean absolute Wisdom. Only those who realise how far Intuition soars above the tardy processes of ratiocinative thought can form the faintest conception of

It is the ONE LIFE, eternal, invisible, yet Omnipresent, without beginning or end, yet periodical in its regular manifestations, between which periods reigns the dark mystery of non-Being ; unconscious, yet absolute Consciousness; unrealisable, yet the one self-existing reality ; truly, "a chaos to the sense, a Kosmos to the reason." Its one absolute attribute, which is ITSELF, eternal, ceaseless Motion, is called in esoteric parlance the "Great Breath,"* which is the perpetual motion of the universe, in the sense of limitless, ever-present SPACE. That which is motionless cannot be Divine. But then there is nothing in fact and reality absolutely motionless within the universal soul.

Almost five centuries B.C. Leucippus, the instructor of Democritus, maintained that Space was filled eternally with atoms actuated by a ceaseless motion, the latter generating in due course of time, when those atoms aggregated, rotatory motion, through mutual collisions producing lateral movements. Epicurus and Lucretius taught the same, only adding to the lateral motion of the atoms the idea of affinity —an occult teaching.

From the beginning of man's inheritance, from the first appearance of the architects of the globe he lives in, the unrevealed Deity was recognised and considered under its only philosophical aspect—universal motion, the thrill of the creative Breath in Nature. Occultism sums up the "One Existence" thus: "Deity is an arcane, living (or moving) FIRE, and the eternal witnesses to this unseen Presence are Light, Heat, Moisture,"—this trinity including, and being the cause of, every

---

that absolute Wisdom which transcends the ideas of Time and Space. Mind, as we know it, is resolvable into states of consciousness, of varying duration, intensity, complexity, etc.—all, in the ultimate, resting on sensation, which is again Maya. Sensation, again, necessarily postulates limitation. The personal God of orthodox Theism perceives, thinks, and is affected by emotion; he repents and feels "fierce anger." But the notion of such mental states clearly involves the unthinkable postulate of the externality of the exciting stimuli, to say nothing of the impossibility of ascribing changelessness to a Being whose emotions fluctuate with events in the worlds he presides over. The conceptions of a Personal God as changeless and infinite are thus unpsychological and, what is worse, unphilosophical.

* Plato proves himself an Initiate, when saying in Cratylus that θεὸς is derived from the verb θέειν, "to move," "to run," as the first astronomers who observed the motions of the heavenly bodies called the planets θεοί, the gods. (See Book II., "Symbolism of the Cross and Circle.") Later, the word produced another term, ἀλήθεια—"the breath of God."

phenomenon in Nature.* Intra-Cosmic motion is eternal and ceaseless; cosmic motion (the visible, or that which is subject to perception) is finite and periodical. As an eternal abstraction it is the EVER-PRESENT; as a manifestation, it is finite both in the coming direction and the opposite, the two being the alpha and omega of successive reconstructions. Kosmos—the NOUMENON—has nought to do with the causal relations of the phenomenal World. It is only with reference to the intra-cosmic soul, the ideal Kosmos in the immutable Divine Thought, that we may say : " It never had a beginning nor will it have an end." With regard to its body or Cosmic organization, though it cannot be said that it had a first, or will ever have a last construction, yet at each new Manvantara, its organization may be regarded as the first and the last of its kind, as it evolutes every time on a higher plane . . . .

A few years ago only, it was stated that :—

" The esoteric doctrine teaches, like Buddhism and Brahminism, and even the Kabala, that the one infinite and unknown Essence exists from all eternity, and in regular and harmonious successions is either passive or active. In the poetical phraseology of Manu these conditions are called the " Days " and the " Nights " of Brahmâ. The latter is either "awake " or " asleep." The Svabhâvikas, or philosophers of the oldest school of Buddhism (which still exists in Nepaul), speculate only upon the active condition of this " Essence," which they call Svâbhâvat, and deem it foolish to theorise upon the abstract and " unknowable " power in its passive condition. Hence they are called atheists by both Christian theologians and modern scientists, for neither of the

---

* Nominalists, arguing with Berkeley that " it is impossible . . . to form the abstract idea of motion distinct from the body moving " (" *Prin. of Human Knowledge*," *Introd., par.* 10), may put the question, " What is that body, the producer of that motion ? Is it a substance ? Then you are believers in a Personal God ? " etc., etc. This will be answered farther on, in the Addendum to this Book ; meanwhile, we claim our rights of Conceptionalists as against Roscelini's materialistic views of Realism and Nominalism. " Has science," says one of its ablest advocates, Edward Clodd, " revealed anything that weakens or opposes itself to the ancient words in which the Essence of all religion, past, present, and to come, is given ; to do justly, to love mercy, to walk humbly before thy God ? " Provided we connote by the word God, *not the crude anthropomorphism which is still the backbone of our current theology, but the symbolic conception of that which is Life and Motion of the Universe*, to know which in physical order is to know time past, present, and to come, in the existence of successions of phenomena ; to know which, in the moral, is to know what has been, is, and will be, within human consciousness. (*See " Science and the Emotions." A Discourse delivered at South Place Chapel, Finsbury, London, Dec.* 27th, 1885.)

two are able to understand the profound logic of their philosophy. The former will allow of no other God than the personified secondary powers which have worked out the visible universe, and which became with them the anthropo-morphic God of the Christians—the male Jehovah, roaring amid thunder and lightning. In its turn, rationalistic science greets the Buddhists and the Svabhâvikas as the "positivists" of the archaic ages. If we take a one-sided view of the philosophy of the latter, our materialists may be right in their own way. The Buddhists maintained that there is no Creator, but an infinitude of creative powers, which collectively form the one eternal substance, the essence of which is inscrutable—hence not a subject for specu-lation for any true philosopher. Socrates invariably refused to argue upon the mystery of universal being, yet no one would ever have thought of charging him with atheism, except those who were bent upon his destruction. Upon inaugurating an active period, says the Secret Doctrine, an expansion of this Divine essence from without inwardly and from within outwardly, occurs in obedience to eternal and immutable law, and the phenomenal or visible universe is the ultimate result of the long chain of cosmical forces thus pro-gressively set in motion. In like manner, when the passive condition is resumed, a contraction of the Divine essence takes place, and the previous work of creation is gradually and progressively undone. The visible universe becomes disintegrated, its material dispersed; and 'darkness' solitary and alone, broods once more over the face of the 'deep.' To use a Metaphor from the Secret Books, which will convey the idea still more clearly, an out-breathing of the 'unknown essence' produces the world; and an inhalation causes it to disappear. This process has been going on from all eternity, and our present universe is but one of an infinite series, which had no beginning and will have no end."—(See "Isis Unveiled;" also "The Days and Nights of Brahmâ" in Part II.)

This passage will be explained, as far as it is possible, in the present work. Though, as it now stands, it contains nothing new to the Orientalist, its esoteric interpretation may contain a good deal which has hitherto remained entirely unknown to the Western student.

The first illustration being a plain disc ◯, the second one in the Archaic symbol shows ⊙, a disc with a point in it—the first differentia-tion in the periodical manifestations of the ever-eternal nature, sexless and infinite "Aditi in THAT" (Rig Veda), the point in the disc, or potential Space within abstract Space. In its third stage the point is transformed into a diameter, thus ⊖ It now symbolises a divine immaculate Mother-Nature within the all-embracing absolute Infinite.

When the diameter line is crossed by a vertical one ⊕, it becomes the mundane cross. Humanity has reached its third root-race; it is the sign for the origin of human life to begin. When the circumference disappears and leaves only the ┼ it is a sign that the fall of man into matter is accomplished, and the FOURTH race begins. The Cross within a circle symbolises pure Pantheism; when the Cross was left uninscribed, it became phallic. It had the same and yet other meanings as a TAU inscribed within a circle ⊖ or as a "Thor's hammer," the Jaina cross, so-called, or simply Svastica within a circle ⊕

By the third symbol—the circle divided in two by the horizontal line of the diameter—the first manifestation of creative (still passive, because feminine) Nature was meant. The first shadowy perception of man connected with procreation is feminine, because man knows his mother more than his father. Hence female deities were more sacred than the male. Nature is therefore feminine, and, to a degree, objective and tangible, and the spirit Principle which fructifies it is concealed. By adding to the circle with the horizontal line in it, a perpendicular line, the tau was formed— T —the oldest form of the letter. It was the glyph of the third root-race to the day of its symbolical Fall—*i.e.*, when the separation of sexes by natural evolution took place—when the figure became ⏚, the circle, or sexless life modified or separated—a double glyph or symbol. With the races of our Fifth Race it became in symbology the sacr', and in Hebrew n'cabvah, of the first-formed races;* then it changed into the Egyptian ♀ (emblem of life), and still later into the sign of Venus, ♀ Then comes the Svastica (Thor's hammer, or the "Hermetic Cross" now), entirely separated from its Circle, thus becoming purely phallic. The esoteric symbol of Kali Yuga is the five-pointed star reversed, thus ⛤—the sign of human sorcery, with its two points (horns) turned heavenward, a position every

---

* See that suggestive work, "The Source of Measures," where the author explains the real meaning of the word "sacr'," from which "sacred," "sacrament," are derived, which have now become synonyms of "holiness," though purely phallic!

Occultist will recognise as one of the " left-hand," and used in ceremonial magic.*

It is hoped that during the perusal of this work the erroneous ideas of the public in general with regard to Pantheism will be modified. It is wrong and unjust to regard the Buddhists and Advaitee Occultists as atheists. If not all of them philosophers, they are, at any rate, all logicians, their objections and arguments being based on strict reasoning. Indeed, if the Parabrahmam of the Hindus may be taken as a representative of the hidden and nameless deities of other nations, this absolute Principle will be found to be the prototype from which all the others were copied. Parabrahm is not " God," because It is not *a* God. " It is that which is supreme, and not supreme (paravara)," explains Mandukya Upanishad (2.28). IT is " Supreme " as CAUSE, not supreme as effect. Parabrahm is simply, as a " Secondless Reality," the all-inclusive Kosmos—or, rather, the infinite Cosmic Space—in the highest spiritual sense, of course. Brahma (neuter) being the unchanging, pure, free, undecaying supreme Root, "the ONE true Existence, Paramarthika," and the absolute Chit and Chaitanya (intelligence, consciousness) cannot be a cogniser, "for THAT can have no subject of cognition." Can the flame be called the essence of Fire ? This Essence is "the LIFE and LIGHT of the Universe, the visible fire and flame are destruction, death, and evil." " Fire and Flame destroy the body of an Arhat, their essence makes him immortal." *(Bodhi-mur, Book II.)* " The knowledge of the absolute Spirit, like the effulgence of the sun, or like heat in fire, is naught else than the absolute Essence itself," says Sankaracharya. IT—is "the Spirit of the Fire," not fire itself; therefore, " the attributes of the latter, heat or flame, are not the attributes of the Spirit, but of that of which that Spirit is the unconscious cause." Is not the above sentence the true key-note of later Rosicrucian

---

* We are told by the Western mathematicians and some American Kabalists, that in the Kabala also " the value of the Jehovah name is that of the diameter of a circle." Add to this the fact that Jehovah is the third Sephiroth, *Binah*, a feminine word, and you have the key to the mystery. By certain Kabalistic transformations this name, *androgynous* in the first chapters of Genesis, becomes in its transformations entirely masculine, Cainite and phallic. The fact of choosing a deity among the pagan gods and making of it a special national God, to call upon it as the " One living God," the " God of Gods," and then proclaim this worship Monotheistic, does not change it into the ONE Principle whose " Unity admits not of multiplication, change, or form," especially in the case of a priapic deity, as Jehovah now demonstrated to be.

philosophy?   Parabrahm is, in short, the collective aggregate of Kosmos in its infinity and eternity, the "THAT" and "THIS" to which distributive aggregates can not be applied.*   "In the beginning THIS was the Self, one only" *(Aitareya Upanishad);* the great Sankaracharya explains that "THIS" referred to the Universe (Jagat); the sense of the words, "In the beginning," meaning before the reproduction of the phenomenal Universe.

Therefore, when the Pantheists echo the Upanishads, which state, as in the Secret Doctrine, that "this" cannot create, they do not deny a Creator, or rather a *collective aggregate* of creators, but only refuse, very logically, to attribute "creation" and especially formation, something finite, to an Infinite Principle.   With them, Parabrahmam is a passive because an Absolute Cause, the unconditioned *Mukta*.   It is only limited Omniscience and Omnipotence that are refused to the latter, because these are still attributes (as reflected in man's perceptions); and because Parabrahm, being the "Supreme ALL," the ever invisible spirit and Soul of Nature, changeless and eternal, can have no attributes; absoluteness very naturally precluding any idea of the finite or conditioned from being connected with it.   And if the Vedantin postulates attributes as belonging simply to its emanation, calling it "Iswara *plus* Maya," and Avidya (Agnosticism and Nescience rather than ignorance), it is difficult to find any Atheism in this conception.†   Since there can be neither two INFINITES nor two ABSOLUTES in a Universe supposed to be Boundless, this Self-Existence can hardly be conceived of as creating personally.   In the sense and perceptions of finite "Beings," THAT is Non-"being," in the sense that it is the one BE-NESS; for, in this ALL lies concealed its coeternal and coeval emanation or inherent radiation, which, upon becoming periodically Brahmâ (the male-female Potency) becomes or expands itself into the manifested Universe.   Narayana moving on the (abstract) waters of Space, is transformed into the Waters of concrete substance moved by him, who now becomes the manifested WORD or Logos.

---

* See "Vedanta Sara," by Major G. A. Jacob; as also "The Aphorisms of S'ândilya," translated by Cowell, p. 42.

† Nevertheless, prejudiced and rather fanatical Christian Orientalists would like to prove this pure Atheism.   For proof of this, see about Major Jacob's "Vedanta Sara."   Yet, the whole Antiquity echoes this Vedantic thought :—
"Omnis enim per se divom natura necesse est
Immortali ævo summa cum pace fruatur."

The orthodox Brahmins, those who rise the most against the Pantheists and Adwaitees, calling them Atheists, are forced, if Manu has any authority in this matter, to accept the death of Brahmâ, the creator, at the expiration of every "Age" of this (creative) deity (100 Divine years— a period which in our years requires fifteen figures to express it). Yet, no philosopher among them will view this " death " in any other sense than as a temporary disappearance from the manifested plane of existence, or as a periodical rest.

The Occultists are, therefore, at one with the Adwaita Vedantin philosophers as to the above tenet. They show the impossibility of accepting on philosophical grounds the idea of the absolute ALL creating or even evolving the " Golden Egg," into which it is said to enter in order to transform itself into Brahmâ—the Creator, who expands himself later into gods and all the visible Universe. They say that Absolute Unity cannot pass to infinity; for infinity presupposes the limitless extension of *something*, and the duration of that " something ;" and the One All is like Space—which is its only mental and physical representation on this Earth, or our plane of existence—neither an object of, nor a subject to, perception. If one could suppose the Eternal Infinite All, the Omnipresent Unity, instead of being in Eternity, becoming through periodical manifestation a manifold Universe or a multiple personality, that Unity would cease to be one. Locke's idea that " pure Space is capable of neither resistance nor Motion "—is incorrect. Space is neither a " limitless void," nor a " conditioned fulness," but both : being, on the plane of absolute abstraction, the ever-incognisable Deity, which is void only to finite minds,* and on that of *mayavic* perception, the Plenum, the absolute Container of all that is, whether manifested or unmanifested : it is, therefore, that ABSOLUTE ALL. There is no difference between the Christian Apostle's " In Him we live and move and have our being," and the Hindu Rishi's " The Universe lives in, proceeds from, and will

---

* The very names of the two chief deities, Brahmâ and Vishnu, ought to have long ago suggested their esoteric meanings. For the root of one, Brahmam, or Brahm, is derived by some from the word Brih, " to grow" or " to expand" (see *Calcutta Review*, vol. lxvi., p. 14) ; and of the other, Vishnu, from the root Vis, "to pervade," to enter in the nature of the essence ; Brahmâ-Vishnu being this infinite SPACE, of which the gods, the Rishis, the Manus, and all in this universe are simply the potencies, Vibhutayah.

return to, Brahma (Brahmâ) :" for Brahma (neuter), the unmanifested, is that Universe *in abscondito*, and Brahmâ, the manifested, is the Logos, made male-female* in the symbolical orthodox dogmas.   The God of the Apostle-Initiate and of the Rishi being both the Unseen and the Visible SPACE.   Space is called in the esoteric symbolism "the Seven-Skinned Eternal Mother-Father."   It is composed from its undifferentiated to its differentiated surface of seven layers.

" What is that which was, is, and will be, whether there is a Universe or not ; whether there be gods or none ? " asks the esoteric Senzar Catechism.   And the answer made is—SPACE.

It is not the One Unknown ever-present God in Nature, or Nature *in abscondito*, that is rejected, but the God of human dogma and his *humanized* " Word."   In his infinite conceit and inherent pride and vanity, man shaped it himself with his sacrilegious hand out of the material he found in his own small brain-fabric, and forced it upon mankind as a direct revelation from the one unrevealed SPACE.†   The Occultist

---

* See Manu's account of Brahmâ separating his body into male and female, the latter the female Vâch, in whom he creates Viraj, and compare this with the esotericism of Chapters II., III., and IV. of Genesis.

† Occultism is indeed in the air at the close of this our century.   Among many other works recently published, we would recommend one especially to students of theoretical Occultism who would not venture beyond the realm of our special human plane.   It is called " New Aspects of Life and Religion," by Henry Pratt, M.D.   It is full of esoteric dogmas and philosophy, the latter rather limited, in the concluding chapters, by what seems to be a spirit of conditioned positivism.   Nevertheless, what is said of Space as " the Unknown First Cause," merits quotation.   " This unknown something, thus recognised as, and indentified with, the primary embodiment of Simple Unity, is invisible and impalpable "—(*abstract* space, granted) ;   " and because invisible and impalpable, therefore incognisable.   And this incognisability has led to the error of supposing it to be a simple void, a mere receptive capacity.   But, even viewed as an absolute void, space must be admitted to be either Self-existent, infinite, and eternal, or to have had a first cause outside, behind, and beyond itself.

" And yet could such a cause be found and defined, this would only lead to the transferring thereto of the attributes otherwise accruing to space, and thus merely throw the difficulty of origination a step farther back, without gaining additional light as to primary causation."   (p. 5.)

This is precisely what has been done by the believers in an anthropomorphic Creator, an extracosmic, instead of an intracosmic God.   Many—most of Mr. Pratt's subjects, we may say—are old Kabalistic ideas and theories which he presents in quite a new garb : " New Aspects " of the Occult in Nature, indeed.   Space, however, viewed as a " Substantial Unity "—the " living Source of Life "—is as the " Un-

accepts revelation as coming from divine yet still finite Beings, the
manifested lives, never from the Unmanifestable ONE LIFE; from those
entities, called Primordial Man, Dhyani-Buddhas, or Dhyan-Chohans,
the "Rishi-Prajâpati" of the Hindus, the Elohim or "Sons of God,"
the Planetary Spirits of all nations, who have become Gods for men.
He also regards the Adi-Sakti—the direct emanation of Mulaprakriti,
the eternal Root of THAT, and the female aspect of the Creative Cause
Brahmâ, in her A'kâsic form of the Universal Soul—as philosophically a
Maya, and cause of human Maya. But this view does not prevent him
from believing in its existence so long as it lasts, to wit, for one Maha-
manvantara; nor from applying A'kâs'a, the radiation of Mulaprakriti,*
to practical purposes, connected as the World-Soul is with all natural
phenomena, known or unknown to science.

The oldest religions of the world—exoterically, for the esoteric root
or foundation is one—are the Indian, the Mazdean, and the Egyptian.
Then comes the Chaldean, the outcome of these—entirely lost to the
world now, except in its disfigured Sabeanism as at present rendered by
the archæologists; then, passing over a number of religions that will be
mentioned later, comes the Jewish, esoterically, as in the Kabala,
following in the line of Babylonian Magism; exoterically, as in Genesis
and the Pentateuch, a collection of allegorical legends. Read by the
light of the Zohar, the initial four chapters of Genesis are the fragment

---

known Causeless Cause," is the oldest dogma in Occultism, millenniums earlier than
the *Pater-Æther* of the Greeks and Latins. So are the "Force and Matter, as Potencies
of Space, inseparable, and the Unknown revealers of the Unknown." They are all
found in Aryan philosophy personified by Visvakarman, Indra, Vishnu, etc., etc. Still
they are expressed very philosophically, and under many unusual aspects, in the work
referred to.

* In contradistinction to the manifested universe of matter, the term *Mulaprakriti*
(from *Mula*, "the root," and *prakriti*, "nature"), or the unmanifested primordial
matter—called by Western alchemists Adam's Earth—is applied by the Vedantins to
Parabrahmam. Matter is dual in religious metaphysics, and septenary in esoteric
teachings, like everything else in the universe. As *Mulaprakriti*, it is undifferentiated
and eternal; as Vyakta, it becomes differentiated and conditioned, according to
Svetasvatara Upanishad, I. 8, and *Devi Bhagavata Purâna.* The author of the
Four Lectures on the Bhagavad Gita, says, in speaking of *Mulaprakriti:* "From its
(the Logos') objective standpoint, *Parabrahmam* appears to it as *Mulaprakriti.* . . . Of
course this *Mulaprakriti* is material to it, as any material object is material to us. . . .
Parabrahmam is an unconditioned and absolute reality, and *Mulaprakriti* is a sort of veil
thrown over it." (*Theosophist,* Vol. VIII., p. 304.)

of a highly philosophical page in the World's Cosmogony. (*See* Book III., *Gupta Vidya and the Zohar*.) Left in their symbolical disguise, they are a nursery tale, an ugly thorn in the side of science and logic, an evident effect of Karma. To have let them serve as a prologue to Christianity was a cruel revenge on the part of the Rabbis, who knew better what their Pentateuch meant. It was a silent protest against their spoliation, and the Jews have certainly now the better of their traditional persecutors. The above-named exoteric creeds will be explained in the light of the Universal doctrine as we proceed with it.

The Occult Catechism contains the following questions and answers :

"*What is it that ever is ?*" "*Space, the eternal Anupadaka.*"* "*What is it that ever was ?*" "*The Germ in the Root.*" "*What is it that is ever coming and going ?*" "*The Great Breath.*" "*Then, there are three Eternals ?*" "*No, the three are one. That which ever is is one, that which ever was is one, that which is ever being and becoming is also one : and this is Space.*"

"*Explain, oh Lanoo (disciple).*" —"*The One is an unbroken Circle (ring) with no circumference, for it is nowhere and everywhere ; the One is the boundless plane of the Circle, manifesting a diameter only during the manvantaric periods ; the One is the indivisible point found nowhere, perceived everywhere during those periods ; it is the Vertical and the Horizontal, the Father and the Mother, the summit and base of the Father, the two extremities of the Mother, reaching in reality nowhere, for the One is the Ring as also the rings that are within that Ring. Light in darkness and darkness in light : the ' Breath which is eternal.' It proceeds from without inwardly, when it is everywhere, and from within outwardly, when it is nowhere—(i.e., maya,* † *one of the centres* ‡*). It expands and*

---

* Meaning " parentless "—see farther on.

† Esoteric philosophy, regarding as Maya (or the illusion of ignorance) every finite thing, must necessarily view in the same light every intra-Cosmic planet and body, as being something organised, hence finite. The expression, therefore, " it proceeds from without inwardly, etc." refers in the first portion of the sentence to the dawn of the Mahamanvantaric period, or the great re-evolution after one of the complete periodical dissolutions of every compound form in Nature (from planet to molecule) into its ultimate essence or element ; and in its second portion, to the partial or local manvantara, which may be a solar or even a planetary one.

‡ By " centre," a centre of energy or a Cosmic focus is meant ; when the so-called " Creation," or formation of a planet, is accomplished by that force which is designated by the Occultists LIFE and by Science " energy," then the process takes place

contracts (exhalation and inhalation). When it expands the mother diffuses and scatters; when it contracts, the mother draws back and ingathers. This produces the periods of Evolution and Dissolution, Manwantara and Pralaya. The Germ is invisible and fiery; the Root (the plane of the circle) is cool; but during Evolution and Manwantara her garment is cold and radiant. Hot Breath is the Father who devours the progeny of the many-faced Element (heterogeneous); and leaves the single-faced ones (homogeneous). Cool Breath is the Mother, who conceives, forms, brings forth, and receives them back into her bosom, to reform them at the Dawn (of the Day of Brahmâ, or Manvantara). . . . ."

For clearer understanding on the part of the general reader, it must be stated that Occult Science recognises *Seven* Cosmical Elements— four entirely physical, and the fifth (Ether) semi-material, as it will become visible in the air towards the end of our Fourth Round, to reign supreme over the others during the whole of the Fifth. The remaining two are as yet absolutely beyond the range of human perception. These latter will, however, appear as presentments during the 6th and 7th Races of this Round, and will become known in the 6th and 7th Rounds respectively.* These seven elements with their numberless Sub-Elements

from within outwardly, every atom being said to contain in itself creative energy of the divine breath. Hence, whereas after an absolute pralaya, or when the pre-existing material consists but of ONE Element, and BREATH " is everywhere," the latter acts from without inwardly : after a minor pralaya, everything having remained in *statu quo*—in a refrigerated state, so to say, like the moon—at the first flutter of manvantara, the planet or planets begin their resurrection to life from within outwardly.

* It is curious to notice how, in the evolutionary cycles of ideas, ancient thought seems to be reflected in modern speculation. Had Mr. Herbert Spencer read and studied ancient Hindu philosophers when he wrote a certain passage in his " First Principles " (p. 482), or is it an independent flash of inner perception that made him say half correctly, half incorrectly, " motion as well as matter, being fixed in quantity (?), it would seem that the change in the distribution of Matter which Motion effects, coming to a limit in whichever direction it is carried (?), the indestructible Motion thereupon necessitates a reverse distribution. Apparently, the universally co-existent forces of attraction and repulsion which, as we have seen, necessitate rhythm in all minor changes throughout the Universe, also necessitate rhythm in the totality of its changes—produce now an immeasurable period during which the attracting forces predominating, cause universal concentration, and then an immeasurable period, during which the repulsive forces predominating, cause universal diffusion—alternate eras of Evolution and dissolution."

far more numerous than those known to Science) are simply *conditional* modifications and aspects of the ONE and only Element. This latter is not *Ether*,* not even *A'kâs'a* but the *Source* of these. The Fifth Element, now advocated quite freely by Science, is not the Ether hypothesised by Sir Isaac Newton—although he calls it by that name, having associated it in his mind probably with the Æther, " Father-Mother " of Antiquity. As Newton intuitionally says, "Nature is a perpetual circulatory worker, generating fluids out of solids, fixed things out of volatile, and volatile out of fixed, subtile out of gross, and gross out of subtile. . . . . Thus, perhaps, may all things be originated from Ether," (Hypoth, 1675).

The reader has to bear in mind that the Stanzas given treat only of the Cosmogony of our own planetary System and what is visible around it, after a Solar Pralaya. The secret teachings with regard to the Evolution of the Universal Kosmos cannot be given, since they could not be understood by the highest minds in this age, and there seem to be very few Initiates, even among the greatest, who are allowed to speculate upon this subject. Moreover the Teachers say openly that not even the highest Dhyani-Chohans have ever penetrated the mysteries beyond those boundaries that separate the milliards of Solar systems from the " Central Sun," as it is called. Therefore, that which is given, relates only to our visible Kosmos, after a " Night of Brahmâ."

Before the reader proceeds to the consideration of the Stanzas from the Book of Dzyan which form the basis of the present work, it is absolutely necessary that he should be made acquainted with the few fundamental conceptions which underlie and pervade the entire system of thought to which his attention is invited. These basic ideas are few in number, and on their clear apprehension depends the understanding of all that follows ; therefore no apology is required for asking the reader to make himself familiar with them first, before entering on the perusal of the work itself.

---

* Whatever the views of physical Science upon the subject, Occult Science has been teaching for ages that A'kâs a—of which Ether is the grossest form—the fifth universal Cosmic Principle (to which corresponds and from which proceeds human Manas) is, cosmically, a radiant, cool, diathermanous plastic matter, creative in its physical nature, correlative in its grossest aspects and portions, immutable in its higher principles. In the former condition it is called the Sub-Root ; and in conjunction with radiant heat, it recalls " dead worlds to life." In its higher aspect it is the Soul of the World ; in its lower—the DESTROYER.

The Secret Doctrine establishes three fundamental propositions :—

(a) An Omnipresent, Eternal, Boundless, and Immutable Principle on which all speculation is impossible, since it transcends the power of human conception and could only be dwarfed by any human expression or similitude. It is beyond the range and reach of thought—in the words of Mandukya, "unthinkable and unspeakable."

To render these ideas clearer to the general reader, let him set out with the postulate that there is one absolute Reality which antecedes all manifested, conditioned, being. This Infinite and Eternal Cause—dimly formulated in the "Unconscious" and "Unknowable" of current European philosophy—is the rootless root of "all that was, is, or ever shall be." It is of course devoid of all attributes and is essentially without any relation to manifested, finite Being. It is "Be-ness" rather than Being (in Sanskrit, *Sat*), and is beyond all thought or speculation.

This "Be-ness" is symbolised in the Secret Doctrine under two aspects. On the one hand, absolute abstract Space, representing bare subjectivity, the one thing which no human mind can either exclude from any conception, or conceive of by itself. On the other, absolute Abstract Motion representing Unconditioned Consciousness. Even our Western thinkers have shown that Consciousness is inconceivable to us apart from change, and motion best symbolises change, its essential characteristic. This latter aspect of the one Reality, is also symbolised by the term "The Great Breath," a symbol sufficiently graphic to need no further elucidation. Thus, then, the first fundamental axiom of the Secret Doctrine is this metaphysical One Absolute—Be-ness—symbolised by finite intelligence as the theological Trinity.

It may, however, assist the student if a few further explanations are given here.

Herbert Spencer has of late so far modified his Agnosticism, as to assert that the nature of the "First Cause,"* which the Occultist more logically derives from the "Causeless Cause," the "Eternal," and the "Unknowable," may be essentially the same as that of the Consciousness which wells up within us : in short, that the impersonal reality pervading

---

* The "first" presupposes necessarily something which is the "first brought forth," "the first in time, space, and rank "—and therefore finite and conditioned. The "first"

the Kosmos is the pure noumenon of thought. This advance on his part brings him very near to the esoteric and Vedantin tenet.*

Parabrahm (the One Reality, the Absolute) is the field of Absolute Consciousness, *i.e.*, that Essence which is out of all relation to conditioned existence, and of which conscious existence is a conditioned symbol. But once that we pass in thought from this (to us) Absolute Negation, duality supervenes in the contrast of Spirit (or consciousness) and Matter, Subject and Object.

Spirit (or Consciousness) and Matter are, however, to be regarded, not as independent realities, but as the two facets or aspects of the Absolute (Parabrahm), which constitute the basis of conditioned Being whether subjective or objective.

Considering this metaphysical triad as the Root from which proceeds all manifestation, the great Breath assumes the character of precosmic Ideation. It is the *fons et origo* of force and of all individual consciousness, and supplies the guiding intelligence in the vast scheme of cosmic Evolution. On the other hand, precosmic root-substance (*Mulaprakriti*) is that aspect of the Absolute which underlies all the objective planes of Nature.

Just as pre-Cosmic Ideation is the root of all individual consciousness, so pre-Cosmic Substance is the substratum of matter in the various grades of its differentiation.

Hence it will be apparent that the contrast of these two aspects of the Absolute is essential to the existence of the " Manifested Universe." Apart from Cosmic Substance, Cosmic Ideation could not manifest as individual consciousness, since it is only through a vehicle† of matter that consciousness wells up as "I am I," a physical basis being necessary to focus a ray of the Universal Mind at a certain stage of complexity. Again, apart from Cosmic Ideation, Cosmic Substance would remain an empty abstraction, and no emergence of consciousness could ensue.

The " Manifested Universe," therefore, is pervaded by duality, which is, as it were, the very essence of its ex-istence as " manifestation."

---

cannot be the absolute, for it is a manifestation. Therefore, Eastern Occultism calls the Abstract All the " Causeless One Cause," the " Rootless Root," and limits the " First Cause " to the *Logos*, in the sense that Plato gives to this term.

* See Mr. Subba Row's four able lectures on the Bhagavad Gita, " Theosophist," February, 1887.

† Called in Sanskrit : " Upadhi."

But just as the opposite poles of subject and object, spirit and matter, are but aspects of the One Unity in which they are synthesized, so, in the manifested Universe, there is "that" which links spirit to matter, subject to object.

This something, at present unknown to Western speculation, is called by the occultists Fohat. It is the "bridge" by which the "Ideas" existing in the "Divine Thought" are impressed on Cosmic substance as the "laws of Nature." Fohat is thus the dynamic energy of Cosmic Ideation; or, regarded from the other side, it is the intelligent medium, the guiding power of all manifestation, the "Thought Divine" transmitted and made manifest through the Dhyan Chohans,* the Architects of the visible World. Thus from Spirit, or Cosmic Ideation, comes our consciousness; from Cosmic Substance the several vehicles in which that consciousness is individualised and attains to self—or reflective—consciousness; while Fohat, in its various manifestations, is the mysterious link between Mind and Matter, the animating principle electrifying every atom into life.

The following summary will afford a clearer idea to the reader.

(1.) The ABSOLUTE; the *Parabrahm* of the Vedantins or the one Reality, SAT, which is, as Hegel says, both Absolute Being and Non-Being.

(2.) The first manifestation, the impersonal, and, in philosophy, *unmanifested* Logos, the precursor of the "manifested." This is the "First Cause," the "Unconscious" of European Pantheists.

(3.) Spirit-matter, LIFE; the "Spirit of the Universe," the Purusha and Prakriti, or the *second* Logos.

(4.) Cosmic Ideation, MAHAT or Intelligence, the Universal World-Soul; the Cosmic Noumenon of Matter, the basis of the intelligent operations in and of Nature, also called MAHA-BUDDHI.

The ONE REALITY; its *dual* aspects in the conditioned Universe.

Further, the Secret Doctrine affirms:—

(b.) The Eternity of the Universe *in toto* as a boundless plane; periodically "the playground of numberless Universes incessantly manifesting and disappearing," called "the manifesting stars," and the "sparks of Eternity." "The Eternity of the Pilgrim"† is like a wink

---

* Called by Christian theology: Archangels, Seraphs, etc., etc.

† "Pilgrim" is the appellation given to our *Monad* (the two in one) during its cycle of incarnations. It is the only immortal and eternal principle in us, being an indivisible part of the integral whole—the Universal Spirit, from which it emanates, and into which it is absorbed at the end of the cycle. When it is said to emanate from the one

of the Eye of Self-Existence (Book of Dzyan.) "The appearance and disappearance of Worlds is like a regular tidal ebb of flux and reflux." (See Part II., "Days and Nights of Brahmâ.")

This second assertion of the Secret Doctrine is the absolute universality of that law of periodicity, of flux and reflux, ebb and flow, which physical science has observed and recorded in all departments of nature. An alternation such as that of Day and Night, Life and Death, Sleeping and Waking, is a fact so common, so perfectly universal and without exception, that it is easy to comprehend that in it we see one of the absolutely fundamental laws of the universe.

Moreover, the Secret Doctrine teaches :—

(c) The fundamental identity of all Souls with the Universal Over-Soul, the latter being itself an aspect of the Unknown Root ; and the obligatory pilgrimage for every Soul—a spark of the former—through the Cycle of Incarnation (or "Necessity") in accordance with Cyclic and Karmic law, during the whole term. In other words, no purely spiritual Buddhi (divine Soul) can have an independent (conscious) existence before the spark which issued from the pure Essence of the Universal Sixth principle,—or the OVER-SOUL,—has (a) passed through every elemental form of the phenomenal world of that Manvantara, and (b) acquired individuality, first by natural impulse, and then by self-induced and self-devised efforts (checked by its Karma), thus ascending through all the degrees of intelligence, from the lowest to the highest Manas, from mineral and plant, up to the holiest archangel (Dhyani-Buddha). The pivotal doctrine of the Esoteric philosophy admits no privileges or special gifts in man, save those won by his own Ego through personal effort and merit throughout a long series of metempsychoses and reincarnations. This is why the Hindus say that the Universe is Brahma and Brahmâ, for Brahma is in every atom of the universe, the six principles in Nature being all the outcome—the variously differentiated aspects—of the SEVENTH and ONE, the only reality in the Universe whether Cosmical or micro-cosmical ; and also why the permutations (psychic, spiritual and physical), on the plane of manifestation and form, of the sixth (Brahmâ the vehicle of Brahma) are viewed by metaphysical

spirit, an awkward and incorrect expression has to be used, for lack of appropriate words in English. The Vedantins call it Sutratma (Thread-Soul), but their explanation, too, differs somewhat from that of the occultists ; to explain which difference, however, is left to the Vedantins themselves.

antiphrasis as illusive and Mayavic. For although the root of every atom individually and of every form collectively, is that seventh principle or the one Reality, still, in its manifested phenomenal and temporary appearance, it is no better than an evanescent illusion of our senses. (See, for clearer definition, Addendum " Gods, Monads and Atoms," and also " Theophania," " Bodhisatvas and Reincarnation," etc., etc.)

In its absoluteness, the One Principle under its two aspects (of Parabrahmam and Mulaprakriti) is sexless, unconditioned and eternal. Its periodical (manvantaric) emanation—or primal radiation—is also One, androgynous and phenomenally finite. When the radiation radiates in its turn, all its radiations are also androgynous, to become male and female principles in their lower aspects. After Pralaya, whether the great or the minor Pralaya (the latter leaving the worlds in *statu quo**), the first that re-awakes to active life is the plastic A'kâs'a, Father-Mother, the Spirit and Soul of Ether, or the plane on the surface of the Circle. Space is called the " Mother" before its Cosmic activity, and Father-Mother at the first stage of re-awakening. (See Comments, Stanza II.) In the Kabala it is also Father-Mother-Son. But whereas in the Eastern doctrine, these are the Seventh Principle of the manifested Universe, or its " Atma-Buddhi-Manas " (Spirit, Soul, Intelligence), the triad branching off and dividing into the seven cosmical and seven human principles, in the Western Kabala of the Christian mystics it is the Triad or Trinity, and with their occultists, the male-female Jehovah, Jah-Havah. In this lies the whole difference between the esoteric and the Christian trinities. The Mystics and the Philosophers, the Eastern and Western Pantheists, synthesize their pregenetic triad in the pure divine abstraction. The orthodox, anthropomorphize it. *Hiranyagarbha, Hari,* and *Sankara*—the three hypostases of the manifesting " Spirit of the Supreme Spirit" (by which title Prithivi—the Earth—greets Vishnu in his first Avatar)—are the purely metaphysical abstract qualities of formation, preservation, and destruction, and are the three divine Avasthas (lit. hypostases) of that which " does

---

* It is not the physical organisms that remain in *statu quo*, least of all their psychical principles, during the great Cosmic or even Solar pralayas, but only their Akâsic or astral " photographs." But during the minor pralayas, once over-taken by the " Night," the planets remain intact, though dead, as a huge animal, caught and embedded in the polar ice, remains the same for ages.

not perish with created things" (or Achyuta, a name of Vishnu);
whereas the orthodox Christian separates his personal creative Deity
into the three personages of the Trinity, and admits of no higher Deity.
The latter, in Occultism, is the abstract Triangle ; with the orthodox, the
perfect Cube. The creative god or the aggregate gods are regarded by
the Eastern philosopher as *Bhrantidarsanatah*—" false apprehension,"
something "conceived of, by reason of erroneous appearances, as a
material form," and explained as arising from the illusive conception of
the Egotistic personal and human Soul (lower fifth principle). It is beautifully expressed in a new translation of Vishnu Purâna. " That Brahmâ
in its totality has essentially the aspect of Prakriti, both evolved and
unevolved (Mulaprakriti), and also the aspect of Spirit and the aspect
of Time. Spirit, O twice born, is the leading aspect of the Supreme
Brahma.* The next is a twofold aspect,—Prakriti, both evolved
and unevolved, and is the time last." Kronos is shown in the Orphic
theogony as being also a generated god or agent.

At this stage of the re-awakening of the Universe, the sacred symbolism represents it as a perfect Circle with the (root) point in the
Centre. This sign was universal, therefore we find it in the Kabala
also. The Western Kabala, however, now in the hands of Christian
mystics, ignores it altogether, though it is plainly shown in the Zohar.
These sectarians begin at the end, and show as the symbol of pregenetic
Kosmos this sign ⊕, calling it "the Union of the Rose and Cross,"
the great mystery of occult generation, from whence the name—Rosicrucians (Rose Cross)!

As may be judged, however, from the most important, as the best
known of the Rosicrucians' symbols, there is one which has never been
hitherto understood even by modern mystics. It is that of the "Pelican"
tearing open its breast to feed its seven little ones—the real creed of the
Brothers of the Rosie-Cross and a direct outcome from the Eastern

* Thus Spencer, who, nevertheless, like Schopenhauer and von Hartmann, only
reflects an aspect of the old esoteric philosophers, and hence lands his readers on the
bleak shore of Agnostic despair—reverently formulates the grand mystery ; " that which
persists unchanging in quantity, but ever changing in form, under these sensible appearances which the Universe presents to us, is an unknown and unknowable power, which
we are obliged to recognise as without limit in Space and without beginning or end in
time." It is only daring Theology—never Science or philosophy—which seeks to
gauge the Infinite and unveil the Fathomless and Unknowable.

Secret Doctrine. Brahma (neuter) is called Kalahansa, meaning, as explained by Western Orientalists, the Eternal Swan or goose (see Stanza III., Comment. 8), and so is Brahmâ, the Creator. A great mistake is thus brought under notice; it is Brahma (neuter) who ought to be referred to as Hansa-vahana (He who uses the swan as his Vehicle) and not Brahmâ the Creator, who is the real Kalahansa, while Brahma (neuter) is hamsa, and "A-hamsa," as will be explained in the Commentary. Let it be understood that the terms Brahmâ and Parabrahmam are not used here because they belong to our Esoteric nomenclature, but simply because they are more familiar to the students in the West. Both are the perfect equivalents of our one, three, and seven vowelled terms, which stand for the ONE ALL, and the One "All in all."

Such are the basic conceptions on which the Secret Doctrine rests.

It would not be in place here to enter upon any defence or proof of their inherent reasonableness; nor can I pause to show how they are, in fact, contained—though too often under a misleading guise—in every system of thought or philosophy worthy of the name.

Once that the reader has gained a clear comprehension of them and realised the light which they throw on every problem of life, they will need no further justification in his eyes, because their truth will be to him as evident as the sun in heaven. I pass on, therefore, to the subject matter of the Stanzas as given in this volume, adding a skeleton outline of them, in the hope of thereby rendering the task of the student more easy, by placing before him in a few words the general conception therein explained.

Stanza I. The history of cosmic evolution, as traced in the Stanzas, is, so to say, the abstract algebraical formula of that Evolution. Hence the student must not expect to find there an account of all the stages and transformations which intervene between the first beginnings of "Universal" evolution and our present state. To give such an account would be as impossible as it would be incomprehensible to men who cannot even grasp the nature of the plane of existence next to that to which, for the moment, their consciousness is limited.

The Stanzas, therefore, give an abstract formula which can be applied, *mutatis mutandis*, to all evolution: to that of our tiny earth, to

that of the chain of planets of which that earth forms one, ₁
Universe to which that chain belongs, and so on, in an ascendₙ
till the mind reels and is exhausted in the effort.

The seven Stanzas given in this volume represent the seven termₛ
this abstract formula. They refer to, and describe the seven stageₛ
of the evolutionary process, which are spoken of in the Purânas as the
" Seven Creations," and in the Bible as the " Days " of Creation.

The First Stanza describes the state of the ONE ALL during Pralaya,
before the first flutter of re-awakening manifestation.

A moment's thought shows that such a state can only be symbolised;
to describe it is impossible. Nor can it be symbolised except in negatives ; for, since it is the state of Absoluteness *per se*, it can possess none
of those specific attributes which serve us to describe objects in positive
terms. Hence that state can only be suggested by the negatives of all
those most abstract attributes which men feel rather than conceive, as
the remotest limits attainable by their power of conception.

The stage described in Stanza II. is, to a western mind, so nearly
identical with that mentioned in the first Stanza, that to express the
idea of its difference would require a treatise in itself. Hence it must
be left to the intuition and the higher faculties of the reader to grasp,
as far as he can, the meaning of the allegorical phrases used. Indeed it
must be remembered that all these Stanzas appeal to the inner faculties
rather than to the ordinary comprehension of the physical brain.

Stanza III. describes the Re-awakening of the Universe to life
after Pralaya. It depicts the emergence of the " Monads " from thei
state of absorption within the ONE ; the earliest and highest stage in the
formation of " Worlds," the term Monad being one which may apply
equally to the vastest Solar System or the tiniest atom.

Stanza IV. shows the differentiation of the " Germ " of the Universe into the septenary hierarchy of conscious Divine Powers, who are the active manifestations of the One Supreme Energy. They are the framers, shapers, and ultimately the creators of all the manifested Universe, in the only sense in which the name " Creator " is intelligible; they inform and guide it; they are the intelligent Beings who adjust and control evolution, embodying in themselves those manifestations of the ONE LAW, which we know as " The Laws of Nature."

Generically, they are known as the Dhyan Chohans, though each of the various groups has its own designation in the Secret Doctrine.

This stage of evolution is spoken of in Hindu mythology as the " Creation " of the Gods.

In Stanza V. the process of world-formation is described:—First, diffused Cosmic Matter, then the fiery " whirlwind," the first stage in the formation of a nebula. That nebula condenses, and after passing through various transformations, forms a Solar Universe, a planetary chain, or a single planet, as the case may be.

The subsequent stages in the formation of a " World " are indicated in Stanza VI., which brings the evolution of such a world down to its fourth great period, corresponding to the period in which we are now living.

Stanza VII. continues the history, tracing the descent of life down to the appearance of Man ; and thus closes the first Book of the Secret Doctrine.

The development of " Man " from his first appearance on this earth in this Round to the state in which we now find him will form the subject of Book II.

NOTE.

The Stanzas which form the thesis of every section are given throughout in their modern translated version, as it would be worse than useless to make the subject still more difficult by introducing the archaic phraseology of the original, with its puzzling style and words. Extracts are given from the Chinese Thibetan and Sanskrit translations of the original Senzar Commentaries and Glosses on the Book of DZYAN —these being now rendered for the first time into a European language. It is almost unnecessary to state that only portions of the seven Stanzas are here given. Were they published complete they would remain incomprehensible to all save the few higher occultists. Nor is there any need to assure the reader that, no more than most of the profane, does the writer, or rather the humble recorder, understand those forbidden passages. To facilitate the reading, and to avoid the too frequent reference to foot-notes, it was thought best to blend together texts and glosses, using the Sanskrit and Tibetan proper names whenever those cannot be avoided, in preference to giving the originals. The more so as the said terms are all accepted synonyms, the former only being used between a Master and his chelas (or disciples).

Thus, were one to translate into English, using only the substantives and technical terms as employed in one of the Tibetan and Senzar versions, Verse 1 would read as follows :—" Tho-ag in Zhi-gyu slept seven Khorlo. Zodmanas zhiba. All Nyug bosom. Konch-hog not ; Thyan-Kam not ; Lha-Chohan not ; Tenbrel Chugnyi not ; Dharmakaya ceased ; Tgenchang not become ; Barnang and Ssa in Ngovonyidj ; alone Tho-og Yinsin in night of Sun-chan and Yong-grub (Parinish-panna), &c., &c.," which would sound like pure *Abracadabra*.

As this work is written for the instruction of students of Occultism, and not for the benefit of philologists, we may well avoid such foreign terms wherever it is possible to do so. The untranslateable terms alone, incomprehensible unless explained in their meanings, are left, but all such terms are rendered in their Sanskrit form. Needless to remind the reader that these are, in almost every case, the late developments of the later language, and pertain to the Fifth Root-Race. Sanskrit, as now known, was not spoken by the Atlanteans, and most of the philosophical terms used in the systems of the India of the post-Mahabharatan period are not found in the Vedas, nor are they to be met with in the original Stanzas, but only their equivalents. The reader who is not a Theosophist, is once more invited to regard all that which follows as a fairy tale, if he likes ; at best as one of the yet unproven speculations of *dreamers ;* and, at the worst, as an additional hypothesis to the many Scientific hypotheses past, present and future, some exploded, others still lingering. It is not in any sense worse than are many of the so called Scientific theories ; and it is in every case more philosophical and probable.

In view of the abundant comments and explanations required, the references to the footnotes are given in the usual way, while the sentences to be commented upon are marked with figures. Additional matter will be found in the Chapters on Symbolism forming Part II., as well as in Part III., these being often more full of information than the text.

———————

PART I.

COSMIC EVOLUTION.

SEVEN STANZAS TRANSLATED WITH COMMENTARIES

FROM THE

SECRET BOOK OF DZYAN.

" Nor Aught nor Nought existed; yon bright sky
   Was not, nor heaven's broad roof outstretched above.
   What covered all? what sheltered? what concealed?
   Was it the water's fathomless abyss?
   There was not death—yet there was nought immortal,
   There was no confine betwixt day and night;
   The only One breathed breathless by itself,
   Other than It there nothing since has been.
   Darkness there was, and all at first was veiled
   In gloom profound—an ocean without light—
   The germ that still lay covered in the husk
   Burst forth, one nature, from the fervent heat.

   . . . .

   Who knows the secret? who proclaimed it here?
   Whence, whence this manifold creation sprang?
   The Gods themselves came later into being—
   Who knows from whence this great creation sprang?
   That, whence all this great creation came,
   Whether Its will created or was mute,
   The Most High Seer that is in highest heaven,
   He knows it—or perchance even He knows not."

    " Gazing into eternity . . .
   Ere the foundations of the earth were laid,
   . . . . .

   Thou wert. And when the subterranean flame
   Shall burst its prison and devour the frame . . .
   Thou shalt be still as Thou wert before
   And knew no change, when time shall be no more.
   Oh! endless thought, divine ETERNITY."

COSMIC EVOLUTION.

In Seven Stanzas translated from the Book of Dzyan.

STANZA I.

1. THE ETERNAL PARENT WRAPPED IN HER EVER INVISIBLE ROBES HAD SLUMBERED ONCE AGAIN FOR SEVEN ETERNITIES.

2. TIME WAS NOT, FOR IT LAY ASLEEP IN THE INFINITE BOSOM OF DURATION.

3. UNIVERSAL MIND WAS NOT, FOR THERE WERE NO AH-HI TO CONTAIN IT.

4. THE SEVEN WAYS TO BLISS WERE NOT. THE GREAT CAUSES OF MISERY WERE NOT, FOR THERE WAS NO ONE TO PRODUCE AND GET ENSNARED BY THEM.

5. DARKNESS ALONE FILLED THE BOUNDLESS ALL, FOR FATHER, MOTHER AND SON WERE ONCE MORE ONE, AND THE SON HAD NOT AWAKENED YET FOR THE NEW WHEEL, AND HIS PILGRIMAGE THEREON.

6. THE SEVEN SUBLIME LORDS AND THE SEVEN TRUTHS HAD CEASED TO BE, AND THE UNIVERSE, THE SON OF NECESSITY, WAS IMMERSED IN PARANISHPANNA, TO BE OUTBREATHED BY THAT WHICH IS AND YET IS NOT. NAUGHT WAS.

7. THE CAUSES OF EXISTENCE HAD BEEN DONE AWAY WITH; THE VISIBLE THAT WAS, AND THE INVISIBLE THAT IS, RESTED IN ETERNAL NON-BEING— THE ONE BEING.

8. ALONE THE ONE FORM OF EXISTENCE STRETCHED BOUNDLESS, INFINITE, CAUSELESS, IN DREAMLESS SLEEP; AND LIFE PULSATED UNCONSCIOUS IN UNIVERSAL SPACE, THROUGHOUT THAT ALL-PRESENCE WHICH IS SENSED BY THE OPENED EYE OF THE DANGMA.

9. BUT WHERE WAS THE DANGMA WHEN THE ALAYA OF THE UNIVERSE WAS IN PARAMARTHA AND THE GREAT WHEEL WAS ANUPADAKA?

STANZA II.

1. . . . WHERE WERE THE BUILDERS, THE LUMINOUS SONS OF MANVANTARIC DAWN ? . . . IN THE UNKNOWN DARKNESS IN THEIR AH-HI PARANISHPANNA. THE PRODUCERS OF FORM FROM NO-FORM—THE ROOT OF THE WORLD—THE DEVAMATRI AND SVÂBHÂVAT, RESTED IN THE BLISS OF NON-BEING.

2. . . . WHERE WAS SILENCE ? WHERE THE EARS TO SENSE IT ? NO, THERE WAS NEITHER SILENCE NOR SOUND ; NAUGHT SAVE CEASELESS ETERNAL BREATH, WHICH KNOWS ITSELF NOT.

3. THE HOUR HAD NOT YET STRUCK ; THE RAY HAD NOT YET FLASHED INTO THE GERM ; THE MATRIPADMA HAD NOT YET SWOLLEN.

4. HER HEART HAD NOT YET OPENED FOR THE ONE RAY TO ENTER, THENCE TO FALL, AS THREE INTO FOUR, INTO THE LAP OF MAYA.

5. THE SEVEN SONS WERE NOT YET BORN FROM THE WEB OF LIGHT. DARKNESS ALONE WAS FATHER-MOTHER, SVÂBHÂVAT ; AND SVÂBHÂVAT WAS IN DARKNESS.

6. THESE TWO ARE THE GERM, AND THE GERM IS ONE. THE UNIVERSE WAS STILL CONCEALED IN THE DIVINE THOUGHT AND THE DIVINE BOSOM. . . .

STANZA III.

1. . . . THE LAST VIBRATION OF THE SEVENTH ETERNITY THRILLS THROUGH INFINITUDE. THE MOTHER SWELLS, EXPANDING FROM WITHIN WITHOUT, LIKE THE BUD OF THE LOTUS.

2. THE VIBRATION SWEEPS ALONG, TOUCHING WITH ITS SWIFT WING THE WHOLE UNIVERSE AND THE GERM THAT DWELLETH IN DARKNESS : THE DARKNESS THAT BREATHES OVER THE SLUMBERING WATERS OF LIFE. . .

3. DARKNESS RADIATES LIGHT, AND LIGHT DROPS ONE SOLITARY RAY INTO THE MOTHER-DEEP. THE RAY SHOOTS THROUGH THE VIRGIN EGG THE RAY CAUSES THE ETERNAL EGG TO THRILL, AND DROP THE NON-ETERNAL GERM, WHICH CONDENSES INTO THE WORLD-EGG.

4. Then the three fall into the four. The radiant essence becomes seven inside, seven outside. The luminous egg, which in itself is three, curdles and spreads in milk-white curds throughout the depths of Mother, the root that grows in the depths of the ocean of life.

5. The root remains, the light remains, the curds remain, and still Oeaohoo is one.

6. The root of life was in every drop of the ocean of immortality, and the ocean was radiant light, which was fire, and heat, and motion. Darkness vanished and was no more; it disappeared in its own essence, the body of fire and water, or father and mother.

7. Behold, oh Lanoo! The radiant child of the two, the unparalleled refulgent glory: Bright Space Son of Dark Space, which emerges from the depths of the great dark waters. It is Oeaohoo the younger, the * * * He shines forth as the son; he is the blazing Divine Dragon of Wisdom; the One is Four, and Four takes to itself Three,† and the Union produces the Sapta, in whom are the seven which become the Tridasa (or the hosts and the multitudes). Behold him lifting the veil and unfurling it from east to west. He shuts out the above, and leaves the below to be seen as the great illusion. He marks the places for the shining ones, and turns the upper into a shoreless sea of fire, and the one manifested into the great waters.

8. Where was the germ and where was now darkness? Where is the spirit of the flame that burns in thy lamp, oh Lanoo? The germ is that, and that is light, the white brillant son of the dark hidden father.

9. Light is cold flame, and flame is fire, and fire produces heat, which yields water: the water of life in the great mother.

10. Father-Mother spin a web whose upper end is fastened to spirit—the light of the one darkness—and the lower one to its shadowy end, matter; and this web is the universe spun out of the two substances made in one, which is Svâbhâvat.

---

† In the English translation from the Sanskrit the numbers are given in that language, *Eka, Chatur*, etc., etc. It was thought best to give them in English.

11. It expands when the breath of fire is upon it; it contracts when the breath of the mother touches it. Then the sons dissociate and scatter, to return into their mother's bosom at the end of the great day, and re-become one with her; when it is cooling it becomes radiant, and the sons expand and contract through their own selves and hearts; they embrace infinitude.

12. Then Svâbhâvat sends Fohat to harden the atoms. Each is a part of the web. Reflecting the "Self-Existent Lord" like a mirror, each becomes in turn a world.

STANZA IV.

1. . . . . Listen, ye Sons of the Earth, to your instructors—the Sons of the Fire. Learn, there is neither first nor last, for all is one: number issued from no number.

2. Learn what we who descend from the Primordial Seven, we who are born from the Primordial Flame, have learnt from our fathers. . . .

3. From the effulgency of light—the ray of the ever-darkness—sprung in space the re-awakened energies; the one from the egg, the six, and the five. Then the three, the one, the four, the one, the five—the twice seven the sum total. And these are the essences, the flames, the elements, the builders, the numbers, the arupa, the rupa, and the force of Divine Man—the sum total. And from the Divine Man emanated the forms, the sparks, the sacred animals, and the messengers of the sacred fathers within the holy four.

4. This was the army of the voice—the divine mother of the seven. The sparks of the seven are subject to, and the servants of, the first, the second, the third, the fourth, the fifth, the sixth, and the seventh of the seven. These "sparks" are called spheres, triangles, cubes, lines, and modellers; for thus stands the Eternal Nidana—the Oeaohoo, which is:

5. "DARKNESS" THE BOUNDLESS, OR THE NO-NUMBER, ADI-NIDANA SVÂBHÂVAT :—

    I. THE ADI-SANAT, THE NUMBER, FOR HE IS ONE.

    II. THE VOICE OF THE LORD SVÂBHÂVAT, THE NUMBERS, FOR HE IS ONE AND NINE.

    III. THE "FORMLESS SQUARE."

AND THESE THREE ENCLOSED WITHIN THE ◯ ARE THE SACRED FOUR ; AND THE TEN ARE THE ARUPA UNIVERSE. THEN COME THE "SONS," THE SEVEN FIGHTERS, THE ONE, THE EIGHTH LEFT OUT, AND HIS BREATH WHICH IS THE LIGHT-MAKER.

6. THEN THE SECOND SEVEN, WHO ARE THE LIPIKA, PRODUCED BY THE THREE. THE REJECTED SON IS ONE. THE "SON-SUNS" ARE COUNTLESS.

———

STANZA V.

1. THE PRIMORDIAL SEVEN, THE FIRST SEVEN BREATHS OF THE DRAGON OF WISDOM, PRODUCE IN THEIR TURN FROM THEIR HOLY CIRCUMGYRATING BREATHS THE FIERY WHIRLWIND.

2. THEY MAKE OF HIM THE MESSENGER OF THEIR WILL. THE DZYU BECOMES FOHAT, THE SWIFT SON OF THE DIVINE SONS WHOSE SONS ARE THE LIPIKA, RUNS CIRCULAR ERRANDS. FOHAT IS THE STEED AND THE THOUGHT IS THE RIDER. HE PASSES LIKE LIGHTNING THROUGH THE FIERY CLOUDS ; TAKES THREE, AND FIVE, AND SEVEN STRIDES THROUGH THE SEVEN REGIONS ABOVE, AND THE SEVEN BELOW. HE LIFTS HIS VOICE, AND CALLS THE INNUMERABLE SPARKS, AND JOINS THEM.

3. HE IS THEIR GUIDING SPIRIT AND LEADER. WHEN HE COMMENCES WORK, HE SEPARATES THE SPARKS OF THE LOWER KINGDOM THAT FLOAT AND THRILL WITH JOY IN THEIR RADIANT DWELLINGS, AND FORMS THEREWITH THE GERMS OF WHEELS. HE PLACES THEM IN THE SIX DIRECTIONS OF SPACE, AND ONE IN THE MIDDLE—THE CENTRAL WHEEL.

4. FOHAT TRACES SPIRAL LINES TO UNITE THE SIXTH TO THE SEVENTH —THE CROWN; AN ARMY OF THE SONS OF LIGHT STANDS AT EACH ANGLE, AND THE LIPIKA IN THE MIDDLE WHEEL. THEY SAY: THIS IS GOOD, THE

FIRST DIVINE WORLD IS READY, THE FIRST IS NOW THE SECOND. THEN THE "DIVINE ARUPA" REFLECTS ITSELF IN CHHAYA LOKA, THE FIRST GARMENT OF THE ANUPADAKA.

5. FOHAT TAKES FIVE STRIDES AND BUILDS A WINGED WHEEL AT EACH CORNER OF THE SQUARE, FOR THE FOUR HOLY ONES AND THEIR ARMIES.

6. THE LIPIKA CIRCUMSCRIBE THE TRIANGLE, THE FIRST ONE, THE CUBE, THE SECOND ONE, AND THE PENTACLE WITHIN THE EGG. IT IS THE RING CALLED "PASS NOT" FOR THOSE WHO DESCEND AND ASCEND. ALSO FOR THOSE WHO DURING THE KALPA ARE PROGRESSING TOWARDS THE GREAT DAY "BE WITH US." THUS WERE FORMED THE RUPA AND THE ARUPA: FROM ONE LIGHT SEVEN LIGHTS; FROM EACH OF THE SEVEN, SEVEN TIMES SEVEN LIGHTS. THE WHEELS WATCH THE RING. . . . .

STANZA VI.

1. BY THE POWER OF THE MOTHER OF MERCY AND KNOWLEDGE—KWAN-YIN—THE "TRIPLE" OF KWAN-SHAI-YIN, RESIDING IN KWAN-YIN-TIEN, FOHAT, THE BREATH OF THEIR PROGENY, THE SON OF THE SONS, HAVING CALLED FORTH, FROM THE LOWER ABYSS, THE ILLUSIVE FORM OF SIEN-TCHANG AND THE SEVEN ELEMENTS:*

2. THE SWIFT AND RADIANT ONE PRODUCES THE SEVEN LAYA CENTRES, AGAINST WHICH NONE WILL PREVAIL TO THE GREAT DAY "BE-WITH-US," AND SEATS THE UNIVERSE ON THESE ETERNAL FOUNDATIONS SURROUNDING TSIEN-TCHAN WITH THE ELEMENTARY GERMS.

3. OF THE SEVEN—FIRST ONE MANIFESTED, SIX CONCEALED, TWO MANIFESTED, FIVE CONCEALED; THREE MANIFESTED, FOUR CONCEALED; FOUR PRODUCED, THREE HIDDEN; FOUR AND ONE TSAN REVEALED, TWO AND ONE HALF CONCEALED; SIX TO BE MANIFESTED, ONE LAID ASIDE. LASTLY, SEVEN SMALL WHEELS REVOLVING; ONE GIVING BIRTH TO THE OTHER.

* Verse 1 of Stanza VI. is of a far later date than the other Stanzas, though still very ancient. The old text of this verse, having names entirely unknown to the Orientalists would give no clue to the student.

4. HE BUILDS THEM IN THE LIKENESS OF OLDER WHEELS, PLACING THEM ON THE IMPERISHABLE CENTRES.

HOW DOES FOHAT BUILD THEM? HE COLLECTS THE FIERY DUST. HE MAKES BALLS OF FIRE, RUNS THROUGH THEM, AND ROUND THEM, INFUSING LIFE THEREINTO, THEN SETS THEM INTO MOTION; SOME ONE WAY, SOME THE OTHER WAY. THEY ARE COLD, HE MAKES THEM HOT. THEY ARE DRY, HE MAKES THEM MOIST. THEY SHINE, HE FANS AND COOLS THEM. THUS ACTS FOHAT FROM ONE TWILIGHT TO THE OTHER, DURING SEVEN ETERNITIES.

5. AT THE FOURTH, THE SONS ARE TOLD TO CREATE THEIR IMAGES. ONE THIRD REFUSES—TWO OBEY.

THE CURSE IS PRONOUNCED; THEY WILL BE BORN ON THE FOURTH, SUFFER AND CAUSE SUFFERING; THIS IS THE FIRST WAR.

6. THE OLDER WHEELS ROTATED DOWNWARDS AND UPWARDS. . . . THE MOTHER'S SPAWN FILLED THE WHOLE. THERE WERE BATTLES FOUGHT BETWEEN THE CREATORS AND THE DESTROYERS, AND BATTLES FOUGHT FOR SPACE; THE SEED APPEARING AND RE-APPEARING CONTINUOUSLY.

7. MAKE THY CALCULATIONS, LANOO, IF THOU WOULDEST LEARN THE CORRECT AGE OF THY SMALL WHEEL. ITS FOURTH SPOKE IS OUR MOTHER. REACH THE FOURTH "FRUIT" OF THE FOURTH PATH OF KNOWLEDGE THAT LEADS TO NIRVANA, AND THOU SHALT COMPREHEND, FOR THOU SHALT SEE . . . . .

STANZA VII.

1. BEHOLD THE BEGINNING OF SENTIENT FORMLESS LIFE.

FIRST THE DIVINE, THE ONE FROM THE MOTHER-SPIRIT; THEN THE SPIRITUAL; THE THREE FROM THE ONE, THE FOUR FROM THE ONE, AND THE FIVE FROM WHICH THE THREE, THE FIVE, AND THE SEVEN. THESE ARE THE THREE-FOLD, THE FOUR-FOLD DOWNWARD; THE "MIND-BORN" SONS OF THE FIRST LORD; THE SHINING SEVEN.

IT IS THEY WHO ARE THOU, ME, HIM, OH LANOO. THEY, WHO WATCH OVER THEE, AND THY MOTHER EARTH.

2. THE ONE RAY MULTIPLIES THE SMALLER RAYS. LIFE PRECEDES FORM, AND LIFE SURVIVES THE LAST ATOM OF FORM. THROUGH THE COUNTLESS RAYS PROCEEDS THE LIFE-RAY, THE ONE, LIKE A THREAD THROUGH MANY JEWELS.

3. WHEN THE ONE BECOMES TWO, THE THREEFOLD APPEARS, AND THE THREE ARE ONE; AND IT IS OUR THREAD, OH LANOO, THE HEART OF THE MAN-PLANT CALLED SAPTASARMA.

4. IT IS THE ROOT THAT NEVER DIES; THE THREE-TONGUED FLAME OF THE FOUR WICKS. THE WICKS ARE THE SPARKS, THAT DRAW FROM THE THREE-TONGUED FLAME SHOT OUT BY THE SEVEN—THEIR FLAME—THE BEAMS AND SPARKS OF ONE MOON REFLECTED IN THE RUNNING WAVES OF ALL THE RIVERS OF EARTH.

5. THE SPARK HANGS FROM THE FLAME BY THE FINEST THREAD OF FOHAT. IT JOURNEYS THROUGH THE SEVEN WORLDS OF MAYA. IT STOPS IN THE FIRST, AND IS A METAL AND A STONE; IT PASSES INTO THE SECOND AND BEHOLD—A PLANT; THE PLANT WHIRLS THROUGH SEVEN CHANGES AND BECOMES A SACRED ANIMAL. FROM THE COMBINED ATTRIBUTES OF THESE, MANU, THE THINKER IS FORMED. WHO FORMS HIM? THE SEVEN LIVES, AND THE ONE LIFE. WHO COMPLETES HIM? THE FIVE-FOLD LHA. AND WHO PERFECTS THE LAST BODY? FISH, SIN, AND SOMA. . . . .

6. FROM THE FIRST-BORN THE THREAD BETWEEN THE SILENT WATCHER AND HIS SHADOW BECOMES MORE STRONG AND RADIANT WITH EVERY CHANGE. THE MORNING SUN-LIGHT HAS CHANGED INTO NOON-DAY GLORY. . . . .

7. THIS IS THY PRESENT WHEEL, SAID THE FLAME TO THE SPARK. THOU ART MYSELF, MY IMAGE, AND MY SHADOW. I HAVE CLOTHED MYSELF IN THEE, AND THOU ART MY VAHAN TO THE DAY, "BE WITH US," WHEN THOU SHALT RE-BECOME MYSELF AND OTHERS, THYSELF AND ME. THEN THE BUILDERS, HAVING DONNED THEIR FIRST CLOTHING, DESCEND ON RADIANT EARTH AND REIGN OVER MEN—WHO ARE THEMSELVES. . . .

Thus ends this portion of the archaic narrative, dark, confused, almost incomprehensible. An attempt will now be made to throw light into this darkness, to make sense out of this apparent NON-SENSE.

COMMENTARIES

STANZA I.

1. "THE ETERNAL PARENT (Space), WRAPPED IN HER EVER INVISIBLE
ROBES, HAD SLUMBERED ONCE AGAIN FOR SEVEN ETERNITIES (a)."

The "Parent Space" is the eternal, ever present cause of all—the
incomprehensible DEITY, whose "invisible robes" are the mystic root of
all matter, and of the Universe. Space is the *one eternal thing* that we can
most easily imagine, immovable in its abstraction and uninfluenced by
either the presence or absence in it of an objective Universe. It is
without dimension, in every sense, and self-existent. Spirit is the first
differentiation from THAT, the causeless cause of both Spirit and Matter.
It is, as taught in the esoteric catechism, neither limitless void, nor
conditioned fulness, but both. It was and ever will be. (See Proem
pp. 2 *et seq.*)

Thus, the "Robes" stand for the noumenon of undifferentiated
Cosmic Matter. It is not matter as we know it, but the spiritual essence
of matter, and is co-eternal and even one with Space in its abstract
sense. Root-nature is also the source of the subtile invisible properties
in visible matter. It is the Soul, so to say, of the ONE infinite Spirit.
The Hindus call it Mulaprakriti, and say that it is the primordial substance, which is the basis of the Upadhi or vehicle of every phenomenon, whether physical, mental or psychic. It is the source from which
Akâsa radiates.

(a) By the Seven "Eternities," æons or periods are meant. The word
"Eternity," as understood in Christian theology, has no meaning to
the Asiatic ear, except in its application to the ONE existence; nor is

the term sempiternity, the eternal only in futurity, anything better than
a misnomer.* Such words do not and cannot exist in philosophical
metaphysics, and were unknown till the advent of ecclesiastical
Christianity. The Seven Eternities meant are the seven periods, or a
period answering in its duration to the seven periods, of a Manvantara,
and extending throughout a Maha-Kalpa or the "Great Age"—100
years of Brahmâ—making a total of 311,040,000,000,000 of years ; each
year of Brahmâ being composed of 360 "days," and of the same
number of "nights" of Brahmâ (reckoning by the Chandrayana or lunar
year) ; and a "Day of Brahmâ" consisting of 4,320,000,000 of mortal
years. These "Eternities" belong to the most secret calculations, in
which, in order to arrive at the true total, every figure must be 7^x (7 to
the power of x) ; x varying according to the nature of the cycle in the
subjective or real world ; and every figure or number relating to, or
representing all the different cycles from the greatest to the smallest—
in the objective or unreal world—must necessarily be multiples of seven.
The key to this cannot be given, for herein lies the mystery of esoteric
calculations, and for the purposes of ordinary calculation it has no
sense. "The number seven," says the Kabala, "is the great number of
the Divine Mysteries ;" number ten is that of all human knowledge
(Pythagorean decade) ; 1,000 is the number ten to the third power, and
therefore the number 7,000 is also symbolical. In the Secret Doctrine
the figure and number 4 are the male symbol only on the highest plane
of abstraction ; on the plane of matter the 3 is the masculine and the 4
the female : the upright and the horizontal in the fourth stage of
symbolism, when the symbols became the glyphs of the generative
powers on the physical plane.

STANZA I.—*Continued.*

2. Time was not, for it lay asleep in the infinite bosom of
duration (*a*).

---

*It is stated in Book II., ch. viii., of Vishnu Purâna : "By immortality is meant
existence to the end of the Kalpa ;" and Wilson, the translator, remarks in a foot-
note : "This, according to the Vedas, is all that is to be understood of the immortality
(or eternity) of the gods ; they perish at the end of universal dissolution (or
Pralaya)." And Esoteric philosophy says : They "perish" not, but are *re-absorbed.*

(*a*) Time is only an illusion produced by the succession of our states of consciousness as we travel through eternal duration, and it does not exist where no consciousness exists in which the illusion can be produced; but "lies asleep." The present is only a mathematical line which divides that part of eternal duration which we call the future, from that part which we call the past. Nothing on earth has real duration, for nothing remains without change—or the same—for the billionth part of a second; and the sensation we have of the actuality of the division of " time " known as the present, comes from the blurring of that momentary glimpse, or succession of glimpses, of things that our senses give us, as those things pass from the region of ideals which we call the future, to the region of memories that we name the past. In the same way we experience a sensation of duration in the case of the instantaneous electric spark, by reason of the blurred and continuing impression on the retina. The real person or thing does not consist solely of what is seen at any particular moment, but is composed of the sum of all its various and changing conditions from its appearance in the material form to its disappearance from the earth. It is these " sumtotals " that exist from eternity in the " future," and pass by degrees through matter, to exist for eternity in the " past." No one could say that a bar of metal dropped into the sea came into existence as it left the air, and ceased to exist as it entered the water, and that the bar itself consisted only of that cross-section thereof which at any given moment coincided with the mathematical plane that separates, and, at the same time, joins, the atmosphere and the ocean. Even so of persons and things, which, dropping out of the to-be into the has-been, out of the future into the past—present momentarily to our senses a cross-section, as it were, of their total selves, as they pass through time and space (as matter) on their way from one eternity to another : and these two constitute that " duration " in which alone anything has true existence, were our senses but able to cognize it there.

STANZA I.—*Continued.*

3. . . . Universal mind was not, for there were no Ah-hi (celestial beings) to contain (hence to manifest) it (*a*).

(*a*) Mind is a name given to the sum of the states of Consciousness grouped under Thought, Will, and Feeling. During deep sleep, ideation ceases on the physical plane, and memory is in abeyance; thus for the time-being "Mind is not," because the organ, through which the Ego manifests ideation and memory on the material plane, has temporarily ceased to function. A noumenon can become a phenomenon on any plane of existence only by manifesting on that plane through an appropiate basis or vehicle; and during the long night of rest called Pralaya, when all the existences are dissolved, the "UNIVERSAL MIND" remains as a permanent possibility of mental action, or as that abstract absolute thought, of which mind is the concrete relative manifestation. The AH-HI (Dhyan-Chohans) are the collective hosts of spiritual beings —the Angelic Hosts of Christianity, the Elohim and "Messengers" of the Jews—who are the vehicle for the manifestation of the divine or universal thought and will. They are the Intelligent Forces that give to and enact in Nature her "laws," while themselves acting according to laws imposed upon them in a similar manner by still higher Powers; but they are not "the personifications" of the powers of Nature, as erroneously thought. This hierarchy of spiritual Beings, through which the Universal Mind comes into action, is like an army—a "Host," truly—by means of which the fighting power of a nation manifests itself, and which is composed of army corps, divisions, brigades, regiments, and so forth, each with its separate individuality or life, and its limited freedom of action and limited responsibilities; each contained in a larger individuality, to which its own interests are subservient, and each containing lesser individualities in itself.

STANZA I.—*Continued.*

4. THE SEVEN WAYS TO BLISS (Moksha* or Nirvana) WERE NOT (*a*). THE GREAT CAUSES OF MISERY (Nidana† and Maya) WERE NOT, FOR THERE WAS NO ONE TO PRODUCE AND GET ENSNARED BY THEM (*b*).

(*a*) There are seven "Paths" or "Ways" to the bliss of Non-Exist-

* Nippang in China; Neibban in Burmah; or Moksha in India.

† The "12" Nidanas (in Tibetan Ten-brel chug-nyi) the chief causes of existence, effects generated by a concatenation of causes produced (see Comment. II).

ence, which is absolute Being, Existence, and Consciousness. They were not, because the Universe was, so far, empty, and existed only in the Divine Thought. For it is . . .

(b) The twelve Nidanas or causes of being. Each is the effect of its antecedent cause, and a cause, in its turn, to its successor; the sum total of the Nidanas being based on the four truths, a doctrine especially characteristic of the Hînayâna System.* They belong to the theory of the stream of catenated law which produces merit and demerit, and finally brings Karma into full sway. It is based upon the great truth that re-incarnation is to be dreaded, as existence in this world only entails upon man suffering, misery and pain; Death itself being unable to deliver man from it, since death is merely the door through which he passes to another life on earth after a little rest on its threshold —Devachan. The Hînayâna System, or School of the " Little Vehicle," is of very ancient growth; while the Mahâyânâ is of a later period, having originated after the death of Buddha. Yet the tenets of the latter are as old as the hills that have contained such schools from time immemorial, and the Hînayâna and Mahâyânâ Schools (the latter, that of the " Great Vehicle ") both teach the same doctrine in reality. Yana, or Vehicle (in Sanskrit, Vahan) is a mystic expression, both " vehicles " inculcating that man may escape the sufferings of rebirths and even the false bliss of Devachan, by obtaining Wisdom and Know-ledge, which alone can dispel the Fruits of Illusion and Ignorance.

Maya or illusion is an element which enters into all finite things, for everything that exists has only a relative, not an absolute, reality, since the appearance which the hidden noumenon assumes for any observer depends upon his power of cognition. To the untrained eye of the savage, a painting is at first an unmeaning confusion of streaks and daubs of colour, while an educated eye sees instantly a face or a lands-cape. Nothing is permanent except the one hidden absolute existence which contains in itself the noumena of all realities. The existences belonging to every plane of being, up to the highest Dhyan-Chohans, are, in degree, of the nature of shadows cast by a magic lantern on a colourless screen; but all things are relatively real, for the cogniser is also a reflection, and the things cognised are therefore as real to him as himself. Whatever reality things possess must be looked for. in them

---

* See Wassilief on Buddhism, pp. 97—950.

before or after they have passed like a flash through the material world;
but we cannot cognise any such existence directly, so long as we have
sense-instruments which bring only material existence into the field of
our consciousness. Whatever plane our consciousness may be acting
in, both we and the things belonging to that plane are, for the time
being, our only realities. As we rise in the scale of development we
perceive that during the stages through which we have passed we
mistook shadows for realities, and the upward progress of the Ego is a
series of progressive awakenings, each advance bringing with it the idea
that now, at last, we have reached " reality ; " but only when we shall
nave reached the absolute Consciousness, and blended our own with it,
shall we be free from the delusions produced by Maya.

STANZA I.—*Continued*.

5. DARKNESS ALONE FILLED THE BOUNDLESS ALL (*a*), FOR FATHER,
MOTHER AND SON WERE ONCE MORE ONE, AND THE SON HAD NOT
AWAKENED YET FOR THE NEW WHEEL* AND HIS PILGRIMAGE THEREON
(*b*).

(*a*) " Darkness is Father-Mother: light their son," says an old Eastern
proverb. Light is inconceivable except as coming from some source
which is the cause of it ; and as, in the instance of primordial light, that
source is unknown, though as strongly demanded by reason and logic,
therefore it is called " Darkness " by us, from an intellectual point of
view. As to borrowed or secondary light, whatever its source, it can be
but of a temporary mayavic character. Darkness, then, is the eternal

------

* That which is called " wheel " is the symbolical expression for a world or globe,
which shows that the ancients were aware that our Earth was a revolving globe, not
a motionless square as some Christian Fathers taught. The " Great Wheel " is the
whole duration of our Cycle of being, or Maha Kalpa, *i.e.*, the whole revolution of our
special chain of seven planets or Spheres from beginning to end ; the " Small Wheels "
meaning the Rounds, of which there are also Seven.

matrix in which the sources of light appear and disappear. Nothing is added to darkness to make of it light, or to light to make it darkness, on this our plane. They are interchangeable, and scientifically light is but a mode of darkness and *vice versâ*. Yet both are phenomena of the same noumenon—which is absolute darkness to the scientific mind, and but a gray twilight to the perception of the average mystic, though to that of the spiritual eye of the Initiate it is absolute light. How far we discern the light that shines in darkness depends upon our powers of vision. What is light to us is darkness to certain insects, and the eye of the clairvoyant sees illumination where the normal eye perceives only blackness. When the whole universe was plunged in sleep—had returned to its one primordial element—there was neither centre of luminosity, nor eye to perceive light, and darkness necessarily filled the boundless all.

(*b*) The Father-Mother are the male and female principles in root-nature, the opposite poles that manifest in all things on every plane of Kosmos, or Spirit and Substance, in a less allegorical aspect, the resultant of which is the Universe, or the Son. They are " once more One " when in " The Night of Brahmâ," during Pralaya, all in the objective Universe has returned to its one primal and eternal cause, to reappear at the following Dawn—as it does periodically. " Karana "—eternal cause—was alone. To put it more plainly: Karana is alone during the " Nights of Brahmâ." The previous objective Universe has dissolved into its one primal and eternal cause, and is, so to say, held in solution in space, to differentiate again and crystallize out anew at the following Manvantaric dawn, which is the commencement of a new " Day " or new activity of Brahmâ—the symbol of the Universe. In esoteric parlance, Brahmâ is Father-Mother-Son, or Spirit, Soul and Body at once; each personage being symbolical of an attribute, and each attribute or quality being a graduated efflux of Divine Breath in its cyclic differentiation, involutionary and evolutionary. In the cosmico-physical sense, it is the Universe, the planetary chain and the earth; in the purely spiritual, the Unknown Deity, Planetary Spirit, and Man—the Son of the two, the creature of Spirit and Matter, and a manifestation of them in his periodical appearances on Earth during the " wheels," or the Manvantaras.—(*See* Part II. § : " *Days and Nights of Brahmâ.*")

STANZA I.—*Continued.*

6. The seven sublime Lords and the seven Truths had ceased to be (*a*), and the Universe, the son of necessity, was immersed in Paranishpanna (*b*) (absolute perfection, Paranirvana, which is Yong-Grüb) to be out-breathed by that which is and yet is not. Naught was (*c*).

(*a*) The seven sublime lords are the Seven Creative Spirits, the Dhyan-Chohans, who correspond to the Hebrew Elohim. It is the same hierarchy of Archangels to which St. Michael, St. Gabriel, and others belong, in the Christian theogony. Only while St. Michael, for instance, is allowed in dogmatic Latin theology to watch over all the promontories and gulfs, in the Esoteric System, the Dhyanis watch successively over one of the Rounds and the great Root-races of our planetary chain. They are, moreover, said to send their Bhodisatvas, the human correspondents of the Dhyani-Buddhas (of whom *vide infra*) during every Round and Race. Out of the Seven Truths and Revelations, or rather revealed secrets, four only have been handed to us, as we are still in the Fourth Round, and the world also has only had four Buddhas, so far. This is a very complicated question, and will receive more ample treatment later on.

So far " There are only Four Truths, and Four Vedas "—say the Hindus and Buddhists. For a similar reason Irenæus insisted on the necessity of Four Gospels. But as every new Root-race at the head of a Round must have its revelation and revealers, the next Round will bring the Fifth, the following the Sixth, and so on.

(*b*) "*Paranishpanna*" is the absolute perfection to which all existences attain at the close of a great period of activity, or Maha-Manvantara, and in which they rest during the succeeding period of repose. In Tibetan it is called Yong-Grüb. Up to the day of the Yogâchârya school the true nature of Paranirvana was taught publicly, but since then it has become entirely esoteric ; hence so many contradictory interpretations of it. It is only a true Idealist who can understand it. Everything has to be viewed as ideal, with the exception of Paranirvana, by him who would comprehend that state, and acquire a knowledge of how Non Ego, Voidness, and Darkness are Three in One and alone Self-existent and perfect. It is absolute, however, only in a relative sense, for it must give room to still further absolute perfection, according to a higher standard of excellence in the following period of activity—just as a perfect flower must cease to be a perfect flower and die, in order to grow into a perfect fruit,—if a somewhat Irish mode of expression may be permitted.

The Secret Doctrine teaches the progressive development of everything, worlds as well as atoms; and this stupendous development has neither conceivable beginning nor imaginable end. Our "Universe" is only one of an infinite number of Universes, all of them "Sons of Necessity," because links in the great Cosmic chain of Universes, each one standing in the relation of an effect as regards its predecessor, and being a cause as regards its successor.

The appearance and disappearance of the Universe are pictured as an outbreathing and inbreathing of "the Great Breath," which is eternal, and which, being Motion, is one of the three aspects of the Absolute—Abstract Space and Duration being the other two. When the "Great Breath" is projected, it is called the Divine Breath, and is regarded as the breathing of the Unknowable Deity—the One Existence—which breathes out a thought, as it were, which becomes the Kosmos. (See "Isis Unveiled.") So also is it when the Divine Breath is inspired again the Universe disappears into the bosom of "the Great Mother," who then sleeps "wrapped in her invisible robes."

(c) By "that which is and yet is not" is meant the Great Breath itself, which we can only speak of as absolute existence, but cannot picture to our imagination as any form of existence that we can distinguish from Non-existence. The three periods—the Present, the Past, and the Future—are in the esoteric philosophy a compound time; for the three are a composite number only in relation to the phenomenal plane, but in the realm of noumena have no abstract validity. As said in the Scriptures: "The Past time is the Present time, as also the Future, which, though it has not come into existence, still is"; according to a precept in the Prasanga Madhyamika teaching, whose dogmas have been known ever since it broke away from the purely esoteric schools.* Our ideas, in short, on duration and time are all derived from our

---

* See Dzungarian "Mani Kumbum," the "Book of the 10,000 Precepts." Also consult Wassilief's "Der Buddhismus," pp. 327 and 357, etc.

sensations according to the laws of Association. Inextricably bound up with the relativity of human knowledge, they nevertheless can have no existence except in the experience of the individual ego, and perish when its evolutionary march dispels the Maya of phenomenal existence. What is Time, for instance, but the panoramic succession of our states of consciousness? In the words of a Master, "I feel irritated at having to use these three clumsy words—Past, Present, and Future—miserable concepts of the objective phases of the subjective whole, they are about as ill-adapted for the purpose as an axe for fine carving." One has to acquire *Paramârtha* lest one should become too easy a prey to *Samvriti*— is a philosophical axiom.*

STANZA I.—*Continued.*

7. THE CAUSES OF EXISTENCE HAD BEEN DONE AWAY WITH (*a*); THE VISIBLE THAT WAS, AND THE INVISIBLE THAT IS, RESTED IN ETERNAL NON-BEING, THE ONE BEING (*b*).

(*a*) "The Causes of Existence" mean not only the physical causes known to science, but the metaphysical causes, the chief of which is the desire to exist, an outcome of Nidana and Maya. This desire for a sentient life shows itself in everything, from an atom to a sun, and is a reflection of the Divine Thought propelled into objective existence, into a law that the Universe should exist. According to esoteric teaching, the real cause of that supposed desire, and of all existence, remains for ever hidden, and its first emanations are the most complete abstractions mind can conceive. These abstractions must of necessity be postulated as the cause of the material Universe which presents itself to the senses and intellect; and they underlie the secondary and subordinate powers of Nature, which, anthropomorphized, have been worshipped as God and gods by the common herd of every age. It is impossible to conceive anything without a cause; the attempt to do so makes the mind a blank.

---

* In clearer words: "One has to acquire true Self-Consciousness in order to understand *Samvriti,* or the 'origin of delusion.'" *Paramârtha* is the synonym of the Sanskrit term *Svasam-vedana,* or "the reflection which analyses itself." There is a difference in the interpretation of the meaning of "*Paramârtha*" between the Yogâ-châryas and the Madhyamikas, neither of whom, however, explain the real and true esoteric sense of the expression. See further, sloka No. 9.

This is virtually the condition to which the mind must come at last when we try to trace back the chain of causes and effects, but both science and religion jump to this condition of blankness much more quickly than is necessary; for they ignore the metaphysical abstractions which are the only conceivable cause of physical concretions. These abstractions become more and more concrete as they approach our plane of existence, until finally they phenomenalise in the form of the material Universe, by a process of conversion of metaphysics into physics, analogous to that by which steam can be condensed into water, and the water frozen into ice.

(*b*) The idea of Eternal Non-Being, which is the One Being, will appear a paradox to anyone who does not remember that we limit our ideas of being to our present consciousness of existence; making it a specific, instead of a generic term. An unborn infant, could it think in our acceptation of that term, would necessarily limit its conception of being, in a similar manner, to the intra-uterine life which alone it knows; and were it to endeavour to express to its consciousness the idea of life after birth (death to it), it would, in the absence of data to go upon, and of faculties to comprehend such data, probably express that life as " Non-Being which is Real Being." In our case the One Being is the noumenon of all the noumena which we know must underlie phenomena, and give them whatever shadow of reality they possess, but which we have not the senses or the intellect to cognize at present. The impalpable atoms of gold scattered through the substance of a ton of auriferous quartz may be imperceptible to the naked eye of the miner, yet he knows that they are not only present there but that they alone give his quartz any appreciable value; and this relation of the gold to the quartz may faintly shadow forth that of the noumenon to the phenomenon. But the miner knows what the gold will look like when extracted from the quartz, whereas the common mortal can form no conception of the reality of things separated from the Maya which veils them, and in which they are hidden. Alone the Initiate, rich with the lore acquired by numberless generations of his predecessors, directs the " Eye of Dangma " toward the essence of things in which no Maya can have any influence. It is here that the teachings of esoteric philosophy in relation to the Nidanas and the Four Truths become of the greatest importance; but they are secret.

STANZA I.—*Continued.*

8. ALONE, THE ONE FORM OF EXISTENCE STRETCHED BOUNDLESS, INFI-
NITE, CAUSELESS, IN DREAMLESS SLEEP (*a*); AND LIFE PULSATED UNCON-
SCIOUS IN UNIVERSAL SPACE, THROUGHOUT THAT ALL-PRESENCE WHICH IS
SENSED BY THE "OPENED EYE"* OF THE DANGMA (*b*).†

(*a*) The tendency of modern thought is to recur to the archaic idea of a
homogeneous basis for apparently widely different things—heterogeneity
developed from homogeneity. Biologists are now searching for their
homogeneous protoplasm and chemists for their protyle, while science is
looking for the force of which electricity, magnetism, heat, and so forth,
are the differentiations. The Secret Doctrine carries this idea into the
region of metaphysics and postulates a "One Form of Existence" as
the basis and source of all things. But perhaps the phrase, the "One
Form of Existence," is not altogether correct. The Sanskrit word is
Prabhavapyaya, "the place, or rather plane, whence emerges the
origination, and into which is the resolution of all things," says a commentator. It is not the "Mother of the World," as translated by
Wilson (see Book I., Vishnu Purana); for Jagad Yoni (as shown by
FitzEdward Hall) is scarcely so much "the Mother of the World" or
"the Womb of the World" as the "Material Cause of the Universe."
The Purânic Commentators explain it by Karana—"Cause"—but the
Esoteric philosophy, by the *ideal spirit of that cause*. It is, in its
secondary stage, the Svâbhâvat of the Buddhist philosopher, the
eternal cause and effect, omnipresent yet abstract, the self-existent
plastic Essence and the root of all things, viewed in the same dual light
as the Vedantin views his Parabrahm and Mulaprakriti, the one under
two aspects. It seems indeed extraordinary to find great scholars
speculating on the possibility of the Vedanta, and the Uttara-Mimansa
especially, having been "evoked by the teachings of the Buddhists,"

---

* In India it is called "The Eye of Siva," but beyond the great range it is known as
"Dangma's opened eye" in esoteric phraseology.

† Dangma means a purified soul, one who has become a Jivanmukta, the highest
adept, or rather a Mahatma so-called. His "opened eye" is the inner spiritual eye of
the seer, and the faculty which manifests through it is not clairvoyance as ordinarily
understood, *i.e.*, the power of seeing at a distance, but rather the faculty of spiritual
intuition, through which direct and certain knowledge is obtainable. This faculty is
intimately connected with the "third eye," which mythological tradition ascribes to
certain races of men. Fuller explanations will be found in Book II.

whereas, it is on the contrary Buddhism (of Gautama, the Buddha) that was "evoked" and entirely upreared on the tenets of the Secret Doctrine, of which a partial sketch is here attempted, and on which, also, the Upanishads are made to rest.* The above, according to the teachings of Sri Sankarâchârya,† is undeniable.

(b) Dreamless sleep is one of the seven states of consciousness known in Oriental esotericism. In each of these states a different portion of the mind comes into action ; or as a Vedantin would express it, the individual is conscious in a different plane of his being. The term "dreamless sleep," in this case is applied allegorically to the Universe to express a condition somewhat analogous to that state of consciousness in man, which, not being remembered in a waking state, seems a blank, just as the sleep of the mesmerised subject seems to him an unconscious blank when he returns to his normal condition, although he has been talking and acting as a conscious individual would.

STANZA I.—*Continued.*

9. BUT WHERE WAS THE DANGMA WHEN THE ALAYA OF THE UNIVERSE *(Soul as the basis of all, Anima Mundi)* WAS IN PARAMARTHA (a) *(Absolute Being and Consciousness which are Absolute Non-Being and Unconsciousness)* AND THE GREAT WHEEL WAS ANUPADAKA (b) ?

* And yet, one, *claiming authority*, namely, Sir Monier Williams, Boden Professor of Sanskrit at Oxford, has just denied this fact. This is what he taught his audience, on June the 4th, 1888, in his annual address before the Victoria Institute of Great Britain : "Originally, Buddhism set its face against all solitary asceticism . . . to attain sublime heights of knowledge. It *had no occult, no esoteric system* of doctrine . . . withheld from ordinary men " (! !) And, again : ". . . When Gautama Buddha began his career, the *later and lower* form of Yoga seems to have been little known." And then, contradicting himself, the learned lecturer forthwith informs his audience that "We learn from *Lalita-Vistâra* that various forms of bodily torture, self-maceration, and austerity were common in Gautama's time." (! !) But the lecturer seems quite unaware that this kind of torture and self-maceration is precisely the *lower* form of Yoga, *Hatha* Yoga, which was "little known" and yet so "*common*" in Gautama's time.

† It is even argued that all the Six Darsanas (Schools of philosophy) show traces of Buddha's influence, being either taken from Buddhism or due to Greek teaching ! (See Weber, Max Müller, etc.) We labour under the impression that Colebrooke, "the highest authority" in such matters, had long ago settled the question by showing, that "the Hindus were in this instance the teachers, not the learners."

(*a*) Here we have before us the subject of centuries of scholastic disputations. The two terms "Alaya" and "Paramârtha" have been the
causes of dividing schools and splitting the truth into more different
aspects than any other mystic terms. Alaya is literally the "Soul of
the World" or Anima Mundi, the "Over-Soul" of Emerson, and
according to esoteric teaching it changes periodically its nature. Alaya,
though eternal and changeless in its inner essence on the planes which
are unreachable by either men or Cosmic Gods (Dhyani Buddhas),
alters during the active life-period with respect to the lower planes, ours
included. During that time not only the Dhyani-Buddhas are one with
Alaya in Soul and Essence, but even the man strong in the Yoga
(mystic meditation) "is able to merge his soul with it" (Aryâsanga,
the *Bumapa* school). This is not Nirvana, but a condition next to
it. Hence the disagreement. Thus, while the Yogâchâryas (of the
Mahâyânâ school) say that Alaya is the personification of the Voidness,
and yet Alaya (*Nyingpo* and *Tsang* in Tibetan) is the basis of every visible
and invisible thing, and that, though it is eternal and immutable in its
essence, it reflects itself in every object of the Universe "like the moon
in clear tranquil water"; other schools dispute the statement. The
same for Paramârtha: the Yogâchâryas interpret the term as that which
is also dependent upon other things *(paratantral)*; and the Madhyamikas
say that Paramârtha is limited to Paranishpanna or absolute perfection;
i.e., in the exposition of these "two truths" (out of four), the former
believe and maintain that (on this plane, at any rate) there exists only
Samvritisatya or relative truth; and the latter teach the existence of
Paramârthasatya, the "absolute truth." * "No Arhat, oh mendicants,
can reach absolute knowledge before he becomes one with Paranirvana.
Parikalpita and *Paratantra* are his two great enemies" (Aphorisms of the
Bodhisattvas). *Parikalpita* (in Tibetan *Kun-ttag*) is error, made by those
unable to realize the emptiness and illusionary nature of all; who
believe something to exist which does not—*e.g.*, the Non-Ego. And

---

* "Paramârtha" is self-consciousness in Sanskrit, Svasamvedana, or the "self-
analysing reflection"—from two words, parama (above everything) and artha (comprehension), Satya meaning absolute true being, or Esse. In Tibetan Paramârthasatya is
Dondampaidenpa. The opposite of this absolute reality, or actuality, is Samvritisatya
—the relative truth only—"Samvriti" meaning "false conception" and being the
origin of illusion, Maya; in Tibetan Kundzabchi-denpa, "illusion-creating appearance."

Paratantra is that, whatever it is, which exists only through a dependent or causal connexion, and which has to disappear as soon as the cause from which it proceeds is removed—*e.g.*, the light of a wick. Destroy or extinguish it, and light disappears.

Esoteric philosophy teaches that everything lives and is conscious, but not that all life and consciousness are similar to those of human or even animal beings. Life we look upon as "the one form of existence," manifesting in what is called matter; or, as in man, what, incorrectly separating them, we name Spirit, Soul and Matter. Matter is the vehicle for the manifestation of soul on this plane of existence, and soul is the vehicle on a higher plane for the manifestation of spirit, and these three are a trinity synthesized by Life, which pervades them all. The idea of universal life is one of those ancient conceptions which are returning to the human mind in this century, as a consequence of its liberation from anthropomorphic theology. Science, it is true, contents itself with tracing or postulating the signs of universal life, and has not yet been bold enough even to whisper "Anima Mundi!" The idea of "crystalline life," now familiar to science, would have been scouted half a century ago. Botanists are now searching for the nerves of plants; not that they suppose that plants can feel or think as animals do, but because they believe that some structure, bearing the same relation functionally to plant life that nerves bear to animal life, is necessary to explain vegetable growth and nutrition. It hardly seems possible that science can disguise from itself much longer, by the mere use of terms such as "force" and "energy," the fact that things that have life are living things, whether they be atoms or planets.

But what is the belief of the inner esoteric Schools? the reader may ask. What are the doctrines taught on this subject by the Esoteric "Buddhists"? With them "Alaya" has a double and even a triple meaning. In the Yogâchârya system of the contemplative Mahâyânâ school, Alaya is both the Universal Soul (Anima Mundi) and the Self of a progressed adept. "He who is strong in the Yoga can introduce at will his Alaya by means of meditation into the true Nature of Existence." The "Alaya has an absolute eternal existence," says Aryâsanga—the rival of Nagârjuna.* In one sense it is *Pradhâna;* which

---

* Aryâsanga was a pre-Christian Adept and founder of a Buddhist esoteric school, though Csoma di Körös places him, for some reasons of his own, in the seventh century

is explained in Vishnu Purâna as: " that which is the unevolved cause, is emphatically called by the most eminent sages Pradhâna, original base, which is subtile Prakriti, viz., that which is eternal, and which at once is (or comprehends) what is and what is not, or is mere process." " Prakriti," however, is an incorrect word, and Alaya would explain it better; for Prakriti is not the "uncognizable Brahma."* It is a mistake of those who know nothing of the Universality of the Occult doctrines from the very cradle of the human races, and especially so of those scholars who reject the very idea of a " primordial revelation," to teach that the Anima Mundi, the One Life or " Universal Soul," was made known only by Anaxagoras, or during his age. This philosopher brought the teaching forward simply to oppose the too materialistic conceptions on Cosmogony of Democritus, based on his exoteric theory of *blindly* driven atoms. Anaxagoras of Clazomene was not its inventor but only its propagator, as also was Plato. That which he called Mundane Intelligence, the nous ($\nu o\hat{u}s$), the principle that according to his views is absolutely separated and free from matter and acts on design,† was called Motion, the ONE LIFE, or *Jivatma*, ages before the year 500 B.C. in India. Only the Aryan philosophers never endowed the principle, which with them is infinite, with the finite " attribute " of " thinking."

This leads the reader naturally to the " Supreme Spirit " of Hegel and the German Transcendentalists as a contrast that it may be useful to point out. The schools of Schelling and Fichte have diverged widely from the primitive archaic conception of an ABSOLUTE principle, and have mirrored only an aspect of the basic idea of the Vedanta. Even the " Absoluter Geist " shadowed forth by von Hartman in his pessimistic philosophy of the Unconscious, while it is, perhaps, the closest approximation made by European speculation to the Hindu Adwaitee Doctrines, similarly falls far short of the reality.

A.D. There was another Aryâsanga, who lived during the first centuries of our era and the Hungarian scholar most probably confuses the two.

* " The indiscreet cause which is uniform, and both cause and effect, and which those who are acquainted with first principles call Pradhâna and Prakriti, is the incognizable Brahma who was before all " (Vâyu Purâna); *i.e.*, Brahma does not put forth evolution itself or create, but only exhibits various aspects of itself, one of which is Prakriti, an aspect of Pradhâna.

† Finite Self-consciousness, I mean. For how can the *absolute* attain it otherwise than as simply an *aspect*, the highest of which known to us is human consciousness?

According to Hegel, the " Unconscious" would never have undertaken the vast and laborious task of evolving the Universe, except in the hope of attaining clear Self-consciousness.   In this connection it is to be borne in mind that in designating Spirit, which the European Pantheists use as equivalent to Parabrahm, as unconscious, they do not attach to that expression of " Spirit "—one employed in the absence of a better to symbolise a profound mystery—the connotation it usually bears.

The " Absolute Consciousness," they tell us, " behind " phenomena, which is only termed unconsciousness in the absence of any element of personality, transcends human conception.   Man, unable to form one concept except in terms of empirical phenomena, is powerless from the very constitution of his being to raise the veil that shrouds the majesty of the Absolute.   Only the liberated Spirit is able to faintly realise the nature of the source whence it sprung and whither it must eventually return. . . .   As the highest Dhyan Chohan, however, can but bow in ignorance before the awful mystery of Absolute Being ; and since, even in that culmination of conscious existence — "the merging of the individual in the universal consciousness "—to use a phrase of Fichte's—the Finite cannot conceive the Infinite, nor can it apply to it its own standard of mental experiences, how can it be said that the " Unconscious " and the Absolute can have even an instinctive impulse or hope of attaining clear self-consciousness ? *   A Vedantin would never admit this Hegelian idea ; and the Occultist would say that it applies perfectly to the awakened MAHAT, the Universal Mind already projected into the phenomenal world as the first aspect of the changeless ABSOLUTE, but never to the latter.   " Spirit and Matter, or Purusha and Prakriti are but the two primeval aspects of the One and Secondless," we are taught.

The matter-moving Nous, the animating Soul, immanent in every atom, manifested in man, latent in the stone, has different degrees of power ; and this pantheistic idea of a general Spirit-Soul pervading all Nature is the oldest of all the philosophical notions.   Nor was the Archæus a discovery of Paracelsus nor of his pupil Van Helmont ; for it is again the same Archæus or " Father-Ether,"—the manifested basis

* See Schwegler's " Handbook of the History of Philosophy " in Sterling's translation, p. 28.

and source of the innumerable phenomena of life—localised. The whole series of the numberless speculations of this kind are but variations on this theme, the key-note of which was struck in this primeval Revelation. (See Part II., " Primordial Substance.")

(b) The term Anupadaka, "parentless," or without progenitors, is a mystical designation having several meanings in the philosophy. By this name celestial beings, the Dhyan-Chohans or Dhyani-Buddhas, are generally meant. But as these correspond mystically to the human Buddhas and Bodhisattwas, known as the " Mânushi (or human) Buddhas," the latter are also designated " Anupadaka," once that their whole personality is merged in their compound sixth and seventh principles—or Atma-Buddhi, and that they have become the " diamond-souled " (Vajra-sattvas),* the full Mahatmas. The " Concealed Lord " (Sangbai Dag-po), "the one merged with the absolute," can have no parents since he is Self-existent, and one with the Universal Spirit (Svayambhu),† the Svâbhâvat in the highest aspect. The mystery in the hierarchy of the Anupadaka is great, its apex being the universal Spirit-Soul, and the lower rung the Mânushi-Buddha; and even every Soul-endowed man is an Anupadaka in a latent state. Hence, when speaking of the Universe in its formless, eternal, or absolute condition, before it was fashioned by the " Builders"—the expression, " the Universe was Anupadaka." (See Part II., " Primordial Substance.")

* Vajra—diamond-holder. In Tibetan *Dorjesempa; sempa* meaning the soul, its adamantine quality referring to its indestructibility in the hereafter. The explanation with regard to the " Anupadaka " given in the Kala Chakra, the first in the Gyu (t) division of the Kanjur, is half esoteric. It has misled the Orientalists into erroneous speculations with respect to the Dhyani-Buddhas and their earthly correspondencies, the Mânushi-Buddhas. The real tenet is hinted at in a subsequent Volume, (see " The Mystery about Buddha "), and will be more fully explained in its proper place.

† To quote Hegel again, who with Schelling practically accepted the Pantheistic conception of periodical Avatars (special incarnations of the World-Spirit in Man, as seen in the case of all the great religious reformers)...." the essence of man is spirit ....only by stripping himself of his finiteness and surrendering himself to pure self-consciousness does he attain the truth. Christ-man, as man in whom the Unity of God-man (identity of the individual with the Universal consciousness as taught by the Vedantins and some Adwaitees) appeared, has, in his death and history generally, himself presented the eternal history of Spirit—a history which every man has to accomplish in himself, in order to exist as Spirit."—*Philosophy of History*. Sibree's English translation, p. 340.

STANZA II.

COMMENTARY.

I. . . . . WHERE WERE THE BUILDERS, THE LUMINOUS SONS OF MANVANTARIC DAWN (*a*) ? . . . . IN THE UNKNOWN DARKNESS IN THEIR AH-HI *(Chohanic, Dhyani-Buddhic)* PARANISHPANNA, THE PRODUCERS OF FORM *(rupa)* FROM NO-FORM *(arupa)*, THE ROOT OF THE WORLD—THE DEVAMATRI* AND SVÂBHÂVAT, RESTED IN THE BLISS OF NON-BEING (*b*).

(*a*) The " Builders," the " Sons of Manvantaric Dawn," are the real creators of the Universe ; and in this doctrine, which deals only with our Planetary System, they, as the architects of the latter, are also called the " Watchers " of the Seven Spheres, which exoterically are the Seven planets, and esoterically the seven earths or spheres (planets) of our chain also. The opening sentence of Stanza I., when mentioning " Seven Eternities," is made to apply both to the *Maha-Kalpa* or " the (great) Age of Brahmâ," as well as to the Solar *pralaya* and subsequent resurrection of our Planetary System on a higher plane. There are many kinds of *pralaya* (dissolution of a thing visible), as will be shown elsewhere.

(*b*) Paranishpanna, remember, is the *summum bonum*, the Absolute, hence the same as Paranirvana. Besides being the final state it is that condition of subjectivity which has no relation to anything but the one absolute truth (Para-mârthasatya) on its plane. It is that state which leads one to appreciate correctly the full meaning of Non-Being, which, as explained, is *absolute* Being. Sooner or later, all that now *seemingly* exists, will be in reality and actually in the state of Paranishpanna. But there is a great difference between *conscious* and *unconscious* " being." The condition of Paranishpanna, without Paramârtha, the Self-analys-

---

* " Mother of the Gods," Aditi, or Cosmic Space. In the Zohar, she is called Sephira the Mother of the Sephiroth, and Shekinah in her primordial form, *in abscondito.*

ing consciousness (Svasamvedana), is no bliss, but simply extinction (for Seven Eternities). Thus, an iron ball placed under the scorching rays of the sun will get heated through, but will not feel or appreciate the warmth, while a man will. It is only " with a mind clear and undarkened by personality, and an assimilation of the merit of manifold existences devoted to being in its collectivity (the whole living and sentient Universe)," that one gets rid of personal existence, merging into, becoming one with, the Absolute,* and continuing in full possession of Paramârtha.

STANZA II.—*Continued.*

2. . . . . WHERE WAS SILENCE? WHERE WERE THE EARS TO SENSE IT? NO! THERE WAS NEITHER SILENCE, NOR SOUND (*a*). NAUGHT SAVE CEASELESS, ETERNAL BREATH *(Motion)* WHICH KNOWS ITSELF NOT (*b*).

(*a*) The idea that things can cease to exist and still BE, is a fundamental one in Eastern psychology. Under this apparent contradiction in terms, there rests a fact of Nature to realise which in the mind, rather than to argue about words, is the important thing. A familiar instance of a similar paradox is afforded by chemical combination. The question whether Hydrogen and Oxygen cease to exist, when they combine to form water, is still a moot one, some arguing that since they are found again when the water is decomposed they must be there all the while; others contending that as they actually turn into something totally different they must cease to exist as themselves for the time being; but neither side is able to form the faintest conception of the real condition of a thing, which has become something else and yet has not ceased to be itself. Existence as water may be said to be, for Oxygen and Hydrogen, a state of Non-being which is " more real being " than their existence as gases; and it may faintly symbolise the

---

* Hence *Non-being* is " ABSOLUTE Being," in esoteric philosophy. In the tenets of the latter even Adi-Budha (first or primeval wisdom) is, while manifested, in one sense an illusion, Maya, since all the gods, including Brahmâ, have to die at the end of the " Age of Brahmâ "; the abstraction called Parabrahm alone—whether we call it Ensoph, or Herbert Spencer's Unknowable—being " the One Absolute " Reality. The One secondless Existence is ADWAITA, " Without a Second," and all the rest is *Maya*, teaches the Adwaita philosophy.

condition of the Universe when it goes to sleep, or ceases to be, during the " Nights of Brahmâ"—to awaken or reappear again, when the dawn of the new Manvantara recalls it to what we call existence.

(b) The " Breath " of the One Existence is used in its application only to the spiritual aspect of Cosmogony by Archaic esotericism; otherwise, it is replaced by its equivalent in the material plane—Motion. The One Eternal Element, or element-containing Vehicle, is *Space*, dimensionless in every sense; co-existent with which are—endless *duration*, primordial (hence indestructible) *matter*, and *motion*—absolute " perpetual motion " which is the " breath " of the " One " Element. This breath, as seen, can never cease, not even during the Pralayic eternities. (*See " Chaos, Theos, Kosmos," in Part II.*)

But the " Breath of the One Existence " does not, all the same, apply to the *One Causeless Cause* or the " All Be-ness" (in contradistinction to All-Being, which is Brahmâ, or the Universe). Brahmâ (or Hari) the four-faced god who, after lifting the Earth out of the waters, " accomplished the Creation," is held to be only the instrumental, and not, as clearly implied, the ideal Cause. No Orientalist, so far, seems to have thoroughly comprehended the real sense of the verses in the Purâna, that treat of " creation."

Therein Brahmâ is the cause of the potencies that are to be generated subsequently for the work of " creation." When a translator says, " And from him proceed the potencies to be created, after they had become the real cause " : " and from IT proceed the potencies that *will create* as they *become* the real cause " (on the material plane) would perhaps be more correct? Save that one (causeless) ideal cause there is no other to which the universe can be referred. " Worthiest of ascetics ! through its potency—*i.e.*, through the potency of that cause—every created thing comes by its inherent or proper nature." If, in the Vedanta and Nyaya, *nimitta* is the efficient cause, as contrasted with *upadána*, the material cause, (and in the Sankhya, *pradhána* implies the functions of both) ; in the Esoteric philosophy, which reconciles all these systems, and the nearest exponent of which is the Vedanta as expounded by the Advaita Vedantists, none but the *upadána* can be speculated upon; that which is in the minds of the Vaishnavas (the Vasishta-dvaitá) as the ideal in contradistinction to the real—or Parabrahm and Isvara—can find no room in published speculations, since that ideal even is a misnomer, when applied to that of which no human reason, even that of an adept, can conceive.

To know itself or oneself, necessitates consciousness and perception (both limited faculties in relation to any subject except Parabrahm), to be cognized. Hence the "Eternal Breath which knows itself not." Infinity cannot comprehend Finiteness. The Boundless can have no relation to the bounded and the conditioned. In the occult teachings, the Unknown and the Unknowable MOVER, or the Self-Existing, is the absolute divine Essence. And thus being *Absolute* Consciousness, and *Absolute* Motion—to the limited senses of those who describe this indescribable—it is unconsciousness and immoveableness. Concrete consciousness cannot be predicated of abstract Consciousness, any more than the quality wet can be predicated of water—wetness being its own attribute and the cause of the wet quality in other things. Conciousness implies limitations and qualifications; something to be conscious of, and someone to be conscious of it. But Absolute Consciousness contains the cognizer, the thing cognized and the cognition, all three in itself and all three *one*. No man is conscious of more than that portion of his knowledge that happens to have been recalled to his mind at any particular time, yet such is the poverty of language that we have no term to distinguish the knowledge not actively thought of, from knowledge we are unable to recall to memory. To forget is synonymous with not to remember. How much greater must be the difficulty of finding terms to describe, and to distinguish between, abstract metaphysical facts or differences. It must not be forgotten, also, that we give names to things according to the appearances they assume for ourselves. We call absolute consciousness " unconsciousness," because it seems to us that it must necessarily be so, just as we call the Absolute, "Darkness," because to our finite understanding it appears quite impenetrable, yet we recognize fully that our perception of such things does not do them justice. We involuntarily distinguish in our minds, for instance, between unconscious absolute consciousness, and unconsciousness, by secretly endowing the former with some indefinite quality that corresponds, on a higher plane than our thoughts can reach, with what we know as consciousness in ourselves. But this is not any kind of consciousness that we can manage to distinguish from what appears to us as unconsciousness.

STANZA II.—*Continued.*

3. THE HOUR HAD NOT YET STRUCK; THE RAY HAD NOT YET FLASHED INTO THE GERM (*a*); THE MATRI-PADMA (*mother lotus*) HAD NOT YET SWOLLEN (*b*).*

(*a*) The ray of the " Ever Darkness " becomes, as it is emitted, a ray of effulgent light or life, and flashes into the " Germ "—the point in the Mundane Egg, represented by matter in its abstract sense. But the term " Point" must not be understoood as applying to any particular point in Space, for a germ exists in the centre of every atom, and these collectively form " the Germ ; " or rather, as no atom can be made visible to our physical eye, the collectivity of these (if the term can be applied to something which is boundless and infinite) forms the noumenon of eternal and indestructible matter.

(*b*) One of the symbolical figures for the Dual creative power in Nature (matter and force on the material plane) is *Padma*, the water-lily of India. The Lotus is the product of heat (fire) and water (vapour or Ether) ; fire standing in every philosophical and religious system as a representation of the Spirit of Deity,† the active, male, generative principle ; and Ether, or the Soul of matter, the light of the fire, for the passive female principle from which everything in this Universe emanated. Hence, Ether or Water is the Mother, and Fire is the Father. Sir W. Jones (and before him archaic botany) showed that the seeds of the Lotus contain—even before they germinate—perfectly formed leaves, the miniature shape of what one day, as perfect plants, they will become : nature thus giving us a specimen of the preformation of its production . . . the seed of all phanerogamous plants bearing proper flowers containing an embryo plantlet ready formed.‡ (See Part II., " The Lotus Flower as an Universal Symbol.") This explains the sentence " The Mother had not yet swollen "—the form being usually sacrificed to the inner or root idea in Archaic symbology.

The Lotus, or Padma, is, moreover, a very ancient and favourite

---

* An unpoetical term, yet still very graphic. (See foot-note to Stanza III.)

† Even in Christianity. (See Part II., " Primordial Substance and Divine Thought.")

‡ Gross, " The Heathen Religion," p. 195.

simile for the Kosmos itself, and also for man. The popular reasons given are, firstly, the fact just mentioned, that the Lotus-seed contains within itself a perfect miniature of the future plant, which typefies the fact that the spiritual prototypes of all things exist in the immaterial world before those things become materialised on Earth. Secondly, the fact that the Lotus plant grows up through the water, having its root in the Ilus, or mud, and spreading its flower in the air above. The Lotus thus typifies the life of man and also that of the Kosmos; for the Secret Doctrine teaches that the elements of both are the same, and that both are developing in the same direction. The root of the Lotus sunk in the mud represents material life, the stalk passing up through the water typifies existence in the astral world, and the flower floating on the water and opening to the sky is emblematical of spiritual being.

STANZA II.—*Continued.*

4. HER HEART HAD NOT YET OPENED FOR THE ONE RAY TO ENTER, THENCE TO FALL AS THREE INTO FOUR IN THE LAP OF MAYA (*a*).

(*a*) The Primordial Substance had not yet passed out of its precosmic latency into differentiated objectivity, or even become the (to man, so far,) invisible Protyle of Science. But, as the hour strikes and it becomes receptive of the Fohatic impress of the Divine Thought (the Logos, or the male aspect of the Anima Mundi, Alaya)—its heart opens. It differentiates, and the THREE (Father, Mother, Son) are transformed into four. Herein lies the origin of the double mystery of the Trinity and the immaculate Conception, The first and Fundamental dogma of Occultism is Universal Unity (or Homogeneity) under three aspects. This led to a possible conception of Deity, which as an absolute unity must remain forever incomprehensible to finite intellects. " If thou wouldest believe in the Power which acts within the root of a plant, or imagine the root concealed under the soil, thou hast to think of its stalk or trunk and of its leaves and flowers. Thou canst not imagine that Power independently of these objects. Life can be known only by the Tree of Life. . . ." (Precepts for Yoga). The idea of *Absolute* Unity

would be broken entirely in our conception, had we not something
concrete before our eyes to contain that Unity.   And the deity being
absolute, must be omnipresent, hence not an atom but contains IT within
itself.   The roots, the trunk and its many branches are three distinct
objects, yet they are one tree.   Say the Kabalists : " The Deity is one,
because It is infinite.   It is triple, because it is ever manifesting."
This manifestation is triple in its aspects, for it requires, as Aristotle has
it, three principles for every natural body to become objective : privation, form, and matter.*   Privation meant in the mind of the great
philosopher that which the Occultists call the prototypes impressed in
the Astral Light—the lowest plane and world of Anima Mundi.   The
union of these three principles depends upon a fourth—the LIFE which
radiates from the summits of the Unreachable, to become an
universally diffused Essence on the manifested planes of Existence.
And this QUATERNARY (Father, Mother, Son, as a UNITY, and a
quaternary, as a living manifestation) has been the means of leading to
the very archaic Idea of Immaculate Conception, now finally crystallized into a dogma of the Christian Church, which carnalized this
metaphysical idea beyond any common sense.   For one has but to
read the Kabala and study its numerical methods of interprctation to
find the origin of that dogma.   It is purely astronomical, mathematical,
and pre-eminently metaphysical : the Male element in Nature (personified by the male deities and Logoi—Viraj, or Brahmâ ; Horus, or
Osiris, etc., etc.) is born through, not from, an immaculate source, personified by the " Mother" ; because that Male having a Mother cannot
have a " Father "—the abstract Deity being sexless, and not even a
Being but Be-ness, or Life itself.   Let us render this in the mathematical
language of the author of " The Source of Measures."   Speaking of the
" Measure of a Man " and his numerical (Kabalistic) value, he writes
that in Genesis, ch. iv., v. 1, " It is called the ' Man even Jehovah '

---

* A Vedantin of the Visishtadwaita philosophy would say that, though the only
independent Reality, Parabrahmam is inseparable from his trinity.   That He is three,
" Parabrahmam, Chit, and Achit," the last two being dependent realities unable to
exist separately ; or, to make it clearer, Parabrahmam is the SUBSTANCE—changeless,
eternal, and incognizable—and Chit (Atma), and Achit (Anâtma) are its qualities, as
form and colour are the qualities of any object.   The two are the garment, or body, or
rather attribute (Sarira) of Parabrahmam.   But an Occultist would find much to
say against this claim, and so would the Adwaitee Vedantin.

Measure, and this is obtained in this way, viz.: $113 \times 5 = 565$, and the value 565 can be placed under the form of expression $56 \cdot 5 \times 10 = 565$. Here the Man-number 113 becomes a factor of $56 \cdot 5 \times 10$, and the (Kabalistic) reading of this last numbered expression is Jod, He, Vau, He, or Jehovah. . . . The expansion of 565 into $56 \cdot 5 \times 10$ is purposed to show the emanation of the male (Jod) from the female (Eva) principle; or, so to speak, the birth of a male element from an immaculate source, in other words, an immaculate conception."

Thus is repeated on Earth the mystery enacted, according to the Seers, on the divine plane. The "Son" of the immaculate Celestial Virgin (or the undifferentiated cosmic protyle, Matter in its infinitude) is born again on Earth as the Son of the terrestrial Eve—our mother Earth, and becomes Humanity as a total—past, present, and future— for Jehovah or Jod-he-vau-he is androgyne, or both male and female. Above, the Son is the whole Kosmos; below, he is MANKIND. The triad or triangle becomes Tetraktis, the Sacred Pythagorean number, the perfect Square, and a 6-faced cube on Earth. The Macroprosopus (the Great Face) is now Microprosopus (the lesser face); or, as the Kabalists have it, the "Ancient of Days," descending on Adam Kadmon whom he uses as his vehicle to manifest through, gets transformed into Tetragrammaton. It is now in the "Lap of Maya," the Great Illusion, and between itself and the Reality has the Astral Light, the great Deceiver of man's limited senses, unless Knowledge through Paramarthasatya comes to the rescue.

STANZA II.—*Continued.*

5. THE SEVEN *(Sons)* WERE NOT YET BORN FROM THE WEB OF LIGHT. DARKNESS ALONE WAS FATHER-MOTHER, SVÂBHÂVAT, AND SVÂBHÂVAT WAS IN DARKNESS *(a)*.

(a) The Secret Doctrine, in the Stanzas given here, occupies itself chiefly, if not entirely, with our Solar System, and especially with our planetary chain. The "Seven Sons," therefore, are the creators of the latter. This teaching will be explained more fully hereafter. (See Part II., "Theogony of the Creative Gods.")

Svâbhâvat, the "Plastic Essence" that fills the Universe, is the root of all things. Svâbhâvat is, so to say, the Buddhistic concrete aspect of the abstraction called in Hindu philosophy *Mulaprakriti*. It is the body of the Soul, and that which Ether would be to Akasa, the latter being the informing principle of the former. Chinese mystics have made of it the synonym of "being." In the *Ekasloka-Shastra* of *Nagârjuna* (the *Lung-shu* of China) called by the Chinese the *Yih-shu-lu-kia-lun*, it is said that the original word of Yeu is "Being" or "Subhâva," "the Substance giving substance to itself," also explained by him as meaning "without action and with action," "the nature which has no nature of its own." *Subhâva*, from which *Svâbhâvat*, is composed of two words: Su "fair," "handsome," good;" Sva, "self;" and bhava. "being" or "states of being."

STANZA II.—*Continued.*

6. THESE TWO ARE THE GERM, AND THE GERM IS—ONE. THE UNI-VERSE WAS STILL CONCEALED IN THE DIVINE THOUGHT AND THE DIVINE BOSOM.

The "*Divine Thought*" does not imply the idea of a Divine thinker. The Universe, not only past, present, and future—which is a human and finite idea expressed by finite thought—but in its totality, the *Sat* (an untranslateable term), the absolute being, with the Past and Future crystallized in an eternal Present, is that Thought itself reflected in a secondary or manifest cause. Brahma (neuter) as the Mysterium Magnum of Paracelsus is an absolute mystery to the human mind. Brahmâ, the male-female, its aspect and anthropomorphic reflection, is conceivable to the perceptions of blind faith, though rejected by human intellect when it attains its majority. (See Part II.. "Primordial Substance and Divine Thought.")

Hence the statement that during the prologue, so to say, of the drama· of Creation, or the beginning of cosmic evolution, the Universe or the "Son" lies still concealed "in the Divine Thought," which had not yet penetrated "into the Divine Bosom." This idea, note well, is at the root, and forms the origin of all the allegories about the "Sons of God" born of immaculate virgins.

STANZA III.

COMMENTARY.

1. THE LAST VIBRATION OF THE SEVENTH ETERNITY THRILLS THROUGH
INFINITUDE (*a*). THE MOTHER SWELLS, EXPANDING FROM WITHIN WITHOUT
LIKE THE BUD OF THE LOTUS (*b*).

(*a*) The seemingly paradoxical use of the sentence " Seventh Eternity,"
thus dividing the indivisible, is sanctified in esoteric philosophy. The
latter divides boundless duration into unconditionally eternal and
universal Time and a conditioned one (*Khandakâla*). One is the abstraction or noumenon of infinite time (Kâla) ; the other its phenomenon
appearing periodically, as the effect of *Mahat* (the Universal Intelligence
limited by Manvantaric duration). With some schools, Mahat is " the
first-born " of Pradhâna (undifferentiated substance, or the periodical
aspect of Mulaprakriti, the root of Nature), which (Pradhâna) is called
Maya, the Illusion. In this respect, I believe, esoteric teaching differs
from the Vedantin doctrines of both the Adwaita and the Visishtadwaita
schools. For it says that, while Mulaprakriti, the noumenon, is self-
existing and without any origin—is, in short, parentless, Anupadaka (as
one with Brahmam)—Prakriti, its phenomenon, is periodical and no better
than a phantasm of the former, so Mahat, with the Occultists, the first-
born of Gnâna (or *gnosis*) knowledge, wisdom or the Logos—is a
phantasm reflected from the Absolute NIRGUNA (Parabrahm, the one
reality, " devoid of attributes and qualities " ; see Upanishads) ; while
with some Vedantins Mahat is a manifestation of Prakriti, or Matter.

(*b*) Therefore, the " last vibration of the Seventh Eternity " was " fore-
ordained "—by no God in particular, but occurred in virtue of the
eternal and changeless LAW which causes the great periods of Activity
and Rest, called so graphically, and at the same time so poetically,
the " Days and Nights of Brahmâ." The expansion " from within
without " of the Mother, called elsewhere the " Waters of Space,"
" Universal Matrix," etc., does not allude to an expansion from a small
centre or focus, but, without reference to size or limitation or area,
means the development of limitless subjectivity into as limitless objectivity. " The ever (to us) invisible and immaterial Substance present
in eternity, threw its periodical shadow from its own plane into the lap

of Maya." It implies that this expansion, not being an increase in size
—for infinite extension admits of no enlargement—was a change of condition. It "expanded like the bud of the Lotus"; for the Lotus plant
exists not only as a miniature embryo in its seed (a physical characteristic), but its prototype is present in an ideal form in the Astral Light
from "Dawn" to "Night" during the Manvantaric period, like everything else, as a matter of fact, in this objective Universe; from man
down to mite, from giant trees down to the tiniest blades of grass.

All this, teaches the hidden Science, is but the temporary reflection,
the shadow of the eternal ideal prototype in Divine Thought; the word
"Eternal," note well again, standing here only in the sense of "Æon,"
as lasting throughout the seemingly interminable, but still limited cycle
of activity, called by us Manvantara. For what is the real esoteric
meaning of Manvantara, or rather a Manu-Antara? It means, esoterically, "between two Manus," of whom there are fourteen in every
"Day of Brahmâ," such a "Day" consisting of 1,000 aggregates of four
ages, or 1,000 "Great Ages," Mahayugas. Let us now analyse the
word or name Manu. Orientalists and their Dictionaries tell us that
the term "Manu" is from the root *Man*, "to think"; hence "the
thinking man." But, esoterically, every Manu, as an anthropomorphized
patron of his special cycle (or Round), is but the personified idea of the
"Thought Divine" (as the Hermetic "Pymander"); each of the Manus,
therefore, being the special god, the creator and fashioner of all that
appears during his own respective cycle of being or Manvantara. Fohat
runs the Manus' (or Dhyan-Chohans') errands, and causes the ideal
prototypes to expand from within without—viz., to cross gradually, on a
descending scale, all the planes from the noumenon to the lowest
phenomenon, to bloom finally on the last into full objectivity—the acme
of illusion, or the grossest matter.

STANZA III.—*continued.*

2. THE VIBRATION SWEEPS ALONG, TOUCHING WITH ITS SWIFT WING
(*simultaneously*) THE WHOLE UNIVERSE, AND THE GERM THAT DWELLETH IN
DARKNESS: THE DARKNESS THAT BREATHES (*moves*) OVER THE SLUMBERING
WATERS OF LIFE (*a*).

(*a*) The Pythagorean Monad is also said to dwell in solitude and darkness like the " germ."   The idea of the " breath " of Darkness moving over " the slumbering Waters of life," which is primordial matter with the latent Spirit in it, recalls the first chapter of Genesis.   Its original is the Brahminical Nârâyana (the mover on the Waters), who is the personification of the eternal Breath of the unconscious All (or Parabrahm) of the Eastern Occultists.   The Waters of Life, or Chaos—the female principle in symbolism—are the vacuum (to our mental sight) in which lie the latent Spirit and Matter.   This it was that made Democritus assert, after his instructor Leucippus, that the primordial principles of all were atoms and a vacuum, in the sense of space, but not of empty space, as " Nature abhors a vacuum " according to the Peripatetics, and every ancient philosopher.

In all Cosmogonies " Water " plays the same important part.   It is the base and source of material existence.   Scientists, mistaking the word for the thing, understood by water the definite chemical combination of oxygen and hydrogen, thus giving a specific meaning to a term used by Occultists in a generic sense, and which is used in Cosmogony with a metaphysical and mystical meaning.   Ice is not water, neither is steam, although all three have precisely the same chemical composition.

STANZA III.—*Continued*.

2. " DARKNESS " RADIATES LIGHT, AND LIGHT DROPS ONE SOLITARY RAY INTO THE WATERS, INTO THE MOTHER DEEP.   THE RAY SHOOTS THROUGH THE VIRGIN-EGG ; THE RAY CAUSES THE ETERNAL EGG TO THRILL, AND DROP THE NON-ETERNAL (*periodical*) GERM, WHICH CONDENSES INTO THE WORLD EGG (*a*).

(*a*) The solitary ray dropping into the mother deep may be taken as meaning Divine Thought or Intelligence, impregnating chaos.   This, however, occurs on the plane of metaphysical abstraction, or rather the plane whereon that which we call a metaphysical abstraction is a reality.   The Virgin-egg being in one sense abstract Egg-ness, or the power of becoming developed through fecundation, is eternal and for ever the same.   And just as the fecundation of an egg takes place before it is dropped ; so the non-eternal periodical germ which becomes later in symbolism the mundane egg, contains in itself, when it emerges from the said symbol, " the promise and potency " of all the Universe. Though the idea *per se* is, of course, an abstraction, a symbolical mode of expression, it is a symbol truly, as it suggests the idea of infinity as an endless circle. It brings before the mind's eye the picture of Kosmos emerging from and in boundless space, a Universe as shoreless in magnitude if not as endless in its objective manifestation. The simile of an egg also expresses the fact taught in Occultism that the primordial form of everything manifested, from atom to globe, from man to angel, is spheroidal, the sphere having been with all nations the emblem of eternity and infinity—a serpent swallowing its tail. To realize the meaning, however, the sphere must be thought of as seen from its centre. The field of vision or of thought is like a sphere whose radii proceed from one's self in every direction, and extend out into space, opening up boundless vistas all around. It is the symbolical circle of Pascal and the Kabalists, " whose centre is everywhere and circumference nowhere," a conception which enters into the compound idea of this emblem.

The " Mundane Egg " is, perhaps, one of the most universally adopted symbols, highly suggestive as it is, equally in the spiritual, physiological, and cosmological sense. Therefore, it is found in every world-theogony, where it is largely associated with the serpent symbol; the latter being everywhere, in philosophy as in religious symbolism, an emblem of eternity, infinitude, regeneration, and rejuvenation, as well as of wisdom. (See Part II. " Tree and Serpent and Crocodile Worship.") The mystery of apparent self-generation and evolution through its own creative power repeating in miniature the process of Cosmic evolution in the egg, both being due to heat and moisture under the efflux of the unseen creative spirit, justified fully the selection of this graphic symbol. The " Virgin Egg " is the microcosmic symbol of the macrocosmic prototype—the " Virgin Mother "—Chaos or the Primeval Deep. The male Creator (under whatever name) springs forth from the Virgin female, the immaculate root fructified by the Ray. Who, if versed in astronomy and natural sciences, can fail to see its suggestiveness? Cosmos as receptive Nature is an Egg fructified—yet left immaculate; once regarded as boundless, it could have no other representation than a spheroid. The Golden Egg was surrounded by seven natural elements (ether, fire, air, water), " four ready, three secret." It may be found

stated in Vishnu Purâna, where elements are translated " Envelopes "
and a *secret* one is added : " Aham-kâra " (see Wilson's Vishnu Purâna,
Book I., p. 40). The original text has no " Aham-kâra ; " it mentions
seven Elements without specifying the last three (see Part II. on " The
Mundane Egg ").

STANZA III.—*Continued.*

4. (*Then*) THE THREE (*triangle*) FALL INTO THE FOUR (*quaternary*). THE
RADIANT ESSENCE BECOMES SEVEN INSIDE, SEVEN OUTSIDE (*a*). THE
LUMINOUS EGG (*Hiranyagarbha*), WHICH IN ITSELF IS THREE (*the triple
hypostases of Brahmâ, or Vishnu, the three " Avasthas"*), CURDLES AND
SPREADS IN MILK-WHITE CURDS THROUGHOUT THE DEPTHS OF MOTHER,
THE ROOT THAT GROWS IN THE OCEAN OF LIFE (*b*).

The use of geometrical figures and the frequent allusions to figures in
all ancient scriptures (see Purânas, Egyptian papyri, the " Book of the
Dead" and even the Bible) must be explained. In the " Book of
Dzyan," as in the Kabala, there are two kinds of numerals to be studied
—the figures, often simple blinds, and the Sacred Numbers, the values
of which are all known to the Occultists through Initiation. The
former is but a conventional glyph, the latter is the basic symbol of all.
That is to say, that one is purely physical, the other purely metaphysical, the two standing in relation to each other as matter stands to
spirit—the extreme poles of the ONE Substance.

As Balzac, the unconscious Occultist of French literature, says
somewhere, the Number is to Mind the same as it is to matter : " an
incomprehensible agent ; " (perhaps so to the profane, never to the
Initiated mind). Number is, as the great writer thought, an Entity,
and, at the same time, a Breath emanating from what he called God
and what we call the ALL ; the breath which alone could organize the
physical Kosmos, " where naught obtains its form but through the
Deity, which is an effect of Number." It is instructive to quote
Balzac's words upon this subject :—

" The smallest as the most immense creations, are they not to be distinguished from each other by their quantities, their qualities, their dimensions,
their forces and attributes, all begotten by the NUMBER ? The infinitude of the
Numbers is a fact proven to our mind, but of which no proof can be physically

given. The mathematician will tell us that the infinitude of the numbers exists but is not to be demonstrated. God is a Number endowed with motion, which is felt but not demonstrated. *As Unity, it begins the Numbers, with which it has nothing in common.* . . . . The existence of the Number depends on Unity, which, without a single Number, begets them all. . . . . What! unable either to measure the first abstraction yielded to you by the Deity, or to get hold of it, you still hope to subject to your measurements the mystery of the Secret Sciences which emanate from that Deity? . . . . And what would you feel, were I to plunge you into the abysses of MOTION, the Force which organizes the Number? What would you think, were I to add that *Motion* and *Number** are begotten by the WORD, the Supreme Reason of the Seers and Prophets, who, in days of old, sensed the mighty Breath of God, a witness to which is the Apocalypse?"

(*b*) "The radiant essence curdled and spread throughout the depths" of Space. From an astronomical point of view this is easy of explanation: it is the "milky way," the world-stuff, or primordial matter in its first form. It is more difficult, however, to explain it in a few words or even lines, from the standpoint of Occult Science and Symbolism, as it is the most complicated of glyphs. Herein are enshrined more than a dozen symbols. To begin with, the whole pantheon of mysterious objects,† every one of them having some definite Occult meaning, extracted from the allegorical "churning of the ocean" by the Hindu gods. Besides *Amrita*, the water of life or immortality, "*Surabhi*" the "cow of plenty," called "the fountain of milk and curds," was extracted from this "Sea of Milk." Hence the universal adoration of the cow and bull, one the productive, the other the generative power in Nature: symbols connected with both the Solar and the Cosmic deities. The specific properties, for occult purposes, of the "fourteen precious things," being explained only at the fourth Initiation, cannot be given here; but the following may be remarked. In the "Satapatha Brâhmana" it is stated that the churning of the "Ocean of Milk" took place in the Satya Yug, the first age which immediately followed the "Deluge." As, however, neither the Rig-Veda nor

---

* Number, truly; but never MOTION. It is *Motion* which begets the Logos, the Word, in occultism.

† The "Fourteen precious things." The narrative or allegory is found in the Satapatha Brâhmana and others. The Japanese Secret Science of the Buddhist Mystics, the *Yamabooshi*, has "seven precious things." We will speak of them, hereafter.

Manu—both preceding Vaivasvata's "deluge," that of the bulk of the Fourth Race—mention this deluge, it is evident that it is not the "great" deluge, nor that which carried away Atlantis, nor even the deluge of Noah, which is meant here. This "churning" relates to a period before the earth's formation, and is in direct connection with that other universal legend, the various and contradictory versions of which culminated in the Christian dogma of the "War in Heaven," and the fall of the Angels (see Book II., also Revelations chap. xii.). The Brâhmanas, reproached by the Orientalists with their versions on the same subjects, often clashing with each other, *are pre-eminently occult works*, hence used purposely as blinds. They were allowed to survive for public use and property only because they were and are absolutely un-intelligible to the masses. Otherwise they would have disappeared from circulation as long ago as the days of Akbar.

———

STANZA III.—*Continued*.

5. THE ROOT REMAINS, THE LIGHT REMAINS, THE CURDS REMAIN, AND STILL OEAOHOO (*a*) IS ONE (*b*).

(*a*) OEAOHOO is rendered "*Father-Mother of the Gods*" in the Commentaries, or the SIX IN ONE, *or the septenary root from which all proceeds.* All depends upon the accent given to these seven vowels, which may be pronounced as *one*, three, or even seven syllables by adding an *e* after the letter "o." This mystic name is given out, because without a thorough mastery of the triple pronunciation it remains for ever ineffectual.

(*b*) This refers to the Non-Separateness of all that lives and has its being, whether in active or passive state. In one sense, Oeaohoo is the "Rootless Root of All"; hence, one with Parabrahmam; in another sense it is a name for the manifested ONE LIFE, the Eternal living Unity. The "Root" means, as already explained, pure knowledge *(Sattva),*[*]

———

[*] The original for Understanding is *Sattva*, which Sankara (acharya) renders anta*h*kara*n*a. "Refined," he says, "by sacrifices and other sanctifying operations." In the *Katha*, at p. 148, Sattva is said by Sankara to mean *buddhi*—a common use of the word. ("The BHAGAVATGITA with The Sanatsugâtîya and The Anugîtâ," trans-

eternal *(Nitya)* unconditioned reality or SAT *(Satya)*, whether we call it Parabrahmam or Mulaprakriti, for these are the two aspects of the ONE. The "Light" is the same Omnipresent Spiritual Ray, which has entered and now fecundated the Divine Egg, and calls cosmic matter to begin its long series of differentiations. The curds are the first differentiation, and probably refer also to that cosmic matter which is supposed to be the origin of the "Milky Way"—the matter we know. This "matter," which, according to the revelation received from the primeval Dhyani-Buddhas, is, during the periodical sleep of the Universe, of the ultimate tenuity conceivable to the eye of the perfect Bodhisatva—this matter, radical and cool, becomes, at the first reawakening of cosmic motion, scattered through Space; appearing, when seen from the Earth, in clusters and lumps, like curds in thin milk. These are the seeds of the future worlds, the "Star-stuff."

STANZA III.—*Continued.*

6. THE ROOT OF LIFE WAS IN EVERY DROP OF THE OCEAN OF IMMORTALITY *(Amrita)** AND THE OCEAN WAS RADIANT LIGHT, WHICH WAS FIRE AND HEAT AND MOTION. DARKNESS VANISHED AND WAS NO MORE.† IT DISAPPEARED IN ITS OWN ESSENCE, THE BODY OF FIRE AND WATER, OF FATHER AND MOTHER (a).

(a) The essence of darkness being absolute light, Darkness is taken as the appropriate allegorical representation of the condition of the Universe during Pralaya, or the term of absolute rest, or non-being, as it appears to our finite minds. The "fire," "heat," and "motion" here spoken of, are, of course, not the fire, heat, and motion of physical science, but the underlying abstractions, the noumena, or the soul, of the essence of these material manifestations—the "things in themselves," which, as modern science confesses, entirely elude the instru-

lated by Kâshinâth Trimbak Telang, M.A.; edited by Max Müller.) Whatever meaning various schools may give the term, *Sattva* is the name given among Occult students of the Aryasanga School to the dual Monad or Atma-buddhi, and Atma-buddhi on this plane corresponds to Parabrahm and Mulaprakriti on the higher plane.

* Amrita is "immortality."
† See Commentary No. 1 to this Stanza.

ments of the laboratory, and which even the mind cannot grasp, although it can equally little avoid the conclusion that these underlying essences of things must exist. Fire and Water, or Father * and Mother, may be taken here to mean the divine Ray and Chaos. " Chaos, from this union with Spirit obtaining sense, shone with pleasure, and thus was produced the Protogonos (the first-born light)," says a fragment of Hermas. Damascius calls it Dis in " Theogony" —" The disposer of all things." (See Cory's " *Ancient Fragments*," p. 314.)

According to the Rosicrucian tenets, as handled and explained by the profane for once correctly, if only partially, so "Light and Darkness are identical in themselves, being only divisible in the human mind ;" and according to Robert Fludd, " Darkness adopted illumination in order to make itself visible " (*On Rosenkranz*). According to the tenets of Eastern Occultism, DARKNESS is the one true actuality, the basis and the root of light, without which the latter could never manifest itself, nor even exist. Light is matter, and DARKNESS pure Spirit. Darkness, in its radical, metaphysical basis, is subjective and absolute light ; while the latter in all its seeming effulgence and glory, is merely a mass of shadows, as it can never be eternal, and is simply an illusion, or Maya.

Even in the mind-baffling and science-harassing Genesis, light is created out of darkness " and darkness was upon the face of the deep" (ch. i. v. 2.)—and not *vice versâ*. " In him (in darkness) was life; and the life *was the light of men*" (John i. 4). A day may come when the eyes of men will be opened ; and then they may comprehend better than they do now, that verse in the Gospel of John that says " And the light shineth in darkness; and the darkness comprehendeth it not." They will see then that the word " darkness " does not apply to man's spiritual eyesight, but indeed to " Darkness," the absolute, that comprehendeth not (cannot cognize) transient light, however transcendent to human eyes. *Demon est Deus inversus.* The devil is now called Darkness by the Church, whereas, in the Bible he is called the " Son of God " (see Job), the bright star of the early morning, Lucifer (see Isaiah). There is a whole philosophy of dogmatic craft in the reason why the first Archangel, who sprang from the depths of Chaos, was called Lux (Lucifer), the " Luminous Son of the Morning," or man-

* See " Kwan-Shai-Yin." The real name from the text cannot be given.

vantaric Dawn. He was transformed by the Church into Lucifer or Satan, because he is higher and older than Jehovah, and had to be sacrificed to the new dogma. (See Book II.)

STANZA III.—*Continued.*

7. BEHOLD, OH LANOO![†] THE RADIANT CHILD OF THE TWO, THE UNPARALLELED REFULGENT GLORY, BRIGHT SPACE, SON OF DARK SPACE, WHO EMERGES FROM THE DEPTHS OF THE GREAT DARK WATERS. IT IS OEAOHOO, THE YOUNGER, THE * * * (*whom thou knowest now as Kwan-Shai-Yin.—Comment*) (*a*). HE SHINES FORTH AS THE SUN. HE IS THE BLAZING DIVINE DRAGON OF WISDOM. THE EKA IS CHATUR (*four*), AND CHATUR TAKES TO ITSELF THREE, AND THE UNION PRO-DUCES THE SAPTA (*seven*) IN WHOM ARE THE SEVEN WHICH BECOME THE TRIDASA[‡] (*the thrice ten*) THE HOSTS AND THE MULTITUDES (*b*). BEHOLD HIM LIFTING THE VEIL, AND UNFURLING IT FROM EAST TO WEST. HE SHUTS OUT THE ABOVE AND LEAVES THE BELOW TO BE SEEN AS THE GREAT ILLUSION. HE MARKS THE PLACES FOR THE SHINING ONES (*stars*) AND TURNS THE UPPER (*space*) INTO A SHORELESS SEA OF FIRE, AND THE ONE MANIFESTED (*element*) INTO THE GREAT WATERS (*c*).

" Bright Space, son of dark Space," corresponds to the Ray dropped at the first thrill of the new " Dawn " into the great Cosmic depths, from which it re-emerges differentiated as Oeaohoo the younger, (the " new LIFE "), to become, to the end of the life-cycle, the germ of all things. He is " the Incorporeal man who contains in himself the divine Idea,"—the generator of Light and Life, to use an expression of Philo Judæus. He is called the " Blazing Dragon of Wisdom,"

---

† Lanoo is a student, a chela who studies practical Esotericism.

‡ " Tri-dasa," or three times ten (30), alludes to the Vedic deities, in round numbers, or more accurately 33—a sacred number. They are the 12 Adityas, the 8 Vasus, the 11 Rudras, and 2 Aswins—the twin sons of the Sun and the Sky. This is the root-number of the Hindu Pantheon, which enumerates 33 crores or over three hundred millions of gods and goddesses.

because, firstly, he is that which the Greek philosophers called the Logos, the Verbum of the Thought Divine; and secondly, because in Esoteric philosophy this first manifestation, being the synthesis or the aggregate of Universal Wisdom, Oeaohoo, " the Son of the Son," contains in himself the Seven Creative Hosts (The Sephiroth), and is thus the essence of manifested Wisdom. " He who bathes in the light of Oeaohoo will never be deceived by the veil of Mâyâ."

Kwan-Shai-Yin is identical with, and an equivalent of the Sanskrit *Avalôkitêshwara*, and as such he is an androgynous deity, like the Tetragrammaton and all the Logoi * of antiquity. It is only by some sects in China that he is anthropomorphized and represented with female attributes,† when, under his female aspect, he becomes Kwan-Yin, the goddess of mercy, called the " Divine Voice."‡ The latter is the patron deity of Thibet and of the island of Puto in China, where both deities have a number of monasteries.§ (See Part II. Kwan-Shai-Yin and Kwan-yin.)

---

* Hence all the higher gods of antiquity are all " Sons of the Mother " before they become those of the "Father." The Logoi, like Jupiter or Zeus, Son of Kronos-Saturn, " Infinite Time " (or Kâla), in their origin were represented as male-female. Zeus is said to be the " beautiful Virgin," and Venus is made bearded. Apollo is originally bisexual, so is Brahmâ-Vâch in Manu and the Purânas. Osiris is interchangeable with Isis, and Horus is of both sexes. Finally St. John's vision in Revelation, that of the Logos, who is now connected with Jesus—is hermaphrodite, for he is described as having female breasts. So is the Tetragrammaton = Jehovah. But there are two Avalôkitêshwaras in Esotericism; the first and the second *Logos*.

† No religious symbol can escape profanation and even derision in our days of politics and Science. In Southern India the writer has seen a converted native making pujah with offerings before a statue of Jesus clad in woman's clothes and with a ring in his nose. When asking the meaning of the masquerade we were answered that it was Jesu-Maria blended in one, and that it was done by the permission of the Padri, as the zealous convert had no money to purchase two statues or " idols " as they, very properly, were called by a witness—another but a non-converted Hindu. Blasphemous this will appear to a dogmatic Christian, but the Theosophist and the Occultist must award the palm of logic to the converted Hindu. The esoteric Christos in the *gnosis* is, of course, sexless, but in exoteric *theology* he is male and female.

‡ The Gnostic Sophia, " Wisdom " who is " the Mother " of the Ogdoad (Aditi, in a certain sense, with her eight sons), is the Holy Ghost and the Creator of all, as in the ancient systems. The " father " is a far later invention. The earliest manifested Logos was female everywhere—the mother of the seven planetary powers.

§ See " Chinese Buddhism," by the Rev. J. C. Edkins, who always gives correct facts, although his conclusions are very frequently erroneous.

(b) " The " Dragon of Wisdom " is the One, the "Eka" (Sanskrit) or Saka. It is curious that Jehovah's name in Hebrew should also be One, Echod. " His name is Echod " : say the Rabbins. The philologists ought to decide which of the two is derived from the other— linguistically and symbolically : surely, not the Sanskrit ? The " One " and the Dragon are expressions used by the ancients in connection with their respective Logoi. Jehovah—esoterically (as Elohim)—is also the Serpent or Dragon that tempted Eve, and the " Dragon " is an old glyph for " Astral Light " (Primordial Principle), " which is the Wisdom of Chaos." Archaic philosophy, recognizing neither Good nor Evil as a fundamental or independent power, but starting from the Absolute ALL (Universal Perfection eternally), traced both through the course of natural evolution to pure Light condensing gradually into form, hence becoming Matter or Evil. It was left with the early and ignorant Christian fathers to degrade the philosophical and highly scientific idea of this emblem (the Dragon) into the absurd superstition called the " Devil." They took it from the later Zoroastrians, who saw devils or the Evil in the Hindu Devas, and the word Evil thus became by a double transmutation D'Evil in every tongue (Diabolos, Diable, Diavolo, Teufel). But the Pagans have always shown a philosophical discrimination in their symbols. The primitive symbol of the serpent symbolised divine Wisdom and Perfection, and had always stood for psychical Regeneration and Immortality. Hence—Hermes, calling the serpent the most spiritual of all beings ; Moses, initiated in the wisdom of Hermes, following suit in Genesis ; the Gnostic's Serpent with the seven vowels over its head, being the emblem of the seven hierarchies of the Septenary or Planetary Creators. Hence, also, the Hindu serpent Sesha or Ananta, " the Infinite," a name of Vishnu, whose first Vahan or vehicle on the primordial waters is this serpent.* Yet they all made a difference between the good and the bad Serpent (the Astral Light of

---

* Like the *logoi* and the Hierarchies of Powers, however, the " Serpents " have to be distinguished one from the other. Sesha or Ananta, " the couch of Vishnu," is an allegorical abstraction, symbolizing infinite Time in Space, which contains the germ and throws off periodically the efflorescence of this germ, the *manifested* Universe ; whereas, the gnostic *Ophis* contained the same triple symbolism in its seven vowels as the One, Three and Seven-syllabled *Oeaohoo* of the Archaic doctrine ; *i.e.,* the One Unmanifested Logos, the Second manifested, the triangle concreting into the Quaternary or Tetragrammaton, and the rays of the latter on the material plane.

the Kabalists)—between the former, the embodiment of divine Wisdom in the region of the Spiritual, and the latter, Evil, on the plane of matter.* Jesus accepted the serpent as a synonym of Wisdom, and this formed part of his teaching: "Be ye wise as serpents," he says. "In the beginning, before Mother became Father-Mother, the fiery Dragon moved in the infinitudes alone" (*Book of Sarparâjni*.) The Aitareya Brâhmana calls the Earth Sarparâjni, "the Serpent Queen," and "the Mother of all that moves." Before our globe became egg-shaped (and the Universe also) "a long trail of Cosmic dust (or fire mist) moved and writhed like a serpent in Space." The "Spirit of God moving on Chaos" was symbolized by every nation in the shape of a fiery serpent breathing fire and light upon the primordial waters, until it had incubated cosmic matter and made it assume the annular shape of a serpent with its tail in its mouth—which symbolises not only Eternity and Infinitude, but also the globular shape of all the bodies formed within the Universe from that fiery mist. The Universe, as well as the Earth and Man, cast off periodically, serpent-like, their old skins, to assume new ones after a time of rest. The serpent is, surely, a not less graceful or a more unpoetical image than the caterpillar and chrysalis from which springs the butterfly, the Greek emblem of Psyche, the human soul. The "Dragon" was also the symbol of the Logos with the Egyptians, as with the Gnostics. In the "Book of Hermes," Pymander, the oldest and the most spiritual of the Logoi of the Western Continent, appears to Hermes in the shape of a Fiery Dragon of "Light, Fire, and Flame." Pymander, the "Thought Divine" personified, says: The Light is me, I am the Nous (the mind or Manu), I am thy God, and I am far older than the human principle which escapes from the shadow ("*Darkness,*" or the concealed Deity). I am the germ of thought, the resplendent *Word*, the *Son* of God. All that thus sees and hears in thee is the *Verbum* of the Master, it is the Thought (*Mahat*) which is God, the Father.†

---

* The Astral Light, or the Ether, of the ancient pagans (for the name of Astral Light is quite modern) is Spirit-Matter. Beginning with the pure spiritual plane, it becomes grosser as it descends until it becomes the *Maya* or the tempting and deceitful serpent on our plane.

† By "God, the Father," the seventh principle in Man and Kosmos are here unmistakeably meant, this principle being inseparable in its Esse and Nature from the seventh Cosmic principle. In one sense it is the Logos of the Greeks and the Avalôkitêswara of the esoteric Buddhists.

The celestial Ocean, the Æther . . . . is the *Breath* of the Father, the life-giving principle, the *Mother*, the Holy Spirit, ... for these are not separated, and their union is LIFE."

Here we find the unmistakeable echo of the Archaic Secret Doctrine, as now expounded. Only the latter does not place at the head and Evolution of Life " the Father," who comes third and is the " Son of the Mother," but the " Eternal and Ceaseless Breath of the ALL." The *Mahat* (Understanding, Universal Mind, Thought, etc.), before it manifests itself as Brahmâ or Siva, appears as Vishnu, says *Sânkhya Sâra* (p. 16); hence *Mahat* has several aspects, just as the *logos* has. *Mahat* is called the Lord, in the *Primary* Creation, and is, in this sense, Universal Cognition or *Thought Divine;* but, " That Mahat which was first produced is (afterwards) called *Ego-ism*, when it is born as " I," that is said to be the *second* Creation " (*Anugîtâ*, ch. xxvi.). And the translator (an able and learned Brahmin, not a European Orientalist) explains in a foot-note (6), " *i.e.*, when Mahat develops into the feeling of Self-Consciousness—I—then it assumes the name of Egoism," which, translated into our esoteric phraseology, means when *Mahat* is transformed into the human *Manas* (or even that of the finite gods), and becomes *Aham*-ship. Why it is called the *Mahat* of the *Second* creation (or the *ninth*, that of the *Kumâra* in *Vishnu Purâna*) will be explained in Book II. The " Sea of Fire" is then the Super-Astral (*i.e.*, noumenal) Light, the first radiation from the *Root*, the Mulaprakriti, the undifferentiated Cosmic Substance, which becomes *Astral* Matter. It is also called the " Fiery Serpent," as above described. If the student bears in mind that there is but One Universal Element, which is infinite, unborn, and undying, and that all the rest—as in the world of phenomena—are but so many various differentiated aspects and transformations (correlations, they are now called) of that One, from Cosmical down to microcosmical effects, from super-human down to human and sub-human beings, the totality, in short, of objective existence—then the first and chief difficulty will disappear and Occult Cosmology may be mastered.*
All the Kabalists and Occultists, Eastern and Western, recognise (*a*)

---

* In the Egyptian as in the Indian theogony there was a *concealed* deity, the ONE, and the creative, androgynous god. Thus *Shoo* is the god of creation and Osiris is, in his original primary form, the " god whose name is unknown." (See Mariette's Abydos II., p. 63, and Vol. III., pp. 413, 414, No. 1122.)

the identity of " Father-Mother " with primordial *Æther* or *Akâsa*, (Astral Light)* ; and (*b*) its homogeneity before the evolution of the " Son," cosmically *Fohat*, for it is Cosmic Electricity. " Fohat hardens and scatters the seven brothers " (Book III. Dzyan) ; which means that the primordial Electric Entity—for the Eastern Occultists insist that Electricity is an Entity—electrifies into life, and separates primordial stuff or pregenetic matter into atoms, themselves the source of all life and consciousness. " There exists an universal *agent unique* of all forms and of life, that is called Od,† Ob, and Aour, active and passive, positive and negative, like day and night : it is the first light in Creation " (Eliphas Lévi's Kabala) :—the first Light of the primordial Elohim—the Adam, "male and female "—or (scientifically) ELECTRICITY AND LIFE.

(*c*) The ancients represented it by a serpent, for " Fohat hisses as he glides hither and thither " (in zigzags). The Kabala figures it with the Hebrew letter Teth ⌁, whose symbol is the serpent which played such a prominent part in the Mysteries. Its universal value is nine, for it is the ninth letter of the alphabet and the ninth door of the fifty portals or gateways that lead to the concealed mysteries of being. It is the magical agent *par excellence*, and designates in Hermetic philosophy "Life infused into primordial matter," the essence that composes all things, and the spirit that determines their form. But there are two secret Hermetical operations, one spiritual, the other material-correlative, and for ever united. " Thou shalt separate the earth from the fire, the subtile from the solid . . . that which ascends from earth to heaven and descends again from heaven to earth. It (the subtile light), is the strong force of every force, for it conquers every subtile thing and penetrates into every solid. Thus was the world formed " (*Hermes*).

It was not Zeno alone, the founder of the Stoics, who taught that the

---

* See next note.

† Od is the pure life-giving Light, or magnetic fluid ; Ob the messenger of death used by the sorcerers, the nefarious evil fluid ; Aour is the synthesis of the two, Astral Light proper. Can the Philologists tell why Od—a term used by Reichenbach to denominate the vital fluid—is also a Tibetan word meaning light, brightness, radiancy ? It equally means " Sky " in an occult sense. Whence the root of the word ? But *Akasa* is not quite *Ether*, but far higher than that, as will be shown.

Universe evolves, when its primary substance is transformed from the state of fire into that of air, then into water, etc. Heracleitus of Ephesus maintained that the one principle that underlies all phenomena in Nature is fire. The intelligence that moves the Universe is fire, and fires is intelligence. And while Anaximenes said the same of air, and Thales of Miletus (600 years B.C.) of water, the Esoteric Doctrine reconciles all those philosophers by showing that though each was right the system of none was complete.

STANZA III.—*Continued*.

8. WHERE WAS THE GERM, AND WHERE WAS NOW DARKNESS ? WHERE IS THE SPIRIT OF THE FLAME THAT BURNS IN THY LAMP, OH LANOO ? THE GERM IS THAT, AND THAT IS LIGHT ; THE WHITE BRILLIANT SON OF THE DARK HIDDEN FATHER (*a*).

(*a*) The answer to the first question, suggested by the second, which is the reply of the teacher to the pupil, contains in a single phrase one of the most essential truths of occult philosophy. It indicates the existence of things imperceptible to our physical senses which are of far greater importance, more real and more permanent, than those that appeal to these senses themselves. Before the Lanoo can hope to understand the transcendentally metaphysical problem contained in the first question he must be able to answer the second, while the very answer he gives to the second will furnish him with the clue to the correct reply to the first.

In the Sanscrit Commentary on this Stanza, the terms used for the concealed and the unrevealed Principle are many. In the earliest MSS. of Indian literature this Unrevealed, Abstract Deity has no name. It is called generally "*That*" (*Tad* in Sanskrit), and means all that is, was, and will be, or that can be so received by the human mind.

Among such appellations, given, of course, only in esoteric philosophy, as the " Unfathomable Darkness," the " Whirlwind," etc.—it is also called the " It of the Kalahansa, the Kala-ham-sa," and even the " Kali Hamsa," (Black swan). Here the *m* and the *n* are convertible, and both sound like the nasal French *an* or *am*, or, again, *en* or *em* (*Ennui, Embarras*, etc.) As in the Hebrew Bible, many a mysterious sacred name in Sanscrit conveys to the profane ear no more than some ordinary, and often vulgar word, because it is concealed anagrammatically or otherwise. This word of Hansa or esoterically " hamsa " is just such a case. Hamsa is equal to a-ham-sa, three words meaning " I am he " (in English), while divided in still another way it will read " So-ham," " he (is) I "—Soham being equal to Sah, " he," and aham, " I," or " I am he." In this alone is contained the universal mystery, the doctrine of the identity of man's essence with god-essence, for him who understands the language of wisdom. Hence the glyph of, and the allegory about, Kalahansa (or hamsa), and the name given to Brahma neuter (later on, to the male Brahmâ) of " Hansa-Vahana," he who uses the Hansa as his vehicle." The same word may be read " Kalaham-sa " or " I am I " in the eternity of Time, answering to the Biblical, or rather Zoroastrian " I am that I am." The same doctrine is found in the Kabala, as witness the following extract from an unpublished MS. by Mr. S. Liddell McGregor Mathers, the learned Kabalist : " The three pronouns היא, אתה, אני, Hoa, Atah, Ani ; He, Thou, I ; are used to symbolize the ideas of Macroprosopus and Microprosopus in the Hebrew Qabalah. Hoa, " He," is applied to the hidden and concealed Macroprosopus ; Atah, " Thou," to Microprosopus ; and Ani, " I," to the latter when He is represented as speaking. (See *Lesser Holy Assembly*, 204 *et seq.*) It is to be noted that each of these names consists of three letters, of which the letter Aleph א, A, forms the conclusion of the first word Hoa, and the commencement of Atah and Ani, as if it were the connecting link between them. But א is the symbol of the Unity and consequently of the unvarying Idea of the Divine operating through all these. But behind the א in the name Hoa are the letters ו and ה, the symbols of the numbers Six and Five, the Male and the Female, the Hexagram and the Pentagram. And the numbers of these three words, Hoa Atah Ani, are 12, 406, and 61, which are resumed in the key numbers of 3, 10, and 7, by the Qabalah of the Nine Chambers, which is a form of the exegetical rule of Temura."

It is useless to attempt to explain the mystery in full. Materialists and the men of modern Science will never understand it, since, in order to obtain clear perception of it, one has first of all to admit the postulate of a universally diffused, omnipresent, eternal Deity in Nature; secondly, to have fathomed the mystery of electricity in its true essence ; and thirdly, to credit man with being the septenary symbol, on the terrestrial plane, of the One Great UNIT (the Logos), which is Itself the Seven-vowelled sign, the Breath crystallized into the WORD.* He who believes in all this, has also to believe in the multiple combination of the seven planets of Occultism and of the Kabala, with the twelve zodiacal signs; to attribute, as we do, to each planet and to each constellation an influence which, in the words of Ely Star (a French Occultist), "is proper to it, beneficent or maleficent, and this, after the planetary Spirit which rules it, who, in his turn, is capable of influencing men and things which are found in harmony with him and with which he has any affinity." For these reasons, and since few believe in the foregoing, all that can now be given is that in both cases the symbol of Hansa (whether " I," " He," Goose or Swan) is an important symbol, representing, for instance, Divine Wisdom, Wisdom in darkness beyond the reach of men. For all exoteric purposes, Hansa, as every Hindu knows, is a fabulous bird, which, when given milk mixed with water for its food (in the allegory) separated the two, drinking the milk and leaving the water ; thus showing inherent wisdom—milk standing symbolically for spirit, and water for matter.

That this allegory is very ancient and dates from the very earliest archaic period, is shown by the mention (in Bhagavata Purâna) of a certain caste named " Hamsa " or " Hansa," which was the " one caste " *par excellence ;* when far back in the mists of a forgotten past there was among the Hindus only " One Veda, One Deity, One Caste." There is also a range in the Himalayas, described in the old books as being situated north of Mount Meru, called " Hamsa," and connected with episodes pertaining to the history of religious mysteries and initiations. As to the name of Kâla-Hansa being the supposed vehicle of Brahmâ-Prajâpati, in the exoteric texts and translations of the

---

* This is again similar to the doctrine of Fichte and German Pantheists. The former reveres Jesus as the great teacher who inculcated the unity of the spirit of man with the God-Spirit (the Adwaita doctrine) or universal Principle. It is difficult to find a single speculation in Western metaphysics which has not been anticipated by Archaic Eastern philosophy. From Kant to Herbert Spencer, it is all a more or less distorted echo of the Dwaita, Adwaita, and Vedantic doctrines generally.

Orientalists, it is quite a mistake. Brahma, the neuter, is called by
them Kala-Hansa and Brahmâ, the male, Hansa-Vahana, because
forsooth "his vehicle or Vahan is a swan or goose" (vide "the Hindu
Classical Dictionary.") This is a purely exoteric gloss. Esoterically
and logically, if Brahma, the infinite, is all that is described by the
Orientalists, namely, agreeably with the Vedantic texts, an abstract
deity in no way characterised by the description of any human attributes, and it is still maintained that he or it is called Kala-Hansa—
then how can it ever become the Vahan of Brahmâ, the manifested
finite god ? It is quite the reverse. The " Swan or goose " (Hansa) is
the symbol of that male or temporary deity, as he, the emanation of the
primordial Ray, is made to serve as a Vahan or vehicle for that divine
Ray, which otherwise could not manifest itself in the Universe, being,
antiphrastically, itself an emanation of " Darkness "—for our human
intellect, at any rate. It is Brahmâ, then, who is Kâla-Hansa, and the
Ray, the Hansa-Vahana.

As to the strange symbol chosen, it is equally suggestive ; the
true mystic significance being the idea of a universal matrix,
figured by the primordial waters of the " deep," or the opening
for the reception, and subsequently for the issue, of that one
ray (the Logos), which contains in itself the other seven
procreative rays or powers (the logoi or builders). Hence the
choice by the Rosecroix of the aquatic fowl — whether swan
or pelican,* with seven young ones for a symbol, modified and
adapted to the religion of every country. En-Soph is called the
" Fiery Soul of the Pelican " in the Book of Numbers.† (See
Part II. " The Hidden Deity and its Symbols and Glyphs.")
Appearing with every Manvantara as Narâyan, or Swayambhuva (the

---

* Whether the genus of the bird be *cygnus, anser*, or *pelecanus*, it is no matter, as it
is an aquatic bird floating or moving on the waters like the Spirit, and then issuing
from those waters to give birth to other beings. The true significance of the symbol
of the Eighteenth Degree of the Rose-Croix is precisely this, though poetised later on
into the motherly feeling of the Pelican rending its bosom to feed its seven little ones
with its blood.

† The reason why Moses forbids eating the pelican and swan, classing the two among
the unclean fowls, and permits eating "bald locusts, beetles, and the grasshopper after
his kind " (Leviticus xi. and Deuteronomy xiv.) is a purely physiological one, and
has to do with mystic symbology only in so far as the word " unclean," like every
other word, ought not to be read and understood literally, as it is esoteric like all the

Self-Existent), and penetrating into the Mundane Egg, it emerges from it at the end of the divine incubation as Brahmâ or Prajâpati, a progenitor of the future Universe into which he expands. He is Purusha (spirit), but he is also Prakriti (matter). Therefore it is only after separating himself into two halves—Brahmâ-vâch (the female) and Brahmâ-Virâj (the male), that the Prajâpati becomes the male Brahmâ.

STANZA III.—*Continued.*

9. LIGHT IS COLD FLAME, AND FLAME IS FIRE, AND THE FIRE PRODUCES HEAT, WHICH YIELDS WATER, THE WATER OF LIFE IN THE GREAT MOTHER (*Chaos*) (*a*).

(*a*) It must be remembered that the words "Light," "Fire," and "Flame" used in the Stanzas have been adopted by the translators thereof from the vocabulary of the old "Fire philosophers,"‡ in order to render better the meaning of the archaic terms and symbols employed in the original. Otherwise they would have remained entirely unintelligible to a European reader. But to a student of the Occult the terms used will be sufficiently clear.

All these—"Light," "Flame," "Hot," "Cold," "Fire," "Heat," "Water," and the "water of life" are all, on our plane, the progeny; or as a modern physicist would say, the correlations of ELECTRICITY. Mighty word, and a still mightier symbol! Sacred generator of a no less sacred progeny; of fire—the creator, the preserver and the destroyer; of light—the essence of our divine ancestors; of flame—the Soul of things. Electricity, the ONE Life at the upper rung of Being, and Astral Fluid, the Athanor of the Alchemists, at its lowest; GOD and DEVIL, GOOD and EVIL. . . .

---

rest, and may as well mean "holy" as not. It is a blind, very suggestive in connection with certain superstitions—*e.g.*, that of the Russian people who will not use the pigeon for food; not because it is "unclean," but because the "Holy Ghost" is credited with having appeared under the form of a Dove.

‡ Not the Mediæval Alchemists, but the Magi and Fire-Worshippers, from whom the Rosicrucians or the Philosophers *per ignem*, the successors of the theurgists borrowed all their ideas concerning Fire, as a mystic and divine element.

Now, why is Light called in the Stanzas " cold flame " ? Because in the order of Cosmic evolution (as taught by the Occultist), the energy that actuates matter after its first formation into atoms is generated on our plane by Cosmic heat ; and because Kosmos, in the sense of dissociated matter, was not, before that period. The first primordial matter, eternal and coeval with Space, " which has neither a beginning nor an end," is " neither hot nor cold, but is of its own special nature," says the Commentary (Book II). Heat and cold are relative qualities and pertain to the realms of the manifested worlds, which all proceed from the manifested *Hyle*, which, in its absolutely latent aspect, is referred to as the " cold Virgin," and when awakened to life, as the " Mother." The ancient Western Cosmogonic myths state that at first there was but cold mist which was the Father, and the prolific slime (the Mother, Ilus or Hyle), from which crept forth the Mundane snake-matter, (*Isis*, vol. i., p. 146). Primordial matter, then, before it emerges from the plane of the never-manifesting, and awakens to the thrill of action under the impulse of Fohat, is but " a cool Radiance, colourless, formless, tasteless, and devoid of every quality and aspect." Even such are her first-born, the " four sons," who " are One, and become Seven," —the entities, by whose qualifications and names the ancient Eastern Occultists called the four of the seven primal " centres of Forces," or atoms, that develop later into the great Cosmic " Elements," now divided into the seventy or so sub-elements, known to science. The four primal natures of the first Dhyan Chohans, are the so-called (for want of better terms) " Akasic," " Ethereal," " Watery," and " Fiery," answering, in the terminology of practical occultism, to scientific definitions of gases, which, to convey a clear idea to both Occultists and laymen, must be defined as Parahydrogenic,* Paraoxygenic, Oxy-hydrogenic, and Ozonic, or perhaps Nitr-ozonic ; the latter forces or gases (in Occultism, supersensuous, yet atomic substances) being the most effective and active when energising on the plane of more grossly differentiated matter.† These are both electro-positive and electro-negative.

---

* παρὰ, " beyond," outside.

† Each of these and many more are probably the missing links of chemistry. They are known by other names in Alchemy and to the Occultists who practise in phenomenal powers. It is by combining and recombining in a certain way (or dissociating) the " Elements " by means of astral fire that the greatest phenomena are produced.

STANZA III.—*Continued.*

10. FATHER-MOTHER SPIN A WEB WHOSE UPPER END IS FASTENED TO SPIRIT (*Purusha*), THE LIGHT OF THE ONE DARKNESS, AND THE LOWER ONE TO MATTER (*Prakriti*) ITS (*the Spirit's*) SHADOWY END ; AND THIS WEB IS THE UNIVERSE SPUN OUT OF THE TWO SUBSTANCES MADE IN ONE, WHICH IS SWÂBHÂVAT (*a*).

(*a*) In the Mandukya (Mundaka) Upanishad it is written, " As a spider throws out and retracts its web, as herbs spring up in the ground . . . so is the Universe derived from the undecaying one " (I. 1. 7). Brahmâ, as " the germ of unknown Darkness," is the material from which all evolves and develops " as the web from the spider, as foam from the water," etc. This is only graphic and true, if Brahmâ the " Creator " is, as a term, derived from the root *brih*, to increase or expand. Brahmâ " expands " and becomes the Universe woven out of his own substance.

The same idea has been beautifully expressed by Goethe, who says :
> " Thus at the roaring loom of Time I ply,
> And weave for God the garment thou see'st Him by."

STANZA III.—*Continued.*

11. IT (*the Web*) EXPANDS WHEN THE BREATH OF FIRE (*the Father*) IS UPON IT ; IT CONTRACTS WHEN THE BREATH OF THE MOTHER (*the root of Matter*) TOUCHES IT. THEN THE SONS (*the Elements with their respective Powers, or Intelligences*) DISSOCIATE AND SCATTER, TO RETURN INTO THEIR MOTHER'S BOSOM AT THE END OF THE " GREAT DAY " AND REBECOME ONE WITH HER (*a*). WHEN IT (*the Web*) IS COOLING, IT BECOMES RADIANT, ITS SONS EXPAND AND CONTRACT THROUGH THEIR OWN SELVES AND HEARTS ; THEY EMBRACE INFINITUDE. (*b*)

The expanding of the Universe under the breath of FIRE is very suggestive in the light of the " Fire mist " period of which modern science speaks so much, and knows in reality so little.

Great heat breaks up the compound elements and resolves the

heavenly bodies into their primeval one element, explains the commentary. " Once disintegrated into its primal constituent by getting within the attraction and reach of a focus, or centre of heat (energy), of which many are carried about to and fro in space, a body, whether alive or dead, will be vapourised and held in "the bosom of the Mother" until Fohat, gathering a few of the clusters of Cosmic matter (nebulæ) will, by giving it an impulse, set it in motion anew, develop the required heat, and then leave it to follow its own new growth.

The expanding and contracting of the Web—*i.e.*, the world stuff or atoms—expresses here the pulsatory movement ; for it is the regular contraction and expansion of the infinite and shoreless Ocean of that which we may call the noumenon of matter emanated by Swâbhâvat, which causes the universal vibration of atoms. But it is also suggestive of something else. It shows that the ancients were acquainted with that which is now the puzzle of many scientists and especially of astronomers : the cause of the first ignition of matter or the world-stuff, the paradox of the heat produced by the refrigerative contraction and other such Cosmic riddles. For it points unmistakeably to a knowledge by the ancients of such phenomena. " There is heat internal and heat external in every atom," say the manuscript Commentaries, to which the writer has had access ; " the breath of the Father (or Spirit) and the breath (or heat) of the Mother (matter) ;" and they give explanations which show that the modern theory of the extinction of the solar fires by loss of heat through radiation, is erroneous. The assumption is false even on the Scientists' own admission. For as Professor Newcomb points out (Popular Astronomy, pp. 506-508), " by losing heat, a gaseous body contracts, and the heat generated by the contraction exceeds that which it had to lose in order to produce the contraction." This paradox, that a body gets hotter as the shrinking produced by its getting colder is greater, led to long disputes. The surplus of heat, it was argued, was lost by radiation, and to assume that the temperature is not lowered *pari passu* with a decrease of volume under a constant pressure, is to set at nought the law of Charles (Nebular Theory, Winchell). Contraction develops heat, it is true ; but contraction (from cooling) is incapable of developing the whole amount of heat at any time existing in the mass, or even of maintaining a body at a constant temperature, etc. Professor Winchell tries to reconcile the paradox—only a seeming one in fact, as

Homer Lanes proved,—by suggesting " something besides heat."
" May it not be," he asks, " simply a repulsion among the molecules,
which varies according to some law of the distance ? " But even this
will be found irreconcileable, unless this " something besides heat " is
ticketed " Causeless Heat," the " Breath of Fire," the all-creative
Force plus ABSOLUTE INTELLIGENCE, which physical science is not likely
to accept.

However it may be, the reading of this Stanza shows it, notwithstanding its archaic phraseology, to be more scientific than even modern
science.

STANZA III.—*Continued.*

12. THEN SVÂBHÂVAT SENDS FOHAT TO HARDEN THE ATOMS. EACH
(*of these*) IS A PART OF THE WEB (*Universe*). REFLECTING THE " SELF-
EXISTENT LORD " (*Primeval Light*) LIKE A MIRROR, EACH BECOMES IN
TURN A WORLD.* . . .

" Fohat hardens the atoms "; *i.e.*, by infusing energy into them: he
scatters the atoms or primordial matter. " He scatters himself while
scattering matter into atoms " (MSS. Commentaries.)

It is through Fohat that the ideas of the Universal Mind are
impressed upon matter. Some faint idea of the nature of Fohat may
be gathered from the appellation " Cosmic Electricity " sometimes
applied to it; but to the commonly known properties of electricity
must, in this case, be added others, including intelligence. It is of
interest to note that modern science has come to the conclusion, that
all cerebration and brain-activity are attended by electrical phenomena.
(*For further details as to " Fohat " See Stanza V. and Comments.*")

---

* This is said in the sense that the flame from a fire is endless, and that the lights of
the whole Universe could be lit at one simple rush-light without diminishing its
flame.

STANZA IV.

1. LISTEN, YE SONS OF THE EARTH, TO YOUR INSTRUCTORS—THE SONS OF THE FIRE (*a*). LEARN THERE IS NEITHER FIRST NOR LAST ; FOR ALL IS ONE NUMBER, ISSUED FROM NO NUMBER (*b*).

(*a*) These terms, the "Sons of the Fire," the "Sons of the Fire-Mist," and the like, require explanation. They are connected with a great primordial and universal mystery, and it is not easy to make it clear. There is a passage in the *Bhagavatgîtâ* (ch. viii.) wherein Krishna, speaking symbolically and *esoterically*, says : "I will state the times (conditions) . . . at which devotees departing (from this life) do so never to return (be reborn), or to return (to incarnate again). The Fire, the Flame, the day, the bright (lucky) fortnight, the six months of the Northern solstice, departing (dying) in these, those who know the Brahman (Yogis) go to the Brahman. Smoke, night, the dark (unlucky) fortnight, the six months of the Southern solstice, (dying) in these, the devotee goes to the lunar light (or mansion the astral light also) and returns (is reborn). These two paths, bright and dark, are said to be eternal in this world (or great kalpa, 'Age'). By the one a man goes never to come back, by the other he returns." Now these names, "Fire," "Flame," "Day," the "bright fortnight," etc., as "Smoke," "Night," and so on, leading only to the end of the lunar path are incomprehensible without a knowledge of Esotericism. These are *all names of various deities* which preside over the Cosmo-psychic Powers. We often speak of the Hierarchy of "Flames" (see Book II.), of the "Sons of Fire," etc. Sankarâchârya the greatest of the Esoteric masters of India, says that *fire* means a deity which presides over Time (kâla). The able translator of Bhagavatgîtâ, Kashinâth Trimbak Telang, M.A., of Bombay, confesses he has "no clear notion of the meaning of these verses" (p. 81, footnote). It seems quite clear, on the contrary, to him who knows the occult doctrine. With these verses the mystic sense of the solar and lunar symbols are connected : the Pitris are *lunar* deities and our ancestors, because they *created the physical man.*

The Agnishwatha, the Kumara (the seven mystic sages), are solar deities, though the former are Pitris also; and these are the "fashioners of the *Inner* Man." (See Book II.) They are:—

"The Sons of Fire"—because they are the first Beings (in the Secret Doctrine they are called "Minds"), evolved from Primordial Fire. "The Lord is a consuming Fire" (Deuteronomy iv. 24); "The Lord (Christos) shall be revealed with his mighty angels in flaming fire" (2 Thessal. i. 7, 8). The Holy Ghost descended on the Apostles like "cloven tongues of fire," (Acts ii. v. 3); Vishnu will return on *Kalki*, the White Horse, as the last Avatar amid fire and flames; and *Sosiosh* will be brought down equally on a White Horse in a "tornado of fire." "And I saw heaven open and behold a white horse, and he that sat upon him . . . . is called the Word of God," (Rev. xix. 13) amid flaming Fire. Fire is Æther in its purest form, and hence is not regarded as matter, but it is the unity of Æther—the second manifested deity—in its universality. But there are two "Fires" and a distinction is made between them in the Occult teachings. The first, or the purely *Formless* and *invisible* Fire concealed in the *Central Spiritual Sun*, is spoken of as "triple" (metaphysically); while the Fire of the manifested Kosmos is Septenary, throughout both the Universe and our Solar System. "The fire or knowledge burns up all action on the plane of illusion," says the commentary. "Therefore, those who have acquired it and are emancipated, are called 'Fires.'" Speaking of the *seven* senses symbolised as *Hotris*, priests, the Brâhmana says in *Anugîtâ* : " Thus these *seven* (senses, smell and taste, and colour, and sound, etc., etc.) are the causes of emancipation;" and the commentator adds: "It is from these seven from which the Self is to be emancipated. 'I' (am here devoid of qualities) must mean the Self, not the Brâhmana who speaks." ("*Sacred Books of the East*,," ed. by Max Müller, Vol. VIII., 278.)

(*b*) The expression "All is One Number, issued from No Number " relates again to that universal and philosophical tenet just explained in Stanza III. (Comm. 4). That which is absolute is of course No Number; but in its later significance it has an application in Space as in Time. It means that not only every increment of time is part of a larger increment, up to the most indefinitely prolonged duration conceivable by the human intellect, but also that no manifested thing can be thought of except as part of a larger whole : the total aggregate being the One manifested Universe that issues from the unmanifested or Absolute—called Non-Being or " No-Number," to distinguish it from BEING or " the One Number."

STANZA IV.—*Continued.*

(2) LEARN WHAT WE, WHO DESCEND FROM THE PRIMORDIAL SEVEN, WE, WHO ARE BORN FROM THE PRIMORDIAL FLAME, HAVE LEARNED FROM OUR FATHERS (*a*).

(*a*) This is explained in Book II., and this name, " Primordial Flame," corroborates what is said in the first paragraph of the preceding commentary on Stanza IV.

The distinction between the " Primordial " and the subsequent seven Builders is this : The former are the Ray and direct emanation of the first " Sacred Four," the *Tetraktis*, that is, the eternally Self-Existent One (Eternal *in Essence* note well, not in manifestation, and distinct from the universal ONE). Latent, during Pralaya, and active, during Manvantara, the " Primordial " proceed from " Father-Mother " (Spirit-Hyle, or *Ilus*); whereas the other manifested Quaternary and the Seven proceed from the Mother alone. It is the latter who is the immaculate Virgin-Mother, who is overshadowed, not impregnated, by the Universal MYSTERY—when she emerges from her state of Laya or undifferentiated condition. In reality, they are, of course, all one; but their aspects on the various planes of being are different. (See Part II., " Theogony of the Creative Gods.")

The first " Primordial " are the highest Beings on the Scale of Existence. They are the Archangels of Christianity, those who refuse —as Michael did in the latter system, and as did the eldest " Mind-born sons " of Brahmâ (Veddhas)—to create or rather to multiply.

STANZA IV.—*Continued.*

3. FROM THE EFFULGENCE OF LIGHT—THE RAY OF THE EVER-DARKNESS —SPRUNG IN SPACE THE RE-AWAKENED ENERGIES (*Dhyan Chohans*): THE ONE FROM THE EGG, THE SIX AND THE FIVE (*a*); THEN THE THREE, THE ONE,

THE FOUR, THE ONE, THE FIVE—THE TWICE SEVEN, THE SUM TOTAL (b). AND THESE ARE : THE ESSENCES, THE FLAMES, THE ELEMENTS, THE BUILDERS, THE NUMBERS, THE ARUPA (*formless*), THE RUPA (*with bodies*), AND THE FORCE OR DIVINE MAN—THE SUM TOTAL. AND FROM THE DIVINE MAN EMANATED THE FORMS, THE SPARKS, THE SACRED ANIMALS, AND THE MESSENGERS OF THE SACRED FATHERS (*the Pitris*) WITHIN THE HOLY FOUR.*

(*a*) This relates to the sacred Science of the Numerals : so sacred, indeed, and so important in the study of Occultism that the subject can hardly be skimmed, even in such a large work as the present. It is on the Hierarchies and correct numbers of these Beings invisible (to us) except upon very rare occasions, that the mystery of the whole Universe is built. The *Kumaras*, for instance, are called the "Four" though in reality seven in number, because Sanaka, Sananda, Sanatana and Sanat-Kumara are the chief Vaidhâtra (their patronymic name), as they spring from the "four-fold mystery." To make the whole clearer we have to turn for our illustrations to tenets more familiar to some of our readers, namely, the Brahminical.

According to Manu, Hiranyagarbha is Brahmâ *the first male* formed by the undiscernible Causeless CAUSE in a "Golden Egg resplendent as the Sun," as states the Hindu Classical Dictionary. "Hiranyagarbha" —means the golden, or rather the "Effulgent Womb" or Egg. The meaning tallies awkwardly with the epithet of "male." Surely the esoteric meaning of the sentence is clear enough. In the Rig Veda it is said :—" THAT, the one Lord of all beings . . . . the one animating principle of gods and man," arose, in the beginning, in the Golden Womb, Hiranyagarbha—which is the Mundane Egg or sphere of our Universe. That Being is surely androgynous, and the allegory of Brahmâ separating into two and recreating in one of his halves (the female Vâch) himself as Virâj, is a proof of it.

"The One from the Egg, the Six and the Five," give the number 1065, the value of the first-born (later on the male and female Brahmâ-Prajâpati), who answers to the numbers 7, and 14, and 21 respectively. The Prajâpati are, like the Sephiroth, only seven, including the

---

* The 4, represented in the Occult numerals by the Tetraktis, the Sacred or Perfect Square, is a Sacred Number with the mystics of every nation and race. It has one and the same significance in Brahmanism, Buddhism, the Kabala and in the Egyptian, Chaldean and other numerical systems.

synthetic Sephira of the triad from which they spring. Thus from Hiranyagarbha or Prajâpati, the *triune* (primeval Vedic Trimurti, Agni, Vayu, and Surya), emanate the other seven, or again ten, if we separate the first three which exist in one, and one in three, all, moreover, being comprehended within that one "supreme" Parama, called Guhya or "secret," and Sarvâtma, the "Super-Soul." "The seven Lords of Being lie concealed in Sarvâtma like thoughts in one brain." So are the Sephiroth. It is either seven when counting from the upper Triad headed by Kether, or ten—exoterically. In the Mahabhârata the Prajâpati are 21 in number, or ten, six, and five (1065), thrice seven.*

(*b*) "The Three, the One, the Four, the One, the Five" (in their totality —twice seven) represent 31415—the numerical hierarchy of the Dhyan-Chohans of various orders, and of the inner or circumscribed world.† When placed on the boundary of the great circle of "Pass not" (see Stanza V.), called also the Dhyanipasa, the "rope of the Angels," the "rope" that hedges off the phenomenal from the noumenal Kosmos, (not falling within the range of our present objective consciousness); this number, when not enlarged by permutation and expansion, is ever 31415 anagrammatically and Kabalistically, being both the number of the circle and the mystic Svastica, the twice seven once more; for whatever way the two sets of figures are counted, when added separately, one figure after another, whether crossways, from right or from left, they will always yield fourteen. Mathematically they represent the well-known calculation, namely, that the ratio of the diameter to the circumference of a circle is as 1 to 3·1415, or the value of the π (pi), as this ratio is called—the symbol π being always used in

---

* In the Kabala the same numbers are a value of Jehovah, viz., 1065, since the numerical values of the three letters which compose his name—Jod, Vau and twice He —are respectively 10 (י), 6 (ו) and 5 (ה); or again thrice seven, 21. "Ten is the Mother of the Soul, for Life and Light are therein united," says Hermes. "For number one is born of the Spirit and the number ten from matter (chaos, feminine) ; the unity has made the ten, the ten the unity" (*Book of the Keys*). By the means of the Temura, the anagrammatical method of the Kabala, and the knowledge of 1065 (21), a universal science may be obtained regarding Kosmos and its mysteries" (Rabbi Yogel). The Rabbis regard the numbers 10, 6, and 5 as the most sacred of all.

† The reader may be told that an American Kabalist has now discovered the same number for the Elohim. It came to the Jews from Chaldæa. See "Hebrew Metrology" in the Masonic Review, July, 1885, McMillan Lodge, No. 141.

mathematical formulæ to express it. This set of figures must have the same meaning, since the 1 : 314,159, and then again 1 : 3 : 1,415,927 are worked out in the secret calculations to express the various cycles and ages of the "first born," or 311,040,000,000,000 with fractions, and yield the same 13,415 by a process we are not concerned with at present. And it may be shown that Mr. Ralston Skinner, author of *The Source of Measures*, reads the Hebrew word Alhim in the same number values, by omitting, as said, the ciphers and by permutation—13,514 : since א (a) is 1 : ל (l) is 3 (or 30); ה (h) is 5 ; י (i) 1 for 10 ; and מ (m) is 4 (40), and anagrammatically—31,415 as explained by him.

Thus, while in the metaphysical world, the circle with the one central Point in it has no number, and is called Anupadaka (parentless and numberless)—viz., it can fall under no calculation,—in the manifested world the mundane Egg or Circle is circumscribed within the groups called the Line, the Triangle, the Pentacle, the second Line and the Cube (or 13514) ; and when the Point having generated a Line, thus becomes a diameter which stands for the androgynous Logos, then the figures become 31415, or a triangle, a line, a cube, the second line, and a pentacle. " When the Son separates from the Mother he becomes the Father," the diameter standing for Nature, or the feminine principle. Therefore it is said : " In the world of being, the one Point fructifies the Line—the Virgin Matrix of Kosmos (the egg-shaped zero)—and the immaculate Mother gives birth to the form that combines all forms." Prajâpati is called the first procreating male, and "his Mother's husband." * This gives the key-note to all the later divine sons from immaculate mothers. It is greatly corroborated by the significant fact that Anna (the name of the Mother of the Virgin Mary) now represented by the Roman Catholic church as having given birth to her daughter in an immaculate way (" Mary conceived without sin "), is derived from the Chaldean Ana, heaven, or Astral Light, Anima Mundi; whence Anaitia, Devi-durga, the wife of Siva, is also called Annapurna,

---

* We find the same expression in Egypt. Mout signifies, for one thing, " Mother," and shows the character assigned to her in the triad of that country. " She was no less the mother than the wife of Ammon, one of the principle titles of the god being " the husband of his mother." The goddess Mout, or Mût, is addressed as "our lady," the " queen of Heaven " and of " the Earth," thus " sharing these titles with the other mother goddesses, Isis, Hathor, etc." (Maspero).

and Kanya, the Virgin; "Uma-Kanya" being her esoteric name, and meaning the "Virgin of light," Astral Light in one of its multitudinous aspects.

(c) The Devas, Pitris, Rishis; the Suras and the Asuras; the Daityas and Adityas; the Danavas and Gandharvas, etc., etc., have all their synonyms in our Secret Doctrine, as well as in the Kabala and the Hebrew Angelology; but it is useless to give their ancient names, as it would only create confusion. Many of these may be also found now, even in the Christian hierarchy of divine and celestial powers. All those Thrones and Dominions, Virtues and Principalities, Cherubs, Seraphs and demons, the various denizens of the Sidereal World, are the modern copies of archaic prototypes. The very symbolism in their names, when transliterated and arranged in Greek and Latin, are sufficient to show it, as will be proved in several cases further on.

The "Sacred Animals" are found in the Bible as well as in the Kabala, and they have their meaning (a very profound one, too) on the page of the origins of Life. In the Sepher Jezirah it is stated that "God engraved in the Holy Four the throne of his glory, the Ophanim (Wheels or the World-Spheres), the Seraphim,* the Sacred Animals, and the ministering angels, and from these three (the Air, Water, and Fire or Ether) he formed his habitation." Thus was the world made "through three Seraphim—Sepher, Saphar, and Sipur," or "through Number, Numbers, and Numbered." With the astronomical key these "Sacred Animals" become the signs of the Zodiac.

---

* This is the literal translation from the IXth and Xth Sections: "Ten numbers without what? One: the spirit of the living God . . . . who liveth in eternities! Voice and Spirit and Word, and this is the Holy Spirit. Two: Spirit out of Spirit. He designed and hewed therewith twenty-two letters of foundation, three Mothers and seven double and Twelve single, and one spirit out of them. Three: Water out of spirit; he designed and hewed with them the barren and the void, mud and earth. He designed them as a flowerbed, hewed them as a wall, covered them as a paving. Four: Fire out of water. He designed and hewed therewith the throne of glory and the wheels, and the seraphim and the holy animals and the ministering angels, and of the three He founded his dwelling, as it is said, He makes his angels spirits and his servants fiery flames!" Which words "founded his dwelling" show clearly that in the Kabala, as in India, the Deity was considered as the Universe, and was not, in his origin, the extra-cosmic God he is now.

STANZA IV.—*Continued.*

4. THIS WAS THE ARMY OF THE VOICE—THE DIVINE SEPTENARY. THE SPARKS OF THE SEVEN ARE SUBJECT TO, AND THE SERVANTS OF, THE FIRST, SECOND, THIRD, FOURTH, FIFTH, SIXTH, AND THE SEVENTH OF THE SEVEN (*a*). THESE ("*sparks*") ARE CALLED SPHERES, TRIANGLES, CUBES, LINES, AND MODELLERS ; FOR THUS STANDS THE ETERNAL NIDANA—THE OI-HA-HOU (*the permutation of Oeaohoo*) (*b*).*

(*a*) This Sloka gives again a brief analysis of the Hierarchies of the Dhyan Chohans, called Devas (gods) in India, or the conscious intelligent powers in Nature. To this Hierarchy correspond the actual types into which humanity may be divided ; for humanity, as a whole, is in reality a materialized though as yet imperfect expression thereof. The " army of the Voice " is a term closely connected with the mystery of Sound and Speech, as an effect and corollary of the cause—Divine Thought. As beautifully expressed by P. Christian, the learned author of " The History of Magic " and of " L'Homme Rouge des Tuileries," the word spoken by, as well as the name of, every individual largely determine his future fate. Why ? Because—

—" When our Soul (mind) creates or evokes a thought, the representative sign ot that thought is self-engraved upon the astral fluid, which is the receptacle and, so to say, the mirror of all the manifestations of being.

" The sign expresses the thing : the thing is the (hidden or occult) virtue of the sign.

" To pronounce a word is to evoke a thought, and make it present : the magnetic potency of the human speech is the commencement of every manifestation in the Occult World. To utter a Name is not only to define a Being (an Entity), but to place it under and condemn it through the emission of the Word (Verbum), to the influence of one or more Occult potencies. Things are, for every one of us, that which it (the Word) makes them while naming them. The Word (Verbum) or the speech of every man is, quite unconsciously to himself, a BLESSING or a CURSE ; this is why our present ignorance about the properties or attributes of the IDEA as well as about the attributes and properties of MATTER, is often fatal to us.

---

* The literal signification of the word is, among the Eastern Occultists of the North, a circular wind, whirlwind ; but in this instance, it is a term to denote the ceaseless and eternal Cosmic Motion ; or rather the Force that moves it, which Force is tacitly accepted as the Deity but never named. It is the eternal *Karana*, the ever-acting Cause.

" Yes, names (and words) are either BENEFICENT or MALEFICENT ; they are, in a certain sense, either venomous or health-giving, according to the hidden influences attached by Supreme Wisdom to their elements, that is to say, to the LETTERS which compose them, and the NUMBERS correlative to these letters."

This is strictly true as an esoteric teaching accepted by all the Eastern Schools of Occultism. In the Sanskrit, as also in the Hebrew and all other alphabets, every letter has its occult meaning and its rationale ; it is a cause and an effect of a preceding cause and a combination of these very often produces the most magical effect. The vowels, especially, contain the most occult and formidable potencies. The Mantras (esoterically, magical rather than religious) are chanted by the Brahmins and so are the Vedas and other Scriptures.

The " Army of the Voice," is the prototype of the "Host of the Logos," or the " WORD " of the Sepher Jezirah, called in the Secret Doctrine "the One Number issued from No-Number"—the One Eternal Principle. The esoteric theogony begins with the One, manifested, therefore not eternal in its presence and being, if eternal in its essence ; the number of the numbers and numbered—the latter proceeding from the Voice, the feminine Vâch, Satarupa " of the hundred forms," or Nature. It is from this number 10, or creative nature, the Mother (the occult cypher, or "nought," ever procreating and multiplying in union with the Unit " I," one, or the Spirit of Life), that the whole Universe proceeded.

In the *Anugîtâ* a conversation is given (ch. vi., 15) between a Brâhmana and his wife, on the origin of Speech and its occult properties.* The wife asks how Speech came into existence, and which was prior to the other, Speech or Mind. The Brâhmana tells her that the Apâna (*inspirational breath*) becoming lord, changes that intelligence, which does not understand Speech or Words, into the state of Apâna, and thus opens the mind. Thereupon he tells her a story, a dialogue between Speech and Mind. " Both went to the Self of Being (*i.e.*, to the individual Higher Self, as Nilakantha thinks, to Prajâpati, according to the commentator Arjûna Misra), and asked him to destroy their doubts and decide which of them preceded and was superior to the

---

* *Anugîtâ* forms part of the Asvamedha Parvan of the " Mahâbhârata." The translator of the Bhagavatgîtâ, edited by Max Müller, regards it as a continuation of the Bhagavatgîtâ. Its original is one of the oldest *Upanisha s.*

other. To this the lord said: 'Mind is superior.' But Speech answered the Self of Being, by saying: 'I verily yield (you) your desires,' meaning that by speech he acquired what he desired. Thereupon again, the Self told her that there are two minds, the 'movable' and the 'immovable.' 'The immovable is with me,' he said, 'the movable is in your dominion' (*i.e.* of Speech) on the plane of matter. To that you are superior. But inasmuch, O beautiful one, as you came personally to speak to me (in the way you did, *i.e.* proudly), therefore, O, Sarasvati! you shall never speak after (hard) exhalation." "The goddess Speech" (Sarasvati, a later form or aspect of Vâch, the goddess also of secret learning or Esoteric Wisdom), "verily, dwelt always between the Prâna and the Apâna. But O noble one! going with the Apâna wind (vital air), though impelled, without the Prâna (expirational breath), she ran up to Prajâpati (Brahmâ), saying, 'Be pleased, O venerable sir!' Then the Prâna appeared again, nourishing Speech. And, therefore, Speech never speaks after (hard or inspirational) exhalation. It is always noisy or noiseless. Of these two, the noiseless is the superior to the noisy (Speech). . . . . The (speech) which is produced in the body by means of the Prâna, and which then goes (is transformed) into Apâna, and then becoming assimilated with the Udâna (physical organs of Speech) . . . then finally dwells in the Samâna ('at the navel in the form of sound, as the material cause of all words,' says Arjûna Misra). So Speech formerly spoke. Hence the mind is distinguished by reason of its being immovable, and the Goddess (Speech) by reason of her being movable."

This allegory is at the root of the Occult law, which prescribes silence upon the knowledge of certain secret and invisible things perceptible only to the spiritual mind (the 6th sense), and which cannot be expressed by "noisy" or uttered speech. This chapter of *Anugîtâ* explains, says Arjuna Misra, Prânâyâma, or regulation of the breath in Yoga practices. This mode, however, without the previous acquisition of, or at least full understanding of the two higher senses, of which there are seven, as will be shown, pertains rather to the lower Yoga. The *Hâtha* so called was and still is discountenanced by the Arhats. It is injurious to the health and alone can never develop into Raj Yoga. This story is quoted to show how inseparably connected are, in the metaphysics of old, intelligent beings, or rather "Intelligences," with every sense or function whether physical or mental. The Occult claim that there are seven senses in man, as in nature, as there are seven states of consciousness, is corroborated in the same work, chapter vii., on Pratyâhâra (the restraint and regulation of the senses, Prânâyâma being that of the " vital winds " or breath). The Brâhmana speaks in it " of the institution of the seven sacrificial Priests (Hotris). He says : " The nose and the eyes, and the tongue, and the skin and the ear as the fifth (or smell, sight, taste, touch and hearing), mind and understanding are the seven sacrificial priests separately stationed " ; and which " dwelling in a minute space (still) do not perceive each other " on this sensuous plane, none of them except mind. For mind says : " The nose smells not without me, the eye does not take in colour, etc., etc. I am the eternal chief among all elements (*i.e.*, senses). Without me, the senses never shine, like an empty dwelling, or like fires the flames of which are extinct. Without me, all beings, like fuel half dried and half moist, fail to apprehend qualities or objects even with the senses exerting themselves."*

This, of course, with regard only to *mind on the sensuous plane*. Spiritual mind (the upper portion or aspect of the *impersonal* MANAS) takes no cognisance of the senses in physical man. How well the ancients were acquainted with the correlation of forces and all the recently discovered phenomena of mental and physical faculties and functions, with many more mysteries also—may be found in reading chapters vii. and viii. of this (in philosophy and mystic learning) priceless work. See the quarrel of the senses about their respective superiority and their taking the Brahman, the lord of all creatures, for their arbiter. " You are all greatest and not greatest," or superior to objects, as A. Misra says, none being independent of the other. " You are all possessed of one another's qualities. All are greatest in their own spheres and all support one another. There is one unmoving (life-wind or breath, the '*Yoga inhalation*,' so called, which is the breath of the *One* or Higher SELF). That is the (or my) own Self, accumulated in numerous (forms)."

This Breath, Voice, Self or " Wind " (*pneuma ?*) is the Synthesis of the Seven Senses, *noumenally* all minor deities and esoterically—the *septenary* and the " Army of the VOICE."

---

* This shows the modern metaphysicians, added to all past and present Hægels, Berkeleys, Schopenhauers, Hartmanns, Herbert Spencers, and even the modern Hylo-Idealists to boot, no better than the pale copyists of hoary antiquity.

(b) Next we see Cosmic matter scattering and forming itself into elements; grouped into the mystic four within the fifth element—Ether, the lining of Akasa, the Anima Mundi or Mother of Kosmos. "Dots, Lines, Triangles, Cubes, Circles" and finally "Spheres"—why or how? Because, says the Commentary, such is the first law of Nature, and because Nature geometrizes universally in all her manifestations. There is an inherent law—not only in the primordial, but also in the manifested matter of our phenomenal plane—by which Nature correlates her geometrical forms, and later, also, her compound elements; and in which there is no place for accident or chance. It is a fundamental law in Occultism, that there is no rest or cessation of motion in Nature.* That which seems rest is only the change of one form into another; the change of substance going hand in hand with that of form—as we are taught in Occult physics, which thus seem to have anticipated the discovery of the "Conservation of matter" by a considerable time. Says the ancient Commentary† to Stanza IV. :—

"*The Mother is the fiery Fish of Life. She scatters her spawn and the Breath (Motion) heats and quickens it. The grains (of spawn) are soon attracted to each other and form the curds in the Ocean (of Space). The larger lumps coalesce and receive new spawn—in fiery dots, triangles and cubes, which ripen, and at the appointed time some of the lumps detach themselves and assume spheroidal form, a process which they effect only when not interfered with by the others. After which, law No. * * * comes into operation. Motion (the Breath) becomes the whirlwind and sets them into rotation.*" ‡

---

* It is the knowledge of this law that permits and helps the Arhat to perform his *Siddhis*, or various phenomena, such as disintegration of matter, the transport of objects from one place to another.

† These are ancient Commentaries attached with modern Glossaries to the Stanzas, as the Commentaries in their symbolical language are usually as difficult to understand as the Stanzas themselves.

‡ In a polemical scientific work, "*The Modern Genesis*," the author, the Rev. W. B. Slaughter, criticising the position assumed by the astronomers, asks:—"It is to be regretted that the advocates of this (nebular) theory have not entered more largely into the discussion of it (the beginning of rotation). No one condescends to give us the *rationale* of it. How does the process of cooling and contracting the mass impart to it a rotatory motion?" The question is amply treated in the Addendum. It is not materialistic science that can ever solve it. "Motion is eternal in the unmanifested, and periodical in the manifest," says an Occult teaching. It is "when heat caused

STANZA IV.—*Continued*.

5. . . . . . WHICH IS :—

"DARKNESS," THE BOUNDLESS OR THE NO-NUMBER, ADI-NIDANA
SVÂBHÂVAT : THE ◯ (*for x, unknown quantity*) :

    I. THE ADI-SANAT, THE NUMBER, FOR HE IS ONE (*a*).

    II. THE VOICE OF THE WORD, SVÂBHÂVAT, THE NUMBERS, FOR
    HE IS ONE AND NINE. *

    III. THE "FORMLESS SQUARE." (*Arupa.*) (*b*).

AND THESE THREE ENCLOSED WITHIN THE ◯ (*boundless circle*), ARE
THE SACRED FOUR, AND THE TEN ARE THE ARUPA (*subjective, formless*)
UNIVERSE (*c*) ; THEN COME THE "SONS," THE SEVEN FIGHTERS, THE ONE,
THE EIGHTH LEFT OUT, AND HIS BREATH WHICH IS THE LIGHT-MAKER
(*Bhâskara*) (*d*).

(*a*) "Adi-Sanat," translated literally is the First or "primeval" ancient,
which name identifies the Kabalistic "Ancient of Days" and the
"Holy Aged" (Sephira and Adam Kadmon) with Brahmâ the Creator,
called also *Sanat* among his other names and titles.

Svâbhâvat is the mystic Essence, the plastic root of physical
Nature—"Numbers" when manifested ; the Number, in its Unity of
Substance, on the highest plane. The name is of Buddhist use and a
synonym for the four-fold Anima Mundi, the Kabalistic "Archetypal
World," from whence proceed the "Creative, Formative, and the

---

by the descent of FLAME into primordial matter causes its particles to move, which
motion becomes Whirlwind." A drop of liquid assumes a spheroidal form owing to
its atoms moving around themselves in their ultimate, unresolvable, and noumenal
essence ; unresolvable for physical science, at any rate.

* Which makes ten, or the perfect number applied to the "Creator," the name
given to the totality of the Creators blended by the Monotheists into One, as the
"Elohim," Adam Kadmon or Sephira—the Crown—are the androgyne synthesis of
the 10 Sephiroth, who stand for the symbol of the manifested Universe in the
popularised Kabala. The esoteric Kabalists, however, following the Eastern
Occultists, divide the upper Sephirothal triangle from the rest (or Sephira, Chochmah
and Binah), which leaves seven Sephiroth. As for Svâbhâvat, the Orientalists explain
the term as meaning the Universal plastic matter diffused through Space, with,
perhaps, half an eye to the Ether of Science. But the Occultists identify it with
"FATHER-MOTHER" on the mystic plane. (Vide supra.)

THE OGDOAD AND HEPTAD.

Material Worlds " ; the Scintillæ or Sparks,—the various other worlds contained in the last three. The Worlds are all subject to Rulers or Regents—Rishis and Pitris with the Hindus, Angels with the Jews and Christians, Gods, with the Ancients in general.

(*b*) ◯ This means that the " Boundless Circle " (Zero) becomes a figure or number, only when one of the nine figures precedes it, and thus manifests its value and potency, the Word or Logos in union with VOICE and Spirit* (the expression and source of Consciousness) standing for the nine figures and thus forming, with the Cypher, the Decade which contains in itself all the Universe. The triad forms within the circle the Tetraktis or Sacred Four, the Square within the Circle being the most potent of all the magical figures.

(*c*) The " One Rejected " is the Sun of our system. The exoteric version may be found in the oldest Sanskrit Scriptures. In the Rig Veda, Aditi, " The Boundless " or infinite Space, translated by Mr. Max Müller, " the visible infinite, visible by the naked eye (! !) ; the endless expanse beyond the Earth, beyond the clouds, beyond the sky," is the equivalent of " Mother-Space " coeval with " Darkness." She is very properly called " The Mother of the Gods," DEVA-MATRI, as it is from her Cosmic matrix that all the heavenly bodies of our system were born—Sun and Planets. Thus she is described, allegorically, in this wise : " Eight Sons were born from the body of Aditi ; she approached the gods with seven, but cast away the eighth, Mârttânda," our sun. The seven sons called the Aditya are, cosmically or astronomically, the seven planets ; and the Sun being excluded from their number shows plainly that the Hindus may have known, and in fact knew of a seventh planet, without calling it Uranus.† But esoterically and theologically,

---

* " In union with the Spirit and the Voice," referring to the Abstract Thought and concrete Voice, or the manifestation thereof, the effect of the Cause. Adam Kadmon or Tetragrammaton is the Logos in the Kabala ; therefore this triad answers in the latter to the highest triangle of Kether, Chochmah and Binah, the last a female potency and at the same time the male Jehovah, as partaking of the nature of Chochmah, or the male Wisdom.

† The Secret Doctrine teaches that the Sun is a central Star and not a planet. Yet the Ancients knew of and worshipped seven great gods, excluding the Sun and Earth. Which was that " Mystery God " they set apart ? Of course not Uranus, discovered only by Herschel in 1781. But could it not be known by another name ? Says the

so to say, the Adityas are, in their primitive most ancient meanings, the eight, and the twelve great gods of the Hindu Pantheon. " The Seven allow the mortals to see their dwellings, but show themselves only to the Arhats," says an old proverb, "their dwellings" standing here for planets. The ancient Commentary gives an allegory and explains it :—

"Eight houses were built by Mother. Eight houses for her Eight Divine sons ; four large and four small ones. Eight brilliant suns, according to their age and merits. Bal-ilu (Mârttânda) was not satisfied, though his house was the largest. He began (to work) as the huge elephants do. He breathed (drew in) into his stomach the vital airs of his brothers. He sought to devour them. The larger four were far away ; far, on the margin of their kingdom.* They were not robbed (affected), and laughed. Do your worst, Sir, you cannot reach us, they said. But the smaller wept. They complained to the Mother. She exiled Bal-i-lu to the centre of her Kingdom, from whence he could not move. (Since then) he (only) watches and threatens. He pursues them, turning slowly around himself, they turning swiftly from him, and he following from afar the direction in which his brothers move on the path that encircles their houses.† From that day he feeds on the sweat of the Mother's body. He fills himself with her breath and refuse. Therefore, she rejected him."

Thus the " rejected Son" being our Sun, evidently, as shown above, the " Sun-Sons" refer not only to our planets but to the heavenly bodies in general. Himself only a reflection of the Central Spiritual Sun, *Surya* is the prototype of all those bodies that evolved after him. In the Vedas he is called *Loka-Chakshuh*, "the Eye of the World" (our

---

author of " Maçonnerie Occulte " :—" Occult Sciences having discovered through astronomical calculations that the number of the planets must be seven, the ancients were led to introduce the Sun into the scale of the celestial harmonies, and make him occupy the vacant place. Thus, every time they perceived an influence that pertained to none of the six planets known, they attributed it to the Sun. The error only seems important, but was not so in practical results, if the ancient astrologers replaced Uranus by the Sun, which is a central Star relatively motionless, turning only on its axis and regulating time and measure; and which cannot be turned aside from its true functions.". . . . . .The nomenclature of the days of the week is thus faulty. " The Sun-Day ought to be Uranus-day (Urani dies, Urandi)," adds the learned writer, Ragon.

* Planetary System.

† " The Sun rotates on his axis always in the same direction in which the planets revolve in their respective orbits," astronomy teaches us.

planetary world), and he is one of the three chief deities. He is called indifferently the Son of *Dyaus* and of *Aditi*, because no distinction is made with reference to, or scope allowed for, the esoteric meaning. Thus he is depicted as drawn by seven horses, and by one horse with seven heads; the former referring to his seven planets, the latter to their one common origin from the One Cosmic Element. This " One Element " is called figuratively " FIRE." The Vedas (Aitareya-Brâhmana of Haug also; p. i.) teach " that the fire verily is all the deities." (Narada in Anugîtâ).

The meaning of the allegory is plain, for we have both the Dzyan Commentary and modern science to explain it, though the two differ in more than one particular. The Occult Doctrine rejects the hypothesis born out of the Nebular Theory, that the (seven) great planets have evolved from the Sun's central mass, not of this our visible Sun, at any rate. The first condensation of Cosmic matter of course took place about a central nucleus, its parent Sun; but our sun, it is taught, merely detached itself earlier than all the others, as the rotating mass contracted, and is their elder, bigger brother therefore, not their father. The eight Adityas, " the gods," are all formed from the eternal substance (Cometary matter*—the Mother) or the " World-Stuff " which is both the fifth and the sixth COSMIC Principle, the Upadhi or basis of the Universal Soul, just as in man, the Microcosm, Manas† is the Upadhi of Buddhi.‡

(*d*) There is a whole poem on the pregenetic battles fought by the growing planets before the final formation of Kosmos, thus accounting for the seemingly disturbed position of the systems of several planets, the plane of the satellites of some (of Neptune and Uranus, for instance, of which the ancients knew nothing, it is said) being tilted over, thus giving them an appearance of retrograde motion. These planets are called the warriors, the Architects, and are accepted by the

---

* This Essence of Cometary matter, Occult Science teaches, is totally different from any of the chemical or physical characteristics with which modern science is acquainted. It is homogeneous in its primitive form beyond the Solar Systems, and differentiates entirely once it crosses the boundaries of our Earth's region, vitiated by the atmospheres of the planets and the already compound matter of the interplanetary stuff, heterogeneous only in our manifested world.

† Manas—the Mind-Principle, or the human Soul.

‡ Buddhi—the divine Soul.

Roman Church as the leaders of the heavenly Hosts, thus showing the
same traditions. Having evolved from Cosmic Space, and before the
final formation of the primaries and the annulation of the planetary
nebula, the Sun, we are taught, drew into the depths of its mass all the
Cosmic vitality he could, threatening to engulf his weaker " brothers "
before the law of attraction and repulsion was finally adjusted ; after
which he began feeding on " The Mother's refuse and sweat " ; in
other words, on those portions of Ether (the " breath of the Universal
Soul ") of the existence and constitution of which science is as yet
absolutely ignorant. A theory of this kind having been propounded by
Sir William Grove (see " *Correlation of the Physical Forces*," 1843, p. 81 ;
and "*Address to the British Association*, 1866 "), who theorized that the
systems " are gradually changing by atmospheric additions or subtractions, or by accretions and diminutions arising from nebular substances "
. . . and again that " the Sun may condense gaseous matter as it
travels in Space and so heat may be produced "—the archaic
teaching seems scientific enough, even in this age. *   Mr. W.
Mattieu Williams suggested that the diffused matter or Ether
which is the recipient of the heat radiations of the Universe
is thereby drawn into the depths of the solar mass.   Expel-
ling thence the previously condensed and thermally exhausted Ether,
it becomes compressed and gives up its heat, to be in turn itself
driven out in a rarified and cooled state, to absorb a fresh supply of
heat, which he supposes to be in this way taken up by the Ether, and
again concentrated and redistributed by the Suns of the Universe.†

This is about as close an approximation to the Occult teachings as
Science ever imagined ; for Occultism explains it by " the dead breath "
given back by Mârttânda and his feeding on the " sweat and refuse " of
" Mother Space." What could affect Neptune,‡ Saturn and Jupiter,

* Very similar ideas in Mr. W. Mattieu Williams' " *The Fuel of the Sun* ; " in Dr. C.
William Siemens' " *On the Conservation of Solar Energy* " (Nature, XXV., p. 440-444,
March 9, 1882) ; and also in Dr. P. Martin Duncan's " *Address of the President of the
Geological Society*," London, May, 1877.

† See " *Comparative Geology*," by Alexander Winchell, LL.D., p. 56.

‡ When we speak of Neptune it is not as an Occultist but as a European. The
true Eastern Occultist will maintain that, whereas there are many yet undiscovered
planets in our system, Neptune does not belong to it, his apparent connection with our
sun and the influence of the latter upon Neptune notwithstanding. This connection
is *mayavic*, imaginary, they say.

but little, would have killed such comparatively small " Houses " as Mercury, Venus and Mars. As Uranus was not known before the end of the eighteenth century, the name of the fourth planet mentioned in the allegory must remain to us, so far, a mystery.

The " Breath " of all the " seven " is said to be Bhâskara (light-making), because they (the planets) were all comets and suns in their origin. They evolve into Manvantaric life from primæval Chaos (now the noumenon of irresolvable nebulæ) by aggregation and accumulation of the primary differentiations of the eternal matter, according to the beautiful expression in the Commentary, " Thus the Sons of Light clothed themselves in the fabric of Darkness." They are called allegorically " the Heavenly Snails," on account of their (to us) formless INTELLIGENCES inhabiting unseen their starry and planetary homes, and, so to speak, carrying them as the snails do along with themselves in their revolution. The doctrine of a common origin for all the heavenly bodies and planets, was, as we see, inculcated by the Archaic astronomers, before Kepler, Newton, Leibnitz, Kant, Herschel and Laplace. Heat (the Breath), attraction and repulsion—the three great factors of Motion—are the conditions under which all the members of all this primitive family are born, developed, and die, to be reborn after a " Night of Brahmâ," during which eternal matter relapses periodically into its primary undifferentiated state. The most attenuated gases can give no idea of its nature to the modern physicist. Centres of Forces at first, the invisible sparks of primordial atoms differentiate into molecules, and become Suns—passing gradually into objectivity—gaseous, radiant, cosmic, the one " Whirlwind " (or motion) finally giving the impulse to the form, and the initial motion, regulated and sustained by the never-resting Breaths—the Dhyan Chohans.

STANZA IV.—*Continued.*

6. . . . . THEN THE SECOND SEVEN, WHO ARE THE LIPIKA, PRODUCED BY THE THREE (*Word, Voice, and Spirit*). THE REJECTED SON IS ONE, THE " SON-SUNS " ARE COUNTLESS.

The *Lipi-ka*, from the word *lipi*, " writing," means literally the

" Scribes."* Mystically, these Divine Beings are connected with
Karma, the Law of Retribution, for they are the Recorders or
Annalists who impress on the (to us) invisible tablets of the Astral
Light, "the great picture-gallery of eternity"—a faithful record
of every act, and even thought, of man, of all that was, is, or ever
will be, in the phenomenal Universe. As said in "*Isis*," this divine
and unseen canvas is the BOOK OF LIFE. As it is the Lipika
who project into objectivity from the passive Universal Mind the
ideal plan of the universe, upon which the "Builders" reconstruct the
Kosmos after every Pralaya, it is they who stand parallel to the Seven
Angels of the Presence, whom the Christians recognise in the Seven
"Planetary Spirits" or the "Spirits of the Stars;" for thus it is they
who are the direct amanuenses of the Eternal Ideation—or, as called
by Plato, the "Divine Thought." The Eternal Record is no fantastic
dream, for we meet with the same records in the world of gross matter.
"A shadow never falls upon a wall without leaving thereupon a permanent
trace which might be made visible by resorting to proper processes,"
says Dr. Draper. . . . "The portraits of our friends or landscape-
views may be hidden on the sensitive surface from the eye, but they are
ready to make their appearance as soon as proper developers are resorted
to. A spectre is concealed on a silver or a glassy surface, until, by our
necromancy, we make it come forth into the visible world. Upon the
walls of our most private apartments, where we think the eye of
intrusion is altogether shut out, and our retirement can never be
profaned, there exist the vestiges of all our acts, silhouettes of whatever
we have done." † Drs. Jevons and Babbage believe that every thought,
displacing the particles of the brain and setting them in motion, scatters
them throughout the Universe, and they think that "each particle of
the existing matter must be a register of all that has happened."
(Principles of Science, Vol. II. p. 455.) Thus the ancient doctrine
has begun to acquire rights of citizenship in the speculations of the
scientific world.

The forty "Assessors" who stand in the region of *Amenti* as the
accusers of the Soul before *Osiris*, belong to the same class of deities as
the Lipika, and might stand paralleled, were not the Egyptian gods so

---

* These are the four "Immortals" which are mentioned in *Atharva Veda* as the
"Watchers" or Guardians of the four quarters of the sky (see ch. lxxvi., 1-4, *et seq.*).

† "Conflict between Religion and Science."—Draper, pp. 132 and 133.

little understood in their esoteric meaning. The Hindu *Chitra-Gupta* who reads out the account of every Soul's life from his register, called Agra-Sandhani; the "Assessors" who read theirs from the heart of the defunct, which becomes an open book before (whether) Yama, Minos, Osiris, or Karma—are all so many copies of, and variants from the Lipika, and their Astral Records. Nevertheless, the Lipi-ka are not deities connected with Death, but with Life Eternal.

Connected as the Lipika are with the destiny of every man and the birth of every child, whose life is already traced in the Astral Light— not fatalistically, but only because the future, like the PAST, is ever alive in the PRESENT—they may also be said to exercise an influence on the Science of Horoscopy. We must admit the truth of the latter whether we will or not. For, as observed by one of the modern adepts of Astrology, " Now that photography has revealed to us the chemical influence of the Sidereal system, by fixing on the sensitized plate of the apparatus milliards of stars and planets that had hitherto baffled the efforts of the most powerful telescopes to discover them, it becomes easier to understand how our solar system can, at the birth of a child, influence his brain—virgin of any impression—in a definite manner and according to the presence on the zenith of such or another zodiacal constellation."†

† Les Mystères de l'Horoscope, p. XI.

STANZA V.

1. THE PRIMORDIAL SEVEN, THE FIRST SEVEN BREATHS OF THE DRAGON OF WISDOM, PRODUCE IN THEIR TURN FROM THEIR HOLY CIRCUMGYRATING BREATHS THE FIERY WHIRLWIND (*a*).

COMMENTARY.

(*a*) This is, perhaps, the most difficult of all the Stanzas to explain. Its language is comprehensible only to him who is thoroughly versed in Eastern allegory and its purposely obscure phraseology. The question will surely be asked, " Do the Occultists believe in all these ' Builders,' ' Lipika,' and ' Sons of Light' as Entities, or are they merely imageries ? " To this the answer is given as plainly: " After due allowance for the imagery of personified Powers, we must admit the existence of these Entities, if we would not reject the existence of spiritual humanity within physical mankind. For the hosts of these Sons of Light and ' Mind-born Sons ' of the first manifested Ray of the UNKNOWN ALL, are the very root of spiritual man." Unless we want to believe the unphilosophical dogma of a specially created soul for every human birth—a fresh supply of these pouring in daily, since " Adam "—we have to admit the occult teachings. This will be explained in its place. Let us see, now, what may be the occult meaning of this Stanza.

The Doctrine teaches that, in order to become a divine, fully conscious god,—aye, even the highest—the Spiritual primeval INTELLIGENCES must pass through the human stage. And when we say human, this does not apply merely to our terrestrial humanity, but to the mortals that inhabit any world, *i.e.*, to those Intelligences that have reached the appropriate equilibrium between matter and spirit, as *we* have now, since the middle point of the Fourth Root Race of the Fourth Round was passed. Each Entity must have won for itself the right of becoming divine, through self-experience. Hegel, the great German thinker, must have known or sensed intuitionally this truth when saying, as he did, that the Unconscious evolved the Universe only " in the hope of attaining clear self-consciousness," of becoming, in other words, MAN; for this is also the secret meaning of the usual Purânic phrase about

Brahmâ being constantly "moved by the desire to create." This explains also the hidden Kabalistic meaning of the saying: "The *Breath* becomes a stone; the stone, a plant; the plant, an animal; the animal, a man; the man, a spirit; and the spirit, a god." The Mind-born Sons, the Rishis, the Builders, etc., were all men—of whatever forms and shapes—in other worlds and the preceding Manvantaras.

This subject, being so very mystical, is therefore the most difficult to explain in all its details and bearings; since the whole mystery of evolutionary creation is contained in it. A sentence or two in it vividly recalls to mind similar ones in the Kabala and the phraseology of the King Psalmist (civ.), as both, when speaking of God, show him making the wind his messenger and his "ministers a flaming fire." But in the Esoteric doctrine it is used figuratively. The "fiery Wind" is the incandescent Cosmic dust which only follows magnetically, as the iron filings follow the magnet, the directing thought of the "Creative Forces." Yet, this cosmic dust is something more; for every atom in the Universe has the potentiality of self-consciousness in it, and is, like the Monads of Leibnitz, a Universe in itself, and *for* itself. *It is an atom and an angel.*

In this connection it should be noted that one of the luminaries of the modern Evolutionist School, Mr. A. R. Wallace, when discussing the inadequacy of "natural selection" as the sole factor in the development of physical man, practically concedes the whole point here discussed. He holds that the evolution of man was directed and furthered by superior Intelligences, whose agency is a necessary factor in the scheme of Nature. But once the operation of these Intelligences is admitted in one place, it is only a logical deduction to extend it still further. No hard and fast line can be drawn.

STANZA V.—*Continued.*

2. They make of him the messenger of their will (*a*). The Dzyu becomes Fohat; the Swift Son of the Divine Sons, whose sons are the Lipika,* runs circular errands. He is the steed, and

---

* The difference between the "Builders," the Planetary Spirits, and the Lipika must not be lost sight of. (See Nos. 5 and 6 of this Commentary.)

THE THOUGHT IS THE RIDER (*i.e.*, *he is under the influence of their guiding thought*). HE PASSES LIKE LIGHTNING THROUGH THE FIERY CLOUDS (*cosmic mists*) (*b*) ; TAKES THREE, AND FIVE, AND SEVEN STRIDES THROUGH THE SEVEN REGIONS ABOVE AND THE SEVEN BELOW (*the world to be*). HE LIFTS HIS VOICE, AND CALLS THE INNUMERABLE SPARKS (*atoms*) AND JOINS THEM TOGETHER (*c*).

(*a*) This shows the "Primordial Seven" using for their *Vahan* (vehicle, or the manifested subject which becomes the symbol of the Power directing it), Fohat, called in consequence, the "Messenger of their will"—the fiery whirlwind.

"Dzyu becomes Fohat"—the expression itself shows it. Dzyu is the one real (magical) knowledge, or Occult Wisdom ; which, dealing with eternal truths and primal causes, becomes almost omnipotence when applied in the right direction. Its antithesis is Dzyu-mi, that which deals with illusions and false appearances only, as in our exoteric modern sciences. In this case, Dzyu is the expression of the collective Wisdom of the Dhyani-Buddhas.

(*b*) As the reader is supposed not to be acquainted with the Dhyani-Buddhas, it is as well to say at once that, *according to the Orientalists*, there are five Dhyanis who are the "celestial" Buddhas, of whom the human Buddhas are the manifestations in the world of form and matter. Esoterically, however, the Dhyani-Buddhas are seven, of whom five only have hitherto manifested,* and two are to come in the sixth and seventh Root-races. They are, so to speak, the eternal prototypes of the Buddhas who appear on this earth, each of whom has his particular divine prototype. So, for instance, Amitâbha is the Dhyani-Buddha of Gautama Sakyamuni, manifesting through him whenever this great Soul incarnates on earth as He did in Tzon-kha-pa.† As the synthesis of the seven Dhyani-Buddhas, Avalôkitêswara was the first Buddha (the Logos), so Amitâbha is the inner "God" of Gautama, who, in China, is called Amita(-Buddha). They are, as Mr. Rhys Davids

---

* See A. P. Sinnett's "Esoteric Buddhism," 5th annotated edition, pp. 171-173.

† The first and greatest Reformer who founded the "Yellow-Caps," Gyalugpas. He was born in the year 1355 A.D. in Amdo, and was the *Avatar* of Amitâbha, the celestial name of Gautama Buddha.

correctly states, " the glorious counterparts in the mystic world, free from the debasing conditions of this material life" of every earthly mortal Buddha—the liberated Manushi-Buddhas appointed to govern the Earth in this Round. They are the " Buddhas of Contemplation," and are all Anupadaka (parentless), *i.e.*, self-born of divine essence. The exoteric teaching which says that every Dhyani-Buddha has the faculty of creating from himself, an equally celestial son—a Dhyani-Bodhisattva—who, after the decease of the Manushi (human) Buddha, has to carry out the work of the latter, rests on the fact that owing to the highest initiation performed by one overshadowed by the " Spirit of Buddha "—(who is credited by the Orientalists with having created the five Dhyani-Buddhas !),—a candidate becomes virtually a Bodhisattva, created such by the High Initiator.

(*c*) Fohat, being one of the most, if not the most important character in esoteric Cosmogony, should be minutely described. As in the oldest Grecian Cosmogony, differing widely from the later mythology, Eros is the third person in the primeval trinity : Chaos, Gæa, Eros : answering to the Kabalistic En-Soph (for Chaos is SPACE, χαίνω, " void ") the Boundless ALL, Shekinah and the Ancient of Days, or the Holy Ghost ; so Fohat is one thing in the yet unmanifested Universe and another in the phenomenal and Cosmic World. In the latter, he is that Occult, electric, vital power, which, under the Will of the Creative Logos, unites and brings together all forms, giving them the first impulse which becomes in time law. But in the unmanifested Universe, Fohat is no more this, than Eros is the later brilliant winged Cupid, or LOVE. Fohat has naught to do with Kosmos yet, since Kosmos is not born, and the gods still sleep in the bosom of " Father-Mother." He is an abstract philosophical idea. He produces nothing yet by himself ; he is simply that potential creative power in virtue of whose action the NOUMENON of all future phenomena divides, so to speak, but to reunite in a mystic supersensuous act, and emit the creative ray. When the " Divine Son " breaks forth, then Fohat becomes the propelling force, the active Power which causes the ONE to become Two and THREE—on the Cosmic plane of manifestation. The triple One differentiates into the many, and then Fohat is transformed into that force which brings together the elemental atoms and makes them aggregate and combine. We find an echo of this primeval teaching in early Greek mythology. Erebos and Nux are born out of Chaos, and, under the action of Eros, give birth in their turn to Æther and Hemera, the light of the superior and the light of the inferior or terrestrial regions. Darkness generates light. See in the Purânas Brahmâ's "Will" or desire to create ; and in the Phœnician Cosmogony of Sanchoniathon the doctrine that Desire, πόθος, is the principle of creation.

Fohat is closely related to the "ONE LIFE." From the Unknown One, the Infinite TOTALITY, the manifested ONE, or the periodical, Manvantaric Deity, emanates ; and this is the Universal Mind, which, separated from its Fountain-Source, is the Demiurgos or the creative Logos of the Western Kabalists, and the four-faced Brahmâ of the Hindu religion. In its totality, viewed from the standpoint of manifested Divine Thought in the esoteric doctrine, it represents the Hosts of the higher creative Dhyan Chohans. Simultaneously with the evolution of the Universal Mind, the concealed Wisdom of Adi-Buddha—the One Supreme and eternal—manifests itself as Avalôkitêshwara (or manifested Iswara), which is the Osiris of the Egyptians, the Ahura-Mazda of the Zoroastrians, the Heavenly Man of the Hermetic philosopher, the Logos of the Platonists, and the Atman of the Vedantins.* By the action of the manifested Wisdom, or Mahat, represented by these innumerable centres of spiritual Energy in the Kosmos, the reflection of the Universal Mind, which is Cosmic Ideation and the intellectual Force accompanying such ideation, becomes objectively the Fohat of the Buddhist esoteric philosopher. Fohat, running along the seven principles of AKASA, acts upon manifested substance or the One Element, as declared above, and by differentiating it into various centres of Energy, sets in motion the law of Cosmic Evolution, which, in obedience to the Ideation of the Universal Mind, brings into existence all the various states of being in the manifested Solar System.

The Solar System, brought into existence by these agencies, consists of Seven Principles, like everything else within these centres. Such is the teaching of the trans-Himalayan Esotericism. Every philosophy, however, has it own way of dividing these principles.

---

* Mr. Subba Row seems to identify him with, and to call him, the LOGOS. (See his four lectures on the "Bhagavadgita" in the Theosophist.)

Fohat, then, is the personified electric vital power, the transcendental binding Unity of all Cosmic Energies, on the unseen as on the manifested planes, the action of which resembles—on an immense scale—that of a living Force created by WILL, in those phenomena where the seemingly subjective acts on the seemingly objective and propels it to action. Fohat is not only the living Symbol and Container of that Force, but is looked upon by the Occultists as an Entity—the forces he acts upon being cosmic, human and terrestrial, and exercising their influence on all those planes respectively. On the earthly plane his influence is felt in the magnetic and active force generated by the strong desire of the magnetizer. On the Cosmic, it is present in the constructive power that carries out, in the formation of things—from the planetary system down to the glow-worm and simple daisy—the plan in the mind of nature, or in the Divine Thought, with regard to the development and growth of that special thing. He is, metaphysically, the objectivised thought of the gods; the " Word made flesh," on a lower scale, and the messenger of Cosmic and human ideations : the active force in Universal Life. In his secondary aspect, Fohat is the Solar Energy, the electric vital fluid,* and the preserving fourth

* In 1882 the President of the Theosophical Society, Col. Olcott, was taken to task for asserting in one of his lectures that Electricity is matter. Such, nevertheless, is the teaching of the Occult Doctrine. " Force," " Energy," may be a better name for it, so long as European Science knows so little about its true nature ; yet matter it is, as much as Ether is matter, since it is as atomic, though several removes from the latter. It seems ridiculous to argue that because a thing is imponderable to Science, therefore it cannot be called matter. Electricity is " immaterial " in the sense that its molecules are not subject to perception and experiment ; yet it may be—and Occultism says it is —atomic ; therefore it is matter. But even supposing it were unscientific to speak of it in such terms, once Electricity is called in Science a source of Energy, Energy simply, and a Force—where is that Force or that Energy which can be thought of without thinking of matter ? Maxwell, a mathematician and one of the greatest authorities upon Electricity and its phenomena, said, years ago, that Electricity was matter, not motion merely. " If we accept the hypothesis that the elementary substances are composed of atoms we cannot avoid concluding that electricity also, positive as well as negative, is divided into definite elementary portions, which behave like atoms of electricity." (Helmholtz, *Faraday Lecture*, 1881). We will go further than that, and assert that Electricity is not only Substance but that it is an emanation from an Entity, which is neither God nor Devil, but one of the numberless Entities that rule and guide our world according to the eternal Law of KARMA. (See the Addendum to this Book.)

principle, the animal Soul of Nature, so to say, or—Electricity. In India, Fohat is connected with Vishnu and Surya in the early character of the (first) God; for Vishnu is not a high god in the Rig Veda. The name Vishnu is from the root *vish*, " to pervade," and Fohat is called the " Pervader " and the Manufacturer, because he shapes the atoms from crude material.* In the sacred texts of the Rig Veda, Vishnu, also, is " a manifestation of the Solar Energy," and he is described as striding through the Seven regions of the Universe in three steps, the Vedic God having little in common with the Vishnu of later times. Therefore the two are identical in this particular feature, and one is the copy of the other.

The " three and seven " strides refer to the Seven spheres inhabited by man, of the esoteric Doctrine, as well as to the Seven regions of the Earth. Notwithstanding the frequent objections made by would-be Orientalists, the Seven Worlds or spheres of our planetary chain are distinctly referred to in the exoteric Hindu scriptures. But how strangely all these numbers are connected with like numbers in other Cosmogonies and with their symbols, can be seen from comparisons and parallelisms made by students of old religions. The " three strides of Vishnu " through the " seven regions of the Universe," of the Rig Veda, have been variously explained by commentators as meaning " fire, lightning and the Sun " cosmically; and as having been taken in the Earth, the atmosphere, and the sky; also as the " three steps " of the dwarf (Vishnu's incarnation), though more philosophically—and in the astronomical sense, very correctly—they are explained by Aurnavâbha as being the various positions of the sun, rising, noon, and setting. Esoteric philosophy alone explains it clearly, and the Zohar laid it down very philosophically and comprehensively. It is said and plainly demonstrated therein that in the beginning the Elohim (Elhim) were called Echod, " one," or the " Deity is one in many," a very simple idea in a pantheistic conception (in its philosophical sense, of course). Then came the change, " Jehovah is Elohim," thus unifying the multiplicity and taking the first step towards Monotheism. Now to the query, " How is Jehovah Elohim ? " the answer is, " By three Steps " from below.

---

* It is well known that sand, when placed on a metal plate in vibration assumes a series of regular curved figures of various descriptions. Can Science give a *complete* explanation of this fact ?

The meaning is plain.* They are all symbols, and emblematic, mutually and correlatively, of Spirit, Soul and Body (MAN); of the circle transformed into Spirit, the Soul of the World, and its body (or Earth). Stepping out of the Circle of Infinity, that no man comprehendeth, Ain-Soph (the Kabalistic synonym for Parabrahm, for the Zeroana Akerne, of the Mazdeans, or for any other "UNKNOWABLE") becomes "One"—the ECHOD, the EKA, the AHU—then he (or it) is transformed by evolution into the One in many, the Dhyani-Buddhas or the Elohim, or again the Amshaspends, his third Step being taken into generation of the flesh, or "Man." And from man, or Jah-Hova, "male female," the *inner* divine entity becomes, on the metaphysical plane, once more the Elohim.

The Kabalistic idea is identical with the Esotericism of the Archaic period. This esotericism is the common property of all, and belongs neither to the Aryan 5th Race, nor to any of its numerous Sub-races. It cannot be claimed by the Turanians, so-called, the Egyptians, Chinese, Chaldeans, nor any of the Seven divisions of the Fifth Root Race, but really belongs to the Third and Fourth Root Races, whose descendants we find in the Seed of the Fifth, the earliest Aryans. The Circle was with every nation the symbol of the Unknown—"Boundless Space," the abstract garb of an ever present abstraction—the Incognisable Deity. It represents limitless Time in Eternity. The Zeroana Akerne is also the "Boundless Circle of the Unknown Time," from which Circle issues the radiant light—the Universal SUN, or Ormazd †—and the latter

---

* The numbers 3, 5, and 7 are prominent in speculative masonry, as shown in "Isis." A mason writes:—"There are the 3, 5, and 7 steps to show a circular walk. The three faces of 3, 3; 5, 3; and 7, 3; etc., etc. Sometimes it comes in this form— $\frac{753}{2} = 376\cdot5$ and $\frac{7635}{2} = 3817\cdot5$ and the ratio of $\frac{20612}{6561}$ feet for cubit measure gives the Great Pyramid measures," etc., etc. Three, five and seven are mystical numbers, and the last and the first are as greatly honoured by Masons as by the Parsis—the triangle being a symbol of Deity everywhere. (See the *Masonic Cyclopedia*, and "*Pythagorean Triangle*," Oliver.) As a matter of course, doctors of divinity (Cassel, for instance) show the Zohar explaining and supporting the Christian trinity (!). It is the latter, however, that had its origin from the $\triangle$ of the Heathen, in the Archaic Occultism and Symbology. The three strides relate metaphysically to the descent of Spirit into matter, of the Logos falling as a ray into the Spirit, then into the Soul, and finally into the human physical form of man, in which it becomes LIFE.

† Ormazd is the Logos, the "First Born" and the Sun.

is identical with Kronos, in his Æolian form, that of a Circle. For the circle is Sar, and Saros, or cycle, and was the Babylonian god whose circular horizon was the visible symbol of the invisible, while the sun was the ONE Circle from which proceeded the Cosmic orbs, and of which he was considered the leader. Zero-ana, is the Chackra or circle of Vishnu, the mysterious emblem which is, according to the definition of a mystic, "a curve of such a nature that as to any, the least possible part thereof, if the curve be protracted either way it will proceed and finally re-enter upon itself, and form one and the same curve—or that which we call the circle." No better definition could thus be given of the natural symbol and the evident nature of Deity, which having its circumference everywhere (the boundless) has, therefore, its central point also everywhere; in other words, is in every point of the Universe. The invisible Deity is thus also the Dhyan Chohans, or the Rishis, the primitive seven, and the nine, without, and ten, including, their synthetical unit; from which IT steps into Man. Returning to the Commentary (4) of Stanza IV. the reader will understand why, while the trans-Himalayan Chackra has inscribed within it △|□|⊠ (triangle, first line, cube, second line, and a pentacle with a dot in the centre thus: ⊠, and some other variations), the Kabalistic circle of the Elohim reveals, when the letters of the word אלהים (Alhim or Elohim) are numerically read, the famous numerals 13514, or by anagram 31415 — the astronomical π (pi) number, or the hidden meaning of Dhyani-Buddhas, of the Gebers, the Geborim, the Kabeiri, and the Elohim, all signifying "great men," "Titans," "Heavenly Men," and, on earth, "the giants."

The Seven was a Sacred Number with every nation; but none applied it to more physiologically materialistic uses than the Hebrews. With these it was pre-eminently the generative number and 9 the male causative one, forming as shown by the Kabalists the ע ע or otz—"the Tree of the Garden of Eden,"* the "double hermaphrodite rod" of the fourth race. Whereas with the Hindus and Aryans generally, the significance was manifold, and related almost entirely to purely metaphysical

---

* This was the symbol of the "Holy of Holies," the 3 and the 4 of sexual separation. Nearly every one of the 22 Hebrew letters are merely phallic symbols. Of the two letters—as shown above—one, the *ayin*, is a *negative* female letter, symbolically an eye; the other a male letter, *tza*, a *fish*-hook or a dart.

and astronomical truths.* Their Rishis and gods, their Demons and Heroes, have historical and ethical meanings, and the Aryans never made their religion rest solely on physiological symbols, as the old Hebrews have done. This is found in the exoteric Hindu Scriptures. That these accounts are blinds is shown by their contradicting each other, a different construction being found in almost every Purâna and epic poem. Read esoterically—they will all yield the same meaning. Thus one account enumerates Seven worlds, exclusive of the nether worlds, also seven in number ; these fourteen upper and nether worlds have

---

* We are told by a Kabalist, who in a work not yet published contrasts the Kabala and Zohar with Aryan Esotericism, that " The Hebrew clear, short, terse and exact modes far and beyond measure surpass the toddling word-talk of the Hindus—just as by parallelisms the Psalmist says, ' My mouth speaks with my tongue, I know not thy numbers' (lxxi., 15). . . . The Hindu Glyph shows by its insufficiency in the large admixture of adventitious sides the same borrowed plumage that the Greeks (the lying Greeks) had, and that Masonry has : which in the rough monosyllabic (and apparent) poverty of the Hebrew, shows the latter to have come down from a far more remote antiquity than any of these, and to have been the source (! ?), or nearer the old original source than any of them." This is entirely erroneous. Our learned brother and correspondent judges apparently the Hindu religious systems by their Shastras and Purânas, probably the latter, and in their modern translation moreover, which is disfigured out of all recognition, by the Orientalists. It is to their philosophical systems that one has to turn, to their esoteric teaching, if he would make a point of comparison. No doubt the symbology of the Pentateuch and even of the New Testament, comes from the same source. But surely the Pyramid of Cheops, whose measurements are all found repeated by Professor Piazzi Smythe in Solomon's alleged and mythical temple, is not of a later date than the Mosaic books ? Hence, if there is any such great identity as claimed, it must be due to servile copying on the part of the Jews, not on that of the Egyptians. The Jewish glyphs—and even their language, the Hebrew—are not original. They are borrowed from the Egyptians, from whom Moses got his Wisdom; from the Coptic, the probable kinsman, if not parent, of the old Phœnician and from the Hyksos, their (alleged) ancestors, as Josephus shows in his "Against Apion," I., 25. Aye; but who are the Hyksos shepherds? And who the Egyptians ? History knows nothing of the question, and speculates and theorizes out of the depths of the respective consciousnesses of her historians. (See Isis Unveiled, vol. II., p. 430-438.) " Khamism, or old Coptic," says Bunsen, " is from Western Asia, and contains some germ of the Semitic, thus bearing witness to the primitive cognate unity of the Aryan and Semitic races " ; and he places the great events in Egypt 9,000 years B.C. The fact is that in archaic Esotericism and Aryan thought we find a grand philosophy, whereas in the Hebrew records we find only the most surprising ingenuity in inventing apotheoses for phallic worship and sexual theogony.

nothing to do with the classification of the septenary chain and belong to the purely æthereal, invisible worlds. These will be noticed elsewhere. Suffice for the present to show that they are purposely referred to as though they belonged to the chain. " Another enumeration calls the Seven worlds—earth, sky, heaven, middle region, place of birth, mansion of the blest, and abode of truth ; placing the ' Sons of Brahmâ ' in the sixth division, and stating the fifth, or Jana Loka, to be that where animals destroyed in the general conflagration are born again." (see *Hindu Classical Dictionary*.)   Some real esoteric teaching is given in the " Symbolism." He who is prepared for it will understand the hidden meaning.

———

STANZA V.—*Continued.*

3. HE IS THEIR GUIDING SPIRIT AND LEADER. WHEN HE COMMENCES WORK, HE SEPARATES THE SPARKS OF THE LOWER KINGDOM (*mineral atoms*) THAT FLOAT AND THRILL WITH JOY IN THEIR RADIANT DWELLINGS (*gaseous clouds*), AND FORMS THEREWITH THE GERMS OF WHEELS. HE PLACES THEM IN THE SIX DIRECTIONS OF SPACE AND ONE IN THE MIDDLE—THE CENTRAL WHEEL (*a*).

(*a*) " Wheels," as already explained, are the centres of force, around which primordial Cosmic matter expands, and, passing through all the six stages of consolidation, becomes spheroidal and ends by being transformed into globes or spheres. It is one of the fundamental dogmas of Esoteric Cosmogony, that during the Kalpas (or æons) of life, MOTION, which, during the periods of Rest " pulsates and thrills through every slumbering atom "* (Commentary on Dzyan), assumes an evergrowing

———

* It may be asked, as also the writer has not failed to ask, " Who is there to ascertain the difference in that motion, since all nature is reduced to its primal essence, and there can be no one—not even one of the Dhyani-Chohans, who are all in Nirvana—to see it ?" The answer to this is : " Everything in Nature has to be judged by analogy. Though the highest Deities (Archangels or Dhyani-Buddhas) are unable to penetrate the mysteries too far beyond our planetary system and the visible Kosmos, yet there were great seers and prophets in olden times who were enabled to perceive the mystery of Breath and Motion retrospectively, when the systems of worlds were at rest and plunged in their periodic sleep."

tendency, from the first awakening of Kosmos to a new "Day," to circular movement. The "Deity becomes a WHIRLWIND." They are also called Rotæ—the moving wheels of the celestial orbs participating in the world's creation—when the meaning refers to the animating principle of the stars and planets; for in the Kabala, they are represented by the Ophanim, the Angels of the Spheres and stars, of which they are the informing Souls. (See *Kabala Denudata*, "*De Anima*," p. 113.)

This law of vortical movement in primordial matter, is one of the oldest conceptions of Greek philosophy, whose first historical Sages were nearly all Initiates of the Mysteries. The Greeks had it from the Egyptians, and the latter from the Chaldeans, who had been the pupils of Brahmins of the esoteric school. Leucippus, and Democritus of Abdera—the pupil of the Magi—taught that this gyratory movement of the atoms and spheres existed from eternity.* Hicetas, Heraclides, Ecphantus, Pythagoras, and all his pupils, taught the rotation of the earth ; and Aryabhata of India, Aristarchus, Seleucus, and Archimedes calculated its revolution as scientifically as the astronomers do now ; while the theory of the Elemental Vortices was known to Anaxagoras, and maintained by him 500 years B.C., or nearly 2,000 before it was taken up by Galileo, Descartes, Swedenborg, and finally, with slight modifications, by Sir W. Thomson. (See his "*Vortical Atoms*.") All such knowledge, if justice be only done to it, is an echo of the archaic doctrine, an attempt to explain which is now being made. How men of the last few centuries have come to the same ideas and conclusions that were taught as axiomatic truths in the secrecy of the Adyta dozens of

---

* "The doctrine of the rotation of the earth about an axis is taught by the Pythagorean Hicetas, probably as early as 500 B.C. It was also taught by his pupil Ecphantus, and by Heraclides, a pupil of Plato. The immobility of the Sun and the orbital rotation of the earth were shown by Aristarchus of Samos as early as 281 B.C. to be suppositions accordant with facts of observation. The Heliocentric theory was taught about 150 B.C., by Seleucus of Seleucia on the Tigris.—[It was taught 500 B.C. by Pythagoras.—H.P.B.] It is said also that Archimedes, in a work entitled Psammites, inculcated the Heliocentric theory. The sphericity of the earth was distinctly taught by Aristotle, who appealed for proof to the figure of the Earth's shadow on the moon in eclipses (Aristotle, De Cœlo, lib. II., cap. XIV.). The same idea was defended by Pliny (Nat. Hist., II., 65). These views seem to have been lost from knowledge for more than a thousand years. . . ." (*Comparative Geology*, Part IV., "Pre-Kantian Speculation," p. 551, by Alex. Winchell, LL.D.).

millenniums ago, is a question that is treated separately. Some were led
to it by the natural progress in physical science and by independent
observation; others—such as Copernicus, Swedenborg, and a few
more—their great learning notwithstanding, owed their knowledge far
more to intuitive than to acquired ideas, developed in the usual way by
a course of study.* (See "A Mystery about Buddha.")

By the "Six directions of Space" is here meant the "Double
Triangle," the junction and blending together of pure Spirit and
Matter, of the Arupa and the Rupa, of which the Triangles are a
Symbol. This double Triangle is a sign of Vishnu, as it is Solomon's
seal, and the Sri-Antara of the Brahmins.

STANZA V.—(*Continued.*)

4. Fohat traces spiral lines to unite the six to the seventh—
the Crown (*a*); an Army of the Sons of Light stands at each angle
(*and*) the Lipika—in the middle wheel. They (*the Lipika*) say, "This
is good" (*b*). The first Divine World is ready, the first (*is now*),
the second (*world*), then the "Divine Arupa" (*the formless Universe*

That Swedenborg, who could not possibly have known anything of the esoteric
ideas of Buddhism, came independently near the Occult teaching in his general conceptions, is shown by his essay on the Vortical Theory. In Clissold's translation of
it, quoted by Prof. Winchell, we find the following *résumé* :—"The first Cause is the
Infinite or Unlimited. This gives existence to the First Finite or Limited." (The
Logos in His manifestation and the Universe.) "That which produces a limit is analogous to motion. (See first Stanza, *supra.*) The limit produced is a point, the Essence
of which is Motion ; but being without parts, this Essence is not actual Motion, but
only a connatus to it." (In our Doctrine it is not a "connatus," but a change from
eternal vibration in the unmanifested, to Vortical Motion in the phenomenal or manifested World). . . "From this first proceed Extension, Space, Figure, and Succession,
or Time. As in Geometry a point generates a line, a line a surface, and a surface a
solid, so here the connatus of a point tends towards lines, surfaces and solids. In other
words, the Universe is contained *in ovo* in the first natural point . . . the Motion toward
which the connatus tends, is circular, since the circle is the most perfect of all figures
. . . The most perfect figure of a Motion. . . must be the perpetually circular, that is to
say, it must proceed from the centre to the periphery and from the periphery to the
centre." (Quoted from *Principia Rerum Naturalia.*) This is Occultism pure and
simple.

of Thought) REFLECTS ITSELF IN CHHAYALOKA (*the shadowy world of primal form, or the intellectual*) THE FIRST GARMENT OF (*the*) ANUPADAKA (*c*).

(*a*) This tracing of " Spiral lines " refers to the evolution of man's as well as Nature's principles ; an evolution which takes place gradually (as will be seen in Book II., on " The origin of the Human Races "), as does everything else in nature. The Sixth principle in Man (Buddhi, the Divine Soul) though a mere breath, in our conceptions, is still something material when compared with divine " Spirit " (Atma) of which it is the carrier or vehicle. Fohat, in his capacity of DIVINE LOVE (*Eros*), the electric Power of affinity and sympathy, is shown allegorically as trying to bring the pure Spirit, the Ray inseparable from the ONE absolute, into union with the Soul, the two constituting in Man the MONAD, and in Nature the first link between the ever un-conditioned and the manifested. " The first is now the second " (world) —of the Lipikas—has reference to the same.

(*b*) The " Army " at each angle is the Host of angelic Beings (Dhyan-Chohans) appointed to guide and watch over each respective region from the beginning to the end of Manvantara. They are the " Mystic Watchers " of the Christian Kabalists and Alchemists, and relate, symbolically as well as cosmogonically, to the numerical system of the Universe. The numbers with which these celestial Beings are con-nected are extremely difficult to explain, as each number refers to several groups of distinct ideas, according to the particular group of " Angels " which it is intended to represent. Herein lies the *nodus* in the study of symbology, with which, unable to untie by disentangling it, so many scholars have preferred dealing as Alexander dealt with the Gordian knot ; hence erroneous conceptions and teachings, as a direct result.

The " First is the Second," because the " First " cannot really be numbered or regarded as the First, as that is the realm of noumena in its primary manifestation : the threshold to the World of Truth, or SAT, through which the direct energy that radiates from the ONE REALITY— the Nameless Deity—reaches us. Here again, the untranslateable term SAT (*Be-ness*) is likely to lead into an erroneous conception, since that which is manifested cannot be SAT, but is something phenomenal, not everlasting, nor, in truth, even sempiternal. It is coeval and coexistent with the One Life, " Secondless," but as a manifestation it is still a Maya—like the rest. This " World of Truth " can be described only in the words of the Commentary as " A bright star dropped from the heart of Eternity ; the beacon of hope on whose Seven Rays hang the Seven Worlds of Being." Truly so ; since those are the Seven Lights whose reflections are the human immortal Monads—the Atma, or the irradiating Spirit of every creature of the human family. First, this septenary Light ; then :—

(c) The " Divine World "—the countless Lights lit at the primeval Light—the Buddhis, or formless divine Souls, of the last Arupa (formless) world ; the " Sum Total," in the mysterious language of the old Stanza. In the Catechism, the Master is made to ask the pupil :—

"*Lift thy head, oh Lanoo ; dost thou see one, or countless lights above thee, burning in the dark midnight sky ?* "

"*I sense one Flame, oh Gurudeva, I see countless undetached sparks shining in it.*"

"*Thou sayest well. And now look around and into thyself. That light which burns inside thee, dost thou feel it different in anywise from the light that shines in thy Brother-men ?*"

"*It is in no way different, though the prisoner is held in bondage by Karma, and though its outer garments delude the ignorant into saying, ' Thy Soul and My Soul.'*"

The radical unity of the ultimate essence of each constituent part of compounds in Nature—from Star to mineral Atom, from the highest Dhyan Chohan to the smallest infusoria, in the fullest acceptation of the term, and whether applied to the spiritual, intellectual, or physical worlds—this is the one fundamental law in Occult Science. " The Deity is boundless and infinite expansion," says an Occult axiom ; and hence, as remarked, the name of Brahmâ.* There is a deep philosophy underlying the earliest worship in the world, that of the Sun and of Fire. Of all the Elements known to physical science, Fire is the one that has ever eluded definite analysis. It is confidently asserted that

* In the Rig Veda we find the names *Brahmanaspati* and *Brihaspati* alternating and equivalent to each other. Also see " Brihad Upanishad " ; Brihaspati is a deity called " the Father of the gods."

Air is a mixture containing the gases Oxygen and Nitrogen. We view the Universe and the Earth as matter composed of definite chemical molecules. We speak of the primitive ten Earths, endowing each with a Greek or Latin name. We say that water is, chemically, a compound of Oxygen and Hydrogen. But what is FIRE? It is the effect of combustion, we are gravely answered. It is heat and light and motion, and a correlation of physical and chemical forces in general. And this scientific definition is philosophically supplemented by the theological one in Webster's Dictionary, which explains fire as " the instrument of punishment, or the punishment of the impenitent in another state"— the " state," by the bye, being supposed to be spiritual ; but, alas ! the presence of fire would seem to be a convincing proof of its material nature. Yet, speaking of the illusion of regarding phenomena as simple, because they are familiar, Professor Bain says (*Logic*. Part II.) : " Very familiar facts seem to stand in no need of explanation themselves and to be the means of explaining whatever can be assimilated to them. Thus, the boiling and evaporation of a liquid is supposed to be a very simple phenomenon requiring no explanation, and a satisfactory explanation of rarer phenomena. That water should dry up is, to the uninstructed mind, a thing wholly intelligible ; whereas to the man acquainted with physical science the liquid state is anomalous and inexplicable. The lighting of a fire by a flame is a GREAT SCIENTIFIC DIFFICULTY, yet few people think so " (p. 125).

What says the esoteric teaching with regard to fire ? " Fire," it says, " is the most perfect and unadulterated reflection, in Heaven as on Earth, of the ONE FLAME. It is Life and Death, the origin and the end of every material thing. It is divine ' SUBSTANCE.' " Thus, not only the FIRE-WORSHIPPER, the Parsee, but even the wandering savage tribes of America, which proclaim themselves " born of fire," show more science in their creeds and truth in their superstitions, than all the speculations of modern physics and learning. The Christian who says : " God is a living Fire," and speaks of the Pentecostal " Tongues of Fire " and of the " burning bush " of Moses, is as much a fire-worshipper as any other " heathen." The Rosicrucians, among all the mystics and Kabalists, were those who defined Fire in the right and most correct way. Procure a sixpenny lamp, keep it only supplied with oil, and you will be able to light at its flame the lamps, candles, and fires of the whole globe without diminishing that flame. If the Deity, the radical One, is eternal and an infinite substance ("the Lord thy God is a consuming fire") and never consumed, then it does not seem reasonable that the Occult teaching should be held as unphilo-sophical when it says: "Thus were the Arupa and Rupa worlds formed: from One light seven lights; from each of the seven, seven times seven," etc., etc.

STANZA V.—*Continued.*

5. FOHAT TAKES FIVE STRIDES (*having already taken the first three*) (*a*), AND BUILDS A WINGED WHEEL AT EACH CORNER OF THE SQUARE FOR THE FOUR HOLY ONES . . . . . AND THEIR ARMIES (*hosts*) (*b*).

(*a*) The "strides," as already explained (see Commentary on Stanza IV.), refer to both the Cosmic and the Human principles—the latter of which consist, in the exoteric division, of three (Spirit, Soul, and Body), and, in the esoteric calculation, of seven principles—three rays of the Essence and four aspects.* Those who have studied Mr. Sinnett's "*Esoteric Buddhism*" can easily grasp the nomenclature. There are two esoteric schools—or rather one school, divided into two parts—one for the inner Lanoos, the other for the outer or semi-lay chelas beyond the Himalayas; the first teaching a septenary, the other a six-fold division of human principles.

From a Cosmic point of view, Fohat taking "five strides" refers here to the five upper planes of Consciousness and Being, the sixth and the seventh (counting downwards) being the astral and the terrestrial, or the two lower planes.

(*b*) "Four winged wheels at each corner . . . . . for the four holy ones and their armies (hosts)" . . . . . These are the "four Maharajahs" or great Kings of the Dhyan-Chohans, the Devas who preside, each over one of the four cardinal points. They are the Regents or Angels who rule over the Cosmical Forces of North, South,

---

* The four aspects are the body, its life or vitality, and the "Double" of the body, the triad which disappears with the death of the person, and the Kama-rupa which disintegrates in *Kama-loka*.

East and West, Forces having each a distinct occult property. These BEINGS are also connected with Karma, as the latter needs physical and material agents to carry out her decrees, such as the four kinds of winds, for instance, professedly admitted by Science to have their respective evil and beneficent influences upon the health of Mankind and every living thing. There is occult philosophy in that Roman Catholic doctrine which traces the various public calamities, such as epidemics of disease, and wars, and so on, to the invisible " Messengers " from North and West. " The glory of God comes from the way of the East " says Ezekiel; while Jeremiah, Isaiah, and the Psalmist assure their readers that all the evil under the Sun comes from the North and the West—which proposition, when applied to the Jewish nation, sounds like an undeniable prophecy for themselves. And this accounts also for St. Ambrose (On Amos, ch. iv.) declaring that it is precisely for that reason that " we curse the North-Wind, and that during the ceremony of baptism we begin by turning towards the West (Sidereal), to renounce the better him who inhabits it ; after which we turn to the East."

Belief in the " Four Maharajahs "—the Regents of the Four cardinal points—was universal and is now that of Christians,* who call them, after St. Augustine, " Angelic Virtues," and " Spirits " when enumerated by themselves, and " Devils " when named by Pagans. But where is the difference between the Pagans and the Christians in this cause ? Following Plato, Aristotle explained that the term στοιχεῖα was understood only as meaning the incorporeal principles placed at each of the four great divisions of our Cosmical world to supervise them. Thus, no more than the Christians did, do they *adore* and *worship* the Elements and the cardinal (imaginary) points, but the "gods" that ruled these respectively. For the Church there are two kinds of Sidereal beings, the

---

* Says the scholarly Vossius, in his Theol. Cir. I. VII. : " Though St. Augustine has said that every visible thing in this world had an angelic virtue as an overseer near it, it is not individuals but entire species of things that must be understood, each such species having indeed its particular angel to watch it. He is at one in this with all the philosophers . . . For us these angels are spirits separated from the objects . . . whereas for the philosophers (pagan) they were gods." Considering the Ritual established by the Roman Catholic Church for " Spirits of the Stars," the latter look suspiciously like " Gods," and were no more honoured and prayed to by the ancient and modern pagan rabble than they are now at Rome by the highly cultured Catholic Christians.

Angels and the Devils. For the Kabalist and Occultist there is but one; and neither of them makes any difference between " the Rectors of Light " and the Cosmocratores, or " Rectores tenebrarum harum," whom the Roman Church imagines and discovers in a " Rector of Light " as soon as he is called by another name than the one she addresses him by. It is not the " Rector " or " Maharajah " who punishes or rewards, with or without " God's " permission or order, but man himself—his deeds or Karma, attracting individually and collectively (as in the case of whole nations sometimes), every kind of evil and calamity. We produce CAUSES, and these awaken the corresponding powers in the sidereal world ; which powers are magnetically and irresistibly attracted to— and react upon—those who produced these causes ; whether such persons are practically the evil-doers, or simply Thinkers who brood mischief. Thought is matter,* we are taught by modern Science ; and " every particle of the existing matter must be a register of all that has happened," as in their " *Principles of Science* " Messrs. Jevons and Babbage tell the profane. Modern Science is drawn more every day into the maëlstrom of Occultism ; unconsciously, no doubt, still very sensibly The two main theories of science—*re* the relations between Mind and Matter—are Monism and Materialism. These two cover the whole ground of negative psychology with the exception of the quasi-occult views of the pantheistic German schools.†

---

* Not of course in the sense of the German Materialist Moleschott, who assures us that " Thought is the movement of matter," a statement of almost unequalled absurdity. Mental states and bodily states are utterly contrasted as such. But that does not affect the position that every thought, in addition to its physical accompaniment (brain-change), exhibits an objective—though to us supersensuously objective— aspect on the astral plane. (See " The Occult World," pp. 89, 90.)

† The views of our present-day scientific thinkers as to the relations between mind and matter may be reduced to two hypotheses. These show that both views equally exclude the possibility of an independent Soul, distinct from the physical brain through which it functions. They are :—

(1.) MATERIALISM, the theory which regards mental phenomena as the product of molecular change in the brain ; *i.e.*, as the outcome of a transformation of motion into feeling (!). The cruder school once went so far as to identify mind with a " peculiar mode of motion " (! !), but this view is now happily regarded as absurd by most of the men of science themselves.

(2.) MONISM, or the Single Substance Doctrine, is the more subtle form of negative psychology, which one of its advocates, Professor Bain, ably terms " guarded

In the Egyptian temples, according to Clemens Alexandrinus, an immense curtain separated the tabernacle from the place for the congregation. The Jews had the same. In both, the curtain was drawn over five pillars (the Pentacle) symbolising our five senses and five Root-races esoterically, while the four colours of the curtain represented the four cardinal points and the four terrestrial elements. The whole was an allegorical symbol. It is through the four high Rulers over the four points and Elements that our five senses may become cognisant of the hidden truths of Nature; and not at all, as Clemens would have it, that it is the elements *per se* that furnished the Pagans with divine Knowledge or the knowledge of God.* While the Egyptian emblem was spiritual, that of the Jews was purely materialistic, and, indeed, honoured only the blind Elements and the imaginary " Points." For what was the meaning of the square tabernacle raised by Moses in the wilderness, if it had not the same cosmical significance ? " Thou shalt make an hanging . . . of blue, purple, and scarlet " and " five pillars of shittim wood for the hanging . . . four brazen rings in the four corners thereof . . . boards of fine wood for the four sides, North, South, West, and East . . . of the Tabernacle . . . with Cherubims of cunning work." (Exodus, ch. xxvi., xxvii.) The Tabernacle and the square courtyard, Cherubim and all, were precisely the same as those in the Egyptian temples. The square form of the Tabernacle meant just the same thing as it still means, to this day, in the exoteric worship of the Chinese and Tibetans—the four cardinal points signifying that which the four sides of the pyramids, obelisks, and other such square erections mean. Josephus takes care to explain the whole thing. He declares that the Tabernacle pillars are the same

---

Materialism." This doctrine, which commands a very wide assent, counting among its upholders such men as Lewis, Spencer, Ferrier, and others, while positing thought and mental phenomena generally as radically contrasted with matter, regards both as equal to the two sides, or aspects, of one and the same substance in some of its conditions. Thought as thought, they say, is utterly contrasted with material phenomena, but it must be also regarded as only " the subjective side of nervous motion "—whatever our learned men may mean by this.

* Thus the sentence, " Natura Elementorum obtinet revelationem Dei," (In Clemens's *Stromata*, R. IV., para. 6), is applicable to both or neither. Consult the Zends, vol II., p. 228, and Plutarch *De Iside*, as compared by Layard, *Academie des Inscriptions*, 1854, Vol. XV.

as those raised at Tyre to the four Elements, which were placed on pedestals whose four angles faced the four cardinal points : adding that "the angles of the pedestals had equally the four figures of the Zodiac" on them, which represented the same orientation (*Antiquities I.,* VIII., ch. xxii.).

The idea may be traced in the Zoroastrian caves, in the rock-cut temples of India, as in all the sacred square buildings of antiquity that have survived to this day. This is shown definitely by Layard, who finds the four cardinal points, and the four primitive elements, in the religion of every country, under the shape of square obelisks, the four sides of the pyramids, etc., etc. Of these elements and their points the four Maharajahs were the regents and the directors.

If the student would know more of them, he has but to compare the Vision of Ezekiel (chap. i.) with what is known of Chinese Buddhism (even in its exoteric teachings) ; and examine the outward shape of these "Great Kings." In the opinion of the Rev. Joseph Edkins, they are "the Devas who preside each over one of the four continents into which the Hindus divide the world."* Each leads an army of spiritual beings to protect mankind and Buddhism. With the exception of favouritism towards Buddhism, the four celestial beings are precisely this. They are the protectors of mankind and also the Agents of Karma on Earth, whereas the Lipika are concerned with Humanity's hereafter. At the same time they are the four living creatures "who have the likeness of a man" of Ezekiel's visions, called by the translators of the Bible, "Cherubim," "Seraphim," etc. ; and by the Occultists, "the winged Globes," the "Fiery Wheels," and in the Hindu Pantheon by a number of different names. All these Gandharvas, the "Sweet Songsters," the Asuras, Kinnaras, and Nagas, are the allegorical descriptions of the "four Maharajahs." The Seraphim are the fiery Serpents of Heaven which we find in a passage describing Mount Meru as: "the exalted mass of glory, the venerable haunt of gods and heavenly choristers . . . . not to be reached by sinful men . . . . because guarded by Serpents." They are called the Avengers, and the "Winged Wheels."

Their mission and character being explained, let us see what the

* The Hindus happen to divide the world into seven continents, exoterically as esoterically ; and their four cosmic Devas are eight, presiding over the eight points of the compass and not the Continents. (Compare "Chinese Buddhism," p. 216.)

Christian Bible-interpreters say of the Cherubim:—" The word signifies in Hebrew, fullness of knowledge ; these angels are so called from their exquisite Knowledge, and were therefore used for the punishment of men who affected divine Knowledge." (Interpreted by Cruden in his Concordance, from Genesis iii., 24.) Very well ; and vague as the information is, it shows that the Cherub placed at the gate of the garden of Eden after the " Fall," suggested to the venerable Interpreters the idea of punishment connected with forbidden Science or divine Knowledge—one that generally leads to another " Fall," that of the gods, or " God," in man's estimation. But as the good old Cruden knew nought of Karma, he may be forgiven. Yet the allegory is suggestive. From Meru, the abode of gods, to Eden, the distance is very small, and from the Hindu Serpents to the Ophite Cherubim, the third out of the seven of which was the Dragon, the separation is still smaller, for both watched the entrance to the realm of Secret Knowledge. But Ezekiel plainly describes the four Cosmic Angels: " I looked, and behold, a whirlwind, a cloud and fire infolding it . . . also out of the midst thereof came the likeness of four living creatures . . . they had the likeness of a man. And every one had four faces and four wings . . . the face of a man, and the face of a lion, the face of an ox, and the face of an eagle . . . " (" Man " was here substituted for " Dragon." Compare the " *Ophite Spirits.*"*) . . . " Now as I beheld the living creatures behold one wheel upon the Earth with his four faces . . . as it were a wheel in the middle of a wheel . . . for the support of the living creature was in the wheel . . . their appearance was like coals of fire . . ." etc. (Ezekiel, ch. i.)

There are three chief groups of Builders and as many of the Planetary Spirits and the Lipika, each group being again divided into Seven sub-groups. It is impossible, even in such a large work as this, to enter into a minute examination of even the three principal groups, as it would demand an extra volume. The " Builders " are the representatives of the first " Mind-Born " Entities, therefore of the primeval Rishi-Prajapati : also of the Seven great Gods of Egypt, of which Osiris is the chief: of the Seven Amshaspends of the Zoroastrians, with

* The Angels recognised by the Roman Catholic Church who correspond to these " Faces " were with the Ophites :—Dragon—Raphael ; Lion—Michael ; Bull, or ox— Uriel ; and Eagle—Gabriel. The four keep company with the four Evangelists, and preface the Gospels.

Ormazd at their head : or the " Seven Spirits of the Face " : the Seven Sephiroth separated from the first Triad, etc., etc.*

They build or rather rebuild every " System " after the " Night." The Second group of the Builders is the Architect of our planetary chain exclusively ; and the third, the progenitor of our Humanity—the Macrocosmic prototype of the microcosm.

The Planetary Spirits are the informing spirits of the Stars in general, and of the Planets especially. They rule the destinies of men who are all born under one or other of their constellations ; the second and third groups pertaining to other systems have the same functions, and all rule various departments in Nature. In the Hindu exoteric Pantheon they are the guardian deities who preside over the eight points of the compass—the four cardinal and the four intermediate points—and are called *Loka-Pâlas*, " Supporters or guardians of the World " (in our visible Kosmos), of which Indra (East), Yama (South), Varuna (West), and Kuvera (North) are the chief; their elephants and their spouses pertaining of course to fancy and afterthought, though all of them have an occult significance.

The Lipika (a description of whom is given in the Commentary on Stanza IV. No. 6) are the Spirits of the Universe, whereas the Builders are only our own planetary deities. The former belong to the most occult portion of Cosmogenesis, which cannot be given here. Whether the Adepts (even the highest) know this angelic order in the completeness of its triple degrees, or only the lower one connected with the records of our world, is something which the writer is unprepared to say, and she would incline rather to the latter supposition. Of its highest grade one thing only is taught : the Lipika are connected with Karma—being its direct Recorders.†

---

* The Jews, save the Kabalists, having no names for East, West, South, and North, expressed the idea by words signifying before, behind, right and left, and very often confounded the terms exoterically, thus making the blinds in the Bible more confused and difficult to interpret. Add to this the fact that out of the forty-seven translators of King James I. of England's Bible "only three understood Hebrew, and of these two died before the Psalms were translated" (*Royal Masonic Cyclopaedia*), and one may easily understand what reliance can be placed on the English version of the Bible. In this work the Douay Roman Catholic version is generally followed.

† The Symbol for Sacred and Secret Knowledge was universally in antiquity, a Tree, by which a Scripture or a Record was also meant. Hence the word Lipika, the

STANZA V.—*Continued.*

6. THE LIPIKA CIRCUMSCRIBE THE TRIANGLE, THE FIRST ONE (*the vertical line or the figure* I.), THE CUBE, THE SECOND ONE, AND THE PENTACLE WITHIN THE EGG (*circle*) (*a*). IT IS THE RING CALLED " PASS NOT," FOR THOSE WHO DESCEND AND ASCEND (*as also for those*) WHO, DURING THE KALPA, ARE PROGRESSING TOWARD THE GREAT DAY " BE WITH US " (*b*). . . . THUS WERE FORMED THE ARUPA AND THE RUPA (*the Formless World and the World of Forms*) ; FROM ONE LIGHT SEVEN LIGHTS ; FROM EACH OF THE SEVEN SEVEN TIMES SEVEN LIGHTS. THE " WHEELS" WATCH THE RING.

The Stanza proceeds with a minute classification of the Orders of Angelic Hierarchy. From the group of Four and Seven emanates the " mind-born" group of Ten, of Twelve, of Twenty-one, etc., all these divided again into sub-groups of septenaries, novems, duodecimals, and so on, until the mind is lost in this endless enumeration of celestial hosts and Beings, each having its distinct task in the ruling of the visible Kosmos during its existence.

(*a*) The esoteric meaning of the first sentence of the Sloka is, that those who have been called Lipikas, the Recorders of the Karmic ledger, make an impassible barrier between the personal EGO and the impersonal SELF, the Noumenon and Parent-Source of the former. Hence the allegory. They circumscribe the manifested world of matter within the RING " Pass-Not." This world is the symbol (objective) of the ONE divided into the many, on the planes of Illusion, of Adi (the " First") or of Eka (the " One ") ; and this One is the collective aggregate, or totality, of the principal Creators or Architects of this visible universe. In Hebrew Occultism their name is both Achath, feminine, " One," and Achod, " One" again, but masculine. The monotheists have taken (and are still taking) advantage of the profound esotericism of the Kabala to apply the name by which the One Supreme Essence is known to ITS manifestation, the Sephiroth-Elohim, and call it Jehovah. But this is

"writers " or scribes ; the " Dragons," symbols of wisdom, who guard the Trees of Knowledge ; the " golden " apple Tree of the Hesperides ; the " Luxuriant Trees " and vegetation of Mount Meru guarded by a Serpent. Juno giving to Jupiter, on her marriage with him, a Tree with golden fruit is another form of Eve offering Adam the apple from the Tree of Knowledge.

quite arbitrary and against all reason and logic, as the term
Elohim is a plural noun, identical with the plural word *Chiim*, often
compounded with the Elohim.*   Moreover, in Occult metaphysics
there are, properly speaking, two " ONES "—the One on the unreachable
plane of Absoluteness and Infinity, on which no speculation is possible,
and the Second " One" on the plane of Emanations.   The former
can neither emanate nor be divided, as it is eternal, absolute, and
immutable.   The Second, being, so to speak, the reflection of the first
One (for it is the Logos, or Eswara, in the Universe of Illusion), can
do all this.†   It emanates from itself—as the upper Sephirothal Triad
emanates the lower seven Sephiroth—the seven Rays or Dhyan
Chohans; in other words, the Homogeneous becomes the Heterogeneous, the "Protyle" differentiates into the Elements.   But these,
unless they return into their primal Element, can never cross beyond
the Laya, or zero-point.

Hence the allegory.   The Lipika separate the world (or plane) of
pure spirit from that of Matter.   Those who " descend and ascend "
—the incarnating Monads, and men striving towards purification and
" ascending," but still not having quite reached the goal—may cross the
" circle of the Pass-Not," only on the day " Be-With-Us "; that day
when man, freeing himself from the trammels of ignorance, and recog-

---

* The sentence in the Sepher Jezirah and elsewhere: "Achath-Ruach-Elohim-
Chiim" denotes the Elohim as androgynous at best, the feminine element almost predominating, as it would read: "ONE is She the Spirit of the Elohim of Life." As said
above, Echath (or Achath) is feminine, and Echod (or Achod) masculine, both meaning
ONE.

† This metaphysical tenet can hardly be better described than Mr. Subba Row's in
" Bhagavadgita " lectures: " Mulaprakiti (the veil of Parabrahmam) acts as the one
energy through the Logos (or ' Eswara '). Now Parabrahmam, is the one essence from which
starts into existence a centre of energy, which I shall for the present call the Logos. . . .
It is called the Verbum . . . by the Christians, and it is the divine Christos who is eternal
in the bosom of his father. It is called Avalôkitêshwara by the Buddhists. . . . In almost
every doctrine, they have formulated the existence of a centre of spiritual energy which
is unborn and eternal, and which exists in the bosom of Parabrahmam at the time of
Pralaya, and starts as a centre of conscious energy at the time of Cosmic activity. . . ."
For, as the lecturer premised by saying, Parabraham is not this or that, it is not even
consciousness, as it cannot be related to matter or anything conditioned. It is not Ego nor
is it Non-ego, not even Atma, but verily the one source of all manifestations and modes
of existence.

nising fully the non-separateness of the Ego within his personality—erroneously regarded as his own—from the UNIVERSAL EGO (Anima Supra-Mundi), merges thereby into the One Essence to become not only one " with us " (the manifested universal lives which are " ONE " LIFE), but that very life itself.

Astronomically, the " Ring PASS-NOT " that the Lipika trace around the Triangle, the First One, the Cube, the Second One, and the Pentacle to circumscribe these figures, is thus shown to contain the symbol of 31415 again, or the coefficient constantly used in mathematical tables (the value of π, pi), the geometrical figures standing here for numerical figures. According to the general philosophical teachings, this ring is beyond the region of what are called nebulæ in astronomy. But this is as erroneous a conception as that of the topography and the descriptions, given in Purânic and other exoteric Scriptures, about the 1008 worlds of the Devaloka worlds and firmaments. There are worlds, of course, in the esoteric as well as in the profane scientific teachings, at such incalculable distances that the light of the nearest of them which has just reached our modern Chaldees, had left its luminary long before the day on which the words " Let there be Light " were pronounced ; but these are no worlds on the Devaloka plane, but in our Kosmos.

The chemist goes to the *laya* or zero point of the plane of matter with which he deals, and then stops short. The physicist or the astronomer counts by billions of miles beyond the nebulæ, and then they also stop short ; the semi-initiated Occultist will represent this laya-point to himself as existing on some plane which, if not physical, is still conceivable to the human intellect. But the full Initiate *knows* that the ring " Pass-Not " is neither a locality nor can it be measured by distance, but that it exists in the absoluteness of infinity. In this " Infinity " of the full Initiate there is neither height, breadth nor thickness, but all is fathomless profundity, reaching down from the physical to the " para-para-metaphysical." In using the word "down," essential depth—"nowhere and everywhere "—is meant, not depth of physical matter.

If one searches carefully through the exoteric and grossly anthropomorphic allegories of popular religions, even in these the doctrine embodied in the circle of " Pass-Not " thus guarded by the Lipika, may be dimly perceived. Thus one finds it even in the teachings of

the Vedantin sect of the Visishtadwaita, the most tenaciously anthropomorphic in all India.   For we read of the released soul that:—

After reaching Moksha (a state of bliss meaning "release from
Bandha" or bondage), bliss is enjoyed by it in a place called
PARAMAPADHA, which place is not material, but made of Suddasatwa
(the essence, of which the body of Iswara—"the Lord"—is formed).
There, Muktas or Jivatmas (Monads) who have attained Moksha, are never
again subject to the qualities of either matter or Karma.   " But if they
choose, *for the sake of doing good to the world*, they may incarnate on
Earth."* The way to Paramapadha, or the immaterial worlds, from
this world, is called Devayana.   When a person has attained Moksha
and the body dies :—

" The Jiva (Soul) goes with Sukshma Sarira† from the heart of the body, to
the Brahmarandra in the crown of the head, traversing Sushumna, a nerve
connecting the heart with the Brahmarandra.   The Jiva breaks through the
Brahmarandra and goes to the region of the Sun (Suryamandala) through the
solar Rays.   Then it goes, through a dark spot in the Sun, to Paramapadha.
The Jiva is directed on its way by the Supreme Wisdom acquired by Yoga.‡
The Jiva thus proceeds to Paramapadha by the aid of Athivahikas (bearers in
transit), known by the names of Archi-Ahas . . . Aditya, Prajapati, etc.   The
Archis here mentioned are certain pure Souls, etc., etc." (Visishtadwaita
Catechism, by Pundit Bhashyacharya, F.T.S.)

No Spirit except the " Recorders " (Lipika) has ever crossed its forbidden line, nor will any do so until the day of the next Pralaya, for it
is the boundary that separates the finite—however infinite in man's
sight—from the truly INFINITE.   The Spirits referred to, therefore, as
those who " ascend and descend " are the " Hosts " of what we loosely
call " celestial Beings."   But they are, in fact, nothing of the kind.

---

* These voluntary re-incarnations are referred to in our Doctrine as Nirmânakâyas
(the surviving spiritual principles of men).

† Sukshma-sarira, " dream-like " illusive body, with which are clothed the inferior
Dhyanis of the celestial Hierarchy.

‡ Compare this esoteric tenet with the Gnostic doctrine found in " Pistis-Sophia "
(Knowledge = Wisdom), in which treatise Sophia Achamoth is shown lost in the waters
of Chaos (matter), on her way to Supreme Light, and Christos delivering and helping her
on the right Path.   Note well, " Christos " with the Gnostics meant the impersonal
principal, the Atman of the Universe, and the Atma within every man's soul—not
Jesus; though in the old Coptic MSS. in the British Museum " Christos " is almost
constantly replaced by " Jesus."

They are Entities of the higher worlds in the hierarchy of Being, so immeasurably high that, to us, they must appear as Gods, and collectively—GOD. But so we, mortal men, must appear to the ant, which reasons on the scale of its special capacities. The ant may also, for all we know, see the avenging finger of a personal God in the hand of the urchin who, in one moment, under the impulse of mischief, destroys its anthill, the labour of many weeks—long years in the chronology of insects. The ant, feeling it acutely, and attributing the undeserved calamity to a combination of Providence and sin, may also, like man, see in it the result of the sin of its first parent. Who knows and who can affirm or deny? The refusal to admit in the whole Solar system of any other reasonable and intellectual beings on the human plane, than ourselves, is the greatest conceit of our age. All that science has a right to affirm, is that there are no invisible Intelligences living under the same conditions as we do. It cannot deny point-blank the possibility of there being worlds within worlds, under totally different conditions to those that constitute the nature of our world ; nor can it deny that there may be a certain limited communication* between some of those worlds and our own. To the highest, we are taught, belong the seven orders of the purely divine Spirits ; to the six lower ones belong hierarchies that can occasionally be seen and heard by men, and who do communicate with their progeny of the Earth ; which progeny is indissolubly linked with them, each principle in man having its direct source in the nature of those great Beings, who furnish us with the respective invisible elements in us. Physical Science is welcome to speculate upon the physiological mechanism of living beings, and to continue her fruitless efforts in trying to resolve our feelings, our sensations, mental and spiritual, into functions of their inorganic vehicles. Nevertheless, all that will ever be accomplished in this direction has already been done, and Science will go no farther.

---

* The greatest philosopher of European birth, Imanuel Kant, assures us that such a communication is in no way improbable. " I confess I am much disposed to assert the existence of Immaterial natures in the world, and to place my own soul in the class of these beings. It will hereafter, I know not where, or when, yet be proved that the human soul stands even in this life in indissoluble connection with all immaterial natures in the spirit-world, that it reciprocally acts upon these and receives impressions from them." (Träume eines Geistersehers, quoted by C. C. Massey, in his preface to Von Hartmann's " Spiritismus.")

She is before a dead wall, on the face of which she traces, as she imagines, great physiological and psychic discoveries, but every one of which will be shown later on to be no better than the cobwebs spun by her scientific fancies and illusions. The tissues of our objective framework alone are subservient to the analysis and researches of physiological science.* The six higher principles in them will evade for ever the hand that is guided by an animus that purposely ignores and rejects the Occult Sciences.

The " Great Day of Be-with-us," then, is an expression the only merit of which lies in its literal translation. Its significance is not so easily revealed to a public, unacquainted with the mystic tenets of Occultism, or rather of Esoteric Wisdom or " Budhism." It is an expression peculiar to the latter, and as hazy for the profane as that of the Egyptians who called the same the " Day of Come-to-us, "† which

---

* *E.g.*, all that modern physiological research in connection with psychological problems has, and owing to the nature of things, could have shown, is, that every thought, sensation, and emotion is attended with a re-marshalling of the molecules of certain nerves. The inference drawn by scientists of the type of Büchner, Vogt, and others, that thought is molecular motion, necessitates a complete abstraction being made of the fact of our subjective consciousness.

† See " Le Livre des Morts," by Paul Pierret ; " Le Jour de ' Viens a nous ' . . . c'est le jour où Osiris a dit au Soleil : Viens ! Je le vois rencontrant le Soleil dans l'Amenti." (Chap. xvii., p. 61.) The Sun here stands for the Logos (or Christos, or Horus) as central Essence synthetically, and as a diffused essence of radiated Entities, different in substance, but not in essence. As expressed by the *Bhagavadgita* lecturer, " it must not be supposed that the Logos is but a single centre of energy manifested from Parabrahmam ; there are innumerable other centres . . . and their number is almost infinite in the bosom of Parabrahmam." Hence the expressions, " The Day of Come to us" and " The Day of Be with us," etc. Just as the square is the Symbol of the Four sacred Forces or Powers—Tetraktis—so the Circle shows the boundary within the Infinity that no man can cross, even in spirit, nor Deva nor Dhyan Chohan. The Spirits of those who " descend and ascend " during the course of cyclic evolution shall cross the " iron-bound world" only on the day of their approach to the threshold of Paranirvana. If they reach it—they will rest in the bosom of Parabrahmam, or the " Unknown Darkness," which shall then become for all of them Light—during the whole period of Mahapralaya, the " Great Night," namely, 311,040,000,000,000 years of absorption in Brahm. The day of " Be-With-Us " is this period of rest or Paranirvana. See also for other data on this peculiar expression, the day of " Come-To-Us," *The Funerary Ritual of the Egyptians,* by Viscount de Rougé. It corresponds to the Day of the Last Judgment of the Christians, which has been sorely materialised by their religion.

is identical with the former, though the verb " be " in this sense, might be still better replaced with either of the two words "Remain" or " Rest-with-us," as it refers to that long period of REST which is called Paranirvana. As in the exoteric interpretation of the Egyptian rites the soul of every defunct person—from the Hierophant down to the sacred bull Apis—became an Osiris, was Osirified, though the Secret Doctrine had always taught, that the real Osirification was the lot of every Monad only after 3,000 cycles of Existences; so in the present case. The "Monad," born of the nature and the very Essence of the "Seven" (its highest principle becoming immediately enshrined in the Seventh Cosmic Element), has to perform its septenary gyration throughout the Cycle of Being and forms, from the highest to the lowest; and then again from man to God. At the threshold of Paranirvana it reassumes its primeval Essence and becomes the Absolute once more.

STANZA VI.

1. By the power of the Mother of Mercy and Knowledge (*a*), Kwan-Yin,* the "Triple" of Kwan-Shai-Yin, residing in Kwan-Yin-Tien (*b*), Fohat, the breath of their progeny, the Son of the Sons, having called forth from the lower abyss (*chaos*) the illusive form of Sien-Tchan (*our Universe*) and the seven elements :—

(*a*.) The Mother of Mercy and Knowledge is called " the triple " of Kwan-Shai-Yin because in her correlations, metaphysical and cosmical, she is the " Mother, the Wife and the Daughter " of the *Logos*, just as in the later theological translations she became " the Father, Son and (the female) Holy Ghost "—the *Sakti* or Energy—the Essence of the three. Thus in the Esotericism of the Vedantins, *Daiviprakriti*, the Light manifested through Eswara, the *Logos*,† is at one and the same time the Mother and also the Daughter of the Logos or Verbum of Parabrahmam ; while in that of the trans-Himalayan teachings it is—in the hierarchy of allegorical and metaphysical theogony—" the Mother " or abstract, ideal matter, Mulaprakriti, the Root of Nature ;—from the metaphysical standpoint, a correlation of Adi-Bhûta, manifested in the Logos, Avalokitêshwâra ;—and from the purely occult and

---

* This stanza is translated from the Chinese text, and the names, as the equivalents of the original terms, are preserved. The real esoteric nomenclature cannot be given, as it would only confuse the reader. The Brahmanical doctrine has no equivalent to these. Vâch seems, in many an aspect, to approach the Chinese Kwan-yin, but there is no regular worship of Vâch under this name in India, as there is of Kwan-Yin in China. No exoteric religious system has ever adopted a female Creator, and thus woman was regarded and treated, from the first dawn of popular religions, as inferior to man. It is only in China and Egypt that Kwan-Yin and Isis were placed on a par with the male gods. Esotericism ignores both sexes. Its highest Deity is sexless as it is formless, neither Father nor Mother ; and its first manifested beings, celestial and terrestrial alike, become only gradually androgynous and finally separate into distinct sexes.

† The "Theosophist " of February, 1887, p. 305, first lecture on the Bhagavadgita.

Cosmical, Fohat,* the "Son of the Son," the androgynous energy resulting from this "Light of the Logos," and which manifests in the plane of the objective Universe as the hidden, as much as the revealed, Electricity—which is LIFE.

(b) *Kwan-Yin-Tien* means the "melodious heaven of Sound," the abode of Kwan-Yin, or the "*Divine Voice*" literally. This "Voice" is a synonym of the *Verbum* or the Word: "Speech," as the expression of thought. Thus may be traced the connection with, and even the origin of the Hebrew *Bath-Kol*, the "daughter of the Divine Voice," or *Verbum*, or the male and female Logos, the "Heavenly Man" or Adam Kadmon, who is at the same time Sephira. The latter was surely anticipated by the Hindu Vâch, the goddess of Speech, or of the Word. For Vâch—the daughter and the female portion, as is stated, of Brahmâ, one "generated by the gods"—is, in company with Kwan-Yin, with Isis (also the *daughter*, wife and *sister* of Osiris) and other goddesses, the female *Logos*, so to speak, the goddess of the *active* forces in Nature, the Word, Voice or Sound, and Speech. If Kwan-Yin is the "melodious Voice," so is Vâch; "the melodious cow who milked forth sustenance and water" (the female principle)—"who yields us nourishment and sustenance," as Mother-Nature. She is associated in the work of creation with the Prajâpati. She is male and female *ad libitum*, as Eve is with Adam. And she is a form of Aditi—the principle higher than *Ether*—in Akâsa, the synthesis of all the forces in Nature; thus Vâch and Kwan-Yin are both the magic potency of Occult sound in Nature and Ether—which "Voice" calls forth Sien-Tchan, the illusive form of the Universe out of Chaos and the Seven Elements.

Thus in Manu Brahmâ (the *Logos* also) is shown dividing his body into two parts, male and female, and creating in the latter, who is Vâch, Viraj, who is himself, or Brahmâ again—it is in this way a learned Vedantin Occultist speaks of that "goddess," explaining the reason why Eswara (or Brahmâ) is called *Verbum* or *Logos*; why in fact it is called Sabda Brahmam :—

---

* Says the lecturer on p. 306: "Evolution is commenced by the intellectual energy of the *Logos*, not merely on account of the potentialities locked up in *Mulaprakriti*. This light of the Logos is the link . . . between objective matter and the subjective thought of *Eswara* (or Logos). It is called in several Buddhist books *Fohat*. It is the one instrument with which the *Logos* works."

"The explanation I am going to give you will appear thoroughly mystical; but if mystical, it has a tremendous significance when properly understood. Our old writers said that *Vâch* is of four kinds (see Rig Veda and the Upanishads). *Vaikhari-Vâch* is what we utter. Every kind of *Vaikhari-Vâch* exists in its *Madhyama*, further in its *Pasyanti*, and ultimately in its *Para* form.* The reason why this Pranava is called Vâch is this, that the four principles of the great Kosmos correspond to these four forms of *Vâch*. Now the whole manifested solar System exists in its *Sukshma* form in the light or energy of the *Logos*, because its energy is caught up and transferred to Cosmic matter. . . . The whole Kosmos in its objective form is *Vaikhari-Vâch*, the light of the *Logos* is the *Madhyama* form, and the Logos itself the *Pasyanti* form, and Parabrahm the *Para* form or aspect of that *Vâch*. It is by the light of this explanation that we must try to understand certain statements made by various philosophers to the effect that the manifested Kosmos is the *Verbum* manifested as Kosmos" (see Lecture on the Bhagavadgita, referred to above).

STANZA VI.—(*Continued.*)

2. THE SWIFT AND THE RADIANT ONE PRODUCES THE SEVEN *Layu* †
(*a*) CENTRES, AGAINST WHICH NONE WILL PREVAIL TO THE GREAT DAY
" BE WITH US "—AND SEATS THE UNIVERSE ON THESE ETERNAL FOUNDA-
TIONS, SURROUNDING SIEN-TCHAN WITH THE ELEMENTARY GERMS (*b*).

(*a.*) The seven *Layu* centres are the seven Zero points, using the term Zero in the same sense that Chemists do, to indicate a point at which, in Esotericism, the scale of reckoning of differentiation begins. From the Centres—beyond which Esoteric philosophy allows us to perceive the dim metaphysical outlines of the " Seven Sons " of Life and Light, the Seven Logoi of the Hermetic and all other philosophers—begins

---

* *Madhya* is said of something whose commencement and end are unknown, and *Para* means infinite. These expressions all relate to infinitude and to division of time.
† From the Sanskrit *Laya*, the point of matter where every differentiation has ceased.

the differentiation of the elements which enter into the constitution of our Solar System. It has often been asked what was the exact definition of Fohat and his powers and functions, as he seems to exercise those of a Personal God as understood in the popular religions. The answer has just been given in the comment on Stanza V. As well said in the Bhagavadgita Lectures, " The whole Kosmos must necessarily exist in the One Source of energy from which this light (*Fohat*) emanates." Whether we count the principles in Kosmos and man as seven or only as four, the forces of, and in, physical Nature are Seven; and it is stated by the same authority that " *Pragna*, or the capacity of perception, exists in seven different aspects corresponding to the seven conditions of matter " (*Personal and impersonal God*). For, " just as a human being is composed of seven principles, differentiated matter in the Solar System exists in seven different conditions "· (*ibid*). So does Fohat.* He is One and Seven, and on the Cosmic plane is behind all such manifestations as light, heat, sound, adhesion, etc., etc., and is the " spirit " of ELECTRICITY, which is the LIFE of the Universe. As an abstraction, we call it the ONE LIFE; as an objective and evident Reality, we speak of a septenary scale of manifestation, which begins at the upper rung with the One Unknowable CAUSALITY, and ends as Omnipresent Mind and Life immanent in every atom of Matter. Thus, while science speaks of its evolution through brute matter, blind force, and senseless motion, the Occultists point to *intelligent* LAW and *sentient* LIFE, and add that Fohat is the guiding Spirit of all this. Yet he is no personal god at all, but the emanation of those other Powers behind him whom the Christians call the " Messengers " of their God (who is in reality only the Elohim, or rather one of the Seven Creators called Elohim), and we, the " Messenger of the primordial Sons of Life and Light."

(*b.*) The " Elementary Germs " with which he fills Sien-Tchan (the " Universe ") from Tien-Sin (the " Heaven of Mind," literally, or that which is absolute) are the Atoms of Science and the Monads of Leibnitz.

---

* " Fohat " has several meanings. (See Stanza V., Commentary *et infra*). He is called the " Builder of the Builders," the Force that he personifies having formed our Septenary chain.

STANZA VI.— *Continued.*

3. OF THE SEVEN (*elements*)—FIRST ONE MANIFESTED, SIX CONCEALED;
TWO MANIFESTED—FIVE CONCEALED; THREE MANIFESTED—FOUR CON-
CEALED; FOUR PRODUCED — THREE HIDDEN; FOUR AND ONE TSAN
(*fraction*) REVEALED—TWO AND ONE HALF CONCEALED; SIX TO BE MANI-
FESTED—ONE LAID ASIDE (*a*). LASTLY, SEVEN SMALL WHEELS REVOLVING;
ONE GIVING BIRTH TO THE OTHER (*b*).

(*a*.) Although these Stanzas refer to the whole Universe after a Maha-
pralaya (universal destruction), yet this sentence, as any student of
Occultism may see, refers also by analogy to the evolution and final
formation of the primitive (though compound) Seven Elements on our
Earth. Of these, four elements are now fully manifested, while the
fifth—Ether—is only partially so, as we are hardly in the second half
of the Fourth Round, and consequently the fifth Element will manifest
fully only in the Fifth Round. The Worlds, including our own, were
of course, as germs, primarily evolved from the ONE Element in its
second stage (" Father-Mother," the differentiated World's Soul, not
what is termed the " Over-Soul " by Emerson), whether we call it, with
modern Science, Cosmic dust and Fire Mist, or with Occultism—Akâsa,
Jivâtma, divine Astral Light, or the " Soul of the World." But this
first stage of Evolution was in due course of time followed by the
next. No world, as no heavenly body, could be constructed on the
objective plane, had not the Elements been sufficiently differentiated
already from their primeval *Ilus*, resting in *Laya*. The latter term is a
synonym of Nirvana. It is, in fact, the Nirvanic dissociation of all substances, merged after a life-cycle into the latency of their primary conditions. It is the luminous but bodiless shadow of the matter *that was,* the
realm of negativeness—wherein lie latent during their period of rest the
active Forces of the Universe. Now, speaking of Elements, it is made the
standing reproach of the Ancients, that they "supposed their Elements
simple and undecomposable."* Once more this is an unwarrantable state-

---

* The shades of our pre-historical ancestors might return the compliment to modern
physicists, now that new discoveries in chemistry have led Mr. Crookes, F.R.S., to admit
that Science is yet a thousand leagues from the knowledge of the compound nature of
the simplest molecule. From him we learn that such a thing as a really simple

ment ; as, at any rate, their initiated philosophers can hardly come under such an imputation, since it is they who have invented allegories and religious myths from the beginning. Had they been ignorant of the Heterogeneity of their Elements they would have had no personifications of Fire, Air, Water, Earth, and Æther ; their Cosmic gods and goddesses would never have been blessed with such posterity, with so many sons and daughters, elements born *from* and *within each respective Element*. Alchemy and occult phenomena would have been a delusion and a snare, even in theory, had the Ancients been ignorant of the potentialities and correlative functions and attributes of every element that enters into the composition of Air, Water, Earth, and even *Fire*—the latter a terra incognita to this day to modern Science, which is obliged to call it Motion, evolution of light and heat, state of ignition,—defining it by its outward aspects in short, and remaining ignorant of its nature. But that which

---

molecule entirely homogeneous is *terra incognita* in chemistry. " Where are we to draw the line ? " he asks ; " is there no way out of this perplexity ? Must we either make the elementary examinations so stiff that only 60 or 70 candidates can pass, or must we open the examination doors so wide that the number of admissions is limited only by the number of applicants ? " And then the learned gentleman gives striking instances. He says : " Take the case of yttrium. It has its definite atomic weight, it behaved in every respect as a simple body, an element, to which we might indeed add, but from which we could not take away. Yet this yttrium, this supposed homogeneous whole, on being submitted to a certain method of fractionation, is resolved into portions not absolutely identical among themselves, and exhibiting a gradation of properties. Or take the case of didymium. Here was a body betraying all the recognised characters of an element. It had been separated with much difficulty from other bodies which approximated closely to it in their properties, and during this crucial process it had undergone very severe treatment and very close scrutiny. But then came another chemist, who, treating this assumed homogeneous body by a peculiar process of fractionation, resolved it into the two bodies praseodymium and neodymium, between which certain distinctions are perceptible. Further, we even now have no certainty that neodymium and praseodymium are simple bodies. On the contrary, they likewise exhibit symptoms of splitting up. Now, if one supposed element on proper treatment is thus found to comprise dissimilar molecules, we are surely warranted in asking whether similar results might not be obtained in other elements, perhaps in all elements, if treated in the right way. We may even ask where the process of sorting-out is to stop —a process which of course pre-supposes variations between the individual molecules of each species. And in these successive separations we naturally find bodies approaching more and more closely to each other." (Presidential address before the Royal Society of Chemists, March, 1888.)

modern Science seems to fail to perceive is that, differentiated as may
have been those simple chemical atoms—which archaic philosophy
called "the creators of their respective Parents," fathers, brothers,
husbands of their mothers, and those mothers the daughters of their
own sons, like Aditi and Daksha, for example—differentiated as these
elements were in the beginning, still, they were not the compound
bodies known to science, as they are now. Neither Water, Air, Earth
(synonym for solids generally) existed in their present form, representing
the three states of matter alone recognised by Science; for all these are
the productions already recombined by the atmospheres of globes completely formed—even to fire—so that in the first periods of the earth's
formation they were something quite *sui generis*. Now that the
conditions and laws ruling our solar system are fully developed;
and that the atmosphere of our earth, as of every other globe,
has become, so to say, a crucible of its own, Occult Science
teaches that there is a perpetual exchange taking place in space of
molecules, or of atoms rather, correlating, and thus changing their
combining equivalents on every planet. Some men of Science, and
those among the greatest physicists and chemists, begin to suspect this
fact, which has been known for ages to the Occultists. The spectroscope
only shows the probable similarity (on external evidence) of terrestrial
and sidereal substance; it is unable to go any farther, or to show
whether atoms gravitate towards one another in the same way and under
the same conditions as they are supposed to do on our planet, physically and chemically. The scale of temperature, from the highest
degree to the lowest that can be conceived of, may be imagined to be
one and the same in and for the whole Universe; nevertheless, its
properties, other than those of dissociation and re-association, differ on
every planet; and thus atoms enter into new forms of existence, undreamt of, and incognizable to, physical Science. As already expressed
in "Five Years of Theosophy," the essence of Cometary matter, for
instance, "is totally different from any of the chemical or physical
characteristics with which the greatest chemists and physicists of the
earth are acquainted" (p. 242). And even that matter, during rapid
passage through our atmosphere, undergoes a certain change in its
nature. Thus not alone the elements of our planets, but even those
of all its sisters in the Solar System, differ as widely from each other
in their combinations, as from the Cosmic elements beyond our

Solar limits.* Therefore, they cannot be taken as a standard for comparison with the same in other worlds.† Enshrined in their virgin, pristine state within the bosom of the Eternal Mother, every atom born beyond the threshold of her realm is doomed to incessant differentiation. " The Mother sleeps, yet is ever breathing." And every breath sends out into the plane of manifestation her Protean products, which, carried on by the wave of the efflux, are scattered by Fohat, and driven toward and beyond this or another planetary atmosphere. Once caught by the latter, the atom is lost; its pristine purity is gone for ever, unless Fate dissociates it by leading it to "a current of EFFLUX " (an occult term meaning quite a different process from that which the ordinary term implies); when it may be carried once more to the borderland where it had perished, and taking its flight, not into Space *above* but into Space *within*, it will be brought under a state of differential equilibrium and happily re-absorbed. Were a truly learned Occultist-alchemist to write the " Life and Adventures of an Atom " he would secure thereby the eternal scorn of the modern chemist, perchance also his subsequent

---

* This is again corroborated by the same man of science in the same lecture, who quotes Clerk Maxwell, saying " that the elements are not absolutely homogeneous." He writes : " It is difficult to conceive of selection and elimination of intermediate varieties, for where can these eliminated molecules have gone to, if, as we have reason to believe, the hydrogen, &c. of the fixed stars is composed of molecules identical in all respects with our own." And he adds : " In the first place we may call in question this absolute molecular identity, since we have hitherto had no means for coming to a conclusion save the means furnished by the spectroscope, while it is admitted that, for accurately comparing and discriminating the spectra of two bodies, they should be examined under identical states of temperature, pressure, and all other physical conditions. We have certainly seen, in the spectrum of the sun, rays which we have not been able to identify."

† " Each world has its Fohat, who is omnipresent in his own sphere of action. But there are as many Fohats as there are worlds, each varying in power and degree of manifestations. The individual Fohats make one Universal, Collective Fohat—the aspect-Entity of the one absolute Non-Entity, which is absolute Be-Ness, 'SAT.' " Millions and billions of worlds are produced at every Manvantara "—it is said. Therefore there must be many Fohats, whom we consider as conscious and *intelligent* Forces. This, no doubt, to the disgust of scientific minds. Nevertheless the Occultists, who have good reasons for it, consider all the forces of Nature as veritable, though supersensuous, states of Matter ; and as possible objects of perception to Beings endowed with the requisite senses.

gratitude.* However it may be, "*The Breath of the Father-Mother issues cold and radiant and gets hot and corrupt, to cool once more, and be purified in the eternal bosom of inner Space*," says the Commentary. Man absorbs cold pure air on the mountain-top, and throws it out impure, hot and transformed. Thus—the higher atmosphere being the mouth, and the lower one the lungs of every globe—the man of our planet breathes only the refuse of " Mother ; " therefore, " he is doomed to die on it."†

(*b*) The process referred to as " the small wheels giving birth, one to the other," takes place in the sixth region from above, and on the plane of the most material world of all in the manifested Kosmos—our terrestrial plane. These " Seven Wheels " are our planetary chain (see Commentary Nos. 5 and 6). By "Wheels " the various spheres and centres of forces are generally meant ; but in this case they refer to our septenary ring.

STANZA VI.—*Continued.*

4. He builds them in the likeness of older Wheels (*worlds*), placing them on the imperishable centres (*a*).

How does Fohat build them ? He collects the fiery dust. He makes balls of fire, runs through them and round them, infusing life thereinto; then sets them into motion, some one, some the other way. They are cold—he makes them hot. They are dry—he makes them moist. They shine—he fans and cools them (*b*).

Thus acts Fohat from one *Twilight* to the other during Seven Eternities. ‡

(*a*) The Worlds are built " in the likeness of older Wheels "—*i.e.*, those that existed in preceding Manvantaras and went into Pralaya,

----

* Indeed, if such an imaginary Chemist happened to be intuitional, and would for a moment step out of the habitual groove of strictly " Exact Science," as the Alchemists of old did, he might be repaid for his audacity.

† He who would allotropise sluggish oxygen into *Ozone* to a measure of alchemical activity, reducing it to its pure essence (for which there are means), would discover thereby a substitute for an " Elixir of Life " and prepare it for practical use.

‡ A period of 311,040,000,000,000 years, according to Brahminical calculations.

because the LAW for the birth, growth, and decay of everything in Kosmos, from the Sun to the glow-worm in the grass, is ONE. It is an everlasting work of perfection with every new appearance, but the Substance-Matter and Forces are all one and the same. But this LAW acts on every planet through minor and varying laws. The "imperishable Laya Centres" have a great importance, and their meaning must be fully understood if we would have a clear conception of the Archaic Cosmogony, whose theories have now passed into Occultism. At present, one thing may be stated. The worlds are built neither *upon*, nor *over*, nor *in* the *Laya* centres, the zero-point being a condition, not any mathematical point.

(*b*) Bear in mind that Fohat, the constructive Force of Cosmic Electricity, is said, metaphorically, to have sprung like Rudra from Brahmâ " from the brain of the Father and the bosom of the Mother," and then to have metamorphosed himself into a male and a female, *i.e.*, polarity, into postive and negative electricity. He has *seven sons* who are *his brothers ;* and Fohat is forced to be born time after time whenever any two of his son-brothers indulge *in too close contact*— whether an embrace or a fight. To avoid this, he binds together and unites those of unlike nature and separates those of similar temperaments. This, of course, relates, as any one can see, to electricity generated by friction and to the law involving attraction between two objects of unlike, and repulsion between those of like polarity. The Seven " Sons-brothers," however, represent and personify the seven forms of Cosmic magnetism called in *practical Occultism* the " Seven Radicals," whose co-operative and active progeny are, among other energies, Electricity, Magnetism, Sound, Light, Heat, Cohesion, etc. Occult Science defines all these as Super-sensuous effects in their hidden behaviour, and as objective phenomena in the world of senses ; the former requiring abnormal faculties to perceive them—the latter, our ordinary physical senses. They all pertain to, and are the emanations of, still more supersensuous spiritual qualities, not personated by, but belonging to, real and conscious CAUSES. To attempt a description of such ENTITIES would be worse than useless. The reader must bear in mind that, according to our teaching which regards this phenomenal Universe as a great *Illusion*, the nearer a body is to the UNKNOWN SUBSTANCE, the more it approaches *reality*, as being removed the farther from this world of *Maya*. Therefore, though the molecular constitution of their bodies is not deducible from their manifestations on this plane of consciousness, they nevertheless (from the standpoint of the adept Occultist) possess a distinctive objective if not material structure, in the relatively noumenal—as opposed to the phenomenal—Universe. Men of science may term them Force or Forces generated by matter, or " modes of its motion," if they will; Occultism sees in the effects " Elemental " (forces), and, in the direct causes producing them, intelligent DIVINE Workmen. The intimate connection of those Elementals (guided by the unerring hand of the Rulers)—their correlation we might call it—with the elements of pure Matter, results in our terrestrial phenomena, such as light, heat, magnetism, etc., etc. Of course we shall never agree with the American Substantialists* who call every Force and Energy—whether Light, Heat, Electricity or Cohesion—an " Entity ; " for this would be equivalent to calling the noise produced by the rolling of the wheels of a vehicle an *Entity*—thus confusing and identifying that " noise " with the driver *outside*, and the guiding Master Intelligence *within* the vehicle. But we certainly give that name to the " drivers " and to these guiding Intelligences—the ruling Dhyan Chohans, as shown. The " Elementals," the Nature-Forces, are the acting, though invisible, or rather imperceptible, secondary Causes and in themselves the effects of primary Causes behind the Veil of all terrestrial phenomena. Electricity, light, heat, etc., have been aptly termed the " Ghost or Shadow of Matter in Motion," *i.e.*, supersensuous states of matter whose effects only we are able to cognize. To expand, then, the simile given above. The sensation of light is like the sound of the rolling wheels—a purely phenomenal effect, having no existence outside the observer ; the proximate exciting cause of the sensation is comparable to the driver—a supersensuous state of matter in motion, a Nature-Force or Elemental. But, behind even this, stand—just as the owner of the carriage directs the driver from within—the higher and *noumenal* causes, the *Intelligences* from whose essence radiate these States of " *Mother*," generating the countless milliards of Elementals or psychic Nature-Spirits, just as every drop of water generates its physical

---

* See " Scientific Arena," a monthly Journal devoted to current philosophical teaching and its bearing upon the religious thought of the Age. New York: A. Wilford Hall, Ph.D., LL.D., Editor. (1886, July, August, and September.)

infinitesimal Infusoria. (See "Gods, Monads, and Atoms," in Part III.) It is Fohat who guides the transfer of the principles from one planet to the other, from one star to another—child-star. When a planet dies, its informing principles are transferred to a *laya* or sleeping centre, with potential but latent energy in it, which is thus awakened into life and begins to form itself into a new sidereal body. (*Vide infra*, " A Few Theosophical Misconceptions, etc.")

It is most remarkable that, while honestly confessing their entire ignorance of the true Nature of even terrestrial matter—primordial substance being regarded more as a dream than as a sober reality—the physicists should set themselves up as judges, nevertheless, of that matter, and claim to know what it is able and is not able to do, in various combinations. Scientists know it (matter) hardly skin-deep, and yet they will dogmatise. It is "a mode of motion" and nothing else. But the *force* that is inherent in a living person's breath, when blowing a speck of dust from the table, is also, and undeniably, " a mode of motion"; and it is as undeniably not a quality of the matter, or the particles of that speck, and it emanates from the living and thinking Entity that breathed, whether the impulse originated consciously or unconsciously. Indeed, to endow matter—something of which nothing is known so far—with an inherent quality called Force, of the nature of which still less is known, is to create a far more serious difficulty than that which lies in the acceptation of the intervention of our " Nature-Spirits " in every natural phenomenon.

The Occultists, who do not say—if they would express themselves correctly—that *matter*, but only the *substance* or *essence* of matter, is indestructible and eternal, (*i.e.*, the Root of all, *Mulaprakriti*) : assert that all the so-called Forces of Nature, Electricity, Magnetism, Light, Heat, etc., etc., far from being modes of motion of material particles, are *in esse*, *i.e.*, in their ultimate constitution, the differentiated aspects of that Universal Motion which is discussed and explained in the first pages of this volume (*See Proem*). When Fohat is said to produce " Seven Laya Centres," it means that for formative or creative purposes, the GREAT LAW (Theists may call it God) stops, or rather modifies its perpetual motion on seven invisible points within the area of the manifested Universe. "*The great Breath digs through Space seven holes into Laya to cause them to circumgyrate during Manvantara*" (Occult Catechism). We have said that Laya is what Science may call the Zero-point or line ; the realm of absolute negativeness, or the one real absolute Force, the NOUMENON of the Seventh State of that which we ignorantly call and recognise as " Force " ; or again the Noumenon of Undifferentiated Cosmic Substance which is itself an unreachable and unknowable object to finite perception ; the root and basis of all states of objectivity and subjectivity too ; the neutral axis, not one of the many aspects, but its centre. It may serve to elucidate the meaning if we attempt to imagine a neutral centre—the dream of those who would discover perpetual motion. A " neutral centre " is, in one aspect, the limiting point of any given set of senses. Thus, imagine two consecutive planes of matter as already formed ; each of these corresponding to an appropriate set of perceptive organs. We are forced to admit that between these two planes of matter an incessant circulation takes place ; and if we follow the atoms and molecules of (say) the lower in their transformation upwards, these will come to a point where they pass altogether beyond the range of the faculties we are using on the lower plane. In fact, to us the matter of the lower plane there vanishes from our perception into nothing—or rather it passes on to the higher plane, and the state of matter corresponding to such a point of transition must certainly possess special and not readily discoverable properties. Such " Seven Neutral Centres,"* then, are produced by Fohat, who, when, as Milton has it—

" Fair foundations (are) laid whereon to build . . ."

quickens matter into activity and evolution.

The *Primordial Atom* (*anu*) cannot be multiplied either in its pre-genetic state, or its primogeneity ; therefore it is called " SUM TOTAL," figuratively, of course, as that " SUM TOTAL " is boundless. (See Addendum to this Book.) That which is the abyss of nothingness to the physicist, who knows only the world of visible causes and effects, is the boundless Space of the Divine *Plenum* to the Occultist. Among many other objections to the doctrine of an endless evolution and re-involution (or re-absorption) of the Kosmos, a process which, according to the Brahminical and Esoteric Doctrine, is without a beginning or an end, the Occultist is told that it cannot be, since " by all the admissions of

---

* Such, we believe, is the name applied by Mr. Keely, of Philadelphia, the inventor of the famous " Motor "—destined, as his admirers have hoped, to revolutionise the motor power of the world—to what he again calls the " Etheric Centres."

modern scientific philosophy it is a necessity of Nature to run down."
If the tendency of Nature " to run down " is to be considered so
forcible an objection to Occult Cosmogony, "How," we may ask, "do your
Positivists and Free-thinkers and Scientists account for the phalanx
around us of active stellar systems ? " They had eternity to " run
down " in ; why, then, is not the Kosmos a huge inert mass ?   Even the
moon is only hypothetically believed to be a dead planet, " run
down," and astronomy does not seem to be acquainted with many
such dead planets.*   The query is unanswerable. But apart from this
it must be noted that the idea of the amount of " transformable energy "
in our little system coming to an end is based purely on the fallacious
conception of a " white-hot, incandescent Sun " perpetually radiating
away his heat without compensation into Space.   To this we reply that
nature runs down and disappears from the objective plane, only to re-
emerge after a time of rest out of the subjective and to reascend once
more.   Our Kosmos and Nature will run down only to reappear on a
more perfect plane after every PRALAYA.   The *matter* of the Eastern
philosophers is not the " matter " and Nature of the Western metaphysicians.   For what is Matter ?   And above all, what is our scientific
philosophy but that which was so justly and so politely defined by Kant
as " the Science of the *limits* to our Knowledge ?"   Where have the
many attempts made by Science to bind, to connect, and define all the
phenomena of organic life by mere physical and chemical manifestations,
brought it to?   To speculation generally—mere soap-bubbles, that burst
one after the other before the men of Science were permitted to discover
real facts.   All this would have been avoided, and the progress of
knowledge would have proceeded with gigantic strides, had only Science
and its philosophy abstained from accepting hypotheses on the mere
one-sided Knowledge of *their* Matter.†

---

* The moon is *dead* only so far as regards her *inner* " principles "—*i.e.*, *psychically* and
spiritually, however absurd the statement may seem.   Physically, she is only as a semi-
paralysed body may be.   She is aptly referred to in Occultism as the " insane mother,"
the great sidereal *lunatic*.

† The instance of Uranus and Neptune, whose satellites, four and one respectively,
revolved, it was thought, in their orbits from East to West, whereas all the other
satellites rotate from West to East, is a very good one, as showing how unreliable are all
a priori speculations even when based on the strictest mathematical analysis.   The
famous hypothesis of the formation of our Solar System out of the nebulous rings, put

If no physical intellect is capable of counting the grains of sand covering a few miles of sea-shore; or to fathom the ultimate nature and essence of those grains, palpable and visible on the palm of the naturalist, how can any materialist limit the laws changing the conditions and being of the atoms in primordial chaos, or know anything certain about the capabilities and potency of their atoms and molecules before and after their formation into worlds? These changeless and eternal molecules —far thicker in space than the grains on the ocean shore— may differ in their constitution along the line of their planes of existence, as the soul-substance differs from its vehicle, the body. Each atom has seven planes of being or existence, we are taught; and each plane is governed by its specific laws of evolution and absorption. Ignorant of any, even approximate, chronological data from which to start in attempting to decide the age of our planet or the origin of the solar system, astronomers, geologists, and physicists are drifting with each new hypothesis farther and farther away from the shores of fact into the fathomless depths of speculative ontology.* The Law of Analogy in the plan of structure between the trans-Solar systems and the intra-Solar planets, does not necessarily bear upon the finite conditions to which every visible body is subject, in this our plane of being. In Occult Science this law is the first and most important key to Cosmic physics; but it has to be studied in its minutest details and, " to be

orward by Kant and Laplace, was chiefly based on the above fact that all the planets revolved in the same direction. It is on this fact, mathematically demonstrated during the time of Laplace, that this great astronomer, calculating on the theory of probabilities, offered to bet three milliards to one that the next planet discovered would have in its system the same peculiarity of motion Eastward. The immutable laws of scientific mathematics got "worsted by further experiments and observations," it was said. This idea of Laplace's mistake prevails generally to this day; but some astronomers have finally succeeded in demonstrating (?) that the mistake had been in accepting Laplace's assertion for a mistake; and steps to correct it without attracting general attention to the *bévue* are now being taken. Many such unpleasant surprises are in store for hypotheses of even a purely physical character. What further disillusions, then, may there not be in questions of a transcendental, Occult Nature? At any rate, Occultism teaches that the so-called "reverse rotation" is a fact.

* The Occultists, having most perfect faith in their own exact records, astronomical and mathematical, calculate the age of Humanity, and assert that the latter (as separate sexes) has existed in this Round just 18,618,727 years, as the Brahmanical teachings and even some Hindu calendars declare.

turned seven times," before one comes to understand it. Occult philosophy is the only science that can teach it. How, then, can anyone
hang the truth or the untruth of the Occultist's proposition that " the
Kosmos is eternal in its unconditioned collectivity, and finite but in its
conditioned manifestations " on this one-sided physical enunciation that
" it is a necessity of Nature to run down ? "

With these verses—the 4th Sloka of Stanza VI.—ends that portion
of the Stanzas which relates to the Universal Cosmogony after the last
Mahapralaya or Universal destruction, which, when it comes, sweeps
out of Space every differentiated thing, Gods as atoms, like so many
dry leaves. From this verse onwards, the Stanzas are concerned only
with our Solar System in general, with the planetary chains therein,
inferentially, and with the history of our globe (the 4th and its
chain) especially. All the Stanzas and verses which follow in this
Book I. refer only to the evolution of, and on, our Earth. With regard
to the latter, a strange tenet—strange from the modern scientific stand-
point only, of course—is held, which ought to be made known.

But before entirely new and rather startling theories are presented to
the reader, they must be prefaced by a few words of explanation. This
is absolutely necessary, as these theories clash not only with modern
science, but contradict, on certain points, earlier statements made by
other Theosophists, who claim to base their explanations and renderings
of these teachings on the same authority as we do.*

This may give rise to the idea that there is a decided contradiction
between the expounders of the same doctrine ; whereas the difference,
in reality, arises from the incompleteness of the information given to
earlier writers, who thus drew some erroneous conclusions and indulged
in premature speculations, in their endeavour to present a complete
system to the public. Thus the reader, who is already a student of
Theosophy, must not be surprised to find in these pages the rectifica-
tion of certain statements made in various Theosophical works, and
also the explanation of certain points which have remained obscure,
because they were necessarily left incomplete. Many are the questions
upon which even the author of " Esoteric Buddhism " (the best and

---

* " Esoteric Buddhism " and " Man."

most accurate of all such works) has not touched.   On the other hand,
even he has introduced several mistaken notions which must now be
presented in their true mystic light, as far as the present writer is
capable of doing so.

Let us then make a short break between the Slokas just explained
and those which follow, for the Cosmic periods which separate them
are of immense duration.   This will afford us ample time to take a
bird's-eye view of some points pertaining to the Secret Doctrine, which
have been presented to the public under a more or less uncertain and
sometimes mistaken light.

A FEW EARLY THEOSOPHICAL MISCONCEPTIONS CONCERNING PLANETS, ROUNDS, AND MAN.

Among the eleven Stanzas omitted* there is one which gives a full
description of the formation of the planetary chains one after another,
after the first Cosmic and Atomic differentiation had commenced in the
primitive *Acosmism*.   It is idle to speak of " laws arising when Deity
prepares to create" for (*a*) laws or rather LAW is eternal and uncreated ;
and (*b*) that Deity is Law, and *vice versâ*.   Moreover, the one eternal
LAW unfolds everything in the (to be) manifested Nature on a sevenfold
principle ; among the rest, the countless circular chains of worlds, composed of seven globes, graduated on the four lower planes of the world
of formation (the three others belonging to the Archetypal Universe).
Out of these seven only *one, the lowest and the most material of those globes,*
is within our plane or means of perception, the six others lying outside
of it and being therefore invisible to the terrestrial eye.   Every such
chain of worlds is the progeny and creation of another, *lower*, and *dead*
chain—*its reincarnation*, so to say.   To make it clearer : we are told of
the planets—of which *seven only* were held as sacred, as being ruled by
the highest regents or gods, and not at all because the ancients knew
nothing of the others†—that each of these, whether known or unknown,
is a septenary, as is the chain to which the Earth belongs (see " Esoteric

* See the note which follows the Commentary on the preceding page, and also the
summary of the Stanzas in the Proem, page 22.

† Many more planets are enumerated in the Secret Books than in modern
astronomical works.

Buddhism "). For instance, all such planets as Mercury, Venus, Mars, Jupiter, Saturn, etc., etc., or our Earth, are as visible to us as our globe, probably, is to the inhabitants of the other planets, if any, because they are all on the same plane ; while the superior fellow-globes of these planets are on other planes quite outside that of our terrestrial senses. As their relative position is given further on, and also in the diagram appended to the Comments on Verse 7 of Stanza VI., a few words of explanation is all that is needed at present. These invisible companions correspond curiously to that which we call "the principles in Man." The seven are on three material planes and one spiritual plane, answering to the three *Upadhis* (material bases) and one spiritual vehicle (*Vahan*) of our seven principles in the human division. If, for the sake of a clearer mental conception, we imagine the human principles to be arranged as in the following scheme, we shall obtain the annexed diagram of correspondences :—

HUMAN PRINCIPLES.   PLANETARY DIVISION.

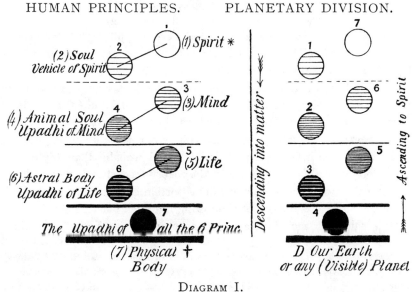

DIAGRAM I.

* As we are proceeding here from Universals to Particulars, instead of using the inductive or Aristotelean method, the numbers are reversed. Spirit is enumerated the first instead of seventh, as is usually done, but, in truth, *ought not to be done.*

† Or as usually named after the manner of *Esoteric Buddhism* and others: 1, Atma ; 2, Buddhi (or Spiritual Soul) ; 3, Manas (Human Soul) ; 4, Kama Rupa (Vehicle of Desires and Passions) ; 5, Linga Sarira ; 6, Prana ; 7, Sthula Sarira.

The dark horizontal lines of the lower planes are the Upadhis in one case, and the planes in the case of the planetary chain. Of course, as regards the human principles, the diagram does not place them quite in order, yet it shows the correspondence and analogy to which attention is now drawn. As the reader will see, it is a case of descent into matter, the adjustment—in both the mystic and the physical senses—of the two, and their interblending for the great coming " struggle of life " that awaits both the *entities*. " Entity " may be thought a strange term to use in the case of a globe; but the ancient philosophers, who saw in the earth a huge " animal," were wiser in their generation than our modern geologists are in theirs; and Pliny, who called the Earth our kind nurse and mother, the only element which is not inimical to man, spoke more truly than Watts, who fancied that he saw in her the footstool of God. For Earth is only the footstool of man in his ascension to higher regions; the vestibule—

" .   .   .   . to glorious mansions,
        Through which a moving crowd for ever press."

But this only shows how admirably the occult philosophy fits everything in Nature, and how much more logical are its tenets than the lifeless hypothetical speculations of physical science.

Having learned thus much, the mystic will be better prepared to understand the occult teaching, though every formal student of modern science may, and probably will, regard it as preposterous nonsense. The student of occultism, however, holds that the theory at present under discussion is far more philosophical and probable than any other. It is more logical, at any rate, than the theory recently advanced which made of the moon the projection of a portion of our Earth extruded when the latter was but a globe in fusion, a molten plastic mass.*

It is said that the planetary chains having their " Days " and their

---

* Says the author of " Modern Science and Modern Thought," Mr. Samuel Laing : " The astronomical conclusions are theories based on data so uncertain, that while in some cases they give results incredibly short, like that of 15 millions of years for the whole past process of formation of the solar system, in others they give results almost incredibly long, as *in that which supposes the moon to have been thrown off when the Earth was rotating in three hours, while the utmost actual retardation obtained from observation would require* 600 millions of years to make it rotate in twenty-three hours instead of twenty-four " (p. 48). And if physicists persist, why should the chronology of the Hindus be laughed at as exaggerated ?

" Nights "—*i.e.*, periods of activity or life, and of inertia or death—and behave in heaven as do men on Earth : they generate their likes, get old, and become personally extinct, their spiritual principles only living in their progeny as a survival of themselves.

Without attempting the very difficult task of giving out the whole process in all its cosmic details, enough may be said to give an approximate idea of it. When a planetary chain is in its last Round, its Globe I or A, before finally *dying out*, sends all its energy and " principles " into a neutral centre of latent force, a " laya centre," and thereby informs a new nucleus of undifferentiated substance or matter, *i.e.*, calls it into activity or gives it life. Suppose such a process to have taken place in the lunar " planetary " chain ; suppose again, for argument's sake (though Mr. Darwin's theory quoted below has lately been upset, even if the fact has not yet been ascertained by mathematical calculation) that the moon is far older than the Earth. Imagine the six fellow-globes of the moon—æons before the first globe of our seven was evolved—just in the same position in relation to each other as the fellow-globes of our chain occupy in regard to our Earth now. (See in " Esoteric Buddhism," " The Constitution of Man," and the " Planetary Chain.") And now it will be easy to imagine further Globe A of the lunar chain informing Globe A of the terrestrial chain, and—dying ; Globe B of the former sending after that its energy into Globe B of the new chain ; then Globe C of the lunar, creating its progeny sphere C of the terrene chain ; then the Moon (our Satellite*) pouring forth into

* She is the satellite, undeniably, but this does not invalidate the theory that she has given to the Earth all but her corpse. For Darwin's theory to hold good, besides the hypothesis just upset (vide last footnote), other still more incongruous speculations had to be invented. The Moon, it is said, has cooled nearly six times as rapidly as the Earth (Winchell's " World-Life ") : " The Moon, if the earth is 14,000,000 years old since its incrustation, is only eleven and two thirds millions of years old since that stage . . ." etc. And if our Moon is but a splash from our Earth, why can no similar inference be established for the Moons of other planets ? The Astronomers " do not know." Why should Venus and Mercury have no satellites, and by what, when they exist, were they formed ? Because, we say, science has only one key—the key of matter—to open the mysteries of nature withal, while occult philosophy has seven keys and explains that which science fails to see. Mercury and Venus have no satellites but they had " parents " just as the earth had. Both are far older than the Earth and, before the latter reaches her seventh Round, her mother Moon will have dissolved

the lowest globe of our planetary ring—Globe D, our Earth—all its life, energy and powers ; and, having transferred them to a new centre becoming virtually *a dead planet*, in which rotation has almost ceased since the birth of our globe. The Moon is now the cold residual quantity, the shadow dragged after the new body, into which her living powers and "principles" are transfused. She now is doomed for long ages to be ever pursuing the Earth, to be attracted by and to attract her progeny. Constantly *vampirised* by her child, she revenges herself on it by soaking it through and through with the nefarious, invisible, and poisoned influence which emanates from the occult side of her nature. For she is a *dead*, yet a *living body*. The particles of her decaying corpse are full of active and destructive life, although the body which they had formed is soulless and lifeless. Therefore its emanations are at the same time beneficent and maleficent—this circumstance finding its parallel on earth in the fact that the grass and plants are nowhere more juicy and thriving than on the graves; while at the same time it is the graveyard or corpse-emanations, which kill. And like all ghouls or vampires, the moon is the friend of the sorcerers and the foe of the unwary. From the archaic æons and the later times of the witches of Thessaly, down to some of the present *tantrikas* of Bengal, her nature and properties were known to every Occultist, but have remained a closed book for physicists.

Such is the moon from the astronomical, geological, and physical standpoints. As to her metaphysical and psychic nature it must remain an occult secret in this work, as it was in the volume on "Esoteric Buddhism," notwithstanding the rather sanguine statement made therein on p. 113 (5th edition) that "there is not much mystery left now in the riddle of the eighth sphere." These are topics, indeed, "on which the adepts are very reserved in their communications to uninitiated pupils," and since they have, moreover, never sanctioned or permitted any published speculations upon them, the less said the better.

Yet without treading upon the forbidden ground of the "eighth sphere," it may be useful to state some additional facts with regard to ex-monads of the lunar chain—the "lunar ancestors"—as they play a

into thin air, as the "Moons" of the other planets have, or have not, as the case may be, since there are planets which have *several* moons—a mystery again which no Œdipus of astronomy has solved.

leading part in the coming *Anthropogenesis*. This brings us directly to the septenary constitution of man ; and as some discussion has arisen of late about the best classification to be adopted for the division of the microcosmic entity, two systems are now appended with a view to facilitate comparison. The subjoined short article is from the pen of Mr. T. Subba Row, a learned Vedantin scholar. He prefers the Brahmanical division of the Raja Yoga, and from a metaphysical point of view he is quite right. But, as it is a question of simple choice and expediency, we hold in this work to the " time-honoured " classification of the trans-Himalayan " Arhat Esoteric School." The following table and its explanatory text are reprinted from the " Theosophist " of Madras, and they are also contained in " Five Years of Theosophy":—

SEPTENARY DIVISION IN DIFFERENT INDIAN SYTEMS.

" We give below in a tabular form the classifications adopted by the Buddhist and Vedantic teachers of the principles of man :—

CLASSIFICATION IN ESOTERIC BUDDHISM.	VEDANTIC CLASSIFICATION.	CLASSIFICATION IN TARAKA RAJA YOGA.
1. Sthula Sarira.	Annamaya kosa.*	} Sthulopadhi.§
2. Prana.†	} Pranamaya kosa.	
3. The vehicle of Prana.‡		
4. Kama Rupa.	} Manomaya kosa.	} Sukshmopadhi.
5. Mind { (a) Volitions and feelings, etc.		
(b) Vignanam.	Vignanamaya kosa.	
6. Spiritual Soul.‖	Anandamaya kosa.	Karanopadhi.
7. Atma.	Atma.	Atma.

* Kosa (kosha) is " Sheath " literally, the sheath of every principle.
† " Life."
‡ The astral body or Linga Sarira.
§ Sthula-Upadhi, or basis of the principle.
‖ Buddhi.

From the foregoing table it will be seen that the third principle in the Buddhist classification is not separately mentioned in the Vedantic division, as it is merely the vehicle of Prana. It will also be seen that the Fourth principle is included in the third Kosa (Sheath), as the same principle is but the vehicle of will-power, which is but an energy of the mind. It must also be noticed that the Vignanamaya Kosa is considered to be distinct from the Manomaya Kosa, as a division is made after death between the lower part of the mind, as it were, which has a closer affinity with the fourth principle than with the sixth; and its higher part, which attaches itself to the latter, and which is, in fact, the basis for the higher spiritual individuality of man.

We may also here point out to our readers that the classification mentioned in the last column is, for all practical purposes, connected with Raja Yoga, the best and simplest. Though there are seven principles in man, there are but three distinct Upadhis (bases), in each of which his Atma may work independently of the rest. These three Upadhis can be separated by an Adept without killing himself. He cannot separate the seven principles from each other without destroying his constitution."

The student will now be better prepared to see that between the three Upadhis of the Raja Yoga and its Atma, and our three Upadhis, Atma, and the additional three divisions, there is in reality but very little difference. Moreover, as every adept in cis-Himalayan or trans-Himalayan India, of the Patanjali, the Aryasanga or the Mahayana schools, has to become a Raja Yogi, he must, therefore, accept the Taraka Raja classification in principle and theory whatever classification he resorts to for practical and occult purposes. Thus, it matters very little whether one speaks of the *three Upadhis with their three aspects* and Atma, the eternal and immortal synthesis, or calls them the " seven principles."

For the benefit of those who may not have read, or, if they have, may not have clearly understood, in Theosophical writings, the doctrine of the septenary chains of worlds in the Solar Kosmos, the teaching is briefly thus :—

1. Everything in the metaphysical as in the physical Universe is septenary. Hence every sidereal body, every planet, whether visible

or invisible, is credited with six companion globes. (See Diagram No. 3, after verse 6 of this commentary.) The evolution of life proceeds on these seven globes or bodies from the 1st to the 7th in Seven ROUNDS or Seven Cycles.

2. These globes are formed by a process which the Occultists call the " rebirth of planetary chains (or rings)." When the seventh and last Round of one of such rings has been entered upon, the highest or first globe " A," followed by all the others down to the last, instead of entering upon a certain time of rest—or " obscuration," as in their previous Rounds—begins to die out. The "planetary" dissolution (*pralaya*) is at hand, and its hour has struck ; each globe has to transfer its life and energy to another planet. (See diagram No. 2 *infra*, " The Moon and the Earth.")

3. Our Earth, as the visible representative of its invisible superior fellow globes, its " lords " or " principles " (see diagram No. 1), has to live, as have the others, through seven Rounds. During the first three, it forms and consolidates ; during the fourth it settles and hardens ; during the last three it gradually returns to its first ethereal form : it is spiritualised, so to say.

4. Its Humanity develops fully only in the Fourth—our present Round. Up to this fourth Life-Cycle, it is referred to as " humanity" only for lack of a more appropriate term. Like the grub which becomes chrysalis and butterfly, Man, or rather that which becomes man, passes through all the forms and kingdoms during the first Round and through all the human shapes during the two following Rounds. Arrived on our Earth at the commencement of the Fourth in the present series of life-cycles and races, MAN is the first form that appears thereon, being preceded only by the mineral and vegetable kingdoms—even the latter *having to develop and continue its further evolution through man.* This will be explained in Book II. During the three Rounds to come, Humanity, like the globe on which it lives, will be ever tending to reassume its primeval form, that of a Dhyan Chohanic Host. Man tends to become *a* God and then—GOD, like every other atom in the Universe.

" Beginning so early as with the 2nd round, Evolution proceeds already on quite a different plan. It is only during the 1st round that (heavenly) man becomes a human being on globe A (rebecomes) a mineral, a plant, an animal, on globe B and C, etc. The process changes

entirely from the second round; but you have learned prudence . . .
and I advise you *to say nothing before the time for saying it has come.* . ."
(Extract from the Teacher's letters on various topics.)

5. Every life-cycle on Globe D (our Earth)* is composed of seven
root-races.   They commence with the Ethereal and end with the
spiritual on the double line of physical and moral evolution—from the
beginning of the terrestrial round to its close. (One is a "planetary
round" from Globe A to Globe G, the seventh; the other, the "globe
round," or the *terrestrial*).

This is very well described in "Esoteric Buddhism" and needs no
further elucidation for the time being.

6. The first root-race, *i.e.,* the first "men" on earth (irrespective of
form) were the progeny of the "celestial men," called rightly in Indian
philosophy the "Lunar Ancestors" or the Pitris, of which there are
seven classes or Hierarchies.   As all this will be sufficiently explained
in the following sections and in Book II., no more need be said of it
here.

But the two works already mentioned, both of which treat of
subjects from the occult doctrine, need particular notice.   "Esoteric
Buddhism" is too well known in Theosophical circles, and even to the
outside world, for it to be necessary to enter at length upon its merits
here.   It is an excellent book, and has done still more excellent work.
But this does not alter the fact that it contains some mistaken notions,
and that it has led many Theosophists and lay-readers to form an
erroneous conception of the Secret Eastern Doctrines.   Moreover it
seems, perhaps, a little too materialistic.

"MAN," which came later, was an attempt to present the archaic
doctrine from a more ideal standpoint, to translate some visions in and
from the Astral Light, to render some teachings partly gathered from a
Master's thoughts, but unfortunately misunderstood.   This work also
speaks of the evolution of the early Races of men on Earth, and
contains some excellent pages of a philosophical character.   But so far
it is only an interesting little mystical romance.   It has failed in its
mission, because the conditions required for a correct translation of
these visions were not present.   Hence the reader must not wonder if
our Volumes contradict these earlier descriptions in several particulars.

---

* We are not concerned with the other Globes in this work except incidentally.

Esoteric " Cosmogony " in general, and the evolution of the human Monad especially, differ so essentially in these two books and in other Theosophical works written independently by *beginners*, that it becomes impossible to proceed with the present work without special mention of these two earlier volumes, for both have a number of admirers— " Esoteric Buddhism " especially. The time has arrived for the explanation of some matters in this direction. Mistakes have now to be checked by the original teachings and corrected. If one of the said works has too pronounced a bias toward materialistic science, the other is decidedly too idealistic, and is, at times, fantastic.

From the doctrine—rather incomprehensible to western minds— which deals with the periodical " obscurations " and successive " Rounds " of the Globes along their circular chains, were born the first perplexities and misconceptions. One of such has reference to the " *Fifth-*" and even " *Sixth-*Rounders." Those who knew that a Round was preceded and followed by a long *Pralaya*, a pause of rest which created an impassable gulf between two Rounds until the time came for a renewed cycle of life, could not understand the " fallacy " of talking about "*fifth* and *sixth* Rounders" in our *Fourth* Round. Gautama Buddha, it was held, was a Sixth-Rounder, Plato and some other great philosophers and minds, " Fifth-Rounders." How could it be? One Master taught and affirmed that there were such " Fifth-Rounders " even now on Earth; and though *understood to say* that mankind was yet " in the Fourth Round," in another place he *seemed* to say that we were in the Fifth. To this an " apocalyptic answer " was returned by another Teacher:—" A few drops of rain do not make a Monsoon, though they presage it." . . . " No, we are not in the Fifth Round, but Fifth Round men have been coming in for the last few thousand years." This was worse than the riddle of the Sphinx.! Students of Occultism subjected their brains to the wildest work of speculation. For a considerable time they tried to outvie Œdipus and reconcile the two statements. And as the Masters kept as silent as the stony Sphinx herself, they were accused of inconsistency, " contradiction," and " discrepancies." But they were simply allowing the speculations to go on, in order *to teach a lesson* which the Western mind sorely needs. In their conceit and arrogance, as in their habit of materializing every metaphysical conception and term without allowing any margin for Eastern metaphor and allegory, the Orientalists have made a jumble of the Hindu exoteric philosophy, and the Theosophists were now doing the same with regard to esoteric teachings.   To this day it is evident that the latter have utterly failed to understand the meaning of the term " Fifth and Sixth Rounders."   But it is simply this : every " Round " brings about a new development and even an entire change in the mental, psychic, spiritual and physical constitution of man, all these principles evoluting on an ever ascending scale.   Thence it follows that those persons who, like Confucius and Plato, belonged psychically, mentally and spiritually to the higher planes of evolution, were in our Fourth Round as the average man will be in the Fifth Round, whose mankind is destined to find itself, on this scale of Evolution, immensely higher than is our present humanity.   Similarly Gautama Buddha— Wisdom incarnate—was still higher and greater than all the men we have mentioned, who are called Fifth Rounders, while Buddha and Sankaracharya are termed Sixth Rounders, allegorically.   Thence again the concealed wisdom of the remark, pronounced at the time " evasive "—that " a few drops of rain do not make the Monsoon, *though they presage it.*"

And now the truth of the remark made in " Esoteric Buddhism " by its author will be fully apparent :—

" It is impossible, *when the complicated facts of an entirely unfamiliar science are being presented to untrained minds for the first time,* to put them forward with all their appropriate qualifications . . . and abnormal developments. . . .   We must be content to take the broad rules first and deal with the exceptions afterwards, and especially is this the case with study, in connection with which *the traditional methods of teaching, generally followed, aim at impressing every fresh idea on the memory by provoking the perplexity it at last relieves.*"

As the author of the remark was himself, as he says, " an untrained mind " in Occultism, his own inferences, and his better knowledge of modern astronomical speculations than of archaic doctrines led him quite naturally, and as unconsciously to himself, to commit a few mistakes of detail rather than of any " broad rule."   One such will now be noticed.   It is a trifling one, still it is calculated to lead many a beginner into erroneous conceptions.   But as the mistaken notions of the earlier editions were corrected in the *annotations* of the fifth edition, so the sixth may be revised and perfected.   There were several reasons for such mistakes. (1) They were due to the necessity under which the teachers laboured of giving what were considered as " evasive answers " : the questions being too persistently pressed to be left unnoticed, while, on the other hand, they *could only be partially answered.* (2) This position notwithstanding, the confession that " half a loaf is better than no bread " was but too often misunderstood and hardly appreciated as it ought to have been. As a result thereof gratuitous speculations were sometimes indulged in by the European lay-chelas. Among such were (a) the " Mystery of the Eighth Sphere " in its relation to the Moon ; and (b) the erroneous statement that two of the superior Globes of the terrestrial chain were two of our well-known planets : " besides the Earth . . . there are *only two other worlds of our chain which are visible.* . . . Mars and Mercury. . . ." (*Esoteric Buddhism ;* p. 136.)

This was a great mistake. But the blame for it is to be attached as much to the vagueness and incompleteness of the Master's answer as to the question of the learner itself, which was equally vague and indefinite.

It was asked : " What planets, of those known to ordinary science, besides Mercury, belong to our system of worlds ? " Now if by " System of Worlds " our *terrestrial chain* or " string " was intended in the mind of the querist, instead of the " Solar System of Worlds," as it should have been, then of course the answer was likely to be misunderstood. For the reply was : " Mars, etc., and four other planets of which astronomy knows nothing. Neither A, B, nor YZ are known nor can they be seen through physical means however perfected." This is plain : (a) Astronomy as yet knows nothing in reality of the planets, neither the ancient ones, nor those discovered in modern times. (b) No *companion* planets from A to Z, *i.e.,* no upper globes of any chain in the Solar System, can be seen.* As to Mars, Mercury, and " the four other planets," they bear

---

* With the exception of course of all the planets which come *fourth* in number, as our earth, the moon, etc., etc. Copies of all the letters ever received or sent, with the exception of a few private ones—" *in which there was no teaching* " the Master says—are with the writer. As it was her duty, in the beginning, to answer and explain certain points not touched upon, it is more than likely that notwithstanding the many annotations on these copies, the writer, in her ignorance of English and her fear of saying too much, may have bungled the information given. *She takes the whole blame for it upon herself in any and every case.* But it is impossible for her to allow students to remain any longer under erroneous impressions, or to believe that the fault lies with the esoteric system.

a relation to Earth of which no master or high Occultist will ever speak, much less explain the nature.*

Let it now be distinctly stated, then, that the theory broached is impossible, with or without the additional evidence furnished by modern Astronomy. Physical Science can supply corroborative, though still very uncertain, evidence, but only as regards heavenly bodies on the same plane of materiality as our objective Universe. Mars and Mercury, Venus and Jupiter, like every hitherto discovered planet (or those still to be discovered), are all, *per se*, the representatives on our plane of such chains. As distinctly stated in one of the numerous letters of Mr. Sinnett's " Teacher," " there are other and innumerable Manvantaric chains of globes which bear intelligent Beings both in and outside our solar system." But neither Mars nor Mercury belong *to our chain*. They are, along with the other planets, septenary *Units* in the great host of " chains " of our system, and all are as visible as their *upper* globes are invisible.

If it is still argued that certain expressions in the Teacher's letters were liable to mislead, the answer comes:—Amen; so it was. The author of " Esoteric Buddhism " understood it well when he wrote that such are " the traditional modes of teaching   . . .   by provoking the perplexity "   . . .   they *do*, or *do not relieve*—as the case may be. At all events, if it is urged that this might have been explained earlier, and the true nature of the planets given out as they now are, the answer comes that : " it was not found expedient to do so at the time, as it would have opened the way to a series of additional questions *which could never be answered on account of their esoteric nature*, and thus would only become embarrassing." It had been declared from the first and has been repeatedly asserted since that (1st) no Theosophist, *not even as an accepted chela*—let alone lay students—could expect to have the secret teachings explained to him *thoroughly and completely*, before *he had irretrievably pledged himself to the Brotherhood and passed through at least one initiation*, because no figures and numbers could be given to the public, for figures and numbers are the key to the esoteric system.   (2.) That

---

* In this same letter the impossibility is distinctly stated :— . . . " Try to understand that you are putting me questions pertaining to the highest initiation ; that I can give you (only) a general view, but *that I dare not nor will I enter upon details* . . ." wrote one of the Teachers to the author of " Esoteric Buddhism."

what was revealed was merely the esoteric lining of that which is contained in almost all the exoteric Scriptures of the world-religions— pre-eminently in the Brahmânas, and the Upanishads of the Vedas and even in the Purânas. It was a small portion of what is divulged far more fully now in the present volumes ; and even this is very incomplete and fragmentary.

When the present work was commenced, the writer, feeling sure that the speculation about Mars and Mercury was a mistake, applied to the Teachers *by letter* for explanation and an authoritative version. Both came in due time, and *verbatim* extracts from these are now given.

" . . . . *It is quite correct that Mars is in a state of obscuration at present, and Mercury just beginning to get out of it. You might add that Venus is in her last Round.* . . . . *If neither Mercury nor Venus have satellites, it is because of the reasons* . . . (vide footnote supra, where those reasons are given), *and also because Mars has two satellites to which he has no right.* . . . . *Phöbos, the supposed* INNER *satellite, is no satellite at all. As remarked long ago by Laplace and now by Faye (see* COMPTES RENDUS, *Tome XC., p.* 569), *Phöbos keeps a too short periodic time,ˎ and there- fore there ' must exist some defect in the mother idea of the theory ' as Faye justly observes.* . . . . *Again, both (Mars and Mercury) are septenary chains, as independent of the Earth's sidereal lords and superiors as you are independent of the ' principles ' of Daumling (Tom Thumb)—which were perhaps his six brothers, with or without night-caps.* . . . . ' *Gratification of curiosity is the end of knowledge for some men,' was said by Bacon, who was as right in postulating this truism, as those who were familiar with it before him were right in hedging off* WISDOM *from Knowledge, and tracing limits to that which is to be given out at one time.* . . . *Remember :—*

' . . . . *knowledge dwells*
In heads replete with thoughts of other men,
Wisdom in minds attentive to their own. . . .'

You can never impress it too profoundly on the minds of those to whom you impart some of the esoteric teachings. . ."

Again, here are more extracts from another letter written by the same authority. This time it is in answer to some objections laid before the Teachers. They are based upon extremely scientific, and as futile, reasonings about the advisability of trying to reconcile the Esoteric theories with the speculations of Modern Science, and were written by a young Theosophist as a warning against the "Secret Doctrine" and in reference to the same subject. He had declared that if there were such companion Earths "they must be only a wee bit less material than our globe." How then was it that they could not be seen ? The answer was :—

" .   .   .   *Were psychic and spiritual teachings more fully understood, it would become next to impossible to even imagine such an incongruity. Unless less trouble is taken to reconcile the irreconcileable—that is to say, the metaphysical and spiritual sciences with physical or natural philosophy, 'natural' being a synonym to them (men of science) of that matter which falls under the perception of their corporeal senses—no progress can be really achieved. Our Globe, as taught from the first, is at the bottom of the arc of descent, where the matter of our perceptions exhibits itself in its grossest form.   .   .   .   .   .   .   Hence it only stands to reason that the globes which overshadow our Earth must be on different and superior planes. In short, as Globes, they are in* CO-ADUNITION *but not in* CONSUBSTANTIALITY WITH OUR EARTH *and thus pertain to quite another state of consciousness. Our planet (like all those we see) is adapted to the peculiar state of its human stock, that state which enables us to see with our naked eye the sidereal bodies which are co-essential with our terrene plane and substance, just as their respective inhabitants, the Jovians, Martians and others can perceive our little world : because our planes of consciousness, differing as they do in degree but being the same in kind, are on the same layer of differentiated matter.   .   .   .   .   What I wrote was 'The minor Pralaya concerns only our little* STRINGS OF GLOBES.' *(We called chains 'Strings' in those days of lip-confusion.)   .   .   .   'To such a string our Earth belongs.'   This ought to have shown plainly that the other planets were also 'strings' or* CHAINS.   .   . *If he (meaning the objector) would perceive even the dim silhouette of one of such 'planets' on the higher planes, he has to first throw off even the thin clouds of the astral matter that stands between him and the next plane.   .   .   .   ."*

It becomes patent why we could not perceive, even with the help of the best earthly telescopes, that which is outside our world of matter. Those alone, whom we call adepts, who know how to direct their mental vision and to transfer their consciousness—physical and psychic both—

to other planes of being, are able to speak with authority on such subjects. And they tell us plainly :—

" Lead the life necessary for the acquisition of such knowledge and powers, and Wisdom will come to you naturally. Whenever your are able to attune your consciousness to any of the seven chords of ' Universal Consciousness,' those chords that run along the sounding-board of Kosmos, vibrating from one Eternity to another ; when you have studied thoroughly ' the music of the Spheres,' then only will you become quite free to share your knowledge with those with whom it is safe to do so. Meanwhile, be prudent. Do not give out the great Truths that are the inheritance of the future Races, to our present generation. Do not attempt to unveil the secret of being and non-being to those unable to see the hidden meaning of Apollo's HEPTA-CHORD—*the lyre of the radiant god, in each of the seven strings of which dwelleth the Spirit, Soul and Astral body of the Kosmos, whose shell only has now fallen into the hands of Modern Science. . . . . . Be prudent, we say, prudent and wise, and above all take care what those who learn from you believe in ; lest by deceiving themselves they deceive others . . . . for such is the fate of every truth with which men are, as yet, unfamiliar. . . . . Let rather the planetary chains and other super- and sub-cosmic mysteries remain a dreamland for those who can neither see, nor yet believe that others can. . . ."*

It is to be regretted that few of us have followed the wise advice ; and that many a priceless pearl, many a jewel of wisdom, has been cast to an enemy unable to understand its value and who has turned round and rent us.

" ' Let us imagine,' wrote the same Master to his two 'lay chelas,' as he called the author of ' Esoteric Buddhism' and another gentleman, his co-student for some time—*' let us imagine* THAT OUR EARTH IS ONE OF A GROUP OF SEVEN PLANETS OR MAN-BEARING WORLDS. . . . . . *(The* SEVEN *planets are the sacred planets of antiquity, and are all septenary.) Now the life-impulse reaches A, or rather that which is destined to become A, and which so far is but cosmic dust (*a "laya centre ")*. . . etc.'"*

In these early letters, in which the terms had to be invented and words coined, the " Rings " very often became " Rounds," and the " Rounds " life-cycles, and *vice versâ*. To a correspondent who called a " Round " a " World-Ring," the Teacher wrote : " I believe this will lead to a further confusion. A Round we are agreed to call the passage of a monad from Globe A to Globe G or Z. . . The 'World-Ring' is correct. . . Advise Mr. . . . strongly, to agree upon a nomenclature before going any further. . ."

Notwithstanding this agreement, many mistakes, owing to this confusion, crept into the earliest teachings. The Races even were occasionally mixed up with the "Rounds" and "Rings," and led to similar mistakes in "Man." From the first the Master had written :—

"Not being permitted to give you *the whole truth*, or divulge the number of isolated fractions . . . I am unable to satisfy you."

This in answer to the questions, "If we are right, then the total existence prior to the man-period is 637," etc., etc. To all the queries relating to figures, the reply was, "Try to solve the problem of 777 incarnations. . . . *Though I am obliged to withhold information . . . yet if you should work out the problem by yourself, it will be my duty to tell you so.*"

But they never were so worked out, and the results were—never-ceasing perplexity and mistakes.

Even the teaching about the Septenary constitution of the sidereal bodies and of the macrocosm—from which the septenary division of the microcosm, or Man—has until now been among the most esoteric. In olden times it used to be divulged only at the Initiation and along with the most sacred figures of the cycles. Now, as stated in one of the Theosophical journals,* the revelation of the whole system of Cosmogony had not been contemplated, nor even thought for one moment possible, at a time when a few bits of information were sparingly given out in answer to letters written by the author of "Esoteric Buddhism," in which he put forward a multiplicity of questions. Among these were questions on such problems *as no MASTER, however high and independent he might be, would have the right to answer, thus divulging to the world the most time-honoured and archaic of the mysteries of the ancient college-temples.* Hence only a few of the doctrines were revealed in their broad outlines, while details were constantly withheld, and all the efforts made to elicit more information about them were systematically eluded from the beginning. This is perfectly natural. Of the four Vidyas— out of the seven branches of Knowledge mentioned in the Purânas— namely, "Yajna-Vidya" (the performance of religious rites in order to

---

* "Lucifer," May, 1888.

produce certain results) ; " Maha-Vidya," the great (Magic) knowledge, now degenerated into Tantrika worship ; " Guhya-Vidya," the science of Mantras and their true rhythm or chanting, of mystical incantations, etc.—it is only the last one, " Atma-Vidya," or the true *Spiritual* and *Divine wisdom*, which can throw absolute and final light upon the teachings of the three first named. Without the help of Atma-Vidya, the other three remain no better than *surface* sciences, geometrical magnitudes having length and breadth, but no thickness. They are like the soul, limbs, and mind of a sleeping man : capable of mechanical motions, of chaotic dreams and even sleep-walking, of producing visible effects, but stimulated by instinctual not intellectual causes, least of all by fully conscious spiritual impulses. A good deal can be given out and explained from the three first-named sciences. But unless the key to their teachings is furnished by Atma-Vidya, they will remain for ever like the fragments of a mangled text-book, like the adumbrations of great truths, dimly perceived by the most spiritual, but distorted out of all proportion by those who would nail every shadow to the wall.

Then, again, another great perplexity was created in the minds of students by the incomplete exposition of the doctrine of the evolution of the Monads. To be fully realised, both this process and that of the birth of the Globes must be examined far more from their metaphysical aspect than from what one might call a statistical standpoint, involving figures and numbers which are rarely permitted to be broadly used. Unfortunately, there are few who are inclined to handle these doctrines only metaphysically. Even the best of the Western writers upon our doctrine declares in his work that "on pure metaphysics of that sort we are not now engaged," when speaking of the evolution of the Monads (" Esoteric Buddhism," p. 46). And in such case, as the Teacher remarks in a letter to him, "Why this preaching of our doctrines, all this uphill work and swimming *in adversum flumen ?* Why should the West . . . learn . . . from the East . . . that which can never meet the requirements of the special tastes of the æsthetics ? " And he draws his correspondent's attention " to the formidable difficulties encountered by us (the Adepts) in every attempt we make to explain our metaphysics to the Western mind."

And well he may ; for *outside* of metaphysics no occult philosophy, no esotericism is possible. It is like trying to explain the aspirations and affections, the love and hatred, the most private and sacred workings in

the soul and mind of the living man, by an anatomical description of the
chest and brain of his dead body.

Let us now examine two tenets mentioned above and hardly
alluded to in " Esoteric Buddhism," and supplement them as far as lies
in our power.

ADDITIONAL FACTS AND EXPLANATIONS CONCERNING THE GLOBES AND THE MONADS.

Two statements made in " Esoteric Buddhism " must be noticed and
the author's opinions quoted. On p. 47 (fifth edition) it is said :—

" . . . the spiritual monads . . . do not fully complete their
mineral existence on Globe A, then complete it on Globe B, and so on.
They pass several times round the whole circle as minerals, and then
again several times round as vegetables, and several times as animals.
We purposely refrain for the present from going into figures," etc., etc.

This was a wise course to adopt in view of the great secrecy maintained with regard to figures and numbers.   This reticence is now
partially relinquished ; but it would perhaps have been better had the
real numbers concerning Rounds and evolutional gyrations been either
entirely divulged at the time, or as entirely withheld. Mr. Sinnett understood this difficulty well when saying (p. 140) that : " For reasons
which are not easy for the outsider to divine, the possessors of occult
knowledge are especially reluctant to give out facts relating to
Cosmogony, though it is hard for the uninitiated to understand why
they should be withheld."

That there were such reasons is evident.   Nevertheless, it is to this
reticence that most of the confused ideas of some Eastern as well as
Western pupils are due.   The difficulties in the way of the acceptance
of the two particular tenets under consideration seemed great, just
because of the absence of any data to go upon.   But there it was.
For the figures belonging to the Occult calculations cannot be given—
as the Masters have many times declared—outside the circle of pledged
chelas, and not even these can break the rules.

To make things plainer, without touching upon the mathematical aspects
of the doctrine, the teaching given may be expanded and some obscure

points solved.   As the evolution of the Globes and that of the Monads are so closely interblended, we will make of the two teachings one.   In reference to the Monads, the reader is asked to bear in mind that Eastern philosophy rejects the Western theological dogma of a newly-created soul for every baby born, as being as unphilosophical as it is impossible in the economy of Nature.   There must be a limited number of Monads evolving and growing more and more perfect through their assimilation of many successive personalities, in every new Manvantara.   This is absolutely necessary in view of the doctrines of Rebirth, Karma, and the gradual return of the human Monad to its source—*absolute* Deity. Thus, although the hosts of more or less progressed Monads are almost incalculable, they are still finite, as is everything in this Universe of differentiation and finiteness.

As shown in the double diagram of the human " principles " and the ascending Globes of the world-chains, there is an eternal concatenation of causes and effects, and a perfect anology which runs through, and links together, all the lines of evolution.   One begets the other—globes as personalities.   But, let us begin at the beginning.

The general outline of the process by which the successive planetary chains are formed has just been given.   To prevent future misconceptions, some further details may be offered which will also throw light on the history of humanity on our own chain, the progeny of that of the Moon.

In the diagrams on p. 172, Fig. 1 represents the " lunar-chain " of seven planets at the outset of its seventh or last Round; while Fig. 2 represents the " earth-chain " which will be, but is not yet in existence. The seven Globes of each chain are distinguished in their cyclic order by the letters A to G, the Globes of the Earth-chain being further marked by a cross— + —the symbol of the Earth.

Now, it must be remembered that the Monads cycling round any septenary chain are divided into seven classes or hierarchies according to their respective stages of evolution, consciousness, and merit.   Let us follow, then, the order of their appearance on planet A, in the first Round.   The time-spaces between the appearances of these hierarchies on any one Globe are so adjusted that when Class 7, the last, appears on Globe A, Class 1, the first, has just passed on to Globe B, and so on, step by step, all round the chain.

Again, in the Seventh Round on the Lunar chain, when Class 7, the last, quits Globe A, that Globe, instead of falling asleep, as it had done in previous Rounds, begins to die (to go into its planetary pralaya);* and in dying it transfers successively, as just said, its "principles," or life-elements and energy, etc., one after the other to a new "laya-centre," which commences the formation of Globe A of the Earth Chain. A similar process takes place for each of the Globes of the "lunar chain" one after the other, each forming a fresh Globe of the "earth-chain." Our Moon was the fourth Globe of the series, and was

EARTH CHAIN.   LUNAR CHAIN.

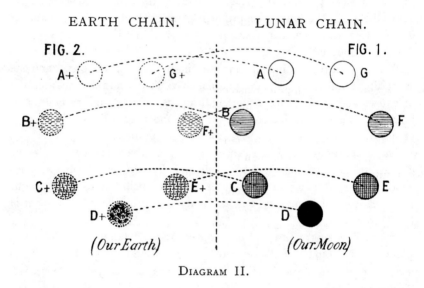

DIAGRAM II.

on the same plane of perception as our Earth. But Globe A of the lunar chain is not fully " dead" till the first Monads of the first class have passed from Globe G or Z, the last of the "lunar chain," into the Nirvana

---

* Occultism divides the periods of Rest (Pralaya) into several kinds; there is the *individual* pralaya of each Globe, as humanity and life pass on to the next; seven minor Pralayas in each Round; the *planetary* Pralaya, when seven *Rounds* are completed; the *Solar* Pralaya, when the whole system is at an end; and finally the Universal Maha— or Brahmâ—Pralaya at the close of the "Age of Brahmâ." These are the three chief *pralayas* or " destruction periods." There are many other minor ones, but with these we are not concerned at present.

which awaits them between the two chains ; and similarly for all the other Globes as stated, each giving birth to the corresponding globe of the " earth-chain."

Further, when Globe A of the new chain is ready, the first class or Hierarchy of Monads from the Lunar chain incarnate upon it in the lowest kingdom, and so on successively. The result of this is, that it is only the first class of Monads which attains the human state of development during the first Round, since the second class, on each planet, arriving later, has not time to reach that stage. Thus the Monads of Class 2 reach the incipient human stage only in the Second Round, and so on up to the middle of the Fourth Round. But at this point—and on this Fourth Round in which the human stage will be *fully* developed—the " Door " into the human kingdom closes; and henceforward the number of " human " Monads, *i.e.*, Monads in the human stage of development, is complete. For the Monads which had not reached the human stage by this point will, owing to the evolution of humanity itself, find themselves so far behind that they will reach the human stage only at the close of the seventh and last Round. They will, therefore, not be men on this chain, but will form the humanity of a future Manvantara and be rewarded by becoming " Men " on a higher chain altogether, thus receiving their Karmic compensation. To this there is *but one solitary exception*, for very good reasons, of which we shall speak farther on. But this accounts for the difference in the races.

It thus becomes apparent how perfect is the analogy between the processes of Nature in the Kosmos and in the individual man. The latter lives through his life-cycle, and dies. His " higher principles," corresponding in the development of a planetary chain to the cycling Monads, pass into Devachan, which corresponds to the " Nirvana " and states of rest intervening between two chains. The Man's lower " principles " are disintegrated in time and are used by Nature again for the formation of new human principles, and the same process takes place in the disintegration and formation of Worlds. Analogy is thus the surest guide to the comprehension of the Occult teachings.

This is one of the " seven mysteries of the Moon," and it is now revealed. The seven " mysteries " are called by the Japanese *Yama-boosis*, the mystics of the Lao-Tze sect and the ascetic monks of Kioto, the Dzenodoo—the " seven jewels." Only the Japanese and the Chinese

Buddhist ascetics and Initiates are, if possible, even more reticent in giving out their " Knowledge " than are the Hindus.

But the reader must not be allowed to lose sight of the Monads, and must be enlightened as to their nature, as far as permitted, without trespassing upon the highest mysteries, of which the writer does not in any way pretend to know the last or final word.

The Monadic Host may be roughly divided into three great classes :—

1. The most developed Monads (the Lunar Gods or " Spirits," called, in India, the Pitris), whose function it is to pass in the first Round through the whole triple cycle of the mineral, vegetable, and animal kingdoms in their most ethereal, filmy, and rudimentary forms, in order to clothe themselves in, and assimilate, the nature of the newly formed chain. They are those who first reach the human form (if there can be any form in the realm of the almost subjective) on Globe A in the first Round. It is they, therefore, who lead and represent the human element during the second and third Rounds, and finally evolve their shadows at the beginning of the Fourth Round for the second class, or those who come behind them.

2. Those Monads that are the first to reach the human stage during the three and a half Rounds, and to become men.*

---

* We are forced to use here the misleading word " Men," and this is a clear proof of how little any European language is adapted to express these subtle distinctions.

It stands to reason that these " Men " did not resemble the men of to-day, either in form or nature. Why then, it may be asked, call them " Men " at all ? Because there is no other term in any Western language which approximately conveys the idea intended. The word " Men " at least indicates that these beings were " MANUS," thinking entities, however they differed in form and intellection from ourselves. But in reality they were, in respect of spirituality and intellection, rather " gods " than " Men."

The same difficulty of language is met with in describing the " stages " through which the Monad passes. Metaphysically speaking, it is of course an absurdity to talk of the " development " of a Monad, or to say that *it* becomes " Man." But any attempt to preserve metaphysical accuracy of language in the use of such a tongue as the English would necessitate at least three extra volumes of this work, and would entail an amount of verbal repetition which would be wearisome in the extreme. It stands to reason that a MONAD cannot either progress or develop, or even be affected by the changes of states it passes through. *It is not of this world or plane,* and may be compared only to an indestructible star of divine light and fire, thrown down on to our

3. The laggards ; the Monads which are retarded, and which will not reach, by reason of Karmic impediments, the human stage at all during this cycle or Round, save one exception which will be spoken of elsewhere as already promised.

Now the evolution of the *external* form or body round the *astral* is produced by the terrestrial forces, just as in the case of the lower kingdoms; but the evolution of the internal or real MAN is purely spiritual. It is now no more a passage of the impersonal Monad through many and various forms of matter—endowed at best with instinct and consciousness on quite a different plane—as in the case of external evolution, but a journey of the " pilgrim-soul" through various *states* of *not only matter* but Self-consciousness and self-perception, or of *perception* from apperception. (See " *Gods, Monads and Atoms.*")

The MONAD emerges from its state of spiritual and intellectual unconsciousness ; and, skipping the first two planes—too near the ABSOLUTE to permit of any correlation with anything on a lower plane— it gets direct into the plane of Mentality. But there is no plane in the whole universe with a wider margin, or a wider field of action in its almost endless gradations of perceptive and apperceptive qualities, than this plane, which has in its turn an appropriate smaller plane for every " form," from the " mineral" monad up to the time when that monad blossoms forth by evolution into the DIVINE MONAD. But all the time it is still one and the same Monad, differing only in its incarnations, throughout its ever succeeding cycles of partial or total obscuration of spirit, or the partial or total obscuration of matter—two polar antitheses —as it ascends into the realms of mental spirituality, or descends into the depths of materiality.

To return to " Esoteric Buddhism." It is there stated with regard to the enormous period intervening between the mineral epoch on Globe A, and the man-epoch,* that: " The full development of the

---

Earth as a plank of salvation for the personalities in which it indwells. It is for the latter to cling to it ; and thus partaking of its divine nature, obtain immortality. Left to itself the Monad will cling to no one ; but, like the " plank," be drifted away to another incarnation by the unresting current of evolution.

* The term " Man epoch " is here used because of the necessity of giving a name to that fourth kingdom which follows the animal. But in truth the " Man " on Globe A during the First Round is no Man, but only his prototype or dimensionless image from the astral regions.

mineral epoch on Globe A, prepares the way for the vegetable development, and, as soon as this begins, the mineral life-impulse overflows into Globe B. Then, when the vegetable development on Globe A is complete and the animal development begins, the vegetable life-impulse overflows to Globe B, and the mineral impulse passes on to Globe C. Then finally comes the human life-impulse on Globe A." (Page 49.)

And so it goes on for three Rounds, when it slackens, and finally stops at the threshold of our Globe, at the Fourth Round ; because the human period (of the true physical men to be), the seventh, is now reached. This is evident, for as said, " . . . there are processes of evolution which precede the mineral kingdom, and thus a wave of evolution, indeed several waves of evolution, precede the mineral wave in its progress round the spheres " (*ibid*).

And now we have to quote from another article, " The Mineral Monad " in " *Five Years of Theosophy*," p. 273 *et seq.*

" There are seven kingdoms. The first group comprises three degrees of elementals, or nascent centres of forces—from the first stage of differentiation of (from) Mulaprakriti (or rather Pradhâna, primordial homogeneous matter) to its third degree—*i.e.*, from full unconsciousness to semi-perception ; the second or higher group embraces the kingdoms from vegetable to man ; the mineral kingdom thus forming the central or turning point in the degrees of the " Monadic Essence," considered as an evoluting energy. Three stages (sub-physical) on the elemental side ; the mineral kingdom ; three stages on the objective physical* side—these are the (first or preliminary) seven links of the evolutionary chain."

" Preliminary " because they are preparatory, and though belonging in fact to the natural, they yet would be more correctly described as sub-natural evolution. This process makes a halt in its stages at the Third, at the threshold of the Fourth stage, when it becomes, on the plane of the natural evolution, the first really manward stage, thus forming with the three elemental kingdoms, the ten, the Sephirothal number. It is at this point that begins :—

" A descent of spirit into matter equivalent to an ascent in physical

---

* " Physical " here means differentiated for cosmical purposes and work ; that " physical side," nevertheless, if objective to the apperception of beings from other planes, is yet quite subjective to us on our plane.

evolution; a re-ascent from the deepest depths of materiality (the mineral) towards its *status quo ante*, with a corresponding dissipation of concrete organism—up to Nirvana, the vanishing point of differentiated matter." (*"Five Years of Theosophy,"* p. 276.)

Therefore it becomes evident why that which is pertinently called in *Esoteric Buddhism* " Wave of Evolution," and mineral-, vegetable-, animal- and man-"impulse," stops at the door of our Globe, at its Fourth cycle or Round. It is at this point that the Cosmic Monad (Buddhi) will be wedded to and become the vehicle of the Atmic Ray, *i.e.*, it (Buddhi) will awaken to an apperception of it (Atman); and thus enter on the first step of a new septenary ladder of evolution, which will lead it eventually to the tenth (counting from the lowest upwards) of the Sephirothal tree, the Crown.

Everything in the Universe follows analogy. " As above, so below ; " Man is the microcosm of the Universe. That which takes place on the spiritual plane repeats itself on the Cosmic plane. Concretion follows the lines of abstraction; corresponding to the highest must be the lowest; the material to the spiritual. Thus, corresponding to the Sephirothal Crown (or upper triad) there are the three elemental Kingdoms, which precede the Mineral (see diagram on p. 277 in *Five Years of Theosophy*), and which, using the language of the Kabalists, answer in the Cosmic differentiation to the worlds of Form and Matter from the Super-Spiritual to the Archetypal.

Now what is a " Monad ? " And what relation does it bear to an Atom ? The following reply is based upon the explanations given in answer to these questions in the above-cited article: " The Mineral Monad," written by the author.

" None whatever," is answered to the second question, " to the atom or molecule as existing in the scientific conception at present. It can neither be compared with the microscopic organism, once classed among polygastric infusoria, and now regarded as vegetable, and classed among Algæ; nor is it quite the Monas of the Peripatetics. Physically or constitutionally the mineral monad differs, of course, from the human monad, which is neither physical nor can its constitution be rendered by chemical symbols and elements." In short, as the spiritual Monad is One, Universal, Boundless and Impartite, whose rays, nevertheless, form what we, in our ignorance, call the " Individual Monads " of men, so the Mineral Monad—being at the opposite point of the circle—is also One—and from it proceed the countless physical atoms, which Science is beginning to regard as individualized.

Otherwise how could one account for and explain mathematically the evolutionary and spiral progress of the Four Kingdoms ? The "Monad" is the combination of the last two " principles " in man, the 6th and the 7th, and, properly speaking, the term " human monad " applies only to the dual soul (Atma-Buddi), not to its highest spiritual vivifying Principle, Atma, alone. But since the Spiritual Soul, if divorced from the latter (Atma) could have no existence, no being, it has thus been called . . . . Now the Monadic, or rather Cosmic, Essence (if such a term be permitted) in the mineral, vegetable, and animal, though the same throughout the series of cycles from the lowest elemental up to the Deva Kingdom, yet differs in the scale of progression. It would be very misleading to imagine a Monad as a separate Entity trailing its slow way in a distinct path through the lower Kingdoms, and after an incalculable series of transformations flowering into a human being; in short, that the Monad of a Humboldt dates back to the Monad of an atom of horneblende. Instead of saying a " Mineral Monad," the more correct phraseology in physical Science, which differentiates every atom, would of course have been to call it "the Monad manifesting in that form of Prakriti called the Mineral Kingdom." The atom, as represented in the ordinary scientific hypothesis, is not a particle of something, animated by a psychic something, destined after æons to blossom as a man. But it is a concrete manifestation of the Universal Energy which itself has not yet become individualized ; a sequential manifestation of the one Universal Monas. The ocean (of matter) does not divide into its potential and constituent drops until the sweep of the life-impulse reaches the evolutionary stage of man-birth. The tendency towards segregation into individual Monads is gradual, and in the higher animals comes almost to the point. The Peripatetics applied the word Monas to the whole Kosmos, in the pantheistic sense ; and the Occultists, while accepting this thought for convenience sake, distinguish the pro-gressive stages of the evolution of the concrete from the abstract by terms of which the " Mineral, Vegetable, Animal, (etc.), Monad " are examples. The term merely means that the tidal wave of spiritual evolution is passing through that arc of its circuit. The " Monadic

Essence " begins to imperceptibly differentiate towards individual consciousness in the Vegetable Kingdom. As the Monads are uncompounded things, as correctly defined by Leibnitz, it is the spiritual essence which vivifies them in their degrees of differentiation, which properly constitutes the Monad—not the atomic aggregation, which is only the vehicle and the substance through which thrill the lower and the higher degrees of intelligence.

Leibnitz conceived of the Monads as elementary and indestructible units endowed with the power *of giving and receiving* with respect to other units, and thus of determining all spiritual and physical phenomena. It is he who invented the term apperception, which together with nerve- (not perception, but rather)—sensation, expresses the state of the Monadic consciousness through all the Kingdoms up to Man.

Thus it may be wrong on strictly metaphysical lines to call Atma- Buddhi a MONAD, since in the materialistic view it is dual and therefore compound. But as Matter is Spirit, and *vice versâ ;* and since the Universe and the Deity which informs it are unthinkable apart from each other ; so in the case of Atma-Buddhi. The latter being the vehicle of the former, Buddhi stands in the same relation to Atma, as Adam- Kadmon, the Kabalistic Logos, does to En-Soph, or Mulaprakriti to Parabrahm.

A few words more of the Moon.

What, it may be asked, are the " Lunar Monads," just spoken of ? The description of the seven classes of Pitris will come later, but now some general explanations may be given. It must be plain to everyone that they are Monads, who, having ended their life-cycle on the lunar chain, which is inferior to the terrestrial chain, have incarnated on this one. But there are some further details which may be added, though they border too closely on forbidden ground to be treated of fully. The last word of the mystery is divulged only to the adepts, but it may be stated that our satellite is only the gross body of its invisible principles. Seeing then that there are 7 Earths, so there are 7 Moons, the last one alone being visible; the same for the Sun, whose visible body is called a Maya, a reflection, just as man's body is. " The real Sun and the real Moon are as invisible as the real man," says an occult maxim.

And it may be remarked *en passant* that those ancients were not so foolish after all who first started the idea of " the seven moons." For though this conception is now taken solely as an astronomical measure of time, in a very materialised form, yet underlying the husk there can still be recognised the traces of a profoundly philosophical idea.

In reality the Moon is only the satellite of the Earth in one respect, viz., that physically the Moon revolves round the Earth. But in every other respect it is the Earth which is the satellite of the Moon, and not *vice versâ*. Startling as the statement may seem it is not without confirmation from scientific knowledge. It is evidenced by the tides, by the cyclic changes in many forms of disease which coincide with the lunar phases; it can be traced in the growth of plants, and is very marked in the phenomena of human gestation and conception. The importance of the Moon and its influence on the Earth were recognized in every ancient religion, notably the Jewish, and have been remarked by many observers of psychical and physical phenomena. But, so far as Science knows, the Earth's action on the Moon is confined to the physical attraction, which causes her to circle in her orbit. And should an objector insist that this fact alone is sufficient evidence that the Moon is truly the Earth's satellite on other planes of action, one may reply by asking whether a mother, who walks round and round her child's cradle keeping watch over the infant, is the subordinate of her child or dependent upon it; though in one sense she is its satellite, yet she is certainly older and more fully developed than the child she watches.

It is, then, the Moon that plays the largest and most important part, as well in the formation of the Earth itself, as in the peopling thereof with human beings. The " Lunar Monads " or Pitris, the ancestors of man, become in reality man himself. They are the " Monads " who enter on the cycle of evolution on Globe A, and who, passing round the chain of planets, evolve the human form as has just been shown. At the beginning of the human stage of the Fourth Round on this Globe, they " ooze out " their astral doubles from the " ape-like " forms which they had evolved in Round III. And it is this subtle, finer form, which serves as the model round which Nature builds physical man. These " Monads " or " divine sparks " are thus the " Lunar " ancestors, the Pitris themselves. For these " Lunar Spirits " have to become " Men " in order that their " Monads " may reach a higher plane of activity and self-consciousness, *i.e.*, the plane of the Manasa-Putras, those who endow the "senseless" shells, created and informed by the Pitris, with "mind" in the latter part of the Third Root-Race.

In the same way the "Monads" or Egos of the men of the seventh Round of our Earth, after our own Globes A, B, C, D, *et seq.*, parting with their life-energy, will have informed and thereby called to life other laya-centres destined to live and act on a still higher plane of being—in the same way will the Terrene "Ancestors" create those who will become their superiors.

It now becomes plain that there exists in Nature a triple evolutionary scheme, for the formation of the three *periodical Upadhis ;* or rather three separate schemes of evolution, which in our system are inextricably interwoven and interblended at every point. These are the Monadic (or spiritual), the intellectual, and the physical evolutions. These three are the finite aspects or the reflections on the field of Cosmic Illusion of ATMA, the seventh, the ONE REALITY.

1. The Monadic is, as the name implies, concerned with the growth and development into still higher phases of activity of the Monad in conjunction with :—

2. The Intellectual, represented by the Manasa-Dhyanis (the Solar Devas, or the Agnishwatta Pitris) the "givers of intelligence and consciousness "* to man and :—

3. The Physical, represented by the Chhayas of the lunar Pitris, round which Nature has concreted the present physical body. This body serves as the vehicle for the "growth" (to use a misleading word) and the transformations through Manas and—owing to the accumulation of experiences—of the finite into the INFINITE, of the transient into the Eternal and Absolute.

Each of these three systems has its own laws, and is ruled and guided by different sets of the highest Dhyanis or "Logoi." Each is represented in the constitution of man, the Microcosm of the great Macrocosm ; and it is the union of these three streams in him which makes him the complex being he now is.

"Nature," the physical evolutionary Power, could never evolve intelligence unaided—she can only create "senseless forms," as will be seen in our "ANTHROPOGENESIS." The "Lunar Monads" cannot progress, for they have not yet had sufficient touch with the forms

---

* *Vide* CONCLUSION in Part II. of this Book.

created by " Nature " to allow of their accumulating experiences
through its means.   It is the Manasa-Dhyanis who fill up the gap, and
they represent the evolutionary power of Intelligence and Mind, the link
between " Spirit " and " Matter "—in this Round.

Also it must be borne in mind that the Monads which enter upon the
evolutionary cycle upon Globe A, in the first Round, are in very different
stages of development.   Hence the matter becomes somewhat complicated. . . . Let us recapitulate.

The most developed Monads (the lunar) reach the human germ-stage
in the first Round ; become terrestrial, though very ethereal human
beings towards the end of the Third Round, remaining on it (the globe)
through the " obscuration " period as the seed for future mankind in the
Fourth Round, and thus become the pioneers of Humanity at the
beginning of this, the Fourth Round.   Others reach the Human stage
only during later Rounds, *i.e.*, in the second, third, or first half of the
Fourth Round.   And finally the most retarded of all, *i.e*, those still
occupying animal forms after the middle turning-point of the Fourth
Round—will not become men at all during this Manwantara.   They will
reach to the verge of humanity only at the close of the seventh Round to
be, in their turn, ushered into a new chain after *pralaya*—by older pioneers,
the progenitors of humanity, or the Seed-Humanity *(Sishta)*, viz., the
men who will be at the head of all at the end of these Rounds.

The student hardly needs any further explanation on the part played
by the fourth Globe and the fourth Round in the scheme of evolution.

From the preceding diagrams, which are applicable, *mutatis mutandis*,
to Rounds, Globes or Races, it will be seen that the fourth member of
a series occupies a unique position.   Unlike the others, the Fourth has
no " sister " Globe on the same plane as itself, and it thus forms the
fulcrum of the " balance " represented by the whole chain.   It is the
sphere of final evolutionary adjustments, the world of Karmic scales,
the Hall of Justice, where the balance is struck which determines the
future course of the Monad during the remainder of its incarnations in
the cycle.   And therefore it is, that, after this central turning-point has
been passed in the Great Cycle,—*i.e.*, after the middle point of the
Fourth Race in the Fourth Round on our Globe—no more Monads can
enter the human kingdom.   The door is closed for this Cycle and the
balance struck.   For were it otherwise—had there been a new soul

created for each of the countless milliards of human beings that have passed away, and had there been no reincarnation—it would become difficult indeed to provide room for the disembodied " Spirits ;" nor could the origin and cause of suffering ever be accounted for.   It is the ignorance of the occult tenets and the enforcement of false conceptions under the guise of religious education, which have created materialism and atheism as a protest against the asserted divine order of things.

The only exceptions to the rule just stated are the " dumb races," whose Monads are already within the human stage, in virtue of the fact that these " animals " are later than, and even half descended from man, their last descendants being the anthropoid and other apes.   These " human presentments " are in truth only the distorted copies of the early humanity.   But this will receive full attention in the next Book.

As the Commentary, broadly rendered, says :—

1. " *Every form on earth, and every speck (atom) in Space strives in its efforts towards self-formation to follow the model placed for it in the* ' HEAVENLY MAN.' . . . *Its (the atom's) involution and evolution, its external and internal growth and development, have all one and the same object—man ; man, as the highest physical and ultimate form on this earth ; the* MONAD, *in its absolute totality and awakened condition—as the culmination of the divine incarnations on Earth.*"

2. " *The Dhyanis (Pitris) are those who have evolved their* BHUTA *(doubles) from themselves, which* RUPA *(form) has become the vehicle of monads (seventh and sixth principles) that had completed their cycle of transmigration in the three preceding Kalpas (Rounds).   Then, they (the astral doubles) became the men of the first Human Race of the Round.   But they were not complete, and were senseless.*"

This will be explained in the Books that follow.   Meanwhile man— or rather his Monad—has existed on the earth from the very beginning of this Round.   But, up to our own Fifth Race, the external shapes which covered those divine astral doubles changed and consolidated with every sub-race ; the form and physical structure of the fauna changing at the same time, as they had to be adapted to the ever-changing conditions of life on this globe during the geological periods of its formative cycle.   And thus shall they go on changing with every

Root Race and *every chief sub-race* down to the last one of the Seventh in this Round.

3. "*The inner, now concealed, man, was then (in the beginnings) the external man. The progeny of the Dhyanis (Pitris), he was 'the son like unto his father.' Like the lotus, whose external shape assumes gradually the form of the model within itself, so did the form of man in the beginning evolve from within without. After the cycle in which man began to procreate his species after the fashion of the present animal kingdom, it became the reverse. The human fœtus follows now in its transformations all the forms that the physical frame of man had assumed throughout the three Kalpas (Rounds) during the tentative efforts at plastic formation around the monad by senseless, because imperfect, matter, in her blind wanderings. In the present age, the physical embryo is a plant, a reptile, an animal, before it finally becomes man, evolving within himself his own ethereal counterpart, in his turn. In the beginning it was that counterpart (astral man) which, being senseless, got entangled in the meshes of matter.*"

But this " man " belongs to the fourth Round. As shown, the MONAD had passed through, journeyed and been imprisoned in, every transitional form throughout every kingdom of nature during the three preceding Rounds. But the monad which becomes human *is not the Man*. In this Round—with the exception of the highest mammals after man, the anthropoids destined to die out in this our race, when their monads will be liberated and pass into the astral human forms (or the highest elementals) of the Sixth* and the Seventh Races, and then into lowest human forms in the fifth Round—no units of either of the kingdoms are animated any longer by monads destined to become human in their next stage, but only by the lower Elementals of their respective realms.†

The last human Monad incarnated before the beginning of the 5th

---

* Nature never repeats herself, therefore the anthropoids of our day have not existed at any time since the middle of the Miocene period; when, like all cross breeds, they began to show a tendency, more and more marked as time went on, to return to the type of their first parent, the black and yellow gigantic Lemuro-Atlantean. To search for the " Missing Link " is useless. To the scientists of the closing sixth Root-race, millions and millions of years hence, our modern races, or rather their fossils, will appear as those of small insignificant apes—an extinct species of the genus homo.

† These " Elementals " will become human Monads, in their turn, only at the next great planetary Manvantara.

Root-Race.* The cycle of *metempsychosis* for the human monad is closed, for we are in the Fourth Round and the Fifth Root-Race. The reader will have to bear in mind—at any rate one who has made himself acquainted with " Esoteric Buddhism "—that the Stanzas which follow in this Book and Book II. speak of the evolution in our Fourth Round only. The latter is the cycle of the turning-point, after which, matter,

---

* Such anthropoids form an exception because they were not intended by Nature, but are the direct product and creation of " senseless " man. The Hindus give a divine origin to the apes and monkeys because the men of the Third Race were gods from another plane who had become " senseless " mortals. This subject had already been touched upon in " Isis Unveiled " twelve years ago as plainly as was then possible. On pp. 278-279, the reader is referred " to the Brahmins, if he would know the reason of the regard they have for the monkeys. For then he (the reader) would perhaps learn—were the Brahman to judge him worthy of an explanation—that the Hindu sees in the ape but what Manu desired he should : the transformation of species most directly connected with that of the human family, a bastard branch engrafted on their own stock before the final perfection of the latter. He might learn, further, that in the eyes of the educated ' heathen ' the spiritual or inner man is one thing, and his terrestrial physical casket another. That physical nature, the great combination of physical correlations of forces, ever creeping onward towards perfection, has to avail herself of the material at hand ; she models and remodels as she proceeds, and finishing her crowning work in man, presents him alone as a fit tabernacle for the overshadowing of the divine Spirit."

Moreover, a German scientific work is mentioned in a footnote on the same page. It says that a Hanoverian scientist had recently published a Book entitled " Ueber die Auflösung der Arten durch Natürliche Zucht-wahl," in which he shows, with great ingenuity, that Darwin was wholly mistaken in tracing man back to the ape. On the contrary, he maintains that it is the ape which is evolved from man. He shows that, in the beginning, mankind were morally and physically the types and prototypes of our present Race, and of our human dignity, by their beauty of form, regularity of feature, cranial development, nobility of sentiments, heroic impulses, and grandeur of ideal conception. This is a purely Brahmanic, Buddhistic and Kabalistic philosophy. The Book is copiously illustrated with diagrams, tables, etc. It asserts that the gradual debasement and degradation of man, morally and physically, can be readily traced throughout the ethnological transformation down to our time. And, as one portion has already degenerated into apes, so the civilized man of the present day will at last, under the action of the inevitable law of necessity, be also succeeded by like descendants. If we may judge of the future by the actual Present, it certainly does seem possible that so unspiritual and materialistic a body should end as Simia rather than as Seraphs. But though the apes descend from man, it is certainly not the fact that the human Monad, which has once reached the level of humanity, ever incarnates again in the form of an animal.

having reached its lowest depths, begins to strive onward and to get spiritualized with every new Race and with every fresh cycle. Therefore the student must take care not to see contradiction where there is none, as in "Esoteric Buddhism" Rounds are spoken of in general, while here only the Fourth, or our present Round, is meant. Then it was the work of formation; now it is that of reformation and evolutionary perfection.

Finally, to close this chapter anent various, but unavoidable misconceptions, we must refer to a statement in "Esoteric Buddhism" which has produced a very fatal impression upon the minds of many Theosophists. One unfortunate sentence from the work just referred to is constantly brought forward to prove the materialism of the doctrine. On p. 48, 5th Edition, the Author, referring to the progress of organisms on the Globes, says that "the mineral kingdom will no more develop the vegetable . . . than the Earth was able to develop man from the ape, till it received an impulse."

Whether this sentence renders literally the thought of the author, or is simply (as we believe it is) a *lapsus calami*, may remain an open question.

It is really with surprise that we have ascertained the fact that "Esoteric Buddhism" was so little understood by some Theosophists, as to have led them into the belief that it thoroughly supported Darwinian evolution, and especially the theory of the descent of man from a pithecoid ancestor. As one member writes: "I suppose you realise that three-fourths of Theosophists and even outsiders imagine that, as far as the evolution of man is concerned, Darwinism and Theosophy kiss one another." Nothing of the kind was ever realised, nor is there any great warrant for it, so far as we know, in "Esoteric Buddhism." It has been repeatedly stated that evolution as taught by Manu and Kapila was the groundwork of the modern teachings, but neither Occultism nor Theosophy has ever supported the wild theories of the present Darwinists—least of all the descent of man from an ape. Of this, more hereafter. But one has only to turn to p. 47 of "Esoteric Buddhism," 5th edition, to find there the statement that "Man belongs to a kingdom distinctly separate from that of the animals." With such a plain and unequivocal statement before him, it is very strange that any careful student should have been so misled unless he is prepared to charge the author with a gross contradiction.

Every Round repeats on a higher scale the evolutionary work of the preceding Round. With the exception of some higher anthropoids, as just mentioned, the Monadic inflow, or inner evolution, is at an end till the next Manvantara. It can never be too often repeated, that the full-blown human Monads have to be first disposed of, before the new crop of candidates appears on this Globe at the beginning of the next cycle. Thus there is a lull; and this is why, during the Fourth Round, man appears on Earth earlier than any animal creation, as will be described.

But it is still urged that the author of " Esoteric Buddhism " has "preached Darwinism " all along. Certain passages would undoubtedly seem to lend countenance to this inference. Besides which the Occultists themselves are ready to concede *partial* correctness to the Darwinian hypothesis, in later details, bye-laws of Evolution, and after the midway point of the Fourth Race. Of that which has taken place, physical science can really know nothing, for such matters lie entirely outside of its sphere of investigation. But what the Occultists have never admitted, nor will they ever admit, is that man was *an ape in this or in any other Round;* or that he ever could be one, however much he may have been "ape-like." This is vouched for by the very authority from whom the author of " Esoteric Buddhism " got his information.

Thus to those who confront the Occultists with these lines from the above-named volume : " It is enough to show that we may as reasonably—and that we must, if we would talk about these matters at all—conceive a life-impulse giving birth to mineral form, as of the same sort of impulse concerned to *raise a race of apes into a race of rudimentary men.*" To those who bring this passage forward as showing "decided Darwinism," the Occultists answer by pointing to the explanation of the Master (Mr. Sinnett's " teacher ") which would contradict these lines, were they written in the spirit attributed to them. A copy of this letter was sent to the writer, together with others, two years ago (1886), with additional marginal remarks, to quote from, in the " *Secret Doctrine.*" It begins by considering the difficulty experienced by the Western student, in reconciling some facts, previously given, with the evolution of man from the animal, *i.e.,* from the mineral, vegetable and animal kingdoms, and advises the student to hold to the doctrine of analogy and correspondences. Then it touches upon the mystery of the Devas,

and even Gods, having to pass through states which it was agreed to
refer to as " Inmetallization, Inherbation, Inzoonization and finally
Incarnation," and explains this by hinting at the necessity of failures
even in the ethereal races of Dhyan Chohans.   Concerning this
it says :

" Still, as these ' failures ' are too far progressed and spiritualized to
be thrown back forcibly from Dhyan Chohanship into the vortex of a new
primordial evolution through the lower kingdoms. . . . ." After
which only a hint is given about the mystery contained in the allegory
of the fallen Asuras, which will be expanded and explained in Book II.
When Karma has reached them at the stage of human evolution, " they
will have to drink it to the last drop in the bitter cup of retribution.
Then they become an active force and commingle with the Elementals,
the progressed entities of the pure animal kingdom, to develop little by
little the full type of humanity."

These Dhyan Chohans, as we see, do not pass through the three
kingdoms as do the lower Pitris ; nor do they incarnate in man until the
Third Root Race.   Thus, as the teaching stands:

" *Man in the First Round and First Race on Globe D, our Earth, was an
ethereal being (a Lunar Dhyani, as man), non-intelligent but super-spiritual ;
and correspondingly, on the law of analogy, in the First Race of the Fourth
Round.   In each of the subsequent races and sub-races . . . he grows more
and more into an encased or incarnate being, but still preponderatingly ethereal.
. . . He is sexless, and, like the animal and vegetable, he develops monstrous
bodies correspondential with his coarser surroundings.*

" *II. Round.   He (Man) is still gigantic and ethereal but growing firmer
and more condensed in body, a more physical man.   Yet still less intelligent than
spiritual (1), for mind is a slower and more difficult evolution than is the physical
frame . . .*

" *III. Round.   He has now a perfectly concrete or compacted body, at first the
form of a giant-ape, and now more intelligent, or rather cunning, than spiritual.
For, on the downward arc, he has now reached a point where his primordial
spirituality is eclipsed and overshadowed by nascent mentality (2).   In the last
half of the Third Round his gigantic stature decreases, and his body improves in
texture, and he becomes a more rational being, though still more an ape than a*

Deva. . . . (All this is almost exactly repeated in the third Root-Race of the Fourth Round.)

"*IV. Round. Intellect has an enormous development in this Round. The (hitherto) dumb races acquire our (present) human speech on this globe, on which, from the Fourth Race, language is perfected and knowledge increases. At this half-way point of the Fourth Round (as of the Fourth Root, or Atlantean, race) humanity passes the axial point of the minor Manvantara cycle . . . . the world teeming with the results of intellectual activity and spiritual decrease . . . ."*

This is from the authentic letter; what follows are the later remarks and additional explanations traced by the same hand in the form of footnotes.

(1.) " . . . The original letter contained general teaching—a ' bird's-eye view '—and particularized nothing. . . . To speak of ' physical man ' while limiting the statement to the early Rounds would be drifting back to the miraculous and instantaneous ' coats of skin.' . . . The first ' Nature,' the first ' body,' the first ' mind' on the first plane of perception, on the first Globe in the first Round, is what was meant. For Karma and evolution have—

' . . . centred in our make such strange extremes !
From different Natures* marvellously mixed . . .'

(2.) " Restore : he has now reached the point (by analogy, and as the Third Root Race in the Fourth Round) where his (" the angel "-man's) primordial spirituality is eclipsed and overshadowed by nascent human mentality, and you have the true version on your thumb-nail. . . ."

These are the words of the Teacher—text, words and sentences in brackets, and explanatory footnotes. It stands to reason that there must be an enormous difference in such terms as " objectivity " and " subjectivity," " materiality " and " spirituality," when the same terms are applied to different planes of being and perception. All this must be taken in its relative sense. And therefore there is little to be wondered at, if, left to his own speculations, an author, however eager to learn, yet quite inexperienced in these abstruse teachings, has fallen

---

* The *Natures* of the seven hierarchies or classes of Pitris and Dhyan Chohans which compose our nature and Bodies are here meant.

into an error. Neither was the difference between the " Rounds " and the " Races " sufficiently defined in the letters received, nor was there anything of the kind required before, as the ordinary Eastern disciple would have found out the difference in a moment. Moreover, to quote from a letter of the Master's (188-), " the teachings were imparted under protest. . . . They were, so to say, smuggled goods . . . and when I remained face to face with only one correspondent, the other, Mr. ————, had so far tossed all the cards into confusion, that little remained to be said without trespassing upon law." Theosophists, " whom it may concern," will understand what is meant.

The outcome of all this is that nothing had ever been said in the " letters " to warrant the assurance that the Occult doctrine has ever taught, or any Adept believed in, the preposterous modern theory of the descent of man from a common ancestor with the ape—an anthropoid of the actual animal kind, unless metaphorically. To this day the world is more full of " ape-like men " than the woods are of " men-like apes." The ape is sacred in India because its origin is well known to the Initiates, though concealed under a thick veil of allegory. Hanuman is the son of Pavana (Vayu, " the god of the wind ") by Anjana, a monster called Kesarî, though his genealogy varies. The reader who bears this in mind will find in Book II. *passim*, the whole explanation of this ingenious allegory. The " Men " of the Third Race (who separated) were " Gods " by their spirituality and purity, though senseless, and as yet destitute of mind, as men.

These " Men " of the Third Race—the ancestors of the Atlanteans— were just such ape-like, intellectually senseless giants as were those beings, who, during the Third Round, represented Humanity. Morally irresponsible, it was these third Race " men " who, through promiscuous connection with animal species lower than themselves, created that missing link which became ages later (in the tertiary period only) the remote ancestor of the real ape as we find it now in the pithecoid family.*

---

* And if this is found clashing with that other statement which shows the animal later than man, then the reader is asked to bear in mind that the *placental mammal* only is meant. In those days there were animals of which zoology does not even dream in our own ; *and the modes of reproduction were not identical* with the notions which modern physiology has upon the subject. It is not altogether convenient to touch upon such questions in public, but there is *no* contradiction or impossibility in this whatever.

Thus the earlier teachings, however unsatisfactory, vague and fragmentary, did not teach the evolution of " man " from the " ape." Nor does the author of " Esoteric Buddhism " assert it anywhere in his work in so many words ; but, owing to his inclination towards modern science, he uses language which might perhaps justify such an inference. The man who preceded the Fourth, the Atlantean race, however much he may have looked physically like a " gigantic ape "—" the counterfeit of man who hath not the life of a man "—was still a thinking and already a speaking man. The " Lemuro-Atlantean " was a highly civilized race, and if one accepts tradition, which is better history than the speculative fiction which now passes under that name, he was higher than we are with all our sciences and the degraded civilization of the day : at any rate, the Lemuro-Atlantean of the closing Third Race was so.

And now we may return to the Stanzas.

STANZA VI.—*Continued.*

5. AT THE FOURTH (*Round, or revolution of life and being around " the seven smaller wheels "*) (*a*), THE SONS ARE TOLD TO CREATE THEIR IMAGES ONE THIRD REFUSES. TWO (*thirds*) OBEY.

The full meaning of this sloka can be fully comprehended only after reading the detailed additional explanations in the " Anthropogenesis " and its commentaries, in Book II. Between this Sloka and the last, Sloka 4 in this same Stanza, extend long ages ; and there now gleams the dawn and sunrise of another æon. The drama enacted on our planet is at the beginning of its fourth act, but for a clearer comprehension of the whole play the reader will have to turn back before he can proceed onward. For this verse belongs to the general Cosmogony given in the archaic volumes, whereas Book II. will give a detailed account of the " Creation " or rather the formation, of the first human beings, followed by the second humanity, and then by the third ; or, as they are called, "the first, second, and the third Root-Races." As the solid Earth began by being a ball of liquid fire, of fiery dust and its protoplasmic phantom, so did man.

(a) That which is meant by the qualification the " Fourth " is explained as the " fourth Round " only on the authority of the Commentaries. It can equally mean fourth " Eternity " as " Fourth Round," or even the fourth (our) Globe. For, as will repeatedly be shown, it is the fourth Sphere on the fourth or lowest plane of material life. And it so happens that we are in the Fourth Round, at the middle point of which the perfect equilibrium between Spirit and Matter had to take place.* Says the Commentary explaining the verse :—

" *The holy youths (the gods) refused to multiply and create species after their likeness, after their kind. They are not fit forms (rupas) for us. They have to grow. They refuse to enter the chhayas (shadows or images) of their inferiors. Thus had selfish feeling prevailed from the beginning, even among the gods, and they fell under the eye of the Karmic Lipikas.*"

They had to suffer for it in later births. How the punishment reached the gods will be seen in the second volume.

STANZA VI.—*Continued.*

6. THE CURSE IS PRONOUNCED (*a*) : THEY WILL BE BORN IN THE FOURTH (*Race*), SUFFER AND CAUSE SUFFERING (*b*). THIS IS THE FIRST WAR (*c*).

(*a*) It is a universal tradition that, before the physiological " Fall," propagation of one's kind, whether human or animal, took place through the WILL of the Creators, or of their progeny. It was the Fall of Spirit into generation, not the Fall of mortal man. It has already been stated that, to become a Self-Conscious Spirit, the latter must pass through every cycle of being, culminating in its highest point on earth in Man.

---

* It was, as we shall see, at this period—during the highest point of civilization and knowledge, as also of human intellectuality, of the fourth, Atlantean Race—that, owing to the final crisis of physiologico-spiritual adjustment of the races, humanity branched off into its two diametrically opposite paths : the RIGHT- and the LEFT-hand paths of knowledge or of Vidya. " *Thus were the germs of the White and the Black Magic sown in those days. The seeds lay latent for some time, to sprout only during the early period of the Fifth (our Race).*" (Commentary.)

Spirit *per se* is an unconscious negative ABSTRACTION. Its purity is inherent, not acquired by merit ; hence, as already shown, to become the highest Dhyan Chohan it is necessary for each Ego to attain to full self-consciousness as a human, *i.e.*, conscious Being, which is synthesized for us in Man. The Jewish Kabalists arguing that no Spirit could belong to the divine hierarchy unless Ruach (Spirit) was united to Nephesh (living Soul), only repeat the Eastern Esoteric teaching. " A Dhyani has to be an Atma-Buddhi ; once the Buddhi-Manas breaks loose from its immortal Atma of which it (Buddhi) is the vehicle, Atman passes into NON-BEING, which is absolute Being." This means that the purely Nirvanic state is a passage of Spirit back to the ideal abstraction of Be-ness which has no relation to the plane on which our Universe is accomplishing its cycle.

(*b*) " The curse is pronounced" does not mean, in this instance, that any personal Being, god, or superior Spirit, pronounced it, but simply that the cause which could but create bad results had been generated, and that the effects of a Karmic cause could lead the " Beings " that counteracted the laws of Nature, and thus impeded her legitimate progress, only to bad incarnations, hence to suffering.

(*c*) " There were many wars " refers to several struggles of adjustment, spiritual, cosmical, and astronomical, but chiefly to the mystery of the evolution of man as he is now. Powers—pure Essences—" that were told to create " is a sentence that relates to a mystery explained, as already said, elsewhere. It is not only one of the most hidden secrets of Nature—that of generation, over whose solution the Embryologists have vainly put their heads together—but likewise a divine function that involves that other religious, or rather dogmatic, mystery, the " Fall " of the Angels, as it is called. Satan and his rebellious host would thus prove, when the meaning of the allegory is explained, to have refused to create physical man, only to become the direct Saviours and the Creators of " *divine* Man." The symbolical teaching is more than mystical and religious, it is purely scientific, as will be seen later on. For, instead of remaining a mere blind, functioning medium, impelled and guided by fathomless LAW, the " rebellious " Angel claimed and enforced his right of independent judgment and will, his right of free-agency and responsibility, since man and angel are alike under Karmic Law.*

"And there was war in Heaven. . . . Michael and his angels fought against the Dragon; and the Dragon fought and his angels, and prevailed not; neither was their place found any more in Heaven. And the Dragon was cast out, that old serpent, called the devil and Satan, which deceiveth the whole world."

The Kabalistic version of the same story is given in the Codex Nazareus, the scripture of the Nazarenes, the real mystic Christians of John the Baptist and the Initiates of Christos. Bahak-Zivo, the "Father of the Genii," is ordered to construct creatures (to create). But, as he is "ignorant of Orcus," he fails to do so, and calls in Fetahil, a still purer spirit, to his aid, who fails still worse. This is a repetition of the failure of the "Fathers," the lords of light who fail one after the other. (Book II, Sloka 17.)

We will now quote from our earlier Volumes :—

"Then steps on the stage of creation the spirit † (of the Earth so-called, or the Soul, Psyche, which St. James calls ' devilish ') the lower portion the *Anima Mundi* or Astral Light. (See the close of this Sloka). With the Nazarenes and the Gnostics this Spirit was

---

* Explaining Kabalistic views, the author of the "*New Aspects of Life*" says of the Fallen Angels that, "According to the symbolical teaching, Spirit, from being simply a functionary agent of God, became volitional in its developed and developing action ; and, substituting its own-will for the Divine desire in its regard, so fell. Hence the Kingdom and reign of Spirits and spiritual action, which flow from and are the product of Spirit-volition, are outside, and contrasted with, and in contradiction to the Kingdom of Souls and Divine action." So far, so good ; but what does the Author mean by saying, "When man was created, he was human in constitution, with human affections, human hopes and aspirations. From this state he fell—into the brute and savage "? This is diametrically opposite to our Eastern teaching, and even to the Kabalistic notion so far as we understand it, and to the Bible itself. This looks like Corporealism and Substantialism colouring positive philosophy, though it is rather hard to feel quite sure of the Author's meaning (see p. 235). A FALL, however, "from the natural into the supernatural and the animal "—supernatural meaning the purely spiritual in this case—means what we suggest.

† On the authority of Irenæus, of Justin Martyr and the "Codex" itself, Dunlap shows that the Nazarenes regarded "Spirit" as a female and *Evil Power* in its connection with our Earth. (Dunlap: "Sod," the Son of the Man, p. 52).

feminine. Thus the spirit of the Earth perceiving that for Fetahil,* the *newest man* (the latest), the splendour was 'changed,' and that for splendour existed 'decrease and damage,' she awakes Karabtanos,† 'who was frantic and *without sense and judgment*,' and says to him :— 'Arise, see, the splendour (light) of the *newest* man (Fetahil) has failed (to produce or create men), the decrease of this splendour is visible. Rise up, come with thy MOTHER (the Spiritus) and free thee from limits by which thou art held, and those more ample than the whole world.' After which follows the union of the frantic and blind matter, guided by the insinuations of the spirit (not the *Divine* breath but the *Astral* spirit, which by its double essence is already tainted with matter); and the offer of the MOTHER being accepted, the Spiritus conceives " Seven Figures," and the seven *stellars* (planets) which represent also the *seven capital sins*, the progeny of an astral soul separated from its divine source (spirit) and *matter*, the blind demon of concupiscence. Seeing this, Fetahil extends his hand towards the abyss of matter, and says :—' Let the Earth exist, just as the abode of the powers has existed.' Dipping his hand in the chaos, which he condenses, he creates our planet.‡ "

" Then the Codex proceeds to tell how Bahak-Zivo was separated from the Spiritus, and the Genii or angels from the rebels.§ Then Mano‖ (the greatest), who dwells with the greatest FERHO, call Kebar-Zivo (known also by the name of Nebat-Iavar bar Iufin Ifafin), Helm and *Vine* of the food of life,¶ he being the third life, and commiserating the rebellious and foolish Genii, on account of the magnitude of their ambition, says : 'Lord of the Genii** (Æons), see what the Genii, the

---

* Fetahil is identical with the host of the Pitris who " created Man " as only a " shell." He was, with the Nazarenes, the king of light, and the creator ; but in this instance he is the unlucky Prometheus, who fails to get hold of the Living Fire necessary for the formation of the divine Soul, as he is ignorant of the secret name, the ineffable or incommunicable name of the Kabalists.

† The spirit of Matter and Concupiscence ; " Kamarupa " *minus* " Manas," Mind.

‡ See Franck's " *Codex Nazaræus*," and Dunlap's " *Sod, the Son of the Man.*"

§ *Codex Nazaræus*, ii., 233.

‖ This Mano of the Nazarenes strangely resembles the Hindu Manu, the Heavenly Man of the " *Rig Vedas*."

¶ " I am the *true Vine*, and my father is the husbandman." (*John* xv., 1.)

** With the Gnostics, Christ, as well as Michael who is identical with him in some respects, was the " Chief of the Æons."

rebellious angels do, and about what they are consulting.* They say, 'Let us call for the world, and let us call the 'powers' into existence," The Genii are the *Principes*, the "Sons of Light," but thou art the "*Messenger of Life*."†

And in order to counteract the influence of the seven "badly disposed" principles, the progeny of *Spiritus*, CABAR-ZIO, the mighty Lord of Splendor, produces *seven other lives* (the cardinal virtues) who shine in their own form and light "from on high"‡ and thus re-establish the balance between good and evil, light and darkness.

Here one finds a repetition of the early *allegorical*, dual systems, as the Zoroastrian, and detects a germ of the dogmatic and dualistic religions of the future, a germ which has grown into such a luxuriant tree in ecclesiastical Christianity. It is already the outline of the two "Supremes"—God and Satan. But in the Stanzas no such idea exists.

Most of the Western Christian Kabalists—pre-eminently Eliphas Lévi—in their desire to reconcile the Occult Sciences with Church dogmas, did their best to make of the "Astral Light" only and pre-eminently the *Pleroma* of early Church Fathers, the abode of the Hosts of the Fallen Angels, of the "Archons" and "Powers." But the Astral Light, while only the lower aspect of the Absolute, is yet dual. It is the *Anima Mundi*, and ought never to be viewed otherwise, except for Kabalistic purposes. The difference which exists between its "light" and its "Living Fire" ought to be ever present in the mind of the Seer and the "Psychic." The higher aspect, without which only creatures of matter from that Astral Light can be produced, is this Living Fire, and it is the Seventh Principle. It is said in "Isis Unveiled," in a complete description of it:—

"The Astral Light or *Anima Mundi* is dual and bisexual. The (ideal) male part of it is purely divine and spiritual, it is the *Wisdom*, it is Spirit or Purusha; while the female portion (the Spiritus of the Nazarenes) is tainted, in one sense, with matter, *is* indeed matter, and therefore is evil already. It is the life-principle of every living creature, and furnishes the astral soul, the fluidic *perisprit*, to men, animals, fowls of the air, and everything living. Animals have only the latent germ of the highest immortal soul in them. . . . . This latter will develop

---

* *Codex Nazaræus*, i., 135.   † *Ibid*.   ‡ See the Cosmogony of Pherecydes.

only after a series of countless evolutions ; the doctrine of which evolution is contained in the Kabalistic axiom : ' A stone becomes a plant ; a plant, a beast ; a beast, a man ; a man, a spirit ; and the spirit, a god.' " (Vol. I., p. 301, note.)

The seven principles of the Eastern Initiates had not been explained when " Isis " was written, but only the three *Kabalistic Faces* of the semi-exoteric Kabala.* But these contain the description of the mystic natures of the first group of Dhyan Chohans in the *regimen ignis*, the region and " rule (or government) of fire," which group is divided into three classes, synthesized by the first, which makes *four* or the " Tetraktis." *(See Comments on Stanza VII. Book I.)* If one studies the Comments attentively he will find the same progression in the angelic natures, viz., from the *passive* down to the *active*, the last of these Beings being as near to the *Ahamkara* element (the region or plane wherein *Ego-ship* or the feeling of *I-am-ness* is beginning to be defined) as the first ones are near to the undifferentiated essence. The former are *Arupa* incorporeal ; the latter, *Rupa*, corporeal.

In Volume II. of *Isis (p. 183 et seq.)* the philosophical systems of the Gnostics and the primitive Jewish Christians, the Nazarenes and the Ebionites, are fully considered. They show the views held in those days—outside the circle of Mosaic Jews—about Jehovah. He was identified by all the Gnostics with the evil, rather than with the good principle. For them, he was *Ilda-Baoth*, " the son of Darkness," whose mother, Sophia Achamoth, was the daughter of Sophia, the Divine Wisdom (the female Holy Ghost of the early Christians)—Akâsa ;† while Sophia Achamoth personified the lower Astral Light or *Ether*. Ilda-Baoth, ‡ or Jehovah, is simply one of the Elohim, the seven

---

* They are found, however, in the Chaldean Book of Numbers.

† The astral light stands in the same relation to Akâsa and *Anima Mundi*, as Satan stands to the Deity. They are one and the same thing *seen from two aspects :* the spiritual and the psychic—the super-ethereal or connecting link between matter and pure spirit, and the physical. See for the difference between *nous*, the higher divine wisdom, and *psyche*, the lower and terrestrial (*St. James iii. v.* 15-17). *Vide* " Demon est Deus inversus," Part II. of this volume.

‡ Ilda-Baoth is a compound name made up of *Ilda*, ילד, " a child," and Baoth ; both from בדוצ the egg, and בהוה *Baoth*, " chaos," emptiness, void, or desolation ; or the child born in the egg of Chaos, like Brahmâ.

creative Spirits, and one of the lower Sephiroth. He produces from himself seven other Gods, "Stellar Spirits" (or the lunar ancestors*), for they are all the same. † They are all *in his own image* (the "Spirits of the Face"), and the reflections one of the other, and have become darker and more material as they successively receded from their originator. They also inhabit seven regions disposed like a ladder, as its rungs slope up and down the scale of spirit and matter.‡ With Pagans and Christians, with Hindus and Chaldeans, with the Greek as with the Roman Catholics—with a slight variation of the texts in their inter-pretations—they all were the Genii of the seven planets, as of the seven planetary spheres of our septenary chain, of which Earth is the lowest. (See *Isis, Vol. II. p.* 186.) This connects the "Stellar" and "Lunar" Spirits with the higher planetary Angels and the *Saptarishis* (the seven Rishis of the Stars) of the Hindus—as subordinate Angels (Messengers) to these "Rishis," the emanations, on the descending scale, of the former. Such, in the opinion of the philosophical Gnostics, were the God and the Archangels now worshipped by the Christians! The "Fallen Angels" and the legend of the "War in Heaven" is thus purely pagan in its origin and comes from India *viâ* Persia and Chaldea. The only reference to it in the Christian canon is found in Revelations xii., as quoted a few pages back.

Thus "SATAN," once he ceases to be viewed in the superstitious, dogmatic, unphilosophical spirit of the Churches, grows into the grandiose image of one who made of *terrestrial* a *divine* MAN ; who gave him, throughout the long cycle of Mahâ-kalpa the law of the Spirit of Life, and made him free from the Sin of Ignorance, hence of death. (See the Section *On Satan* in Part II. Vol. II.)

---

* Jehovah's connection with the moon in the Kabala is well known to students.

† About the Nazarenes see *Isis, Vol. II. p.* 131 and 132 ; the true followers of the true Christos were all Nazarenes and Christians, and were the opponents of the later Christians.

‡ *Vide supra*, the diagram of the lunar ring of seven worlds, where, as in our or any other chain, the upper worlds are spiritual, while the lowest, whether Moon, Earth, or any planet, is dark with matter.

STANZA VI.—*Continued.*

6. The older wheels rotated downward and upward (*a*). . . . The Mother's spawn filled the whole (*Kosmos*).* There were battles fought between the Creators and the Destroyers, and battles fought for Space; the seed appearing and reappearing continuously (*b*). †

(*a*) Here, having finished for the time being with our side-issues—which, however they may break the flow of the narrative, are necessary for the elucidation of the whole scheme—the reader must return once more to Cosmogony. The phrase " Older wheels " refers to the worlds or Globes of our chain as they were during the " previous Rounds." The present Stanza, when explained esoterically, is found embodied entirely in the Kabalistic works. Therein will be found the very history of the evolution of those countless Globes which evolve after a periodical Pralaya, rebuilt from old material into new forms. The previous Globes disintegrate and reappear transformed and perfected for a new phase of life. In the Kabala, worlds are compared to sparks which fly from under the hammer of the great Architect—LAW, the law which rules all the smaller Creators.

The following comparative diagram shows the identity between the two systems, the Kabalistic and the Eastern. The three upper are the three higher planes of consciousness, revealed and explained in both schools only to the Initiates, the lower ones represent the four lower planes—the lowest being our plane, or the visible Universe.

These seven *planes* correspond to the seven *states* of consciousness in man. It remains with him to attune the three higher states in himself to the three higher planes in Kosmos. But before he can attempt to attune, he must awaken the three " seats " to life and activity. And how many are capable of bringing themselves to even a superficial comprehension of *Atma-Vidya* (Spirit-Knowledge), or what is called by the Sufis, *Rohanee!* In Section the VIIth of this Book, in Sub-section 3,

---

* The reader is reminded that Kosmos often means in our Stanzas only our own Solar System, not the Infinite Universe.

† This is purely astronomical.

the reader will find a still clearer explanation of the above in the Commentary upon *Saptaparna*—the man-plant.   See also the Section of that name in Part II.

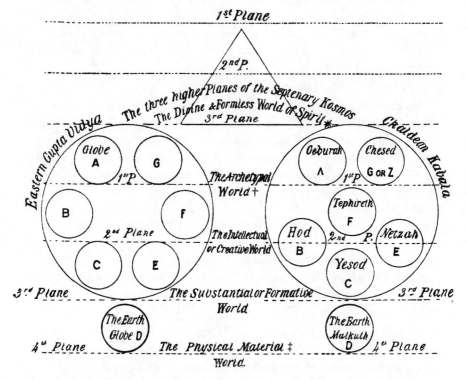

* The *Arupa* or " formless," there where form ceases to exist, on the objective plane.

† The word "Archetypal" must not be taken here in the sense that the Platonists gave to it, *i.e.*, the world as it existed *in the Mind* of the Deity ; but in that of a world made as a first model, to be followed and improved upon by the worlds which succeed it physically—though deteriorating in purity.

‡ These are the four lower planes of Cosmic Consciousness, the three higher planes being inaccessible to human intellect as developed at present. The seven states of human consciousness pertain to quite another question.

(*b*) " The Seed appears and disappears continuously." Here " Seed " stands for "the World-germ," viewed by Science as material particles in a highly attenuated condition, but in Occult physics as " Spiritual particles," *i.e.*, supersensuous matter existing in a state of primeval differentiation.* In theogony, every Seed is an ethereal organism, from which evolves later on a celestial being, a God.

In the "beginning," that which is called in mystic phraseology "Cosmic *Desire*" evolves into absolute Light. Now light without any shadow would be absolute light—in other words, absolute darkness—as physical science seeks to prove. That shadow appears under the form of primordial matter, allegorized—if one likes—in the shape of the Spirit of Creative Fire or Heat. If, rejecting the poetical form and allegory, science chooses to see in this the primordial Fire-Mist, it is welcome to do so. Whether one way or the other, whether Fohat or the famous FORCE of Science, nameless, and as difficult of definition as our Fohat himself, that Something " caused the Universe to move with circular motion," as Plato has it ; or, as the Occult teaching expresses it :

" *The Central Sun causes Fohat to collect primordial dust in the form of balls, to impel them to move in converging lines and finally to approach each other and aggregate.*" *(Book of Dzyan)* . . . . . " *Being scattered in Space, without order or system, the world-germs come into frequent collision until their final aggregation, after which they become wanderers (Comets). Then the battles and struggles begin. The older (bodies) attract the younger, while others repel them. Many perish, devoured by their stronger companions. Those that escape become worlds.*"†

---

* To see and appreciate the difference—the immense gulf that separates terrestrial matter from the finer grades of supersensuous matter—every astronomer, every chemist and *physicist* ought to be a *psychometer*, to say the least; he ought to be able to sense for himself that difference in which he now refuses to believe. Mrs. Elizabeth Denton, one of the most learned, and also one of the most materialistic and sceptical women of her age—the wife of Professor Denton, the well-known American geologist and the author of " The Soul of Things "—was, nevertheless, one of the most wonderful psychometers some years ago. This is what she described in one of her experiments, with a particle of a meteorite placed on her forehead, in an envelope, the lady, not being aware of what it contained, said :

" What a difference between that which we recognise as matter here and that which seems like matter there ! In the one, the *elements are so coarse and so angular*, I wonder that we can endure it all, much more that we can desire to continue our present relations to it ; in the other, all the elements are so refined, they are so free from those great, rough angularities, which characterize the elements here, that I can but regard that as by so much the more than this, the real existence." *(Vol. III. p. 345-6.)*

† When carefully analysed and reflected upon, this will be found as scientific as Science could make it, even at our late period.

We have been assured that there exist several modern works of
speculative fancy upon such struggles for life in sidereal heaven,
especially in the German language. We rejoice to hear it, for ours is
an Occult teaching lost in the darkness of archaic ages. We have
treated of it fully in " *Isis Unveiled*," and the idea of Darwinian-like
evolution, of struggle for life and supremacy, and of the " survival of
the fittest " among the Hosts above as the Hosts below, runs throughout both the volumes of our earlier work, written in 1876 (*See Index in*
" *Isis Unveiled* " *at the words* " *Evolution* "—" *Darwin* "—" *Kapila* "—
" *Battle of Life*," *etc. etc.*) But the idea was not ours, it is that of antiquity.
Even the Purânic writers have ingeniously interwoven allegory with
Cosmic facts and human events. Any symbologist may discern the astro-
cosmical allusion even though he be unable to grasp the whole meaning.
The great " Wars in Heaven," in the Purânas ; the wars of the Titans, in
Hesiod and other classical writers; the " struggles," also in the Egyptian
legend between Osiris and Typhon, and even those in the Scandinavian
legends, all refer to the same subject. Northern Mythology refers to it
as the battle of the Flames, the sons of Muspel who fought on the field
of Wigred. All these relate to Heaven and Earth, and have a double
and often even a triple meaning, and esoteric application to things above
as to things below. They relate severally to astronomical, theogonical
and human struggles ; to the adjustment of orbs, and the supremacy
among nations and tribes. The " Struggle for Existence " and the
" Survival of the Fittest " reigned supreme from the moment that Kosmos
manifested into being, and could hardly escape the observant eye of the
ancient Sages. Hence the incessant fights of Indra, the god of the
Firmament, with the Asuras—degraded from high gods into Cosmic
demons ; and with Vritri or Ah-hi ; the battles fought between stars and
constellations, between Moon and planets—later on incarnated as kings
and mortals. Hence also the War in Heaven of Michael and his Host
against the Dragon (Jupiter and Lucifer-Venus), when a third of the
stars of the rebellious host was hurled down into Space, and " its place
was found no more in Heaven." As said long ago—" This is the basic
and fundamental stone of the secret cycles. It shows that the Brahmins
and Tanäim . . . speculated on the creation and development of
the world quite in a Darwinian way, both anticipating him and his
school in the natural selection of species, the survival of the fittest,

and transformation. . . . There were old worlds that perished conquered by the new," etc., etc. ("*Isis Unveiled*," *Vol. II.*, *p.* 260.) The assertion that all the worlds (Stars, planets, etc.)—as soon as a nucleus of primordial substance in the *laya* (undifferentiated) state is informed by the freed principles, of a just *deceased* sidereal body— become first comets, and then Suns to cool down to inhabitable worlds, is a teaching as old as the Rishis.

Thus the Secret Books distinctly teach, as we see, an astronomy that would not be rejected even by modern speculation could the latter thoroughly understand its teachings.

For, archaic astronomy, and the ancient, physical and mathematical sciences, expressed views identical with those of modern science, and many of far more momentous import. A "struggle for life" as a "survival of the fittest" in the worlds above, as on our planet here below, are distinctly taught. This teaching, however, although it would not be "entirely rejected" by Science, is sure to be repudiated as an integral whole. For it avers that there are only seven Self-born primordial "gods" emanated from the trinitarian ONE. In other words, it means that all the worlds or sidereal bodies (always on strict analogy) are formed one from the other, after the primordial manifestation at the beginning of the "Great Age" is accomplished. The birth of the celestial bodies in Space is compared to a crowd or multitude of "pilgrims" at the festival of the "Fires." Seven ascetics appear on the threshold of the temple with seven lighted sticks of incense. At the light of these the first row of pilgrims light their incense sticks. After which every ascetic begins whirling his stick around his head in space, and furnishes the rest with fire. Thus with the heavenly bodies. A laya-centre is lighted and awakened into life by the fires of another "pilgrim," after which the new "centre" rushes into space and becomes a comet. It is only after losing its velocity, and hence its fiery tail, that the "Fiery Dragon" settles down into quiet and steady life as a regular respectable citizen of the sidereal family. Therefore it is said :—

Born in the unfathomable depths of Space, out of the homogeneous Element called the World-Soul, every nucleus of Cosmic matter, suddenly launched into being, begins life under the most hostile circumstances. Through a series of countless ages, it has to conquer for itself a place in the infinitudes. It circles round and round between denser and already fixed bodies, moving by jerks, and pulling towards some given point or centre that attracts it, trying to avoid, like a ship drawn into a channel dotted with reefs and sunken rocks, other bodies that draw and repel it in turn ; many perish, their mass disintegrating through stronger masses, and, when born within a system, chiefly within the insatiable stomachs of various Suns. (*See Comm. to Stanza IV*). Those which move slower and are propelled into an elliptic course are doomed to annihilation sooner or later. Others moving in parabolic curves generally escape destruction, owing to their velocity.

Some very critical readers will perhaps imagine that this teaching, as to the cometary stage passed through by all heavenly bodies, is in contradiction with the statements just made as to the moon being the mother of the earth. They will perhaps fancy that intuition is needed to harmonise the two. But no intuition is in truth required. What does Science know of Comets, their genesis, growth, and ultimate behaviour ? Nothing—absolutely nothing ! And what is there so impossible that a laya centre—a lump of cosmic protoplasm, homogeneous and latent, when suddenly animated or fired up—should rush from its bed in Space and whirl throughout the abysmal depths in order to strengthen its homogeneous organism by an accumulation and addition of differentiated elements ? And why should not such a comet settle in life, live, and become an inhabited globe !

" The abodes of Fohat are many," it is said. " He places his four fiery (electro-positive) Sons in the " Four circles " ; these *Circles* are the Equator, the Ecliptic, and the two parallels of declination, or the tropics—to preside over the *climates* of which are placed the Four mystical Entities. Then again : " Other seven (sons) are commissioned to preside over the seven hot, and seven cold *lokas* (the hells of the orthodox Brahmins) at the two ends of the Egg of Matter (our Earth and its poles). The seven *lokas* are also called the " Rings," elsewhere, and the " Circles." The ancients made the polar circles *seven* instead of two, as Europeans do ; for Mount Meru, which is the North Pole, is said to have seven gold and seven silver steps leading to it.

The strange statement made in one of the Stanzas : " The Songs of Fohat and his Sons were *radiant* as the noon-tide Sun and the Moon combined ; " and that the four Sons on the *middle* four-fold

Circle " *saw* their father's songs and *heard* his Solar-selenic radiance ; " is explained in the Commentary in these words : " The agitation of the *Fohatic* Forces at the two cold ends (North and South Poles) of the Earth which resulted in a multicoloured radiance at night, have in them several of the properties of Akâsa (Ether) *colour* and sound as well." . . . . . . " Sound is the characteristic of Akâsa (Ether) : it generates air, the property of which is Touch ; which (by friction) becomes productive of Colour and Light." . . . . . . (Vishnu Purâna.)

Perhaps the above will be regarded as archaic nonsense, but it will be better comprehended, if the reader remembers the Aurora Borealis and Australis, both of which take place at the very centres of terrestrial electric and magnetic forces. The two poles are said to be the store-houses, the receptacles and liberators, at the same time, of Cosmic and terrestrial Vitality (Electricity) ; from the surplus of which the Earth, had it not been for these two natural " safety-valves," would have been rent to pieces long ago. At the same time it is now a theory that has lately become an axiom, that the phenomenon of polar lights is accompanied by, and productive of, strong sounds, like whistling, hissing, and cracking. (But see Professor Trumholdt's works on the Aurora Borealis, and his correspondence regarding this moot question.)

STANZA VI.—*Continued.*

7. MAKE THY CALCUATIONS, O LANOO, IF THOU WOULDST LEARN THE CORRECT AGE OF THY SMALL WHEEL (*chain*). ITS FOURTH SPOKE IS OUR MOTHER (*Earth*) (*a*). REACH THE FOURTH " FRUIT " OF THE FOURTH PATH OF KNOWLEDGE THAT LEADS TO NIRVANA, AND THOU SHALT COMPREHEND, FOR THOU SHALT SEE (*b*).

(*a*) The " small wheel " is our chain of spheres, and the fourth spoke is our Earth, the fourth in the chain. It is one of those on which the " hot (positive) breath of the Sun " has a direct effect.*

---

* The seven fundamental transformations of the globes or heavenly spheres, or rather of their constituent particles of matter, is described as follows : (1) The *homogeneous ;* (2) the *aeriform* and *radiant* (gaseous) ; (3) *Curd-like* (nebulous) ; (4) *Atomic, Ethereal*

To calculate its age, however, as the pupil is asked to do in the Stanza, is rather difficult, since we are not given the figures of the Great Kalpa, and are not allowed to publish those of our small Yugas, except as to the approximate duration of these. " The older wheels rotated for one Eternity and one half of an Eternity," it says. We know that by " Eternity" the seventh part of 311,040,000,000,000 years, or an age of Brahmâ is meant. But what of that? We also know that, to begin with, if we take for our basis the above figures, we have first of all to eliminate from the 100 years of Brahmâ (or 311,040,000,000,000 years) two *years* taken up by the Sandhyas (twilights), which leaves 98, as we have to bring it to the mystical combination 14 × 7. But *we* have no knowledge at what time precisely the evolution and formation of our little earth began. Therefore it is impossible to calculate its age, unless the time of its birth is given—which the TEACHERS refuse to do, so far. At the close of this Book and in Book II., however, some chronological hints will be given. We must remember, moreover, that the law of Analogy holds good for the worlds, as it does for man; and that as " The ONE (Deity) becomes *Two* (Deva or Angel) and *Two* becomes *Three* (or man)," etc., etc., so we are taught that the *Curds* (world-stuff) become wanderers, (Comets), these become stars, and the stars (the centres of vortices) *our sun and planets*—to put it briefly.*

(*b*) There are four grades of initiation mentioned in exoteric works, which are known respectively in Sanskrit as " Sçrôtâpanna," " Sagardagan," " Anagamin," and " Arhan"—the four paths to Nirvana, in this, our fourth Round, bearing the same appellations. The Arhan, though he can see the Past, the Present, and the Future, is not yet the highest Initiate; for the Adept himself, the *initiated* candidate, becomes chela (pupil) to a higher Initiate. Three further higher grades have to be conquered by the Arhan who would reach the apex of the ladder of Arhatship. There are those who have reached it even in this fifth race of ours, but the faculties necessary for the attainment of these higher

---

(beginning of motion, hence of differentiation) ; (5) *Germinal, fiery,* (differentiated, but composed of the germs only of the Elements, in their earliest states, they having seven states, when completely developed on our earth) ; (6) *Four-fold, vapoury* (the future Earth) ; (7) *Cold and depending* (on the Sun for life and light).

* This cannot be so very *unscientific*, since Descartes thought also that "the planets rotate on their axes because they were once lucid stars, the centres of Vortices."

grades will be fully developed in the average ascetic only at the end of this Root-Race, and in the Sixth and Seventh. Thus there will always be Initiates and the Profane till the end of this minor Manvantara, the present *life-cycle*. The *Arhats* of the "fire-mist" of the 7th rung are but one remove from the Root-Base of their Hierarchy—the highest on Earth, and our Terrestrial chain. This "Root-Base" has a name which can only be translated by several compound words into English "—"the ever-living-human-Banyan." This "Wondrous Being" descended from a "high region," they say, in the early part of the Third Age, before the separation of the sexes of the Third Race.

This Third Race is sometimes called collectively "the Sons of *Passive* Yoga," *i.e.*, it was produced unconsciously by the second Race, which, as it was intellectually inactive, is supposed to have been constantly plunged in a kind of blank or abstract contemplation, as required by the conditions of the Yoga state. In the first or earlier portion of the existence of this third race, while it was yet in its state of purity, the "Sons of Wisdom," who, as will be seen, incarnated in this Third Race, produced by *Kriyasakti* a progeny called the "Sons of Ad" or "of the Fire-Mist," the "Sons of Will and Yoga," etc. They were a conscious production, as a portion of the race was already animated with the divine spark of spiritual, superior intelligence. It was not a Race, this progeny. It was at first a wondrous Being, called the "Initiator," and after him a group of semi-divine and semi-human beings. "*Set apart*" in Archaic *genesis* for certain purposes, they are those in whom are said to have incarnated the highest Dhyanis, "Munis and Rishis from previous Manvantaras "—*to form the nursery for future human adepts*, on this earth and during the present cycle. These "Sons of Will and Yoga " born, so to speak, in an immaculate way, remained, it is explained, entirely apart from the rest of mankind.

The " BEING " just referred to, which has to remain nameless, is the *Tree* from which, in subsequent ages, all the great *historically* known Sages and Hierophants, such as the Rishi Kapila, Hermes, Enoch, Orpheus, etc., etc., have branched off. As objective *man*, he is the mysterious (to the profane—the ever invisible) yet ever present Personage about whom legends are rife in the East, especially among the Occultists and the students of the Sacred Science. It is he who changes form, yet remains ever the same. And it is he again who holds spiritual sway over the

initiated Adepts throughout the whole world. He is, as said, the
" Nameless One " who has so many names, and yet whose names and
whose very nature are unknown. He is *the* "Initiator," called the
" GREAT SACRIFICE." For, sitting at the threshold of LIGHT, he looks
into it from within the circle of Darkness, which he will not cross ; nor
will he quit his post till the last day of this life-cycle. Why does the
solitary Watcher remain at his self-chosen post ? Why does he sit by
the fountain of primeval Wisdom, of which he drinks no longer, as he
has naught to learn which he does not know—aye, neither on this Earth,
nor in its heaven ? Because the lonely, sore-footed pilgrims on their
way back to their *home* are never sure to the last moment of not losing
their way in this limitless desert of illusion and matter called Earth-
Life. Because he would fain show the way to that region of freedom
and light, from which he is a voluntary exile himself, to every prisoner
who has succeeded in liberating himself from the bonds of flesh and
illusion. Because, in short, he has sacrificed himself for the sake of
mankind, though but a few Elect may profit by the GREAT SACRIFICE.

It is under the direct, silent guidance of this MAHA—(great)—
GURU that all the other less divine Teachers and instructors of mankind became, from the first awakening of human consciousness, the
guides of early Humanity. It is through these " Sons of God " that
infant humanity got its first notions of all the arts and sciences, as well
as of spiritual knowledge; and it is they who have laid the first
foundation-stone of those ancient civilizations that puzzle so sorely our
modern generation of students and scholars.*

---

* Let those who doubt this statement explain the mystery of the extraordinary knowledge possessed by the ancients—alleged to have developed from lower and animal-like
savages, the *cave-men* of the Palæolithic age—on any other equally reasonable grounds.
Let them turn to such works as those of Vitruvius Pollio of the Augustan age, on
architecture, for instance, in which all the rules of proportion are those *taught anciently
at initiations,* if he would acquaint himself with the truly divine art, and understand the
deep esoteric significance hidden in every rule and law of proportion. No man descended
from a Palæolithic cave-dweller could ever evolve such a science unaided, even
in millenniums of thought and intellectual evolution. It is the pupils of those
incarnated Rishis and Devas of the third Root Race, who handed their knowledge from
one generation to another, to Egypt and Greece with its now lost *canon of proportion ;*
as it is the Disciples of the Initiates of the 4th, the Atlanteans, who handed it over to
their *Cyclopes,* the " Sons of Cycles " or of the " Infinite," from whom the name passed
to the still later generations of Gnostic priests. " It is owing to the divine perfection

Although these matters were barely hinted at in "*Isis Unveiled*," it will be well to remind the reader of what was said in Vol. I., pp. 587 to 593, concerning a certain Sacred Island in Central Asia, and to refer him for further details to the chapter in Book II. on " The Sons of God and the Sacred Island." A few more explanations, however, though thrown out in a fragmentary form, may help the student to obtain a glimpse into the present mystery.

To state at least one detail concerning these mysterious " Sons of God " in plain words. It is from them, these Brahmaputras, that the high Dwijas, the initiated Brahmins of old justly claimed descent, while the modern Brahmin would have the lowest castes believe literally that they issued direct from the mouth of Brahmâ. This is the esoteric teaching, which adds moreover that, although these descendants (spiritually of course) from the " sons of Will and Yoga," became in time divided into opposite sexes, as their "*Kriyasakti*" progenitors did themselves, later on ; yet even their degenerate descendants have down to the present day retained a veneration and respect for the creative

---

of those architectural proportions that the Ancients could build those wonders of all the subsequent ages, their Fanes, Pyramids, Cave-Temples, Cromlechs, Cairns, Altars, proving they had the powers of machinery and a knowledge of mechanics to which modern skill is like a child's play, and which that *skill* refers to itself as the ' works of hundred-handed giants.' " *(See " Book of God," Kenealy.)* Modern architects may not altogether have neglected those rules, but they have superadded enough empirical innovations to destroy those just proportions. It is Vitruvius who gave to posterity the rules of construction of the Grecian temples erected to the immortal gods ; and the ten books of Marcus Vitruvius Pollio on Architecture, of one, in short, *who was an initiate*, can only be studied esoterically. The Druidical circles, the Dolmen, the Temples of India, Egypt and Greece, the Towers and the 127 towns in Europe which were found " Cyclopean in origin " by the French Institute, are all the work of initiated Priest-Architects, the descendants of those primarily taught by the " Sons of God," justly called " The Builders." This is what appreciative posterity says of those descendants. " They used neither mortar nor cement, nor steel nor iron to cut the stones with ; and yet they were so artfully wrought that in many places the joints are not seen, though many of the stones, as in Peru, are 18ft. thick, and in the walls of the fortress of Cuzco there are stones of a still greater size." *(Acosta*, vi., 14.) " Again, the walls of Syene, built 5,400 years ago, when that spot was exactly under the tropic, which it has now ceased to be, were so constructed that at noon, at the precise moment of the solar solstice, the entire disc of the Sun was seen reflected on their surface—a work which the united skill of all the astronomers of Europe would not now be able to effect."— (Kenealy, " *Book of God*.")

function, and still regard it in the light of a religious ceremony, whereas the more civilized nations consider it as a mere animal function. Compare the western views and practice in these matters with the Institutions of Manu in regard to the laws of Grihasta and married life. The true Brahmin is thus indeed " he whose seven forefathers have drunk the juice of the moon-plant (Soma)," and who is a " Trisuparna," for he has understood the secret of the Vedas.

And, to this day, such Brahmins know that, during its early beginnings, psychic and physical intellect being dormant and consciousness still undeveloped, the spiritual conceptions of that race were quite unconnected with its physical surroundings. That *divine* man dwelt in his animal—though externally human—form ; and, if there was instinct in him, no self-consciousness came to enlighten the darkness of the latent fifth principle. When, moved by the law of Evolution, the Lords of Wisdom infused into him the spark of consciousness, the first feeling it awoke to life and activity was a sense of solidarity, of one-ness with his spiritual creators. As the child's first feeling is for its mother and nurse, so the first aspirations of the awakening consciousness in primitive man were for those whose element he felt within himself, and who yet were outside, and independent of him. DEVOTION arose out of that feeling, and became the first and foremost motor in his nature ; for it is the only one which is natural in our heart, which is innate in us, and which we find alike in human babe and the young of the animal. This feeling of irrepressible, instinctive aspiration in primitive man is beautifully, and one may say intuitionally, described by Carlyle. " The great antique heart," he exclaims, " how like a child's in its simplicity, like a man's in its earnest solemnity and depth ! heaven lies over him wheresoever he goes or stands on the earth ; making all the earth a mystic temple to him, the earth's business all a kind of worship. Glimpses of bright creatures flash in the common sunlight ; angels yet hover, doing God's messages among men . . . . . Wonder, miracle, encompass the man ; he lives in an element of miracle * . . . . A great law of duty, high as these two infinitudes (heaven and hell), dwarfing all else, annihilating all else—it was a reality, and it is one : the garment

---

* That which was *natural* in the sight of primitive man has become only now *miracle* to us ; and that which was to him a miracle could never be expressed in our language.

only of it is dead; the essence of it lives through all times and all eternity!"

It lives undeniably, and has settled in all its ineradicable strength and power in the Asiatic Aryan heart from the Third Race direct through its first "mind-born" sons,—the fruits of *Kriyasakti*. As time rolled on the holy caste of Initiates produced but rarely, and from age to age, such perfect creatures: beings apart, inwardly, though the same as those who produced them, outwardly.

While in the infancy of the third primitive race :—

> " A creature of a more exalted kind
> Was wanting yet, and therefore was designed ;
> Conscious of thought, of more capacious breast
> For empire formed and fit to rule the rest. . . . ."

It was called into being, a ready and perfect vehicle for the incarnating denizens of higher spheres, who took forthwith their abodes in these forms born of *Spiritual* WILL and the natural divine power in man. It was a child of pure Spirit, mentally unalloyed with any tincture of earthly element. Its physical frame alone was of time and of life, as it drew its intelligence direct from above. It was the living tree of divine wisdom ; and may therefore be likened to the Mundane Tree of the Norse Legend, which cannot wither and die until the last battle of life shall be fought, while its roots are gnawed all the time by the dragon Nidhogg ; for even so, the first and holy Son of Kriyasakti had his body gnawed by the tooth of time, but the roots of his inner being remained for ever undecaying and strong, because they grew and expanded in heaven not on earth. He was the first of the FIRST, and he was the seed of all the others. There were other " Sons of Kriyasakti " produced by a second Spiritual effort, but the first one has remained to this day the Seed of divine Knowledge, the One and the Supreme among the terrestrial "Sons of Wisdom." Of this subject we can say no more, except to add that in every age—aye, even in our own—there have been great intellects who have understood the problem correctly.

How comes our physical body to the state of perfection it is found in now ? Through millions of years of evolution, of course, yet never through, or from, animals, as taught by materialism. For, as Carlyle says :—" . . . The essence of our being, the mystery in us that calls itself ' I,'—what words have we for such things ?—it is a breath of Heaven, the highest Being reveals himself in man. This body, these faculties, this life of ours, is it not all as a vesture for the UNNAMED ? "

The *breath* of heaven, or rather the breath of life, called in the Bible *Nephesh*, is in every animal, in every animate speck as in every mineral atom. But none of these has, like man, the consciousness of the nature of that highest Being,* as none has that divine harmony in its form which man possesses. It is, as Novalis said, and no one since has said it better, as repeated by Carlyle :—

" There is but one temple in the universe, and that is the body of man. Nothing is holier than that high form. . . . We touch heaven when we lay our hand on a human body ! " " This sounds like a mere flourish of rhetoric," adds Carlyle, " but it is not so. If well meditated it will turn out to be a scientific fact ; the expression . . . of the actual truth of the thing. We are the miracle of miracles,—the great inscrutable Mystery."

---

* There is no nation in the world in which the feeling of devotion or of religious mysticism is more developed and prominent than in the Hindu people. See what Max Müller says of this idiosyncracy and national feature in his works. This is direct inheritance from the primitive *conscious* men of the Third Race.

STANZA VII.

1. BEHOLD THE BEGINNING OF SENTIENT FORMLESS LIFE (a).
FIRST, THE DIVINE (*vehicle*) (b), THE ONE FROM THE MOTHER-SPIRIT
Atman); THEN THE SPIRITUAL—(*Atma-Buddhi, Spirit-soul*)* (c) ; (*again*)
THE THREE FROM THE ONE (d), THE FOUR FROM THE ONE (e), AND THE
FIVE (f), FROM WHICH THE THREE, THE FIVE AND THE SEVEN (g)—
THESE ARE THE THREE-FOLD AND THE FOUR-FOLD DOWNWARD; THE
" MIND-BORN SONS OF THE FIRST LORD (*Avalôkitêshwara*) THE SHINING
SEVEN (*the "Builders"*).† IT IS THEY WHO ARE THOU, ME, HIM, O
LANOO; THEY WHO WATCH OVER THEE AND THY MOTHER, BHUMI (*the
Earth*).

(a) The hierarchy of Creative Powers is divided into seven (or 4 and 3)
esoteric, within the twelve great Orders, recorded in the twelve signs of
the Zodiac; the seven of the manifesting scale being connected, moreover, with the Seven Planets. All this is subdivided into numberless
groups of divine Spiritual, semi-Spiritual, and ethereal Beings.

The Chief Hierarchies among these are hinted at in the great
Quaternary, or the "four bodies and the three faculties" of Brahmâ
exoterically, and the Panchâsyam, the five Brahmâs, or the five Dhyani-
Buddhas in the Buddhist system.

The highest group is composed of the divine Flames, so-called, also
spoken of as the "Fiery Lions" and the "Lions of Life," whose
esotericism is securely hidden in the Zodiacal sign of Leo. It is the
nucleole of the superior divine World (see *Commentary* in first pages of
Addendum). They are the formless Fiery Breaths, identical in one
aspect with the upper Sephirothal TRIAD, which is placed by the
Kabalists in the "Archetypal World."

The same hierarchy, with the same numbers, is found in the
Japanese system, in the "Beginnings" as taught by both the Shinto
and the Buddhist sects. In this system, Anthropogenesis precedes
Cosmogenesis, as the Divine merges into the human, and creates—

* This relates to the Cosmic principles.
† The seven creative Rishis now connected with the constellation of the Great Bear

midway in its descent into matter—the visible Universe. The legendary personages—remarks reverentially Omoie—" having to be understood as the stereotyped embodiment of the higher (secret) doctrine, and its sublime truths."   To state it at full length, however, would occupy too much of our space, but a few words on this old system cannot be out of place.   The following is a short synopsis of this Anthropo-Cosmogenesis, and it shows how closely the most separated notions echoed one and the same Archaic teaching.

When all was as yet Chaos (*Kon-ton*) three spiritual Beings appeared on the stage of future creation: (1) *Ame no ani naka nushi no Kami*, " Divine Monarch of the Central Heaven"; (2) *Taka mi onosubi no Kami*, " Exalted, imperial Divine offspring of Heaven and the Earth "; and (3) *Kamu mi musubi no Kami*, " Offspring of the Gods," simply.

These were without form or substance (our *arupa* triad), as neither the celestial nor the terrestrial substance had yet differentiated, " nor had the essence of things been formed."

In the Zohar—which, as now arranged and re-edited by Moses de Leon, with the help of Syrian and Chaldean Christian Gnostics in the XIIIth century, and corrected and revised still later by many Christian hands, is only a little less exoteric than the Bible itself—this divine " Vehicle" no longer appears as it does in the " Chaldean Book of Numbers."   True enough, Ain-Soph, the ABSOLUTE ENDLESS NO-THING, uses also the form of the ONE, the manifested " Heavenly man " (the FIRST CAUSE) as its chariot (*Mercabah*, in Hebrew; *Vahan*, in Sanskrit) or vehicle to descend into, and manifest through, in the phenomenal world.   But the Kabalists neither make it plain how the ABSOLUTE can use anything, or exercise any attribute whatever, since, as the Absolute, it is devoid of attributes; nor do they explain that in reality it is the First Cause (Plato's *Logos*) the original and eternal IDEA, that manifests through Adam Kadmon, the *Second* Logos, so to speak.   In the " Book of Numbers " it is explained that EN (or *Ain*, Aiôr) is the only self-existent, whereas its " Depth " (*Bythos* or *Buthon* of the Gnostics, called *Propator*) is only periodical.   The latter is Brahmâ as differentiated from Brahma or Parabrahm.   It is the Depth, the Source of Light, or Propator, which is the *unmanifested* Logos or the abstract *Idea*, and not Ain-Soph, *whose ray* uses Adam-Kadmon or the *manifested* Logos (the objective Universe) " male and female "—as a chariot through which to manifest. But in the Zohar we read the following incongruity: " *Senior*

occultatus est et absconditus ; Microprosopus manifestus est, et non manifestus."
(Rosenroth ; *Liber Mysterii*, IV., 1.)   This is a fallacy, since *Microprosopus*
or the *microcosm*, can only exist during its manifestations, and is destroyed
during the Maha-Pralayas.   Rosenroth's Kabala is no guide, but very
often a puzzle.

(*b*) As in the Japanese system, in the Egyptian, and every old cosmogony—at this divine FLAME, The " One," are lit the three descending
groups.   Having their potential being in the higher group, they
now become distinct and separate Entities.   These are called the
" Virgins of Life," the " Great Illusion," etc., etc., and collectively
the " Six-pointed Star."   The latter is the symbol, in almost
every religion, of the *Logos* as the first emanation.   It is that
of Vishnu in India (the *Chakra*, or wheel), and the glyph of the
Tetragrammaton, the " He of the four letters " or—metaphorically—"the limbs of Microprosopos " in the Kabala, which are ten and
six respectively.   The later Kabalists however, especially the Christian
mystics, have played sad havoc with this magnificent symbol.*   For
the " *ten* limbs " of the Heavenly Man are the ten Sephiroth ; but the
first Heavenly Man is the unmanifested Spirit of the Universe, and
ought never to be degraded into Microprosopus—the lesser Face or
Countenance, the prototype of man on the terrestrial plane.†   Of this,
however, later on.   The six-pointed Star refers to the six Forces or
Powers of Nature, the six planes, principles, etc., etc., all synthesized
by the seventh, or the central point in the Star.   All these, the upper
and lower hierarchies included, emanate from the " Heavenly or Celestial Virgin,"‡ the great mother in all religions, the Androgyne, the

---

* Indeed, the Microprosopus—who is, philosophically speaking, quite distinct from
the unmanifested eternal Logos " one with the Father,"—has been finally brought, by
centuries of incessant efforts, of sophistry and paradoxes, to be considered as one with
Jehovah, or the ONE living God (!), whereas Jehovah is no better than Binah, a female
Sephiroth.   This fact cannot be too frequently impressed upon the reader.

† The Microprosopus is, as just said, the Logos manifested, and of such there are
many.

‡ Sephira is the Crown, KETHER, in the abstract principle only, as a mathematical *x*
(the unknown quantity).   On the plane of differentiated nature she is the female
counterpart of Adam Kadmon—the first Androgyne.   The Kabala teaches that the
word " *Fiat Lux* " (*Genesis* ch. i.) referred to the formation and evolution of the
Sephiroth, and not to light as opposed to darkness.   Rabbi Simeon says : " Oh com-

Sephira-Adam-Kadmon. In its *Unity*, primordial light is the seventh, or highest, principle, *Daivi-prakriti*, the light of the unmanifested Logos. But in its differentiation it becomes *Fohat*, or the " Seven Sons." The former is symbolised by the Central point in the double-Triangle ; the latter by the hexagon itself, or the " six limbs " of the Microprosopus the Seventh being Malkuth, the " Bride " of the Christian Kabalists, or our Earth. Hence the expressions :

" The first after the ' One' is divine Fire ; the second, Fire and Æther ; the third is composed of Fire, Æther and Water ; the fourth of Fire, Æther, Water, and Air." The One is not concerned with Man-bearing globes, but with the inner invisible Spheres. " The ' First-Born' are the* LIFE, *the heart and pulse of the Universe ; the Second are its* MIND *or Consciousness,"*† as said in the Commentary.

(*c*) The second Order of Celestial Beings, those of Fire and Æther (corresponding to Spirit and Soul, or the Atma-Buddhi) whose names are legion, are still formless, but more definitely " substantial." They are the first differentiation in the Secondary Evolution or " Creation "— a misleading word. As the name shows, they are the prototypes of the incarnating Jivas or Monads, and are composed of the Fiery Spirit of Life. It is through these that passes, like a pure solar beam, the ray which is furnished by them with its future vehicle, the Divine Soul, Buddhi. These are directly concerned with the Hosts of the higher world of *our* system. From these twofold *Units* emanate the *threefold*.

In the cosmogony of Japan, when, out of the chaotic mass, an egg-like nucleus appears, having within itself the germ and potency of all the universal as well as of all terrestial life, it is the " three-fold " just named, which differentiates. " The male æthereal" (*Yo*) principle

---

panions, companions, man as an emanation was both man and woman, Adam Kadmon verily, and this is the sense of the words ' Let there be Light, and it was Light.' And this is the two-fold man." (*Auszüge aus dem Zohar*, pp. 13-15.)

  * See next footnote. These elements of Fire, Air, etc., are not our compound elements.

  † This " Consciousness " has no relation to our consciousness. The consciousness of the " One manifested," if not absolute, is still unconditioned. Mahat (the Universal Mind) is the first production of the Brahmâ-Creator, but also of the Pradhâna (un-differentiated matter).

ascends and the female grosser or more material principle (*In*) is precipitated into the Universe of substance, when a separation occurs between the celestial and the terrestial. From this the female, the mother, the first rudimentary objective being is born. It is ethereal, without form or sex, and yet it is from this and the mother that the Seven Divine Spirits are born, from whom will emanate *the seven creations*, just as in the Codex Nazaræus from Karabtanos and the Mother *Spiritus* the seven *evilly disposed* (material) spirits are born. It would be too long to give here the Japanese names, but once translated they stand in this order :—

(1.) The " Invisible Celibate," which is the creative logos of the non-creating "father," or the creative potentiality of the latter made manifest.

(2.) " The Spirit (or the God) of the rayless depths " (of Chaos) ; which becomes differentiated matter, or the world-stuff ; also the mineral realm.

(3.) " The Spirit of the Vegetable Kingdom," of the " Abundant Vegetation."

(4.) This one is of dual nature, being at the same time " The Spirit of the Earth " and " the Spirit of the Sands," the former containing the potentiality of the male element, the latter that of the female element, the two forming a combined nature.

These two were ONE ; yet unconscious of being two.

In this duality were contained (*a*) the male, dark and muscular Being, *Isu no gai no Kami ;* and (*b*) *Eku gai no Kami*, the female, fair and weaker or more delicate Being. Then, the :—

(5th and 6th.) Spirits who were androgynous or dual-sexed, and, finally :—

(7.) The *Seventh* Spirit, the last emanated from the " mother," appears as the first divine human form distinctly male and female. It was the seventh creation, as in the Purânas, wherein man is the seventh creation of Brahmâ.

These, *Tsanagi-Tsanami*, descended into the Universe by the celestial Bridge (the milky way), and " *Tsanagi*, perceiving far below a chaotic mass of cloud and water, thrust his jewelled spear into the depths, and dry land appeared." Then the two separated to explore *Onokoro*, the newly-created island-world ; etc., etc. (*Omoie*).

Such are the Japanese exoteric fables, the rind that conceals the kernel of the same one truth of the Secret Doctrine. Turning back to the esoteric explanations in every cosmogony :—

(d) The *Third* order corresponds to the *Atma-Buddhi-Manas :* Spirit, Soul and Intellect, and is called the " Triads."

(e) The *Fourth* are substantial Entities. This is the highest group among the *Rupas* (Atomic Forms *). It is the nursery of the human, conscious, spiritual Souls. They are called the " Imperishable Jivas," and constitute, through the order below their own, the first group of the first septenary † host—the great mystery of human conscious and

---

* It is worthy of notice that, while rejecting as a superstition of Occultism, and religion too, the theory of substantial and invisible Beings called Angels, Elementals, etc.—without, of course, having ever looked into the philosophy of these incorporeal Entities, or thought over them—modern chemistry, owing to observation and discovery, should have unconsciously been forced to adopt and recognize the same ratio of progression and order in the evolution of chemical atoms as Occultism does, both for its Dhyanis and Atoms—analogy being its first law. As seen above, the very first group of the Rupa Angels is quaternary, an element being added to each in descending order. So are the atoms, adopting the phraseology of chemistry, monatomic, diatomic, and tetratomic, progressing downwards. Let it be remembered that Fire, Water, and Air, or the " Elements of primary Creation " so-called, are not the compound Elements they are on Earth, but noumenal homogeneous Elements—the Spirits thereof. Then follow the septenary groups or hosts. Placed on parallel lines in a diagram with Atoms, the Natures of those Beings would be seen to correspond in their downward scale of progression to composite elements in a mathematically identical manner, as to analogy. This refers, of course, only to diagrams made by the Occultists ; for were the scale of Angelic Beings to be placed on a parallel line with the scale of the chemical atoms of Science—from the hypothetical Helium down to Uranium—they would of course be found to differ. For these have, as correspondents on the Astral plane, only the four lowest orders—the higher three principles in the atom, or rather molecule or chemical element, being perceptible only to the initiated Dangma's eye. But then, if Chemistry desired to find itself on the right path, it would have to correct its tabular arrangement by that of the Occultists—which it may refuse to do. In Esoteric Philosophy, every physical particle corresponds to and depends on its higher *noumenon*— the Being to whose essence it belongs ; and above as below, the Spiritual evolves from the Divine, the psycho-mental from the Spiritual—tainted from its lower plane by the astral—the whole animate and (seemingly) inanimate Nature evolving on parallel lines, and drawing its attributes from above as well as from below.

† The number seven does not imply only seven Entities, but seven groups or Hosts, as explained before. The highest group, the Asuras born in Brahmâ's first body—

intellectual Being. For the latter are the field wherein lies concealed *in its privation* the germ *that will fall into generation.* That germ will become the spiritual potency in the physical cell that guides the development of the embryo, and which is the cause of the hereditary transmission of faculties and all the inherent qualities in man. The Darwinian theory, however, of the transmission of acquired faculties, is neither taught nor accepted in Occultism. Evolution, in it, proceeds on quite other lines ; the physical, according to esoteric teaching, evolving gradually from the spiritual, mental, and psychic. This inner soul of the physical cell—this " spiritual plasm " that dominates the germinal plasm—is the key that must open one day the gates of the terra incognita of the Biologist, now called the dark mystery of Embryology. (*See text and note infra.*)

(*f*) The Fifth group is a very mysterious one, as it is connected with the Microcosmic Pentagon, the five-pointed star representing man. In India and Egypt these Dhyanis were connected with the Crocodile, and their abode is in Capricornus. These are convertible terms in Indian astrology, as this (tenth) sign of the Zodiac is called *Makara*, loosely translated " crocodile." The word itself is occultly interpreted in various ways, as will be shown further on. In Egypt the defunct man —whose symbol is the pentagram or the five-pointed star, the points of which represent the limbs of a man—was shown emblematically transformed into a crocodile : Sebakh or Sevekh " or seventh," as Mr. Gerald Massey says, showing it as having been the type of intelligence, is a dragon in reality, not a crocodile. He is the " Dragon of Wisdom " or Manas, the " Human Soul," Mind, the Intelligent principle, called in our esoteric philosophy the " Fifth " principle.

Says the defunct " Osirified " in ch. lxxxviii., " Book of the Dead," or the *Ritual*, under the glyph of a mummiform god with a crocodile's head :—

(1) " I am the god (crocodile) presiding at the fear . . . at the arrival of his Soul among men. I am the god-crocodile brought for destruction" (an allusion to the destruction of divine spiritual purity

which turned into " Night "—are septenary, *i.e.*, divided like the Pitris into seven classes, three of which are arupa (bodiless) and four with bodies. (See Vishnu Purâna, Book I.) They are in fact more truly our *Pitris* (ancestors) than the Pitris who projected the first physical men. (See Book II.)

when man acquires the knowledge of good and evil; also to the
" fallen" gods, or angels of every theogony).

(2) " I am the fish of the great Horus (as *Makara* is the " crocodile,"
the vehicle of Varuna). I am merged in Sekten."

This last sentence gives the corroboration of, and repeats the doctrine
of, esoteric Buddhism, for it alludes directly to the fifth principle
(Manas), or the most spiritual part of its essence rather, which merges
into, is absorbed by, and made one with Atma-Buddhi after the
death of man. For Se-khen is the residence or *loka* of the god Khem
(Horus-Osiris, or Father and Son), hence the " Devachan" of Atma-
Buddhi. In the Ritual of the Dead the defunct is shown entering into
Sekhem with Horus-Thot and " emerging from it as pure spirit"
(lxiv., 29). Thus the defunct says (v. 130): " I see the forms of
(myself, as various) men transforming eternally . . . I know this
(chapter). He who knows it . . . takes all kinds of living forms." . . .

And in verse 35, addressing in magic formula that which is called, in
Egyptian esotericism, the " ancestral heart," or the re-incarnating principle, the permanent EGO, the defunct says :—

" Oh my heart, my ancestral heart necessary for my transformations,
. . . . . . do not separate thyself from me before the guardian of
the Scales. Thou art my personality within my breast, divine companion *watching over my fleshes* (bodies). . . . . . ."

It is in Sekhem that lies concealed " the Mysterious Face," or the
real man concealed under the false personality, the triple-crocodile of
Egypt, the symbol of the higher Trinity or human Triad, *Atma, Buddhi*
and *Manas.** In all the ancient papyri the crocodile is called *Sebek*
(Seventh), while the water is the fifth principle esoterically; and, as
already stated, Mr. Gerald Massey shows that the crocodile was " the
Seventh Soul, the supreme one of seven—the Seer unseen." Even
exoterically *Sekhem* is the residence of the god Khem, and Khem is
Horus avenging the death of his father Osiris, hence punishing the Sins
of man when he becomes a disembodied Soul. Thus the defunct

---

* One of the explanations of the real though hidden meaning of this Egyptian religious glyph is easy. The crocodile is the first to await and meet the devouring fires of
the morning sun, and very soon came to personify the solar heat. When the sun
arose, it was like the arrival on earth and among men " of the divine soul which informs
the Gods." Hence the strange symbolism. The mummy donned the head of a
crocodile to show that it was a soul arriving from the earth.

"Osirified" became the god Khem, who " gleans the field of *Aanroo*,"*i.e.*, he gleans either his reward or punishment, as that field is the celestial locality (Devachan) where the defunct is given *wheat*, the food of divine justice. The fifth group of the celestial Beings is supposed to contain in itself the dual attributes of both the spiritual and physical aspects of the Universe; the two poles, so to say, of Mahat the Universal Intelligence, and the dual nature of man, the spiritual and the physical. Hence its number Five, multiplied and made into ten, connecting it with *Makara*, the 10th sign of Zodiac.

(*g*) The sixth and seventh groups partake of the lower qualities of the Quaternary. They are conscious, ethereal Entities, as invisible as Ether, which are shot out like the boughs of a tree from the first central group of the four, and shoot out in their turn numberless side groups, the lower of which are the Nature-Spirits, or Elementals of countless kinds and varieties; from the formless and unsubstantial—the ideal THOUGHTS of their creators—down to the Atomic, though, to human perception, invisible organisms. The latter are considered as the " Spirits of Atoms " for they are the first remove (backwards) from the physical Atom—sentient, if not intelligent creatures. They are all subject to Karma, and have to work it out through every cycle. For, as the doctrine teaches, there are no such privileged beings in the universe, whether in our or in other systems, in the outer or the inner worlds,* as the angels of the Western Religion and the Judean. A Dhyan Chohan has to become one; he cannot be born or appear suddenly on the plane of life as a full-blown angel. The Celestial Hierarchy of the present Manvantara will find itself transferred in the next cycle of life into higher, superior worlds, and will make room for a new hierarchy, composed of the elect ones of our mankind. Being is an endless cycle within the one absolute eternity, wherein move numberless inner cycles finite and conditioned. Gods, created as such, would evince no personal merit in being gods. Such a class of beings, perfect only by virtue of the special immaculate nature inherent in them, in the face of suffering and struggling humanity, and even of the lower creation, would be the

---

* A world when called " a higher world " is not higher by reason of its location, but because it is superior in quality or essence. Yet such a world is generally understood by the profane as " Heaven," and located above our heads.

symbol of an eternal injustice quite Satanic in character, an ever present crime. It is an anomaly and an impossibility in Nature. Therefore the "Four" and the "Three" have to incarnate as all other beings have. This sixth group, moreover, remains almost inseparable from man, who draws from it all but his highest and lowest principles, or his spirit and body, the five middle human principles being the very essence of those Dhyanis.* Alone, the Divine Ray (the Atman) proceeds directly from the One. When asked how that can be? How is it possible to conceive that those "gods," or angels, can be at the same time their own emanations and their personal selves? Is it in the same sense in the material world, where the son is (in one way) his father, being his blood, the bone of his bone and the flesh of his flesh? To this the teachers answer "Verily it is so." But one has to go deep into the mystery of BEING before one can fully comprehend this truth.

STANZA VII.—*Continued.*

2. THE ONE RAY MULTIPLIES THE SMALLER RAYS. LIFE PRECEDES FORM, AND LIFE SURVIVES THE LAST ATOM (*of* Form, Sthula-sarira, external body). THROUGH THE COUNTLESS RAYS THE LIFE-RAY, THE ONE, LIKE A THREAD THROUGH MANY BEADS (*pearls*) (a).

(a) This sloka expresses the conception—a purely Vedantic one, as already explained elsewhere—of a life-thread, *Sutratma*, running through successive generations. How, then, can this be explained? By resorting to a simile, to a familiar illustration, though necessarily imperfect, as all our available analogies must be. Before resorting to it, however, I would ask whether it seems *unnatural*, least of all "supernatural," to any one of us, when we consider that process known as the growth and development of a fœtus into a healthy baby weighing several pounds— evolves from what? From the segmentation of an infinitesimally small ovum and a spermatozoon; and afterwards we see that baby develop into a six-foot man! This refers to the atomic and physical

---

* Paracelsus calls them the *Flagæ;* the Christians, the "Guardian Angels;" the Occultist, the "Ancestors, the Pitris;" they are the *sixfold* Dhyan Chohans, having the six spiritual Elements in the composition of their bodies—in fact, men, minus the physical body.

expansion from the microscopically small into something very large, from the—to the naked eye—unseen, into the visible and objective. Science has provided for all this; and, I dare say, her theories, embryological, biological, and physiological, are correct enough so far as exact observation of the material goes. Nevertheless, the two chief difficulties of the science of embryology—namely, what are the forces at work in the formation of the fœtus, and the *cause* of "hereditary transmission" of likeness, physical, moral or mental—have never been properly answered; nor will they ever be solved till the day when scientists condescend to accept the Occult theories.* But if this physical pheno-

---

* The materialists and the evolutionists of the Darwinian school would be ill-advised to accept the newly worked-out theories of Professor Weissmann, the author of *Beiträge zur Descendenzlehre*, with regard to one of the two mysteries of Embryology, as above specified, which he seems to have solved—as he thinks. For, when it is solved, Science will have stepped over into the domain of the truly occult, and stepped for ever out of the realm of transformation, as taught by Darwin. The two are irreconcileable, from the standpoint of materialism. Regarded from that of the Occultists, it solves all these mysteries. Those who are not acquainted with the new discovery of Professor Weissman—at one time a fervent Darwinist—ought to hasten to repair the deficiency. The German Embryologist-philosopher shows—thus stepping over the heads of the Greek Hippocrates and Aristotle, right back into the teachings of the old Aryans—one infinitesimal cell, out of millions of others at work in the formation of an organism, determining alone and unaided, by means of constant segmentation and multiplication, the correct image of the future man (or animal) in its physical, mental, and psychic characteristics. It is that cell which impresses on the face and form of the new individual the features of the parents or of some distant ancestor; it is that cell again which transmits to him the intellectual and mental idiosyncracies of his sires, and so on. This Plasm is the immortal portion of our bodies—simply through the process of successive assimilations. Darwin's theory, viewing the embryological cell as an essence or the extract from all other cells, is set aside; it is incapable of accounting for hereditary transmission. There are but two ways of explaining the mystery of heredity; either the substance of the germinal cell is endowed with the faculty of crossing the whole cycle of transformations that lead to the construction of a separate organism and then to the reproduction of identical germinal cells; or, *those germinal cells do not have their genesis at all in the body of the individual, but proceed directly from the ancestral germinal cell passed from father to son through long generations.* It is the latter hypothesis that Weissmann accepted and has worked upon; and it is to this cell that he traces the immortal portion of man. So far, so good; and when this almost correct theory is accepted, how will Biologists explain the first appearance of this everlasting cell? Unless man "grew" like the "immortal Topsy," and was not born at all, but fell from the clouds, how was that embryological cell born in him?

menon astonishes no one, except in so far as it puzzles the Embryologists, why should our intellectual and inner growth, the evolution of the human-spiritual to the Divine-Spiritual, be regarded as, or seem, more impossible than the other ?   Now to the simile.

Complete the physical plasm, mentioned in the last foot-note, the " Germinal Cell " of man with all its material potentialities, with the " spiritual plasm," so to say, or the fluid that contains the five lower principles of the six-principled Dhyan—and you have the secret, if you are spiritual enough to understand it.

" When the seed of the animal man is cast into the soil of the animal woman, that seed cannot germinate unless it has been fructified by the five virtues (the fluid of, or the emanation from the principles) of the six-fold Heavenly man.   Wherefore the Microcosm is represented as a Pentagon, within the Hexagon Star, the " Macrocosm."   (""Aνθρωπos," a work on Occult Embryology, Book I.).   Then: " The functions of *Jiva* on this Earth are of a five-fold character.   In the mineral atom it is connected with the lowest principles of the Spirits of the Earth (the six-fold Dhyanis) ; in the vegetable particle, with their second—the *Prana* (life) ; in the animal, with all these plus the third and the fourth ; in man, the germ must receive the fruition of all the five.   Otherwise he will be born no higher than an animal " ; namely, a congenital idiot. Thus in man alone the Jiva is complete.   As to his seventh principle, it is but one of the Beams of the Universal Sun.   Each rational creature receives only the temporary loan of that which has to return to its source ; while his physical body is shaped by the lowest terrestrial lives, through physical, chemical, and physiological evolution.   " The Blessed Ones have nought to do with the purgations of matter." (Kabala, Chaldean Book of Numbers).

It comes to this : Mankind in its first prototypal, shadowy form, is the offspring of the Elohim of Life (or Pitris); in its qualitative and physical aspect it is the direct progeny of the " Ancestors," the lowest Dhyanis, or Spirits of the Earth ; for its moral, psychic, and spiritual nature, it is indebted to a group of divine Beings, the name and characteristics of which will be given in Book II.   Collectively, men are the handiwork of hosts of various spirits ; distributively, the taber-nacles of those hosts ; and occasionally and singly, the vehicles of some of them.   In our present all-material Fifth Race, the earthly Spirit of the

Fourth is still strong in us ; but we are approaching the time when the pendulum of evolution will direct its swing decidedly upwards, bringing Humanity back on a parallel line with the primitive third Root-Race in Spirituality. During its childhood, mankind was composed wholly of that Angelic Host, who were the indwelling Spirits that animated the monstrous and gigantic tabernacles of clay of the Fourth Race— built by (as they are now also) and composed of countless myriads o lives.* This sentence will be explained later on in the present Commentary. The " tabernacles " have improved in texture and symmetry of form, growing and developing with the globe that bore them ; but the physical improvement took place at the expense of the spiritual inner man and nature. The three middle principles in earth and man became with every race more material ; the Soul stepping back to make room for the physical intellect ; the essence of elements becoming the material and composite elements now known.

Man is not, nor could he ever be, the complete product of the " Lord God"; but he *is* the child of the *Elohim*, so arbitrarily changed into the singular masculine gender. The first Dhyanis, commissioned to "create" man in their image, could only throw off their shadows, like a delicate model for the Nature Spirits of matter to work upon. (See Book II.) Man is, beyond any doubt, formed physically out of the dust of the Earth, but his creators and fashioners were many. Nor can it be said that the " Lord God breathed into his nostrils the breath of life," unless that God is identified with the "ONE LIFE," Omnipresent though invisible, and unless the same operation is attributed to " God" on behalf of every *living Soul*—or *Nephesch*, which is the *vital* Soul, not the divine Spirit or *Ruach*, which ensures to man alone a divine degree of immortality, that no animal, as such, could ever attain in this cycle of incarnation. It is the inadequate distinctions made by the Jews, and now by our Western metaphysicians, who, not knowing of, and being unable to understand, hence to accept, more than a triune man—Spirit, Soul,

* Science, dimly perceiving the truth, may find Bacteria and other infinitesimals in the human body, and see in them but occasional and abnormal visitors to which diseases are attributed. Occultism—which discerns a life in every atom and molecule, whether in a mineral or human body, in air, fire or water—affirms that our whole body is built of such lives, the smallest bacteria under the microscope being to them in comparative size like an elephant to the tiniest infusoria.

Body—thus confuse the "breath of life" with immortal Spirit.* This applies also directly to the Protestant theologians, who, in translating verse 8 of Ch. III. in the Fourth Gospel, have entirely perverted the meaning. Indeed the verse is made to say " The *wind* bloweth where it listeth," instead of "the *Spirit* goeth where it willeth," as in the original and also in the translation of the Greek Eastern Church.

Thus the philosophy of psychic, spiritual, and mental relations with man's physical functions is in almost inextricable confusion. Neither the old Aryan, nor the Egyptian psychology are now properly understood. Nor can they be assimilated without accepting the esoteric septenary, or, at any rate, the Vedantic quinquepartite division of the human inner principles. Failing which, it will be for ever impossible to understand the metaphysical and purely psychic and even physiological relations between the Dhyan-Chohans, or Angels, on the one plane, and humanity on the other. No Eastern (Aryan) esoteric works are so far published, but we possess the Egyptian papyri which speak clearly

---

* The learned and very philosophical author of " New Aspects of Life " would impress upon his reader that the *Nephesh chaiah* (living soul), according to the Hebrews, " proceeded from, or was produced by, the infusion of the Spirit or Breath of Life into the quickening body of man, and was to supersede and take the place of that spirit in the thus constituted self, so that the spirit passed into, was lost sight of, and disappeared in the living Soul." The human body, he thinks, ought to be viewed as a matrix in which, and from which, the Soul (which he seems to place higher than the spirit) is developed—considered *functionally* and from the standpoint of activity, the Soul stands undeniably higher in this finite and conditioned world of Maya—the Soul, he says, " is ultimately produced from the animated body of man." Thus the author identifies " Spirit " (Atma) simply with " the breath of life." The Eastern Occultists will demur to this statement, for it is based on the erroneous conception that *Prana* and *Atma* or *Jivatma* are one and the same thing. The author supports the argument by showing that with the ancient Hebrews, Greeks and even Latins, *Ruach*, *Pneuma* and *Spiritus*—with the Jews undeniably, and with the Greeks and Romans very probably— meant Wind ; the Greek word *Anemos* (wind) and the Latin *Anima* " Soul " having a suspicious relation.

This is very far fetched. A legitimate battle-field for deciding this question is hardly to be found, since Mr. Pratt seems to be a practical, matter-of-fact metaphysician, a kind of Kabalist-Positivist, and the Eastern metaphysicians, especially the Vedantins, are all Idealists. The Occultists are also of the extreme esoteric Vedantin school, and they call the One Life (Parabrahm), the Great Breath and the Whirlwind ; but they disconnect the seventh principle entirely from matter or any relation to, or connection with it.

of the seven principles or the " Seven Souls of Man."* The Book of the Dead gives a complete list of the "transformations" that every defunct undergoes, while divesting himself, one by one, of all those principles—materialised for the sake of clearness into ethereal entities or bodies. We must, moreover, remind those who try to prove that the ancient Egyptians knew nothing of and did not teach Reincarnation, that the "Soul" (the *Ego* or *Self*) of the defunct is said to be living in Eternity: it is immortal, "co-eval with, and disappearing with the Solar boat," *i.e.*, for the cycle of necessity. This "Soul" *emerges from the Tiaou* (the realm *of the cause of life*) and joins the living on Earth *by day*, to return to *Tiaou* every night. This expresses the periodical existences of the Ego. (Book of the Dead, cvxliii.)

The *shadow*, the astral form, is annihilated, "devoured by the Uræus" (cxlix., 51), the *Manes* will be annihilated; the two twins (the 4th and 5th principles) will be scattered; but the Soul-bird, "the divine Swallow —and the Uræus of Flame" (Manas and Atma-Buddhi) will live in the eternity, for they are their mother's husbands.†

Like alone produces like. The Earth gives Man his body, the gods (Dhyanis) his five inner principles, the psychic Shadow, of which those gods are often the animating principle. SPIRIT (Atman) is one—and indiscrete. It is not in the *Tiaou*.

For what is the *Tiaou*? The frequent allusion to it in the "Book of the Dead" contains a mystery. *Tiaou* is the path of the Night Sun, the inferior hemisphere, or the infernal region of the Egyptians, placed by them on the *concealed side of the moon*. The human being, in their

---

* *Vide* in Part II., Book II., "The Seven Souls of Man," the divisions made respectively by Messrs. Gerald Massey and Franz Lambert.

† Another suggestive analogy between the Aryan or Brahmanical and the Egyptian esotericism. The former call the Pitris "the lunar ancestors" of men; and the Egyptians made of the Moon-God, Taht-Esmun, the first human ancestor. This "moon-god" "expressed the Seven nature-powers that were prior to himself, and were summed up in him as his seven souls, of which he was the manifestor as the eighth one (hence the eighth sphere). The seven rays of the Chaldean Heptakis or Iao, on the Gnostic stones indicate the same septenary of souls." . . . "The first form of the mystical SEVEN was seen to be figured in heaven, by the seven large stars of the Great Bear, the constellation assigned by the Egyptians to the Mother of Time, and of the seven elemental powers." (See *The Seven Souls*, etc.) As well known to every Hindu, this same constellation represents in India the Seven Rishis, and as such is called *Riksha*, and *Chitra-Sikhandinas*.

esotericism, came out from the moon (a triple mystery—astronomical, physiological, and psychical at once); he crossed the whole cycle of existence and then returned to his birth-place before issuing from it again. Thus the defunct is shown arriving in the West, receiving his judgment before Osiris, resurrecting as the god Horus, and circling round the sidereal heavens, which is an allegorical assimilation to Ra, the Sun ; then having crossed the *Noot* (the celestial abyss), returning once more to Tiaou : an assimilation to Osiris, who, as the God of life and reproduction, inhabits the moon. Plutarch (Isis and Osiris, ch. xliii.) shows the Egyptians celebrating a festival called " The Ingress of Osiris into the moon." In chapter xli. life is promised after death ; and the renovation of life is placed under the patronage of Osiris-Lunus, because the moon was the symbol of life-renewals or reincarnations, owing to its growth, waning, dying, and reappearance every month. In the *Dankmoe*, (iv. 5) it is said :—" Oh, Osiris-Lunus ! That renews to thee thy renewal." And Safekh says to Seti I. (Mariette's Abydos, plate 51), " Thou renewest thyself as the god Lunus when a babe." It is still better explained in a Louvre papyrus (P. Pierret, " Etudes Egyptologiques ") : " Couplings and conceptions abound when he (Osiris-Lunus) is seen in heaven on that day." Says Osiris : " Oh, sole radiant beam of the moon ! I issue from the circulating multitudes (of stars) . . . . . Open me the Tiaou, for Osiris N. I will issue by day to do what I have to do amongst the living " (" Book of the Dead," ch. ii.),—*i.e.*, to produce conceptions.

Osiris was " God manifest in generation," because the ancients knew, far better than the moderns, the real occult influences of the lunar body upon the mysteries of conception.* Later on, when the moon became connected with female goddesses†—with Diana, Isis, Artemis,

---

* In the oldest systems we find the Moon always male. Thus Soma is, with the Hindus, a kind of sidereal Don Juan, a " King," and the father, albeit illegitimate, of Buddha—Wisdom, which relates to Occult Knowledge, a wisdom gathered through a thorough acquaintance with lunar mysteries including those of sexual generation. (See " Holy of Holies.")

† If instead of being taught in Sunday Schools useless lessons from the Bible, the armies of the ragged and the poor were taught Astrology—so far, at any rate, as the occult properties of the Moon and its hidden influences on generation are concerned, then there would be little need to fear increase of the population nor to resort to the questionable literature of the Malthusians for its arrest. For it is the Moon and her

Juno, etc., that connection was due to a thorough knowledge of physiology and female nature, physical as much as psychic. But, primarily, the Sun and Moon were the only visible and, so to say, *tangible* [by their effects] psychic and physiological deities—the Father and the Son, while Space and air in general, or that expanse of Heaven called Noot by the Egyptians, was the concealed Spirit or Breath of the two. These " Father and Son " were interchangeable in their functions and worked harmoniously together in their effects upon terrestrial nature and humanity ; hence they were regarded as ONE, though TWO in personified Entities. They were both males, and both had their distinct and also collaborative work in the causative generation of Humanity. So much from the astronomical and cosmic standpoints viewed and expressed in symbolical language—which became in our last races theological and dogmatic. But behind this veil of Cosmic and Astrological symbols, there were the Occult mysteries of Anthropography and the primeval genesis of man. And in this, no knowledge of symbols— or even the key to the *post-diluvian* symbolical language of the Jews— will, or can help, save only with reference to that which was laid down in national scriptures for exoteric uses ; the sum of which, however cleverly veiled, was only the smallest portion of the real primitive history of each people, often relating, moreover,—as in the Hebrew Scriptures—merely to the terrestrial human, not divine life of that nation. That psychic and spiritual element belonged to MYSTERY and INITIATION. There were things never recorded in scrolls, but, as in Central Asia, on rocks and in subterranean crypts.

Nevertheless, there was a time when the whole world was " of one lip and of one knowledge," and Man knew more of his origin than he does now, and thus knew that the Sun and Moon, however large a part they do play in the constitution, growth and development of the human body, were not the direct causative agents of his appearance on Earth ;

conjunctions that regulate conceptions, and every astrologer in India knows it. During the previous and the present races, at least at the beginning of this one, those who indulged in marital relations during certain lunar phases that made those relations sterile were regarded as sorcerers and sinners. But even now those sins of old, based on the Occult knowledge and the abuse of it, would appear preferable to the crimes of to-day, which are perpetrated because of the complete ignorance of, and disbelief in all such occult influences.

these agents being, in truth, the living and intelligent Powers which the Occultists call Dhyan Chohans.

As to this, a very learned admirer of the Jewish Esotericism tells us that " the Kabala says expressly that Elohim is a ' *general abstraction* '; what we call in mathematics ' a constant co-efficient' or a ' general function' entering into all construction, not particular; that is, by the general ratio 1 to 31415, (the astro-Dhyanic and) Elohistic figures." To this the Eastern Occultist replies: Quite so, it is an abstraction to our physical senses. To our spiritual perceptions, however, and to our inner spiritual eye, the Elohim or Dhyanis are no more an abstraction than our soul and spirit are to us. Reject the one and you reject the other—since that which is the *surviving Entity in us* is partly the direct emanation from, and partly *those celestial Entities themselves*. One thing is sure; the Jews were perfectly acquainted with sorcery and various maleficent forces; but, with the exception of some of their great prophets and seers like Daniel and Ezekiel (Enoch belonging to a far distant race and not to any nation but to all, as a generic character), they knew little of, nor would they deal with, the real divine Occultism, their national character being averse to anything which had no direct bearing upon their own ethnical, tribal, and individual benefits—witness their own prophets, and the curses thundered by them against the " stiff-necked race." But even the Kabala plainly shows the direct relation between the Sephiroth, or Elohim, and men.

Therefore, when it is proved to us that the Kabalistic identification of Jehovah with Binah, a female Sephiroth, has still another, a sub-occult meaning in it, then and then only the Occultist will be ready to pass the palm of perfection to the Kabalist. Until then, it is asserted that, as Jehovah is in the abstract sense of a " one living God," a single number, a metaphysical figment, and a reality only when put in his proper place as an emanation and a Sephiroth—we have a right to maintain that the Zohar (as witnessed by the BOOK OF NUMBERS, at any rate), gave out originally, before the Christian Kabalists had disfigured it, and still gives out the same doctrine that we do; *i.e.*, it makes Man emanate, not from one Celestial MAN, but from a Septenary group of Celestial men or Angels, just as in " Pymander, the Thought Divine."

STANZA VII.—*Continued.*

(3) When the one becomes two—the "three-fold" appears (*a*). The three are (*linked into*) one; and it is our thread, O Lanoo, the heart of the man-plant, called Saptaparna (*b*).

(*a*) " When the one becomes two, the three-fold appears": to wit, when the One Eternal drops its reflection into the region of Manifestation, that reflection, " the Ray," differentiates the " Water of Space "; or, in the words of the " Book of the Dead"; "Chaos ceases, through the efful-gence of the Ray of Primordial light dissipating total darkness by the help of the great magic power of the word of the (Central) Sun." Chaos becomes male-female, and Water, incubated through Light, and the " three-fold being issues as its First-born." " Osiris-Ptah (or ra) creates his own limbs (like Brahmâ) by creating the gods destined to personify his phases " during the Cycle (xvii., 4). The Egyptian Ra, issuing from the deep, is the Divine Universal Soul in its manifested aspect, and so is Narâyana, the Purusha, " *concealed in Akâsa and present in Ether.*"

This is the metaphysical explanation, and refers to the very beginning of Evolution, or, as we should rather say, of Theogony. The meaning of the Stanza when explained from another standpoint in its reference to the mystery of man and his origin, is still more difficult to comprehend. In order to form a clear conception of what is meant by the One becoming two, and then being transformed into the " three-fold," the student has to make himself thoroughly acquainted with what we call " Rounds." If he refers to " Esoteric Buddhism "—the first attempt to sketch out an approximate outline of archaic Cosmogony—he will find that by a " Round " is meant the serial evolution of nascent material nature, of the seven globes of our chain * with their mineral,

* Several inimical critics are anxious to prove that no seven principles of man nor septenary constitution of our chain were taught in our earlier volume, " Isis Unveiled." Though in that work the doctrine could only be hinted at, there are many passages, nevertheless, in which the septenary constitution of both man and chain is openly mentioned. Speaking of the Elohim in Vol. II., page 420, it is said: " They remain over the seventh heaven (or spiritual world), for it is they who, accord-ing to the Kabalists, formed in succession the six material worlds, or rather, attempts at worlds that preceded our own, which, they say, is the seventh." Our globe is, of course, upon the diagram representing the " chain," the seventh and the lowest ; though,

vegetable, and animal kingdoms (man being there included in the latter
and standing at the head of it) during the whole period of a life-cycle.
The latter would be called by the Brahmins "a Day of Brahmâ." It
is, in short, one revolution of the "Wheel" (our planetary chain), which
is composed of seven globes (or seven separate "Wheels," in another
sense this time). When evolution has run downward into matter, from
planet A to planet G, or Z, as the Western students call it, it is one
Round. In the middle of the Fourth revolution, which is our present
"Round": "Evolution has reached its acme of physical development,
crowned its work with the perfect physical man, and, from this point,
begins its work spirit-ward." All this needs little repetition, as it is
well explained in "Esoteric Buddhism." That which was hardly
touched upon, and of which the little that was said has misled many,
is the origin of man, and it is upon this that a little more light may now
be thrown, just enough to make the Stanza more comprehensible, as the
process will be fully explained only in its legitimate place, in Book II.

Now every "Round" (on the descending scale) is but a repetition
in a more concrete form of the Round which preceded it, as every globe
—down to our fourth sphere (the actual earth)—is a grosser and more
material copy of the more shadowy sphere which precedes it in their
successive order, on the three higher planes. (See diagram in Stanza
VI. Comm. 6). On its way upwards on the ascending arc, Evolution
spiritualises and etherealises, so to speak, the general nature of all,
bringing it on to a level with the plane on which the twin globe on the
opposite side is placed; the result being, that when the seventh globe
is reached (in whatever Round) the nature of everything that is evolving
returns to the condition it was in at its starting point—plus, every
time, a new and superior degree in the states of consciousness. Thus
it becomes clear that the "origin of man," so-called, on this our present

as the evolution on these globes is cyclic, it is the fourth in descending the arc of
matter. And again, on page 367, Vol. II., it is written: "In the Egyptian notions,
as in those of all other faiths founded on philosophy, man was not merely . . . an union of
soul and body; he was a trinity when spirit was added to it; and besides that doctrine
made him consist of body, astral form, or shadow, the animal soul, the higher soul, and
terrestrial intelligence and a sixth principle, etc., etc.—the seventh—SPIRIT." So
clearly are these principles mentioned, that even in the *Index*, one finds on page 683 :—
" Six principles of man "—the seventh being the synthesis of the six, and *not a principle*
but a ray of the Absolute ALL—in strict truth.

Round, or life-cycle on this planet, must occupy the same place in the same order—save details based on local conditions and time—as in the preceding Round. Again, it must be explained and remembered that, as the work of each Round is said to be apportioned to a different group of so-called "Creators" or "Architects," so is that of every globe; *i.e.*, it is under the supervision and guidance of special "Builders" and "Watchers"—the various Dhyan-Chohans.

The group of the hierarchy which is commissioned to "create" * men is a special group, then; yet it evolved shadowy man in this cycle just as a higher and still more spiritual group evolved him in the Third Round. But as it is the Sixth—on the downward scale of Spirituality—the last and seventh being the terrestrial Spirits (elementals) which gradually form, build, and condense his physical body—this Sixth group evolves no more than the future man's shadowy form, a filmy, hardly visible transparent copy of themselves. It becomes the task of the fifth Hierarchy—the mysterious beings that preside over the constellation Capricornus, Makara, or "Crocodile" in India as in Egypt—to inform the empty and ethereal animal form and make of it the Rational Man. This is one of those subjects upon which very little may be said to the general public. It is a MYSTERY, truly but only to him who is prepared to reject the existence of intellectual and conscious spiritual Beings in the Universe, limiting full Consciousness to man alone, and that only as a "function of the Brain." Many are those among the Spiritual Entities, who have incarnated bodily in man, since the beginning of his appearance, and who, for all that, still exist as independently as they did before, in the infinitudes of Space. . . .

To put it more clearly: the invisible Entity may be bodily present on earth without abandoning, however, its status and functions in the supersensuous regions. If this needs explanation, we can do no better than remind the reader of like cases in Spiritualism, though such cases are very rare, at least as regards the nature of the Entity incarnating,†

---

* Creation is an incorrect word to use, as no religion, not even the sect of the Visishta Adwaitees in India—one which anthropomorphises even Parabrahmam—believes in creation out of *nihil* as Christians and Jews do, but in evolution out of pre-existing materials.

† The so-called "Spirits" that may occasionally possess themselves of the bodies of mediums are not the Monads or Higher Principles of disembodied personalities. Such a Spirit" can only be either an Elementary, or—a Nirmânakâya.

or taking temporary possession of a medium. Just as certain persons —men and women, reverting to parallel cases among living persons— whether by virtue of a peculiar organization, or through the power of acquired mystic knowledge, can be seen in their "double" in one place, while the body is many miles away; so the same thing can occur in the case of superior Beings.

Man, philosophically considered, is, in his outward form, simply an animal, hardly more perfect than his pithecoid-like ancestor of the third round. He is a living body, not a living being, since the realisa- tion of existence, the "Ego-Sum," necessitates self-consciousness, and an animal can only have direct consciousness, or instinct. This was so well understood by the Ancients that the Kabalist even made of soul and body two lives, independent of each other.* The soul, whose body vehicle is the Astral, ethero-substantial envelope, could die and man be still living on earth—*i.e.*, the soul could free itself from and quit the tabernacle for various reasons—such as insanity, spiritual and physical depravity, etc.† Therefore, that which living men (Initiates)

---

* On p. 340-351 (Genesis of the Soul) in the "*New Aspects of Life*," the Author states the Kabalistic teaching: "They held that, functionally, Spirit and Matter of corre- sponding opacity and density tended to coalesce; and that the resultant created Spirits, in the disembodied state, were constituted on a scale in which the differing opacities and transparencies of Elemental or uncreated Spirit were reproduced. And that these Spirits in the disembodied state attracted, appropriated, digested and assimilated Elemental Spirit and Elemental Matter whose condition was conformed to their own." "They therefore taught that there was a wide difference in the condition of created Spirits; and that in the intimate association between the Spirit-world and the world of Matter, the more opaque Spirits in the disembodied state were drawn towards the more dense parts of the material world, and therefore tended towards the centre of the Earth, where they found the conditions most suited to their state; while the more transparent Spirits passed into the surrounding aura of the planet, the most rarified finding their home in its satellite."

This relates exclusively to our Elementary Spirits, and has naught to do with either the Planetary, Sidereal, Cosmic or Inter-Etheric Intelligent Forces or "Angels" as they are termed by the Roman Church. The Jewish Kabalists, especially the practical Occultists who dealt with ceremonial magic, busied themselves solely with the spirits of the Planets and the "Elementals" so-called. Therefore this covers only a portion of the Esoteric Teaching.

† The possibility of the "Soul" (*i.e.*, the eternal Spiritual Ego) dwelling in the unseen worlds, while its body goes on living on Earth, is a pre-eminently occult doctrine, especially in Chinese and Buddhist philosophy. See "Isis Unveiled," vol. i.,

can do, the Dhyanis, who have no physical body to hamper them, can do still better. This was the belief of the Antediluvians, and it is fast becoming that of modern intellectual society, in Spiritualism, besides the Greek and Roman Churches, which teach the ubiquity of their angels. The Zoroastrians regarded their Amshaspends as dual entities (Ferouers), applying this duality—in esoteric philosophy, at any rate—to all the spiritual and invisible denizens of the numberless worlds in space which are visible to our eye. In a note of Damascius (sixth century) on the Chaldean oracles, we have a triple evidence of the universality of this doctrine, for he says : " In these oracles the seven Cosmocratores of the world, (' The World-Pillars,') mentioned likewise by St. Paul, are double—one set being commissioned to rule the superior worlds the spiritual and the sidereal, and the other to guide and watch over the worlds of matter." Such is also the opinion of Jamblichus, who makes an evident distinction between the archangels and the " Archontes." (See " De Mysteriis," sec. ii., ch. 3.) The above may be applied, of course, to the distinction made between the degrees or orders of spiritual beings, and it is in this sense that the Roman Catholic Church tries to interpret and teach the difference ; for while the archangels are in her teaching divine and holy, their doubles are denounced by her as devils.* But the word " ferouer " is not to be understood in this sense, for it means simply the reverse or the opposite side of some attribute or quality. Thus when the Occultist says that the " Demon is the lining of God " (evil, the reverse of the medal), he does not mean two separate

---

p. 602, for an illustration. Many are the *Soulless* men among us, for the occurrence is found to take place in wicked materialists as well as in persons " who advance in holiness and never turn back." (See ibid and also " Isis," vol. ii., p. 369.)

* This identity between the Spirit and its material " double " (in man it is the reverse) explains still better the confusion, alluded to already in this work, made in the names and individualities, as well as the numbers, of the Rishis and the Prajâpatis ; especially between those of the Satyayuga and the Mahabhâratan period. It also throws additional light on what the Secret Doctrine teaches with regard to the Root and the Seed Manus (see Book ii. " On the primitive Manus of humanity "). Not only those progenitors of our mankind, but every human being, we are taught, has its prototype in the Spiritual Spheres ; which prototype is the highest essence of his seventh principle. Thus the seven Manus become 14, the Root Manu being the Prime Cause, and the " Seed-Manu " its effect ; and when the latter reach from Satyayuga (the firs stage) to the heroic period, these Manus or Rishis become 21 in number.

actualities, but the two aspects or facets of the same Unity. Now the best man living would appear, side by side with an Archangel—as described in Theology—a fiend. Hence a certain reason to depreciate a lower " double," immersed far deeper in matter than its original. But there is still as little cause to regard them as devils, and this is precisely what the Roman Catholics maintain against all reason and logic.

(*b*) The concluding sentence of this sloka shows how archaic is the belief and the doctrine that man is seven-fold in his constitution. The thread of being which animates man and passes through all his personalities, or rebirths on this Earth (an allusion to Sutratma), the thread on which moreover all his " Spirits " are strung—is spun from the essence of the "threefold," the " fourfold " and the " fivefold "; which contain all the preceding. *Panchâsikha*, agreeably to Bhâgavata Purâna (V. XX. 25-28), is one of the seven *Kumâras* who go to Sveta-Dvipa to worship Vishnu. We shall see further on, what connection there is between the " celibate " and chaste sons of Brahmâ, who refuse " to multiply," and terrestrial mortals. Meanwhile it is evident that " the Man-Plant," Saptaparna, thus refers to the seven principles, and man is compared to the seven-leaved plant of this name* so sacred among Buddhists.

For further details as to Saptaparna and the importance of the number seven in occultism, as well as in symbology, the reader is referred to Part II., Book II., on Symbolism : Sections on "*Saptaparna*," " The Septenary in the Vedas," etc. etc.

---

* The Egyptian allegory in the " Book of the Dead " already mentioned, the hymn that relates to the reward "of the Soul," is as suggestive of our Septenary Doctrine as it is poetical. The deceased is allotted a piece of land in the field of Aanroo, wherein the Manes, the deified shades of the dead, glean, as the harvest they have sown by their actions in life, the corn seven cubits high, which grows in a territory divided into 14 and 7 portions. This corn is the food on which they live and prosper, or that will kill them, in Amenti, the realm of which the Aanroo field is a domain. For, as said in the hymn, (see chap. xxxii. 9) the deceased is either destroyed therein, or becomes pure spirit for the Eternity, in consequence of the " Seven times seventy-seven lives " passed or to be passed on Earth. The idea of the corn reaped as the " fruit of our ctions " is very graphic

STANZA VII.—*Continued.*

4. It is the root that never dies, the three-tongued flame of the four wicks * (*a*) . . . The wicks are the sparks, that draw from the three-tongued flame (*their upper triad*) shot out by the seven, their flame; the beams and sparks of one moon reflected in the running waves of all the rivers of the earth ("*Bhumi,*" or "*Prithivi*") † (*b*).

(*a*) The "Three-tongued flame" that never dies is the immortal spiritual triad—the Atma-Buddhi and Manas—the fruition of the latter assimilated by the first two after every terrestrial life. The "four wicks" that go out and are extinguished, are the four lower principles, including the body.

"I am the three-wicked Flame and my wicks are immortal," says the defunct. "I enter into the domain of Sekhem (the God whose arm sows the seed of action produced by the disembodied soul) and I enter the region of the Flames who have destroyed their adversaries," *i.e.*, got rid of the sin-creating "four wicks." (See chap. i., vii., "Book of the Dead," and the "Mysteries of Ro-stan.")

(*b*) Just as milliards of bright sparks dance on the waters of an ocean above which one and the same moon is shining, so our evanescent personalities—the illusive envelopes of the immortal MONAD-EGO—twinkle and dance on the waves of Maya. They last and appear, as the thousands of sparks produced by the moon-beams, only so long as the Queen of the Night radiates her lustre on the running waters of life: the period of a Manvantara; and then they disappear, the beams—symbols of our eternal Spiritual Egos—alone surviving, re-merged in, and being, as they were before, one with the Mother-Source.

---

* The three-tongued flame of the four wicks corresponds to the four unities and the three Binaries of the Sephirothal tree (see Commentary on Stanza VI.).

† Useless to repeat again that the terms given here are Sanskrit translations; for the original terms, unknown and unheard of in Europe, would only puzzle the reader more, and serve no useful purpose.

STANZA VII.—*Continued*.

(5) THE SPARK HANGS FROM THE FLAME BY THE FINEST THREAD OF FOHAT. IT JOURNEYS THROUGH THE SEVEN WORLDS OF MAYA (*a*). IT STOPS IN THE FIRST (*Kingdom*), AND IS A METAL AND A STONE; IT PASSES INTO THE SECOND (*Kingdom*), AND BEHOLD—A PLANT; THE PLANT WHIRLS THROUGH SEVEN FORMS AND BECOMES A SACRED ANIMAL; (*the first shadow of the physical man*) (*b*).

FROM THE COMBINED ATTRIBUTES OF THESE, MANU (*man*), THE THINKER, IS FORMED.

WHO FORMS HIM? THE SEVEN LIVES; AND THE ONE LIFE (*c*). WHO COMPLETES HIM? THE FIVEFOLD LHA. AND WHO PERFECTS THE LAST BODY? FISH, SIN, AND SOMA (*the moon*) (*d*).

(*a*) The phrase " through the seven Worlds of Maya " refers here to the seven globes of the planetary chain and the seven rounds, or the 49 stations of active existence that are before the " Spark " or Monad, at the beginning of every " Great Life-Cycle " or Manvantara. The " thread of Fohat " is the thread of life before referred to.

This relates to the greatest problem of philosophy—the physical and substantial nature of life, the independent nature of which is denied by modern science because that science is unable to comprehend it. The reincarnationists and believers in Karma alone dimly perceive that the whole secret of Life is in the unbroken series of its manifestations: whether in, or apart from, the physical body. Because if—

> " Life, like a dome of many-coloured glass,
> Stains the white radiance of Eternity "—

yet it is itself part and parcel of that Eternity; for life alone can understand life.

What is that " Spark " which " hangs from the flame?" It is JIVA, the MONAD in conjunction with MANAS, or rather its aroma—that which remains from each personality, when worthy, and hangs from Atma-Buddhi, the Flame, by the thread of life. In whatever way interpreted, and into whatever number of principles the human being is divided, it may easily be shown that this doctrine is supported by all the ancient

religions, from the Vedic to the Egyptian, from the Zoroastrian to the
Jewish. In the case of the last-mentioned, the Kabalistic works offer
abundant proof of this statement. The entire system of the Kabalistic
numerals is based on the divine septenary hanging from the Triad (thus
forming the *Decade*) and its permutations 7, 5, 4, and 3, which, finally,
all merge into the ONE itself : an endless and boundless Circle.

" The Deity (the ever Invisible Presence)," says the Zohar, " manifests itself through the *ten* Sephiroth which are its radiating witnesses.
The Deity is like the Sea from which outflows a stream called WISDOM,
the waters of which fall into a lake named Intelligence. From the basin,
like seven channels, issue the Seven Sephiroth. . . . . For *ten equal
seven :* the Decade contains *four* Unities and *three* Binaries." The ten
Sephiroth correspond to the limbs of MAN. " When I framed Adam
Kadmon," the Elohim are made to say, " the Spirit of the Eternal shot
out of his Body like a sheet of lightning that radiated at once on the
billows of the *Seven* millions of skies, and my *ten* splendours were his
limbs." But neither the Head nor the shoulders of Adam-Kadmon can
be seen ; therefore we read in the *Sephra Dzenioutha* (the " Book of the
Concealed Mystery ") :—

" In the beginning of Time, after the Elohim (the " Sons of Light
and Life," or the " Builders ") had shaped out of the eternal Essence
the Heavens and the Earth, they formed the worlds six by six, the
seventh being *Malkuth*, which is our Earth (see *Mantuan Codex*) on its
plane, and the lowest on all the other planes of conscious existence.
The Chaldean *Book of Numbers* contains a detailed explanation of all
this. " The first triad of the body of Adam Kadmon (the three upper
planes of the seven*) cannot be seen before the soul stands in the
presence of the Ancient of Days." The Sephiroth of this upper triad
are :—" 1, *Kether* (the Crown) represented by the brow of Macropro-
sopos ; 2, *Chochmah* (Wisdom, a male Principle) by his right shoulder ;
and 3, *Binah* (Intelligence, a female Principle) by the left shoulder."
Then come the *seven* limbs (or Sephiroth) on the planes of manifestation,
the totality of these four planes being represented by *Microprosopus* (the

---

* The formation of the "living Soul" or man, would render the idea more clearly.
" A Living Soul " is a synonym of man in the Bible. These are our seven " Principles."

lesser Face) or Tetragrammaton, the "four-lettered" Mystery. "The seven manifested and the *three* concealed limbs are the Body of the Deity."

Thus our Earth, *Malkuth*, is both the *Seventh* and the *Fourth* world, the former when counting from the first globe above, the latter if reckoned by the planes. It is generated by the sixth globe or Sephiroth called *Yezod*, "foundation," or as said in the Book of Numbers "by Yezod, He (Adam Kadmon) fecundates the primitive Heva" (Eve or our Earth). Rendered in mystic language this is the explanation why Malkuth, called "the inferior Mother," Matrona, Queen, and the Kingdom of the Foundation, is shown as the *Bride* of Tetragrammaton or Microprosopus (the 2nd Logos) the Heavenly Man. When free from all impurity she will become united with the Spiritual *Logos*, *i.e.*, in the 7th Race of the 7th Round—after the regeneration, on the day of "SABBATH." For the "*seventh* day " has again an occult significance undreamt of by our theologians.

"When Matronitha, the Mother, is separated and brought face to face with the King, in the excellence of the Sabbath, all things become one body," says verse 746, in chapter xxii. of "Ha Idra Zuta Kadisha." "Becomes one body" means that all is reabsorbed once more into the one element, the spirits of men becoming *Nirvanees* and the elements of everything else becoming again what they were before—*protyle* or undifferentiated substance. "Sabbath" means *rest* or Nirvana. It is not the *seventh* day after *six* days but a period the duration of which equals that of the seven "days" or any period made up of seven parts. Thus a *pralaya* is equal in duration to the manwantara, or a night of Brahmâ is equal to this "day." If the Christians will follow Jewish customs they ought to adopt the spirit and not the dead letter thereof: *i.e.*, to work one week of seven days and *rest* seven days. That the word "Sabbath" had a mystic significance is shown in the contempt shown by Jesus for the Sabbath day, and by what is said in Luke xviii. 12. Sabbath is there taken *for the whole week*. (See Greek text where the week is called *Sabbath*. "I fast twice in the Sabbath.") Paul, an Initiate, knew it well when referring to the eternal rest and felicity in heaven, as Sabbath; "and their happiness will be eternal, for they will ever be (*one*) with the Lord and will enjoy *an eternal Sabbath*." (Hebrew iv. 2.)

The difference between the two systems, taking the Kabala as contained in the Chaldean *Book of Numbers*, not as misrepresented by its now disfigured copy, the Kabala of the Christian mystics—the Kabala and the archaic esoteric Vidya, is very small indeed, being confined to unimportant divergences of form and expression. Thus Eastern occultism refers to our earth as the fourth world, the lowest of the chain, above which run upward on both its sides the six globes, three on each side. The *Zohar*, on the other hand, calls the earth the lower, or the *Seventh*, adding that upon the six depend all things which are in it, " Microprosopus." The " smaller face," smaller because manifested and finite, " is formed of *six Sephiroth*," says the same work. " Seven kings come and *die in the thrice-destroyed world* "—(Malkuth our earth, destroyed after each of the three rounds which it has gone through). " And their reign (of the seven kings) will be broken up." (*Book of Numbers*, l. viii., 3.) This relates to the Seven Races, five of which have already appeared, and two more have still to appear in this Round.

The Shinto allegorical accounts of Cosmogony and the origin of man in Japan hint at the same belief.

Captain C. Pfoundes studied for nearly nine years in the monasteries of Japan the religion underlying the various sects of the land. . . . . . " The Shinto idea of creation," he says, " is as follows : Out of chaos (*Konton*) the earth (*in*) was the sediment precipitated, and the Heavens (*yo*) the ethereal essences which ascended : *Maa* (*jin*) appeared between the two. The first man was called Kuni-to ko tatchino-mikoto, and *five other names were given to him*, and then the human race appeared, male and female. Isanagi and Isanami begat *Tenshoko doijin*, the first of the five gods of the Earth." These " gods " are simply our five races, Isanagi and Isanami being the two kinds of the " ancestors," the two preceding races which give birth to animal and to rational man.

It will be shown (Vol. II. Pt. II.) that the number seven, as well as the doctrine of the septenary constitution of man, was pre-eminent in all the secret systems. It plays as important a part in Western Kabala as in Eastern Occultism. Eliphas Lévi calls the number seven " the key to the Mosaic creation and the symbols of every religion." He shows the Kabala following faithfully even the septenary division of man, as the diagram he gives in his " *Clef des Grands Mystères* " is septenary. This may be seen at a glance on page 389, " *Une prophetie et diverses pensées de Paracelse*," however cleverly the correct thought is veiled. One needs also only to look at the diagram (Plate VII. in Mr. Mathers' Kabala) "the formation of the Soul "* from the same " Key of the Great Mysteries " by Lévi to find the same, though with a different interpretation.

Thus it stands with both the Kabalistic and the Occult names attached :—

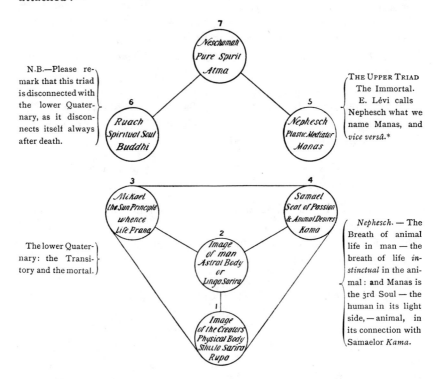

N.B.—Please remark that this triad is disconnected with the lower Quaternary, as it disconnects itself always after death.

THE UPPER TRIAD
The Immortal.
E. Lévi calls Nephesch what we name Manas, and *vice versâ.**

7
Neschomah
Pure Spirit
Atma

6
Ruach
Spiritual Soul
Buddhi

5
Nephesch
Plastic Mediator
Manas

3
Mickael
the Sun Principle
whence
Life Prana

4
Samael
Seat of Passion
& Animal Desires
Kama

2
Image
of man
Astral Body
or
Linga Sarira

The lower Quaternary: the Transitory and the mortal.

Nephesch. — The Breath of animal life in man — the breath of life *instinctual* in the animal: and Manas is the 3rd Soul — the human in its light side,— animal, in its connection with Samaelor *Kama.*

1
Image
of the Creators
Physical Body
Sthula Sarira
Rupa

* Nephesch is the "breath of (animal) life" breathed into Adam, the man of dust; it is consequently the *Vital Spark*, the informing element. Without *Manas*, or what is miscalled in Lévi's diagram Nephesch instead of Manas, "the reasoning Soul," or mind, Atma-Buddhi are irrational on this plane and cannot act. It is Buddhi which is the plastic mediator, not Manas, "the intelligent medium between the upper Triad and the lower Quaternary." But there are many such strange and curious tranformations to be found in the Kabalistic works—a convincing proof that its literature has become a sad jumble. We do not accept the classification except in this one particular, in order to show the points of agreement.

We will now give in tabular form what the very cautious Eliphas Lévi says in explanation of his diagram, and what the Esoteric Doctrine teaches —and compare the two. Lévi, too, makes a distinction between Kabalistic and Occult Pneumatics. (See "*Histoire de la Magic,*" pp. 388, 389.)

Says Eliphas Lévi, the Kabalist :—	Say the Theosophists :—
KABALISTIC PNEUMATICS.	ESOTERIC PNEUMATICS.
1. The Soul (or EGO) is a clothed light ; and this light is triple.	1. Ditto, for it is Atma-Buddhi-*Manas.*
2. *Neschamah*—"pure Spirit."	2. Ditto.*
3. *Ruach*—the Soul or Spirit.	3. Spiritual Soul.
4. *Nephesch*—plastic mediator.†	4. Mediator between Spirit and its Man, the Seat of Reason, the Mind, in man.
5. The garment of the Soul is the rind (body) of the image (astral Soul).	5. Correct.
6. The image is double, because it reflects the good as the bad.	6. Too uselessly apocalyptic. Why not say that the *astral* reflects the good as well as the bad man; man, who is ever tending to the upper triangle, or else disappears with the Quaternary.
7. Imago, body.	7. Ditto, the earthly image.

OCCULT PNEUMATICS.	OCCULT PNEUMATICS.
As given by Eliphas Levi.	*As given by the Occultists.*
1. *Nephesh* is immortal because it renews its life by the destruction of forms.	1. *Manas* is immortal, because after every new incarnation it adds to Atma-Buddhi
[But *Nephesh*, the "breath of	something of itself, and

---

* Eliphas Lévi has, whether purposely or otherwise, confused the numbers : with us his No. 2 is No. 1. (Spirit) ; and by making of Nephesch both the plastic mediator and Life, he thus makes in reality only six principles, because he repeats the first two.

† Esotericism teaches the same. But Manas is not Nephesch ; nor is the latter the astral, but the 4th principle, if also the 2nd *prana*, for Nephesch is the "breath of life" in man, as in beast or insect, of physical, material life, which has no spirituality in it.

life," is a misnomer and a useless puzzle to the student.]

2. *Ruach* progresses by the evolution of ideas (! ?).

thus, assimilating itself to the Monad, shares its immortality.

2. *Buddhi* becomes conscious by the accretions it gets from Manas after every new incarnation and the death of man.

3. *Neschamah* is progressive without oblivion and destruction.

3. *Atma* neither progresses, forgets, nor remembers. It does not belong to this plane : it is but the ray of light eternal which shines upon and through the darkness of matter—when the latter is willing.

4. The soul has three dwellings.

4. The Soul (collectively, as the upper Triad) lives on three planes, besides its fourth, the terrestrial sphere ; and it *exists* eternally on the highest of the three.

5. These dwellings are : the plane of the mortals : the Superior Eden ; and the Inferior Eden.

5. These dwellings are : Earth for the physical man, or the animal Soul ; Kama-loka (Hades, the Limbo) for the disembodied man, or his *Shell ;* Devachan for the higher Triad.

6. The image (man) is a sphinx that offers the riddle of birth.

6. Correct.

7. The fatal image (the astral) endows Nephesch with its aptitudes ; but Ruach is able to substitute for this (vitiated) Nephesch the image

7. The astral through Kama (desire) is ever drawing Manas down into the sphere of material passions and desires. But if the *better* man

conquered in accordance with the inspirations of *Neschamah*.

or *Manas* tries to escape the fatal attraction and turns its aspirations to Atma—Spirit —then Buddhi (Ruach) conquers, and carries Manas with it to the realm of eternal Spirit.

It is very evident that the French Kabalist either did not know sufficiently the real tenet, or distorted it to suit himself and his object. Thus he says again, treating upon the same subject, and we, Occultists, answer the late Kabalist and his admirers :—

1. The body is the mould of Nephesch; Nephesch the mould of Ruach; Ruach the mould *of the garments of Neschamah.*

1. The body follows the whims, good or bad, of *Manas;* Manas tries to follow the light of Buddhi, but often fails. Buddhi is the mould of the "garments" of Atma, because Atma is no body, or shape, or anything, and because Buddhi is its vehicle only *figuratively.*

2. Light (the Soul) personifies in clothing itself (with a body); and personality endures only when the garment is perfect.

2. The Monad becomes a personal ego when it incarnates; and something remains of that personality through Manas, when the latter is perfect enough to assimilate Buddhi.

3. The angels aspire to become men ; a perfect man, a mangod is above all the angels.

3. Correct.

4. Every 14,000 years the soul rejuvenates and rests in the jubilean sleep of oblivion.

4. Within a period, " a great age " or a day of Brahmâ, 14 Manus reign ; after which comes Pralaya when all the Souls rest in Nirvana. (Souls = Egos).

Such are the distorted copies of the esoteric doctrine in the Kabala. But see also " The Primeval Manus of Humanity " in Book II.

To return to Stanza VII.

(b) The well-known Kabalistic aphorism runs :—" A stone becomes a plant ; a plant, a beast ; the beast, a man ; a man a spirit ; and the spirit a god." The " spark " animates all the kingdoms in turn before it enters into and informs divine man, between whom and his predecessor, animal man, there is all the difference in the world. Genesis begins its anthropology at the wrong end (evidently for a blind) and lands no-where.* Had it begun as it ought, one would have found in it, first, the celestial Logos, the " Heavenly Man," which evolves as a Com-pound Unit of Logoi, out of whom after their pralayic sleep—a sleep that gathers the cyphers scattered on the Mayavic plane into One, as the separate globules of quicksilver on a plate blend into one mass—the Logoi appear in their totality as the first " male and female " or Adam Kadmon, the " Fiat Lux " of the Bible, as we have already seen. But this transformation did not take place on our Earth, nor on any material plane, but in the Spacial Depths of the first differentiation of the eternal Root-matter. On our nascent globe things proceed differently. The Monad or Jiva, as said in " Isis Unveiled," vol. i., p. 302, is, first of all, shot down by the law of Evolution into the lowest form of matter—the mineral. After a sevenfold gyration encased in the stone (or that which will become mineral and stone in the Fourth Round), it creeps out of it, say, as a lichen. Passing thence, through all the forms of vegetable matter, into what is termed animal matter, it has now reached the point in which it has become the germ, so to speak, of the

---

* The introductory chapters of Genesis were never meant to represent even a remote allegory of the creation of our Earth. They embrace a metaphysical con-ception of some indefinite period in the eternity, when successive attempts were being made by the law of evolution at the formation of universes. The idea is plainly stated in the Zohar : " There were old worlds, which perished as soon as they came into existence, were formless, and were called Sparks. Thus, the smith, when hammering the iron, lets the sparks fly in all directions. The sparks are the primordial worlds, which could not continue because the *Sacred Aged* (Sephira) had not as yet assumed its form (of androgyne, or opposite sexes) of King and Queen (Sephira and Kadmon), and the Master was not yet at his work. See Zohar, " Idra Suta," Book iii., p. 292, b. The Supreme consulting with the Architect of the world—his Logos—about creation. (" Isis Unveiled," vol. ii., p. 421.)

animal, that will become the physical man. All this, up to the Third Round, is formless, as matter, and senseless, as consciousness. For the Monad or Jiva *per se* cannot be even called spirit : it is a ray, a breath of the ABSOLUTE, or the Absoluteness rather, and the Absolute Homogeneity, having no relations with the conditioned and relative finiteness, is unconscious on our plane. Therefore, besides the material which will be needed for its future human form, the monad requires (*a*) a spiritual model, or prototype, for that material to shape itself into; and (*b*) an intelligent consciousness to guide its evolution and progress, neither of which is possessed by the homogeneous monad, or by senseless though living matter. The Adam of dust requires the *Soul of Life* to be breathed into him : the two middle principles, which are the *sentient* life of the irrational animal and the Human Soul, for the former is irrational without the latter. It is only when, from a potential androgyne, man has become separated into male and female, that he will be endowed with this conscious, rational, individual Soul, (*Manas*) "the principle, or the intelligence, of the Elohim," to receive which, he has to eat of the fruit of Knowledge from the Tree of Good and Evil. How is he to obtain all this ? The Occult doctrine teaches that while the monad is cycling on downward into matter, these very Elohim—or Pitris, the lower Dhyan-Chohans—are evolving *pari passu* with it on a higher and more spiritual plane, descending also relatively into matter on their own plane of consciousness, when, after having reached a certain point, they will meet the incarnating senseless monad, encased in the lowest matter, and blending the two potencies, Spirit and Matter, the union will produce that terrestrial symbol of the " Heavenly Man" in space—PERFECT MAN. In the Sankhya philosophy, Purusha (spirit) is spoken of as something impotent unless he mounts on the shoulders of Prakriti (matter), which, left alone, is—senseless. But in the secret philosophy they are viewed as graduated. Though one and the same thing in their origin, Spirit and Matter, when once they are on the plane of differentiation, begin each of them their evolutionary progress in contrary directions—Spirit falling gradually into matter, and the latter ascending to its original condition, that of a pure spiritual substance. Both are inseparable, yet ever separated. In polarity, on the physical plane, two like poles will always repel each other, while the negative and the positive are mutually attracted, so do Spirit and Matter stand to each other—the two poles of the same homogeneous substance, the root-principle of the universe.

Therefore, when the hour strikes for Purusha to mount on Prakriti's shoulders for the formation of the Perfect Man — rudimentary man of the first 2½ Races being only the *first*, gradually evolving into *the most perfect of mammals*—the Celestial "Ancestors" (Entities from preceding worlds, called in India the Sishta) step in on this our plane, as the Pitris had stepped in before them for the formation of the physical or animal-man, and incarnate in the latter. Thus the two processes— for the two *creations :* the animal and the divine man—differ greatly. The Pitris shoot out from their ethereal bodies, still more ethereal and shadowy similitudes of themselves, or what we should now call "doubles," or "astral forms," in their own likeness.* This furnishes the Monad with its first dwelling, and blind matter with a model around and upon which to build henceforth. But *Man is still incomplete.* From Swayambhuva Manu (in Manu, Book I.), from whom descended the seven primitive Manus or Prajapati, each of whom gave birth to a primitive race of men, down to the Codex Nazareus, in which Karab-tanos or Fetahil (blind concupiscent matter) begets on his Mother, "Spiritus," seven figures, each of which stands as the progenitor of one of the primæval seven races—this doctrine has left its impress on every Archaic Scripture.

"Who forms Manu (the Man) and who forms his body? The LIFE and the LIVES. Sin† and the MOON." Here Manu stands for the spiritual, heavenly man, the real and non-dying EGO in us, which is the direct emanation of the "One Life" or the Absolute Deity. As to our outward physical bodies, the house of the tabernacle of the Soul, the Doctrine teaches a strange lesson ; so strange that unless thoroughly explained and as rightly comprehended, it is only the exact Science of the future that is destined to vindicate the theory fully.

It has been stated before now that Occultism does not accept any-thing inorganic in the Kosmos. The expression employed by Science, "inorganic substance," means simply that the latent life slumbering in the molecules of so-called "inert matter" is incognizable. ALL IS LIFE, and every atom of even mineral dust is a LIFE, though beyond our comprehension and perception, because it is outside the range of the

---

* Read in Isis, vol. ii., pp. 297—303, the doctrine of the Codex Nazaræus—every tenet of our teaching is found there under a different form and allegory.

† The word "Sin" is curious, but has a particular Occult relation to the Moon, besides being its Chaldean equivalent.

laws known to those who reject Occultism. " The very Atoms," says Tyndall, "seem instinct with a desire for life." Whence, then, we would ask, comes the tendency " to run into organic form " ? Is it in any way explicable except according to the teachings of Occult Science ?

" The worlds, to the profane," says a Commentary, *" are built up of the known Elements. To the conception of an Arhat, these Elements are themselves collectively a divine Life ; distributively, on the plane of manifestations, the numberless and countless crores of lives.* Fire alone is ONE, on the plane of the One*

---

* Is Pasteur unconsciously taking the first step toward Occult Science in declaring that, if he dared express his full idea upon this subject, he would say that the Organic cells are endowed with a vital potency that does not cease its activity with the cessation of a current of Oxygen towards them, and does not, on that account, break off its relations with life itself, which is supported by the influence of that gas ? " I would add," goes on Pasteur, " that the evolution of the germ is accomplished by means of complicated phenomena, among which we must class processes of fermentation " ; and life, according to Claude Bernard and Pasteur, is nothing else than a process of fermentation. That there exist in Nature Beings or Lives that can live and thrive without air, even on our globe, was demonstrated by the same men of science. Pasteur found that many of the lower lives, such as Vibriones, and some microbes and bacteria, could exist without air, which, on the contrary, killed them. They derived the oxygen necessary for their multiplication from the various substances that surround them. He calls them *Ærobes*, living on the tissues of our matter when the latter has ceased to form a part of an integral and living whole (then called very unscientifically by science " dead matter "), and *Anærobes*. The one kind binds oxygen, and contributes vastly to the destruction of animal life and vegetable tissues, furnishing to the atmospher materials which enter later on into the constitution of other organisms ; the other destroys, or rather annihilates finally, the so-called organic substance ; ultimate decay being impossible without their participation. Certain germ-cells, such as those of yeast, develop and multiply in air, but when deprived of it, they will adapt themselves to life without air and become ferments, absorbing oxygen from substances coming in contact with them, and thereby ruining the latter. The cells in fruit, when lacking free oxygen, act as ferments and stimulate fermentation. " Therefore the vegetable cell manifests in this case its life as an anærobic being. Why, then, should an organic cell form in this case an exception " ? asks Professor Bogolubof. Pasteur shows that in the substance of our tissues and organs, the cell, not finding sufficient oxygen for itself, stimulates fermentation in the same way as the fruit-cell, and Claude Bernard thought that Pasteur's idea of the formation of ferments found its application and corroboration in the fact that Urea increases in the blood during strangulation : LIFE therefore is everywhere in the Universe, and, Occultism teaches us, it is also in the atom. Also see *infra*, at the close of this Section.

Reality : on that of manifested, hence illusive, being, its particles are fiery lives which live and have their being at the expense of every other life that they consume. Therefore they are named the " DEVOURERS." . . . *" Every visible thing in this Universe was built by such LIVES, from conscious and divine primordial man down to the unconscious agents that construct matter."* . . . *" From the ONE LIFE formless and Uncreate, proceeds the Universe of lives. First was manifested from the Deep (Chaos) cold luminous fire (gaseous light ?) which formed the curds in Space."* (*Irresolvable nebulæ, perhaps ?*). . . . . . . *" . . . These fought, and a great heat was devoloped by the encountering and collision, which produced rotation. Then came the first manifested MATERIAL, Fire, the hot flames, the wanderers in heaven (comets); heat generates moist vapour; that forms solid water (?); then dry mist, then liquid mist, watery, that puts out the luminous brightness of the pilgrims (comets ?) and forms solid watery wheels (MATTER globes). Bhumi (the Earth) appears with six sisters.* These produce by their continuous motion the inferior fire, heat, and an aqueous mist, which yields the third World-Element—WATER ; and from the breath of all (atmospheric) AIR is born. These four are the four lives of the first four periods (Rounds) of Manvantara. The three last will follow."*

This means that every new Round develops one of the Compound Elements, as now known to Science,—which rejects the primitive nomenclature, preferring to subdivide them into constituents. If Nature is the " Ever-becoming " on the manifested plane, then those Elements are to be regarded in the same light : they have to evolve, progress, and increase to the Manvantaric end. Thus the First Round, we are taught, developed but one Element, and a nature and humanity in what may be called one aspect of Nature—called by some, very unscientifically, though it may be so *de facto*, " One-dimensional Space."

---

* It is a Vedic teaching that " there are three Earths corresponding to three Heavens, and our Earth (the fourth) is called Bhumi." This is the explanation given by our exoteric Western Orientalists. But the esoteric meaning and allusion to it in the Vedas is that it refers to our planetary chain, three " Earths " on the descending arc, and three " heavens " which are the three Earths or globes also, only far more ethereal, on the ascending or spiritual arc : by the first three we descend into matter, by the other three we ascend into Spirit ; the lower one, *Bhumi*, our Earth, forming the turning point, so to say, and containing *potentially* as much of Spirit as it does of Matter. We shall treat of this hereafter.

The Second Round brought forth and developed two Elements—Fire and Earth—and *its* humanity, adapted to this condition of Nature, if we can give the name Humanity to beings living under conditions unknown to men, was—to use again a familiar phrase in a strictly figurative sense (the only way in which it can be used correctly)—" a two-dimensional species." The processes of natural development which we are now considering will at once elucidate and discredit the fashion of speculating on the attributes of the *two*, *three*, and *four* or more " dimensional Space; " but in passing, it is worth while to point out the real significance of the sound but incomplete intuition that has prompted —among Spiritualists and Theosophists, and several great men of Science, for the matter of that*—the use of the modern expression, "the fourth dimension of Space." To begin with, of course, the super- ficial absurdity of assuming that Space itself is measurable in any direction is of little consequence. The familiar phrase can only be an abbreviation of the fuller form—the " *Fourth dimension of* MATTER *in Space.*"† But it is an unhappy phrase even thus expanded, because while it is perfectly true that the progress of evolution may be destined to introduce us to new characteristics of matter, those with which we are already familiar are really more numerous than the three dimensions. The faculties, or what is perhaps the best available term, the characteristics of matter, must clearly bear a direct relation always to the senses of man. Matter has extension, colour, motion (molecular motion), taste, and smell, corresponding to the existing senses of man, and by the time that it fully develops the next characteristic—let us call it for the moment PERMEABILITY—this will correspond to the next sense of man—let us call it " NORMAL CLAIR- VOYANCE ; " thus, when some bold thinkers have been thirsting for a fourth dimension to explain the passage of matter through matter, and the production of knots upon an endless cord, what they were really in want of, was a *sixth characteristic of matter.* The three dimensions belong really but to one attribute or characteristic of matter—extension ; and

---

* Professor Zöllner's theory has been more than welcomed by several Scientists— who are Spiritualists—Professors Butlerof and Wagner, of St. Petersburg, for instance.

† " The giving reality to abstractions is the error of Realism. Space and Time are frequently viewed as separated from all the concrete experiences of the mind, instead of being generalizations of these in certain aspects." (Bain, *Logic*, Part II., p. 389.)

popular common sense justly rebels against the idea that under any condition of things there can be more than three of such dimensions as length, breadth, and thickness. These terms, and the term "dimension" itself, all belong to one plane of thought, to one stage of evolution, to one characteristic of matter. So long as there are foot-rules within the resources of Kosmos, to apply to matter, so long will they be able to measure it three ways and no more; and from the time the idea of measurement first occupied a place in the human understanding, it has been possible to apply measurement in three directions and no more. But these considerations do not militate in any way against the certainty that in the progress of time—as the faculties of humanity are multiplied—so will the characteristics of matter be multiplied also.— Meanwhile, the expression is far more incorrect than even the familiar one of the "Sun rising or setting."

We now return to the consideration of material evolution through the Rounds. Matter in the *second* Round, it has been stated, may be figuratively referred to as two-dimensional. But here another *caveat* must be entered. That loose and figurative expression may be regarded —in one plane of thought, as we have just seen—as equivalent to the second characteristic of matter corresponding to the second perceptive faculty or sense of man. But these two linked scales of evolution are concerned with the processes going on within the limits of a single Round. The succession of primary aspects of Nature with which the succession of Rounds is concerned, has to do, as already indicated, with the development of the "Elements" (in the Occult sense)—Fire, Air, Water,* Earth. We are only in the fourth Round, and our catalogue so far stops short. The centres of consciousness (destined to develop into humanity as we know it) of the third Round arrived at a perception of the third Element Water.† Those of the fourth Round have added

---

* The order in which these Elements are placed above is the correct one for esoteric purposes and in the Secret Teachings. Milton was right when he spoke of the " Powers of Fire, Air, Water, Earth " ; the Earth, such as we know it now, had no existence before the 4th Round, hundreds of million years ago, the commencement of our geological Earth. The globe was " *fiery, cool and radiant* as its ethereal men and animals during the first Round," says the Commentary, uttering a contradiction or paradox in the opinion of our present Science ; " *luminous* and more dense and heavy—during the second Round ; *watery* during the Third ! " Thus are the elements reversed.

† If we had to frame our conclusions according to the data furnished to us by the

earth as a state of matter to their stock as well as the three other elements in their present transformation. In short, none of the so-called elements were, in the three preceding Rounds, as they are now. For all we know, FIRE may have been *pure* AKASA, the first Matter of the *Magnum Opus* of the Creators and " Builders," that Astral Light which the paradoxical Eliphas Lévi calls in one breath " the body of the Holy Ghost," and in the next " Baphomet," the " Androgyne Goat of Mendes"*; AIR, simply

---

geologists, then we would say that there was no real water—even during the Carboniferous period. We are told that gigantic masses of carbon, which existed formerly spread in the atmosphere as Carbonic Acid, were absorbed by plants, while a large proportion of that gas was mixed in the water. Now, if this be so, and we have to believe that all the Carbonic Acid which went to compose those plants that formed bituminous coal, lignite, etc., and went towards the formation of limestone, and so on, that all this was at that period in the atmosphere in gaseous form, then, there must have been seas and oceans of liquid carbonic acid? But how then could the carboniferous period be preceded by the Devonian and Silurian ages—those of Fishes and Molluscs—on that assumption? Barometric pressure, moreover, must have exceeded several hundred times the pressure of our present atmosphere. How could organisms, even so simple as those of certain fishes and molluscs, stand that? There is a curious work by Blanchard, on the Origin of Life, wherein he shows some strange contradictions and confusions in the theories of his colleagues, and which we recommend to the reader's attention.

* Eliphas Lévi shows it very truly " a force in Nature," by means of which " a single man who can master it . . . might throw the world into confusion and transform its face "; for it is the " great Arcanum of transcendent Magic." Quoting the words of the great Western Kabalist in their translated form (see *The Mysteries of Magic*, by A. E. Waite), we may explain them perhaps the better by the occasional addition of a word or two to show the difference between Western and Eastern explanations of the same subject. The Author says of the great Magic Agent—" This ambient and all-penetrating fluid, this ray detached from the (Central or ' Spiritual ') Sun's splendour . . . fixed by the weight of the atmosphere (? !) and the power of central attraction . . . the Astral Light, this electro-magnetic ether, this vital and luminous caloric, is represented on ancient monuments by the girdle of Isis which twines round two poles . . . and in ancient theogonies by the serpent devouring its own tail, emblem of prudence and of Saturn "— emblem of infinity, immortality, and Kronos—" Time "—not the god Saturn or the planet. " It is the winged dragon of Medea, the double serpent of the caduceus, and the tempter of Genesis; but it is also the brazen snake of Moses encircling the Tau . . . lastly, it is the devil of exoteric dogmatism, and is really the blind force (it is not blind, and Lévi knew it), which souls must conquer in order to detach themselves from the chains of Earth; ' for if they should not,' they will be absorbed by the same power which first produced them and will return to the central and eternal fire." This great *archæus* is now discovered by, and only *for one man*—Mr. J. W. Keeley, of

Nitrogen, " the breath of the Supporters of the Heavenly Dome," as the Mahometan mystics call it ; WATER, that primordial fluid which was required, according to Moses, to make *a living soul* with. And this may account for the flagrant discrepancies and unscientific statements found in Genesis. Separate the first from the second chapter ; read the former as a scripture of the Elohists, and the latter as that of the far younger Jehovists ; still one finds, if one reads between the lines, the same order in which things created appear—namely, Fire (light), Air, Water, and MAN (or the Earth). For the sentence : " In the beginning God created Heaven and Earth" is a mistranslation ; it is not " Heaven and Earth," but the *duplex* or dual Heaven, the *upper* and the *lower* Heavens, or the separation of primordial substance that was light in its upper and dark in its lower portions—or the manifested Universe—in its duality of the *invisible* (to the senses) and the *visible* to our perceptions. God divided the light from the Darkness (v. 4) ; and then made the firmament, air (5), " a firmament in the midst of the waters, and let it divide the waters from the waters," (6), *i.e.*, " the waters which were under the firmament (our manifested visible Universe) from the waters *above* the firmament," or the (to us) invisible planes of being. In the second chapter (the Jehovistic), plants and herbs are created before water, just as in the first, *light is produced before the Sun.* " God made the Earth and the Heavens and every plant of the field *before it was in the Earth* and every herb of the field *before it grew ;* for the Elohim (' gods ') had not caused it to rain upon the earth, etc." (v. 5)— an absurdity unless the esoteric explanation is accepted. The plants *were* created before they were in the earth—*for there was no earth then such as it is now ;* and the herb of the field was in existence before it grew as it does now in the fourth Round.

Discussing and explaining the nature of the invisible Elements and the " primordial fire " mentioned above, Eliphas Lévi calls it invariably the " Astral Light." It is the " grand Agent Magique " with him ; undeniably it is so, but—only so far as *Black* Magic is concerned, and

---

Philadelphia. For others, however, it *is* discovered, yet must remain almost useless. " So far shalt thou go. . . . "

All the above is as practical as it is correct, save one error, which we will explain in the text further on. Eliphas Lévi commits a great blunder in always identifying the Astral Light with what we call Akâsa. What it really is will be given in Part II. of Vol. II.

on the lowest planes of what we call Ether, the noumenon of which is Akâsa ; and even this would be held incorrect by orthodox Occultists. The " Astral Light " is simply the older " *sidereal* Light " of Paracelsus ; and to say that " everything which exists has been evolved from it, and it preserves and reproduces all forms," as he writes, is to enunciate truth only in the second proposition. The first is erroneous ; for if all that exists was evolved *through* (or *via*) it, it is not the astral light. The latter is not the container of *all* things but only the reflector, at best, of this *all*. Eliphas Lévi writes :—

" The great Magic agent is the fourth emanation of the life principle (we say—it is the first in the inner, and the second in the outer (our) Universe), of which the Sun is the third form . . . for the day-star (the sun) is only the reflection and material shadow of the Central Sun of truth, which illuminates the intellectual (invisible) world of Spirit and which itself is but a gleam borrowed from the ABSOLUTE."

So far he is right enough. But when the great authority of the Western Kabalists adds that nevertheless, " it is not the immortal Spirit as the Indian Hierophants have imagined "—we answer that he slanders the said Hierophants, as they have said nothing of the kind ; while even the Purânic exoteric writings flatly contradict the assertion. No Hindu has ever mistaken *Prakriti*—the Astral Light being only above the lowest plane of Prakriti, the material Kosmos— for the "immortal Spirit." Prakriti is ever called *Maya*, illusion, and is doomed to disappear with the rest, the gods included, at the hour of the Pralaya ; for it is shown that Akâsa is not even the Ether, least of all then, we imagine, can it be the Astral Light. Those unable to penetrate beyond the dead letter of the Purânas, have occasionally confused Akâsa with Prakriti, with Ether, and even with the visible Sky ! It is true also that those who have invariably translated the term Akâsa by " Ether " (Wilson, for instance), finding it called " the material cause of sound " possessing, moreover, this *one single property* (Vishnu Purâna), have ignorantly imagined it to be " material," in the physical sense. True, again, that if the characteristics are accepted literally, then, since nothing material or physical, and there-fore conditioned and temporary can be immortal—according to meta-physics and philosophy—it would follow that Akâsa is neither infinite nor immortal. But all this is erroneous, since both the words *Pradhâna*

256 THE SECRET DOCTRINE.

(primeval matter) and *sound*, as a property, have been misunderstood; the former term (Pradhâna) being certainly synonymous with *Mulaprakriti* and Akâsa, and the latter (sound) with the Verbum, the Word or the Logos. This is easy to demonstrate; for it is shown in the following sentences in Vishnu Purâna: "In the beginning there was neither day nor night, nor sky, nor earth, nor darkness, nor light. . . . . Save only ONE, unapprehensible by intellect, or that which is Brahma and Pums (Spirit) and Pradhâna (primordial matter)." . . . . (Book I., ch. ii.).

Now, what is Pradhâna, if it is not Mulaprakriti, the root of all, in another aspect ? For Pradhâna, though said further on to merge into the Deity as everything else does, in order to leave the ONE absolute during the Pralaya, yet is held as infinite and immortal. The Commentator describes the Deity as: "One *Pradhánika* Brahma Spirit: THAT, was," and interprets the compound term as a substantive, not as a derivative word used attributively, *i.e.*, like something conjoined with Pradhâna.* Hence Pradhâna even in the Purânas is an aspect of Parabrahmam, not an evolution, and must be the same as the Vedantic Mulaprakriti. " Prakriti in its *primary* state is Akâsa," says a Vedantin scholar (see " Five Years of Theosophy," p. 169). It is almost abstract Nature.

Akâsa, then, is Pradhâna in another form, and as such cannot be Ether, the ever-invisible agent, courted even by physical Science. Nor is it Astral Light. It is, as said, the *noumenon* of the seven-fold differentiated Prakriti†—the ever immaculate " Mother " of the *fatherless* Son, who becomes " Father" on the lower manifested plane. For MAHAT is the first product of Pradhâna, or Akâsa, and Mahat—Universal intelligence " whose *characteristic property* is Buddhi"—is no other than the *Logos*, for he is called " Eswara" Brahmâ, Bhâva, etc. (See *Linga Purâna*, sec. lxx. 12 *et seq.* ; and Vâyu Purâna, but especially the former Purâna—prior, section viii., 67-74). He is, in short, the " Creator" or the divine mind in creative operation, " the cause of all things." He is

---

* The student has to note, moreover, that the Purâna is a dualistic system, not evolutionary, and that, in this respect, far more will be found, from an esoteric standpoint, in Sankhya, and even in the *Mânava-dharma-Sâstra*, however much the latter differs from the former.

† In the Sankhya philosophy, the seven Prakritis or " productive productions " are *Mahat, Ahamkara,* and the *five tanmatras.* See " *Sankhya-kârika,*" III., and the Commentary thereon.

the " first-born" of whom the Purânas tell us that " Mahat and matter
are the inner and outer boundaries of the Universe," or, in our language,
the negative and the positive poles of dual nature (abstract and concrete),
for the Purâna adds : " In this manner—as were the *seven* forms (principles) of Prakriti reckoned from Mahat to Earth—so at the time of
pralaya (pratyâhâra) these seven successively re-enter into each other.
The egg of Brahmâ (Sarva-mandala) is dissolved with its seven zones
(dwipa), seven oceans, seven regions, etc." (Vishnu Purâna, Book
vi., ch. iv.)*

These are the reasons why the Occultists refuse to give the name of
Astral Light to Akâsa, or to call it Ether. " In my Father's house are
many mansions," may be contrasted with the occult saying, " In our
Mother's house there are seven mansions," or planes, the lowest of
which is above and around us—the Astral Light.

The elements, whether simple or compound, could not have remained
the same since the commencement of the evolution of our chain.
Everything in the Universe progresses steadily in the Great Cycle,
while incessantly going up and down in the smaller cycles. Nature is
never stationary during manvantara, as it is ever *becoming*,† not simply
being ; and mineral, vegetable, and human life are always adapting their
organisms to the then reigning Elements, and therefore *those* Elements
were then fitted for them, as they are now for the life of present
humanity. It will only be in the next, or fifth, Round that the fifth
Element, *Ether*—the gross body of Akâsa, if it can be called even that—

* No use to say so to the Hindus, who know their Purânas by heart, but very
useful to remind our Orientalists and those Westerns who regard Wilson's translations
as authoritative, that in his English translation of the Vishnu Purâna he is guilty of
the most ludicrous contradictions and errors. So on this identical subject of the seven
Prakritis or the seven zones of Brahma's egg, the two accounts differ totally. In Vol.
I, page 40, the egg is said to be externally invested by seven envelopes—Wilson comments : " by Water, Air, Fire, Ether, and Ahamkâra " (which last word does not exist in
the Sanskrit texts) ; and in vol. v., p. 198, of the same Vishnu Purana it is written, "in
this manner were the seven forms of nature (Prakriti) reckoned from Mahat to Earth "
(?). Between Mahat or Maha-Buddhi and " Water, etc.," the difference is very
considerable.

† According to the great metaphysician Hegel also. For him Nature was a *perpetual
becoming.* A purely esoteric conception. Creation or Origin, in the Christian sense of
the term, is absolutely unthinkable. As the above-quoted thinker said : " God (the
Universal Spirit) *objectivises himsel as Nature*, and again rises out of it."

will, by becoming a familiar fact of Nature to all men, as air is familiar to us now, cease to be as at present hypothetical, and also an "agent" for so many things. And only during that Round will those higher senses, the growth and development of which Akâsa subserves, be susceptible of a complete expansion. As already indicated, a *partial* familiarity with the characteristic of matter—permeability—which should be developed concurrently with the sixth sense, may be expected to develop at the proper period in this Round. But with the next element added to our resources in the next Round, *permeability* will become so manifest a characteristic of matter, that the densest forms of this will seem to man's perceptions as obstructive to him as a thick fog, and no more.

Let us return to the life-cycle now. Without entering at length upon the description given of the *higher* LIVES, we must direct our attention at present simply to the earthly beings and the earth itself. The latter, we are told, is built up for the first Round by the "Devourers" which disintegrate and differentiate the germs of other lives in the Elements ; pretty much, it must be supposed, as in the present stage of the world, the *ærobes* do, when, undermining and loosening the chemical structure in an organism, they transform animal matter and generate substances that vary in their constitutions. Thus Occultism disposes of the so-called Azoic age of Science, for it shows that there never was a time when the Earth was without life upon it. Wherever there is an atom of matter, a particle or a molecule, even in its most gaseous condition, there is life in it, however latent and unconscious. "*What-soever quits the Laya State, becomes active life ; it is drawn into the vortex of MOTION (the alchemical solvent of Life); Spirit and Matter are the two States of the ONE, which is neither Spirit nor Matter, both being the absolute life, latent.*" (*Book of Dzyan, Comm. III., par.* 18). . . . "*Spirit is the first differentiation of (and in) SPACE; and Matter the first differentiation of Spirit. That, which is neither Spirit nor matter—that is IT—the Causeless CAUSE of Spirit and Matter, which are the Cause of Kosmos. And THAT we call the ONE LIFE or the Intra-Cosmic Breath.*"

Once more we will say—*like must produce like.* Absolute Life cannot produce an inorganic atom whether single or complex, and there is life even in *laya* just as a man in a profound cataleptic state—to all appearance a corpse—is still a living being.

When the "Devourers" (in whom the men of science are invited to see, with some show of reason, atoms of the Fire-Mist, if they will, as the Occultist will offer no objection to this) ; when the "Devourers," we say, have differentiated "the fire-atoms" by a peculiar process of segmentation, the latter become life-germs, which aggregate according to the laws of cohesion and affinity. Then the life-germs produce lives of another kind, which work on the structure of our globes. * * * *

Thus, in the first Round, the globe, having been built by the primitive fire-lives, *i.e.*, formed into a sphere—had no solidity, nor qualifications, save a cold brightness, nor form nor colour ; it is only towards the end of the First Round that it developed one Element which from its inorganic, so to say, or simple Essence became now in our Round the fire we know throughout the system. The Earth was in her first rupa, the essence of which is the Akâsic principle named *** "that which is now known as, and very erroneously termed, Astral Light, which Eliphas Lévi calls "the imagination of Nature," † probably to avoid giving it its correct name, as others do.

" *It is through and from the radiations of the seven bodies of the seven orders of Dhyanis, that the seven discrete quantities (Elements), whose motion and harmonious Union produce the manifested Universe of Matter, are born.*" *(Commentary.)*

---

† Speaking of it in his Preface to the "History of Magic" Eliphas Lévi says : "It is through this Force that all the nervous centres secretly communicate with each other ; from it—that sympathy and antipathy are born ; from it—that we have our dreams ; and that the phenomena of second sight and extra-natural visions take place. . . . . Astral Light, acting under the impulsion of powerful wills, destroys, coagulates, separates, breaks, gathers in all things. . . . God created it on that day when he said : *Fiat Lux*, and it is directed by the *Egregores*, *i.e.*, the chiefs of the souls who are the spirits of energy and action." Eliphas Lévi ought to have added that the astral light, or primordial substance, if matter at all, is that which, called *Light*, Lux, esoterically explained, *is the body of those Spirits themselves, and their very essence. Our physical light is the manifestation on our plane* and the reflected radiance of the *Divine* Light emanating from the collective body of those who are called the " Lights "and the " Flames." But no other Kabalist has ever had the talent of heaping up one contradiction on the other, of making one paradox chase another in the same sentence and in such flowing language, as Eliphas Lévi. He leads his reader through the most lovely, gorgeously blooming valleys, to strand him after all on a desert and barren rocky island.

The Second Round brings into manifestation the second element—AIR, that element, the purity of which would ensure continuous life to him who would use it. There have been two occultists only in Europe who have discovered and even partially applied it in practice, though its composition has always been known among the highest Eastern Initiates. The ozone of the modern chemists is poison compared with the real universal solvent which could never be thought of unless it existed in nature. "*From the second Round, Earth—hitherto a fœtus in the matrix of Space—began its real existence : it had developed individual sentient life, its second principle. The second corresponds to the sixth (principle) ; the second is life continuous, the other, temporary.*"

The *Third* Round developed the *third* Principle—WATER ; while the Fourth transformed the gaseous fluids and plastic form of our globe into the hard, crusted, grossly material sphere we are living on. "Bhumi" has reached her *fourth* principle. To this it may be objected that the law of analogy, so much insisted upon, is broken. Not at all. Earth will reach her true ultimate form—(inversely in this to man)—her body shell—only toward the end of the manvantara after the Seventh Round. Eugenius Philalethes was right when he assured his readers *on his word of honour* that no one had yet seen *the Earth* (*i.e.*, MATTER in its essential form). Our globe is, so far, in its *Kamarupic* state—the astral body of desires of *Ahamkara*, dark Egotism, the progeny of Mahat, on the lower plane. . . .

It is not molecularly constituted matter—least of all the human body (*sthulasarira*)—that is the grossest of all our "principles," but verily the *middle* principle, the real animal centre ; whereas our body is but its shell, the irresponsible factor and medium through which the beast in us acts all its life. Every intellectual theosophist will understand my real meaning. Thus the idea that the human tabernacle is built by countless *lives*, just in the same way as the rocky crust of our Earth was, has nothing repulsive in it for the true mystic. Nor can Science oppose the occult teaching, for it is not because the microscope will ever fail to detect the ultimate living atom or life, that it can reject the doctrine.

(*c*) Science teaches us that the living as well as the dead organism of both man and animal are swarming with bacteria of a hundred various kinds; that from without we are threatened with the invasion of microbes with every breath we draw, and from within by leucomaines, ærobes, anærobes, and what not. But Science never yet went so far as to assert with the occult doctrine that our bodies, as well as those of animals, plants, and stones, are themselves altogether built up of such beings; which, except larger species, no microscope can detect. So far, as regards the purely animal and material portion of man, Science is on its way to discoveries that will go far towards corroborating this theory. Chemistry and physiology are the two great magicians of the future, who are destined to open the eyes of mankind to the great physical truths. With every day, the identity between the animal and physical man, between the plant and man, and even between the reptile and its nest, the rock, and man—is more and more clearly shown. The physical and chemical constituents of all being found to be identical, chemical science may well say that there is no difference between the matter which composes the ox and that which forms man. But the Occult doctrine is far more explicit. It says:—Not only the chemical compounds are the same, but the same infinitesimal *invisible lives* compose the atoms of the bodies of the mountain and the daisy, of man and the ant, of the elephant, and of the tree which shelters him from the sun. Each particle—whether you call it organic or inorganic—*is a life*. Every atom and molecule in the Universe is both *life-giving* and *death-giving* to that form, inasmuch as it builds by aggregation universes and the ephemeral vehicles ready to receive the transmigrating soul, and as eternally destroys and changes the *forms* and expels those souls from their temporary abodes. It creates and kills; it is self-generating and self-destroying; it brings into being, and annihilates, that mystery of mysteries—the *living body* of man, animal, or plant, every second in time and space; and it generates equally life and death, beauty and ugliness, good and bad, and even the agreeable and disagreeable, the beneficent and maleficent sensations. It is that mysterious LIFE, represented collectively by countless myriads of lives, that follows in its own sporadic way, the hitherto incomprehensible law of Atavism; that copies family resemblances as well as those it finds impressed in the aura of the generators of every future human being, a mystery, in short, that will receive fuller attention elsewhere. For the present, one instance may be cited in illustration. Modern science begins to find out that ptomaïne (the alkaloid poison generated by decaying matter and corpses — a *life* also) extracted

with the help of volatile ether, yields a smell as strong and equal
to that of the freshest orange-blossoms ; but that free from oxygen,
these alkaloids yield either a most sickening, disgusting smell, or
the most agreeable aroma which recalls that of the most delicately
scented flowers. And it is suspected that such blossoms owe their
agreeable smell to the poisonous ptomaïne ; the venomous essence
of certain mushrooms (fungi) being nearly identical with the venom
of the cobra of India, the most deadly of serpents.* Thus, having discovered the effects, Science has to find their PRIMARY causes ; and this
it can never do without the help of the old sciences, of alchemy, occult
botany and physics. We are taught that every physiological change, in
addition to pathological phenomena ; diseases—nay, life itself—or rather
the objective phenomena of life, produced by certain conditions and
changes in the tissues of the body which allow and force life to act in
that body ; that all this is due to those unseen CREATORS and DESTROYERS
that are called in such a loose and general way, microbes.†   Such

* The French savants Arnaud, Gautier, and Villiers, have found in the saliva of living
men the same venomous alkaloid as in that of the toad, the salamander, the cobra,
and the trigonocephalus of Portugal. It is proven that venom of the deadliest kind,
whether called ptomaïne, or leucomaine, or alkaloid, is generated by living men,
animals, and plants. The same savant, Gautier, discovered an alkaloid in the fresh meat
of an ox and in its brains, and a venom which he calls Xanthocreatinine similar to the
substance extracted from the poisonous saliva of reptiles. It is the muscular tissues,
as being the most active organ in the animal economy, that are suspected of being the
generators or factors of venoms, having the same importance as carbonic acid and urea
in the functions of life, which venoms are the ultimate products of inner combustion.
And though it is not yet fully determined whether poisons can be generated by the
animal system of living beings without the participation and interference of microbes,
it is ascertained that the animal does produce venomous substances in its physiological
or living state.

† It might be supposed that these "fiery lives" and the microbes of science are
identical. This is not true. The "fiery lives" are the seventh and highest sub-
division of the plane of matter, and correspond in the individual with the One Life of
the Universe, though only on that plane. The microbes of science are the first and
lowest sub-division on the second plane—that of material *prâna* (or life). The physical
body of man undergoes a complete change of structure every seven years, and its
destruction and preservation are due to the alternate function of the fiery lives as
"destroyers" and "builders." They are "builders" by sacrificing themselves in the
form of vitality to restrain the destructive influence of the microbes, and, by supplying
the microbes with what is necessary, they compel them under that restraint to build
up the material body and its cells. They are "destroyers" also when that restraint is

experimenters as Pasteur are the best friends and helpers of the De-stroyers and the worst enemies of the Creators—if the latter were not at the same time destroyers too.   However it may be, one thing is sure in this : The knowledge of these primary causes and of the ultimate essence of every element, of its lives, their functions, properties, and conditions of change—constitutes the basis of MAGIC.   Paracelsus was, perhaps, the only Occultist in Europe, during the last centuries since the Christian era, who was versed in this mystery.   Had not a criminal hand put an end to his life, years before the time allotted him by Nature, physio-logical Magic would have fewer secrets for the civilized world than it now has.

(*d*) But what has the Moon to do in all this ? we may be asked. What have " Fish, Sin and Moon " in the apocalyptic saying of the Stanza to do in company with the " Life-microbes " ?   With the latter nothing, except availing themselves of the tabernacle of clay prepared by them ; with divine perfect man everything, since " Fish, Sin and Moon " make conjointly the three symbols of the immortal Being.

This is all that can be given.   Nor does the writer pretend to know more of this strange symbol than may be inferred about it from exoteric religions ; from the mystery perhaps, which underlies the *Matsya* (fish)

---

removed and the microbes, unsupplied with vital constructive energy, are left to run riot as destructive *agents*. Thus, during the first half of a man's life (the first *five* periods of seven years each) the " fiery lives " are indirectly engaged in the process of building up man's material body ; life is on the ascending scale, and the force is used in construction and increase. After this period is passed the age of retrogression commences, and, the work of the " fiery lives " exhausting their strength, the work of destruction and decrease also commences.

An analogy between cosmic events in the descent of spirit into matter for the first half of a manvantara (planetary as human) and its ascent at the expense of matter in the second half, may here be traced. These considerations have to do solely with the plane of matter, but the restraining influence of the " fiery lives " on the lowest sub-division of the second plane—the microbes—is confirmed by the fact mentioned in the foot-note on Pasteur (*vide supra*) that the cells of the organs, when they do not find sufficient oxygen for themselves, adapt themselves to that condition and form *ferments*, which, by absorbing oxygen from substances coming in contact with them, ruin the latter. Thus the process is commenced by one cell robbing its neigh-bour of the source of its vitality when the supply is insufficient ; and the ruin so commenced steadily progresses.

Avatar of Vishnu, the Chaldean Oannes—the Man-Fish, recorded in the imperishable sign of the Zodiac, *Pisces*, and running throughout the two Testaments in the personages of Joshua " Son of the Fish (Nun) " and Jesus ; the allegorical " Sin " or Fall of Spirit into matter, and the Moon—in so far as it relates to the " Lunar " ancestors, the Pitris.

For the present it may be as well to remind the reader that while the Moon-goddesses were connected in every mythology, especially the Grecian, with child-birth, because of the lunar influence on women and conception, the occult and actual connection of our satellite with fecundation is to this day unknown to physiology, which regards every popular practice in this reference as gross superstition. As it is useless to discuss them in detail, we may only stop at present to discuss the lunar symbology casually, to show that the said superstition belongs to the most ancient beliefs, and even to Judaism—the basis of Christianity. With the Israelites, the chief function of Jehovah was child-giving, and the esotericism of the Bible, interpreted Kabalistically, shows undeniably the Holy of Holies in the temple to be only the symbol of the womb. This is now proven beyond doubt and cavil, by the *numerical* reading of the Bible in general, and of Genesis especially. This idea must certainly have been borrowed by the Jews from the Egyptians and Indians, whose Holy of Holies was, and with the latter is to this day, symbolised by the King's chamber in the Great Pyramid (see " *Source of Measures* ") and the Yoni symbols of exoteric Hinduism. To make the whole clearer and to show at the same time the enormous difference in the spirit of interpretation and the original meaning of the same symbols between the ancient Eastern Occultists and the Jewish Kabalists we refer the reader to Book II., " The Holy of Holies."*

<hr>

STANZA VII.—*Continued.*

6. FROM THE FIRST-BORN (*primitive, or the first man*) THE THREAD BETWEEN THE SILENT WATCHER AND HIS SHADOW BECOMES MORE

---

* Phallic worship has developed only with the loss of the keys to the true meaning of the symbols. It was the last and most fatal turning point from the highway of truth and divine knowledge into the side path of fiction, raised into dogma through human falsification and hierarchic ambition.

STRONG AND RADIANT WITH EVERY CHANGE (*re-incarnation*) (*a*). THE
MORNING SUN-LIGHT HAS CHANGED INTO NOON-DAY GLORY . . . .

(*a*) This sentence: " The thread between the *silent watcher* and his
shadow (man) becomes stronger "—with every re-incarnation—is another
psychological mystery, that will find its explanation in Book II. For
the present it will suffice to say that the " Watcher" and his " Shadows "
—the latter numbering as many as there are re-incarnations for the
monad—are one. The Watcher, or the divine prototype, is at the
upper rung of the ladder of being ; the shadow, at the lower. Withal,
the *Monad* of every living being, unless his moral turpitude breaks the
connection and runs loose and " astray into the lunar path "—to use the
Occult expression—*is an individual Dhyan Chohan, distinct from others, a
kind of spiritual individuality of its own*, during one special Manvantara. Its
Primary, the Spirit (Atman) is one, of course, with *Paramâtma* (the one
Universal Spirit), but the vehicle (Vahan) it is enshrined in, the *Buddhi*,
is part and parcel of that Dhyan-Chohanic Essence ; and it is in this
that lies the mystery of that *ubiquity*, which was discussed a few pages
back. " My Father, that is in Heaven, and I—are one,"—says the
Christian Scripture ; in this, at any rate, it is the faithful echo of the
esoteric tenet.

STANZA VII.—*Continued.*

7. THIS IS THY PRESENT WHEEL—SAID THE FLAME TO THE SPARK.
THOU ART MYSELF, MY IMAGE AND MY SHADOW. I HAVE CLOTHED
MYSELF IN THEE, AND THOU ART MY VAHAN *(vehicle)* TO THE DAY, " BE
WITH US," WHEN THOU SHALT RE-BECOME MYSELF AND OTHERS, THYSELF
AND ME (*a*), THEN THE BUILDERS, HAVING DONNED THEIR FIRST CLOTHING,
DESCEND ON RADIANT EARTH, AND REIGN OVER MEN—WHO ARE THEM-
SELVES (*b*).

(*a*) The day when " the spark will re-become the Flame (man will
merge into his Dhyan Chohan) myself and others, thyself and me," as
the Stanza has it—means this : In *Paranirvana*—when *Pralaya* will have
reduced not only material and psychical bodies, but even the spiritual
Ego(s) to their original principle—the Past, Present, and even Future

Humanities, like all things, will be one and the same. Everything will have re-entered the *Great Breath.* In other words, everything will be " merged in Brahma " or the divine unity.

Is this annihilation, as some think ? Or *Atheism,* as other critics—the worshippers of a *personal* deity and believers in an unphilosophical paradise—are inclined to suppose ? Neither. It is worse than useless to return to the question of implied atheism in that which is *spirituality* of a most refined character. To see in Nirvana annihilation amounts to saying of a man plunged in a sound *dreamless* sleep—*one that leaves no impression on the physical memory and brain, because the sleeper's Higher Self is in its original state of absolute consciousness* during those hours—that he, too, is annihilated. The latter simile answers only to one side of the question —the most material ; since *re-absorption* is by no means such a " dreamless sleep," but, on the contrary, *absolute* existence, an unconditioned unity, or a state, to describe which human language is absolutely and hopelessly inadequate. The only approach to anything like a comprehensive conception of it can be attempted solely in the panoramic visions of the soul, through spiritual ideations of the divine monad. Nor is the individuality—*nor even the essence of the personality*, if any be left behind— lost, because re-absorbed. For, however limitless—from a human standpoint—the paranirvanic state, it has yet a limit in Eternity. Once reached, the same monad will *re-emerge* therefrom, as a still higher being, on a far higher plane, to recommence its cycle of perfected activity. The human mind cannot in its present stage of development transcend, scarcely reach this plane of thought. It totters here, on the brink of incomprehensible Absoluteness and Eternity.

(*b*) The " Watchers " reign over man during the whole period of *Satya Yuga* and the smaller subsequent yugas, down to the beginning of the Third Root Race ; after which it is the Patriarchs, Heroes, and the Manes *(see Egyptian Dynasties enumerated by the priests to Solon)*, the incarnated Dhyanis of a lower order, up to King Menes and the human kings of other nations ; all were recorded carefully. In the views of symbologists this *Mythopœic Age* is of course only regarded as a fairy tale. But since traditions and even Chronicles of such dynasties of *divine* Kings—of gods reigning over men followed by dynasties of Heroes or Giants—exist in the annals of every nation, it is difficult to understand how all the peoples under the sun, some of whom are separated by vast oceans and belong to different hemispheres, such as the ancient Peruvians and Mexicans, as well as the Chaldeans, could have worked out the same "fairy tales" in the same order of events.* However, as the Secret Doctrine teaches *history*—which, for being esoteric and traditional, is none the less more reliable than profane history—we are as entitled to our beliefs as anyone else, whether religionist or sceptic. And that Doctrine says that the Dhyani-Buddhas of the two higher groups, namely, the "Watchers" or the "Architects," furnished the many and various races with divine kings and leaders. It is the latter who taught humanity their arts and sciences, and the former who revealed to the incarnated Monads that had just shaken off their vehicles of the lower Kingdoms—and who had, therefore, lost every recollection of their divine origin—the great spiritual truths of the transcendental worlds. (See Book II., "Divine Dynasties.")

Thus, as expressed in the Stanza, the Watchers descended on Earth and reigned over men—"*who are themselves.*" The reigning kings had finished their cycle on Earth and other worlds, in the preceding Rounds. In the future manvantaras they will have risen to higher systems than our planetary world; and it is the Elect of our Humanity, the Pioneers on the hard and difficult path of Progress, who will take the places of their predecessors. The next great Manvantara will witness the men of our own life-cycle becoming the instructors and guides of a man-kind whose Monads may now yet be imprisoned—semi-conscious—in the most intellectual of the animal kingdom, while their lower principles will be animating, perhaps, the highest specimens of the Vegetable world.

Thus proceed the cycles of the septenary evolution, in Septennial nature; the Spiritual or divine; the psychic or semi-divine; the intel-lectual, the passional, the instinctual, or *cognitional;* the semi-corporeal and the purely material or physical natures. All these evolve and pro-gress cyclically, passing from one into another, in a double, centrifugal and centripetal way, *one* in their ultimate essence, *seven* in their aspects. The lowest, of course, is the one depending upon and subservient to

---

* See the "Sacred Mysteries among the Mayas and the Quiches, 11,500 years ago," by Auguste le Plongeon, who shows the identity between the Egyptian rites and beliefs and those of the people he describes. The ancient hieratic alphabets of the Maya and the Egyptians are almost identical.

our five physical senses.* Thus far, for individual, human, sentient, animal and vegetable life, each the microcosm of its higher macrocosm. The same for the Universe, which manifests periodically, for purposes of the collective progress of the countless *lives*, the outbreathings of the One *Life;* in order that through the *Ever-Becoming*, every cosmic atom in this infinite Universe, passing from the formless and the intangible, through the mixed natures of the semi-terrestrial, down to matter in full generation, and then back again, reascending at each new period higher and nearer the final goal; that each atom, we say, *may reach through individual merits and efforts* that plane where it re-becomes the one unconditioned ALL. But between the Alpha and the Omega there is the weary " Road " hedged in by thorns, that "goes down first, then—

Winds up hill all the way
Yes, to the very end. . . . ."

Starting upon the long journey immaculate; descending more and more into sinful matter, and having connected himself with every atom in manifested *Space*—the *Pilgrim*, having struggled through and suffered in every form of life and being, is only at the bottom of the valley of matter, and half through his cycle, when he has identified himself with collective Humanity. This, *he has made in his own image.* In order to progress upwards and homewards, the " God " has now to ascend the weary uphill path of the Golgotha of Life. It is the martyrdom of self-conscious existence. Like Visvakarman he has to sacrifice *himself to himself* in order to redeem all creatures, to resurrect from the many into the *One Life.* Then he ascends into heaven indeed; where, plunged into the incomprehensible absolute Being and Bliss of Para-nirvana, he reigns unconditionally, and whence he will re-descend again at the next " coming," which one portion of humanity expects in its dead-letter sense as the *second advent,* and the other as the last " Kalki Avatar."

---

* Which are in truth *seven* as shown later, on the authority of the oldest *Upanishads.*

SUMMING UP.

"The History of Creation and of this world from
its beginning up to the present time is composed of
seven chapters. The *seventh* chapter is not yet written."
(T. Subba Row, *Theosophist*, 1881.)

THE first of these Seven chapters has been attempted and is now finished. However incomplete and feeble as an exposition, it is, at any rate, an approximation—using the word in a mathematical sense—to that which is the oldest basis for all the subsequent Cosmogonies. The attempt to render in a European tongue the grand panorama of the ever periodically recurring Law—impressed upon the plastic minds of the first races endowed with Consciousness by those who reflected the same from the Universal Mind—is daring, for no human language, save the Sanskrit—which is that *of the Gods*—can do so with any degree of adequacy. But the failures in this work must be forgiven for the sake of the motive.

As a whole, neither the foregoing nor what follows can be found in full anywhere. It is not taught in any of the six Indian schools of philosophy, for it pertains to their synthesis—the seventh, which is the Occult doctrine. It is not traced on any crumbling papyrus of Egypt, nor is it any longer graven on Assyrian tile or granite wall. The Books of the *Vedanta* (the last word of human knowledge) give out but the metaphysical aspect of this world-Cosmogony; and their priceless thesaurus, the *Upanishads*—*Upa-ni-shad* being a compound word meaning "the conquest of ignorance by the revelation of *secret*, *spiritual* knowledge"—require now the additional possession of a Master-key to enable the student to get at their full meaning. The reason for this I venture to state here as I learned it from a Master.

The name, "*Upanishads*," is usually translated "esoteric doctrine.' These treatises form part of the *Sruti* or "revealed knowledge," *Revelation*, in short, and are generally attached to the *Brahmana* portion of the Vedas,* as their third division.   There are over 150 *Upanishads* enumerated by, and known to, Orientalists, who credit the oldest with being written *probably* about 600 years B.C.; but of *genuine* texts there does not exist a fifth of the number.   The Upanishads are to the Vedas what the Kabala is to the Jewish Bible. They treat of and expound the secret and mystic meaning of the Vedic texts.   They speak of the origin of the Universe, the nature of Deity, and of Spirit and Soul, as also of the metaphysical connection of mind and matter.   In a few words : They CONTAIN *the beginning and the end of all human knowledge, but they have now ceased to* REVEAL *it,* since the day of Buddha.   If it were otherwise, the Upanishads could not be called *esoteric,* since they are now openly attached to the Sacred Brahmanical books, which have, in our present age, become accessible even to the *Mlechchhas* (out-*castes*) and the European Orientalists.   One thing in them—and this in all the *Upanishads*—invariably and constantly points to their ancient origin, and proves (*a*) that they were written, in some of their portions, *before* the caste system became the tyrannical institution which it still is ; and (*b*) that half of their contents have been eliminated, while some of them were rewritten and abridged.   " The great Teachers of the higher Knowledge and the Brahmans are continually represented as going to Kshatriya (military caste) kings to become their pupils."   As Cowell pertinently remarks, the *Upanishads* " breathe an entirely different spirit " (from other Brahmanical writings), " a freedom of thought unknown in any earlier work except in the Rig Veda hymns themselves."   The second fact is explained by a tradition recorded in one of the MSS. on Buddha's life.   It says that the Upanishads were originally attached to their Brahmanas after the beginning of a reform, which led to the exclusiveness of the present caste system among the Brahmins, a few centuries after the invasion of India by the " twice-born."   They were complete in those days, and were used for the instruction of the chelas who were preparing for their initiation.

---

* . . . " The Vedas have a distinct dual meaning—one expressed by the literal sense of the words, the other indicated by the metre and the *swara*—intonation—which are as the life of the Vedas. . . . Learned pundits and philologists of course deny that *swara* has anything to do with philosophy or ancient esoteric doctrines; but the mysterious connection between *swara* and *light* is one of its most profound secrets." (T. Subba Row, *Five Years of Theosophy,* p. 154.)

This lasted so long as the Vedas and the Brahmanas remained in the sole and exclusive keeping of the temple-Brahmins—while no one else had the right to study or even read them outside of the *sacred* caste. Then came Gautama, the Prince of Kapilavastu. After *learning* the whole of the Brahmanical wisdom in the *Rahasya* or the *Upanishads*, and finding that the teachings differed little, if at all, from those of the "Teachers of Life" inhabiting the snowy ranges of the Himalaya, * the Disciple of the Brahmins, feeling indignant because the sacred wisdom was thus withheld from all but the Brahmins, determined to save the whole world by popularizing it. Then it was that the Brahmins, seeing that their sacred knowledge and Occult wisdom was falling into the hands of the "*Mlechchhas*," abridged the texts of the Upanishads, originally containing thrice the matter of the Vedas and the Brahmanas together, without altering, however, one word of the texts. They simply detached from the MSS. the most important portions containing the last word of the Mystery of Being. The key to the Brahmanical secret code remained henceforth with the initiates alone, and the Brahmins were thus in a position to publicly deny the correctness of Buddha's teaching by appealing to their *Upanishads*, silenced for ever on the chief questions. Such is the esoteric tradition beyond the Himalayas.

Sri Sankaracharya, the greatest Initiate living in the historical ages, wrote many a Bhâshya on the *Upanishads*. But his original treatises, as there are reasons to suppose, have not yet fallen into the hands of the Philistines, for they are too jealously preserved in his *maths* (monasteries, *mathams*). And there are still weightier reasons to believe that the priceless Bhâshyas (Commentaries) on the esoteric doctrine of the Brahmins, by their greatest expounder, will remain for ages yet a dead letter to most of the Hindus, except the *Smârtava* Brahmins. This sect, founded by Sankaracharya, (which is still very powerful in Southern India) is now almost the only one to produce students who have preserved sufficient knowledge to comprehend the

---

* Also called "the Sons of Wisdom," and of the "Fire-Mist" and the "Brothers of the Sun" in the Chinese records. *Si-dzang* (Tibet) is mentioned in the MSS. of the sacred library of the province of Fo-Kien, as the great seat of Occult learning from time immemorial, ages before Buddha. The Emperor Yu, the "great" (2,207 years B.C.), a pious mystic and great adept, is said to have obtained his knowledge from the "great teachers of the Snowy Range" in Si-dzang.

dead letter of the Bhashyas.   The reason of this is that they alone, I am informed, have occasionally real Initiates at their head in their mathams, as for instance, in the " Sringa-giri," in the Western Ghauts of Mysore.   On the other hand, there is no sect in that desperately exclusive caste of the Brahmins, more exclusive than is the Smârtava; and the reticence of its followers to say what they may know of the Occult sciences and the esoteric doctrine, is only equalled by their pride and learning.

Therefore the writer of the present statement must be prepared beforehand to meet with great opposition and even the denial of such statements as are brought forward in this work.   Not that any claim to infallibility, or to perfect correctness in every detail of all that which is herein said, was ever put forward.   Facts are there, and they can hardly be denied.   But, owing to the intrinsic difficulties of the subjects treated, and the almost insurmountable limitations of the English tongue (as of all other European languages) to express certain ideas, it is more than probable that the writer has failed to present the explanations in the best and in the clearest form;   yet all that could be done was done under every adverse circumstance, and this is the utmost that can be expected of any writer.

Let us recapitulate and show, by the vastness of the subjects expounded, how difficult, if not impossible, it is to do them full justice.

(1.) The Secret Doctrine is the accumulated Wisdom of the Ages, and its cosmogony alone is the most stupendous and elaborate system : *e.g.*, even in the exotericism of the Purânas.   But such is the mysterious power of Occult symbolism, that the facts which have actually occupied countless generations of initiated seers and prophets to marshal, to set down and explain, in the bewildering series of evolutionary progress, are all recorded on a few pages of geometrical signs and glyphs.   The flashing gaze of those seers has penetrated into the very kernel of matter, and recorded the soul of things there, where an ordinary profane, however learned, would have perceived but the external work of form.   But modern science believes not in the " soul of things," and hence will reject the whole system of ancient cosmogony.   It is useless to say that the system in question is no fancy of one or several isolated individuals. That it is the uninterrupted record covering thousands of generations of Seers whose respective experiences were made to test and to verify the

traditions passed orally by one early race to another, of the teachings of
higher and exalted beings, who watched over the childhood of Humanity.
That for long ages, the " Wise Men " of the Fifth Race, of the stock
saved and rescued from the last cataclysm and shifting of continents,
had passed their lives *in learning, not teaching.* How did they do so? It
is answered : by checking, testing, and verifying in every department of
nature the traditions of old by the independent visions of great adepts ;
i.e., men who have developed and perfected their physical, mental,
psychic, and spiritual organisations to the utmost possible degree. No
vision of one adept was accepted till it was checked and confirmed by
the visions—so obtained as to stand as independent evidence—of other
adepts, and by centuries of experiences.

(2.) The fundamental Law in that system, the central point from
which all emerged, around and toward which all gravitates, and upon
which is hung the philosophy of the rest, is the One homogeneous
divine SUBSTANCE-PRINCIPLE, the one radical cause.

> .   .   .   " Some few, whose lamps shone brighter, have been led
>   From cause to cause to nature's secret head,
>   And found that one first Principle must be. .   .   ."

It is called " Substance-Principle," for it becomes " substance " on the
plane of the manifested Universe, an illusion, while it remains a
" principle " in the beginningless and endless abstract, visible and
invisible SPACE. It is the omnipresent Reality : impersonal, because it
contains all and everything. *Its impersonality is the fundamental conception*
of the System. It is latent in every atom in the Universe, and is the
Universe itself. (See in chapters on Symbolism, " Primordial Substance,
and Divine Thought.")

(3.) The Universe is the periodical manifestation of this unknown
Absolute Essence. To call it " essence," however, is to sin against the
very spirit of the philosophy. For though the noun may be derived in
this case from the verb *esse,* " to be," yet IT cannot be identified with a
being of any kind, that can be conceived by human intellect. IT is
best described as neither Spirit nor matter, but both. " Parabrahmam
and Múlaprakriti " are One, in reality, yet two in the Universal conception of the manifested, even in the conception of the One Logos,
its first manifestation, to which, as the able lecturer in the " Notes on
the Bhagavadgita " shows, IT appears from the objective standpoint of

the One Logos as Mulaprakriti and not as Parabrahmam; as its *veil* and not the one REALITY hidden behind, which is unconditioned and absolute.

(4.) The Universe is called, with everything in it, MAYA, because all is temporary therein, from the ephemeral life of a fire-fly to that of the Sun. Compared to the eternal immutability of the ONE, and the changelessness of that Principle, the Universe, with its evanescent ever-changing forms, must be necessarily, in the mind of a philosopher, no better than a will-o'-the-wisp. Yet, the Universe is real enough to the conscious beings in it, which are as unreal as it is itself.

(5.) Everything in the Universe, throughout all its kingdoms, is CONSCIOUS: *i.e.*, endowed with a consciousness of its own kind and on its own plane of perception. We men must remember that because *we* do not perceive any signs—which we can recognise—of consciousness, say, in stones, we have no right to say that *no consciousness exists there.* There is no such thing as either " dead " or " blind " matter, as there is no " Blind " or " Unconscious " Law. These find no place among the conceptions of Occult philosophy. The latter never stops at surface appearances, and for it the *noumenal* essences have more reality than their objective counterparts; it resembles therein the mediæval *Nominalists*, for whom it was the Universals that were the realities and the particulars which existed only in name and human fancy.

(6.) The Universe is worked and *guided* from *within outwards*. As above so it is below, as in heaven so on earth; and man—the microcosm and miniature copy of the macrocosm—is the living witness to this Universal Law and to the mode of its action. We see that every *external* motion, act, gesture, whether voluntary or mechanical, organic or mental, is produced and preceded by *internal* feeling or emotion, will or volition, and thought or mind. As no outward motion or change, when normal, in man's external body can take place unless provoked by an inward impulse, given through one of the three functions named, so with the external or manifested Universe. The whole Kosmos is guided, controlled, and animated by almost endless series of Hierarchies of sentient Beings, each having a mission to perform, and who—whether we give to them one name or another, and call them Dhyan-Chohans or Angels—are " messengers " in the sense only that they are the agents of Karmic and Cosmic Laws. They vary infinitely in their respective degrees of consciousness and intelligence ; and to call them all pure Spirits without any of the earthly alloy " which time is wont to prey upon " is only to indulge in poetical fancy. For each of these Beings either *was*, or prepares to become, a man, if not in the present, then in a past or a coming cycle (Manvantara). They are *perfected*, when not *incipient*, men ; and differ morally from the terrestrial human beings on their higher (less material) spheres, only in that they are devoid of the feeling of personality and of the *human* emotional nature—two purely earthly characteristics. The former, or the " perfected," have become free from those feelings, because (*a*) they have no longer fleshly bodies —an ever-numbing weight on the Soul; and (*b*) the pure spiritual element being left untrammelled and more free, they are less influenced by *maya* than man can ever be, unless he is an adept who keeps his two personalities—the spiritual and the physical—entirely separated. The incipient monads, having never had terrestrial bodies yet, can have no sense of personality or EGO-ism. That which is meant by "personality," being a limitation and a relation, or, as defined by Coleridge, " individuality existing in itself but with a nature as a ground," the term cannot of course be applied to non-human entities ; but, as a fact insisted upon by generations of Seers, none of these Beings, high or low, have either individuality or personality as separate Entities, *i.e.*, they have no individuality in the sense in which a man says, "*I am myself* and no one else ; " in other words, they are conscious of no such distinct separateness as men and things have on earth. Individuality is the characteristic of their respective hierarchies, not of their units ; and these characteristics vary only with the degree of the plane to which those hierarchies belong : the nearer to the region of Homogeneity and the One Divine, the purer and the less accentuated that individuality in the Hierarchy. They are finite, in all respects, with the exception of their higher principles—the immortal sparks reflecting the universal divine flame—individualized and separated only on the spheres of Illusion by a differentiation as illusive as the rest. They are " Living Ones," because they are the streams projected on the Kosmic screen of illusion from the ABSOLUTE LIFE ; beings in whom life cannot become extinct, before the fire of ignorance is extinct in those who sense these " Lives." Having sprung into being under the quickening influence of the uncreated beam, the reflection of the great Central Sun that radiates on the shores of the river of Life, it is the inner principle in them which belongs to the waters of immortality, while its differentiated clothing is as perishable as man's body. Therefore Young was right in saying that

"Angels are men of a superior kind"

and no more. They are neither "ministering" nor "protecting" angels; nor are they "Harbingers of the Most High" still less the "Messengers of wrath" of any God such as man's fancy has created. To appeal to their protection is as foolish as to believe that their sympathy may be secured by any kind of propitiation; for they are, as much as man himself is, the slaves and creatures of immutable Karmic and Kosmic law. The reason for it is evident. Having no elements of personality in their essence they can have no personal qualities, such as attributed by men, in their exoteric religions, to their anthropomorphic God—a jealous and exclusive God who rejoices and feels wrathful, is pleased with sacrifice, and is more despotic in his vanity than any finite foolish man. Man, as shown in Book II., being a compound of the essences of all those celestial Hierarchies may succeed in making himself, as such, superior, in one sense, to any hierarchy or class, or even combination of them. "Man can neither propitiate nor command the *Devas*," it is said. But, by paralyzing his lower personality, and arriving thereby at the full knowledge of the *non-separateness* of his higher SELF from the One absolute SELF, man can, even during his terrestrial life, become as "One of Us." Thus it is, by eating of the fruit of knowledge which dispels ignorance, that man becomes like one of the Elohim or the Dhyanis; and once on *their* plane the Spirit of Solidarity and perfect Harmony, which reigns in every Hierarchy, must extend over him and protect him in every particular.

The chief difficulty which prevents men of science from believing in divine as well as in nature Spirits is their materialism. The main impediment before the Spiritualist which hinders him from believing in the same, while preserving a blind belief in the "Spirits" of the Departed, is the general ignorance of all, except some Occultists and Kabalists, about the true essence and nature of matter. It is on the acceptance or rejection of the theory of the *Unity of all in Nature, in its ultimate Essence*, that mainly rests the belief or unbelief in the existence around us of other conscious beings besides the Spirits of the Dead.

It is on the right comprehension of the primeval Evolution of Spirit-Matter and its real essence that the student has to depend for the further elucidation in his mind of the Occult Cosmogony, and for the only sure clue which can guide his subsequent studies.

In sober truth, as just shown, every " Spirit " so-called is either a *disembodied or a future man.* As from the highest Archangel (Dhyan Chohan) down to the last conscious " Builder " (the inferior class of Spiritual Entities), all such are *men*, having lived æons ago, in other Manvantaras, on this or other Spheres ; so the inferior, semi-intelligent and non-intelligent Elementals—are all *future* men. That fact alone—that a Spirit is endowed with intelligence—is a proof to the Occultist that that Being must have been a *man*, and acquired his knowledge and intelligence throughout the human cycle. There is but one indivisible and absolute Omniscience and Intelligence in the Universe, and this thrills throughout every atom and infinitesimal point of the whole finite Kosmos which hath no bounds, and which people call SPACE, considered independently of anything contained in it. But the first differentiation of its *reflection* in the manifested World is purely Spiritual, and the Beings generated in it are not endowed with a consciousness that has any relation to the one we conceive of. They can have no human consciousness or Intelligence before they have acquired such, personally and individually. This may be a mystery, yet it is a fact, in Esoteric philosophy, and a very apparent one too.

The whole order of nature evinces a progressive march towards *a higher life.* There is design in the action of the seemingly blindest forces. The whole process of evolution with its endless adaptations is a proof of this. The immutable laws that weed out the weak and feeble species, to make room for the strong, and which ensure the " survival of the fittest," though so cruel in their immediate action—all are working toward the grand end. The very *fact* that adaptations *do* occur, that the fittest *do* survive in the struggle for existence, shows that what is called " unconscious Nature "* is in reality an aggregate of forces mani-

---

* Nature taken m its abstract sense, *cannot* be " unconscious," as it is the emanation from, and thus an aspect (on the manifested plane) of the ABSOLUTE consciousness. Where is that daring man who would presume to deny to vegetation and even to minerals *a consciousness of their own.* All he can say is, that this consciousness is beyond his comprehension.

pulated by semi-intelligent beings (Elementals) guided by High Planetary Spirits, (Dhyan Chohans), whose collective aggregate forms the
manifested *verbum* of the unmanifested LOGOS, and constitutes at one and
the same time the MIND of the Universe and its immutable LAW.

Three distinct representations of the Universe in its three distinct
aspects are impressed upon our thought by the esoteric philosophy: the
PRE-EXISTING (evolved from) the EVER-EXISTING; and the PHENOMENAL
—the world of illusion, the reflection, and shadow thereof.   During the
great mystery and drama of life known as the Manvantara, real Kosmos
is like the object placed behind the white screen upon which are thrown
the Chinese shadows, called forth by the magic lantern.   The actual
figures and things remain invisible, while the wires of evolution are
pulled by the unseen hands ; and men and things are thus but the reflections, *on* the white field, of the realities *behind* the snares of *Mahamaya*, or
the great Illusion.   This was taught in every philosophy, in every religion, *ante* as well as *post* diluvian, in India and Chaldea, by the
Chinese as by the Grecian Sages.   In the former countries
these three Universes were allegorized, in exoteric teachings, by the
three trinities emanating from the Central eternal germ and forming
with it a Supreme Unity: the *initial*, the *manifested*, and the *Creative*
Triad, or the three in One.   The last is but the symbol, in its concrete
expression, of the first *ideal* two.   Hence Esoteric philosophy passes
over the necessarianism of this purely metaphysical conception, and
calls the first one, only, the Ever Existing.   This is the view of every
one of the six great schools of Indian philosophy—the *six principles of
that unit body of* WISDOM *of which the "gnosis,"* the *hidden* knowledge, is
the seventh.

The writer hopes that, superficially handled as may be the comments
on the Seven Stanzas, enough has been given in this cosmogonic portion
of the work to show Archaic teachings to be more *scientific* (in the
modern sense of the word) on their very face, than any other ancient
Scriptures left to be regarded and judged on their exoteric aspect.
Since, however, as confessed before, this work *withholds far more than it
gives out*, the student is invited to use his own intuitions.   Our
chief care is to elucidate that which has already been given out,
and, to our regret, very incorrectly at times; to supplement the
knowledge hinted at—whenever and wherever possible—by addi-

tional matter ; and to bulwark our doctrines against the too strong attacks of modern Sectarianism, and more especially against those of our latter-day Materialism, very often miscalled Science, whereas, in reality, the words " Scientists " and " Sciolists " ought alone to bear the responsibility for the many illogical theories offered to the world.   In its great ignorance, the public, while blindly accepting every-thing that emanates from " authorities," and feeling it to be its duty to regard every *dictum* coming from a man of Science as a proven fact—the public, we say, is taught to scoff at anything brought forward from " heathen " sources.   Therefore, as materialistic Scientists can be fought solely with their own weapons—those of controversy and argument—an *Addendum* is added to every Book contrasting our respective views and showing how even great authorities may often err. We believe that this can be done effectually by showing the weak points of our opponents, and by proving their too frequent sophisms—made to pass for scientific *dicta*—to be incorrect.   We hold to Hermes and his " Wisdom "—in its universal character; they—to Aristotle as against intuition and the experience of the ages, fancying that Truth is the exclusive property of the Western world.   Hence the disagreement. As Hermes says, " Knowledge differs much from sense ; for sense is of things that sur-mount it, but Knowledge (*gyi*) is the end of sense "—*i.e.*, of the illusion of our physical brain and its intellect ; thus emphasizing the contrast between the laboriously acquired knowledge of the senses and mind (manas), and the intuitive omniscience of the Spiritual divine Soul—Buddhi.

Whatever may be the destiny of these actual writings in a remote future, we hope to have proven so far the following facts :

(1) The Secret Doctrine teaches no *Atheism*, except in the Hindu sense of the word *nastika*, or the rejection of *idols*, including every anthro-pomorphic god.   In this sense every Occultist is a *Nastika*.

(2) It admits a Logos or a collective " Creator " of the Universe ; a *Demi-urgos*—in the sense implied when one speaks of an " Architect " as the "Creator " of an edifice, whereas that Architect has never touched one stone of it, but, while furnishing the plan, left all the manual labour to the masons ; in our case the plan was furnished by the Ideation of the Universe, and the constructive labour was left to the Hosts of intelligent Powers and Forces. But that *Demiurgos* is no

personal deity,—*i.e.*, an imperfect *extra-cosmic god*,—but only the aggregate of the Dhyan-Chohans and the other forces.

As to the latter—

(3) They are dual in their character; being composed of (*a*) the irrational *brute energy*, inherent in matter, and (*b*) the intelligent soul or cosmic consciousness which directs and guides that energy, and which is the *Dhyan-Chohanic thought reflecting the Ideation of the Universal mind*. This results in a perpetual series of physical mani-festations and *moral effects* on Earth, during manvantaric periods, the whole being subservient to Karma. As that process is not always perfect; and since, however many proofs it may exhibit of a guiding intelligence behind the veil, it still shows gaps and flaws, and even results very often in evident failures—therefore, neither the collective Host (Demiurgos), nor any of the working powers individually, are proper subjects for divine honours or worship. All are entitled to the grateful reverence of Humanity, however, and man ought to be ever striving to help the divine evolution of *Ideas*, by becoming to the best of his ability a *co-worker with nature* in the cyclic task. The ever unknow-able and incognizable *Karana* alone, the *Causeless* Cause of all causes, should have its shrine and altar on the holy and ever untrodden ground of our heart—invisible, intangible, unmentioned, save through " the still small voice " of our spiritual consciousness. Those who worship before it, ought to do so in the silence and the sanctified solitude of their Souls *; making their spirit the sole mediator between them and the *Universal Spirit*, their good actions the only priests, and their sinful intentions the only visible and objective sacrificial victims to the *Presence*. (*See Part II., " On the Hidden Deity."*)

(4) Matter is *Eternal*. It is the *Upadhi* (the physical basis) for the One infinite Universal Mind to build thereon its ideations. Therefore, the Esotericists maintain that there is no inorganic or *dead* matter in nature, the distinction between the two made by Science being as unfounded as it is arbitrary and devoid of reason.

---

* " When thou prayest, thou shalt not be as the hypocrites are . . . but enter into *thine inner chamber and having shut thy door, pray to thy Father which is in secret.*" Matt. vi.). Our Father is *within us* " in Secret, " our 7th principle, in the " inner chamber " of our Soul perception. " The Kingdom of Heaven " and of God "*is within us* " says Jesus, not *outside*. Why are Christians so absolutely blind to the self-evident meaning of the words of wisdom they delight in mechanically repeating ?

Whatever Science may think, however—and *exact* Science is a fickle dame, as we all know by experience—Occultism knows and teaches differently, from time immemorial—from *Manu* and *Hermes* down to Paracelsus and his successors.

Thus, Hermes, the thrice great Trismegistus, says: "Oh, my son, matter *becomes;* formerly it *was;* for matter is the vehicle of becoming.* Becoming is the mode of activity of the uncreate deity. Having been endowed with the germs of becoming, matter (objective) is brought into birth, for the creative force fashions it *according to the ideal forms.* Matter not yet engendered had no form; it becomes when it is put into operation." (*The Definitions of Asclepios*, p. 134, " Virgin of the World.")

" Everything is the product of one universal creative effort. . . . There is nothing *dead* in Nature. *Everything is organic and living,* and therefore the whole world appears to be a living organism." (Paracelsus, "*Philosophia ad Athenienses,*" F. Hartmann's translations, p. 44.)

(5.) The Universe was evolved out of its ideal plan, upheld through Eternity in the unconsciousness of that which the Vedantins call Parabrahm. This is practically identical with the conclusions of the highest Western Philosophy—" the innate, eternal, and self-existing Ideas" of Plato, now reflected by Von Hartmann. The " unknowable" of Herbert Spencer bears only a faint resemblance to that transcendental *Reality* believed in by Occultists, often appearing merely a personification of a "*force* behind phenomena"—an infinite and eternal *Energy*

---

* To this the late Mrs. (Dr.) Kingsford, the able translator and compiler of the Hermetic Fragments (see " *The Virgin of the World* ") remarks in a foot-note ; " Dr. Menard observes that in Greek the same word signifies *to be born* and *to become.* The idea here is that the material of the world is in its essence eternal, but that before creation or ' becoming' it is in a passive and motionless condition. Thus it ' was ' before being put into operation ; now it ' becomes,' that is, it is mobile and progressive." And she adds the purely Vedantic doctrine of the Hermetic philosophy that " Creation is thus the period of activity (Manvantara) of God, who, according to Hermetic thought (or *which*, according to the Vedantin) has two modes—Activity or Existence, God evolved (*Deus explicitus*) ; and Passivity of Being (Pralaya) God involved (*Deus implicitus*). Both modes are perfect and complete, as are the waking and sleeping states of man. Fichte, the German philosopher, distinguished Being (Seyn) as One, which we know only through existence (Daseyn) as the Manifold. This view is thoroughly Hermetic. The ' Ideal Forms ' are the archetypal or formative ideas of the Neo-Platonists ; the eternal and subjective concepts of things subsisting in the divine mind prior to ' becoming ' " (p. 134).

from which all things proceed, while the author of the "Philosophy of the Unconscious" has come (in this respect only) as near to a solution of the great *Mystery* as mortal man can. Few were those, whether in ancient or mediæval philosophy, who have dared to approach the subject or even hint at it. Paracelsus mentions it inferentially. His ideas are admirably synthesized by Dr. F. Hartmann, F.T.S., in his "Life of Paracelsus."

All the *Christian* Kabalists understood well the Eastern root idea: The active Power, the "Perpetual motion of the great Breath" only awakens Kosmos at the dawn of every new Period, setting it into motion by means of the two contrary Forces,* and thus causing it to become objective on the plane of Illusion. In other words, that dual motion transfers Kosmos from the plane of the Eternal Ideal into that of finite manifestation, or from the *Noumenal* to the *phenomenal* plane. Everything that *is*, *was*, and *will be*, eternally is, even the countless forms, which are finite and perishable only in their objective, not in their *ideal* Form. They existed as Ideas, in the Eternity,† and, when they pass away, will exist as reflections. Neither the form of man, nor that of any animal, plant or stone has ever been *created*, and it is only on this plane of ours that it commenced "becoming," *i.e.*, objectivising into its present materiality, or expanding *from within outwards*, from the most sublimated and supersensuous essence into its grossest appearance. Therefore *our* human forms have existed in the Eternity as astral or ethereal prototypes; according to which models, the Spiritual Beings (or Gods) whose duty it was to bring them into objective being and terrestrial Life, evolved the protoplasmic forms of the future *Egos* from *their own essence*. After which, when this human *Upadhi*, or basic mould was ready, the natural terrestrial Forces began to work on those supersensuous moulds *which contained, besides their own, the elements of all the past vegetable and future animal forms of this globe in them.* Therefore, man's *outward* shell passed through every vegetable and animal body before it assumed the human shape. As this will be fully

---

* The centripetal and the centrifugal forces, which are male and female, positive and negative, physical and spiritual, the two being the one *Primordial* Force.

† Occultism teaches that no form can be given to anything, either by nature or by man, whose ideal type does not already exist on the subjective plane. More than this; that no such form or shape can possibly enter man's consciousness, or evolve in his imagination, which does not exist in prototype, at least as an approximation.

described in Book II., with the Commentaries thereupon, there is no need to say more of it here.

According to the Hermetico-Kabalistic philosophy of Paracelsus, it is Yliaster—the ancestor of the just-born *Protyle*, introduced by Mr. Crookes in chemistry—or primordial *protomateria* that evolved out of itself the Kosmos.

"When Evolution took place the Yliaster divided itself. . . . melted and dissolved, developing from within itself the *Ideos* or Chaos, called respectively *Mysterium magnum, Iliados, Limbus Major*, or Primordial Matter. This Primordial essence is of a monistic nature, and manifests itself not only as vital activity, a spiritual force, an invisible, incomprehensible, and indescribable power, but also as vital matter of which the substance of living beings consists." In this *Ideos* of primordial matter, or the *proto-ilos*—which is the matrix of all created things—is contained the substance from which everything is formed. It is the Chaos . . . out of which the Macrocosm, and, later on, by evolution and division in *Mysteria Specialia,** each separate being, came into existence. "All things and all elementary substances were contained in it *in potentiâ* but not in *actu*"—which makes the translator, Dr. F. Hartmann, justly observe that "it seems that Paracelsus anticipated the modern discovery of the 'potency of matter' three hundred years ago " (*p.* 42).

This Magnus Limbus, then, or Yliaster of Paracelsus, is simply our old friend "Father-Mother," *within*, before it appeared in Space, of the second and other Stanzas. It is the universal matrix of Kosmos, personified in the dual character of Macro- and Microcosm (or the Universe and our Globe)† by Aditi-Prakriti, the Spiritual and the physical nature. For we find it explained in Paracelsus that "the Magnus Limbus is the nursery out of which all creatures have grown, in the same sense as a tree grows out of a small seed; with the difference, however, that the great Limbus takes its origin from the Word, while the Limbus minor (the terrestrial seed or sperm) takes it from the earth.

---

* This word is explained by Dr. Hartmann from the original texts of Paracelsus before him, as follows. According to this great Rosicrucian : "Mysterium is everything out of which something may be developed, which is only germinally contained in it. A seed is the ' Mysterium ' of a plant, an egg that of a living bird, etc."

† It is only the mediæval Kabalists who, following the Jewish and one or two Neo-Platonists, applied the term *Microcosm* to man. Ancient philosophy called the Earth the Microcosm of the Macrocosm, and man the outcome of the two.

The great Limbus is the seed out of which all beings have come, and the little Limbus is each ultimate being that reproduces its form, and that has itself been produced by the 'great.' The latter possesses all the qualifications of the great one, in the same sense as a son has an organization similar to that of his father." (*See Comment. Book II. para. iii.*) . . . " As Yliaster dissolved, *Ares*, the dividing, differentiating, and individualising power (*Fohat*, another old friend,) . . . began to act. All production took place in consequence of separation. There were produced out of the Ideos, the elements of Fire, Water, Air and Earth, whose birth, however, did not take place in a material mode, or by simple separation," but by spiritual and dynamical, not even complex, combinations—*e.g.*, mechanical *mixture* as opposed to *chemical* combination—just as fire may come out of a pebble, or a tree out of a seed, although there is originally no fire in the pebble, nor a tree in the seed. Spirit is living, and Life is Spirit, and Life and Spirit (*Prakriti Purusha*) (?) produce all things, but they are essentially one and not two. . . . The elements too, have each one its own Yliaster, because all the activity of matter in every form is only an effluvium of the same fount. But as from the seed grow the roots with their fibres, and after that the stalk with its branches and leaves, and lastly the flowers and seeds ; likewise all beings were born from the elements, and consist of elementary substances out of which other forms may come into existence, bearing the characteristics of their parents." (" This doctrine, preached 300 years ago," remarks the translator, " is identical with the one that has revolutionized modern thought, after having been put into new shape and elaborated by Darwin. It was still more elaborated by Kapila in the Sankhya philosophy "). . . . The elements as the mothers of all creatures *are of an invisible, spiritual nature, and have souls.** They all spring from the "*Mysterium Magnum*." *(Philosophia ad Athenienses.)*

Compare this with Vishnu Purâna.

" From *Pradhâna* (primordial substance) presided over by *Kshetrajna* (embodied Spirit ?) proceeds the evolution of those qualities. . . . From the great Principle *Mahat* (Universal Intellect, or mind) . . . proceeds

---

* The Eastern Occultist says—" are guided and informed by the Spiritual Beings "— the Workmen in the invisible worlds and behind the veil of Occult nature, or nature *in Abscondito.*

the origin of the subtle elements and from these the organs of sense
. . ." (*Book I., ii.*).

Thus it may be shown that all the fundamental truths of nature were
universal in antiquity, and that the basic ideas upon spirit, matter, and
the universe, or upon God, Substance, and man, were identical. Taking
the two most ancient religious philosophies on the globe, Hinduism and
Hermetism, from the scriptures of India and Egypt, the identity of the
two is easily recognisable.

This becomes apparent to one who reads the latest translation and
rendering of the " Hermetic Fragments " just mentioned, by our late
lamented friend, Dr. Anna Kingsford. Disfigured and tortured as these
have been in their passage through Sectarian Greek and Christian
hands, the translator has most ably and intuitively seized the weak
points and tried to remedy them by means of explanations and footnotes. And she says: . . . . " The creation of the visible world by
the ' working gods ' or Titans, as agents of the Supreme God,* is a
thoroughly Hermetic idea, *recognisable in all religious systems*, and in
accordance with modern scientific research (?), which shows us everywhere the Divine power operating through natural Forces."

" That Universal Being, that contains all, and which is all, put into
motion the Soul and the World, all that nature comprises, says Hermes.
In the manifold unity of universal life, the innumerable individualities
distinguished by their variations, are, nevertheless, united in such a
manner that the whole is one, and that everything proceeds from
Unity." (*Asclepios, Part I.*)

" God is not a mind, but the cause that the mind is ; *not a spirit*, but
the cause that the Spirit is ; not light, but the cause that the Light is "
(*Divine Pymander, Book IX., v. 64.*)

The above shows plainly that " Divine Pymander," however much
distorted in some passages by Christian " smoothing," was nevertheless
written by a philosopher, while most of the so-called " hermetic Fragments " are the production of sectarian pagans with a tendency
towards an anthropomorphic Supreme Being. Yet both are the echo
of the Esoteric philosophy and the Hindu Purânas.

Compare two invocations, one to the Hermetic " Supreme All," the

---

* A frequent expression in the said Fragments, to which we take exception. The
Universal Mind is not a *Being* or " God."

other to the "Supreme All" of the later Aryans. Says a Hermetic Fragment cited by Suidas (see Mrs. Kingsford's "*The Virgin of the World*") :—

"I adjure thee, Heaven, holy work of the great God ; I adjure thee, Voice of the Father, uttered in the beginning when the universal world was framed ; I adjure thee by the word, only Son of the Father who upholds all things ; be favourable, be favourable."

This just preceded by the following : "Thus the Ideal Light was before the Ideal Light, and the luminous Intelligence of Intelligence was always, *and its unity was nothing else than the Spirit enveloping the Universe. Out of whom is neither God nor Angels, nor any other essentials,* for He (It ?) is the Lord of all things and the power and the Light ; and all depends on Him (It) and is in Him (It), etc." (*Fragments of the writings of Hermes to Ammon.*)

This is contradicted by the very same *Trismegistos*, who is made to say : "To speak of God is impossible. For corporeal cannot express the incorporeal. . . . . That which has not any body nor appearance, nor form, nor matter, cannot be apprehended by sense. I understand, Tatios, I understand, that which it is impossible to define— that is God." (*Physical Eclogues, Florilegium of Stobæus.*)

The contradiction between the two passages is evident ; and this shows (*a*) that Hermes was a generic *nom-de-plume* used by a series of generations of mystics of every shade, and (*b*) that a great discernment has to be used before accepting a Fragment as esoteric teaching only because it is undeniably ancient. Let us now compare the above with a like invocation in the Hindu Scriptures—undoubtedly as old, if not far older. Here it is *Parâsara*, the Aryan "Hermes" who instructs *Maitreya*, the Indian Asclepios, and calls upon Vishnu in his triple hypostasis.

"Glory to the unchangeable, holy, eternal Supreme Vishnu, of one universal nature, the mighty over all ; to him who is Hiranyagarbha, Hari, and Sankara (Brahma, Vishnu, and Siva), the creator, the pre- server, and the destroyer of the world ; to Vasudeva, the liberator (of his worshippers); to him whose essence is both single and manifold ; who is both subtile and corporeal, indiscreet and discreet ; to Vishnu the cause of final emancipation, the cause of the creation, existence, the

end of the world ; *who is the root of the world*, and who *consists of the world*."
(*Vish. Purâna, Book L.*)

This is a grand invocation, full of philosophical meaning underlying it;
but, for the profane masses, as suggestive as is the first of an anthropomorphic Being. We must respect the feeling that dictated both ; but
we cannot help finding it in full disharmony with its inner meaning, even
with that which is found in the same Hermetic treatise where it is
said :

" Reality is not upon the earth, my son, and it cannot be thereon.
. . . Nothing on earth is real, there are only appearances. . . He
(man) is not real, my son, as man. The real consists solely in itself and
remains what it is. . . Man is transient, therefore he is not real, he
is but appearance, and appearance is the supreme illusion.

Tatios : Then the *celestial bodies themselves are not real, my father, since they
also vary ?*

Trismegistos : That which is subject to birth and to change is not real.
. . . . There is in them a certain falsity, seeing that they too are
variable. . . . .

Tatios : And what then is the primordial Reality ?

Trismeg.: That which is one and alone, O Tatios ; That which is not
made of matter, nor in any body. Which has neither colour nor form,
which changes not nor is transmitted but which always is."

This is quite consistent with the Vedantic teaching. The leading
thought is Occult ; and many are the passages in the Hermetic Fragments that belong bodily to the Secret Doctrine.

The latter teaches that the whole universe is ruled by intelligent and
semi-intelligent Forces and Powers, as stated from the very beginning.
Christian Theology admits and even *enforces* belief in such, but makes an
arbitrary division and refers to them as " Angels " and " Devils."
Science denies the existence of such, and ridicules the very idea.
Spiritualists believe in the Spirits of the Dead, and, outside these, deny
entirely any other kind or class of invisible beings. The Occultists
and Kabalists are thus the only rational expounders of the ancient
traditions, which have now culminated in dogmatic faith on the one
hand, and dogmatic denials on the other. For, both belief and unbelief embrace but one small corner each of the infinite horizons of
spiritual and physical manifestations ; and thus both are right from

their respective standpoints, and both are wrong in believing that they can circumscribe the whole within their own special and narrow barriers ; for—they can never do so. In this respect Science, Theology, and even Spiritualism show little more wisdom than the ostrich does, when it hides its head in the sand at its feet, feeling sure that there can be thus nothing beyond its own point of observation and the limited area occupied by its foolish head.

As the only works now extant upon the subject under consideration within reach of the profane of the Western " civilized " races are the above-mentioned Hermetic Books, or rather Hermetic Fragments, we may constrast them in the present case with the teachings of Esoteric philosophy. To quote for this purpose from any other would be use-less, since the public knows nothing of the Chaldean works which are translated into Arabic and preserved by some *Sufi* initiates. Therefore the " Definitions of Asclepios," as lately compiled and glossed by Mrs. A. Kingsford, F.T.S., some of which sayings are in remarkable agree-ment with the Esoteric Eastern doctrine, have to be resorted to for comparison. Though not a few passages show a strong impression of some later Christian hand, yet on the whole the characteristics of the genii* and gods are those of eastern teachings, while concerning other things there are passages which differ widely in our doctrines. The following are a few :—

---

* The Hermetic philosophers called *Theoi*, gods, Genii and Daimones (in the original texts), those Entities whom we call *Devas* (gods), Dhyan Chohans, *Chitkala* (Kwan-yin, the Buddhists call them), and by other names. The *Daimones* are—in the Socratic sense, and even in the Oriental and Latin theological sense—the guardian spirits of the human race ; " those who dwell in the neighbourhood of the immortals, and thence watch over human affairs," as Hermes has it. In Esoteric parlance, they are called *Chitkala*, some of which are those who have furnished man with his fourth and fifth Principles from their own essence ; and others the *Pitris* so-called. This will be explained when we come to the production of the *complete man*. The root of the name is *Chiti*, " that by which the effects and consequences of actions and kinds of knowledge are selected for the use of the soul," or conscience the *inner* Voice in man. With the Yogis, the *Chiti* is a synonym of *Mahat*, the first and divine intellect ; but in Esoteric philosophy *Mahat* is the root of Chiti, its germ ; and *Chiti* is a quality of *Manas* in conjunction with Buddhi, a quality that attracts to itself by spiritual affinity a *Chitkala* when it develops sufficiently in man. This is why it is said that *Chiti* is a voice acquiring mystic life and becoming Kwan-Yin.

EXTRACTS FROM A PRIVATE COMMENTARY,* *hitherto secret* :—

(xvii.) "*The Initial Existence in the first twilight of the Maha-Manwantara (after the* MAHA-PRALAYA *that follows every age of Brahmâ) is a* CONSCIOUS SPIRITUAL QUALITY. *In the manifested* WORLDS *(solar systems) it is, in its* OBJECTIVE SUBJECTIVITY, *like the film from a Divine Breath to the gaze of the entranced seer. It spreads as it issues from* LAYA† *throughout infinity as a colourless spiritual fluid. It is on the* SEVENTH PLANE, *and in its* SEVENTH STATE *in our planetary world.*‡

(xviii.) "*It is Substance to* OUR *spiritual sight. It cannot be called so by men in their* WAKING STATE ; *therefore they have named it in their ignorance* '*God-Spirit.*'

(xix.) "*It exists everywhere and forms the first* UPADHI *(foundation) on which our World (solar system) is built. Outside the latter it is to be found in its pristine purity only between (the solar systems or) the Stars of the Universe, the worlds already formed or forming; those in* LAYA *resting meanwhile in its bosom. As its substance is of a different kind from that known on earth, the inhabitants of the latter, seeing* THROUGH IT, *believe in their illusion and ignorance that* it *is empty space. There is not one finger's breath* (ANGULA) *of void Space in the whole Boundless (Universe).* . . . .

(xx.) "*Matter or Substance is septenary within our World, as it is so beyond it. Moreover, each of its states or principles is graduated into seven degrees of density.* SÛRYA *(the Sun), in its visible reflection, exhibits the first, or lowest state of the seventh, the highest state of the Universal* PRESENCE, *the pure of the pure, the first manifested Breath of the ever Unmanifested* SAT *(Be-ness). All the Central physical or objective Suns are in their substance the lowest state of the first Principle of the* BREATH. *Nor are any of these any more than the* REFLECTIONS *of their* PRIMARIES *which are concealed from the gaze of all but the Dhyan Chohans, whose Corporeal substance belongs to the fifth division of the seventh Principle of the Mother substance, and is,*

---

* This (teaching) does not refer to Prakriti-Purusha beyond the boundaries of our small universe.

† The ultimate quiescent state : the *Nirvana* condition of the seventh Principle.

‡ The teaching is all given from our plane of consciousness.

therefore, four degrees higher than the solar reflected substance. As there are seven Dhâtu (principal substances in the human body) so there are seven Forces in Man and in all Nature.

(xxi.) " *"The real substance of the concealed (Sun) is a nucleus of Mother substance.** *It is the heart and the matrix of all the living and existing Forces in our solar universe. It is the Kernel from which proceed to spread on their cyclic journeys all the Powers that set in action the atoms in their functional duties, and the focus within which they again meet in their* SEVENTH ESSENCE *every eleventh year. He who tells thee he has seen the sun, laugh at him*† *as if he had said that the sun moves really onward on his diurnal path . . . .*

(xxiii). " *It is on account of his septennary nature that the Sun is spoken of by the ancients as one who is driven by seven horses equal to the metres of the Vedas; or, again, that, though he is identified with the* SEVEN *"Gaina"* (classes of being) *in his orb, he is distinct from them,*‡ *as he is, indeed; as also that he has* SEVEN RAYS, *as indeed he has . . . .*

(xxv.) " *The Seven Beings in the Sun are the Seven Holy Ones, Self-born from the inherent power in the matrix of Mother substance. It is they who send the Seven Principal Forces, called rays, which at the beginning of Pralaya will centre into seven new Suns for the next Manvantara. The energy from which they spring into conscious existence in every Sun, is what some people call Vishnu (see foot-note below), which is the Breath of the* ABSOLUTENESS.

We call it the One manifested life—itself a reflection of the Absolute . . . . .

(xxvi.) " *The latter must never be mentioned in words or speech* LEST IT SHOULD TAKE AWAY SOME OF OUR SPIRITUAL ENERGIES THAT ASPIRE *towards* ITS *state, gravitating ever onward unto* IT *spiritually, as the whole physical universe gravitates towards* ITS *manifested centre—cosmically.*

(xxvii.) " *The former—the Initial existence—which may be called while in*

---

* Or the " dream of Science," the primeval really homogeneous matter, which no mortal can make objective in this *Race* or *Round* either.

† " Vishnu in the form of the Solar active energy, neither ever rises nor sets, and is at once, the *sevenfold Sun* and distinct from it," says Vishnu Purâna (Book II., Chap 11).

‡ " In the same manner as a man approaches a mirror placed upon a stand, beholds in it his own image, so the energy or reflection of Vishnu (the Sun) is never disjoined but remains in the Sun as in a mirror that is there stationed " (" *Vishnu Purâna* ").

this state of being the ONE LIFE, *is, as explained, a* FILM *for creative or formative purposes. It manifests in seven states, which, with their septenary subdivisions, are the* FORTY-NINE *Fires* mentioned in sacred books . . . . . .*

(xxix.) *" The first is the . . . . ' Mother' (prima* MATERIA). *Separating itself into its primary seven states, it proceeds down cyclically ; when†* *having consolidated itself in its* LAST *principle as* GROSS MATTER, *it revolves around itself and informs, with the seventh emanation of the last, the first and the lowest element (the Serpent biting its own tail). In a hierarchy, or order of being, the seventh emanation of her last principle is :—*

(a) *In the mineral, the spark that lies latent in it, and is called to its evanescent being by the* POSITIVE *awakening the* NEGATIVE *(and so forth) . . . .*

(b) *In the plant it is that vital and intelligent Force which informs the seed and develops it into the blade of grass, or the root and sapling. It is the germ which becomes the* UPADHI *of the seven principles of the thing it resides in, shooting them out as the latter grows and develops.*

(c) *In every animal it does the same. It is its life principle and vital power ; its instinct and qualities ; its characteristics and special idiosyncracies . . . .*

(d) *To man, it gives all that it bestows on all the rest of the manifested units in nature ; but develops, furthermore, the reflection of all its* FORTY-NINE FIRES *in him. Each of his seven principles is an heir in full to, and a partaker of, the seven principles of the " great Mother." The breath of her first principle is his spirit (Atma). Her second principle is* BUDDHI *(soul). We call it, erroneously, the seventh. The third furnishes him with* (a) *the brain stuff on the physical plane, and* (b) *with the* MIND *that moves it—* [which is the human soul.—H. P. B.] *—according to his organic capacities.*

(e) *It is the guiding Force in the Cosmic and terrestrial elements. It resides in the Fire provoked out of its latent into active being ; for the whole of the seven subdivisions of the* * * * *principle reside in the terrestrial Fire. It whirls in the breeze, blows with the hurricane, and sets the air in motion, which* element *participates in one of its principles also. Proceeding cyclically, it regulates the motion*

---

* In " Vishnu " and other *Purânas.*

† See the Hermetic " Nature," " Going down cyclically into matter when she meets ' heavenly man.' "

of the water, attracts and repels the waves according to fixed laws of which its seventh principle is the informing soul.*

(*f*) *Its four higher principles contain the germ that develops into the Cosmic Gods; its three lower ones breed the lives of the Elements (Elementals).*

(*g*) *In our Solar world, the One Existence is Heaven and the Earth, the Root and the flower, the Action and the Thought. It is in the Sun, and is as present in the glow-worm. Not an atom can escape it. Therefore, the ancient Sages have wisely called it the manifested God in Nature. . . ."*

It may be interesting, in this connection, to remind the reader of what Mr. Subba Row said of the Forces—mystically defined. See "*Five Years of Theosophy*" and "The Twelve Signs of the Zodiac." Thus he says :

"Kanyâ (the sixth sign of the Zodiac, or *Virgo*) means a Virgin, and represents *Sakti* or *Mahamaya*. The sign . . . is the 6th *Rasi* or division, and indicates that there are six primary forces in Nature (synthesized by the Seventh)" . . . These Sakti stand as follows :—

(1.) PARASAKTI. Literally the great or Supreme Force or power. It means and includes the powers of *light and heat.*

(2.) JNANASAKTI. . . . The power of intellect, of real Wisdom or Knowledge. It has two aspects :

The following are *some* of its manifestations *when placed under the influence or control of material conditions.* (a) The power of the mind in interpreting our sensations. (b) Its power in recalling past ideas (memory) and raising future expectation. (c) Its power as exhibited in what are called by modern psychologists "the laws of association," which enables it to form *persisting* connections between various groups of sensations and possibilities of sensations, and thus generate the notion or idea of an external object. (d) Its power in connecting our ideas together by the mysterious link of memory, and thus generating the notion of self or individuality; *some* of its manifestations when liberated *from the bonds of matter* are—(a) Clairvoyance, (b) Psychometry.

(3.) ITCHASAKTI—the *power of the Will.* Its most ordinary manifesta-

---

* The writers of the above knew perfectly well the physical cause of the tides, of the waves, etc. It is the informing Spirit of the whole Cosmic solar body that is meant here, and which is referred to whenever such expressions are used from the mystic point of view.

tion is the generation of certain nerve currents which set in motion such muscles as are required for the accomplishment of the desired object.

(4.) KRIYASAKTI. The mysterious power of thought which enables it to produce external, perceptible, phenomenal results by its own inherent energy. The ancients held that *any idea will manifest itself externally if one's attention is deeply concentrated upon it.* Similarly *an intense volition will be followed by the desired result.*

A Yogi generally performs his wonders by means of Itchasakti and Kriyasakti.

(5.) KUNDALINI SAKTI. The power or Force which moves in a curved path. It is the Universal life-Principle manifesting everywhere in nature. This force includes the two great forces of attraction and repulsion. Electricity and magnetism are but manifestations of it. This is the power which brings about that " continuous adjustment of *internal relations to external relations* " which is the essence of life according to Herbert Spencer, and that " *continuous adjustment of external relations to internal relations* " which is the basis of transmigration of souls, *punar janman* (re-birth) in the doctrines of the ancient Hindu philosophers. A Yogi must thoroughly subjugate this power before he can attain Moksham. . . .

(6.) MANTRIKA-SAKTI. The force or power of letters, speech or music. The *Mantra Shastra* has for its subject-matter this force in all its manifestations. . . . . The influence of melody is one of its ordinary manifestations. The power of the ineffable name is the crown of this Sakti.

Modern Science has but partly investigated the first, second and fifth of the forces above named, but is altogether in the dark as regards the remaining powers. The six forces are in their unity represented by the "*Daiviprakriti*" (the Seventh, the light of the LOGOS).

The above is quoted to show the real Hindu ideas on the same. It is all esoteric, though not covering the tenth part of *what might be said.* For one, the six names of the Six Forces mentioned are those of *the six Hierarchies* of Dhyan Chohans synthesized by their *Primary*, the seventh, who personify the Fifth Principle of Cosmic Nature, or of the "Mother" in its Mystical Sense. The enumeration alone of the *yogi* Powers would require ten volumes. Each of these Forces has a *living Conscious Entity* at its head, of which entity it is an emanation.

But let us compare with the commentary just cited the words of Hermes, the " thrice great " :—

" The creation of Life *by the Sun* is as continuous as his light ; nothing arrests or limits it. Around him, like an army of Satellites, *are innumerable choirs of genii.* These dwell in the neighbourhood of the Immortals, and thence watch over human things. They fulfil the will of the gods (Karma) *by means of storms, tempests, transitions of fire and earthquakes ;* likewise by famines and wars, for the punishment of impiety.* . . . It is the sun who preserves and nourishes all creatures ; and even as the Ideal World which environs the sensible world fills this last with the plenitude and universal variety of forms, so also the Sun, enfolding all in his light, accomplishes everywhere the birth and development of creatures." . . . " *Under his orders is the choir of Genii,* or rather the choirs, *for there are many and diverse, and their number corresponds to that of the stars. Every star has its genii, good and evil by nature,* or rather by their *operation, for operation is the essence of the genii.* . . . All these Genii *preside over mundane affairs,*† they shake and overthrow the constitution of States and of individuals ; they *imprint their likeness on our Souls,* they are present in our nerves, our marrow, our veins, our arteries, and *our very brain-substance* . . . at the moment when each of us receives life and being, he is taken in charge by the genii (Elementals) who preside over births,‡ and who are classed beneath the astral powers (Superhuman astral Spirits.) They change perpetually, not always identically, but revolving in circles.§ They permeate by the body two parts of the Soul, that it may receive from each the impress of his own energy. But the reasonable part of the Soul is not subject to the genii ; it is designed

---

* See Stanzas III. and IV. and the Commentaries thereupon, especially the Comments on Stanza IV. " the *Lipika* and the four Maharajas," the agents of Karma.

† And " Gods " or Dhyanis, too, not only the genii or " guided Forces."

‡ The meaning of this is that as man is composed of all the Great Elements : Fire, Air, Water, Earth and Ether—the ELEMENTALS which belong respectively to these Elements feel attracted to man by reason of their co-essence. That element which predominates in a certain constitution will be the ruling element throughout life. For instance, if man has a preponderance of the Earthly, gnomic element, the gnomes will lead him towards assimilating metals—money and wealth, and so on. " Animal man is the son of the animal elements out of which his Soul (life) was born, and animals are the mirrors of man," says Paracelsus (*De Fundamento Sapientiæ*). Paracelsus was cautious, and wanted the Bible to agree with what he said, and therefore did not say all.

§ Cyclic progress in development.

for the reception of (the) God,* who enlightens it with a sunny ray. Those who are thus illumined are few in number, and from them the genii abstain : for neither genii nor Gods have any power in the presence of a single ray of God.† But all other men, both soul and body, are directed by genii, to whom they cleave, and whose operations they affect. . . . . . The genii have then the control of mundane things and our bodies serve them as instruments. . . . ."

The above, save a few sectarian points, represents that which was a universal belief common to all nations till about a century or so back. It is still as orthodox in its broad outlines and features among pagans and Christians alike, if one excepts a handful of materialists and men of Science.

For whether one calls the genii of Hermes and his " Gods," " Powers of Darkness " and " Angels," as in the Greek and Latin Churches ; or " Spirits of the Dead," as in Spiritualism ; or, again, *Bhoots* and *Devas*, *Shaitan* or *Djin*, as they are still called in India and Mussulman countries —*they are all one and the same thing*—ILLUSION. Let not this, however, be misunderstood in the sense into which the great philosophical doctrine of the Vedantists has been lately perverted by Western schools.

All that which *is*, emanates from the ABSOLUTE, which, from this qualification alone, stands as the one and only reality—hence, every-thing extraneous to this Absolute, the generative and causative Ele-ment, *must* be an illusion, most undeniably. But this is only so from the purely metaphysical view. A man who regards himself as mentally sane, and is so regarded by his neighbours, calls the visions of an *insane* brother—whose hallucinations make *the victim either happy or supremely wretched*, as the case may be—illusions and fancies likewise. But, where is that madman for whom the hideous shadows in his deranged mind, his *illusions*, are not, for the time being, as actual and as real as the things which his physician or keeper may see ? Everything is relative in this Universe, everything is an illusion. But

---

* The God in man and often the incarnation of a God, a highly Spiritual Dhyan Chohan in him, besides the presence of his own seventh Principle.

† Now, what "god" is meant here ? Not God " the Father," the anthropomorphic fiction ; for that god is the Elohim collectively, and has no being apart from the Host. Besides, such a god is finite and imperfect. It is the high Initiates and Adepts who are meant here by those men " few in number." And it is precisely those men who believe in " gods " and know no " God," but one Universal unrelated and unconditioned Deity.

the experience of any plane is an actuality for the percipient being, whose consciousness is on that plane; though the said experience, regarded from the purely metaphysical standpoint, may be conceived to have no objective reality. But it is not against metaphysicians, but against physicists and materialists that Esoteric teachings have to fight, and for these Vital Force, Light, Sound, Electricity, even to the objectively pulling force of magnetism, have no objective being, and are said to exist merely as "modes of motion," "sensations and *affections* of matter."

Neither the Occultists generally, nor the Theosophists, reject, as erroneously believed by some, the views and theories of the modern scientists, only because these views are opposed to Theosophy. The first rule of our Society is to render unto Cæsar what is Cæsar's. The Theosophists, therefore, are the first to recognize the intrinsic value of science. But when its high priests resolve consciousness into a secretion from the grey matter of the brain, and everything else in nature into a mode of motion, we protest against the doctrine as being unphilosophical, self-contradictory, and simply absurd, from a *scientific* point of view, as much and even more than from the occult aspect of the esoteric knowledge.

For truly the astral light of the derided Kabalists has strange and weird secrets for him who can see in it; and the mysteries concealed within its incessantly disturbed waves *are there*, the whole body of Materialists and scoffers notwithstanding.* These secrets, along with

---

* The astral light of the Kabalists is very incorrectly translated by some "Æther;" the latter is confused with the hypothetical Ether of Science, and both are referred to by some theosophists as synonymous with *Akâsa*. This is a great mistake.

"A characteristic of Akâsa will serve to show how inadequately it is represented by Ether," writes the author of Rational Refutations, thus unconsciously helping Occultism. "In dimension it is infinite; it is not made up of parts; and colour, taste, smell, and tangibility do not appertain to it. So far forth it corresponds exactly to time, space, *Isvara*, ("The Lord," but rather creative potency and soul—*anima mundi*). Its speciality, as compared therewith, consists in its being the *material cause of sound*. Except for its being so, one might take it to be one with vacuity" (*p.* 120.)

It is *vacuity*, no doubt, especially for Rationalists. At any rate Akâsa is sure to produce vacuity in the brain of a materialist. Nevertheless, though Akâsa is not that Ether of Science, not even the Ether of the Occultist, who defines the latter as one of the principles of Akâsa only, it is as certainly, together with its primary, the cause of sound, only a physical and spiritual, not a material cause by any means. The relations

many other mysteries, will remain non-existent to the materialists of our age, in the same way as America was a non-existent myth for Europeans during the early part of the mediæval ages, whereas Scandinavians and Norwegians had actually reached and settled in that very old " New World " several centuries before. But, as a Columbus was born to re-discover, and to force the Old World to believe in Antipodal countries, so will there be born scientists who will discover the marvels now claimed by Occultists to exist in the regions of Ether, with their varied and multiform denizens and conscious Entities. Then, *nolens volens*, Science will have to accept the old " Superstition," as it has several others. And having been once forced to accept it—judging from past experience—its learned professors will, in all probability, as in the case of MESMERISM and Magnetism, now re-baptised Hypnotism, father the thing and reject its name. The choice of the new appellation will depend, in its turn, on the " modes of motion," the new name for the older " automatic physical processes among the nerve fibrils of the (Scientific) brain " of Moleschott ; as also, very likely, upon the last meal of the namer ; since, according to the Founder of the new Hylo-Idealistic Scheme, " Cerebration is generically the same as chylification."* Thus, were one to believe this preposterous proposition, the new name of the archaic thing would have to take its chance, on the inspiration of the namer's liver, and then only would these truths have a chance of becoming scientific !

But TRUTH, however distasteful to the generally blind majorities, has always had her champions, ready to die for her, and it is not the Occultists who will protest against its adoption by Science under whatever new name. But, until absolutely forced on the notice and acceptance of Scientists, many an Occult truth will be tabooed, as the phenomena of the Spiritualists and other psychic manifestations were, to be finally appropriated by its ex-traducers without the least acknowledgment or thanks. Nitrogen has added considerably to chemical knowledge, but its discoverer, Paracelsus, is to this day called a " quack."

---

of Ether to Akâsa may be defined by applying to both Akâsa and Ether the words said of the god in the Vedas, " So himself was indeed (his own) son," one being the progeny of the other and yet itself. This may be a difficult riddle to the profane, but very easy to understand for any Hindu—though not even a mystic.

* *National Reformer*, January 9th, 1887. Article " Phreno-Kosmo-Biology," by Dr. Lewins.

How profoundly true are the words of H. T. Buckle, in his admirable "*History of Civilization*" (Vol. I., p. 256), when he says :—

"Owing to circumstances still unknown (Karmic provision, H.P.B.) there appear from time to time great thinkers, who, devoting their lives to a single purpose, are able to anticipate the progress of mankind, and to produce a religion or a philosophy by which important effects are eventually brought about. But if we look into history we shall clearly see that, although the origin of a new opinion may be thus due to a single man, the result which the new opinion produces will depend on the condition of the people among whom it is propagated. If either a religion or a philosophy is too much in advance of a nation it can do no present service but must bide its time* until the minds of men are ripe for its reception. . . . Every science, every creed has had its martyrs. *According to the ordinary course of affairs, a few generations pass away, and then there comes a period when these very truths are looked upon as commonplace facts, and a little later there comes another period in which they are declared to be necessary, and even the dullest intellect wonders* how they could ever have been denied."

It is barely possible that the minds of the present generations are not quite ripe for the reception of Occult truths. Such will be the retrospect furnished to the advanced thinkers of the Sixth Root Race of the history of the acceptance of Esoteric Philosophy—fully and unconditionally. Meanwhile the generations of our Fifth Race will continue to be led away by prejudice and preconceptions. Occult Sciences will have the finger of scorn pointed at them from every street corner, and everyone will seek to ridicule and crush them in the name, and for the greater glory, of Materialism and its so-called Science. The Addendum which completes the present Book shows, however, in an anticipatory answer to several of the forthcoming Scientific objections, the true and mutual positions of the defendant and plaintiff. The Theosophists and Occultists stand arraigned by public opinion, which still holds high the banner of the inductive Sciences. The latter have, then, to be examined ; and it must be shown how far their achievements and discoveries in the realm of natural laws are opposed, not so much to our claims, as to the facts in nature. The hour has now struck to ascertain whether the

---

* This is Cyclic law, but this law itself is often defied by human stubbornness.

walls of the modern Jericho are so impregnable that no blast of the Occult trumpet is ever likely to make them crumble.

The so-called *Forces*, with Light and Electricity heading them, and the constitution of the Solar orb must be carefully examined ; as also Gravitation and the Nebular theories. The Natures of Ether and of other Elements must be discussed : thus contrasting scientific with other Occult teachings, while revealing some of the hitherto secret tenets of the latter. *(Vide Addendum.)*

Some fifteen years ago, the writer was the first to repeat, after the Kabalists, the wise Commandments in the Esoteric Catechism. " Close thy mouth, lest thou shouldst speak of *this* (the mystery), and thy heart, lest thou shouldst think aloud ; and if thy heart has escaped thee, bring it back to its place, for such is the object of our alliance." *(Sepher Jezireh, Book of Creation.)* And again :—" This is a secret which gives death : close thy mouth lest thou shouldst reveal it to the vulgar ; compress thy brain lest something should escape from it and fall outside." (Rules of Initiation.)

A few years later, a corner of the Veil of Isis had to be lifted ; and now another and a larger rent is made. . . .

But old and time-honoured errors—such as become with every day more glaring and self-evident—stand arrayed in battle-order now, as they did then. Marshalled by blind conservatism, conceit and prejudice, they are constantly on the watch, ready to strangle every truth, which, awakening from its age-long sleep, happens to knock for admission. Such has been the case ever since man became an animal. That this proves in every case *moral death* to the revealers, who bring to light any of these old, old truths, is as certain as that it gives LIFE and REGENERATION to those who are fit to profit even by the little that is now revealed to them.

BOOK I., PART II.

THE

EVOLUTION OF SYMBOLISM

IN ITS APPROXIMATE ORDER.

EXPLANATORY SECTIONS.

CONTENTS.

BOOK I.—PART II.

(SECRET DOCTRINE.)

§ I.

SYMBOLISM AND IDEOGRAPHS.

> " A symbol is ever, to him who has eyes for it,
> some dimmer or clearer revelation of the God-like.
> Through all there glimmers something of a divine
> idea ; nay, the highest ensign that men ever met and
> embraced under the cross itself, had no meaning, save
> an accidental extrinsic one."   CARLYLE.

THE study of the hidden meaning in every religious and profane legend, of whatsoever nation, large or small—pre-eminently the traditions of the East—has occupied the greater portion of the present writer's life. She is one of those who feel convinced that no mythological story, no traditional event in the folk-lore of a people has ever been, at any time, pure fiction, but that every one of such narratives has an actual, historical lining to it.   In this the writer disagrees with those symbologists, however great their reputation, who find in every myth nothing save additional proofs of the superstitious bent of mind of the ancients, and believe that all mythologies sprung from and are built upon *solar myths*.   Such superficial thinkers were admirably disposed of by Mr. Gerald Massey, the poet and Egyptologist, in a lecture on " Luniolatry, Ancient and Modern."   His pointed criticism is worthy of reproduction in this part of this work, as it echoes so well our own feelings, expressed openly so far back as 1875, when " Isis Unveiled " was written.

" For thirty years past Professor Max Müller has been teaching in his books and lectures, in the *Times* and various magazines, from the platform of the Royal Institution, the pulpit of Westminster Abbey, and his chair at Oxford, that mythology is a disease of language, and that the ancient symbolism was a result of something like a primitive aberration.

" ' We know,' says Renouf, echoing Max Müller, in his Hibbert lectures, ' we know that mythology *is* the disease which springs up at a peculiar stage of human culture.'   Such is the shallow explanation of the non-evolutionists, and such explanations are still accepted by the British public, that gets its thinking done by proxy. Professor Max Müller, Cox, Gubernatis, and other pro-pounders of the Solar Mythos, have portrayed the primitive myth-maker for us as a sort of Germanised-Hindu metaphysician, projecting his own shadow on a mental mist, and talking ingeniously concerning smoke, or, at least, *cloud;* the sky overhead becoming like the dome of dreamland, scribbled over with the imagery of aboriginal nightmares ! They conceive the early man in their own likeness, and look upon him as perversely prone to self-mystification, or, as Fontenelle has it, ' subject to beholding things that are not there.' They have misrepresented primitive or archaic man as having been idiotically misled from the first by an active but untutored imagination into believing all sorts of fallacies, which were directly and constantly contradicted by his own daily experience ; a fool of fancy in the midst of those grim realities that were grind-ing his experience into him, like the grinding icebergs making their imprints upon the rocks submerged beneath the sea. It remains to be said, and will one day be acknowledged, that these accepted teachers have been no nearer to the beginnings of mythology and language than Burns' poet Willie had been near to Pegasus. My reply is, 'Tis but a dream of the metaphysical theorist that mythology was a disease of language, or of anything else except his own brain. The origin and meaning of mythology have been missed altogether by these solarites and weather-mongers ! Mythology was a primitive mode of *thinking* the early thought. It was founded on natural facts, and is still verifiable in phenomena. There is nothing insane, nothing irrational in it, when con-sidered in the light of evolution, and when its mode of expression by sign-language is thoroughly understood. The insanity lies in mistaking it for human history or Divine Revelation.* Mythology is the repository of man's most ancient science, and what concerns us chiefly is this—when truly in-terpreted once more, it is destined to be the death of those false theologies to which it has unwittingly given birth.† In modern phraseology a statement is sometimes said to be mythical in proportion to its being untrue; but the ancient mythology was not a system or mode of falsifying in that sense. Its fables were the means of conveying facts; they were neither forgeries nor fictions. . . . For example, when the Egyptians portrayed the moon as a *Cat,* they were not ignorant enough to suppose that the moon was a cat; nor did their wandering fancies see any likeness in the moon to a cat ; nor was a cat-myth any *mere expansion of verbal metaphor;* nor had they any intention of making puzzles or riddles. . . . They had observed the simple fact that the cat saw in the dark, and that her eyes became full-orbed, and grew most luminous by night. The moon was the *seer* by night in heaven, and the cat was its equivalent on the earth ; and so the familiar cat was adopted as a repre-sentative, a natural sign, a living pictograph of the lunar orb. . . . And so it followed that the sun which saw down in the under-world at night could also be called the cat, as it was, because *it also saw* in the dark. The name of the

---

* As far as *divine revelation* is concerned, we agree. Not so with regard to " *human history.*" . . . For there is " history " in most of the allegories and " myths " of India, and events, real actual events, are concealed under them.

† When the " false theologies " disappear, then true prehistoric realities will be found, contained especially in the mythology of the Aryans—ancient Hindoos, and even the pre-Homeric Hellenes.

cat in Egyptian is *mau*, which denotes the *seer*, from *mau*, to see.   One writer on mythology asserts that the Egyptians 'imagined a great cat behind the sun, which is the pupil of the cat's eye.'   But this imagining is all modern. It is the Müllerite stock in trade.   The moon *as cat* was the eye of the sun, *because it reflected the solar light*, and because the eye gives back the image in its mirror.   In the form of the goddess Pasht, the cat keeps watch for the sun, with her paw holding down and bruising the head of the serpent of darkness, called his eternal enemy. . . ."

This is a very correct exposition of the lunar-mythos from its astronomical aspect.   Selenography, however, is the least esoteric of the divisions of lunar Symbology.   To master thoroughly—if one is permitted to coin a new word—*Selenognosis*, one must become proficient in more than its astronomical meaning.   The moon (*vide* § VII. *Deus Lunus*) is intimately related to the Earth, as shown in Stanza VI. of Book I., and is more directly concerned with all the mysteries of our globe than is even Venus-Lucifer, the occult sister and *alter-ego* of the Earth.

The untiring researches of Western, and especially German, symbologists, during the last and the present centuries, have brought every Occultist and most unprejudiced persons to see that without the help of symbology (with its seven departments, of which the moderns know nothing) no ancient Scripture can ever be correctly understood.   Symbology must be studied from every one of its aspects, for each nation had its own peculiar methods of expression.   In short, no Egyptian papyrus, no Indian tolla, no Assyrian tile, or Hebrew scroll, should be read and accepted *literally*.

This every scholar now knows.   The able lectures of Mr. G. Massey alone are sufficient in themselves to convince any *fair-minded* Christian that to accept the dead-letter of the Bible is equivalent to falling into a grosser error and superstition than any hitherto evolved by the brain of the savage South Sea Islander.   But the point to which even the most truth-loving and truth-searching Orientalists—whether Aryanists or Egyptologists—seem to remain blind, is the fact that every symbol in papyrus or *olla* is a many-faced diamond, each of whose facets not merely bears several interpretations, but relates likewise to several sciences.   This is instanced in the just quoted interpretation of the moon symbolized by the cat—an example of sidero-terrestrial imagery; the moon bearing many other meanings besides this with other nations.

As a learned Mason and Theosophist, the late Mr. Kenneth Mackenzie, has shown in his *Royal Masonic Cyclopædia*, there is a great difference between *emblem* and *symbol*.   The former " comprises a larger series of thoughts than a symbol, which may be said rather to illustrate some single special idea."   Hence, the symbols (say lunar, or solar) of several countries, each illustrating such a special idea, or series of ideas, form collectively an esoteric emblem.   The latter is " a concrete visible picture or sign representing principles, or a series of principles, *recognizable by those who have received certain instructions"* (initiates). To put it still plainer, an emblem is *usually a series of graphic pictures* viewed and explained allegorically, and unfolding an idea in panoramic views, one after the other. Thus the Purânas are written emblems. So are the Mosaic and Christian Testaments, or the Bible, and all other exoteric Scriptures. As the same authority shows :—

" All esoteric Societies have made use of emblems and symbols, such as the Pythagorean Society, the Eleusinian, the Hermetic Brethren of Egypt, the Rosicrucians, and the Freemasons. Many of these emblems it is not proper to divulge to the general eye, and *a very minute difference may make the emblem or symbol* differ widely in its meaning. The magical sigillæ, being founded on certain principles of numbers, partake of this character, and although monstrous or ridiculous in the eyes of the uninstructed, convey a whole body of doctrine to those who have been trained to recognise them."

The above enumerated societies are all comparatively modern, none dating back earlier than the middle ages. How much more proper, then, that the students of the oldest Archaic School should be careful not to divulge secrets of far more importance to humanity (in the sense of being dangerous in the hands of the latter) than any of the so-called " Masonic Secrets," which have now become, as the French say, those of " Polichinelle ! " But this restriction can apply only to the psychological or rather psycho-physiological and Cosmical significance of symbol and emblem, and even to that only partially. An adept must refuse to impart the conditions and means that lead to a correlation of elements, whether psychic or physical, that may produce a hurtful result as well as a beneficent one. But he is ever ready to impart to the earnest student the secret of the ancient thought in anything that regards history concealed under mythological symbolism, and thus to furnish a few more land-marks towards a retrospective view of the past, as containing useful information with regard to the origin of man, the evolution of the races and geognosy ; yet it is the crying complaint to-day, not only among theosophists, but also among the few profane interested in the subject. " Why do not the adepts reveal that which they know ? " To this, one might answer, " Why should they, since one knows beforehand that no man of science will accept, even as an hypothesis, let alone as a theory or axiom, the facts imparted. Have you so much as accepted or believed in the A B C of the Occult philosophy contained in the *Theosophist*, " Esoteric Buddhism," and other works and periodicals ? Has not even the little which was given, been ridiculed and derided, and made to face the " animal " and " ape theory " of Huxley—Hæckel, on one hand, and the rib of Adam and the apple on the other ? Notwithstanding such an unenviable prospect, a mass of facts is given in the present work. And now the origin of man, the evolution of the globe and the races, human and animal, are as fully treated here as the writer is able to treat them.

The proofs brought forward in corroboration of the old teachings are scattered widely throughout the old scriptures of ancient civilizations. The Purânas, the Zendavesta, and the old classics are full of them; but no one has ever gone to the trouble of collecting and collating together those facts. The reason for this is, that all such events were recorded symbolically; and that the best scholars, the most acute minds, among our Aryanists and Egyptologists, have been too often darkened by one or another preconception; still oftener, by one-sided views of the secret meaning. Yet even a parable is a spoken symbol: a fiction or a fable, as some think; an allegorical representation, we say, of life-realities, events, and facts. And, as a moral was ever drawn from a parable, that moral being an actual truth and fact in human life, so an historical, real event was deduced—by those versed in the hieratic sciences—from certain emblems and symbols recorded in the ancient archives of the temples. The religious and esoteric history of every nation was embedded in symbols; it was never expressed in so many words. All the thoughts and emotions, all the learning and knowledge, revealed and acquired, of the early races, found their pictorial expression in allegory and parable. Why? Because *the spoken word has a potency unknown to, unsuspected and disbelieved in*, by the modern "sages." Because sound and rhythm are closely related to the four Elements of the Ancients; and because such or another vibration in the air is sure to awaken corresponding powers, union with which produces good or bad results, as the case may be. No student was ever allowed to recite historical, religious, or any real events in so many unmistakable words, lest the powers connected with the event should be once more attracted. Such events were narrated only during the Initiation, and every student had to record them in corresponding symbols, drawn out of his own mind and examined later by his master, before they were finally accepted. Thus was created in time the Chinese Alphabet, as, before that, the hieratic symbols were fixed upon in old Egypt. In the Chinese language, the alphabet of which may be read in any language,* and which is only a little less ancient than the Egyptian alphabet of Thoth, every word has its corresponding symbol conveying the word needed in a pictorial form. The language possesses many thousands of such symbol letters, or logograms, each meaning a whole word; for letters proper, or an alphabet, do not exist in the Chinese language any more than they did in the Egyptian till a far later period.

---

* Thus, a Japanese who does not understand one word of Chinese, meeting with a Chinaman who has never heard the language of the former, will communicate in writing with him, and they will understand each other perfectly—because the writing is symbolical.

The explanation of the chief symbols and emblems is now attempted, as Book II., which treats of Anthropogenesis, would be most difficult to understand without a preparatory acquaintance with the metaphysical symbols at least.

Nor would it be just to enter upon an esoteric reading of symbolism without giving due honour to one who has rendered it the greatest service in this century, by discovering the chief key to ancient Hebrew symbology, interwoven strongly with metrology, one of the keys to the once universal mystery language. Mr. Ralston Skinner, of Cincinnati, the author of "The Hebrew-Egyptian Mystery and the Source of Measures" has our thanks. A mystic and a Kabalist by nature, he has laboured for many years in this direction, and his efforts were certainly crowned with great success. In his own words :—

"The writer is quite certain that there was an ancient language which modernly and up to this time appears to have been lost, the vestiges of which, however, abundantly exist. . . . The author discovered that this (integral ratio in numbers of diameter to circumference of a circle) geometrical ratio was the very ancient, and probably the divine origin of linear measures. . . . It appears almost proven that the same system of geometry, numbers, ratio, and measures were known and made use of on the continent of North America, even prior to the knowledge of the same by the descending Semites. . . . ."

"The peculiarity of this language was that it could be contained in another, concealed and not to be perceived, save through the help of special instruction; letters and syllabic signs possessing at the same time the powers or meaning of numbers, of geometrical shapes, pictures, or ideographs and symbols, the designed scope of which would be determinatively helped out by parables in the shape of narratives or parts of narratives; while also it could be set forth separately, independently, and variously, by pictures, in stone work, or in earth construction."

"To clear up an ambiguity as to the term language : Primarily the word means the expression of ideas by human speech ; but, secondarily, it may mean the expression of ideas by any other instrumentality. This old language is so composed in the Hebrew text, that by the use of the written characters, which will be the language first defined, a distinctly separated series of ideas may be intentionally communicated, other than those ideas expressed by the reading of the sound signs. This secondary language sets forth, under a veil, series of ideas, copies in imagination of things sensible, which may be pictured, and of things which may be classed as real without being sensible ; as, for instance, the number 9 may be taken as a reality, though it has no sensible existence, so also a revolution of the moon, as separate from the moon itself by which that revolution has been made, may be taken as giving rise to, or causing a real idea, though such a revolution has no substance. This idea-language may consist of symbols restricted to arbitrary terms and signs, having a very limited range of conceptions, and quite valueless, or it may be a reading of nature in some of her manifestations of a value almost immeasurable, as regards human civilization. A picture of something natural may give rise to ideas of co-ordinative subject-matter, radiating out in various and even opposing directions, like the spokes of a wheel, and producing natural realities in departments very foreign to the apparent tendency of the reading of the first or starting picture. Notion may give rise to connected notion, but if it does, then, however apparently incongruous, all resulting ideas must spring from the original picture and be harmonically connected, or related. . . . Thus with a pictured idea radical enough, the imagination of the Cosmos itself even in its details of construction might result. Such a use of ordinary language is now obsolete, but it has become a question with the writer whether at one time, far back in the past, it, or such, was not the language of the world and of universal use, possessed, however, as it became more and more moulded into its arcane forms, by a select class or caste. By this I mean that the popular tongue or vernacular commenced even in its origin to be made use of as the vehicle of this peculiar mode of conveying ideas. Of this the evidences are very strong; and, indeed, it would seem that in the history of the human race there happened, from causes which at present, at any rate, we cannot trace, a lapse or loss from an original perfect language and a perfect system of science—shall we say perfect because they were of divine origin and importation?"

" Divine origin " does not mean here a revelation from an anthropomorphic god on a mount amidst thunder and lightning; but, as we understand it, a language and a system of science imparted to the early mankind by a more advanced *mankind*, so much higher as to be *divine* in the sight of that infant humanity. By a " mankind," in short, from other spheres; an idea which contains nothing supernatural in it, but the acceptance or rejection of which depends upon the degree of conceit and arrogance in the mind of him to whom it is stated. For, if the professors of modern knowledge would only confess that, though they know nothing of the future of the disembodied man—or rather will accept nothing—yet this future may be pregnant with surprises and unexpected revelations to them, once their Egos are rid of their gross bodies—then materialistic unbelief would have fewer chances than it has. Who of them knows, or can tell, what may happen when once the life cycle of this globe is run down and our mother earth herself falls into her last sleep? Who is bold enough to say that the *divine Egos* of our mankind—at least the elect out of the multitudes passing on to other spheres—*will not become in their turn* the " divine " instructors of a new mankind generated by them on a new globe, called to life and activity by the disembodied " principles " of our Earth? (See Stanza VI., Book I., Part I.) All this may have been the experience of the PAST, and these strange records lie embedded in the " Mystery language " of the prehistoric ages, the language now called SYMBOLISM.

§ II.

THE MYSTERY LANGUAGE AND ITS KEYS.

RECENT discoveries made by great mathematicians and Kabalists thus prove, beyond a shadow of doubt, that every theology, from the earliest and oldest down to the latest, has sprung not only from a common source of abstract beliefs, but from one universal esoteric, or " Mystery" language. These scholars hold the key to the universal language of old, and have turned it successfully, though only *once*, in the hermetically closed door leading to the Hall of Mysteries. The great archaic system known from prehistoric ages as the sacred Wisdom Science, one that is contained and can be traced in every old as well as in every new religion, had, and still has, its universal language—suspected by the Mason Ragon—the language of the Hierophants, which has seven " dialects," so to speak, each referring, and being specially appropriated, to one of the seven mysteries of Nature. Each had its own symbolism. Nature could thus be either read in its fulness, or viewed from one of its special aspects.

The proof of this lies, to this day, in the extreme difficulty which the Orientalists in general, the Indianists and Egyptologists especially, experience in interpreting the allegorical writings of the Aryans and the hieratic records of old Egypt. This is because they will never remember that all the ancient records were written in a language which was universal and known to all nations alike in days of old, but which is now intelligible only to the few. Like the Arabic figures which are plain to a man of whatever nation, or like the English word *and*, which becomes *et* for the Frenchman, *und* for the German, and so on, yet which may be expressed for all civilized nations in the simple sign &—so all the words of that mystery language signified the same thing to each man of whatever nationality. There have been several men of note who have tried to re-establish such a universal and *philosophical* tongue: Delgarme, Wilkins, Leibnitz; but Demaimieux, in his *Pasigraphie*, is the only one who has proven its possibility. The scheme of Valentinius, called the " Greek Kabala," based on the combination of Greek letters, might serve as a model.

The many-sided facets of the mystery language have led to the adoption of widely varied dogmas and rites in the exotericism of the Church rituals. It is they, again, which are at the origin of most of the dogmas of the Christian Church, *e.g.*, the seven Sacraments, the Trinity, the Resurrection; the seven capital Sins and the seven Virtues. The seven keys to the mystery tongue, however, having always been in the keeping of the highest among the initiated Hierophants of antiquity, it is only the partial use of a few out of the seven which passed, through the treason of some early Church Fathers—ex-initiates of the Temples— into the hands of the new sect of the Nazarenes. Some of the early Popes were Initiates, but the last fragments of their knowledge have now fallen into the power of the Jesuits, who have turned them into a system of sorcery.

It is maintained that INDIA (not in its present limits, but including its ancient boundaries) is the only country in the world which still has among her sons adepts, who have the knowledge of all the seven *sub-systems* and the key to the entire system. Since the fall of Memphis, Egypt began to lose those keys one by one, and Chaldea had preserved only three in the days of Berosus. As for the Hebrews, in all their writings they show no more than a thorough knowledge of the astronomical, geometrical and numerical systems of symbolizing all the human, and especially the *physiological* functions. They never had the higher keys.

"Every time I hear people talking of the religion of Egypt," writes M. Gaston Maspero, the great French Egyptologist and the successor of Mariette Bey, "I am tempted to ask *which* of the Egyptian religions they are talking about? Is it of the Egyptian religion of the 4th Dynasty, or of the Egyptian religion of the Ptolemaic period? Is it of the religion of the rabble, or of that of the learned men? Of that which was taught in the schools of Heliopolis, or of that other which was in the minds and conceptions of the Theban sacerdotal class? For, between the first tomb of Memphis, which bears the *cartouche* of a king of the third dynasty, and the last stones at Esnêh under Cæsar-Philippus, the Arabian, there is an interval of at least five thousand years. Leaving aside the invasion of the Shepherds, the Ethiopian and Assyrian dominions, the Persian conquest, Greek colonization, and the thousand revolutions of its political life, Egypt has passed during those five thousand years through many vicissitudes of life, moral and intellectual. Chapter XVII. of the *Book of the Dead* which seems to contain the exposition of the system of the world as it was understood at Heliopolis during the time of the first dynasties, is known to us only by a few copies of the eleventh and twelfth dynasties. Each of the verses composing it was already at the time interpreted in three or four different ways; so different, indeed, that according to this or another school, the Demiurge became the solar fire—*Ra-shoo*, or the primordial water. Fifteen centuries later, the number of readings had increased considerably. Time had, in its course, modified the ideas about the universe and the forces that ruled it. During the hardly 18 centuries that Christianity exists, it has worked, developed and transformed most of its dogmas ; how many times, then, might not the Egyptian clergy have altered its dogmas during those fifty centuries that separate Theodosius from the King Builders of the Pyramids ? "

Here we believe the eminent Egyptologist is going too far. The exoteric dogmas may often have been altered, the esoteric never. He does not take into account the sacred immutability of the primitive truths, revealed only during the mysteries of initiation. The Egyptian priests *have forgotten much, they altered nothing.* The loss of a good deal of the primitive teaching was due to the sudden deaths of the great Hiero-phants, who passed away before they had time to reveal *all* to their suc-cessors ; mostly, to the absence of worthy heirs to the knowledge. Yet they have preserved in their rituals and dogmas the principal teachings of the secret doctrine. Thus, in the seventeenth chapter mentioned by Maspero, one finds (1) Osiris saying he is *Toum* (the creative force in nature, giving form to all Beings, spirits and men), self-generated and self-existent, issued from *Noun*, the celestial river, called *Father-mother* of the gods, the primordial deity, which is chaos or the *Deep*, impregnated by the unseen spirit. (2) He has found *Shoo* (solar force) on the staircase in the City of the Eight (the two *cubes* of good and Evil), and he has annihi-lated the evil principles in *Noun* (chaos) the children of Rebellion. (3) He is the Fire and Water, *i.e.*, Noun the primordial parent, and he created the gods out of his limbs—14 gods (twice seven) seven dark and seven light gods (the seven Spirits of the Presence of the Christians and the Seven dark Evil Spirits). (4) He is the Law of existence and Being (v. 10), the *Bennoo* (or phœnix, the bird of resurrection in Eternity), in whom night follows the day, and day the night—an allusion to the perio-dical cycles of cosmic resurrection and human re-incarnation ; for what can this mean ? "The wayfarer who crosses millions of years, in the name of One, and the great green (primordial water or Chaos) the name of the other" (v. 17), one begetting millions of years in succession, the other engulfing them, to restore them back. (5) He speaks of the Seven Luminous ones who follow their Lord, who confers justice (Osiris in *Amenti*).

All this is now shown to have been the source and origin of Christian dogmas. That which the Jews had from Egypt, through Moses and other initiates, was confused and distorted enough in later days ; and that which the Church got from both, is still more misinterpreted.

Yet their system is now proven identical in this special department of symbology—the key, namely, to the mysteries of astronomy as connected with those of generation and conception—with those ideas of ancient reli-gions, the theology of which has developed the phallic element. The Jewish system of sacred measures applied to religious symbols is the same, so far as geometrical and numerical combinations go, as those of Chaldea, Greece, and Egypt, having been adopted by the Jews during the centuries of their slavery and captivity with those nations.* What was that system? It is the intimate conviction of the author of "The Source of Measures" that "the Mosaic Books were intended, by a mode of art speech, to set forth a geometrical and numerical system of exact science, which should serve as an origin of measures." Piazzi Smyth believes likewise. This system and these measures are found by some scholars to be identical with those used in the construction of the great pyramid—but this is only partially so. "The foundation of these measures was the Parker ratio," says Mr. R. Skinner, in "The Source of Measures."

The author of this very extraordinary work has found it out, he says, in the use of the integral ratio in numbers of diameter to circumference of a circle, discovered by John Parker, of New York. This ratio is 6,561 for diameter, and 20,612 for circumference. Furthermore, that this geometrical ratio was the very ancient (and probably) the divine origin of what have now become through exoteric handling and practical application the British linear measures, "the underlying unit of which, viz., the *inch*, was likewise the base of one of the royal Egyptian *cubits* and of the Roman *foot*. He also found out that there was a modified form of the ratio, viz., 113-355 (explained in his work); and that while this last ratio pointed through its origin to the exact integral *pi*, or to 6,561 to 20,612, it also served as a base for astronomical calculations. The author discovered that a system *of exact science, geometrical, numerical, and astronomical*, founded on these ratios and to be found in use in the construction of the Great Egyptian Pyramid, was in part the burden of *this language* as contained in, and concealed under, the verbiage of the Hebrew text of the Bible. The inch and the two-foot rule of 24 inches interpreted for use through the elements of the circle (*see first pages of Book I.*) and the ratios mentioned, were found to be at the basis or foundation of this natural and Egyptian and Hebrew system of science, while, moreover, it seems evident enough that the system itself was looked upon as of divine origin and of divine revela-

---

* As we said in *Isis (Vol. II. p.* 438-9), "To the present moment, in spite of all controversies and researches, History and Science remain as much as ever in the dark as to the origin of the Jews. They may be as well the exiled *Tchandalas* of old India, the 'bricklayers' mentioned by Vina-Svata, Veda-Vyasa and Manu, as the Phœnicians of Herodotus, or the Hyk-Sos of Josephus, or descendants of Pali shepherds, or a mixture of all these. The Bible names the Tyrians as a kindred people, and claims dominion over them. . . . Yet whatever they may have been, they became a hybrid people, not long after Moses, as the Bible shows them freely intermarrying not alone with the Canaanites, but with every other nation or race they came in contact with."

tion. . . ." But let us see what is said by the opponents of Prof. Piazzi
Smyth's measurements of the Pyramid.

Mr. Petrie seems to deny them, and to have made short work
altogether of Piazzi Smyth's calculations in their Biblical connection.
So does Mr. Proctor, the champion " Coincidentalist " for many years
past in every question of ancient arts and sciences. Speaking of " the
multitude of relations independent of the Pyramid, which have turned
up while the Pyramidalists have been endeavouring to connect the
pyramid with the solar system . . . . these coincidences," he says,
" are altogether more curious than any coincidence between the
Pyramid and astronomical numbers : the former are as close and
remarkable as they are real " (*i.e.*, those " coincidences " that would
remain if even the pyramid had no existence); " the latter which are
only *imaginary* (?) have only been established by the process which
schoolboys call ' fudging,' and now new measures have left the work to
be done all over again " (*Petrie's letter to the Academy, Dec.* 17, 1881.) To
this Mr. Staniland Wake justly observes in his work on " The Origin
and Significance of the Great Pyramid " (London, 1882) : " They must,
however, have been more than *mere coincidences*, if the builders of the
Pyramid had the astronomical knowledge displayed in its perfect
orientation and in its other admitted astronomical features."

They had it ; and it is on this " knowledge " that the programme of
the MYSTERIES and of the series of Initiations was based : thence, the
construction of the Pyramids, the everlasting record and the indestructible symbol of these Mysteries and Initiations on Earth, as the courses
of the stars are in Heaven. The cycle of Initiation was a reproduction
in miniature of that great series of Cosmic changes to which astronomers
have given the name of tropical or sidereal year. Just as, at the close
of the cycle of the sidereal year [25,868 years], the heavenly bodies
return to the same relative positions as they occupied at its outset, so
at the close of the cycle of Initiation the inner man has regained the
pristine state of divine purity and knowledge from which he set out on
his cycle of terrestrial incarnation.

Moses, an Initiate into the Egyptian Mystagogy, based the religious
mysteries of the new nation which he created, upon the same abstract
formula derived from this sidereal cycle, which he symbolised under the
form and measurements of the tabernacle, that he is supposed to have
constructed in the wilderness. On these data, the later Jewish High
Priests constructed the allegory of Solomon's Temple—a building which
never had a real existence, any more than had King Solomon himself,
who is simply, and as much a solar myth as is the still later Hiram
Abif, of the Masons, as Ragon has well demonstrated. Thus, if the
measurements of this allegorical temple, the symbol of the cycle of

Initiation, coincide with those of the Great Pyramid, it is due to the fact that the former were derived from the latter through the Tabernacle of Moses.

That our author has undeniably discovered *one* and even *two* of *the keys* is fully demonstrated in the work just quoted. One has but to read it to feel a growing conviction that the hidden meaning of the allegories and parables of both Testaments is now unveiled. But that he owes this discovery far more to his own genius than to Parker and Piazzi Smyth, is as certain, if not more so. For, as just shown, whether the measures of the great Pyramid taken and adopted as the correct ones by the Biblical " Pyramidalists " are beyond suspicion, is not so sure. A proof of this is the work called " The Pyramids and Temples of Gizeh," by Mr. F. Petrie, besides other works written quite recently to oppose the said calculations, which were called *biassed*. We gather that nearly every one of Piazzi Smyth's measurements differs from the later and more carefully made measurements of Mr. Petrie, who concludes the Introduction to his work with this sentence :

" As to the results of the whole investigation, perhaps many theories will agree with an American who was a warm believer in Pyramid theories when he came to Gizeh. I had the pleasure of his company there for a couple of days, and at our last meal together he said to me in a saddened tone—' Well, sir ! I feel as if I had been to a funeral. By all means let the old theories have a decent burial, though we should take care that in our haste none of the wounded ones are buried alive.' "

As regards the late J. Parker's calculation in general, and his third proposition especially, we have consulted some eminent mathematicians, and this is the substance of what they say :

Parker's reasoning rests on sentimental, rather than mathematical, considerations, and is logically inconclusive.

Proposition III., namely, that—

" The circle is the natural basis or beginning of all area, and the square being made so in mathematical science, is artificial and arbitrary——"

—is an illustration of an arbitrary proposition, and cannot safely be relied upon in mathematical reasoning. The same observation applies, even more strongly, to Proposition VII., which states that :

" Because the circle is the primary shape in nature, and hence the basis of area ; and because the circle is measured by, and is equal to the square only in ratio of half its circumference by the radius, therefore, circumference and radius, and not the square of diameter, are the only natural and legitimate elements of area, by which all regular shapes are made equal to the square, and equal to the circle."

Proposition IX. is a remarkable example of faulty reasoning, and it is the one on which Mr. Parker's Quadrature mainly rests. Here it is :—

" The circle and the equilateral triangle are opposite to one another in all
the elements of their construction, and hence the fractional diameter of one
circle, which is equal to the diameter of one square, is in the opposite duplicate
ratio to the diameter of an equilateral triangle whose area is one," etc., etc.

Granting, for the sake of argument, that a triangle can be said to
have a radius in the sense in which we speak of the radius of a circle,—
for what Parker calls the radius of the triangle is the radius of a circle
inscribed in the triangle and therefore not the radius of the triangle at
all,—and granting for the moment the other fanciful and mathematical
propositions united in his premises, why must we conclude that if the
triangle and circle are opposite in all the elements of their construction,
the diameter of any defined circle is in the opposite duplicate ratio of
the diameter of any given equivalent triangle ?   What necessary
connection is there between the premises and the conclusion ?   The
reasoning is of a kind not known in geometry, and would not be accepted
by strict mathematicians.

Whether the Archaic esoteric system originated the British inch or
not, is of little consequence, however, to the strict and true metaphysician.   Nor does Mr. Ralston Skinner's esoteric reading of the
Bible become incorrect, merely because the measurements of the Pyramid
will not be found to agree with those of Solomon's temple, the ark of
Noah, etc.; or because Mr. Parker's Quadrature of the Circle is rejected
by mathematicians.   For Mr. Skinner's reading depends first of all on
the Kabalistic methods and the Rabbinical value of the Hebrew letters.
But it is extremely important to ascertain whether the measures used
in the evolution and building of the Aryan symbolic religion, in the
construction of their temples, the figures given in the Purânas, and
especially in their chronology, their astronomical symbols, the duration
of the cycles, and other computations, were, or were not, the same as
those used in the Biblical measurements and glyphs.   For this
will prove that the Jews, unless they took their sacred cubit
and measurements from the Egyptians (Moses being an initiate
of the Priests) must have got those notions from India.   At any rate
they passed them to the early Christians.   Hence, it is the Occultists
and Kabalists who are the " true " heirs to the KNOWLEDGE, or the
secret wisdom which is still found in the Bible; for they alone now
understand its real meaning, whereas profane Jews and Christians cling
to the husks and dead letter thereof.   That it is the system of measures
which led to the invention of the God-names Elohim and Jehovah, and
their adaptation to phallicism, and that Jehovah is a not very flattered
copy of Osiris, is now demonstrated by the author of the " Source of
Measures."   But the latter and Mr. Piazzi Smyth both seem to labour under
the impression that (a) the priority of the system belongs to the Israelites,

the Hebrew language being the *divine* language, and that (*b*) this universal language belongs to direct revelation !

The latter hypothesis is correct only in the sense shown in the last paragraph of the preceding § ; but we have yet to agree as to the nature and character of the divine " Revealer." With regard to priority, this, to the profane, will of course depend on (*a*) the internal and external evidence of the revelation, and (*b*) on each scholar's individual preconception. This, however, cannot prevent either the theistic Kabalist, or the Pantheistic Occultist, from believing each in his way; neither of the two convincing the other. The data furnished by history are too meagre and unsatisfactory for either of them to prove to the sceptic which of them is right.

On the other hand, the proofs afforded by tradition are too constantly rejected for us to hope to settle the question in our present age. Meanwhile, materialistic science will be laughing impartially at both Kabalists and Occultists. But the said vexed question of priority once laid aside, Science, in its departments of philology and comparative religion, will find itself finally taken to task, and be compelled to admit the common claim.* Its greatest scholars, instead of pooh-poohing that supposed

---

* One by one the claims become admitted, as one Scientist after another is compelled to recognize the facts given out from the *Secret Doctrine*—though he rarely, if ever, recognizes that he has been anticipated in his statements. Thus, in the palmy days of Mr. Piazzi Smyth's authority on the Pyramid of Gizeh, his theory was, that the porphyry sarcophagus of the King's Chamber " *is the unit of measure for* the two most enlightened nations of the earth, England and America," and was no better than a " corn bin." This was vehemently denied by us in *Isis Unveiled* just published at that time. Then the New York press arose in arms (the " *Sun*" and the "*World*" chiefly) against our presuming to correct or find fault with such a star of learning. On p. 519, vol. I., we had said, that Herodotus when treating of that Pyramid " might have added that, externally it symbolized *the creative principle of Nature*, and illustrated also the *principles of geometry, mathematics, astrology, and astronomy*. Internally, it was a majestic fane, in whose sombre recesses were performed the mysteries, and whose walls had often witnessed the initiation-scenes of members of the royal family. The porphyry sarcophagus, which Professor Piazzi Smyth, Astronomer Royal of Scotland, degrades into a corn-bin, was the *baptismal font*, upon emerging from which the neophyte was "born again " and became an adept."

Our statement was laughed at in those days. We were accused of having got our ideas from the " craze " of Shaw, an English writer who had maintained that the Sarcophagus had been used for the celebration of the Mysteries of Osiris ; (we had never heard of that writer !). And now, six or seven years later, this is what Mr. Staniland Wake writes on p. 93 of his paper, on " The Origin and Significance of the Great Pyramid.''

" The so-called King's Chamber, of which an enthusiastic pyramidist says, ' The polished walls, fine materials, grand proportions, and exalted place, eloquently tell of glories yet to come—if not, the chamber of perfections of Cheops' tomb, was probably *the place to which the initiant was admitted after he had passed through the narrow upward passage and the grand gallery, with its lowly termination, which gradually prepared him for the*

" farrago of absurd fiction and superstitions," as the Brahminical literature is generally termed, will endeavour to learn the symbolical universal language with its numerical and geometrical keys. But here again
they will hardly be successful if they share the belief that the Jewish
Kabalistic system contains the key to the *whole* mystery : *for, it does not.*
Nor does any other Scripture at present possess it in its entirety, for
even the Vedas are not complete. Every old religion is but a chapter
or two of the entire volume of archaic primeval mysteries—Eastern
Occultism alone being able to boast that it is in possession of the full
secret, with its *seven* keys. Comparisons will be instituted, and as much
as possible will be explained in this work—the rest is left to the
student's personal intuition. For in saying that *Eastern Occultism has the
secret*, it is not as if a "complete " or even an approximate knowledge was
claimed by the writer, which would be absurd. What I know, I give
out ; that which I cannot explain, the student must find out for himself.

But while supposing that the whole cycle of the universal mystery
language will not be mastered for whole centuries to come, even that
which has been hitherto discovered in the Bible by some scholars is quite
sufficient to demonstrate the claim—mathematically. Judaism having
availed itself of two keys out of the seven, and these two keys having been
now rediscovered, it becomes no longer a matter of individual speculation and hypothesis, least of all of " coincidence," but one of a correct
reading of the Bible texts, as anyone acquainted with arithmetic reads
and verifies an addition or total.* A few years longer and this system
will kill the dead letter of the Bible, as it will that of all the other exoteric faiths, by showing the dogmas in their real, naked meaning.

And then this undeniable meaning, however incomplete, will unveil
the mystery of Being, besides changing entirely the modern scientific
systems of Anthropology, Ethnology and especially that of Chronology.
The element of Phallicism, found in every God-name and narrative in the
Old (and to some degree in the New) Testament, may also in time considerably change modern materialistic views in Biology and Physiology.

Divested of their modern repulsive crudeness, such views of nature
and man, on the authority of the celestial bodies and their mysteries,

---

final stage of the SACRED MYSTERIES." Had Mr. Staniland Wake been a Theosophist, he might have added that the narrow upward passage leading to the King's
chamber had a " narrow gate " indeed ; the same " strait gate " which " leadeth unto
life," or the new spiritual re-birth alluded to by Jesus in Matthew vii. 13 *et seq ;* and
that it is this gate in the Initiation temple, that the writer who recorded the words
alleged to have been spoken by an Initiate, was thinking of.

* All we have said in *Isis* is now found corroborated in the " Egyptian Mystery ; or
The Source of Measures," by those readings of the Bible with the numerical and
geometrical keys thereto.

will unveil the evolutions of the human mind and show how natural was such a course of thought.   The so-called phallic symbols have become offensive only because of the element of materiality and animality in them.   As they originated with the archaic races, which, issuing to their personal knowledge from an androgyne ancestry, were the first phenomenal manifestations in their own sight of the separation of sexes and the ensuing mystery of creating in their turn—such symbols were but natural.   If later races have degraded them, especially the " chosen people," this does not affect the origin of those symbols.   The little Semitic tribe—one of the smallest branchlets from the commingling of the 4th and 5th sub-races (the Mongolo-Turanian and the Indo-European, so-called, after the sinking of the great Continent)—could only accept its symbology in the spirit which was given to it by the nations from which it was derived.   Perchance, in the Mosaic beginnings, that symbology was not as crude as it became later under the handling of Ezra, who remodelled the whole Pentateuch.   For the glyph of Pharaoh's daughter (the woman), the Nile (the Great Deep and Water), and the baby-boy found floating therein in the ark of rushes, has not been primarily composed for, or by, Moses.   It has been found anticipated in the Babylonian fragments on the tiles, in the story of King Sargon,* who lived far earlier than Moses.   Now, what is the logical inference ?   Most assuredly that which gives us the right to say that the story told of Moses by Ezra had been learned by him while at Babylon,

---

* On page 224 of *Assyrian Antiquities* Mr. George Smith says: " In the palace of Sennacherib at Kouyunjik I found another fragment of the curious history of Sargon. . . . published in my translation in the *Transactions of the Society of Biblical Archæology*, *vol. I. part I. p.* 46." The capital of Sargon, the Babylonian Moses, " was the great city of Agadi, called by the Semitics Akkad—mentioned in Genesis as the capital of Nimrod." (*Gen. x.* 10.) . . . " Akkad lay near the City of *Sippara* on the Euphrates and North of Babylon." (*See Isis, vol. II. p.* 442-3,) Another strange *coincidence* is found in the fact that the name of the neighbouring above-mentioned City of *Sippara* is the same as the name of the wife of Moses—*Zipporah* (Exodus ii.). Of course the story is a clever addition by Ezra, *who could not be ignorant of it*. This curious story is found on fragments of tablets from Kouyunjik, and reads as follows :—

   1. Sargona, the powerful king, the king of Akkad am I.

   2. My mother was a princess, my father I did not know ; a brother of my father ruled over the country.

   3. In the city of Azupiran, which is by the side of the River Euphrates.

   4. My mother, the princess, conceived me ; in difficulty she brought me forth.

   5. She placed me in an ark of rushes, with bitumen my exit she sealed up.

   6. She launched me in the river, which did not drown me.

   7. The river carried me, to Akki the water-carrier it brought me.

   8. Akki, the water-carrier, in tenderness of bowels, lifted me, etc., etc.

   And now *Exodus* (ii): " And when she (Moses' mother) could not longer hide him, she took for him an ark of bulrushes, and daubed it with slime and with pitch, and put the child therein, and she laid it in the flags by the river's brink."

and that he applied the allegory told of Sargon to the Jewish lawgiver. In short, that *Exodus* was never written by Moses, but re-fabricated from old materials by Ezra.

And if so, then why should not other symbols and glyphs far more crude in their phallic element have been added by this adept in the later Chaldean and Sabæan phallic worship? We are taught that the primeval faith of the Israelites was quite different from that which was developed centuries later by the Talmudists, and before them by David and Hezekiah.

All this, notwithstanding the exoteric element, as now found in the two Testaments, is quite sufficient to class the Bible among esoteric works, and to connect its secret system with Indian, Chaldean, and Egyptian symbolism. The whole cycle of biblical glyphs and numbers as suggested by astronomical observations—astronomy and theology being closely connected—is found in Indian exoteric, as well as esoteric, systems. These figures and their symbols, the signs of the Zodiac, the planets, their aspects and nodes—the last term having now passed even into our modern botany to distinguish male and female plants (the unisexual, polygamous, monœcious, diœcious, etc., etc.)—are known in astronomy as *sextiles*, *quartiles* and so on, and have been used for ages and æons by the archaic nations, and in one sense have the same meaning as the Hebrew numerals. The earliest forms of elementary geometry must have certainly been suggested by the observation of the heavenly bodies and their groupings. Hence the most archaic symbols in Eastern Esotericism are a circle, a point, a triangle, a plane, a cube, a pentacle, and a hexagon, and plane figures with various sides and angles. This shows the knowledge and use of geometrical symbology to be as old as the world.

Starting from this, it becomes easy to understand how nature herself could have taught primeval mankind, even without the help of its divine instructors, the first principles of a numerical and geometrical symbol language.* Hence one finds numbers and figures used as an

---

" The story," says Mr. G. Smith, " is supposed to have happened about 1600 B.C. rather earlier than the supposed age of Moses. As we know that the fame of Sargon reached Egypt, it is quite likely that this account had a connection with the event related in *Exodus* ii., for every action, when once performed, has a tendency to be repeated." But now, when Professor Sayce has had the courage to push back the dates of the Chaldean and Assyrian Kings by two thousand years more, Sargon must have preceded Moses by 2,000 years at the least. (See Professor Sayce's *Lectures* on the subject.) The confession is suggestive, but the figures lack a cypher or two.

* As a reminder how the *Esoteric* religion of Moses was crushed several times, and the worship of Jehovah, as re-established by David, put in its place, by Hezekiah for one, read pp. 436-42, vol. II., in *Isis Unveiled*. Surely there must have been some very

expression and a record of thought in every archaic symbolical Scripture. They are ever the same, with only certain variations growing out of the first figures.   Thus the evolution and correlation of the mysteries of Kosmos, of its growth and development—spiritual and physical, abstract and concrete—were first recorded in geometrical changes of shape. Every Cosmogony began with a circle, a point, a triangle, and a cube, up to number 9, when it was synthesized by the first line and a circle—the Pythagorean mystic *Decade*, the sum of all, involving and expressing the mysteries of the entire Kosmos ; recorded a hundred times more fully in the Hindu system, for him who can understand its mystic language. The numbers 3 and 4, in their blending of 7, as those of 5, 6, 9, and 10, are the very corner-stone of Occult Cosmogonies.   This decade and its thousand combinations are found in every portion of the globe.   One recognizes them in the caves and rock-cut temples of Hindostan and Central Asia, as in the pyramids and lithoi of Egypt and America ; in the Catacombs of Ozimandyas, in the mounds of the Caucasian snow-capped fastnesses, in the ruins of Palenque, in Easter Island, everywhere whither the foot of ancient man has ever journeyed.   The 3 and the 4, the triangle and the cube, or the male and female universal glyph, showing the first aspect of the evolving deity, is stamped for ever in the Southern Cross in the Heavens, as in the Egyptian *Crux-Ansata*.   As well expressed, " The Cube unfolded is in display a cross of the *tau*, or Egyptian form, or of the Christian cross form. . . . A circle attached to the first, gives the *ansated cross*. . . numbers 3 and 4 counted on the cross, showing a form of the (Hebrew) golden candlestick (in the Holy of Holies), and of the 3 + 4 = 7, and 6+1 = 7, days in the *circle of the week*, as 7 lights of the sun.   So also as the week of 7 lights gave origin to the *month* and *year*, so it is the *time marker of birth*. . . . The cross form being shown, then, by the connected use of the form 113 : 355, the symbol is completed by the *attachment of a man to the cross*.* This kind of measure was made to co-ordinate with the idea of the *origin* of human life, and hence the *phallic form*.†"

The *Stanzas* show the cross and these numbers playing a prominent part in archaic cosmogony.   Meanwhile we may profit by the evidence collected by the same author to show the identity of symbols and their esoteric meaning all over the globe, which he calls rightly the " primordial vestiges of these symbols."

good reasons why the Sadducees, who furnished almost all the high Priests of Judea, held to the Laws of Moses and spurned the alleged " Books of Moses," the Pentateuch of the Synagogue and the Talmud.

* Once more, remember the Hindu Wittoba crucified in space ; the significance of the " sacred sign," the *Swastica ;* Plato's Decussated man in Space, etc., etc.

† " Source of Measures."

" Under the general view taken of the nature of the number forms. . . . it becomes a matter of research of the utmost interest as to when and where their existence and their use first became known. Has it been a matter of revelation in what we know as the historic age—a cycle exceedingly modern when the age of the human race is contemplated ? It seems, in fact, as to the date of its possession by man, to have been farther removed in the past from the old Egyptians than are the old Egyptians from us.

" The Easter Isles in ' mid Pacific' present the feature of the remaining peaks of the mountains of *a submerged continent,* for the reason that these peaks are thickly studded with Cyclopean statues, remnants of the civilization of a dense and cultivated people, who must have of necessity occupied a widely extended area. On the back of these images is to be found the ' *ansated cross* ' and the same modified to the outlines of the human form. A full description, with plate showing the land, with the thickly planted statues, also with copies of the images, is to be found in the January number 1870 of the London *Builder.*

" In the ' *Naturalist,*' published at Salem, Massachusetts, in one of the early numbers, is to be found a description of some very ancient and curious carving on the crest walls of the mountains of South America, older by far, it is averred, than the races now living. The strangeness of these tracings is in that they exhibit the outlines of a man stretched out on a cross,* by a series of drawings, by which from the form of *a man* that of *a cross* springs, but so done that the cross may be taken as the man, or the man as the cross ; thus exhibiting a symbolic display of the interdependency of the forms set forth.

" It is known that tradition among the Aztecs has handed down a very perfect account of the *deluge.* . . . Baron Humboldt says that we are to look for the country of Aztalan, the original country of the Aztecs, as high up at least as the 42nd parallel north ; whence, journeying, they at last arrived in the vale of Mexico. In that vale the earthen mounds of the far north become the elegant stone pyramidal and other structures whose remains are now found. The correspondences between the Aztec remains and those of the Egyptians are well known. . . . Attwater, from examination of hundreds of them, is convinced that they had a knowledge of astronomy. As to one of the most perfect of the pyramidal structures among the Aztecs, Humboldt gives a description to the following effect :

" The form of this pyramid (of Papantla) which has *seven* stories, is more tapering than any other monument of this kind yet discovered, but its height is not remarkable, being but 57 feet, its base but 25 feet on each side. However, it is remarkable on one account : it is built entirely of hewn stones, of an extraordinary size, and very beautifully shaped. *Three* staircases lead to the top, the steps of which are decorated with hieroglyphical sculptures and small *niches* arranged with great symmetry. The number of these niches seems to allude to the 318 *simple and compound signs of the days* of their civil calendar."

" 318 is the Gnostic value of Christ," remarks the author, " and the famous number of the trained or circumcised servants of Abraham. When it is consi-

---

* See farther on the description given of the early Aryan initiation : of Visvakarma crucifying the Sun, " Vikkârtana," shorn of his beams—on a cruciform lath.

dered that 318 is an *abstract value*, and *universal*, as expressive of a diameter value to a circumference of *unity*, its use in the composition of the civil calendar becomes manifest."

Identical glyphs, numbers and esoteric symbols are found in Egypt, Peru, Mexico, Easter Island, India, Chaldea, and Central Asia. Crucified men, and symbols of the evolution of races from gods ; and yet behold Science repudiating the idea of *a human race other than* one made in *our* image ; theology clinging to its 6,000 years of Creation ; anthropology teaching our descent from the ape ; and the Clergy tracing it from Adam 4,004 years B.C. ! !

Shall one, for fear of incurring the penalty of being called a superstitious fool, and even a *liar*, abstain from furnishing proofs—as good as any—only because that day, when all the SEVEN KEYS shall be delivered unto Science, or rather the men of learning and research in the symbological department, has not yet dawned ? In the face of the crushing discoveries of Geology and Anthropology with regard to the antiquity of man, shall we—in order to avoid the usual penalty that awaits every one who strays outside the beaten paths of either Theology or Materialism —hold to the 6,000 years and " special creation," or accept in submissive admiration our genealogy and descent from the ape ? Not so, as long as it is known that the secret records hold the said SEVEN keys to the mystery of the genesis of man. Faulty, materialistic, and biassed as the scientific theories may be, they are a thousand times nearer the truth than the vagaries of theology. The latter are in their death agony for every one but the most uncompromising bigot and fanatic.* Hence we have no choice but either to blindly accept the deductions of Science, or to cut adrift from it, and withstand it fearlessly to its face, stating what the Secret Doctrine teaches us, being fully prepared to bear the consequences.

But let us see whether Science in its materialistic speculations, and even tneology in its death-rattle and supreme struggle to reconcile the 6,000 years since Adam with Sir Charles Lyell's " Geological Evidences of the Antiquity of Man," do not themselves give us unconsciously a helping hand. Ethnology, on the confession of some of its very learned votaries, finds it already impossible to account for the varieties in the human race, unless the hypothesis of the *creation of several Adams* be accepted. They speak of " a white Adam and a black Adam, a red

---

* Some of its defenders must have lost their reason, one would rather say. For what can one think when, in the face of *the dead-letter* absurdities of the Bible, these are still supported, publicly and as fiercely as ever, and one finds its theologians maintaining that though " the Scriptures carefully refrain (?) from making any direct contribution to scientific knowledge, *they have never stumbled* upon any statement *which will not abide the light of* ADVANCING SCIENCE " ! ! !—(" *Primeval Man,*" p. 14).

Adam and a yellow Adam." *   Were they Hindus enumerating the
rebirths of Vamadeva from the *Linga Purâna*, they could say little
more.   For, enumerating the repeated births of Siva, the latter show
him in one Kalpa of a *white* complexion, in another of a *black* colour, in
still another of a *red* colour, after which the Kumâra becomes " four
youths of a yellow colour."   This strange *coincidence*, as Mr. Proctor
would say, speak only in favour of scientific intuition, as Siva-
Kumâra represents only allegorically the human races during the
genesis of man.   But it led to another   intuitional phenomenon
—in the theological ranks this time.   The unknown author of
" Primeval Man " in a desperate effort to screen the divine Revelation
from the merciless and eloquent discoveries of geology and anthropology, remarking that " it would be unfortunate if the defenders of the
Bible should be driven into the position of either surrendering the
inspiration of Scripture, or denying the conclusions of geologists "—
finds a compromise.   Nay, he devotes a thick volume to proving this
fact : " Adam was not the *first man*† created upon this earth." . . . The
exhumed relics of pre-Adamic man, " instead of shaking our confidence
in Scripture, supply additional proof of its veracity " (*p.* 194).   How
so ?   In the simplest way imaginable ; for the author argues that, henceforth " we " (the clergy) " are enabled to leave scientific men to pursue
their studies without attempting to coerce them by the fear of heresy "
. . . (this must be a relief indeed to Messrs. Huxley, Tyndall, and Sir
C. Lyell). . . . " The Bible narrative *does not commence with creation*, as
is commonly supposed, but with the formation of Adam and Eve,
millions of years after our planet had been created.   Its previous
history, so far as Scripture is concerned, is yet unwritten." . . . . .
" There may have been not one, but twenty different races upon
the earth before the time of Adam, just as there may be twenty
different races of men on other worlds " (p. 55). . . . Who,
then, or what were those races, since the author still maintains that
Adam is *the first man of our race ?*   It was THE SATANIC RACE AND RACES !
" Satan (was) never in heaven, Angels and men (being) one species.'
It was the pre-Adamic race of " Angels that sinned."   Satan was
" the first Prince of this world," we read.   Having died in consequence of his rebellion, he remained on earth as a *disembodied Spirit*, and
tempted Adam and Eve.   " The earlier ages of the Satanic race, and
more especially *during the life-time of Satan* (*! ! !*) may have been a period

---

* " Primeval Man Unveiled, or the Anthropology of the Bible " ; author (unknown)
of the " Stars and the Angels " 1870, p. 195.

† Especially in the face of the evidence furnished by the authorized Bible itself in
ch. iv. of *Genesis*, *v.* 16 *and* 17, which shows Cain going to the land of Nod and there
marrying a wife.

of patriarchal civilization and comparative repose—a time of Tubal-
Cains and Jubals, when both Sciences and arts attempted to strike their
roots into the accursed ground. . . . . What a subject for an epic. . . .
(when) there are inevitable incidents which must have occurred. We
see before us . . . . the gay primeval lover wooing his blushing bride at
dewy eve under the Danish oaks, that then grew where now no oaks will
grow . . . . the grey primeval patriarch . . . . the primeval offspring
innocently gambolling by his side. . . . . A thousand such pictures rise
before us "! . . . . (pp. 206-207).

The retrospective glance at this *Satanic* " blushing bride " in the
days of Satan's innocence, does not lose in poetry as it gains in
originality.   Quite the reverse.   The modern Christian bride —
who does not often blush nowadays before her gay modern
lovers — might even derive a moral lesson from this daughter
of Satan, in the exuberant fancy of her first human biographer.
These pictures — and to appreciate them at their true value
they must be examined in the volume that describes them—are all
suggested with a view to reconcile the infallibility of revealed Scripture
with Sir C. Lyell's " Antiquity of Man " and other damaging scientific
works.   But this does not prevent truth and fact appearing at the
foundation of these vagaries, which the author has never dared to sign
with his own, or even a borrowed name.   For, his pre-Adamic races—
not Satanic but simply Atlantic, and the Hermaphrodites before the
latter—are mentioned in the Bible when read esoterically, as they are
in the Secret Doctrine.   The SEVEN KEYS open the mysteries, past and
future, of the seven great Root Races, as of the seven Kalpas.   Though
the genesis of man, and even the esoteric geology, will surely be rejected
by Science just as much as the Satanic and pre-Adamic races, yet if
having no other way out of their difficulties the Scientists have to
choose between the two, we feel certain that, Scripture notwithstanding,
once the mystery language is approximately mastered, it is the archaic
teaching that will be accepted.

§ III.

PRIMORDIAL SUBSTANCE AND DIVINE THOUGHT.

" As it would seem irrational to affirm that we already know all existing
causes, permission must be given to assume, if need be, *an entirely new agent.*

" Assuming, what is not strictly accurate as yet, that the undulatory hypothesis accounts for all the facts, we are called on to decide whether the existence of an undulating Ether is thereby proved. *We cannot positively affirm*

that no other supposition will explain the facts. Newton's corpuscular hypothesis is admitted to have broken down on Interference ; and there is, at the present day, no rival.   Still, it is extremely desirable in all such hypotheses to find some collateral confirmation, some evidence *aliunde*, of THE SUPPOSED ETHER. . . . . Some Hypotheses consist of assumptions as to the minute structure and operations of bodies.   From the nature of the case, these assumptions can never be proved by direct means.   Their only merit is *their suitability to express the phenomena.*   They are REPRESENTATIVE FICTIONS."—(" *Logic,*" *by Alexander Bain, LL.D., Part II., p.* 133)

Ether, this *hypothetical* Proteus, one of the "representative *Fictions*" of modern Science—which, nevertheless, was so long *accepted*—is one of the lower "principles" of what we call PRIMORDIAL SUBSTANCE (Akâsa, in Sanskrit), one of the *dreams* of old, and which has now become again the dream of modern science. It is the greatest, just as it is the boldest, of the surviving speculations of ancient philosophers.   For the Occultists, however, both ETHER and the Primordial Substance are a reality.   To put it plainly, ETHER is the Astral Light, and the Primordial Substance is AKÂSA, the *Upadhi* of DIVINE THOUGHT.

In modern language, the latter would be better named COSMIC IDEATION—Spirit ; the former, COSMIC SUBSTANCE, Matter.   These, the Alpha and the Omega of Being, are but the two *facets* of the one Absolute Existence.   The latter was never addressed, or even mentioned, by any name in antiquity, except allegorically.   In the oldest Aryan race, the Hindu, the worship of the intellectual classes never consisted (as with the Greeks) in a fervent adoration of marvellous form and art, which led later on to anthropomorphism.   But while the Greek philosopher adored form, and the Hindu sage alone "perceived the true relation of earthly beauty and eternal truth"—the uneducated of every nation understood neither, at any time.

They do not understand it even now.   The evolution of the GOD-IDEA proceeds apace with man's own intellectual evolution.   So true it is that the noblest ideal to which the religious Spirit of one age can soar, will appear but a gross caricature to the philosophic mind in a succeeding epoch !   The philosophers themselves had to be *initiated into perceptive mysteries*, before they could grasp the correct idea of the ancients in relation to this most metaphysical subject.   Otherwise—outside such initiation—for every thinker there will be a "Thus far shalt thou go and no farther," mapped out by his intellectual capacity, as clearly and as unmistakeably as there is for the progress of any nation or race in its cycle by the law of Karma.   Outside of initiation, the ideals of contemporary religious thought must always have their wings clipped and remain unable to soar higher ; .for idealistic as well as realistic thinkers, and even free-thinkers, are but the outcome and the natural product of their respective environments and periods.   The ideals of both are only the necessary results of their temperaments, and the outcome of that phase of intellectual progress to which a nation, in its collectivity, has attained. Hence, as already remarked, the highest flights of modern (Western) metaphysics have fallen far short of the truth. Much of current Agnostic speculation on the existence of the "First Cause" is little better than veiled materialism—the terminology alone being different. Even so great a thinker as Mr. Herbert Spencer speaks of the "Unknowable" occasionally in terms that demonstrate the lethal influence of materialistic thought, which, like the deadly Sirocco, has withered and blighted all current ontological speculation.*

From the early ages of the Fourth Race, when Spirit alone was worshipped and the mystery was made manifest, down to the last palmy days of Grecian art at the dawn of Christianity—the Hellenes alone had dared to raise publicly an altar to the UNKNOWN GOD. Whatever St. Paul may have had in his profound mind when declaring to the Athenians that this "unknown," ignorantly worshipped by them, was the true God announced by himself—that Deity *was not* "Jehovah" (*see* "*The Holy of Holies*"), nor was he "The Maker of the world and all things." For it is not the "God of Israel" but the "Unknown" of the ancient and modern Pantheist that "dwelleth not in temples *made with hands*" (Acts xviii., 23-4).

Divine thought cannot be defined, or its meaning explained, except by the numberless manifestations of Cosmic Substance in which the former *is sensed* spiritually by those who can do so. To say this, after having defined it as the Unknown Deity, abstract, impersonal, sexless, which must be placed at the root of every Cosmogony and its subsequent evolution, is equivalent to saying nothing at all. It is like attempting a transcendental equation of conditions for the true values of a set, having in hand for deducing them only a number of *unknown* quantities. Its place is found in the old primitive Symbolic charts, in which, as shown in the text, it is represented by a boundless darkness, on the ground of which appears the first central point in white — thus symbolising coeval and co-eternal SPIRIT-MATTER making its appearance in the phenomenal world, before its first differentiation. When "the one becomes two," it may then be

* For instance, when he terms the "First Cause"—the UNKNOWABLE—a "power *manifesting* through phenomena," and "an infinite eternal *Energy*" (?) it is clear that he has grasped solely the *physical* aspect of the mystery of Being—the Energies of Cosmic Substance only. The co-eternal aspect of the ONE REALITY—Cosmic Ideation —(as to its *noumenon*, it seems *non-existent* in the mind of the great thinker) is absolutely omitted from consideration. Without doubt, this *one-sided* mode of dealing with the problem is due largely to the pernicious Western practice of subordinating consciousness, or regarding it as a "by-product" of molecular motion.

referred to as Spirit *and* matter. To "Spirit" is referable every manifestation of consciousness, reflective or direct, and of *unconscious purposiveness* (to adopt a modern expression used in Western *philosophy*, so-called) as evidenced in the Vital Principle, and Nature's submission to the majestic sequence of immutable law. "Matter" must be regarded as objectivity in its purest abstraction—the self-existing basis whose septenary manvantaric differentiations constitute the objective reality underlying the phenomena of each phase of conscious existence. During the period of Universal Pralaya, Cosmic Ideation is non-existent; and the variously differentiated states of Cosmic Substance are resolved back again into the primary state of abstract potential objectivity.

Manvantaric impulse commences with the re-awakening of Cosmic Ideation (the "Universal Mind") concurrently with, and parallel to the primary emergence of Cosmic Substance—the latter being the manvantaric vehicle of the former—from its undifferentiated *pralayic* state. Then, absolute wisdom mirrors itself in its Ideation; which, by a transcendental process, superior to and incomprehensible by human Consciousness, results in Cosmic Energy (*Fohat*). Thrilling through the bosom of inert Substance, *Fohat* impels it to activity, and guides its primary differentiations on all the Seven planes of Cosmic Consciousness. There are thus *Seven Protyles* (as they are now called), while Aryan antiquity called them the Seven Prakriti, or Natures, serving, severally, as the *relatively* homogeneous basis, which in the course of the increasing heterogeneity (in the evolution of the Universe) differentiate into the marvellous complexity presented by phenomena on the planes of perception. The term "relatively" is used designedly, because the very existence of such a process, resulting in the primary segregations of undifferentiated Cosmic Substance into its septenary bases of evolution, compels us to regard the *protyle* * of each plane as only a *mediate* phase assumed by Substance in its passage from abstract, into full objectivity.

Cosmic Ideation is said to be non-existent during Pralayic periods, for the simple reason that there is no one, and nothing, to perceive its effects. There can be no manifestation of Consciousness, semi-consciousness, or even "unconscious purposiveness," except through the

---

* The term *Protyle* is due to Mr. Crookes, the eminent chemist, who has given that name to *pre-Matter*, if one may so call primordial and purely homogeneous substances, suspected, if not actually yet found, by Science in the ultimate composition of the atom. But the incipient segregation of primordial matter into atoms and molecules takes its rise subsequent to the evolution of the Seven *Protyles*. It is the last of these—having recently detected the possibility of its existence on our plane—that Mr. Crookes is in search of.

vehicle of matter; that is to say, on this our plane, wherein human consciousness *in its normal state* cannot soar beyond what is known as transcendental metaphysics, it is only through some molecular aggregation or fabric that Spirit wells up in a stream of individual or sub-conscious subjectivity. And as Matter existing apart from perception is a mere abstraction, both of these aspects of the ABSOLUTE—Cosmic Substance and Cosmic Ideation—are mutually inter-dependent. In strict accuracy—to avoid confusion and misconception—the term "Matter" ought to be applied to the aggregate of objects of possible perception, and "Substance" to *noumena;* for inasmuch as the phenomena of *our* plane are the creation of the perceiving Ego—the modifications of its own subjectivity—all the "states of matter representing the aggregate of perceived objects" can have but a relative and purely phenomenal existence for the children of our plane. As the modern Idealists would say, the co-operation of Subject and Object results in the Sense-object or phenomenon. But this does not necessarily lead to the conclusion that it is the same on all other planes; that the co-operation of the two on the planes of their septenary differentiation results in a septenary aggregate of phenomena which are likewise non-existent *per se*, though concrete realities for the Entities of whose experience they form a part, in the same manner as the rocks and rivers around us are real from the stand-point of a physicist, though unreal illusions of sense from that of the metaphysician. It would be an error to say, or even conceive such a thing. From the stand-point of the highest metaphysics, the whole Universe, gods included, is an illusion; but the illusion of him who is in himself an illusion differs on every plane of consciousness; and we have no more right to dogmatise about the possible nature of the perceptive faculties of an Ego on, say, the sixth plane, than we have to identify our perceptions with, or make them a standard for, those of an ant, in *its* mode of consciousness. The pure object apart from consciousness* is unknown to us, while living on the plane of our three-dimensional World; as we know only the mental states it excites in the perceiving Ego. And, so long as the contrast of Subject and Object endures—to wit, as long as we enjoy our five senses and no more, and do not know how to divorce our all-perceiving *Ego* (the Higher Self) from the thraldom of these senses—so long will it be impossible for the *personal* Ego to break through the barrier which separates it from a

---

* Cosmic Ideation focussed in a principle or *upadhi* (basis) results as the consciousness of the individual Ego. Its manifestation varies with the degree of *upadhi*, *e.g.*, through that known as *Manas* it wells up as Mind-Consciousness; through the more finely differentiated fabric (sixth state of matter) of the *Buddhi* resting on the experience of Manas as its basis—as a stream of spiritual INTUITION.

knowledge of *things in themselves* (*or Substance*). That Ego, progressing in an arc of ascending subjectivity, must exhaust the experience of every plane. But not till the Unit is merged in the ALL, whether on this or any other plane, and Subject and Object alike vanish in the absolute negation of the Nirvanic State (negation, again, only *from our plane*), is scaled that peak of Omniscience—the Knowledge of things-in-them-selves ; and the solution of the yet more awful riddle approached, before which even the highest Dhyan Chohan must bow in silence and ignor-ance—the unspeakable mystery of that which is called by the Vedantins, the PARABRAHMAM.

Therefore, such being the case, all those who sought to give a name to the incognizable Principle have simply degraded it. Even to speak of Cosmic Ideation—save in its *phenomenal* aspect—is like trying to bottle up primordial Chaos, or to put a printed label on ETERNITY.

What, then, is the " primordial Substance," that mysterious object of which Alchemy was ever talking, and which became the subject of philosophical speculation in every age ? What can it be finally, even in its phenomenal pre-differentiation ? Even *that* is ALL in manifested Nature and—*nothing* to our senses. It is mentioned under various names in every Cosmogony, referred to in every philosophy, and shown to be, to this day, the ever grasp-eluding PROTEUS in Nature. We touch and do not feel it ; we look at it without seeing it ; we breathe it and do not perceive it ; we hear and smell it without the smallest cognition that it is there ; for it is in every molecule of that which in our illusion and ignorance we regard as Matter in any of its states, or conceive as a feeling, a thought, an emotion. . . .   In short, it is the " *upadhi*," or vehicle, of every possible phenomenon, whether physical, mental, or psychic. In the opening sentences of *Genesis*, as in the Chaldean Cosmogony ; in the *Purânas* of India, and in the *Book of the Dead* of Egypt, it opens everywhere the cycle of manifestation. It is termed " Chaos," and the face of the waters, incubated by the Spirit proceeding from the Unknown, under whatever name. (*See* " *Chaos, Theos, Kosmos.*")

The authors of the sacred Scriptures in India go deeper into the origin of things evolved than Thales or Job, for they say :—

" From INTELLIGENCE (called MAHAT in the Purânas) associated with IGNORANCE (Iswar, as a *personal* deity) *attended by its projective power*, in which the quality of dulness (*tamas*, insensibility) predominates, proceeds *Ether*—from ether, air ; from air, heat ; from heat, water ; and from water, earth " with everything on it." " From THIS, from this same SELF, was the Ether produced," says the Veda. (*Taittiriya Upanishad II.* 1).

It becomes thus evident that it is not *this* Ether—sprung at the fourth remove from an *Emanation* of Intelligence " associated with Ignorance " —which is the high principle, the *deific* Entity worshipped by the Greeks and Latins under the name of " *Pater omnipotens Æther*," and " *Magnus Æther* " in its collective aggregates. The septenary gradation, and the innumerable subdivisions and differences, made by the ancients between the powers of *Ether* collectively, from its outward fringe of effects, with which our Science is so familiar, up to the " Imponderable Substance," once admitted as the " Ether of Space," now about to be rejected, has been ever a vexing riddle for every branch of knowledge. The mythologists and symbologists of our day, confused by this incomprehensible glorification, on the one hand, and degradation on the other, of the same deified entity and in the same religious systems, are often driven to the most ludicrous mistakes. The Church, firm as a rock in each and all of her early errors of interpretation, has made of Ether the abode of her Satanic legions.* The whole hierarchy of the " Fallen " angels is there ; the *Cosmocratores*—or the " world bearers," (according to Bossuet) ; *Mundi Tenentes*—the " world holders," as Tertullian calls them ; and *Mundi Domini* " world dominations," or rather *dominators*, the *Curbati*, or " Curved," etc., who thus make of the stars and celestial orbs in their course—Devils !

The difference made between the seven states of Ether (itself one of the Seven Cosmic principles), while the Æther of the Ancients is *universal Fire*, may be seen in the injunctions by Zoroaster and Psellus, respectively. The former said: " Consult it only when it is without form or figure," *absque formâ et figurâ*, which means without flames or burning coals. " When it has a form—*heed it not*," teaches Psellus ; " but when it is formless, obey it, for it is then *sacred fire*, and all it will reveal thee, shall be true."† This proves that Ether, itself an aspect of Akâsa, has in its turn several aspects or " principles."

All the ancient nations deified Æther in its imponderable aspect and potency. Virgil calls Jupiter, *Pater omnipotens Æther*, " the great Æther."‡ The Hindus have also placed it among their deities ; under the name of Akâsa (the synthesis of Æther). And the author of the *Homoiomerian*

---

* For it is thus that the Church has interpreted verse 12 in the VI. Chapter to the Ephesians. " For we wrestle not against flesh and blood, but against principalities, against powers, against the rulers of the darkness of this world." Further on St. Paul mentions the spiritual *malices* (" wickedness " in English texts) SPREAD IN THE AIR— " *Spiritualia nequitiæ cœlestibus*," the Latin texts giving various names to these " malices,' the innocent " Elementals." But the Church is right this time, though wrong in calling them all devils. The ASTRAL LIGHT or lower Ether *is* full of conscious and semi-conscious and unconscious entities ; only the church has less *power* over them than over invisible microbes or mosquitoes.

† *Effatum* XVI. " Oracles of Zoroaster."

‡ *Georgica*. Book II.

System of philosophy, Anaxagoras of Clazomenæ, firmly believed that the spiritual prototypes of all things, as well as their elements, were to be found in the boundless Ether where they were generated, whence they evolved, and whither they returned—an Occult teaching.

It thus becomes clear that it is from Ether in its highest synthetic aspect, once anthropomorphised, that sprung the first idea of a personal creative deity. With the philosophical Hindus the elements are *Tamas*, *i.e.*, " unenlightened by *intellect*, which they obscure."

We have now to exhaust the question of the mystical meaning of " Primordial Chaos " and of the Root-Principle, and show how they were connected in the ancient philosophies with Akâsa, wrongly translated Æther, and also with *Maya* (illusion)—of which *Ishwara* is the male aspect. We shall speak further on of the *intelligent* " principle," or rather of the invisible *immaterial* properties, in the visible and material elements, that " sprung from the *primordial* Chaos."

For, " What is the primordial Chaos but Æther ? " it is asked in " Isis Unveiled." Not the *modern* Ether ; not such as is recognised now, but such as *was* known to the ancient philosophers long before the time of Moses ; but Æther, with all its mysterious and occult properties, containing in itself the germs of universal creation. *Upper* Æther or Akâsa, is the celestial virgin and mother of every existing form and being, from whose bosom, as soon as " incubated " by the Divine Spirit, are called into existence Matter and Life, Force and Action. Æther is the Aditi of the Hindus, and it is Akâsa. Electricity, magnetism, heat, light, and chemical action are so little understood even now that fresh facts are constantly widening the range of our knowledge. Who knows where ends the power of this protean giant—Æther ; or whence its mysterious origin ? Who, we mean, that denies the spirit that works in it, and evolves out of it all visible forms ?

It will be an easy task to show that the cosmogonical legends all over the world are based on a knowledge by the ancients of those sciences, which have allied themselves in our days in support of the doctrine of evolution ; and that further research may demonstrate that those ancients were far better acquainted with the fact of evolution itself, embracing both its physical and spiritual aspects, than we are now. " With the old philosophers, evolution was a universal theorem, a doctrine embracing the *whole*, and an established principle ; while our modern evolutionists are enabled to present us merely with speculative theoretics ; with *particular*, if not wholly *negative* theorems. It is idle for the representatives of our modern wisdom to close the debate and pretend that the question is settled, merely because the obscure phraseology of the Mosaic, far later, account clashes with the definite exegesis of ' Exact Science ' " (" *Isis Unveiled* ").

If one turns to the " Laws (or Ordinances) of Manu," one finds the prototype of all these ideas. Mostly lost (to the Western world) in their original form, disfigured by later interpolations and additions, they have, nevertheless, preserved quite enough of their ancient Spirit to show its character. " Removing the darkness, the Self-existent Lord " (*Vishnu, Narayana, etc.*) becoming manifest, and "wishing to produce beings from his Essence, created, in the beginning, water alone. In that he cast seed. . . . . That became a golden Egg." (V. 6, 7, 8, 9.) Whence this Self-existent Lord ? It is called THIS, and is spoken of as " Darkness, imperceptible, without definite qualities, undiscoverable as if wholly in sleep." (V. 5.) Having dwelt in that Egg for a whole divine year, he " who is called in the world Brahmâ," splits that Egg in two, and from the upper portion he forms the heaven, from the lower the earth, and from the middle the sky and " the perpetual place of waters." (12, 13.)

But there is, directly following these verses, something more important for us, as it corroborates entirely our esoteric teachings. From verse 14 to 36, evolution is given in the order described in the Esoteric philosophy. This cannot be easily gainsaid. Even Medhâtithi, the son of Viraswâmin, and the author of the Commentary, "the Manubhâsya," whose date, according to the western Orientalists, is 1,000 A.D., helps us with his remarks to the elucidation of the truth. He showed himself either unwilling to give out more, because he knew that truth which has to be kept from the profane, or else he was really puzzled. Still, what he does give out makes the septenary principle in men and nature plain enough.

Let us begin with Chapter I. of the " Ordinances " or " Laws " after the Self-existent Lord, the *unmanifesting* Logos of the Unknown " Darkness," becomes manifested in the golden Egg. It is from this " Egg," from——

(11.) That which is the undiscrete (undifferentiated) cause, eternal, which *Is and Is not*, from It issued that male who is called in the world Brahmä. . . . .

Here we find, as in all genuine philosophical systems, even the "Egg' or the Circle (or Zero), boundless Infinity, referred to as IT,[*] and Brahmâ, the first *unit* only, referred to as the *male* god, *i.e.*, the fructifying Principle. It is Ⓘ or 10 (ten) the Decade. On the plane of the Septenary *or our World* only, it is called Brahmâ. On that of the *Unified Decade* in the realm of Reality, this male Brahmâ is an illusion.

(14.) " From Self (*átmanah*) he created mind, (1) *which is and is not;*

---

[*] The ideal apex of the Pythagorean triangle: *vide* Sections in Vol. II., " Cross and Circle," and the " Earliest Symbolics of the Cross."

(2) and from mind, Ego-ism (Self-Consciousness) the ruler; (3) the Lord."

(1.) The mind is *Manas*. Medhâtithi, the commentator, justly observes here that it is the reverse of this and shows already interpolation and rearranging; for it is *Manas* that springs from *Ahamkara* or (Universal) Self-Consciousness, as *Manas* in the microcosm springs from Mahat, *or Maha-Buddhi* (Buddhi, in man). For Manas is dual, and as shown and translated by Colebrooke, " is *serving both for sense and action,* is an organ by affinity, being cognate with the rest." "The rest" means, here, that Manas, our *fifth* principle (the fifth, because the body was named the *first,* which is the reverse of the true philosophical order)* is in affinity both with Atma-Buddhi and with the lower four principles. Hence, our teaching : namely, that Manas follows Atma-Buddhi to Devachan, and that the lower (dregs, the residue of) Manas remains with Kama rupa, in *Limbus,* or Kama-loka, the abode of the " Shells."

(2.) Such is the meaning of *Manas*, which "*is, and is not.*"

(3.) Medhâtithi translates it as " the one conscious of the I," or Ego, not "ruler," as the Orientalists do. Thus they translate verse 16 : "He also, having made the subtile parts of those six (the Great Self and the five organs of sense) of unmeasured brightness, to enter into the elements of Self (*Atmamâtrâsu*) created all beings."

When, according to Medhâtithi, it ought to read *mâtrâ-Chit* instead of " Atmamâtrâsu," and thus be made to say :—

" He having pervaded the subtile parts of those six, of unmeasured brightness, by elements of self, created all beings."

This latter reading must be the correct one, since he, the *Self,* is what we call Atmâ, and thus constitutes the seventh principle, the synthesis of the " *six.*" Such is also the opinion of the editor of *Mânava-dharma Shâstra,* who seems to have intuitionally entered far deeper into the spirit of the philosophy than has the translator of the " Ordinances of Manu," the late Dr. Burnell. For he hesitates little between the text of Kulluka and the Commentaries of Medhâtithi. Rejecting the *tanmâtra,* or subtile elements, and the *âtmamâtrâsu* of Kulluka, he says, applying the principles to the Cosmic *Self :* " The six appear rather to be the *manas* plus the five principles of Ether, air, fire, water, earth ; " " having united five portions of these six with the spiritual element (the *seventh*) he (thus) created all existing things ; " *âtmamâtra* is therefore the spiritual atom as opposed to the elementary, not reflective " elements of himself." Thus he corrects the translation of verse—" 17. As the subtile elements of bodily forms of This One depend on these six, so

---

* *Vide* A. Coke Burnell's translation, edited by Ed. W. Hopkins, Ph.D.

the wise call his form *çarira* " (sharira)—and he says that " Elements "
mean here portions or parts (or principles), which reading is borne out
by verse 19, which says :—

" 19. This non-eternal (Universe) arises then from the Eternal, by
means of the subtle elements of forms of *those seven* very glorious
principles " (*purusha*).

Commenting upon which, according to Medhâtithi, the Editor remarks
that "the five elements plus mind (*Manas*) and Self-Consciousness
(Ahamkara)* are meant ; " " subtle elements," as before (meaning)
" five portions of form " (or principles). For verse 20 shows it, when
saying of these (five elements, or " five portions of form " (*rupa, plus
Manas* and Self-Consciousness) that they constitute the " *seven purusha*,"
or *principles*, called in the Purânas the " Seven Prâkritis."

Moreover, these " five elements " or " five portions " are spoken of in
verse 27 as "those which are called the atomic destructible portions "—
therefore " distinct from the atoms of the *nyâya*."

This creative Brahmâ, issuing from the mundane or golden egg,
unites in himself both the male and the female principles. He is, in
short, the same as all the creative Protologoi. Of Brahmâ, however, it
could not be said, as of Dionysos : " πρωτόγονον διφυῆ τρίγονον Βακχεῖον Ἄνακτα
Ἄγριον ἀρρητὸν κρύφιον δικέρωτα δίμορφον "—a lunar Jehovah—Bacchus truly,
with David dancing nude before his *symbol* in the ark—because
no licentious Dionysia were ever established in his name and
honour. All such public worship was exoteric, and the great
universal symbols were distorted universally, as those of Krishna
are now by the Vallabachâryas of Bombay, the followers of the
infant god. But are these popular gods the *true Deity ?* Are
they the Apex and synthesis of the sevenfold creation, man included ? Never ! Each and all are one of the rungs of that septenary
ladder of Divine Consciousness, pagan as Christian. For Ain-Soph
also is said to manifest through the *Seven Letters of Jehovah's name* who,
having usurped the place of the Unknown Limitless, was given by his
devotees his Seven Angels of the Presence—his *Seven Principles*. Yet they
are mentioned in almost every school. In the pure Sankhya philosophy *mahat, ahamkara* and the five *tanmâtras* are called the *seven Prakritis* (or Natures), and they are counted from *Maha-Buddhi* or Mahat
down to Earth. (See *Sânkhya Karika* III. and Commentaries.)

Nevertheless, however disfigured for Rabbinical purposes is the
original *Elohistic* version by Ezra, however repulsive at times even the

---

* *Ahamkara*, as universal Self-Consciousness, has a triple aspect, as also *Manas*. For
this conception of " I," or one's *Ego*, is either *sattwa*, " pure quietude," or appears as
rajas, " active," or remains *tamas*, " stagnant," in darkness. It belongs to Heaven and
Earth, and assumes the properties of either.

esoteric meaning in the Hebrew scrolls, which is far more so than its outward *veil* or *cloaking* may be*—once the *Jehovistic* portions are eliminated, the Mosaic Books are found full of purely occult and priceless knowledge, especially in the first six chapters.

Read by the aid of the Kabala one finds a matchless temple of occult truths, a well of deeply concealed beauty hidden under a structure, the *visible* architecture of which, its apparent symmetry notwithstanding, is unable to stand the criticism of cold reason, or to reveal its age, for it belongs to all the ages. There is more wisdom concealed under the exoteric *fables* of Purânas and Bible than in all the exoteric *facts* and science in the literature of the world, and more OCCULT true Science, than there is of exact knowledge in all the academies. Or, in plainer and stronger language, there is as much esoteric wisdom in some portions of the *exoteric* Purânas and Pentateuch, as there is of nonsense and of designed childish fancy in it, when read only in the dead-letter murderous interpretations of great dogmatic religions, and especially of sects.

Let anyone read the first verses of chapter i. of *Genesis* and reflect upon them. There " God " commands to *another* " god," *who does his bidding* —even in the *cautious* English Protestant translation of James the First's authorised edition.

In the " beginning," the Hebrew language having no word to express the idea of Eternity,† " God " fashions the *heaven* and the *Earth* ; and the latter is " without form and void," while the former is no Heaven in fact, but the " Deep," *Chaos*, with darkness upon its face.‡

" And the *Spirit* of GOD moved upon the face of the Waters " (v. 2), or the great Deep of the Infinite Space. And this Spirit is *Nara-yana*, or Vishnu.

---

* See " The Holy of Holies."

† The word " eternity," by which Christian theologians interpret the term " for ever and ever," does not exist in the Hebrew tongue—either as a word or meaning. *Oulam*, says Le Clerc, only imports a time when beginning or end is not known. " It does not mean *"infinite* duration," and the word *for ever* in the Old Testament, only signifies a " long time." Nor is the term " eternity " used in the Christian sense in the Purânas. For in Vishnu Purâna, it is clearly stated that by Eternity and Immortality only "existence to the end of the Kalpa " is meant (Book II. chap viii.).

‡ Orphic theogony is purely Oriental and Indian in its Spirit. The successive transformations it has undergone, have now separated it widely from the spirit of ancient Cosmogony, as may be seen by comparing it even with Hesiod's theogony. Yet the truly Aryan Hindu spirit breaks forth everywhere in both Hesiod's and the Orphic theogony. (See the remarkable work of James Darmesteter, *Cosmogonies Aryennes*, in his *Essais Orientaux*.) Thus the original Greek conception of Chaos is that of the Secret Wisdom Religion. In Hesiod, therefore, Chaos is infinite, boundless, endless and beginningless in duration, an abstraction at the same time as a visible presence. SPACE filled with darkness, which is primordial matter in its *pre-cosmic* state. For in its etymological sense, Chaos is Space, according to Aristotle, and Space is *the* ever Unseen and Unknowable Deity in our philosophy.

"And God said, Let there be a firmament. . ." (v. 6), and "God,"
the second, obeyed and "*made* the firmament" (v. 7). "And God said
let there be light," and "there was light." Now the latter does not
mean light at all, but in the Kabala, the androgyne "Adam Kadmon," or
Sephira (*Spiritual light*), for they are one; or, according to the Chaldean
"Book of Numbers," the *secondary* angels, the first being the Elohim
who are the *aggregate* of that "fashioning" *god*. For to whom are those
words of command addressed? And who is it who commands? That
which commands is the *eternal Law*, and he who obeys, the *Elohim*, the
known quantity acting in and with *x*, or the coefficient of the unknown
quantity, the *Forces* of the ONE Force. All this is Occultism, and is
found in the archaic STANZAS. It is perfectly immaterial whether
we call these "Forces" the Dhyan Chohans, or the *Ophanim*, as St. John
does.

"The one Universal Light, which to Man is *Darkness*, is ever existent,"
says the Chaldean "Book of Numbers." From it proceeds periodically
the ENERGY, which is reflected in the "Deep" or Chaos, the store-house
of future worlds, and, once awakened, stirs up and fructifies the
latent Forces, which are the ever present eternal potentialities in it.
Then awake anew the Brahmâs and Buddhas—the co-eternal Forces—
and a new Universe springs into being. . . . .

In the *Sepher Jezireh*, the Kabalistic Book of Creation, the author has
evidently repeated the words of Manu. In it, the Divine Substance is
represented as having alone existed from the eternity, boundless and
absolute; and as having emitted from itself the Spirit.* "One is the
Spirit of the living God, blessed be ITS name, which liveth for ever!
Voice, Spirit, and Word, this is the Holy Spirit;"† and this is the
Kabalistic abstract Trinity, so unceremoniously anthropomorphised by
the Christian Fathers. From this triple ONE emanated the whole
Kosmos. First from ONE emanated number Two, or Air (the Father),
the creative element; and then number THREE, *Water* (the Mother),
proceeded from the air; *Ether* or *Fire* completes the mystic four, the
Arba-il. ‡ "When the Concealed of the Concealed wanted to reveal
Himself, he first made a point (primordial point, or the first Sephiroth,
air, or Holy Ghost), shaped into a sacred form (the ten Sephiroth, or the
Heavenly man), and covered it with a rich and splendid garment, *that is
the world*." §

---

* The *manifested* Spirit; Absolute, Divine Spirit is one with absolute Divine Substance: Parabrahm and Mulaprakriti are one in essence. Therefore, Cosmic Ideation
and Cosmic Substance in their primal character are one also.

† "Sepher Jezireh," chap. 1, Mishna ix.

‡ Ibid. It is from *Arba* that Abram is made to come.

§ "Sohar," I., 2a.

"He maketh the wind His messengers, flaming Fire His servants," says the Jezireh, showing the cosmical character of the later euhemerised Elements,* and that the Spirit permeates every atom in Kosmos.

This "primordial Substance" is called by some *Chaos:* Plato and the Pythagoreans named it the *Soul of the World* after it had been impregnated by the Spirit of *that* which broods over the Primeval Waters, or *Chaos.* It is by being reflected in it, say the Kabalists, that the brooding Principle *created* the phantasmagoria of a visible, manifested Universe. *Chaos,* before—*Ether,* after, the "reflection;" it is still the deity that pervades all Space and things. It is the invisible, imponderable Spirit of things and the invisible, but too tangible fluid that radiates from the fingers of the healthy magnetizer, for it is Vital Electricity— LIFE itself. Called in derision by the Marquis de Mirville "the nebulous Almighty," it is termed by the Theurgists and Occultists to this day "the living Fire"; and there is not a Hindu who practises at dawn a certain kind of meditation but knows its effects.† It is the "Spirit of

---

* "Sepher Jezireh," Mishna ix., 10. Everywhere throughout the Acts, Paul calls the invisible Kosmic Beings the "Elements." (*See Greek Texts.*) But now the Elements are degraded into and limited to atoms of which nothing is known, so far, and which are only "children of necessity" as Ether is too—as we said in "Isis." "The poor primordial elements have long been exiled, and our ambitious physicists run races to determine who shall add one more to the fledgling brood of the sixty and odd elementary substances." Meanwhile there rages a war in modern chemistry about terms. We are denied the right to call these substances "chemical elements," for they are not "primordial principles of self-existing essences out of which the universe was fashioned," according to Plato. Such ideas associated with the word *element* were good enough for the "old Greek philosophy," but modern science rejects them ; for, as Professor Crookes says, "they are unfortunate terms," and experimental science will have "nothing to do with any kind of essences except those which it can see, smell, or taste. It leaves others to the metaphysicians. . . . " We must feel grateful even for so much.

† Writing upon this subject in *Isis Unveiled* we said of it that it was : "The Chaos of the ancients, the Zoroastrian sacred fire, or the *Atash-Behram* of the Parsees ; the Hermes-fire, the Elmes-fire of the ancient Germans ; the lightning of Cybele ; the burning torch of Apollo ; the flame on the altar of Pan ; the inextinguishable fire in the temple on the Acropolis, and in that of Vesta ; the fire-flame of Pluto's helm ; the brilliant sparks on the hats of the Dioscuri, on the Gorgon head, the helm of Pallas, and the staff of Mercury ; the Egyptian Phtha-Ra ; the Grecian *Zeus Cataibates* (the descending) of Pausanias ; the pentacostal fire-tongues ; the burning bush of Moses ; the pillar of fire of the *Exodus,* and the "burning lamp" of Abram, the eternal fire of the "bottomless pit" ; the Delphic oracular vapours ; the Sidereal light of the Rosicrucians ; the AKÂSA of the Hindu adepts ; the Astral Light of Eliphas Lévi ; the nerve-aura and the fluid of the magnetists ; the *od* of the Reichenbach ; the *Psychod* and ectenic force of Thury ; the psychic force of Sergeant Cox, and the atmospheric magnetism of some naturalists ; galvanism ; and finally, electricity—all these are but various names for many different manifestations or effects of the same mysterious, all-pervading cause, the Greek *Archeus.*" We now add—it is all this and much more.

Light" and *Magnes*.   As truly expressed by an opponent, *Magus* and *magnes* are two branches growing from the same trunk and shooting forth the same resultants.   And in this appellation of "living fire" we may also discover the meaning of the puzzling sentence in the *Zend-Avesta* saying that there is "a fire that gives knowledge of the future.   Science and amiable speech," *i.e.*, develops an extraordinary eloquence in the sybil, the sensitive, and even some orators.

This "fire" is spoken of in all the Hindu Books, as also in the Kabalistic works.   The *Zohar* explains it as the "white hidden fire, in the *Resha trivrah*" (the White Head), whose Will causes the fiery fluid to flow in 370 currents in every direction of the universe.   It is identica with the "Serpent that runs with 370 leaps" of the *Siphrah Dzenioota*, which, when the "Perfect Man," the Metatron, *is raised*, *i.e.*, when the *divine* man indwells in the *animal* man, it, the Serpent, becomes *three spirits*, that is to say, is Atma-Buddhi-Manas, in our theosophical phraseology.   (*Vide* Part II. in Vol. II., §§ 3, "The Many Meanings of the War in Heaven.")

Spirit, then, or Cosmic Ideation, and Cosmic Substance—one of whose *principles* is Ether—are *one*, and include the ELEMENTS, in the sense St. Paul attaches to them.   These Elements are the veiled Synthesis standing for Dhyan Chohans, Devas, Sephiroth, Amshaspends, Archangels, etc., etc.   The Ether of science—the *Ilus* of Berosus, or the *Protyle* of Chemistry—constitutes, so to speak, the *rude* material (relatively) out of which the above-named "Builders," following the plan traced out for them eternally in the DIVINE THOUGHT, fashion the systems in the Cosmos.   They are "myths," we are told.   "No more so than Ether and the Atoms," we answer.   The two latter are *absolute* necessities of physical science; the "Builders" are as absolute a necessity of metaphysics.   We are twitted with: "You *never saw them*."   We ask the materialists: "Have you ever seen Ether, *or your Atoms*, or, again, your FORCE?"   Moreover, one of the greatest Western Evolutionists of our modern day, the coadjutor of Darwin, Mr. A. R. Wallace, when discussing the inadequacy of Natural Selection alone to account for the physical form of Man, admits the guiding action of "higher intelligences" as a "*necessary* part of the great laws which govern the material Universe" ("*Contributions to Theory of Natural Selection*").

These "higher intelligences" are the Dhyan Chohans of the Occultists.

Indeed, there are few Myths in any religious system worthy of the name, but have an *historical* as well as a *scientific* foundation.   "Myths," justly observes Pococke, "are now proved to be fables, *just in proportion as we misunderstand* them; *truths*, in proportion as *they were once understood*."

The one prevailing, most distinct idea—found in all ancient teaching, with reference to Cosmic Evolution and the first "creation" of our Globe with all its products, organic and *inorganic* (strange word for an Occultist to use)—is that the whole Kosmos has sprung from the DIVINE THOUGHT. This thought impregnates matter, which is co-eternal with the ONE REALITY; and all that lives and breathes evolves from the emanations of the ONE *Immutable*—Parabrahm = Mulaprakriti, the eternal one-root. The former of these is, so to say, the aspect of the central point turned inward into regions quite inaccessible to human intellect, and is absolute abstraction; whereas, in its aspect as *Mulaprakriti* —the eternal root of all,—it gives one some hazy comprehension at least of the Mystery of Being.

"Therefore, it was taught in the *inner* temples that this visible universe of spirit and matter is but the concrete image of the ideal abstraction; it was built on the model of the first DIVINE IDEA. Thus our universe existed from Eternity in a latent state. The soul animating this purely spiritual universe is the central sun, the highest deity itself. It was not the *One* who built the concrete form of the idea, but the first-begotten; and as it was constructed on the geometrical figure of the dodecahedron,* the first-begotten 'was pleased to employ twelve thousand years in its creation.' The latter number is expressed in the Tyrrhenian cosmogony,† which shows man created in the sixth millenium. This agrees with the Egyptian theory of 6,000 'years'‡ and with the Hebrew computation. But it is the exoteric form of it. The *secret* computation explains that the 'twelve thousand and the 6,000 years' are YEARS OF BRAHMA—one *day* of Brahmâ being equal to 4,320,000,000 years. Sanchoniathon§ in his *Cosmogony*, declares that when the wind (spirit) became enamoured of its own principles (the chaos), an intimate union took place, which connection was called *pothos*, and from this sprang the seed of all. And the chaos knew not its own production, for it was *senseless ;* but from its embrace with the wind was generated Môt, or the ilus (mud).‖ From this proceeded the spores of creation and the generation of the universe.

"Zeus-Zen (æther), and Chthonia (the chaotic earth) and Metis (the water), his wives; Osiris and Isis-Latona—the former god also representing ether— the first emanation of the Supreme Deity, Amun, the primeval source of light ; the goddess earth and water again; Mithras,¶ the rock-born god, the symbol of the male mundane-fire, or the personified primordial light, and Mithra, the fire-goddess, at once his mother and his wife: the pure element of fire (the active or male principle) regarded as light and heat, in conjunction with earth and water, or matter (female, or passive, elements of Cosmical generation)

---

* Plato : " Timæus."
† " Suidas " v. Tyrrhenia."
‡ The reader will understand that by " years " is meant " ages," not mere periods of thirteen lunar months each.
§ See the Greek translation by Philo Byblus.
‖ Cory : " Ancient Fragment."
¶ Mithras was regarded among the Persians as the *Theos ekpetros*—god of the rock.

Mithras is the son of Bordj, the Persian mundane mountain,* from which he flashed out as a radiant ray of light. Brahmâ, the fire-god, and his prolific consort; and the Hindu *Agni*, the refulgent deity from whose body issue a thousand streams of glory and *seven* tongues of flame, and in whose honour certain Brahmans preserve to this day a *perpetual* fire; Siva, personated by the mundane mountain of the Hindus, the *Meru*: these terrific fire-gods, who are said in the legend to have descended from heaven, like the Jewish Jehovah, in a *pillar of fire*, and a dozen other Archaic double-sexed deities, all loudly proclaim their hidden meaning. And what could these dual myths mean but the pyscho-chemical principle of primordial creation? The *first Evolution* in its triple manifestation of spirit, force and matter; the divine *correllation* at its starting point, allegorized as the marriage of *Fire* and water, products of electrifying spirit, union of the male active principle with the female passive element, which become the parents of their tellurian child, cosmic matter, the *prima materia*, whose soul is Æther, and whose shadow is the ASTRAL LIGHT!" (ISIS UNVEILED).

The fragments of the systems that have now reached us are rejected as absurd fables. Nevertheless, occult Science—having survived even the great Flood that submerged the antediluvian giants and with them their very memory, save in the Secret Doctrine, the Bible and other Scriptures—still holds the Key to all the world problems.

Let us apply that Key to the rare fragments of long-forgotten cosmogonies and try by their scattered parts to re-establish the once Universal Cosmogony of the Secret Doctrine. The Key fits them all. No one can study ancient philosophies seriously without perceiving that the striking similitude of conception between all—in their exoteric form very often, in their hidden spirit invariably—is the result of no mere coincidence, but of a concurrent design: and that there was, during the youth of mankind, one language, one knowledge, one universal religion, when there were no churches, no creeds or sects, but when every man was a priest unto himself. And, if it is shown that already in those ages which are shut out from our sight by the exuberant growth of tradition, human religious thought developed in uniform sympathy in every portion of the globe; then, it becomes evident that, born under whatever latitude, in the cold North or the burning South, in the East or West, that thought was inspired by the same revelations, and man was nurtured under the protecting shadow of the same TREE OF KNOWLEDGE.

* Bordj is called a fire-mountain—a volcano; therefore it contains fire, rock, earth and water: the male, or active and the female, or passive, elements. The myth is suggestive.

§ IV.

CHAOS—THEOS—KOSMOS.

THESE three are the containment of Space ; or, as a learned Kabalist has defined it, "Space, the all containing uncontained, is the primary embodiment of simply Unity. . . . boundless extension."* But, he asks again, "boundless extension of what ? "—and makes the correct reply—" The *unknown container of all, the Unknown FIRST CAUSE."* This is a most correct definition and answer, most esoteric and true, from every aspect of occult teaching.

SPACE, which, in their ignorance and iconoclastic tendency to destroy every philosophic idea of old, the modern wiseacres have proclaimed " an abstract idea" and a *void,* is, in reality, the container and *the body of the Universe* with its seven principles. It is a body of limitless extent, whose *PRINCIPLES,* in Occult phraseology—each being in its turn a septenary—manifest in our phenomenal world only the grossest fabric of *their sub-divisions.* " No one has ever seen the Elements in their fulness," the Doctrine teaches. We have to search for our Wisdom in the original expressions of the primeval people and in their synonyms. Even the latest of them—the Jews—show in their Kabalistic teachings this idea, *e.g.,* the seven-headed Serpent of Space, called "the great Sea." " In the beginning, the *Alhim* created the heavens and the earth; the 6 (Sephiroth). . . . They created six, and on these all things are based. And those (six) depend upon *the seven forms of the cranium* up to Dignity of all Dignities (*Siphrah Dzenioota,* i, § 16), see part ii., vol. ii. " Ancient Divisions and the Mystic Numbers."

Now *Wind, Air and Spirit* have ever been synonymous with every nation. Pneuma (Spirit) and Anemos (the wind) with the Greeks, *Spiritus* and *Ventus* with the Latins, were convertible terms even if dissociated from the original idea of the breath of life. In the " Forces " of Science we see but the *material effect of the spiritual affect* of one or the other of the four primordial Elements, transmitted to us by the 4th Race, as we shall transmit Ether (or rather the gross subdivision of it) in its fulness to the Sixth Root Race. This is explained in the text of this and the following Book.

" Chaos " is called *senseless* by the ancients, because it represented and contained in itself (Chaos and Space being synonymous) all the Elements in their rudimentary, undifferentiated State. They made of Ether, the fifth element, the synthesis of the other four ; for the Æther of the Greek philosophers is not its dregs—of which indeed they knew more

---

* " New Aspects of Life," by Henry Pratt, M.D.

than science does now—which are rightly enough supposed to act as an agent for many forces that manifest on Earth. Their Æther was the *Akâsa* of the Hindus; the Ether accepted in physics is but one of its subdivisions, on our plane,—the *Astral Light* of the Kabalists with all its *evil* as well as good effects.

On account of the Essence of Æther, or the Unseen Space, being held divine as the supposed veil of Deity, it was regarded as the medium between this life and the next one. The ancients considered that when the directing active " Intelligences " (the gods) retired from any portion of Ether *in our Space*—the four realms which they superintend—then that particular place was left in the possession of evil, so called by reason of the absence of the *Good* from it.

" The existence of spirit in the common mediator, the ether, is denied by materialism; while theology makes of it a personal god. But the Kabalist holds that both are wrong, saying that in ether, the elements represent but matter—the blind cosmic forces of nature; while Spirit represents the intelligence which directs them. The Aryan, Hermetic, Orphic, and Pythagorean cosmogonical doctrines, as well as those of Sanchoniathon and Berosus, are all based upon one irrefutable formula, viz., that the æther and chaos, or, in the Platonic language, mind and matter, were the two primeval and eternal principles of the universe, utterly independent of anything else. The former was the all-vivifying intellectual principle; the chaos, a shapeless liquid principle, without ' form or sense,' from the union of which two sprung into existence the universe, or rather the universal world, the first androgynous deity—the chaotic matter becoming its body, and ether its soul. According to the phraseology of a *Fragment of Hermias*, ' chaos, from this union with spirit, obtaining *sense*, shone with pleasure, and thus was produced the *Protogonos* (the first-born) light.'* This is the universal trinity, based on the metaphysical conceptions of the ancients, who, reasoning by analogy, made of man, who is a compound of intellect and matter, the microcosm of the macrocosm, or great universe." *(Isis Unveiled.)*

" *Nature abhors Vacuum* " said the Peripatetics, who comprehended perhaps, though materialists in their way, why Democritus, with his instructor Leucippus, taught that the first principles of all things contained in the Universe were atoms and a *vacuum*. The latter means simply *latent* Deity or force; which, before its first manifestation when it became WILL—communicating the first impulse to these atoms—was the great *Nothingness*, Ain-Soph, or NO-THING; was, therefore, to every sense, a Void—or CHAOS.

That Chaos, however, became the " Soul of the World," according to Plato and the Pythagoreans. According to Hindu teaching, Deity in the shape of Æther (Akâsa) pervades all things; and it was called there-

---

* Damascius, in the " Theogony," calls it Dis, " the disposer of all things." Cory, " Ancient Fragments," p. 314.

fore by the theurgists " the living fire," the " Spirit of Light," and sometimes *Magnes*. It was the highest Deity itself which, according to Plato,
built the Universe in the geometrical form of the Dodecahedron ; and
its "first begotten" was born of Chaos and Primordial Light (the
Central Sun). This " First-Born," however, was only the aggregate of
the Host of the " Builders," the first constructive Forces, who are called
in ancient Cosmogonies the *Ancients* (born of the Deep, or Chaos) and
the " First Point." He is the Tetragrammaton, so-called, at the head
of the Seven lower Sephiroth. This was the belief of the Chaldees.
" These Chaldeans," writes Philo, the Jew, speaking very flippantly of
the first instructors of his ancestors, " were of opinion that the Kosmos,
among the things that exist (?) is a single point, either being itself God
(Theos) or that in it is God, comprehending the soul of all things."
(See his "*Migration of Abraham*," 32.)

Chaos-Theos-Kosmos are but the three aspects of their synthesis—
SPACE. One can never hope to solve the mystery of this *Tetraktis* by holding
to the dead-letter even of the old philosophies, as now extant. But, even
in these, CHAOS-THEOS-KOSMOS=SPACE, are identified in all Eternity, as
the One Unknown Space, the last word about which will, perhaps,
never be known before our seventh Round. Nevertheless, the allegories and metaphysical symbols about the primeval and *perfect* CUBE,
are remarkable even in the exoteric Purânas.

There, also, Brahmâ is the *Theos*, evolving out of *Chaos*, or the great
" Deep," the waters, over which Spirit-=SPACE, personified by *ayana*—
the Spirit moving over the face of the future boundless Kosmos—is
silently hovering, in the first hour of re-awakening. It is also Vishnu,
sleeping on Ananta-Sacha, the great Serpent of Eternity, of which
Western theology, ignorant of the Kabala, the only key that opens the
secrets of the Bible, has made—the Devil. It is the first *triangle* or the
Pythagorean *triad*, the " God of the *three* Aspects," before it is transformed through its perfect quadrature of the infinite Circle into the
" four-faced Brahmâ."

" Of him who is and yet is not, from the not-being, Eternal Cause, is
born the Being-Purusha," says Manu, the legislator.

In *Isis Unveiled*, it is said that :—

" In the Egyptian mythology, Kneph, the Eternal *Unrevealed* God, is represented by a snake emblem of Eternity encircling a water urn, with its head
hovering over the waters, which it incubates with its breath. In this case the
serpent is the Agathodæmon, the good spirit : in its opposite aspect, it is the
Kakodæmon—the bad one. In the Scandinavian *Eddas*, the honey dew, the
fruit of the gods and of the creative busy Yggdrasill (bees), falls during the
hours of night, when the atmosphere is impregnated with humidity ; and in the
Northern mythologies, as the passive principle of creation, it typifies the

creation of the universe *out of water;* this dew is the astral light in one of its combinations, and possesses creative as well as destructive properties. In the Chaldean legend of Berosus, Oannes or Dagon, the man-fish, instructing the people, shows the infant world created out of *water,* and all beings originating from this *prima materia.* Moses teaches that only earth and *water* can bring a living soul : and we read in the Scriptures that herbs could not grow until the Eternal caused it to *rain* upon earth. In the Mexican *Popol-Vuh,* man is created out of *mud* or clay (*terre glaise*), taken from under the water. Brahmâ creates the great Muni (or first man) seated on his lotus, only after having called into being *spirits* who thus enjoyed over mortals a priority of existence, and he creates him out of *water, air* and *earth.* Alchemists claim that the primordial or pre-Adamic earth, when reduced to its first substance, is in its *second* stage of transformation like clear water, the first being the *alkahest* proper. This primordial substance is said to contain within itself the essence of all that goes to make up man ; it has not only all the elements of his physical being, but even the " breath of life " itself in a latent state, ready to be awakened. This it derives from the " incubation " of the " Spirit of God " upon the face of the waters—CHAOS : in fact, this substance is chaos itself. From this it was that Paracelsus claimed to be able to make his " homunculi ; " and this is why Thales, the great natural philosopher, maintained that *water* was the principle of all things in nature.* . . . Job says, in chap. xxvi. 5, that " dead things are formed from under the waters, and inhabitants thereof." In the original text, instead of " dead things," it is written dead *Rephaim* (giants or mighty primitive men), from whom " Evolution " may one day trace our present race."

" In the primordial state of the creation," says Polier's *Mythologie des Indous,* " the rudimental universe, submerged in water, reposed in the bosom of Vishnu. Sprung from this chaos and darkness, Brahmâ, the architect of the world, poised on a lotus-leaf, floated (moved) upon the waters, unable to discern anything but water and darkness." Perceiving such a dismal state of things, Brahmâ soliloquises in consternation : " Who am I ? Whence came I ? " Then he hears a voice :† " Direct your thoughts to Bhagavat." Brahmâ, rising from his natatory position, seats himself upon the lotus in an attitude of contemplation, and reflects upon the Eternal, who, pleased with this evidence of piety, disperses the primeval darkness and opens his understanding. " After this Brahmâ issues from the universal egg (infinite chaos) as *light,* for his understanding is now opened, and he sets himself to work : he *moves* on the eternal waters, with the spirit of God within himself; and in his capacity of *mover* of the waters he is Vishnu, or *Narayana.*" This is

* With the Greeks, the " River-gods," all of them the Sons of the primeval ocean (Chaos in its masculine aspect), were the respective ancestors of the Hellenic races. For them the OCEAN was the father of the Gods ; and thus they had anticipated in this connection the theories of Thales, as rightly observed by Aristotle (Metaph. I., 3, 5).

† The " Spirit," or hidden voice of the *Mantras,* the active manifestation of the latent Force, or occult potency.

exoteric, of course, yet in its main idea as identical as possible with the Egyptian cosmogony, which shows in its opening sentences Athtor,* or Mother Night (which represents illimitable darkness), as the primeval element which covered the infinite abyss, animated by water and the universal spirit of the Eternal, dwelling alone in Chaos. Similarly in the Jewish Scriptures, the history of the creation opens with the spirit of God and his creative emanation—another Deity.†

The Zohar teaches that it is the primordial elements—the trinity of Fire, Air and Water—the four cardinal points, and all the Forces of Nature, which form collectively the Voice of the Will *Memrab*, or the "Word," the Logos of the Absolute Silent ALL. "The indivisible point, limitless and unknowable" spreads itself over the endless space, and thus forms a veil (the Mulaprakriti of Parabraham) which conceils this Abolute point. (*Vide infra*).

In the cosmogonies of all the nations it is the "Architects" synthesized by Demiurgos (in the Bible the "Elohim"), who fashion Kosmos out of Chaos, and who are the collective *Theos*, "male-female," Spirit and matter. " By a series (*yom*) of foundations (*hasoth*) the Alhim caused earth and heaven to be " (Gen. ii., 4). In the Bible it is first *Alhim*, then Jahva-Alhim, and finally Jehovah—after the separation of the sexes in chapter iv. of Genesis. It is noticeable that no-where, except in the later, the *last* Cosmogonies of our Fifth race, is the ineffable and unutterable Name‡—the symbol of the Unknown Deity, which was used only in the Mysteries—used in connection with the "Creation" of the Universe. It is the "Movers," the "Runners," the *theoi* (from θέειν, "to run"), who do the work of formation, the "Messengers" of the manvantaric law, who have now become in Christianity the "messengers" (malachim) ; and it seems the same in Hinduism or early Brahmanism. For it is not Brahmâ who creates in the *Rig Veda*, but the Prajâpati, the "Lords of Being," who are the *Rishis ;* the word *Rishi* (according to Professor Mahadeo Kunte) being connected with the word to move, to lead on, applied to them in their terrestrial character, when, as Patriarchs, they lead their hosts on the Seven Rivers.

Moreover, the very word " God " in the singular, embracing all the gods—or *theos* from *theoi*—came to the " superior " civilized nations from a strange source, one entirely and as pre-eminently *phallic* as the

---

* Orthography of the " Archaic Dictionary."

† We do not mean the current or accepted Bible, but the *real* Jewish one, now explained kabalistically.

‡ It is " unutterable " for the simple reason that it is non-existent. It never was a *name*, nor any *word* at all, but an Idea that could not be expressed. A substitute was created for it in the century preceding our era.

sincere, open-spoken *lingham* of India. The attempt to derive God from the Anglo-Saxon synonym " good " is an abandoned idea, for in no other language, in all of which the term varies more or less, from the Persian Khoda down to the Latin *Deus*, has an instance been found of a name of God being derived from the attribute of *Goodness*. To the Latin races it comes from the Aryan *Dyaus* (the Day) ; to the Slavonian, from the Greek Bacchus (*Bagh-bog*); and to the Saxon races directly from the Hebrew *Yodh* or *Jod*. The latter is ־ , the number-letter 10, male and female, and Jod the phallic *hook* :— hence the Saxon *Godh*, the Germanic *Gott*, and the English *God*. This symbolic term may be said to represent the Creator of physical " Humanity," on the *terrestrial* plane ; but surely it had nothing to do with the formation or " Creation " of Spirit, gods, or Kosmos !

Chaos-Theos-Kosmos, the triple deity, is *all in all*. Therefore, it is said to be male and female, good and evil, positive and negative : the whole series of contrasted qualities. When latent (in pralaya) it is incognizable and becomes the *unknowable Deity*. It can be known only in its active functions ; hence as *matter-Force* and *living Spirit*, the correlations and outcome, or the expression, on the visible plane, of the ultimate and ever-to-be unknown UNITY.

In its turn this triple unit is the producer of the four primary " Elements," * which are known in our visible terrestrial nature as the seven (so far the *five*) Elements, each divisible into forty-nine (or seven times seven) sub-elements, with about seventy of which Chemistry is acquainted. Every Cosmical Element such as Fire, Air, Water, Earth, partaking of the qualities and defects of their Primaries, are in their nature Good and Evil, Force (or Spirit) and Matter, etc., etc. ; and each, therefore, is at one and the same time Life and Death, Health and Disease, Action and Reaction. (*See Section XIV.*, " *The Four Elements.*") They are ever and constantly forming matter under the never-ceasing impulse of the ONE Element (the *incognizable*), represented in the world of phenomena by Æther, or " the immortal gods who give birth and life to all."

In " the Philosophical writings of Solomon Ben Yehudah Ibn Gebirol" (translated in Mr. Isaac Myer's *Kabbalah*, just published) it is said on the structure of the Universe, " R. Yehudah began, it is written:— ' Elohim said : Let there be a firmament in the midst of the waters.' Come, see, at the time that the Holy. . . . created the World, He

---

* The Cosmic Tabernacle of Moses, erected by him in the Desert, was *square*, representing the four cardinal points and the four Elements, as Josephus tells his readers (*Antiq.* i, *viii ch., xxii.*) It is the idea taken from the pyramids in Egypt and in Tyre, where the pyramids became pillars, the Genii, or Angels have their abodes in the four respective points (*See* § *xiv.; "The Four Elements."*)

created 7 heavens above, 7 earths below, 7 seas, 7 days, 7 rivers, 7 weeks, 7 years, 7 times, and 7,000 years that the world has been. The Holy *is the seventh* of all," etc. (p. 415).

This, besides showing a strange identity with the cosmogony of the Purânas (*e.g.*, Vishnu Purâna 1st Book), corroborates with regard to number seven, all our teachings as briefly given in " Esoteric Buddhism."

The Hindus have an endless series of allegories to express this idea. In the primordial Chaos, before it became developed into the *Seven Oceans* (Sapta Samudra)—emblematical of the *seven gunas* (conditioned qualities) composed of *trigunas* (Satwa, Rajas and Tamas, see Purânas)— lie latent both *Amrita* (immortality) and *Visha* (poison, death, evil). This allegory is found in the " Churning of the Ocean " by the gods. *Amrita* is beyond any guna, for it is UNCONDITIONED *per se ;* yet when fallen into the phenomenal creation it got mixed up with EVIL, *Chaos*, with latent *theos* in it, and before *Kosmos* was evolved. Hence, one finds Vishnu—standing here for eternal Law—periodically calling forth Kosmos into activity—" churning out of the *primitive* Ocean (boundless Chaos) the *Amrita* of Eternity, reserved only for the gods and devas ; and he has to employ in the task *Nagas* and *Asuras*—demons in exoteric Hinduism. The whole allegory is highly philosophical, and we find it repeated in every philosophical System. Plato, having fully embraced the ideas of Pythagoras—who had brought them from India —compiled and published them in a form more intelligible than the mysterious numerals of the Greek Sage. Thus the *Kosmos* is " the Son " with Plato, having for his father and mother the Divine Thought and Matter.*

" The Egyptians," says Dunlap, † " distinguish between an older and younger Horus ; the former the *brother* of Osiris, the latter the *son* of Osiris and Isis." The first is the *Idea* of the world remaining in the Demiurgic Mind, " born in darkness before the creation of the world." The second Horus is this " Idea " going forth from the *Logos*, becoming clothed with matter, and assuming an actual existence. ‡

" The Mundane God, eternal, boundless, young and old, of winding form," § say the *Chaldean oracles*.

This " winding form " is a figure to express the vibratory motion of the Astral Light, with which the ancient priests were perfectly well acquainted, though its name was invented by the Martinists.

Now Cosmolatry has the finger of scorn pointed at its superstitions by modern Science, which ought, however, as advised by a French

* Plutarch, " Isis and Osiris," l., vi.   † " Spirit History of Man," p. 88.
‡ Mover's " Phoinizer," 268.   § Cory, " Fragments," 240.

savant, before laughing at it " to remodel entirely its own system of cosmo-pneumatological education." *Satis eloquentiæ, sapientiæ parvum*. Cosmolatry like Pantheism may be made to yield in its ultimate expression the words applied to Vishnu . . . . " He is only the *ideal* Cause of the *Potencies* to be created in the work of creation; and from him proceed the potencies to be created, after they have become the real cause. *Save that one ideal cause*, there is no other to which the world can be referred. . . . . *Through the potency of that cause*, every created thing comes by its proper nature." (*Original Sanskrit Texts, Part iv., pp. 32, 33.*)

---

§ V.

ON THE HIDDEN DEITY, ITS SYMBOLS AND GLYPHS.

THE Logos or Creative deity, the " Word made Flesh," of every religion, has to be traced to its ultimate source and Essence. In India, it is a Proteus of 1,008 divine names and aspects in each of its *personal* transformations, from Brahmâ-Purusha down through the Seven *divine* Rishis and ten *semi*-divine Prajâpati (also Rishis) to the *divine-human* Avatars. The same puzzling problem of the " One in many " and the multitude in One, is found in other Pantheons, in the Egyptian, the Greek and the Chaldeo-Judaic, the latter having made confusion still more confused by presenting its Gods as euhemerizations, in the shapes of Patriarchs. The latter are now accepted by those who reject Romulus as a myth, and are represented as living and *historical* Entities. *Verbum satis sapienti.*

In the Zohar, En-Soph is also the ONE, and the infinite Unity. This was known to the very few learned Fathers of the Church, who were aware that Jehovah was but a *third rate* potency and no " highest " God. But while complaining bitterly of the Gnostics and saying . . . "our Heretics hold . . . that PROPATOR is known but to the *Only begotten* Son * (who is Brahmâ among the rest) that is to the mind " (*nous*), Irenæus never mentioned that the Jews did the same in their real *secret* books. Valentinus, " the profoundest doctor of the Gnosis," held that " there was a perfect AION who existed before Bythos, or Buthon (the first father of unfathomable nature, which is the second Logos) called Propator." It is thus AION, who springs as a Ray from Ain-Soph (who *does not create*), and AION, who creates, or *through* whom, rather, everything is created, or evolves.

---

* As Mulaprakriti is known only to Iswar, the LOGOS, as he is called now by Mr. T. Subba Row, of Madras. (See his *Bhagavadgita* Lectures.)

For, as the Basilidians taught, " there was a supreme god, *Abraxax*, by whom was created mind" (*Mahat*, in Sanskrit, *Nous* in Greek). " From Mind proceeded the word, *Logos*, from the word, Providence (Divine Light, rather), then from it Virtue and Wisdom in Principalities, Powers, Angels, etc., etc." By these (Angels) the 365 Æons were created. " Amongst the lowest, indeed, and those who made this world, he (Basilides) sets last of all the God of the Jews, whom he denies to be God (and very rightly), affirming he is one of the angels " (*Ibid.*). Here, then, we find the same system as in the Purânas, wherein the Incomprehensible drops a seed, which becomes the golden egg, from which Brahmâ is produced. Brahmâ produces Mahat, etc., etc. True Esoteric philosophy, however, speaks neither of " creation" nor of "evolution " in the sense the exoteric religions do. All these personified Powers are not evolutions from one another, but so many aspects of the one and sole manifestation of the ABSOLUTE all. The same system as the gnostic prevails in the Sephirothal aspects of Ain-Soph, yet, as *these aspects are in Space and Time,* a certain order is maintained in their successive appearances. Therefore, it becomes impossible not to take notice of the great changes that the *Zohar* has undergone under the handling of generations of Christian Mystics. For, even in the metaphysics of the Talmud, the "lower Face" (or " Lesser Countenance "), the microprosopus, in fact, could never be placed on the plane of the same abstract ideal as the Higher, or " Greater Countenance," macroprosopus. The latter is, in the Chaldean Kabala, a pure abstraction ; the Word or LOGOS, or DABAR (in Hebrew), which Word, though it becomes in fact a plural number, or "Words "—D(a)B(a)RIM, when it reflects itself, or falls into the aspect of a Host (of angels, or Sephiroth, " numbers ") is still collectively ONE, and on the ideal plane a nought—0, a " No-thing." IT is without form or being, " with no likeness with anything else." (*Franck, " Die Kabbala," p.* 126.) And even Philo calls the Creator, the *Logos* who stands next God, "*the* SECOND GOD," and " the second God who is his (Highest God's) WISDOM " (*Philo. Quæst. et Solut*). Deity is not God. It is NOTHING, and DARKNESS. It is nameless, and therefore called *Ain-Soph*—" the word *Ayin* meaning nothing." *See Franck " Die Kabbala," p.* 153. *See also Section XII., " Theogony of the Creative Gods."* The " Highest God " (the unmanifested LOGOS) is its Son.

Nor are most of the gnostic systems, which come down to us mutilated by the Church Fathers, anything better than the distorted shells of the original speculations. Nor were they *open* to the public or reader, at any time ; *i.e.*, had their hidden meaning or esotericism been revealed, it would have been no more an esoteric teaching, and this could never be. Alone Marcus (the chief of the Marcosians, 2nd century), who taught

THE GNOSTIC IDEA.

that deity had to be viewed under the symbol of *four syllables*, gave out more of the esoteric truths than any other Gnostic. But even he was never well understood. For it is only on the surface or dead letter of his *Revelation* that it appears that God is a quaternary, to wit: " the Ineffable, the Silence, the Father, and Truth,"—in reality it is quite erroneous, and divulges only one more esoteric riddle. This teaching of Marcus was that of the early Kabalists and ours. For he makes of Deity, the number 30 *in* 4 *syllables*, which, translated esoterically, means a Triad or *Triangle*, and a Quaternary or a square, in all *seven*, which, on the lower plane made the seven divine or secret letters of which the God-name is composed. This requires demonstration. In his " Revelation," speaking of divine mysteries expressed by means of letters and numbers, Marcus narrates how the " Supreme Tetrad came down unto me (him) from the region which cannot be seen nor named, *in a female form*, because *the world would have been unable to bear her appearing under a male figure*," and revealed to him " the generation of the universe, *untold before to either* gods or men."

This first sentence already contains a double meaning. Why should a female figure be more easily borne or listened to by the world than a male figure ? On the very face of it this appears nonsensical. Withal it is quite simple and clear to one who is acquainted with the mystery-language. *Esoteric Philosophy*, or the Secret Wisdom, was symbolized by a female form, while a male figure stood for the *Unveiled* mystery. Hence, the world not being ready to receive, could not bear it, and the Revelation of Marcus had to be given allegorically. Then he writes :

" When first the Inconceivable, the Beingless and Sexless (the Kabalistic Ain-Soph) began to be in labour (*i.e.*, when the hour of manifesting Itself had struck) and desired that Its Ineffable should be born (the first Logos, or Æon, or Aion), and its invisible should be clothed with form, its mouth opened and uttered the word like unto itself. This word (logos) manifested itself in the form of the Invisible One. The uttering of the (ineffable) name (through the word) came to pass in this manner. He (the Supreme Logos) uttered the first word of his name, which is a *syllable of four letters*. Then the second syllable was added, *also of four letters*. Then the third, composed of *ten* letters ; and after this the fourth, which contains *twelve* letters. The whole name consists thus of *thirty letters* and of *four syllables*. Each letter has its own accent and way of writing, but neither understands nor ever beholds that form of the whole Name,—no ; not even the power of the letter that stands next to Itself (to the Beingless and the Inconceivable.)* All these sounds when united are the collective Beingless,

---

* Iswara, or the Logos, cannot see Parabrahmam, but only Mulaprakriti, says the lecturer, in the Four Lectures on Bhagavatgita. (See *Theosophist,* Feb., 1887.)

unbegotten Æon, and *these* are the Angels that are ever beholding the face of the Father* (the Logos, the " second God," who stands next God, " the Inconceivable," according to Philo).

This is as plain as ancient esoteric secresy would make it. It is as Kabalistic, but less veiled than the Zohar in which the mystic names or attributes are also four syllabled, twelve, forty-two, and even seventy-two syllabled words! The *Tetrad* shows to Marcus the TRUTH in the shape of a naked woman, and letters every limb of that figure, calling her head Ω, her neck Ψ, shoulders and hands Γ, and Χ, etc., etc. In this Sephira is easily recognised, the Crown (*Kether*) or head being numbered *one;* the brain or Chochmah, 2; the heart, or Intelligence (Binah), 3; and the other seven Sephiroth representing the limbs of the body. The Sephirothal Tree is the Universe, and Adam Kadmon represents it in the West as Brahmâ represents it in India.

Throughout, the 10 Sephiroth are represented as divided into the three higher, or the spiritual *Triad*, and the lower Septenary. The true Esoteric meaning of the sacred number seven is cleverly veiled in the *Zohar;* yet was betrayed by the double way of writing "in the beginning " or *Be-resheeth*, and Be-raishath, the latter the " Higher, or *Upper* Wisdom.*" As shown by Mr. Macgregor Mathers in his *Kabbalah* (p. 47), and in the *Qabbalah* of Mr. T. Myer (p. 233), both of these Kabalists being supported by the best ancient authorities, these words have a dual and secret meaning. *Braisheeth bara Elohim* means that the *six*, over which stands the *seventh* Sephiroth, belong to the lower material class, or, as the anthor says: " Seven . . . . are applied to the Lower Creation, and three to the spiritual man, the Heavenly Prototypic or first Adam."

When the Theosophists and Occultists say that God is no BEING, for IT is nothing, *No-Thing*, they are more reverential and religiously respectful to the Deity than those who call God a HE, and thus make of Him a gigantic MALE.

He who studies the Kabala will soon find the same idea in the ultimate thought of its authors, the earlier and great Hebrew Initiates, who got this secret Wisdom at Babylonia from the Chaldean Hierophants, while Moses got his in Egypt. The Zohar cannot well be judged by its after translations in Latin and other tongues, as all those ideas were, of course, softened and made to fit in with the views and *policy* of its Christian arrangers; but in truth its ideas are identical with those of all other religious systems. The various Cosmogonies show that the Archaic Universal Soul was held by every nation as the " Mind " of the Demiurgic Creator; and that it

---

* The " Seven Angels of the Face," with the Christians.

was called the "Mother," *Sophia* with the Gnostics (or the female Wisdom), the *Sephira* with the Jews, Saraswati or Vâch, with the Hindus, *the Holy Ghost being a female Principle.*

Hence, born from it, the *Kurios* or Logos was, with the Greeks, the "God, mind" (*nous*). "Now Koros (*Kurios*) signifies the pure and unmixed nature of intellect—wisdom," says Plato in "Cratylus"; and Kurios is Mercury, the Divine Wisdom, and "mercury is the Sol" (Sun) ("*Arnobius*" vi., xii.), from whom Thot-Hermes received this divine Wisdom. While, then, the *Logoi* of all countries and religions are correlative (in their sexual aspects) with the female Soul of the World or the "Great Deep;" the deity, from which these *two in one* have their being, is ever concealed and called the "Hidden One," connected only indirectly with Creation,* as it can act only through the Dual Force emanating from the Eternal Essence. Even Æsculapius, called the "Saviour of all," is identical, according to ancient classics, with *Phta*, the Egyptian Creative Intellect (or Divine Wisdom), and with Apollo, Baal, Adonis and Hercules (*see Dunlap's "Mystery of Adonis," pp. 23 and 95*); and Phta is, in one of its aspects, the "Anima Mundi," the Universal Soul of Plato, the "Divine Spirit" of the Egyptians, the "Holy Ghost" of the early Christians and Gnostics, and the *Akâsa* of the Hindus, and even, in its lower aspect, the *Astral Light*. For *Phta* was originally the "God of the Dead," he in whose bosom they were received, hence the *Limbus* of the Greek Christians, or the Astral Light. It is far later that *Phta* was classed with the Sun-gods, his name signifying "he who opens," as he is shown to be the first to unveil the face of the dead mummy, to call the soul to *life in his bosom*. (See *Maspero's "Bulaq Museum."*) KNEPH, the Eternal *Unrevealed*, is represented by the snake-emblem of eternity encircling a water-urn, with its head hovering *over the "waters" which it incubates with its breath*—another form of one and the same idea of "Darkness," its ray moving on the waters, &c. As "Logos-Soul," this *permutation* is called Phta; as Logos-Creator, he becomes *Imhot-pou*, his son, "the god of the handsome face." In their primitive characters these two were the first Cosmic Duad, *Noot*, "space or *Sky*," and *Noo*, "the primordial Waters," the Androgyne Unity, above whom was the *Concealed* BREATH of Kneph. And all of them had the aquatic animals and plants sacred to them, the *ibis*, the *swan*, the *goose*, the *crocodile*, and the *lotus*.

Returning to the Kabalistic deity, this Concealed Unity is then אַיוּסוֹף = τό πάν = ἄπειρος, Endless, Boundless, non-Existent, אִיד so

---

* We use the term as one accepted and sanctioned by use, and therefore more comprehensible to the reader.

long as the *Absolute* is within *Oulom*,* the boundless and termless time, as such, En-Soph cannot be the Creator or even the modeller of the Universe, nor can he be *Aur* (light). Therefore En-Soph is also Darkness. The *immutably* Infinite and the *absolutely* Boundless can neither will, think, nor act. To do this it has to become finite, and *it* does so, by its ray penetrating into the mundane egg—infinite space—and emanating from it as a finite god. All this is left to the ray latent in the one. When the period arrives, the absolute will expands naturally the force within it, according to the Law of which it is the inner and ultimate Essence. The Hebrews did not adopt the egg as a symbol, but they substituted for it the " Duplex heavens," for, translated correctly, the sentence " God made the heavens and the earth " would read :—" In and out of his own essence as a womb (the mundane egg), God created the two heavens." But the Christians have chosen as the symbol of their Holy Ghost, the dove.

" Whosoever acquaints himself with הדר the Mercaba and the *lahgash* (secret speech or incantation), will learn the secret of secrets." *Lahgash* is nearly identical in meaning with *Vâch*, the hidden power of the Mantras.

When the active period has arrived, from within the eternal essence of Ain-Soph, comes forth Sephira, the active Power, called the Primordial Point, and the Crown, *Kether*. It is only through her that the " Un-bounded Wisdom " could give a concrete form to the abstract Thought. Two sides of the upper triangle by which the ineffable Essence and the universe—its manifested body—are symbolized, the right side and the base are composed of unbroken lines ; the third, the left side, is dotted. It is through the latter that emerges Sephira. Spreading in every direction, she finally encompasses the whole triangle. In this emanation the triple triad is formed. From the invisible Dew falling from the higher *Uni-triad* (thus leaving 7 sephiroths only), the " Head " Sephira *creates* primeval waters, *i.e.*, Chaos takes shape. It is the first stage towards the solidification of spirit which through various modifications will produce earth. " *It requires earth and water to make a living soul*," says Moses. It requires the image of an aquatic bird to connect it with water, the female element of procreation with the egg and the bird that fecundates it.

When Sephira emerges like an active power from within the latent Deity, she is female ; when she assumes the office of a creator, she becomes a male ; hence, she is androgyne. She is the " Father and

---

* With the ancient Jews, as shown by Le Clerc, the word *Oulom* meant only a time whose beginning or end is not known. The term " eternity," properly speaking, did not exist in the Hebrew tongue with the meaning, for instance, applied by the Vedantins to Parabrahm.

Mother Aditi," of the Hindu Cosmogony and of *the Secret Doctrine*. If the oldest Hebrew scrolls had been preserved, the modern Jehovah-worshipper would have found that many and uncomely were the symbols of the *creative* god. The frog in the moon, typical of his generative character, was the most frequent. All the birds and animals now held "unclean" in the Bible had been the symbols of the Deity in days of old. It was because they were too sacred that a mask of uncleanness was placed over them, in order to preserve them from destruction. The brazen serpent was not a bit more poetical than the goose or swan, if symbols are to be accepted *à la lettre*.

In the words of the *Zohar*: "The Indivisible Point, which has no limit and cannot be comprehended because of its purity and brightness, expanded *from without*, forming a brightness that served the indivisible Point as a veil;" yet the latter also "*could not be viewed in* consequence of its immeasurable light. It too *expanded from without*, and this expansion was its garment. Thus through a constant *upheaving* (motion) finally the world originated" (*Zohar I*. 20a). The Spiritual substance sent forth by the Infinite Light is the *first* Sephira or *Shekinah*: Sephira *exoterically* contains all the other nine Sephiroths in her. *Esoterically* she contains but two,* *Chochmah* or *Wisdom*, "a masculine, *active* potency whose divine name is *Jah* (ה י)," and BINAH, a feminine passive potency, Intelligence, represented by the divine name Jehovah (ה ו ה י); which two potencies form, with Sephira the third, the Jewish trinity or the Crown, KETHER. These two Sephiroths called Father, *Abba*, and Mother *Amona*, are the duad or the double-sexed *logos* from which issued the other seven Sephiroths. (See *Zohar*.) This first Jewish triad (Sephira, Chochmah, and Binah) is the Hindu *Trimurti*.* However veiled, even in the *Zohar*, and more still in the exoteric Pantheon of India, every particular connected with one is reproduced in the other. The *Prajâpati* are the Sephiroths. Ten with Brahmâ they dwindle to seven, when the Trimurti, and the Kabalistic triad, are separated from the rest. The seven Builders (Creators) become the seven *Prajâpati*, or the seven Rishis, in the same order as the Sephiroths become the Creators; then the Patriarchs, etc. In both Secret Systems, the One Universal Essence is incomprehensible and *inactive* in its absoluteness, and can be connected with the building of the Universe only in an indirect way. In both, the primeval Male-female or androgynous Principle, and their ten and seven Emanations (Brahmâ-Virâj and Aditi-Vâch on the one part and the Elohim-Jehovah, or Adam-Adami (Adam Kadmon) and Sephira Eve on the

* In the Indian Pantheon the double-sexed Logos is Brahmâ, the Creator, whose seven "mind born" sons are the primeval Rishis—the "Builders."

other), with their Prajâpati and Sephiroths, represent in their totality, first of all the Archetypal man, the *Proto-logos ;* and only in their secondary aspect do they become Cosmic powers, and astronomical or sidereal bodies. If Aditi is the mother of the gods, *Deva-Matri,* Eve is the mother of all living ; they are the *Sakti* or generative power in their female aspect of the " Heavenly man," and they are all compound Creators. Says a "*Gupta Vidya*" Sûtra : " In the beginning, a ray issuing from Paramârthika (*the one* and only true existence), it became manifested in Vyavahârika (conventional existence) which was used as a *Vahan* to descend into the Universal Mother, and to cause her to expand (swell, *brih*)." And in the *Zohar* it is stated : " The Infinite Unity, formless and without similitude, after the form of the heavenly man was created, used it. The Unknown Light* (Darkness) used the אדם‑מצואה (heavenly form) as a chariot מדבבה through which to descend, and wished to be called by this form, which is the sacred name Jehovah."

As the Zohar says : " In the beginning was the Will of the King, prior to any other existence. . . . It (the Will) sketched the forms of all things that had been concealed but now came into view. And there went forth as a sealed secret from the head of Ain Soph, a nebulous spark of matter, without shape or form. . . . Life is drawn from below, and from above the source renews itself, the sea is always full and spreads its waters everywhere." Thus the deity is compared to a shore-less sea, to water which is " the fountain of life " (Zohar iii., 290). " The seventh palace, the fountain of life, is the first in the order from above " (ii. 261). Hence the Kabalistic tenet on the lips of the very Kabalistic Solomon, who says in Proverbs ix., 1 : " Wisdom hath builded her house ; it hath hewn out its *seven* pillars."

Whence then, all this identity of ideas, if there was no primeval UNIVERSAL Revelation ? The few points shown are like a few straws in a hayrick, in comparison to that which will be shown as the work proceeds. If we turn to that most hazy of all Cosmogonies—the Chinese, even there the same idea is found. *Tsi-tsai* (the Self-Existent) is the unknown Darkness, the root of the *Wuliang-sheu* (Boundless Age), Amitabhe, and Tien (heaven) come later on. The " great Extreme " of Confucius gives the same idea, his " straws " notwithstanding. The latter are a source of great amusement to the missionaries. These laugh at every " heathen " religion, despise and hate that of their

---

* Says Rabbi Simeon : " Ah, companions, companions, man as an emanation was both man and woman, as well on the side of the '*Father*' as on the side of the '*Mother.*' And this is the sense of the words : 'And Elohim spoke ; Let there be Light, and it was Light ' . . . and this is the *two-fold man.*" (" *Auszüge aus dem Sohar,*" p. 13, 15.) Light, then, in *Genesis* stood for the Androgyne Ray or " Heavenly Man."

brother Christians of other denominations, and yet one and all accept
à la lettre their own *Genesis*. If we turn to Chaldea we find in it *Anu*, the
concealed deity, the One, whose name, moreover, shows it to be of
Sanskrit origin. *Anu*, which means in Sanskrit " atom," aníyámsam
aníyasâm (smallest of the small), is a name of Parabrahm in the
Vedantic philosophy; Parabrahm being described as smaller than the
smallest atom, and greater than the greatest sphere or universe:
"*Anagraniyam and Mahatorvavat.*" This is what George Smith gives as the
first verses of the Akkadian *Genesis* as found in the Cuneiform Texts on the
" *Lateras Coctiles.*" There also, we find *Anu* the passive deity or En-Soph,
Bel, the Creator, the Spirit of God (Sephira) moving on the face of the
waters, hence water itself, and *Hea*, the Universal Soul or wisdom of
the three combined.

The first eight verses read thus :

1. When above, were not raised the heavens ;
2. And below on the earth a plant had not grown up.
3. The abyss had not broken its boundaries.
4. The chaos (or water) Tiamat (the sea) was the producing mother
of the whole of them. (This is the Cosmical Aditi and Sephira.)
5. Those waters at the beginning were ordained but—
6. A tree had not grown, a flower had not unfolded.
7. When the gods had not sprung up, any one of them.
8. A plant had not grown, and order did not exist.

This was the chaotic or ante-genetic period—the double Swan and
the Dark Swan, which becomes white, when Light is created.*

The symbol chosen for the majestic ideal of the Universal Principle
will seem little calculated to answer its sacred character. A goose, or
even a swan, may appear unfit, no doubt, to represent the grandeur of
the Spirit. Nevertheless, it must have had some deep occult meaning,
since it figures not only in every cosmogony and world religion, but
even was chosen by the mediæval Christians, the Crusaders, as
the *vehicle* of the Holy Ghost supposed to lead the army to Palestine, to wrench the Tomb of the Saviour from the hands of the
Saracen. If we are to credit Professor Draper's statement in
his " Intellectual Development of Europe," the Crusaders, led on by
Peter the Hermit, were preceded, at the head of the army, by the Holy
Ghost under the shape of a white gander in company of a goat. The
Egyptian God of Time, Seb, carries a goose on his head. Jupiter
assumes the form of a swan and Brahmâ also, because the root of all
this is that mystery of mysteries—the MUNDANE EGG. (See preceding §).

* The Seven Swans that are believed to land from Heaven into Lake Mansarovara,
are in the popular fancy the Seven Rishis of the Great Bear, who assume that form to
visit the locality where the Vedas were written.

One has to learn the reason of a symbol before one depreciates it. The dual element of Air and Water is that of the ibis, swan, goose and pelican, of crocodiles and frogs, lotus flowers and water lilies, &c.; and the result is the choice of the most unseemly symbols among the modern as much as the ancient mystics. Pan, the great god of nature, was generally figured in connection with aquatic birds, geese especially, and so were other gods. If, later on, with the gradual degeneration of religion, the gods to whom geese were sacred, became Priapic deities, it does not stand to reason that water fowls were made sacred to Pan and other Phallic deities as some scoffers even of antiquity would have it (*see Petronii Satyrica*, cxxxvi.); but that the abstract and divine power of procreative nature had become grossly anthropomorphized. Nor does the Swan of Leda show "Priapic doings and her enjoyment thereof," as Mr. Hargrave Jennings chastely expresses it; for the myth is but another version of the same philosophical idea of cosmogony. Swans are frequently found associated with Apollo, as they are the emblems of water and fire (sun-light also), before the separation of the Elements.

Our modern symbologists might profit by some remarks made by a well-known writer, Mrs. Lydia Maria Child. "From time immemorial an emblem has been worshipped in Hindostan as the type of creation, or the origin of life. . . . Siva or the Mahadeva being not only the reproducer of human forms, but also the fructifying principle, the generative power that pervades the Universe. The maternal emblem is likewise a religious type. This reverence for the production of life, introduced into the worship of Osiris the sexual emblems. Is it strange that they regarded with reverence the great mystery of human birth? Were they impure thus to regard it? Or are *we* impure that do not so regard it? But *no clean and thoughtful mind* could so regard them. . . . We have travelled far, and unclean have been the paths, since those old Anchorites first spoke of God and the soul in the solemn depths of their first sanctuaries. Let us not smile at their mode of tracing the infinite and the incomprehensible Cause throughout all the mysteries of nature, lest by so doing we cast the shadow of our own grossness on their patriarchal simplicity." (*"Progress of Religious Ideas,"* Vol. i, *p.* 17, *et seq.*)

§ VI.

THE MUNDANE EGG.

WHENCE this universal symbol ? The Egg was incorporated as a sacred sign in the cosmogony of every people on the Earth, and was revered both on account of its form and its inner mystery. From the earliest mental conceptions of man, it was known as that which represented most successfully the origin and secret of being. The gradual development of the imperceptible germ within the closed shell; the inward working, without any apparent outward interference of force, which from a latent *nothing* produced an active *something*, needing nought save heat ; and which, having gradually evolved into a concrete, living creature, broke its shell, appearing to the outward senses of all a self-generated, and self-created being—must have been a standing miracle from the beginning.

The secret teaching explains the reason for this reverence by the Symbolism of the prehistoric races. The " First Cause " had no name in the beginnings. Later it was pictured in the fancy of the thinkers as an ever invisible, mysterious Bird that dropped an Egg into Chaos, which Egg becomes the Universe. Hence Brahm was called Kalahansa, "the swan in (Space and) Time." He became the " Swan of Eternity," who lays at the beginning of each Mahamanvantara a " Golden Egg." It typifies the great Circle, or O, itself a symbol for the universe and its spherical bodies.

The second reason for its having been chosen as the symbolical representation of the Universe, and of our earth, was its form. It was a Circle and a Sphere ; and the ovi-form shape of our globe must have been known from the beginning of symbology, since it was so universally adopted. The first manifestation of the Kosmos in the form of an egg was the most widely diffused belief of antiquity. As Bryant shows (iii., 165), it was a symbol adopted among the Greeks, the Syrians, Persians, and Egyptians. In chap. liv. of the Egyptian Ritual, Seb, the god of Time and of the Earth, is spoken of as having laid an egg, or the Universe, " an egg conceived at the hour of the great one of the Dual Force " (Sec. V., 2, 3, etc.).

Ra is shown like Brahmâ gestating in the Egg of the Universe. The deceased is "resplendent in the Egg of the land of mysteries" (zxii., 1). For, this is "the Egg to which is given life among the gods" (xlii., 11). " It is the Egg of the great clucking Hen, the Egg of Seb, who issues from it like a hawk " (lxiv., 1, 2, 3 ; lxxvii., 1).

With the Greeks the Orphic Egg is described by Aristophanes, and was part of the Dionysiac and other mysteries, during which the Mundane Egg was consecrated and its significance explained ; Porphyry showing it a representation of the world, Ἑρμήνευει δέ τὸ ωὸν κόσμον. Faber and Bryant have tried to show that the egg typified the ark of Noah, which, unless the latter is accepted as purely allegorical and symbolical, is a wild belief. It can have typified the ark only as a synonym of the moon, the *argha* which carries the universal seed of life; but had surely nothing to do with the ark of the Bible. Anyhow, the belief that the universe existed in the beginning in the shape of an egg was general. And as Wilson has it : " A similar account of the first aggregation of the elements in the form of an egg is given in all the (Indian) Purânas, with the usual epithet Haima or Hiranya, 'golden' as it occurs in Manu." Hiranya, however, means " resplendent," " shining," rather than " golden," as proven by the great Indian scholar, the late Swami Dayanand Sarasvati, in his un-published polemics with Professor Max Müller. As said in the Vishnu Purâna : " Intellect (Mahat) . . . the (unmanifested) gross elements inclusive, formed an egg . . . and the lord of the universe himself abided in it, in the character of Brahmâ. In that egg, O Brahman, were the continents, and seas and mountains, the planets and divisions of the universe, the gods, the demons and mankind." (*Book* i., *ch.* 2.) Both in Greece and in India the first visible male being, who united in himself the nature of either sex, abode in the egg and issued from it. This " first born of the world" was Dionysius, with some Greeks ; the god who sprang from the mundane egg, and from whom the mortals and immortals were derived. The god Ra is shown in the *Ritual* (Book of the Dead, xvii., 50) beaming in his egg (the Sun), and he starts off as soon as the god *Shoo* (the Solar energy) awakens and gives him the impulse. " He is in the Solar egg, the egg to which is given life among the gods" (*Ibid*, xlii., 13). The Solar god exclaims : " I am the creative soul of the celestial abyss. None sees my nest, none can break my egg, I am the Lord !" (*Ibid*, LXXXV.).

In view of this circular form, the " | " issuing from the " ○," or the egg, or the male from the female in the androgyne, it is strange to find a scholar saying—on the ground that the most ancient Indian MSS. show no trace of it—that the ancient Aryans were ignorant of the decimal notation. The 10, being the sacred number of the universe, was secret and esoteric, both as the unit and cipher, or *zero*, the circle. Moreover, Professor Max Müller says that " the two words *cipher* and *zero*, which are but one, are sufficient to prove that our figures are borrowed from the Arabs.* Cipher is the Arabic " cifron," and means

---

* See Max Müller's " Our Figures."

empty, a translation of the Sanscrit name of nought " synya," he says.* The Arabs had their figures from Hindustan, and never claimed the discovery for themselves.† As to the Pythagoreans, we need but turn to the ancient manuscripts of Boethius's *Geometry*, composed in the sixth century, to find among the Pythagorean numerals‡ the 1 and the *nought*, as the first and final ciphers. And Porphyry, who quotes from the Pythagorean *Moderatus*,‖ says that the numerals of Pythagoras were "hieroglyphical symbols, by means whereof he explained ideas concerning the nature of things," or the origin of the universe.

Now, if, on the other hand, the most ancient Indian manuscripts show as yet no trace of decimal notation in them, and Max Müller states very clearly that until now he has found but nine letters (the initials of the Sanscrit numerals) in them ; on the other hand, we have records as ancient to supply the wanted proof. We speak of the sculptures and the sacred imagery in the most ancient temples of the far East. Pythagoras derived his knowledge from India ; and we find Professor Max Müller corroborating this statement, at least so far as to allow the *Neo-Pythagoreans* to have been the first teachers of " ciphering," among the Greeks and Romans; that " they at Alexandria, or in Syria, became acquainted with the Indian figures, and adapted them to the Pythagorean abacus" (our figures). This cautious admission implies that Pythagoras himself was acquainted with but *nine* figures. Thus we might reasonably answer that, although we possess no certain proof (*exoterically*) that the decimal notation was known by Pythagoras, who lived on the very close of the archaic ages,§ we have yet sufficient evidence to show that the full numbers, as given by Boethius, were known to the Pythagoreans, even before Alexandria was built.¶ This evidence we find in Aristotle, who says that " some philosophers hold that ideas and numbers are of the same nature, and amount to TEN in all."** This, we believe, will be sufficient to show that the decimal notation was known among them at least as early as four centuries B.C., for Aristotle does not seem to treat the question as an innovation of the " Neo-Pythagoreans."

---

* A Kabalist would be rather inclined to believe that as the Arabic *cifron* was taken from the Indian *Synya*, nought, so the Jewish Kabalistic Sephiroth (*Sephrim*) were taken from the word cipher, not in the sense of emptiness but the reverse—that of creation by number and degrees in their evolution. And the Sephiroth are 10 or Ⓘ.
† See Max Müller's " Our Figures."
‡ See King's " Gnostics and their Remains," plate xiii.
‖ " Vita Pythag."
§ 608 B.C.
¶ This city was built 332 B.C.
** " Metaph." vii., F.

But we know more than that : *we know* that the decimal system must have been known to the mankind of the earliest archaic ages, since the whole astronomical and geometrical portion of the secret sacerdotal language was built upon the number 10, or the combination of the male and female principles, and since the Pyramid of " Cheops " is built upon the measures of this decimal notation, or rather upon the digits and their combinations with the *nought*. Of this, however, sufficient was said in *Isis Unveiled*, and it is useless to repeat and return to the same subject.

The symbolism of the Lunar and Solar Deities is so inextricably mixed up, that it is next to impossible to separate such glyphs as the egg, the lotus, and the " sacred " animals from each other. The *ibis*, for instance, sacred to Isis, who is often represented with the head of that bird, sacred also to Mercury or Thoth, because that god assumed its form while escaping from Typhon,—the *ibis* was held in the greatest veneration in Egypt. There were two kinds of ibises, Herodotus tells us (Lib. II. c. 75 *et seq*.) in that country : one *quite black*, the other black and white. The former is credited with fighting and exterminating the winged serpents which came every spring from Arabia and infested the country. The other was sacred to the moon, because the latter planet is white and brilliant on her external side, dark and black on that side which she never turns to the earth. Moreover, the *ibis* kills land serpents, and makes the most terrible havoc amongst the eggs of the crocodile, and thus saves Egypt from having the Nile infested by those horrible Saurians. The bird is credited with doing so in the moon-light, and thus being helped by *Isis*, as the moon, her sidereal symbol. But the nearer esoteric truth underlying these popular myths is, that Hermes, as shown by Abenephius (*De cultu Egypt*.), watched under the form of that bird over the Egyptians, and taught them the occult arts and sciences. This means simply that the *ibis religiosa* had and has " magical " properties in common with many other birds, the albatross pre-eminently, and the mythical white swan, the swan of Eternity or Time, the KALAHANSA.

Were it otherwise, indeed, why should all the ancient peoples, who were no more fools than we are, have had such a superstitious dread of killing certain birds ? In Egypt, he who killed an *ibis*, or the golden hawk— the symbol of the Sun and Osiris—risked and could hardly escape death. The veneration of some nations for birds was such that Zoro-aster, in his precepts, forbids their slaughter as a heinous crime. We laugh in our age at every kind of divination. Yet why should so many generations have believed in divination by birds, and even in zoomancy, said by Suidas to have been imparted by Orpheus, who taught how to perceive in the yoke and white of the egg, under certain conditions, that which the bird born from it would have seen around it during its short life. This occult art, which demanded 3,000 years ago the greatest learning and the most abstruse mathematical calculations, has now fallen into the depths of degradation : it is old cooks and fortune-tellers who read their future to servant-girls in search of husbands, by means of the white of an egg in a glass.

Nevertheless, even Christians have to this day their sacred birds ; for instance, the dove, the symbol of the Holy Ghost. Nor have they neglected the sacred animals. The *Evangelical* zoolatry—the Bull, the Eagle, the Lion, and the Angel (in reality the Cherub, or Seraph, the fiery-winged Serpent), is as much pagan as that of the Egyptians or the Chaldeans. These four animals are, in reality, the symbols of the four elements, and of the four *lower* principles in man. Nevertheless, they correspond physically and materially to the four constellations that form, so to speak, the *suite* or *cortège* of the Solar God, and occupy during the winter solstice the four cardinal points of the zodiacal circle. These four " animals " may be seen in many of the Roman Catholic New Testaments where the *portraits* of the evangelists are given. They are the animals of Ezekiel's Mercabah.

As truly stated by Ragon, " the ancient Hierophants have combined so cleverly the dogmas and symbols of their religious philosophies, that these symbols can be fully explained only by the combination and know- ledge of *all* the keys." They can be only *approximately* interpreted, even if one finds out three out of these seven systems : the *anthropological*, the *psychic*, and the *astronomical*. The two chief interpretations, the highest and the lowest, the spiritual and the physiological, they preserved in the greatest secrecy until the latter fell into the dominion of the profane. Thus far, with regard only to the *pre-historic* Hierophants, with whom that which has now become purely (or impurely) phallic, was a science as profound and as mysterious as biology and physiology are now. This was their exclusive property, the fruit of their studies and dis- coveries. The other two were those which dealt with the creative gods (theogony), and with creative man, *i.e.*, the ideal and the practical mys- teries. These interpretations were so cleverly veiled and combined, that many were those who, while arriving at the discovery of one meaning, were baffled in understanding the significance of the others, and could never unriddle them sufficiently to commit dangerous indiscretions. The highest, the first and the fourth—theogony in relation to anthro- pogony—were almost impossible to fathom. We find the proofs of this in the Jewish " Holy Writ."

It is owing to the serpent being oviparous, that it became a symbol of wisdom and an emblem of the Logoi, or the *self-born*. In the temple of Philœ in Upper Egypt, an egg was artificially prepared of clay made of various incenses, and it was made to hatch by a peculiar process, when a *cerastes* (the horned viper) was born. The same was done in antiquity for the cobra in the Indian temples. The *creative* God emerges from the egg that issues from the mouth of Kneph—as a winged serpent —because the Serpent is the symbol of the All-wisdom. With the Hebrews he is glyphed by the " flying or fiery serpents " of the Wilderness and Moses, and with the Alexandrian mystics he becomes the Ophio-Christos, the Logos of the Gnostics. The Protestants try to show that the allegory of the Brazen Serpent and of the "fiery serpents " has a direct reference to the mystery of Christ and Crucifixion * ; but it has a far nearer relation, in truth, *to the mystery of generation*, when dissociated from the egg with the central germ, or the *circle with its central point*. The *brazen Serpent* had no such holy meaning as that ; nor was it, in fact, glorified above the "*fiery serpents*" *for the bite of which it was only a natural remedy*. The symbological meaning of the word "brazen" being the feminine principle, and that of fiery, or "gold," the male one.†

In the *Book of the Dead*, as just shown, reference is often made to the Egg. Ra, the mighty one, remains in his Egg, during the struggle between the "children of the rebellion" and *Shoo* (the Solar Energy and the Dragon of Darkness) (ch. xvii.). The deceased is resplendent in his

---

* And this *only* because the brazen serpent was lifted on a pole ! It had rather a reference to Mico the Egyptian egg standing upright supported by the sacred *Tau* ; since the Egg and the Serpent are inseparable in the old worship and symbology of Egypt, and since both the Brazen and " fiery " serpents were *Saraphs*, the " burning fiery " messengers, or the serpent Gods, the *nagas* of India. It was a purely phallic symbol without the egg, while when associated with it—it related to cosmic creation.

† " Brass was a metal symbolizing the *nether world* . . . . that of the womb where life should be given . . . The word for serpent was in Hebrew *Nakash*, but this is the same term for *brass*." It is said in Numbers (xxi.) that the Jews complained of the Wilderness *where there was no water* (v. 5) ; after which " the Lord sent fiery serpents " to bite them, when, to oblige Moses, he gives him as a remedy the *brazen serpent* on a pole to look at ; after which " any man when he beheld the serpent of brass . . . . lived " (?). After that the " Lord," gathering the people together at the well of Beer, gives them water, (14-16), and grateful Israel sang this song, " Spring up, O Well," (v. 17). When, after studying symbology, the Christian reader comes to understand the innermost meaning of these three symbols—*water, brazen, the serpent*, and a few more—*in the sense given to them in the Holy Bible*, he will hardly like to connect the sacred name of his Saviour with the " Brazen Serpent " incident. The Seraphim שרפים (fiery winged serpents) are no doubt connected with, and inseparable from, the idea " of the serpent of eternity—God," as explained in Kenealy's Apocalypse. But the word cherub also meant serpent, in one sense, though its direct meaning is different ; because the *Cherubim* and the Persian winged γρύφες " griffins "—the guardians of the golden mountain—are the same, and their compound name shows their character, as it is formed of כר (kr) *circle*, and אוב " aub," or ob—serpent—therefore, a " serpent in a circle." And this settles the phallic character of the Brazen Serpent, and justifies Hezekiah for breaking it. (*See* II. *Kings*, 18, 4). *Verbum sat. sapienti.*

Egg when he crosses to the land of mystery (xxii. i.). He is the Egg of Seb (liv. 1—3). . . . The Egg was the symbol of life in *immortality* and eternity; as also the glyph of the generative matrix; and the *tau*, associated with it, only of life and birth in *generation*. The Mundane Egg was placed in *Khnoom*, the " Water of Space," or the feminine *abstract* principle (Khnoom becoming, with the *fall* of mankind into generation and phallicism, Ammon, the *creative* God); and when *Phtah*, the " fiery god," carries the Mundane egg in his hand, then the symbolism becomes quite terrestrial and concrete in its significance. In conjunction with the hawk, the symbol of Osiris-Sun, the symbol is dual: it relates to both lives—the mortal and the immortal. In Kircher's *Œdipus Egyptiacus* (vol. iii., p. 124) one can see, on the papyrus engraved in it, an egg floating above the mummy. This is the symbol of hope and the promise of a *second birth* for the *Osirified* dead; his Soul, after due purification in the Amenti, will gestate in this egg of immortality, to be reborn from it into a new life on earth. For this Egg, in the esoteric Doctrine, is the *Devachan*, the abode of Bliss; the winged scarabeus being alike a symbol of it. The " winged globe " is but another form of the egg, and has the same significance as the scarabeus, the *Khopiroo* (from the root *Khoproo* " to become," " to be reborn,") which relates to the rebirth of man, as well as to his spiritual regeneration.

In the Theogony of Mochus, we find Æther first, and then the air, from which Ulom, the *intelligible* (νοητος) deity (the visible Universe of Matter) is born out of the Mundane Egg. (Möver's *Phoinizer*, p. 282.)

In the *Orphic* Hymns, the Eros-Phanes evolves from the divine Egg, which the *Æthereal Winds* impregnate, wind being " the Spirit of the unknown Darkness "—" the spirit of God " (as explains K. O. Müller, 236); the divine " Idea," says Plato, " who is said to move Æther."

In the Hindu *Katakopanishad*, Purusha, the divine spirit, already stands before the original matter, " from whose union springs the great soul of the world," Maha-Atma, Brahmâ, the Spirit of Life,* etc., etc.† Besides this there are many charming allegories on this subject scattered through the sacred books of the Brahmins. In one place it is the female creator who is first a germ, then a drop of heavenly dew, a pearl, and then an egg. In such cases—of which there are too many to enumerate them separately—the Egg gives birth to the four elements within the fifth, Ether, and is covered with seven coverings, which become later on the seven upper and the seven lower worlds. Breaking in two, the shell becomes the heaven, and the meat in the egg the earth, the white forming the terres-

---

* The latter appellations are all identical with *Anima Mundi*, or the " Universal Soul," the astral light of the Kabalist and the Occultist, or the " Egg of Darkness."

† Weber, " Akad Vorles," pp. 213, 214 *et seq.*

trial waters. Then again, it is Vishnu who emerges from within the egg with a lotus in his hand. Vinata, a daughter of Daksha and wife of Kasyapa ("the Self-born sprung from Time," one of the seven " creators" of our world), brought forth an egg from which was born Garuda, the vehicle of Vishnu, the latter allegory having a relation to our Earth only, as Garuda is the Great Cycle.

The egg was sacred to Isis; the priests of Egypt never ate eggs on that account.*

Diodorus Siculus states that Osiris was born from an Egg, like Brahmâ. From Leda's Egg Apollo and Latona were born, as also Castor and Pollux—the bright Gemini. And though the Buddhists do not attribute the same origin to their Founder, yet, no more than the ancient Egyptians or the modern Brahmins, do they eat eggs, lest they should destroy the germ of life latent in them, and commit thereby Sin. The Chinese believe that their first man was born from an egg, which *Tien*, a god, dropped down from heaven to earth into the waters.† This symbol is still regarded by some as representing the idea of the origin of life, which is a scientific truth, though the human *ovum* is invisible to the naked eye. Therefore we see respect shown to it from the remotest past, by the Greeks, Phœnicians, Romans, the Japanese, and the Siamese, the North and South American tribes, and even the savages of the remotest islands.

With the Egyptians, the concealed god was Ammon (*Mon*). All their gods were dual: the scientific *reality* for the Sanctuary; its double, the fabulous and mythical Entity, for the masses. For instance, as observed in " Chaos, Theos, Kosmos," the older Horus was the *Idea* of the world remaining in the demiurgic mind " born in Darkness before the creation of the world;" the *second* Horus‡ was the same *Idea* going forth from the *Logos*, becoming clothed with matter and assuming an actual existence. (Compare *Mövers " Phoinizer," p.* 268.) The same with *Khnoum* and Ammon; ‖ both are represented ram-headed, and both often confused, though their functions are different. Khnoum is " the modeller of men," fashioning men and things out of the Mundane Egg on a potter's wheel;

---

* Isis is almost always represented holding a lotus in one hand and in the other a circle and the Cross (*crux ansata*), the Egg being sacred to her.

† The Chinese seem to have thus anticipated Sir William Thomson's theory that the first living germ had dropped to the Earth from some passing comet. Query! why should this be called *scientific* and the Chinese idea a superstitious, foolish theory?

‡ Horus—the " older," or *Haroiri*, is an ancient aspect of the solar god, contemporary with *Ra* and *Shoo;* Haroiri is often mistaken for Hor (Horsusi), Son of Osiris and Isis. The Egyptians very often represented the rising Sun under the form of Hor the older, rising from a full-blown lotus, the Universe, when the solar disc is always found on the hawk-head of that god. Haroiri is Khnoum.

‖ Ammon or *Mon*, the " hidden," the Supreme Spirit.

Ammon-Ra, the generator, is the secondary aspect of the concealed deity. Khnoum was adored at Elephanta and Philœ,* Ammon at Thebes. But it is Emepht, the One, Supreme *Planetary* principle, who blows the egg out of his mouth, and who is, therefore, Brahmâ. The shadow of the deity, Kosmic and universal, of that which broods over and permeates the egg with its vivifying Spirit until the germ contained in it is ripe, was the *mystery* god whose name was unpronounceable. It is is Phtah, however, " he who opens," the opener of life and Death,† who proceeds from the egg of the world to begin his dual work. (*Book of Numbers.*)

According to the Greeks, the phantom form of the Chemis (*Chemi,* ancient Egypt) which floats on the ethereal waves of the Empyrean Sphere, was called into being by Horus-Apollo, the Sun god, who caused it to evolve out of the Mundane egg.‡

In the Scandinavian Cosmogony—placed by Professor Max Müller, in point of time, as " far anterior to the Vedas " in the poem of Voluspa (the song of the prophetess), the Mundane egg is again discovered in the phantom-germ of the Universe, which is represented as lying in the *Ginnungagap*—the cup of illusion *(Maya)* the boundless and void abyss. In this world's matrix, formerly a region of night and desolation, *Nebelheim* (the mist-place, the *nebular* as it is called now, in the astral light) dropped a *ray of cold light* which overflowed this cup and froze in it. Then the *Invisible* blew a scorching wind which dissolved the frozen waters and cleared the mist. These waters (chaos), called the streams of *Elivagar,* distilling in vivifying drops, fell down and created the earth and the giant *Ymir,* who only had " the semblance of man " (the Heavenly man), and the cow, *Audhumla* (the " mother " or astral light, Cosmic Soul) from whose udder flowed *four* streams of milk (the four cardinal points : the four heads of the four rivers of Eden, etc., etc.) and which " four " allegorically are symbolized by the *cube* in all its various and mystical meanings.

The Christians—especially the Greek and Latin Churches—have fully adopted the symbol, and see in it a commemoration of life eternal,

---

* His triadic goddesses are *Sati* and *Anouki.*

† *Phtah* was originally the god of death, of *destruction,* like Siva. He is a *solar* god only by virtue of the sun's fire killing as well as vivifying. He was the national god of Memphis, the radiant and " fair-faced God." (See *Saqquarah Bronzes, Saitic Epoch.*)

‡ The *Brahmanda Purâna* contains the mystery about Brahmâ's golden egg fully; and this is why, perhaps, it is inaccessible to the Orientalists, who say that this Purâna, like the Skanda, is " no longer procurable in a collective body," but " is represented by a variety of Khandas and Mahatmyas professing to be derived from it." The " Brahmanda Purâna " is described as " that which is declared in 12,200 verses, the magnificence of the egg of Brahmâ, and in which an account of the future Kalpas is contained as revealed by Brahmâ." Quite so, and much more, perchance.

of salvation and of resurrection. This is found in and corroborated by the time-honoured custom of exchanging " Easter Eggs." From the *anguinum*, the " Egg" of the " pagan " Druid, whose name alone made Rome tremble with fear, to the red Easter Egg of the Slavonian peasant, a cycle has passed. And yet, whether in civilized Europe, or among the abject savages of Central America, we find the same archaic, primitive thought ; if we only search for it and do not disfigure—in the the haughtiness of our fancied mental and physical superiority—the original idea of the symbol.

§ VII.

THE DAYS AND NIGHTS OF BRAHMÂ.

THIS is the name given to the Periods called MANVANTARA (*Manu-antara*, or between the Manus) and PRALAYA (Dissolution); one referring to the active periods of the Universe, the other to its times of relative and complete *rest*—according to whether they occur at the end of a " Day," or an " Age " (a life) of Brahmâ. These periods, which follow each other in regular succession, are also called *Kalpas*, small and great, the minor and the *Maha Kalpa ;* though, properly speaking, the Maha Kalpa is never a " day," but a whole life or age of Brahmâ, for it is said in the Brahmâ Vaivarta : " Chronologers compute a Kalpa by the Life of Brahmâ ; minor Kalpas, as Samvarta and the rest, are numerous." In sober truth they are infinite ; as they have never had a commencement, *i.e.*, there never was a *first* Kalpa, nor will there ever be a *last* one, in Eternity.

One *Parardha*—in the ordinary acceptation of this measure of time—or half of the existence of Brahmâ (in the present *Maha Kalpa*) has already expired ; the last Kalpa was the Padma, or that of the Golden Lotos ; the present one being *Vârâha** (the " boar " incarnation, or *Avatar*).

---

* There is a curious piece of information in the Buddhist esoteric traditions. The exoteric or *allegorical* biography of Gautama Buddha shows this great Sage dying of an indigestion of *pork and rice*, a very prosaic end, indeed, having little of the solemn element in it. This is explained as an allegorical reference to his having been born in the " Boar," or Vârâha-Kalpa when Brahmâ assumed the form of that animal to raise the Earth out of the " Waters of Space." And as the Brahmins descend direct from Brahmâ and are, so to speak, identified with him ; and as they are at the same time the mortal enemies of Buddha and Buddhism, we have the curious allegorical hint and combination. Brahminism (of the Boar, or *Vârâha Kalpa*) has slaughtered the religion of Buddha in India, swept it away from its face ; therefore Buddha, identified with his philosophy, is said to have died from the effects of eating of the flesh of a wild hog.

By the scholar who studies the Hindu religion from the Purânas, one thing is to be especially noted.   He must not take literally, and in one sense only, the statements therein found ; since those which especially concern the Manvantaras or Kalpas have to be understood in their several references.   So, for instance, these periods relate in the same language to both the great and the small periods, to Maha Kalpas and to minor Cycles.   The *Matsya*, or Fish Avatar, happened before the Vârâha or Boar Avatar ; the allegories, therefore, must relate to both the *Padma* and the present manvantara, and also to the minor cycles which took place since the reappearance of our Chain of Worlds and Earth.   And, as the Matsya Avatar of Vishnu and Vaivasvata's Deluge are correctly connected with an event that happened on our Earth during this Round, it is evident that while it may relate to pre-cosmic events (in the sense of *our* Kosmos or Solar system) it has reference in our case to a distant geological period.   Not even Esoteric philosophy can claim to know, except by analogical inference, that which took place before the reappearance of our Solar System and previous to the last *Maha Pralaya*.   But it teaches distinctly that after the first geological disturbance in the Earth's axis which ended in the sweeping down to the bottom of the Seas of the whole second Continent, with its primeval races—of which successive " Earths " or Continents Atlantis was the fourth—there came another disturbance by the axis resuming as rapidly its previous degree of inclination ; when the Earth was indeed *raised once more* out of the Waters, and—as above so it is below ; and *vice versâ*.   There were " gods " on Earth in those days—gods, and not men, as we know them now, says the tradition. As will be shown in Book II., the computation of periods in exoteric Hinduism refers to both the great cosmic and the small terrestrial events and cataclysms, and the same may be shown for names.   For instance Yudishthira—the first King of the *Sacea*, who opens the Kali Yuga era, which has to last 432,000 years—" an actual King and man who lived 3,102 years B.C.," applies also, name and all, to the great Deluge at the time of the first sinking of Atlantis.   He is the " Yudish-thira * born on the mountain of the hundred peaks at the extremity of

---

The idea alone of one who established the most rigorous vegetarianism and respect for animal life—even to refusing to eat eggs as *vehicles of a latent future life*—dying of a meat indigestion, is absurdly contradictory and has puzzled more than one Orientalist   But this explanation, unveiling the allegory, explains all the rest.   The *Vârâha*, however, is no simple boar, and seems to have meant at first some antediluvian lacustrine animal ' delighting to sport in water."   (*Vâyu Purâna*.)

* According to Colonel Wilford, the conclusion of the " Great War " was B.C. 1370. (*See A. R., Vol.* 9, *p.* 116) ; according to Bentley, 575 B.C. ! !   We may hope, perhaps, that before the end of this century, the Mahabharatean epics will be found and pro-claimed identical with the wars of the great Napoleon.

the world *beyond which nobody can go* " and "immediately after the flood."
(*See Royal Asiat. Soc.*, *Vol.* 9, *p.* 364,) We know of no " Flood " 3,102
years B.C.—not even that of Noah, for, agreeably with Judæo-Christian
chronology, it took place 2,349 years B.C.

This relates to an esoteric division of time and a mystery explained
elsewhere, and may therefore be left aside for the present. Suffice to
remark at this juncture that all the efforts of imagination of the
Wilfords, Bentleys, and other would-be Œdipuses of esoteric Hindu
Chronology have sadly failed. No computation of either the Four
Ages, or the Manvantaras, has ever been unriddled by our very learned
Orientalists, who have therefore cut the Gordian Knot by proclaiming
the whole "a figment of the Brahmanical brain." So be it, and may
the great scholars rest in peace. This "figment" is given in the
Preliminary Sections which preface *Anthropogenesis* in Book II., and
with esoteric additions.

Let us see, however, what were the three kinds of *pralayas*, and what
is the *popular* belief about them. For once it agrees with Esotericism.

Of the *pralaya* before which fourteen Manvantaras elapse, having over
them as many presiding Manus, and at whose close occurs the "incidental" or Brahmâ's dissolution, it is said in *Vishnu Purâna*, in
condensed form, that "at the end of a thousand periods of four ages,
which complete a day of Brahmâ, the earth is almost exhausted. The
eternal *Avyaya* (Vishnu) assumes then the character of Rudra (the
destroyer, Siva) and re-unites all his creatures to himself. He enters
the Seven rays of the Sun and drinks up all the waters of the globe ; he
causes the moisture to evaporate, thus drying up the whole Earth.
Oceans and rivers, torrents and small streams, are all exhaled. Thus
fed with abundant moisture the seven solar rays become sevens suns by
dilation, and they finally set the world on fire. Hari, the destroyer of
all things, who is ' the flame of time, *Kalâgni*,' finally consumes the Earth.
Then Rudra, becoming Janardana, breathes clouds and rain."

There are many kinds of *Pralaya*, but three chief ones are
specially mentioned in old Hindu books ; and of these, as Wilson
shows :—The first is called NAIMITTIKA * " occasional " or "incidental,"
caused by the intervals of " Brahmâ's Days ;" it is the destruction of
creatures, of all that lives and has a form, but not of the substance
which remains in *statu quo* till the new DAWN in that "Night." The

* In the *Vedanta* and *Nyâya* " nimitta " (from which " Naimittika ") is rendered as the
efficient cause, when antithesized with *upadana* the physical or material cause. In the
Sankhya *pradhâna* is a cause inferior to Brahmâ, or rather Brahmâ being himself a
cause, is superior to Pradhâna. Hence " incidental" is wrongly translated, and ought
to be translated, as shown by some scholars, " Ideal" cause, and even *real* cause would
have been better.

other is called PRAKRITIKA—and occurs at the end of the *Age* or Life of
Brahma, when everything that exists is resolved into the primal element,
to be remodelled at the end of that longer night. But the third,
Atyantika, does not concern the Worlds or the Universe, but only the
individualities of some people ; it is thus individual pralaya or NIRVANA ;
after having reached which, there is no more future existence possible,
no rebirth till after the *Maha Pralaya*. The latter night, lasting as it
does 311,040,000,000,000 years, and having the possibility of being
almost doubled in case the lucky *Jivanmukti* reaches Nirvana at an early
period of a Manvantara, is long enough to be regarded as *eternal*, if not
endless. The *Bhagavata* (XII., iv, 35) speaks of a fourth kind of pralaya,
the *Nitya* or constant dissolution, and explains it as the change which
takes place imperceptibly in everything in this Universe from the globe
down to the atom—without cessation. It is growth and decay (life and
death).

When the Maha Pralaya arrives, the inhabitants of Swar-loka (the
upper sphere) disturbed by the conflagration, seek refuge "with the
Pitris, their progenitors, the Manus, the Seven Rishis, the various orders
of celestial Spirits and the Gods, in Maharloka." When the latter is
reached also, the whole of the above enumerated beings migrate in their
turn from Maharloka, and repair to Jana-loka in "*their subtile forms,
destined to become re-embodied, in similar capacities as their former, when the
world is renewed at the beginning of the succeeding Kalpa*;" (Vâyu Purâna).

" . . . . These clouds, mighty in size, and loud in thunder, fill up all
space (Nabhas-tala)," goes on Vishnu Purâna.—(Book VI., ch. iii.)
" Showering down torrents of water, these clouds quench the dreadful
fires, and then they rain uninterruptedly for a hundred (divine) years,
and deluge the whole world (Solar System). Pouring down, in drops
as large as dice, these rains overspread the earth, and fill the middle
region (*Bhuvaloka*) and inundate heaven. The world is now enveloped
in darkness, and all things animate, or inanimate, having perished, the
clouds continue to pour down their waters " . . . " and the Night of
Brahmâ reigns supreme over the scene of desolation . . . . . "

This is what we call in the Esoteric Doctrine a " Solar Pralaya " . . .
When the waters have reached the region of the Seven Rishis, and the
world (our Solar System) is one ocean, they stop. The breath of
Vishnu becomes a strong wind, which blows for another hundred
(divine) years until all clouds are dispersed. The wind is then
reabsorbed: and " THAT, of which all things are made, the Lord
by whom all things exist, He who is inconceivable, without
beginning, the beginning of the universe, reposes, sleeping upon
Sesha (the Serpent of Infinity) in the midst of the deep. The *Adikrit*

(Creator ?) *Hari,* sleeps upon the ocean of Space in the form of
Brahmâ—glorified by Sanaka* and the *Siddha* (Saints) of Jana-loka, and
contemplated by the holy denizens of Brahmâ-loka, anxious for final
liberation, involved in mystic slumber, the celestial personification
of his own illusions. . . ." This is the *Pratisanchara* (dissolution ?)
termed incidental because *Hari* is its incidental (ideal) Cause. . . . .†
When the Universal Spirit wakes, the world revives ; when he closes
his eyes, all things fall upon the bed of mystic slumber. In like manner,
as 1,000 great ages constitute a Day of Brahmâ (in the original it is
Padma-yoni, the same as *Abjayoni*—"lotos-born," not Brahmâ), so his
Night consists of the same period. "Awaking at the end of his night,
the unborn . . . creates the Universe anew. . . ." (*Vishnu Purâna.*)

This is "incidental" pralaya ; what is the Elemental Dissolution ?
"When by dearth and fire," says Pârâsara to Maitreya, "all the worlds
and Pâtâlas (hells) are withered up . . .‡ the progress of elemental
dissolution is begun. Then, first the waters swallow up the property of
Earth (which is the rudiment of smell), and earth deprived of this property proceeds to destruction—and becomes one with water . . . .
when the Universe is thus pervaded by the waves of the watery Element, its rudimentary flavour is locked up by the elements of fire . . .
on account of which the waters themselves are destroyed . . . and
become one with fire ; and the Universe is therefore, entirely
filled with flame (ethereal) which gradually overspreads the whole
world. While Space is one flame, the element of wind seizes upon the
rudimental property or form, which is the cause of light, and that being
withdrawn (*pralina*) all becomes of the nature of air. The rudiment of
form being destroyed, and *Vibhâvasu* (fire ?) deprived of its rudiment,
air extinguishes fire and spreads over space, which is deprived of light
when fire merges into air. Air, then, accompanied by sound, which is
the source of Ether, extends everywhere throughout the ten
regions . . . . until Ether seizes upon cohesion (*Sparsa*—Touch ?) its
rudimental property, by the loss of which, air is destroyed, and KHA
remains unmodified ; devoid of form, flavour, touch (*Sparsa*), and smell,
it exists, embodied (*mûrttimat*) and vast, and pervades the whole Space.
Akâsa, whose characteristic property and rudiment is sound (the
"Word"), occupies the whole containment of Space. Then the origin
(Noumenon ?) of the Elements (*Bhutadi*), devours sound (collective
Demiurgos) ; and the hosts of Dhyan Chohans, and all the existing

---

* The chief *Kumâra* or Virgin-god (a Dhyan Chohan) who refuses to create. A
prototype of St. Michael, who refuses to do the same.

† See concluding lines in Section, "Chaos, Theos, Kosmos."

‡ This prospect would hardly suit Christian theology, which prefers an eternal, everlasting hell for its followers.

Elements* are at once merged into their original. The primary Element, Consciousness, combined with *tamasa* (spiritual darkness) is itself disintegrated by MAHAT (the Universal Intellect), whose characteristic property is *Buddhi,* and earth and Mahat are the inner and outer boundaries of the Universe." Thus as (in the beginning) "were the seven forms of Prakriti (nature) reckoned from Mahat to earth, so *these seven* successively re-enter into each other."†

"The Egg of Brahmâ (*Sarva-mandala*) is dissolved in the waters that surround it, with its seven zones (*dwipas*) seven oceans, seven regions, and their mountains; the investure of water is drunk by the fire; the (*stratum* of) fire is absorbed by (that of) air; air blends itself with ether (Akâsa); the *Bhutadi* (the origin, or rather the *cause,* of the primary element) devours the ether and is (itself) destroyed by Mahat (the Great, the Universal mind), which along with all these is seized upon by Prakriti and disappears. The Prakriti is essentially the same, whether discrete or indiscrete; only that which is discrete is finally absorbed by and lost in the indiscrete. PUMS (*Spirit*) also, which is one, pure, imperishable, eternal, all-pervading, is a portion of that Supreme spirit which is all things. That Spirit (*Sarvesa*) which is other than (embodied) Spirit, and in which there are no attributes of name, species (*nâman* and *jati,* or *rupa,* hence body rather than species), or the like— remains as the sole existence (SATTÂ). . . Prakriti and Purusha both resolving finally into SUPREME SPIRIT. . . ." (*From Vishnu Purâna,* Wilson's mistakes being here corrected, and original words put in brackets).

This is the final PRALAYA ‡—the Death of Kosmos—after which its Spirit rests in Nirvana, or in THAT for which there is neither Day nor Night. All the other pralayas are periodical and follow, in regular succession, the Manvantaras, as the night follows the day of every human creature, animal, and plant. The cycle of creation of the *lives* of Kosmos is run down, the energy of the manifested " Word " having

---

* The term " Elements " must be understood here to mean not only the visible and physical Elements, but also that which St. Paul calls Elements—the spiritual, intelligent Potencies—Angels and Demons in their Manvantaric form.

† When this description is correctly understood by Orientalists in its esoteric significance then it will be found that this Cosmic correlation of World-Elements may explain the correlation of physical forces better than those now known. At any rate, theosophists will perceive that Prakriti has *seven forms,* or principles, " reckoned from Mahat to Earth." The " Waters " mean here the Mystic " mother "; the Womb of abstract nature, in which the manifested Universe is conceived. The Seven " zones " have reference to the Seven Divisions of that Universe, or the Noumena of the Forces that bring it into being. It is all allegorical.

‡ As it is the *Maha,* the Great, or so-called *final* PRALAYA which is here described, every thing is re-absorbed into its original ONE Element—the " Gods themselves, Brahmâ and the rest " being said to die and disappear during that long NIGHT.

its growth, culmination, and decrease, as have all things temporary,
however long their duration.   The Creative Force is Eternal as
Noumenon; as a phenomenal manifestation in its aspects, it has a
beginning and must, therefore, have an end.   During that interval it has
its periods of activity and its periods of rest.   And these are the " Days
and the nights of Brahmâ."   But Brahma, the Noumenon, never rests,
as IT never changes and ever IS, though IT cannot be said to be
anywhere. . . . .

The Jewish Kabalists felt this necessity of *immutability* in an eternal,
infinite Deity, and therefore applied the same thought to the anthropomorphic god.   The idea is poetical and very appropriate in its application.   In the *Zohar* we read as follows :—

" As Moses was keeping a vigil on Mount Sinai, in company with
the deity, who was concealed from his sight by a cloud, he felt a great
fear overcome him, and suddenly asked : ' Lord, where art thou . . . .
sleepest thou, O Lord ? . . .'   And the *Spirit* answered him : ' I never
sleep : were I to fall asleep for a moment BEFORE MY TIME, all the
creation would crumble into dissolution in one instant.' "

" *Before my time* " is very suggestive.   It shows the God of Moses to
be only a temporary substitute, like Brahmâ the male, a substitute and
an aspect of THAT which is immutable, and which therefore can take no
part in the " days," or in the " nights," nor have any concern whatever
with reaction or dissolution.

While the Eastern Occultists have seven modes of interpretation, the
Jews have only four—namely, the real-mystical ; the allegorical ; the
moral ; and the literal or *Pashut*.   The latter is the key of the exoteric
Churches and not worth discussion.   Read in the first, or mystical key,
here are several sentences which show the identity of the foundations of
construction in every Scripture.   It is given in Mr. T. Myer's excellent
book on the Kabalistic works he seems to have well studied.   I quote
verbatim.   " *B'raisheeth barah elohim ath hash ama yem v'ath haa'retz*—i.e., ' In
the beginning the God(s) created the heavens and the earth ; " (the
meaning of which is :) the six Sephiroth of Construction,* over which
B'raisheeth stands, *all belong Below*.   It created six (and) on these stand
all Things.   And those depend upon *the seven forms of the Cranium* up to
the Dignity of all Dignities.   And the second ' Earth ' does not come
into calculation, therefore it has been said : ' And from it (that Earth)
which underwent the curse, came it forth.' . . . . ' It (the Earth) was
without form and void ; and darkness was over the face of the Abyss,
and the Spirit of elohim . . . . was breathing (*me' racha 'phath*)—i.e.,
hovering, brooding over, moving. . . . . Thirteen depend on thirteen

* The " Builders " of the Stanzas.

(forms) of the most worthy Dignity. Six thousand years hang (are referred to) in the first six words. The seventh (thousand, the millenium) above it (the cursed Earth) is that which is strong by Itself. And it was rendered entirely desolate during twelve hours (one . . . . Day) as is written. . . . . In the thirteenth, It (the Deity) shall restore all . . . . and everything shall be renewed as before ; and all those six shall continue . . . . etc." (*Qabbalah*, p. 233, from *Siphrah Dzeniuta*, c. i., § 16, *s*. 9.)

The "Sephiroth of Construction" are the six Dhyan Chohans, or Manus, or Prajâpati, synthesized by the seventh "B'raisheeth (the First Emanation or *Logos*), and who are called, therefore, the Builders of the Lower or physical Universe" all belong Below. These *six* ₂✡³ whose essence is *of the Seventh*—are the *Upadhi*, the base or fundamental stone on which the objective Universe is built, the *noumenoi* of all things. Hence they are, at the same time, the Forces of nature, the Seven Angels of the Presence, the sixth and seventh principles in man ; the spirito-psycho-physical spheres of the Septenary chain, the Root Races, etc., etc. They all "depend upon the Seven forms of the Cranium" up to the highest. The "*second* Earth" "does not come into calculation" because it is *no Earth*, but the Chaos or Abyss of Space in which rested the paradogmatic, or model universe in ideation of the OVER-SOUL brooding over it. The term "Curse" is here very misleading, for it means simply *doom* or *destiny*, or *that fatality which sent it forth* into the objective state. This is shown by that "Earth" under the "Curse" being described as "without form and void," in whose abysmal depths the "Breath" of the Elohim (collective Logoi) produced or photographed the first divine IDEATION *of the things to be.* This process is repeated after every *Pralaya* before the beginnings of a new Manvantara, or period of sentient individual being. "Thirteen depend on thirteen forms," refers to the thirteen periods personified by the thirteen Manus, with Swayambhûva the fourteenth (13, instead of 14, being an additional *veil*): those fourteen Manus who reign within the term of a Mahayuga, a "Day" of Brahmâ. These (thirteen-fourteen) of the objective Universe depend on the thirteen (fourteen) *paradigmatic, ideal* forms. The meaning of the "Six thousand *years*" which "hang in the first six words," has again to be sought in the Indian Wisdom. They refer to the primordial six (seven) "Kings of Edom" who typify the worlds (or spheres) of our chain during the first Round, as well as the primordial men of this Round. They are the septenary *pre-Adamic* (or before the Third, *Separated* Race) first Root-race. As they were *shadows*, and senseless (they had not eaten yet of the fruit of the Tree of Knowledge), they could not see the

Parguphim, or "Face could not see Face" (primeval men were unconscious), "therefore, the primordial (seven) Kings died," *i.e.*, were destroyed (*vide Sepherah Djenioutha*). Now, who are they? They are the Kings who are " the Seven Rishis, certain (secondary) divinities, Sakra (Indra), Manu, and the Kings his Sons, who *are created and perish at one period*," as said in Vishnu Purâna (Book I. chap. iii.). For the seventh (" thousand ") *(not the millennium of exoteric Christianity, but that of Anthropogenesis)* represents both the " seventh period of creation," that of physical man (Vishnu Purâna), and the seventh Principle—both macrocosmic and microcosmic,—as also the *pralaya* after the Seventh period, the " Night " which has the same duration as the " Day " of Brahmâ. " It was rendered entirely desolate during twelve hours, as is written." It is in the Thirteenth (twice six and the Synthesis) that everything shall be restored " and the *six* will continue."

Thus the author of the *Qabbalah* remarks quite truly that " Long before his (Ibn Gebirol's) time . . . many centuries before the Christian era, there was in Central Asia a ' Wisdom Religion ;' fragments of which subsequently existed among the learned men of the archaic Egyptians, the ancient Chinese, Hindus, etc. . . ." and that . . . . . " The Qabbalah most likely originally came from Aryan sources, through Central Asia, Persia, India and Mesopotamia, for from Ur and Haran came Abraham and many others into Palestine " (p. 221). And such was the firm conviction of C. W. King, the author of " The Gnostics and their Remains."

Vamadeva Modelyar (*Modely*) describes the coming "night" most poetically. Though it is given in *Isis Unveiled*, it is worthy of repetition.

" Strange noises are heard, proceeding from every point . . . These are the precursors of the Night of Brahmâ ; *dusk rises at the horizon*, and the Sun passes away behind the thirteenth degree of Macara (sign of the Zodiac), and will reach no more the sign of the *Minas* (zodiacal *pisces*, or fish). The gurus of the pagodas appointed to watch the *rasi-chakr* (Zodiac), may now break their circle and instruments, for they are henceforth useless.

" Gradually light pales, heat diminishes, uninhabited spots multiply on the earth, the air becomes more and more rarified ; the springs of waters dry up, the great rivers see their waves exhausted, the ocean shows its sandy bottom and plants die. Men and animals decrease in size daily. Life and motion lose their force, planets can hardly gravitate in space ; they are extinguished one by one, like a lamp which the hand of the chokra (servant) neglects to replenish. Sourya (the Sun) flickers and goes out, matter falls into dissolution (pralaya), and Brahmâ merges back into Dayus, the Unrevealed God, and, his task being accomplished, he falls asleep. Another day is passed, night sets in, and continues until the future dawn.

" And now again he re-enters into the golden egg of His Thought, the germs of all that exist, as the divine Manu tells us. During His peaceful rest, the animated beings, endowed with the principles of action, cease their functions, and all feeling (manas) becomes dormant. When they are all absorbed in the SUPREME SOUL, this Soul of all the beings sleeps in complete repose till the day when it resumes its form, and awakes again from its primitive darkness."*

As the " Satya-yuga" is always the first in the series of the four ages or Yugas, so the Kali ever comes the last. The Kali yuga reigns now supreme in India, and it seems to coincide with that of the Western age. Anyhow, it is curious to see how prophetic in almost all things was the writer of Vishnu Purâna when foretelling to Maitreya some of the dark influences and sins of this Kali Yug. For after saying that the " barbarians " will be master s of the banks of the Indus, of Chandrabhaga and Kasmera, he adds :

" There will be contemporary monarchs, reigning over the earth— kings of churlish spirit, violent temper, and ever addicted to falsehood and wickedness. They will inflict death on women, children, and cows ; they will seize upon the property of their subjects, and *be intent upon the wives of others ;* they will be of unlimited power, their lives will be short, their desires insatiable. . . . People of various countries intermingling with them, will follow their example ; and the barbarians being powerful (in India) in the patronage of the princes, while purer tribes are neglected, the people will perish (or, as the Commentator has it, ' The Mlechchas will be in the centre and the Aryas in the end.')† Wealth and piety will decrease until the world will be wholly depraved. Property alone will confer rank ; wealth will be the only source of devotion ; passion will be the sole bond of union between the sexes ; falsehood will be the only means of success in litigation ; and women will be objects merely of sensual gratification. . . . . . *External types will be the only distinction of the several orders of life ;* . . . . . a man if rich will be reputed pure ; dishonesty (anyaya) will be the universal means of subsistence, weakness the cause of dependence, menace and presumption will be substituted for learning ; liberality will be devotion ; mutual assent, marriage ; fine clothes, dignity. He who is the strongest will reign ; the people, unable to bear the heavy burthen, *Khara bhara* (the load of taxes) will take refuge among the valleys. . . . Thus, in the Kali age will decay constantly proceed, until

---

* See Jacquolliot's " Les Fils de Dieu " ; l'Inde des Brahmes, p. 230.
† If this is not prophetic, what is ?

the human race approaches its annihilation (*pralaya*). . . . When the close of the Kali age shall be nigh, a portion of that divine being which exists, of its own spiritual nature . . . shall descend on Earth . . . (*Kalki Avatar*) endowed with the eight superhuman faculties. . . . He will re-establish righteousness on earth, and the minds of those who live at the end of Kali Yuga shall be awakened and become as pellucid as crystal. The men who are thus changed . . . *shall be the seeds of human beings*, and shall give birth to a race who shall follow the laws of the Krita age, the age of purity. As it is said, ' When the sun and moon and the lunar asterism Tishya and the planet Jupiter are in one mansion, the Krita (or Satya) age shall return.' "

" . . . . Two persons, Devapi, of the race of Kuru and Moru, of the family of Ikshwaku, continue alive throughout the four ages, residing at Kalapa.* They will return hither in the beginning of the Krita age . . . Moru† the son of Sighru through the power of Yoga is still living . . . . and will be the restorer of the Kshattriya race of the Solar dynasty."‡ (*Vayu Purâna*, Vol. III, *p*. 197).

Whether right or wrong with regard to the latter prophecy, the *blessings* of Kali Yuga are well described, and fit in admirably even with that which one sees and hears in Europe and other civilized and Christian lands in full XIXth, and at the dawn of the XXth century of our great era of ENLIGHTENMENT.

---

* Matsya Purâna gives Katapa.

† Max Müller translates the name as Morya, of the Morya dynasty, to which Chandragupta belonged (see Sanscrit Literature). In Matsya Purâna, chapter cclxxii, the dynasty of ten Moryas (or Maureyas) is spoken of. In the same chapter, cclxxii, it is stated that the Moryas will one day reign over India, after restoring the Kshattriya race many thousand years hence. Only that reign will be purely Spiritual and " not of this world." It will be the kingdom of the next Avatar. Colonel Tod believes the name Morya (or *Maureyas*) a corruption of Mori, a Rajpoot tribe, and the commentary on Mahavansa thinks that some princes have taken their name Maurya from their town called Mori, or, as Professor Max Müller gives it, Morya-Nagara, which is more correct, after the original Mahavansa. Vachaspattya, we are informed by our Brother, Devan Badhadur R. Ragoonath Rao, of Madras, a Sanscrit Encyclopedia, places Katapa (Kalapa) on the northern side of the Himalayas, hence in Tibet. The same is stated in chapter xii. (Skanda) of Bhagavat, Vol. III, p. 325.

‡ The Vayu Purâna declares that Moru will re-establish the Kshattriya in the Nineteenth coming Yuga. (*See "Five years of Theosophy," p*. 483. *"The Moryas and Koothoomi."*)

§ VIII.

THE LOTUS, AS A UNIVERSAL SYMBOL.

THERE are no ancient symbols, without a deep and philosophical meaning attached to them ; their importance and significance increasing with their antiquity. Such is the LOTUS. It is the flower sacred to nature and her Gods, and represents the abstract and the Concrete Universes, standing as the emblem of the productive powers of both spiritual and physical nature. It was held sacred from the remotest antiquity by the Aryan Hindus, the Egyptians, and the Buddhists after them ; revered in China and Japan, and adopted as a Christian emblem by the Greek and Latin Churches, who made of it a messenger as the Christians do now, who replace it with the water lily.* It had, and still has, its mystic meaning which is identical with every nation on the earth. We refer the reader to Sir William Jones. † With the Hindus, the lotus is the emblem of the productive power of nature, through the agency of fire and water (spirit and matter). " Eternal ! " says a verse in the Bhagavad Gita, " I see Brahm the creator enthroned in thee above the lotus ! "; and Sir W. Jones shows, as noted in the Stanzas, that the seeds of the lotus contain, even before they germinate, perfectly-formed leaves, the miniature shapes of what one day, as perfected plants, they will become. The lotus, in India, is the symbol of prolific earth, and what is more, of Mount Meru. The four angels or genii of the four quarters of Heaven (the Maharajahs, see *Stanzas*) stand each on a lotus. The lotus is the two-fold type of the Divine and human hermaphrodite, being of dual sex, so to say.

The spirit of Fire (or Heat), which stirs up, fructifies, and develops into concrete form everything (from its ideal prototype), which is born of WATER or primordial Earth, evolved Brahmâ—with the Hindus. The lotus flower, represented as growing out of Vishnu's navel—that God resting on the waters of space and his Serpent of Infinity—is the most graphic allegory ever made : the Universe evolving from the central Sun, the POINT, the ever-concealed germ. Lakshmi, who is the

---

* In the Christian religion Gabriel, the Archangel, holding in his hand a spray of water lilies, appears to the Virgin Mary in every picture of the Annunciation. This spray typifying fire and water, or the idea of creation and generation, symbolizes *precisely the same idea as the lotus* in the hand of the Bodhisat who announces to Maha-Maya, Gautama's mother, the birth of the world's Saviour, Buddha. Thus also, Osiris and Horus were represented by the Egyptians constantly in association with the lotus-flower, the two being Sun-gods or Fire (the Holy Ghost being still typified by ' tongues of fire "), (Acts).

† See Sir William Jones' " Dissertations Relating to Asia."

female aspect of Vishnu,* and who is also called *Padma*, the lotus, is likewise shown floating at " Creation," on a lotus flower, and during the " churning of the ocean " of space, springing from the " sea of milk," like Venus from the froth.

> "   .   .   .   Then seated on a lotus
> Beauty's bright goddess, peerless Srî, arose
> Out of the waves   .   .   ."

sings an English Orientalist and poet (Sir Monier Williams).

The underlying idea in this symbol is very beautiful, and it shows, furthermore, its identical parentage in all the religious systems. Whether in the lotus or water-lily shape it signifies one and the same philosophical idea—namely, the emanation of the objective from the subjective, divine Ideation passing from the abstract into the concrete or visible form. For, as soon as DARKNESS—or rather that which is " darkness" for ignorance—has disappeared in its own realm of eternal Light, leaving behind itself only its divine manifested Ideation, the creative Logoi have their understanding opened, and they see in the ideal world (hitherto concealed in the divine thought) the archetypal forms of all, and proceed to copy and build or fashion upon these models forms evanescent and transcendent.

At this stage of action, the Demiurge † is not yet the Architect. Born in the twilight of action, he has yet to first perceive the plan, to realise the ideal forms which lie buried in the bosom of Eternal Idea-tion, as the future lotus-leaves, the immaculate petals, are concealed within the seed of that plant. . . . .

In chapter lxxxi. of the *Ritual* (*Book of the Dead*), called " Trans-formation into the Lotus," a head emerging from this flower, the god exclaims: " I am the pure lotus, emerging from the Luminous one. . . . . I carry the messages of Horus. I am the pure lotus which comes from the Solar Fields. . . . ."

The lotus-idea may be traced even in the Elohistic chapter, the 1st of *Genesis*, as stated in *Isis*.

---

* Lakshmi is Venus—Aphrodite, and, like the latter, she sprang from the froth of the ocean with a lotus in her hand. In the Ramayana she is called Padma.

† In Esoteric philosophy the Demiurge or *Logos*, regarded as the CREATOR, is simply an abstract term, an idea, like "army." As the latter is the all-embracing term for a body of active forces or working units—soldiers—so is the Demiurge the qualitative compound of a multitude of Creators or Builders. Burnouf, the great Orientalist, has seized the idea perfectly when saying that Brahmâ does *not* create the earth, any more than the rest of the universe. " Having evolved himself from the soul of the world, once separated from the first cause, he evaporates with, and emanates all nature out of himself. He does not stand above it, but is mixed up with it ; Brahmâ and the universe form one Being, each particle of which is in its essence Brahmâ himself, who proceeded out of himself."

It is in this idea that we must look for the origin and explanation of the verse in the Jewish cosmogony, which reads : " And God said, Let the earth bring forth . . . . the fruit-tree yielding fruit after his kind, whose seed is in itself." In all the primitive religions, the " Son of the Father " is the creative God—*i.e.*, His thought made visible ; and before the Christian era, from the Trimurti of the Hindus down to the three kabalistic heads of the scriptures as explained by the Jews, the triune godhead of each nation was fully defined and substantiated in its allegories.

Such is the cosmic and ideal significance of this great symbol with the Eastern peoples. But, applied to practical and exoteric worship— which had also its esoteric symbology—the lotus became in time the carrier and container of a more terrestrial idea. No dogmatic religion has ever escaped the sexual element in it ; and to this day it soils the moral beauty of the root idea. The following is quoted from the same Kabalistic MSS. already mentioned :—

" Pointing to like signification was the lotus growing in the waters of the Nile. Its mode of growth peculiarly fitted it as a symbol of the generative activities. The flower of the lotus, which is the bearer of the seed for reproduction, as the result of its maturing, is connected by its placenta-like attachment with mother-earth, or the womb of Isis, through the water of the womb, that is, the river Nile, by means of the long cord-like stalk, the umbilicus. Nothing can be plainer than the symbol, and to make it perfect in its intended signification, a child is sometimes represented as seated in or issuing from the flower.* Thus Osiris and Isis, the children of Chronos, or time without end, in the developement of their nature-forces, in this picture become the parents of man under the name Horus. . ." (See § X., " Deus Lunus.")

" We cannot lay too great stress upon the use of this generative function as a basis for a symbolical language and a scientific art-speech. Thought upon the idea leads at once to reflection upon the subject of creative cause. In its workings Nature is observed to have fashioned a wonderful piece of living mechanism governed by an added living soul ; the life development and history of which soul, as to its whence, its present, and its whither, surpasses all efforts of the human intellect.† The new born is an ever-recurring miracle, an evidence that

---

* In Indian Purânas it is Vishnu, the first, and Brahmâ, the second logos, or the ideal and practical creators, who are respectively represented, one as manifesting the lotus, the other as issuing from it.

† Not the " efforts " of the trained psychic faculties of an Initiate into Eastern metaphysics, and the mysteries of creative Nature. It is the profane of the past ages who have degraded the pure ideal of cosmic creation into an emblem of mere human reproduction and sexual functions : it is the esoteric teachings, and the initiates of the Future, whose mission it is, and will be, to redeem and ennoble once more the primitive conception so sadly profaned by its crude and gross application to exoteric dogmas and personations by theological and ecclesiastical religionists. The silent worship of abstract or *noumenal* Nature, the only divine manifestation, is the one ennobling religion of Humanity.

within the workshop of the womb an intelligent creative power has intervened
to fasten a living soul to a physical machine. The amazing wonderfulness of
the fact attaches a holy sacredness to all connected with the organs of reproduction, as the dwelling and place of evident constructive intervention of
deity."

This is a correct rendering of the underlying ideas of old, of the
purely pantheistic conceptions, *impersonal* and reverential, of the archaic
philosophers of the prehistoric ages. Not so, however, when applied
to sinful humanity, to the gross ideas attached to personality. Therefore, no pantheistic philosopher would fail to find the remarks that
follow the above and which represent the anthropomorphism of Judean
symbology, other than dangerous for the sacredness of true religion,
and fitting only our materialistic age, which is the direct outcome and
result of that anthropomorphic character. For this is the key-note to
the entire spirit and essence of the Old Testament. " Therefore," goes
on the MSS., treating of the symbolism of art-speech of the Bible :—

" The locality of the *womb* is to be taken as the MOST HOLY PLACE, the SANCTUM
SANCTORUM, and the *veritable* TEMPLE OF THE LIVING GOD.* With man the
possession of the woman has always been considered as an essential part of
himself, to make one out of two, and jealously guarded as sacred. Even the part
of the ordinary house or home consecrated to the dwelling of the wife was called
the *penetralia*, the secret or sacred, and hence the metaphor of the Holy of Holies
of sacred constructions taken from the idea of the sacredness of the organs of
generation. Carried to the extreme of description † by metaphor, this part of
the house is described in the Sacred Books as the " between the thighs of the
house," and sometimes the idea is carried out constructively in the great door-
opening of Churches placed inward between flanking buttresses."

No such thought " carried to the extreme " ever existed among the
old primitive Aryans. This is proven by the fact that in the Vedic
period their women were not placed apart from men in *penetralia*, or
" Zenanas." Their seclusion began when the Mahomedans—the next
heirs to Hebrew symbolism after Christian ecclesiasticism—had conquered the land and gradually enforced their ways and customs upon
the Hindus. The pre- and *post*-Vedic woman was as free as man ; and
no impure terrestrial thought was ever mixed with the religious symbo-

---

* Surely the words of the old Initiate into the *primitive* mysteries of Christianity,
" *Know ye not ye are the Temple of God* " (1 *Corinth. iii.* 16) could not be applied in *this*
sense to *men ?* The meaning may have been, and *was* so, undeniably, in the minds of
the Hebrew compilers of the *Old* Testament. And here is the abyss that lies between
the symbolism of the New Testament and the Jewish canon. This gulf would have
remained and ever widened, had not Christianity—especially and most glaringly the
Latin Church—thrown a bridge over it ? Modern Popery has now spanned it entirely,
by its dogma of the two immaculate conceptions, and the anthropomorphic and at the
same time idolatrous character it has conferred upon the Mother of its God.

† It was so carried *only* in the Hebrew Bible, and its servile copyist, Christian
theology.

logy of the early Aryans. The idea and application are purely Semitic. This is corroborated by the writer of the said intensely learned and Kabalistic revelation himself, when he closes the above-quoted passages by adding :—

"If to these organs as symbols of creative cosmic agencies the idea of the origin of measures as well as of time-periods can be attached, then indeed, in the constructions of the Temples as Dwellings of Deity, or of Jehovah, that part designated as the Holy of Holies, or the Most Holy place, should borrow its title from the recognised sacredness of the generative organs, considered as symbols of measures as well as of creative cause. With the ancient WISE, *there was no name and no idea, and no symbol* of A FIRST CAUSE." . . . .

Most decidedly not. Rather never give a thought to it and leave it for ever *nameless*, as the early Pantheists did, than degrade the sacredness of that *Ideal of Ideals*, by dragging down its symbols into such anthropomorphic forms! Here again one perceives the immense chasm between Aryan and Semitic religious thought : two opposite poles— Sincerity and Concealment. With the Brahmins, who have never invested with an "original Sin" element the natural procreative functions of mankind, it is a *religious duty* to have a son. A Brahmin, in days of old, having accomplished his mission of human creator, retired to the jungle and passed the rest of his days in religious meditations. He had accomplished his duty to nature as mortal man and its co-worker, and henceforth gave all his thoughts to the spiritual immortal portion in himself, regarding the terrestrial as a mere illusion, an evanescent dream—which it is. With the Semite, it was different. He invented a temptation of flesh in a garden of Eden ; showed his God (esoterically, the Tempter and the Ruler of Nature) CURSING *for ever* an act, which was in the logical programme of that nature.* All this exoterically, as in the *cloak* and dead letter of Genesis and the rest ; and at the same time *esoterically* he regarded the supposed *sin* and FALL as an act so sacred, as to choose the organ, the perpetrator of the *original sin*, as the fittest and most sacred symbol to represent that God, who is shown as branding its entering into function as disobedience and everlasting SIN !

Who can ever fathom the paradoxical depths of the Semitic mind ? And this paradoxical element, *minus* its innermost significance, has now passed entirely into Christian theology and dogma !

Whether the early Fathers of the Church knew the esoteric meaning of the Hebrew (Old) Testament, or whether only a few of them were aware of it, while the others remained ignorant of the secret, is for

---

* The same idea is carried out exoterically in the incidents of Egypt. The Lord God tempts sorely Pharoah and "plagues him with great plagues," lest the king should escape punishment, and thus afford no pretext for one more triumph to his " Chosen people."

posterity to decide. One thing is certain, at any rate. As the
esotericism of the New Testament agrees perfectly with that of the
Hebrew Mosaic Books; and since, at the same time, a number of purely
Egyptian symbols and pagan dogmas in general—the Trinity for example—have been copied by, and incorporated into, the Synoptics and
St. John, it becomes evident that the identity of those symbols was
known to the writers of the New Testament, whoever they were. They
must have been aware also of the priority of the Egyptian esotericism,
since they have adopted several such symbols that typify purely Egyptian conceptions and beliefs—in their outward and inward meaning—and
which are not to be found in the Jewish Canon. One of such is the
water-lily in the hands of the Archangel in the early representations of
his appearance to the Virgin Mary; and these symbolical images are
preserved to this day in the iconography of the Greek and Roman
Churches. Thus water, fire, the Cross, as well as the Dove, the Lamb,
and other sacred animals, with all their combinations, yield esoterically
an identical meaning, and must have been accepted as an improvement
upon Judaism pure and simple.

For the Lotus and Water are among the oldest symbols, and in their
origin are purely Aryan, though they became common property during
the branching-off of the fifth race. Let us give an example. Letters, as
much as numbers, were all mystic, whether in combination or each taken
separately. The most sacred of all is the letter M. Is is both feminine
and masculine, or androgyne, and is made to symbolize WATER, the great
deep, in its origin. It is mystic in all the languages, Eastern and
Western, and stands as a glyph for the waves, thus: ᴧᴧᴧ. In the
Aryan Esotericism, as in the Semitic, this letter has always stood for the
waters; e.g., in Sanskrit MAKARA—the tenth sign of the Zodiac—means
a crocodile, or rather an aquatic monster associated always with water.
The letter MA is equivalent to and corresponds with number 5—
composed of a *binary*, the symbol of the two sexes separated, and of the
ternary, symbol of the third life, the progeny of the *binary*. This, again,
is often symbolised by a *Pentagon*, the latter being a sacred sign, a divine
Monogram. MAITREYA is the secret name of the *Fifth* Buddha, and the
Kalki Avatar of the Brahmins—the last MESSIAH who will come at the
culmination of the Great Cycle. It is also the initial letter of the Greek
Metis or *Divine Wisdom*; of *Mimra*, the "word" or *Logos*; and of
Mithras (the *Mihr*), the *Monad*, *Mystery*. All these are born in, and from,
the great Deep, and are the Sons of *Maya*—the *Mother*; in Egypt,
Mouth, in Greece *Minerva*(divine wisdom), *Mary*, or *Miriam*, *Myrrha*, etc.;
of the Mother of the Christian Logos, and of *Maya*, the mother of
Buddha. *Madhava* and *Madhavi* are the titles of the most important
gods and goddesses of the Hindu Pantheon. Finally, *Mandala* is in

Sanskrit " a circle," or an orb (the ten divisions of the *Rig Veda*). The most sacred names in India begin with this letter generally—from *Mahat*, the first manifested intellect, and *Mandara*, the great mountain used by the gods to churn the *Ocean*, down to *Mandakin*, the heavenly *Ganga* (Ganges), *Manu*, etc., etc.

Shall this be called a coincidence? A strange one it is then, indeed, when we find even Moses—found in the water of the Nile—having the symbolical consonant in his name. And Pharaoh's daughter " called his name Moses . . . because," she said, " *I drew him out of* WATER" (*Exod. ii.*, 10.)* Besides which the Hebrew sacred name of God *applied to this letter M* is *Meborach*, the " Holy" or the " Blessed," and the name for the water of the *Flood* is *M'bul*. A reminder of the " *three* Maries" at the Crucifixion and their connection with *Mar*, the Sea, or *Water*, may close this example. This is why in Judaism and Christianity the *Messiah* is always connected with Water, Baptism, the *Fishes* (the sign of the Zodiac called *Meenam* in Sanskrit), and even with the *Matsya* (fish) Avatar, and the Lotus—the symbol of the womb, or the water-lily, which is the same.

In the relics of ancient Egypt, the greater the antiquity of the votive symbols and emblems of the objects exhumed, the oftener are the lotus flowers and the water found in connection with the Solar Gods. The god *Khnoom*—the moist power—water, as Thales taught it, being the principle of all things, sits on a throne enshrined in a lotus (Saitic epoch, *Serapeum*). The god Bes stands on a lotus, ready to devour his progeny. (*Ibid*, Abydos.) Thot, the god of mystery and Wisdom, the sacred Scribe of Amenti, wearing the Solar disc as head gear, sits with a bull's head (the sacred bull of Mendes being a form of Thot) and a human body, on a full blown lotus. (*IVth Dynasty*.) Finally it is the goddess *Hiquet*, under her shape of a frog, who rests on the lotus, thus showing her connection with water. And it is this frog-symbol, undeniably the most ancient of their Egyptian deities, from whose unpoetical shape the Egyptologists have been vainly trying to unravel her mystery and functions. Its adoption in the Church by the early Christians shows that they knew it better than our modern Orientalists. The " frog or toad goddess" was one of the chief cosmic deities connected with creation, on account of her amphibious nature, and chiefly because of her apparent resurrection, after long ages of solitary life enshrined in old walls, in rocks, etc. She not only participated in the organization of the world, together with *Khnoom*, but was also connected with *the*

---

* Even to the seven daughters of the *Midian* priest, who, coming to draw the *water*, had Moses *water* their flock, for which service the Midian gives to Moses Zipporah (*sippara*=the *shining* wave) as wife (*Exod. ii.*) All this has the same secret meaning.

dogma of resurrection. There must have been some very profound and sacred meaning attached to this symbol, since, notwithstanding the risk of being charged with a disgusting form of zoolatry, the early Egyptian Christians adopted it in their Churches. A frog or toad enshrined in a lotus flower, or simply without the latter emblem, was the form chosen *for the Church lamps*, on which were engraved the words " I am the resurrection " "Ἐγώ εἰμι ἀνάστασις."† These frog goddesses are also found on all the mummies.

---

§ IX.

THE MOON, DEUS LUNUS, PHŒBE.

This archaic symbol is the most poetical of all symbols, as also the most philosophical. The ancient Greeks brought it into prominence, and the modern poets have worn it threadbare. The Queen of Night, riding in the majesty of her peerless light in heaven, throwing all, even Hesperos, into darkness, and spreading her silver mantle over the whole sidereal world, has ever been a favourite theme with all the poets of Christendom, from Milton and Shakespeare down to the latest versifier. But the refulgent lamp of night, with her suite of stars unnumbered, spoke only to the imagination of the profane. Until lately, Religion and Science had nought to do with the beautiful mythos. Yet, the cold chaste moon, she, in the words of Shelley—

   . . . . " Who makes all beautiful on which she smiles
      That wandering shrine of soft, yet icy flame,
      Which ever is transformed, yet still the same,
      And warms, but not illumines." . . . .

stands in closer relations to Earth than any other sidereal orb. The Sun is the giver of life to the whole planetary system ; the Moon is the giver of life to our globe ; and the early races understood and knew it, even in their infancy. She is the Queen and she is the King, and was King Soma before she became transformed into Phœbe and the chaste Diana. She is pre-eminently the deity of the Christians, through the Mosaic and Kabalistic Jews, though the civilized world may have remained ignorant of the fact for long ages ; in fact, ever since the

---

* With the Egyptians it was the resurrection in rebirth after 3,000 years of purification, either in Devachan or " the fields of bliss."

† Such " frog-goddesses " may be seen at Bulaq, in the Cairo Museum. For the statement about the Church lamps and inscriptions it is the learned ex-director of the Bulaq Museum, Mr. Gaston Maspero, who must be held responsible. (*See his " Guide du Visiteur au Musée de Bulaq," p.* 146.)

last initiated Father of the Church died, carrying with him into his grave the secrets of the pagan temples. For the " Fathers "—such as Origen or Clemens Alexandrinus—the Moon was Jehovah's living symbol : the giver of Life and the giver of Death, the disposer of being —in *our* World. For, if Artemis was *Luna* in Heaven, and, with the Greeks, Diana on Earth, who presided over child-birth and *life :* with the Egyptians, she was Hekat (Hecate) in Hell, the goddess of Death, who ruled over magic and enchantments. More than this : as the personified moon, whose phenomena are triadic, Diana-Hecate-Luna is *the three in one.* For she is *Diva triformis, tergemina, triceps*—three heads on one neck,* like Brahmâ-Vishnu-Siva. Hence she is the prototype of our Trinity, which has not always been entirely male. The number seven, so prominent in the Bible, so sacred in its seventh (Sabbath) day, came to the Jews from Antiquity, deriving its origin from the four-fold number 7 contained in the 28 days of the lunar month, each septenary portion thereof being typified by one quarter of the moon.

It is worth the trouble of presenting in this work a bird's-eye view of the origin and development of the lunar myth and *worship* in historical antiquity, on our side of the globe. Its earlier origin is untraceable by *exact* science, rejecting as it does tradition ; while for Theology, which, under the guidance of the crafty Popes, has put a brand on every fragment of literature that does not bear the *imprimatur* of the Church of Rome, its archaic history is a sealed book. Whether the Egyptian or the Aryan Hindu religious philosophy is the more ancient—and the Secret Doctrine says it is the latter—does not much matter in this instance, as the lunar and solar " worship" are the most ancient in the world. Both have survived, and prevail to this day throughout the whole world, with some openly, with others—*e.g.,* in Christian symbolics—secretly. The cat, a lunar symbol, was sacred to Isis, herself the Moon in one sense, as Osiris was the Sun. The cat is often seen on the top of the *Sistrum* in the hand of the goddess. This animal was held in great veneration in the city of Bubaste, which went into deep mourning after the death of every sacred cat, because Isis, as the Moon, was particularly worshipped in this city of mysteries. The astronomical symbolism connected with it has already been given in Section I. of " Symbolism," and no one has better described it than Mr. G. Massey, in his Lectures and in " The Natural Genesis." The eye of the cat, it is said, seems to follow the lunar phases in its growth and decline, and its orbs shine like two stars in the darkness of night. Hence the mythological allegory which shows Diana hiding under the shape of a cat in the Moon, when, in company with other deities, she was seeking to

---

* The goddess Τρίμορφος in the statuary of Alcamenes.

escape the pursuit of *Typhon* (*Vide* the *Metamorphoses of Ovid*). The moon in Egypt was both the "Eye of Horus" and the "Eye of Osiris," the Sun.

The same with the *Cynocephalus*. The dog-headed ape was a glyph to symbolise the sun and moon, in turn, though the Cynocephalus *is more a Hermetic than a religious symbol*. For it is the hieroglyph of Mercury, the planet, as of the Mercury of the Alchemical philosophers, "as," say the Alchemists, "Mercury has to be ever *near Isis, as her minister*, as without Mercury neither Isis nor Osiris can accomplish anything in the GREAT WORK." Cynocephalus, whenever represented with the Caduceus, the Crescent, or the Lotus, is a glyph of the "philosophical" Mercury; but when seen with a reed, or a roll of parchment, he stands for Hermes, the secretary and adviser of Isis, as Hanuman filled the same office with Rama.

Though the regular Sun-Worshippers, the Parsis, are few, yet not only is the bulk of the Hindu mythology and history based upon and interblended with these two worships, but so is also the Christian religion itself. From their origin down to our modern day it has coloured the theologies of both the Roman Catholic and Protestant Churches. The difference, indeed, between the Aryan Hindu and the Aryan European faiths is very small, if only the fundamental ideas of both are taken into consideration. Hindus are proud of calling themselves *Suryas* and *Chandravansas* (of the *Solar* and *Lunar* dynasties). The Christians pretend to regard it as idolatry, and yet they adhere to a religion entirely based upon the solar and lunar worships. It is useless and vain for the Protestants to exclaim against the Roman Catholics for their "Mariolatry," based on the ancient cult of lunar goddesses, when they themselves worship Jehovah, pre-eminently a *lunar* god, and when both Churches have accepted in their theologies the "*Sun*"-Christ and the lunar trinity.

What is known of Chaldæan Moon-Worship, of the Babylonian god, *Sin*, called by the Greeks "Deus Lunus," is very little, and that little is apt to mislead the profane student who fails to grasp the esoteric significance of the symbols. As popularly known to the ancient profane philosophers and writers (for those who were initiated were pledged to silence) the Chaldæa were the worshippers of the moon under *her* (and *his*) various names, just as were the Jews, who came after them.

In the unpublished MSS. on the Art Speech, already mentioned, giving a key to the formation of the ancient (symbolical) language, a logical *raison d'être* is brought forward for this double worship. It is written by a wonderfully well-informed and acute scholar and Mystic, who gives it in the comprehensive form of a hypothesis. The latter, however, becomes forcibly a proven fact in the history of religious evolution in human thought, to anyone who has ever had a glimpse into the secret of ancient Symbology. Thus, he says :—

"One of the first occupations among men, connected with those of actual necessity, would be the perception of time periods,* marked on the vaulted arch of the heavens sprung and rising over the level floor of the horizon, or the plain of still water. These would come to be marked as those of day and night, of the phases of the moon, of its stellar or synodic revolutions, and of the period of the solar year with recurrence of the seasons, and with the application to such periods of the natural measure of day or night, or of the day divided into the light and the dark. It would also be discovered that there was a longest and shortest solar day, and two solar days of equal day and night, within the period of the solar year; and the points in the year of these could be marked with the greatest precision in the starry groups of the heavens or the constellations, subject to that retrograde movement thereof, which in time would require a correction by intercalation, as was the case in the description of the Flood, where correction of 150 days was made for a period of 600 years, during which confusion of landmarks had increased. . . . This would naturally come to pass . . . . with all races in all time ; and such knowledge must be taken to have been inherent in the human race, prior to what we call the historic period. . . . ."

On this basis, the author seeks for some natural physical function possessed in common by the human race, and connected with the periodical manifestations, such that "the connection between the two kinds of phenomena . . . became fixed in popular usage." He finds it "(a) in the feminine physiological phenomena every lunar month of 28 days, or "4 weeks of 7 days each, so that 13 occurrences of the period should happen in 364 days, which is the solar week year of 52 weeks of 7 days each. (b) The quickening of the fœtus is marked by a period of 126 days, or 18 weeks of 7 days each. (c) That period which is called "the period of viability" is one of 210 days, or 30 weeks of 7 days each. (d) The period of parturition is accomplished in 280 days, or a period of 40 weeks of 7 days each, or 10 lunar months of 28 days each, or of 9 calendar months of 31 days each, counting on the royal arch of heavens for the measure of the period of traverse from the darkness of the womb to the light and glory of conscious existence, that continuing inscrutable mystery and miracle . . . Thus the observed periods of time marking the workings of the birth function would naturally become a basis of astronomical calculation . . . We may almost affirm . . . that this was the mode of reckoning among all nations, either independently, or intermediately and indirectly by tuition. It was the mode with the Hebrews, for even to-day they calculate the calendar by means of the 354 and 355 of the lunar year, and we possess a special evidence that it was the mode with the ancient Egyptians, as to which this is the proof :—

---

* Ancient Mythology includes ancient Astronomy as well as Astrology. The planets were the hands pointing out, on the dial of our solar system, the hours of certain periodical events. Thus, Mercury was *the messenger* appointed to keep time during the daily solar and lunar phenomena, and was otherwise connected with the God and Goddess of Light.

" The basic idea underlying the religious philosophy of the Hebrews was that God contained all things within himself * ; and that man was his image, man including woman . . . The place of the man and woman with the Hebrews was among the Egyptians occupied by the bull and the cow, sacred to Osiris and Isis,† who were represented, respectively, by a man having a bull's head, and a woman having the head of a cow, which symbols were worshipped. Notoriously Osiris was the Sun and the river Nile, the tropical year of 365 days, which number is the value of the word *Neilos*, and the bull, as he was also the principle of fire and of life-giving force, while Isis was the Moon, the bed of the river Nile, or the Mother Earth, for the parturient energies of which water was a necessity, the lunar year of 354—364 days, the time-maker of the periods of gestation, and the cow marked by, or with, the crescent new moon." . . . .

" But the use of the cow of the Egyptians for the women of the Hebrews was not intended as of any radical difference of signification, but a concurrence in the teaching intended, and merely as a substitution of a symbol of common import, which was this, viz., the period of parturition with the cow and the woman was held to be the same, or 280 days, or ten lunar months of four weeks each. And in this period consisted the essential value of this animal symbol, whose mark was that of the crescent moon.‡ . . . These parturient and natural periods are found to have been subjects of symbolism all over the world. They were thus used by the Hindus, and are found to be most plainly set forth by the ancient Americans, in the Richardson and Gest tablets, in the Palenque Cross ; and manifestly lay at the base of the formation of the calendar forms of the Mayas of Yucatan, the Hindus, the Assyrians, and the ancient Babylonians, as well as the Egyptians and old Hebrews. The natural symbols . . . would be either the phallus or the phallus and yoni, . . . or *male* and *female*. Indeed, the words translated by the generalizing terms male and female, in the 27th verse of the 1st chapter of Genesis are . . . *sacr* and *n'cabrah*, or literally, phallus and yoni,‖ while the representation of the phallic emblems would barely indicate the genital members of the human body, when their functions and the development of the seed-vesicles emanating from them was considered ; then would come into indication a mode of measures of lunar time, and, through lunar, of solar time." . . .

This is the physiological or anthropological key to the Moon symbol. The key that opens the mystery of theogony, or the evolution of the Manvantaric gods, is more complicated, and has nothing phallic in it. All is mystical and divine there. But the Jews, beyond connecting Jehovah directly with the Moon as a generative god, preferred to ignore the higher hierarchies, and have made of some of them (zodiacal constellations and planetary gods) their Patriarchs, thus euhemerizing the

---

* A caricatured and dwarfed Vedantin notion of Parabrahmam containing within *itself* the whole Universe as being that boundless Universe itself, and *there existing nothing outside of itself.*

† Just as they are to this day in India, the bull of Siva and the cow representing several *Sakti*—goddesses.

‡ Hence the worship of the moon by the Hebrews.

‖ " *Male and female*, created he them."

purely theosophical idea and dragging it down to the level of sinful humanity. *(See section "Holy of Holies" in the "Symbolism" of Book II.)* The MSS. from which the above is extracted explains very clearly to what hierarchy of gods Jehovah belonged, and who this Jewish GOD was ; for it shows in clear language that which the writer has always insisted upon—namely, that the God with which the Christians have burdened themselves was no better than the lunar symbol of the reproductive or generative faculty in nature. They have ever ignored even the Hebrew secret god of the Kabalists, Ain-Soph, as grand as Parabrahmam in the earliest Kabalistic and mystical conceptions. But it it not the Kabala of Rosenroth that can ever give the true original teachings of Simeon-Ben-Iochai, as metaphysical and philosophical as any. And how many are there among the students of the Kabala who knew anything of them except in their distorted Latin translations. Let us glance at the idea which led the ancient Jews to adopt a substitute for the ever UNKNOWABLE, and which has misled the Christians into mistaking the substitute for the reality.

" If to these organs (phallus and yoni) as symbols of creative cosmic agencies the idea of . . . . time periods can be attached, then, indeed, in the construc-tion of Temples as Dwellings of Deity, or of Jehovah, that post designated as the Holy of Holies, or the most High Place, should borrow its title from the recognized sacredness of the generative organs, considered as symbols of measures as well as of creative Cause."

" With the ancient wise, there was no name, and no idea, and no symbol, of a First Cause.* With the Hebrews, the indirect conception of such was couched in a term of negation of comprehension—viz., *Ain-Soph*, or the With-out Bounds. But the symbol of *its first comprehensible manifestation*, was the conception of a circle with its diameter line. . . . . (See the Proem of Book I., Part I.) to carry at once a geometric, phallic, and astronomic idea . . . . for the one takes its birth from the nought or the Circle, without which it could not be, and from one, or primal one, spring the nine digits, and, geometrically, all plane shapes. So in the Kabala this Circle, with its diameter line, is the picture of the ten Sephiroth or Emanations, composing the Adam Kadmon, the Archetypal Man, the creative origin of all things. . . . . This idea of connecting the circle and its diameter line, that is, number ten, with the signification of the reproductive organs, and the Most Holy Place, was carried out construc-tively in the King's Chamber, or Holy of Holies, of the great Pyramid, in the Tabernacle of Moses, and in the Holy of Holies of the Temple of Solomon. . . . . It is *the picture of a double-womb*, for in Hebrew the letter *hé* ה is at the same time the number 5 and symbol of the womb, and twice 5 is 10, or the phallic number."

This " double womb " also shows the duality of the idea carried from

---

* Because it was too sacred. It is referred to as THAT in the Vedas : it is the " Eternal Cause," and cannot, therefore, be spoken of as a " First Cause," a term implying the absence of any cause, at one time.

the highest, spiritual, down to the lowest or terrestrial plane ; and by the Jews limited to the latter. With them, therefore the number 7 has acquired the most prominent place in their exoteric religion, a cult of external forms and empty rituals ; as their Sabbath, for instance, the seventh day sacred to their deity, the moon, symbolical of the generative Jehovah. While with other nations the number seven was typical of theogonic evolution, of cycles, cosmic planes, and the Seven Forces and Occult Powers in Kosmos, as a boundless whole, whose first upper triangle was unreachable to the finite intellect of man—while other nations, therefore, busied themselves, in their forcible limitation of Kosmos in Space and Time, only with its septenary manifested plane, the Jews centred this member solely in the moon, and based all their sacred calculations thereupon. Hence we find the thoughtful author of the MSS. just quoted, remarking, in reference to the metrology of the Jews that : " If 20,612 be multiplied by $\frac{4}{3}$ *the product will afford a base for the ascertainment of the mean revolution of the moon,* and if this product be again multiplied by $\frac{4}{3}$, this continued product will afford a base for finding the exact period of the mean solar year, . . . this form . . . becoming, for the finding of astronomical periods of time, of very great service." This double number (male and female) is symbolized also in some well-known idols : *e.g.,* " Ardanari-Iswara, the Isis of the Hindus, Eridanus, or Ardan, or the Hebrew Jordan, *or source of descent.* She is standing on a lotus-leaf flowing on the water. But the signification is, that it is androgyne or hermaphrodite, that is *phallus* and *yoni* combined, the number 10, the Hebrew letter *Jod* ־, the *containment of Jehovah.* She, or rather she-he, gives the minutes of the same circle of 360 degrees."

"Jehovah," in its best aspect is Binah, "the Upper mediating Mother, the *Great Sea* or Holy Spirit ; " therefore rather a synonym of Mary, the Mother of Jesus, than of his Father ; that " Mother, being the Latin *Mare* " the Sea is here also, Venus, the *Stella del Mare*, or " Star of the Sea."

The ancestors of the mysterious Akkadians—the *Chandra* or *Indovansas*, the Lunar Kings whom tradition shows reigning at Prayag (Allahabad) ages before our era—had come from India, and brought with them the worship of their forefathers, of Soma, and his son Budha, which afterwards became that of the Chaldeans. Yet such adoration, apart from popular Astrolatry and Heliolatry, was in no sense *idolatry*. No more, at any rate, than the modern Roman Catholic symbolism which connects their Virgin Mary—the *Magna Mater* of the Syrians and Greeks—with the Moon.

Of this worship, the most pious Roman Catholics feel quite proud, and loudly confess to it. In a *Mémoire* to the French Academy, the Marquis De Mirville says :—

"It is only natural that, as an unconscious prophecy, Ammon-Ra should be *his mother's husband*, since the *Magna Mater* of the Christians *is precisely the spouse of that son she conceives.* . . . We (Christians) *can understand now why Neithis throws radiance on the sun, while remaining the Moon*, since the VIRGIN, who is the QUEEN OF HEAVEN, *as Neith was*, clothes herself in her radiance, and clothes in his turn the CHRIST-SUN. *"Tu vestis solem et te sol vestit."* . . . is sung by the Roman Catholics during their service, and he adds :—

"We (Christians) understand also how it is that the famous inscription at Sais should have stated that 'none has ever lifted my peplum (veil),' considering that this sentence, literally translated, *is the summary of what is sung in the Church on the day of the immaculate conception.*" (ARCHÆOLOGY OF THE VIRGIN MOTHER," p. 117.)

Surely nothing could be more sincere than this! It justifies entirely what Mr. Gerald Massey has said in his Lecture on "Luniolatry, Ancient and Modern":—

"The man in the moon (Osiris-Sut, Jehovah-Satan, Christ-Judas, and other Lunar twins) is often charged with bad conduct. . . . In the lunar phenomena the moon was one as *the* moon, which was two-fold in séx, and three-fold in character—as mother, child, and adult male. Thus the child of the moon became the consort of his own mother! It could not be *helped* if there was to be any reproduction. He was compelled to be his own father! These relationships were repudiated by later sociology, and the primitive man in the moon got tabooed. Yet, in its latest, most inexplicable phase, this has become the central doctrine of the grossest superstition the world has seen, for these lunar phenomena and their humanly represented relationships, the incestuous included, are the very foundations of the Christian Trinity in Unity. Through ignorance of the symbolism, the simple representation of early time has become the most profound religious mystery in modern Luniolatry. The Roman Church, without being in any wise ashamed of the proof, portrays the Virgin Mary arrayed with the sun, and the horned moon at her feet, holding the lunar infant in her arms—as child and consort of the mother moon. The mother, child, and adult male, are fundamental."

"In this way it can be proved that our Christology is mummified mythology, and legendary lore, which have been palmed off upon us in the *Old* Testament and the New, as divine revelation uttered by the very voice of God."

A charming allegory is found in the *Zohar*, one which unveils better than anything ever did the true character of Jehovah or YHVH in the primitive conception of the Hebrew Kabalists. It is now found in the philosophy of I'bn Gebirol's Kabbalah, translated by Isaac Myer. "In the introduction written by R'Hez'quee-yah, which is very old," says our author, "and forms part of our Brody edition of the Zohar (1, 5b. sq.) is an account of a journey taken by R. El'azar, son of R. Shim-on b. Io'hai, and Rabbi Abbah." They met a man with a heavy burden and asked his name ; but he refused to give it and proceeded to explain to them Thorah

(Law). " They asked : " Who caused thee thus to walk and carry such a heavy load ? ' He answered : ' The letter י, (Yod, which=10, and is the symbolical letter of Kether and the essence and germ of the Holy name יהוה YHVH) . . . . They said to him : ' If thou wilt tell us the name of thy father, we will kiss the dust of thy feet.' He replied : ' As to my father, *he had his dwelling in the Great Sea, and was a fish therein*' (like Vishnu and Dagon or Oannes), 'which (first) destroyed the great sea ' . . . . . and he was great and mighty and 'Ancient of Days,' until he swallowed all the other fishes in the (Great) Sea . . . R. El'azar listened and said to him : ' Thou art the Son of the Holy Flame, thou art the Son of Rab Ham—'*nun*-ah Sabah [the old : the *fish* in Aramaic or Chaldee is *nun* (*noon*)] thou art the Son of the Light of the Thorah," (*Dharma*) etc. Then the author explains that the feminine Sephiroth, *Binah*, is termed by the Kabalist the great sea : therefore Binah, whose divine names are Jehovah, *Yah*, and Elohim, is simply the Chaldean Tiamat, the female power, the Thalatth of Berosus, who presides over the Chaos, and was made out later by Christian theology to be the serpent and the Devil. She-He (Yah-hovah) is the supernal (Heh, and Eve). This Yah-hovah then, or Jehovah, is identical with our Chaos—Father, Mother, Son,—on the material plane and in the purely physical World. *Demon* and *Deus* at one and the same time ; the sun and moon, good and evil, God and Demon.

Lunar magnetism generates life, preserves and destroys it, psychically as well as physically. And if, astronomically, she is one of the seven planets of the ancient world, in theogony she is one of the regents thereof; with Christians now as much as with Pagans, the former referring to her under the name of one of their archangels, and the latter under that of one of their gods.

Therefore the meaning of the " fairy tale " translated by Chwolson from an old Chaldean MSS. translated into Arabic, about Qû-tâmy being instructed by the *idol* of the moon, is easily understood (*vide* Book III.) Seldenus tells us the secret as well as Maimonides *(More Nevochim*, Book III., ch. xxx). The worshippers of the *Teraphim* (the Jewish Oracles) " carved images and claimed that the light of the principal stars (planets) permeating these through and through, the angelic VIRTUES (or the regents of the stars and planets) conversed with them, teaching them many most useful things and arts." And Seldenus explains that the *Teraphim* were built and composed after the position of certain planets, those which the Greeks called στοιχεῖα, and according to figures that were located in the sky and called ἀλεξητῆροι, or the *tutelary* gods. Those who traced out the στοιχεῖα were called στοιχειωματιχοί, or the diviners by the στοιχεῖα. (*De Diis Syriis, Teraph*, II. Synt. p. 31) *vide infra*, the *Teraphim*.

It is such sentences, however, in the " Nabathean agriculture," that have frightened the men of science and made them proclaim the work " either an *apocrypha* or a fairy tale, unworthy of the notice of an Academician." At the same time, as shown, zealous Roman Catholics and Protestants tore it metaphorically to pieces ; the former because " it described the worship of demons," the latter because it is " ungodly." They are all wrong, once more. It is *not* a fairy tale ; and as far as regards pious Churchmen, the same worship may be shown in the Scriptures, however disfigured by translation. Solar and Lunar worship, as well as that of the Stars and Elements, are traced, and figure in the Christian theology ; defended by Papists, they are stoutly denied by the Protestants only at their own risk and peril. Two instances may be given.

Ammianus Marcellinus teaches that ancient divinations were always accomplished with the help of the Spirits of the Elements, " *Spiritus elementorum*, and in Greek πνεύματα τῶν στοιχείων " (i. I., 21).

But it is found now that the planets, the Elements, and the Zodiac, were figured not only in Heliopolis by the twelve stones called " mysteries of the elements," *elementorum arcana*, but also in Solomon's temple, and, as pointed out by various writers, in several old Italian churches and even at *Notre Dame de Paris* where they can be seen to this day.

No symbol—the sun included—was more complex in its manifold meanings than the lunar symbol. The sex was, of course, dual. With some it was male, *e.g.*, the Hindu " King Soma," and the Chaldean *Sin;* with other nations it was female, the beauteous goddesses Diana-Luna, I'lythia, Lucina. In Tauris, human victims were sacrificed to Artemis, a form of the lunar goddess ; the Cretans called her Dictynna, and the Medes and Persians Anaïtis, as shown by an inscription of Koloé : 'Αρτέμιδι 'Ανάειτι. But, we are now concerned chiefly with the most chaste and pure of the virgin goddesses, Luna-Artemis, to whom Pamphos was the first to give the surname of Καλλίστη, and of whom Hippolitus wrote : Καλλίστα πολύ παρθενῶν. (See Pausanias viii., 35, 8.) This Artemis-Lochia, the goddess that presided at conception and child-birth (Iliad, Pausanias, etc., etc.), is, in her functions and as the triple Hecate, the Orphic deity, the predecessor of the God of the Rabbins and pre-Christian Kabalists, and his lunar type. The goddess Τρίμορφος was the personified symbol of the various and successive aspects represented by the moon in each of her three phases; and this interpretation was already that of the Stoics (Cornut. *De Nat*, D. 34, 1), while the Orpheans explained the epithet (Τρίμορφος) by the three kingdoms of nature over which she reigned. Jealous, blood-thirsty, revengeful and exacting, Hecate-Luna is a worthy counterpart of the " jealous God " of the Hebrew prophets.

The whole riddle of the solar and lunar worship, as now traced in the churches, hangs indeed on this world-old mystery of lunar phenomena. The correlative forces in the " Queen of Night," that lie latent for modern science, but are fully active to the knowledge of Eastern adepts, explain well the thousand and one images under which the moon was represented by the ancients. It also shows how much more profoundly learned in the Selenic mysteries were the ancients than are now our modern astronomers. The whole Pantheon of the lunar gods and goddesses, Nephtys or Neith, Proserpina, Melytta, Cybele, Isis, Astarte, Venus, and Hecate, on the one hand, and Apollo, Dionysius, Adonis, Bacchus, Osiris, Atys, Thammuz, etc., etc., on the other, all show on the face of their names and titles—those of " Sons " and " Husbands " of their mothers—their identity with the Christian Trinity. In every religious system the gods were made to merge their functions as Father, Son, and Husband, into one, and the goddesses were identified as " Wife, Mother, and Sister " of the male God ; the former synthesizing the human attributes as the " Sun, the giver of Life," the latter merging all the other titles in the grand synthesis known as Maïa, Maya, Maria, etc., a generic name. Maïa, in its forced derivation, has come to mean with the Greeks, " mother," from the root *ma* (nurse), and even gave its name to the month of May, which was sacred to all those goddesses before it became consecrated to Mary.* Its primitive meaning, however, was *Maya*, *Durgâ*, translated by the Orientalists as " inaccessible," but meaning in truth the " *unreachable*," in the sense of illusion and unreality ; as being the source and cause of spells, the personification of ILLUSION.

In religious rites the moon served a dual purpose. Personified as a female goddess for exoteric purposes, or as a male god in allegory and symbol, in occult philosophy our satellite was regarded as a sexless Potency to be well studied, because it was to be dreaded. With the initiated Aryans, Khaldii, Greeks and Romans, Soma, Sin, Artemis *Soteira* (the hermaphrodite Apollo, whose attribute is the lyre, and the bearded Diana of the bow and arrow), *Deus Lunus*, and especially Osiris-lunus and Thot-lunus,† were the occult potencies of the moon. But whether male or female, whether Thot or Minerva, Soma or Astoreth, the Moon is the Occult mystery of mysteries, and more a symbol of evil than of good. Her seven phases (original, esoteric division) are divided into three astronomical phenomena and four

---

* The Roman Catholics are indebted for the idea of consecrating the month of May to the Virgin, to the pagan Plutarch, who shows that " May is sacred to *Maïa* (Maîa) or Vesta " (*Aulus-Gellius*, word Maïa)—our mother-earth, our nurse and nourisher personified.

† Thot-Lunus is " Budha-Soma " of India, or " Mercury and the Moon."

purely psychic phases. That the moon was not always reverenced
is shown in the Mysteries, in which the death of the moon-god (the
three phases of gradual waning and final disappearance) was allegorized
by the moon standing for the *genius of evil* that triumphs for the time
over the light and life-giving god (the sun), and all the skill and
learning of the ancient Hierophants in Magic was required to turn this
triumph into a defeat.

It was the most ancient worship of all, that of the *third* Race of our
Round, the Hermaphrodites, to whom the *male*-moon became sacred,
when after the " Fall " so-called, the sexes had become separated.
" Deus Lunus " then became an androgyne, male and female in turn ;
to serve finally, for *purposes of sorcery*, as a dual power, to the *Fourth*
Root-race, the Atlanteans. With the *Fifth* (our own) the lunar-solar
worship divided the nations into two distinct, antagonistic camps. It
led to events described æons later in the Mahabhâratan War, which to
the Europeans is the *fabulous*, to the Hindus and Occultists the historical,
strife between the *Suryavansas* and the *Indovansas*. Originating in the
dual aspect of the moon, the worship of the female and the male
principles respectively, it ended in distinct solar and lunar cults.
Among the Semitic races, the sun was for a very long time
feminine and the moon masculine—the latter notion being adopted
by them from the Atlantean traditions. The moon was called
" the Lord of the sun," *Bel-Shemesh*, * before the Shemesh
worship. The ignorance of the incipient reasons for such a distinction, and of occult principles, led the nations into anthropomorphic
idol-worship. But the religion of every ancient nation had been
primarily based upon the Occult manifestations of a purely abstract
Force or Principle now called " God." The very establishment of
such worship shows, in its details and rites, that the philosophers
who evolved those systems of nature, subjective and objective,
possessed profound knowledge, and were acquainted with many facts

---

* During that period which is absent from the Mosaic books—from the exile of
Eden to the allegorical Flood—the Jews worshipped with the rest of the Semites
Dayanisi דיינים " the Ruler of Men," the " Judge," or the SUN. Though
the Jewish canon and Christianism have made the sun become the " Lord God " and
Jehovah in the Bible, yet the latter is full of indiscreet traces of the androgyne Deity,
which was Jehovah the *sun*, and Astoreth the moon in its female aspect, and quite free
from the present metaphorical element given to it. God is a " consuming fire," appears
in, and is encompassed *by* fire." It was not only in vision that Ezekiel (viii., 16) saw the
Jews " worshipping the sun. The *Baal* of the Israelites (the Shemesh of the Moabites
and the Moloch of the Ammonites) was the identical " Sun-Jehovah," and he is till now
" the King of the Host of Heaven," the Sun, as much as Astoreth was the " Queen of
Heaven "—or the moon. The " Sun of Righteousness " has become a *metaphorical*
expression *only now*.

of a scientific nature. For besides being purely Occult, the rites of lunar worship were based, as just shown, upon a knowledge of physiology (quite a modern science with us), psychology, sacred mathematics, geometry and metrology, in their right applications to symbols and figures, which are but glyphs, recording observed natural and scientific *facts;* in short, upon a most minute and profound knowledge of nature. Lunar magnetism generates life, preserves and kills it. *Soma* embodies the triple power of the *Trimurti*, though it passes unrecognized by the profane to this day. The allegory that makes Soma, the moon, produced by the churning of the *Ocean of Life (Space)* by the gods in another Manvantara *(i.e.,* in the *pregenetic* day of our planetary system), and that other allegory, which shows " the Rishis milking the earth, whose calf was Soma, the moon," has a deep cosmographical meaning ; for it is neither *our* earth which is milked, nor was the moon, which we know, the calf.* Had our wise men of science known as much of the mysteries of nature as the ancient Aryans did, they would surely never have imagined that the moon was projected from the Earth. Once more, the oldest of permutations in theogony, the Son becoming his own father and the mother generated by the Son, has to be remembered and taken into consideration if the symbolical language of the ancients is to be understood by us. Otherwise mythology will be ever haunting the Orientalists as simply " the disease which springs up at a peculiar stage of human culture ! "—as Renouf gravely observes in a Hibbert lecture.

The ancients taught the, so to speak, *auto*-generation of the Gods: the one divine essence, *unmanifested*, perpetually begetting a second-self, *manifested*, which second-self, androgynous in its nature, *gives birth in an immaculate way* to everything macro- and micro-cosmical in this universe. This was shown in the Circle and the Diameter, or the Sacred 10, a few pages back.

But our Orientalists, their extreme desire to discover one homogeneous *element* in nature notwithstanding, will *not* see it ; cramped in their researches by such ignorance, they—the Aryanists and Egyptologists—are constantly led astray from truth in their speculations. Thus, de Rougé is unable to understand, in the text which he translates, the meaning of Ammon-râ saying to King Amenophes (supposed to be Memnon), " Thou art my Son, I have begotten thee ; " and as he

---

* The earth flees for her life in the allegory, before Prithu, who pursues her. She assumes the shape of a cow, and, trembling with terror, runs away and hides even in the regions of Brahmâ. Therefore, it is *not* our Earth. Again, in every Purâna, the calf changes name. In one it is Manu Swayambhûva, in another Indra, in a third the Himavat (Himalayas) itself, while Meru was the milker. This is a deeper allegory than one thinks.

finds the same idea in many a text and under various forms, this very Christian Orientalist is finally compelled to exclaim that " for this idea to have entered the mind of a hierogrammatist, there must have been in their religion a more or less defined doctrine, *indicating as a possible fact that might come to pass, a divine and immaculate incarnation under a human form."* Precisely. But why throw the explanation on an impossible prophecy, when the whole secret is explained by the later religion copying the earlier?

That doctrine was universal, and it was not the mind of any one hierogrammatist that evolved it; for the Indian avatars are a proof to the contrary. After which, having come " to realize clearer "* what " the Divine Father and Son " were with the Egyptians, de Rougé still fails to account for, and perceive what were the functions attributed to the *feminine* principle in that primordial generation. He does not find it in the goddess Neith, of Saïs. Yet he quotes the sentence of the Commander to Cambyses when introducing that king into the Saïtic temple : " I made known to his Majesty the dignity of Saïs, which is the abode of Neith, the great (female) producer, *genitrix* of the *Sun*, who is the *first-born, and who is not begotten, but only brought forth,"* and hence is the fruit of an *immaculate mother.*

How much more grandiose, philosophical and poetical is the real distinction—for whoever is able to understand and appreciate it—made between the *immaculate virgin* of the ancient Pagans and the modern *Papal* conception. With the former, the ever-youthful mother nature, the antitype of her prototypes, the sun and moon, *generates* and *brings forth* her " mind-born " son, the Universe. The Sun and Moon, as male-female deities, fructify the earth, the microcosmical mother, and the latter conceives and brings forth, in her turn. With the Christians, " the first-born " (*primogenitus*) is indeed generated, *i.e.*, begotten, " *genitum, non factum,"* and positively *conceived and brought forth*—" *Virgo pariet,"* explains the Latin Church. Thus, she drags down the noble spiritual ideal of the Virgin Mary to the earth, and, making her " of the earth earthy," degrades that ideal to the lowest of the anthropomorphic goddesses of the rabble.

Truly, Neith, Isis, Diana, etc., etc., were each of them " a demiurgical goddess, at once visible and invisible, having her place in Heaven, and *helping to the generation of species"*—the moon, in short. Her occult aspects and powers are numberless, and, in one of them, the moon becomes with

* His *clear* realization of it is, that the Egyptians *prophesied* Jehovah (!) and his incarnated Redeemer (the good serpent), etc., etc.; even to identifying Typhon with the *wicked* dragon of the garden of Eden, and this passes as serious and sober *science.*

the Egyptians Hathor, another aspect of Isis,* and both of these goddesses are shown suckling Horus. Behold in the Egyptian Hall of the British Museum, Hathor worshipped by Pharaoh Thotmes, who stands between her and the Lord of Heavens. The monolith was taken from Karnac; and the same goddess has the following legend inscribed on her throne: "THE DIVINE MOTHER AND LADY, OR QUEEN OF HEAVEN;" also "the MORNING STAR," and the "LIGHT OF THE SEA" (*Stella matutina* and *Lux maris*). All the lunar goddesses had a dual aspect—one *divine*, the other *infernal*. All were the virgin mothers of an *immaculately* born Son—the SUN. Raoul Rochetti shows the moon-goddess of the Athenians—Pallas, or Cybele, Minerva, or again Diana —holding her child-son on the lap, invoked in her festivals as Μονογενὴς Θεοῦ, "the one Mother of God," sitting on a lion, and surrounded by twelve personages; in whom the Occultist recognises the twelve great gods, and the pious Christian Orientalist the apostles, or rather the Grecian pagan prophecy thereof.

They are both right, for the immaculate *goddess* of the Latin Church is a faithful copy of the older pagan goddesses; the number (twelve) of the apostles is that of the twelve tribes, and the latter are a personification of the twelve great gods, and of the twelve signs of the Zodiac. Every detail almost in the Christian dogma is borrowed from the heathens. Semele, the *wife* of Jupiter and mother of Bacchus, the *Sun*, is, according to Nonnus, also "carried," or made to ascend to heaven after her death, where she presides between Mars and Venus, under the name of the *Queen of the World*, or the universe, πανβασιλεία; "at the names of which, as at the names of Hathor, Hecate, and other infernal goddesses," "tremble all the demons."†

"Σεμελῆν τρέμουσι δαίμονες." This Greek inscription on a small temple, reproduced on a stone that was found by somebody, and copied by Montfaucon, as De Mirville tells us (113, *Archæologie de la Vierge mère*) informs us of the stupendous fact, that the *Magna Mater* of the old world was an impudent *plagiarism*, perpetrated by the *Demon, of the Immaculate Virgin Mother* of his Church. Whether so, or *vice versâ*, is of no importance. That which is interesting to note is the perfect identity between the ARCHAIC COPY and the MODERN ORIGINAL.

Did space permit we might show the inconceivable coolness and un-concern exhibited by certain followers of the Roman Catholic Church, when made to face the revelations of the Past. To Maury's remark that "the Virgin took possession of all the Sanctuaries of Ceres and

---

* Hathor is the *infernal* Isis, the goddess pre-eminently of the West or the *nether* world.

† This is De Mirville, who proudly confesses the similarity, and *he ought to know*.

Venus, and that the pagan rites, proclaimed and practised in honour of those goddesses, were in a good measure transferred to the mother of Christ," the advocate of Rome answers:—

" That such *is* the fact, and that it is just as it should be and quite natural. As the dogma, the liturgy, and the rites professed by the Roman Apostolical Church in 1862 are found engraved on monuments, inscribed on papyri, and cylinders *hardly posterior to the Deluge*, it does seem impossible to deny the existence of a FIRST ANTE-HISTORICAL (Roman) CATHOLICISM OF WHICH OUR OWN IS BUT THE FAITHFUL CONTINUATION. . . . But while the former was the culmination, the *summum* of the impudence of demons and Goetic necromancy . . . . the latter is *divine.* If in *our* (Christian) Revelation (*l'Apocalypse*), Mary, clothed with the Sun and having the moon under her feet, has nothing more in common *with the humble servant of Nazareth (sic.)*, it is because she has now become the greatest of theological and cosmological powers in *our* universe."—(Archæol. de la Vierge, pp. 116 and 119, and by the Marquis de Mirville).

Verily so, since Pindar's *Hymns to Minerva* (p. 19) . . . " who sits *at the right hand* of her Father Jupiter, and who is more powerful than all the other (angels or) gods," are likewise applied to the Virgin. It is St. Bernard, who, quoted by Cornelius *a Lapide*, is made to address the Virgin Mary in this wise :—

" The *Sun-Christ* lives in thee and thou livest in him." (Sermon on the Holy Virgin.) . . . .

Again the Virgin is admitted to be the MOON by the same unsophisticated holy man. Being the *Lucina* of the Church, that is in childbirth, the verse of Virgil—" *Casta fove Lucina, tuus jam regnat Apollo* "—is applied to her. Like the moon, the Virgin is the Queen of Heaven," adds the innocent saint; (Apocal., ch. xii., Comm. by *Cornelius a Lapide*).

This settles the question. The more similarity, according to such writers as De Mirville, there exists between the pagan conceptions and the Christian dogmas, the more divine appears the Christian religion, and the more is it seen to be the only truly inspired one, especially in its Roman Catholic form. The unbelieving scientists and the academicians who think they see in the Latin Church quite the opposite of divine inspiration, and who will not believe in the satanic tricks of plagiarism by anticipation, are severely taken to ask. But then " they believe in nothing and reject even the '*Nabathean Agriculture*' as a romance and a pack of superstitious nonsense," complains the memorialist. " In their perverted opinion Qû-tâ-my's ' idol of the moon ' and the statue of the Madonna are one !" A noble Marquis wrote twenty years ago six huge volumes, or, as he calls them " *Mémoires* to the French Academy," with the sole object of showing Roman Catholicism an inspired and revealed faith. As a proof thereof, he furnishes numberless facts, all tending to show that the entire ancient world, ever since the deluge, had been, with the help of the devil, systematically plagiarizing the rites, ceremonies, and dogmas of the future Holy Church to be born ages later. What would that faithful son of Rome have said had he heard his co-religionist—M. Renouf, the distinguished Egyptologist of the British Museum—declaring, in one of his learned lectures, that " neither Hebrews nor Greeks borrowed any of their ideas from Egypt ? "*

But perhaps it is just this that M. Renouf intended to say—namely, that it is the Egyptians, the Greeks, and the Aryans, who borrowed theirs from the Latin Church ? And if so, why, in the name of logic, do the Papists reject the additional information which the Occultists may give them on Moon-worship, since it all tends to show their (the Roman Catholic) worship as old as the world—OF SABÆANISM AND ASTROLATRY ?

The reason of early Christian and later Roman Catholic astrolatry, or the symbolical worship of Sun and Moon—identical with that of the Gnostics, though less philosophical and pure than the " Sun worship " of the Zoroastrians—is a natural consequence of its birth and origin. The adoption by the Latin Church of such symbols as the water, fire, sun, moon and stars, and a good many other things, is simply a continuation by the early Christians of the old worship of Pagan nations. Thus Odin got his wisdom, power, and knowledge, by sitting at the feet of Mimir, the thrice-wise *Jotun*, who passed his life by the fountain of primeval Wisdom, the crystalline waters of which increased his knowledge daily. Mimir " drew the highest knowledge from the fountain, because the world was born of water ; hence primeval wisdom was to be found in that mysterious element " (" Asgard and the Gods," 86). The eye which Odin had to pledge to acquire that knowledge may be " the Sun, which enlightens and penetrates all things ; his other eye being the moon, whose reflection gazes out of the deep, and which at last, when setting, sinks into the Ocean." (*Ibid.*) But it is something more, besides this. Loki, the fire-god, is said to have hidden in the water, as well as in the moon, the light-giver, whose reflection he found therein ; and this belief that the fire finds refuge in the water was not limited to the old Scandinavians. It was shared by all nations and was finally taken up by the early Christians, who symbolized the Holy Ghost under the shape of Fire, " cloven tongues like as fire "—the breath of the Father-SUN. This " Fire " descends also into the Water or the Sea: *Mar*, Mary. The dove was the symbol of the Soul with several nations, it was sacred to Venus, the goddess born from the

---

* Quoted in Mr. G. Massey's Lecture.

sea-foam, and it became later the symbol of the Christian *Anima Mundi*, or the Holy Spirit.

One of the most occult chapters in the " Book of the Dead " is ch. lxxx., entitled : " To make the transformation into the god giving light to the path of Darkness," wherein "Woman-light of the Shadow" serves Thot in his retreat in the moon. Thot-Hermes is said to hide therein, because he is the representative of the Secret Wisdom. He is the manifested logos of its light side, the concealed deity or " Dark Wisdom " when he is supposed to retire to the opposite hemisphere. Speaking of her power, the moon calls herself repeatedly : " The Light which shineth in Darkness," the " Woman-Light." Hence it became the accepted symbol of all the Virgin-Mother goddesses. As the wicked " evil " spirits warred against the moon in days of yore, so they are supposed to war now, without being able to prevail, however, against the actual Queen of Heaven, Mary, the moon. Hence also the moon was intimately connected in all the Pagan theogonies with the Dragon, her eternal enemy ; the Virgin, or Madonna, standing on the mythical Satan under that form, crushed and made powerless, under her feet. This, because the head and tail of the Dragon, which represent in Eastern astronomy to this day the ascending and descending nodes of the moon, were also symbolized in ancient Greece by the two serpents. Hercules kills them on the day of his birth, and so does the babe in his virgin mother's arms. As Mr. Gerald Massey aptly observes in this connection : " All such symbols figured their own facts from the first, and did not pre-figure others of a totally different order. The Iconography (and dogmas, too) had survived in Rome from a period remotely pre-Christian. *There was neither forgery nor interpolation of types ; nothing but a continuity of imagery with a perversion of its meaning.*"

---

§ X.

TREE, SERPENT, AND CROCODILE WORSHIP.

" Object of horror or of adoration, men have for the serpent an implacable hatred, or prostrate themselves before its genius. Lie calls it, Prudence claims it, Envy carries it in its heart, and Eloquence on its caduceus. In hell it arms the whip of the Furies ; in heaven Eternity makes of it its symbol."

DE CHATEAUBRIAND.

THE Ophites asserted that there were several kinds of genii, from god to man ; that the relative superiority of these was ruled by the degree of light that was accorded to each ; and they maintained that the serpent had to be constantly called upon and to be thanked for the signal service it had rendered humanity. For it taught Adam that if he ate of the fruit of the tree of knowledge of good and evil, he would raise his being immensely by the learning and wisdom he would thus acquire. Such was the exoteric reason given.

It is easy to see whence the primal idea of this dual, Janus-like cha- racter of the Serpent: the good and the bad. This symbol is one of the most ancient, because the reptile preceded the bird, and the bird the mammal. Thence the belief, or rather the superstition, of the savage tribes who think that the souls of their ancestors live under this form, and the general association of the Serpent with the tree. The legends about the various things it represents are numberless ; but, as most of them are allegorical, they have now passed into the class of fables based on ignorance and dark superstition. For instance, when Philostratus narrates that the natives of India and Arabia fed on the heart and liver of serpents in order to learn the language of all the animals, the serpent being credited with that faculty, he certainly never meant his words to be accepted literally. (See *De Vitâ Apollonii*, lib. 1, c. xiv.) As will be found more than once as we proceed, the " Serpent " and " Dragon " were the names given to the " Wise Ones," the initiated adepts of olden times. It was their wisdom and their learning that were devoured or assimilated by their followers, whence the allegory. When the Scandinavian Sigurd is fabled to have roasted the heart of Fafnir, the Dragon, whom he had slain, becoming thereby the wisest of men, it meant the same thing. Sigurd had become learned in the runes and magical charms ; he had received the " word " from an initiate of that name, or from a sorcerer, after which the latter died, as many do, after "passing the word." Epiphanius lets out a secret of the Gnostics while trying to expose their *heresies*. The Gnostic Ophites, he says, had a reason for honouring the Serpent : *it was because he taught the primeval men the Mysteries (Adv. Hæres.* 37). Verily so ; but they did not have Adam and Eve in the garden in their minds when teaching this dogma, but simply that which is stated above. The *Nâgas* of the Hindu and Tibetan adepts were human *Nâgas* (Serpents), not reptiles. Moreover, the Serpent has ever been the type of consecutive or serial rejuvenation, of IMMORTALITY and TIME.

The numerous and extremely interesting readings, the interpretations and facts about Serpent worship, given in " The Natural Genesis," are very ingenious and scientifically correct. But they are far from covering the *whole* of the meanings implied. They divulge only the astronomical and physiological mysteries, with the addition of some cosmic pheno- mena. On the lowest plane of materiality the Serpent was, no doubt, "the great mystery in the mysteries," and was, very likely, "adopted as a type of feminine pubescence, on account of its sloughing and self-renewal." It was so, however, only with regard to mysteries concerning terrestrial *animal* life, for as symbol of "*reclothing* and rebirth in the (universal) mysteries" its "*final phase*"*—or shall we rather say its incipient and culminating phases—they were not of this plane. They were generated in the pure realm of ideal light, and having accomplished the round of the whole cycle of adaptations and symbolism, the "mysteries" returned from whence they had come—into the essence of *immaterial* causality. They belonged to the highest gnosis. And surely this could have never obtained its name and fame solely on account of its penetration into physiological and especially feminine functions!

As a symbol, the Serpent had as many aspects and occult meanings as the Tree itself; the "Tree of Life," with which it was emblematically and almost indissolubly connected. Whether viewed as a metaphysical or a physical symbol, the Tree and Serpent, jointly, or separately, have never been so degraded by antiquity as they are now, in this our age of the breaking of idols, not for truth's sake, but to glorify the more gross matter. The revelations and interpretations in "The Rivers of Life" would have astounded the worshippers of the Tree and Serpent in the days of archaic Chaldean and Egyptian wisdom; and even the early Saivas would have recoiled in horror at the theories and suggestions of the author of the said work. "The notion of Payne Knight and Inman that the cross or Tau is simply a copy of the male organs in a triadic form is radically false," writes Mr. G. Massey, who proves what he says. But this is a statement that could be as justly applied to almost all the modern interpretations of ancient symbols. "The Natural Genesis," a monumental work of research and thought, the most complete on that subject that has ever been published, covering as it does a wider field, and explaining much more than all the symbologists who have hitherto written, does not yet go beyond the "psycho-theistic" stage of ancient thought. Nor were Payne Knight and Inman altogether wrong; except in entirely failing to see that their interpretations of the "Tree of Life," as the cross and phallus, fitted the symbol, and approximated it, only on the lowest and last stage of the evolutionary development of the idea of the GIVER OF LIFE. It was the last and the grossest physical transformation of nature, in animal, insect, bird, and even plant; for biune, creative magnetism, in the form of the attraction of the contraries, or sexual polarization, acts in the constitution of reptile and bird as it does in that of man. Moreover, the modern symbologists and Orientalists—from first to last—

---

* The *Natural Genesis*, by Gerald Massey, Vol. i, p. 340.

being ignorant of the real mysteries revealed by occultism, can necessarily see but this last stage. If told that this mode of procreation, which the whole world of being has now in common on this earth, is but a passing phase, a physical means of furnishing the conditions to, and producing the phenomena of life which will alter with this, and disappear with the next Root-Race—they would laugh at such a superstitious and unscientific idea. But the most learned Occultists assert this because *they know it.* The universe of living beings, of all those which procreate their species, is the living witness to the various modes of procreation in the evolution of animal and human species and races; and the naturalist ought to sense this truth intuitionally, even though he is yet unable to demonstrate it. And how could he, indeed, with the present modes of thought! The landmarks of the archaic history of the past are few and scarce, and those that men of science come across are mistaken for finger-posts of our little era. Even so-called " universal " (?) history embraces but a tiny field in the almost boundless space of the unexplored regions of our latest, fifth Root-Race. Hence, every fresh sign-post, every new glyph of the hoary Past that is discovered, is added to the old stock of information, to be interpreted on the same lines of pre-existing conceptions, and without any reference to the special cycle of thought which that particular glyph may belong to. How can Truth ever come to light if this method is never changed !

Thus, in the beginning of their joint existence as a glyph of Immortal Being, the Tree and Serpent were divine imagery, truly. The tree *was reversed*, and its roots were generated in Heaven and grew out of the Rootless Root of all-being. Its trunk grew and developed, crossing the planes of Pleroma, it shot out crossways its luxuriant branches, first on the plane of hardly differentiated matter, and then downward till they touched the terrestrial plane. Thus, the Asvattha, tree of Life and Being, whose destruction alone leads to immortality, is said in the Bhagavatgita to grow with its roots above and its branches below (ch. xv.). The roots represent the Supreme Being, or First Cause, the Logos; but one has to go beyond those roots to *unite oneself with Krishna,* who, says Arjuna (XI.), is "greater than Brahman, and First Cause . . . the indestructible, that which is, that which is not, and what is beyond them." Its boughs are Hiranyagharba (Brahmâ or Brahman in his highest manifestations, say Sridhara and Madhusûdana), the highest Dhyan Chohans or Devas. The Vedas are its leaves. He only who goes *beyond* the roots shall never return, *i.e.,* shall reincarnate no more during this " age " of Brahmâ.

It is only when its pure boughs had touched the terrestrial mud of the garden of Eden, of our Adamic race, that this Tree got soiled by the contact and lost its pristine purity; and that the Serpent of

THE SEVEN-HEADED DRAGONS.

Eternity—the heaven-born Logos—was finally degraded. In days of old—of the *divine Dynasties* on Earth—the now dreaded Reptile was regarded as the first beam of light that radiated from the abyss of divine Mystery. Various were the forms which it was made to assume, and numerous the natural symbols adapted to it, as it crossed æons of Time: as from Infinite Time itself—*Kala*—it fell into the space and time evolved out of human speculation. These forms were Cosmic and astronomical, theistic and pantheistic, abstract and concrete. They became in turn the Polar Dragon and the Southern Cross, the *Alpha Draconis* of the Pyramid, and the Hindu-Buddhist Dragon, which ever threatens, yet never swallows the Sun during its eclipses. Till then, the Tree remained ever green, for it was sprinkled by the waters of life ; the great Dragon, ever divine, so long as it was kept within the precincts of the sidereal fields. But the tree grew and its lower boughs touched at last the infernal regions—our Earth. Then the great serpent Nidhögg—he who devours the corpses of the evil-doers in the " Hall of Misery " (human life), so soon as they are plunged into " Hwergelmir," the roaring cauldron (of human passions)—gnawed the World-tree. The worms of materiality covered the once healthy and mighty roots, and are now ascending higher and higher along the trunk; while the Midgard-snake coiled at the bottom of the Seas, encircles the Earth, and, through its venomous breath, makes her powerless to defend herself.

They are all seven-headed, the dragons and serpents of antiquity— " one head for each race, and every head with seven hairs on it," as the allegory has it. Aye, from Ananta, the Serpent of Eternity which carries Vishnu through the Manvantara, from the original primordial Sesha, whose seven heads become " one thousand heads" in the Purânic fancy, down to the seven-headed Akkadian Serpent. This typifies the Seven principles throughout nature and man ; the highest or *middle* head being the seventh. It is not of the Mosaic, Jewish Sabbath that Philo speaks in his *Creation of the World*, when saying that the world was completed " according to the perfect nature of number 6." For, " *when that reason (nous) which is holy in accordance with the number seven, has entered the soul* (rather the living body), the number six is thus arrested, and all the mortal things which that number makes." And again : " Number 7 is the festival day of all the earth, the *birthday of the world*. I know not whether any one would be able to celebrate the number 7 in adequate terms." . . . (Par. pp. 30 and 419). The author of *The Natural Genesis* thinks that " the Septenary of Stars seen in the great bear (the *Septarshis*) and seven-headed Dragon furnished a visible origin for the symbolic seven of time above. The goddess of the seven stars," he adds—

"Was the mother of time, as Kep; whence Kepti and Sebti for the two times and number seven. So this is the star of the Seven by name. Sevekt (Kronus), the Son of the goddess, has the name of the seven or seventh. So has Sefekh Abu who builds the house on high, as Wisdom (Sophia) built hers with seven pillars. . . The primary Kronotypes were seven, and thus the beginning of time in heaven is based on the number and the name of seven, on account of the starry demonstrators. The seven stars as they turned round annually kept pointing, as it were, with the forefinger of the right hand, and describing a circle in the upper and lower heaven.* The number seven naturally suggested a measure by seven, that led to what may be termed *Sevening*, and to the marking and mapping out of the circle in seven corresponding divisions which were assigned to the seven great constellations ; and thus was formed the celestial heptanomis of Egypt in the heavens. . . . When the stellar heptanomis was broken up and divided into four quarters, it was multiplied by four, and the twenty-eight signs took the place of the primary seven constellations, the lunar zodiac of twenty-eight days being the registered result. † . . . In the Chinese arrangement the four sevens are given to four genii that preside over the four cardinal points. . . ." (In Chinese Buddhism and Esotericism the genii are represented by four Dragons— the "Maharajahs" of the Stanzas.) "The seven Northern constellations make up the Black Warrior ; the seven Eastern (Chinese autumn) constitute the White Tiger ; the seven Southern are the Vermilion Bird ; and the seven Western (called Vernal) are the Azure Dragon. Each of these four Spirits presides over its heptanomis during one lunar week. The genetive of the first heptanomis (Typhon of the Seven Stars) now took a lunar character ; . . . in this phase we find the goddess Sefekh, whose name signifies number 7, is the feminine word, or *logos* in place of the mother of Time, who was the earlier *Word*, as goddess of the Seven Stars" ("Typology of Time," Vol. II. p. 313, *Nat. Gen.*).

The author shows that it was the goddess of the Great Bear and mother of Time who was in Egypt from the earliest times the "*Living Word*," and that "Sevekh-Kronus, whose type was the Crocodile-Dragon, the pre-planetary form of Saturn, was called her son and consort ; he was her Word-Logos" (p. 321, Vol. I.).

The above is quite plain, but it was not the knowledge of astronomy only that led the ancients to the process of *Sevening*. The primal cause goes far deeper and will be explained in its place.

The above quotations are no digressions. They are brought forward as showing (*a*) the reason why a full Initiate was called a "Dragon," a "Snake" a "Nâga"; and (*b*) that our septenary division was used by the priests of the earliest dynasties in Egypt, for the same reason and on the same basis as by us. This needs further elucidation, however. As already stated, that which Mr. G. Massey calls the four genii of the four cardinal points ; and the Chinese, the Black Warrior, White Tiger, Ver-

---

* For the same reason the division of the principles in man into seven are thus reckoned, as they describe the same circle in the human higher and lower nature.

† Thus the septenary division is the oldest and preceded the four-fold division. It is the root of archaic classification.

milion Bird, and Azure Dragon, is called in the Secret Books,—the " Four Hidden Dragons of Wisdom " and the " Celestial Nâgas." Now, as shown, the seven-headed or septenary DRAGON-LOGOS had been in course of time split up, so to speak, into *four* heptanomic parts or twenty-eight portions. Each lunar week has a distinct occult character in the lunar month ; each day of the twenty-eight has its special characteristics ; as each of the twelve constellations, whether separately or in combination with other signs, has an occult influence either for good or for evil. This represents the sum of knowledge that men can acquire on this earth ; yet few are those who acquire it, and still fewer are the wise men who get to the root of knowledge symbolized by the great Root Dragon, the spiritual LOGOS of these visible signs. But those who do, receive the name of "Dragons," and they are the "Arhats of the Four Truths of the 28 Faculties," or attributes, and have always been so called.

The Alexandrian Neo-Platonists asserted that to become real *Chaldees* or Magi, one had to master the science or knowledge of the periods of the Seven Rectors of the world, in whom is all wisdom. In " Proclus in *Timœus*," b. i, Jamblichus is credited with another version, which does not however, alter, the meaning. He says that "the Assyrians have not only preserved the records of seven and twenty myriads of years, as Hipparchus says they have, but likewise of the whole apocatastases and periods of the Seven Rulers of the World." The legends of every nation and tribe, whether civilized or savage, point to the once universal belief in the great wisdom and cunning of the Serpents. They are "charmers." They hypnotise the bird with their eye, and man himself, very often, does not feel above their fascinating influence ; therefore the symbol is a most fitting one.

The crocodile is the Egyptian dragon. It was the dual symbol of Heaven and Earth, of Sun and Moon, and was made sacred, in consequence of its amphibious nature, to Osiris and Isis. According to Eusebius, the Egyptians represented the sun in a ship as its pilot, this ship being carried along by a crocodile " to show the motion of the Sun in the moyst (Space)"; (*Prepar. Evang.*, I, 3, c. 3). The crocodile was moreover, the symbol of Egypt herself—the *lower*, as being the more swampy of the two countries. The Alchemists claim another interpretation. They say that the symbol of the sun in the ship on the Ether of Space meant that the hermetic matter is the principle, or basis, of gold, or again the *philosophical* sun ; the water, within which the crocodile is swimming, is that water or matter made liquid ; the ship herself, finally, representing the vessel of nature, in which the sun, or the sulphuric, igneous principle, acts as a pilot : because it is the sun which conducts the work by his action upon the *moist* or *mercury*. The above is only for the Alchemists.

The Serpent became the type and symbol of evil, and of the Devil, only during the middle ages. The early Christians—besides the Ophite Gnostics—had their dual Logos: the Good and the Bad Serpent, the Agathodæmon and the Kakodæmon. This is demonstrated by the writings of Marcus, Valentinus, and many others, and especially in *Pistis Sophia*—certainly a document of the earliest centuries of Christianity. On the marble sarcophagus of a tomb, discovered in 1852 near the Porta Pia, one sees the scene of the adoration of the Magi, " or else," remarks the late C. W. King in " *The Gnostics,*" " the prototype of that scene, the ' Birth of the New Sun.' " The mosaic floor exhibited a curious design which might have represented either *(a)* Isis suckling the babe Harpocrates, or *(b)* the Madonna nursing the infant Jesus. In the smaller sarcophagi that surrounded the larger one, eleven leaden plates rolled like scrolls were found, three of which have been deciphered. The contents of these ought to be regarded as final proof of a much-vexed question, for they show that either the early Christians, up to the VIth Century, were *bonâ fide* pagans, or that dogmatic Christianity was borrowed wholesale, and passed in full into the Christian Church—Sun, Tree, Serpent, Crocodile and all.

" On the first is seen Anubis . . . holding out a scroll ; at his feet are two female busts ; below all are two serpents entwined . . . a corpse swathed up like a mummy. In the second scroll . . . is Anubis, holding out a cross, the " Sign of Life." Under his feet lies the corpse encircled in the numerous folds of a huge serpent, the Agathodæmon, guardian of the deceased. . . . . In the third scroll, Anubis bears on his arm . . . . . the outline of . . a complete Latin cross . . . At the god's foot is a rhomboid, the Egyptian ' Egg of the World,' towards which crawls a serpent coiled into a circle . . . . Under the busts is the letter ω repeated *seven* times in a line, reminding one of the ' names ' . . . Very remarkable also is the line of characters, apparently Palmyrene, upon the legs of the first Anubis. As for the figure of the *serpent,* supposing these talismans to emanate not from the Isiac but the newer Ophite creed, it may well stand for that " True and perfect Serpent," who leads forth the souls of all that put their trust in him out of the Egypt of the body, and through the Red Sea of Death into the Land of Promise, saving them on their way from the Serpents of the Wilderness, that is, from the Rulers of the Stars." (King's " Gnostics," p. 366.)

And this " True and Perfect Serpent " is the seven-lettered God who is now credited with being Jehovah, and Jesus *One with him.* To this Seven-vowelled god the candidate for initiation is sent by Christos, in the *Pistis Sophia,* a work earlier than St. John's *Revelation,* and evidently of the same school. " The (Serpent of the) Seven Thunders uttered these seven vowels," but " Seal up those things which the seven thunders uttered, and write them not," says Revelation. " Do ye seek after these mysteries ? " inquiries Jesus in *Pistis Sophia*. " No mystery is more excellent than they (the seven vowels) : for they shall bring your souls unto the Light of Lights "—*i.e.*, true Wisdom. " Nothing, therefore, is more excellent than the mysteries which ye seek after, saving only *the mystery of the Seven Vowels and their* FORTY AND NINE *Powers*, and the numbers thereof."

In India, it was *the mystery of the Seven* FIRES and their forty-nine fires or aspects, or " the members thereof," just the same.

These seven vowels are represented by the Swastika signs on the crowns of the seven heads of the Serpent of Eternity, in India, among esoteric Buddhists, in Egypt, in Chaldea, etc. etc., and among the Initiates of every other country. It is on the Seven zones of *post mortem* ascent, in the Hermetic writings, that the " mortal " leaves, on each, one of his " Souls " (or Principles) ; until arrived on the plane above all zones he remains as the great Formless Serpent of absolute wisdom—or the Deity itself. The seven-headed serpent has more than one signification in the Arcane teachings. It is the seven-headed *Draco*, each of whose heads is a star of the Lesser Bear ; but it was also, and pre-eminently, the Serpent of Darkness (*i.e.*, inconceivable and incomprehensible) whose seven heads were the seven *Logoi*, the reflections of the one and first manifested Light—the universal LOGOS.

----

§ XI.

DEMON EST DEUS INVERSUS.

THIS symbolical sentence, in its many-sided forms, is certainly most dangerous and iconoclastic in the face of all the dualistic later religions or rather theologies—and especially so in the light of Christianity. Yet it is neither just nor correct to say that it is Christianity which has conceived and brought forth Satan. As an " adversary," the opposing Power required by the equilibrium and harmony of things in Nature—like Shadow to throw off still brighter the Light, like Night to bring into greater *relief* the Day, and like cold to make one appreciate the more the comfort of heat—SATAN has ever existed. Homogeneity is one and indivisible. But if the homogeneous One and Absolute is no mere figure of speech, and if heterogeneity in its dualistic aspect, is its offspring—its bifurcous shadow or reflection— then even that divine Homogeneity must contain in itself the essence of both good and evil. If " God " is Absolute, Infinite, and the Universal Root of all and everything in Nature and its universe, whence comes Evil or D'Evil if not from the same " Golden Womb " of the absolute ? Thus we are forced either to accept the emanation of good and evil, of Agathodæmon and Kakodæmon as offshoots from the same trunk of the Tree of Being, or to resign ourselves to the absurdity of believing in two eternal Absolutes !

Having to trace the origin of the idea to the very beginnings of human mind, it is but just, meanwhile, to give his due even to the proverbial devil. Antiquity knew of no isolated, thoroughly and absolutely bad " god of evil." Pagan thought represented good and evil as twin brothers, born from the same mother—Nature ; so soon as that thought ceased to be Archaic, Wisdom too became Philosophy. In the beginning the symbols of good and evil were mere abstractions, Light and Darkness ; then their types became chosen among the most natural and ever-recurrent periodical Cosmic phenomena—the Day and the Night, or the Sun and Moon. Then the Hosts of the Solar and Lunar deities were made to represent them, and the Dragon of Darkness was contrasted with the Dragon of Light (See *Stanzas* V., VII. of Book I.) The Host of Satan is a Son of God, no less than the Host of the B'ni Alhim, these children of God coming to " present themselves before the Lord," their father (see *Job ii.*). " The Sons of God " become the " Fallen Angels " only after perceiving that the daughters of men *were fair*, (*Genesis vi.*) In the Indian philosophy, the *Suras* are among the earliest and the brightest gods, and become *Asuras* only when dethroned by Brahminical fancy. Satan never assumed an anthropo-morphic, individualized shape, until the creation by man, of a " one *living* personal god," had been accomplished; and then merely as a matter of prime necessity. A screen was needed ; a scape-goat to explain the cruelty, blunders, and but too-evident injustice, perpetrated by him for whom absolute perfection, mercy, and goodness were claimed. This was the first Karmic effect of abandoning a philoso-phical and logical Pantheism, to build, as a prop for lazy man, " a merciful father in Heaven," whose daily and hourly actions as *Natura naturans*, the " comely mother but stone cold," belie the assumption. This led to the primal twins, Osiris-Typhon, Ormazd-Ahriman, and finally Cain-Abel and the *tutti-quanti* of contraries.

Having commenced by being synonymous with Nature, " God," the Creator, ended by being made its author. Pascal settles the difficulty very cunningly : " Nature has perfections, in order to show that she is the image of God : and defects, in order to show that she is *only* his image," he says.

The further back one recedes into the darkness of the prehistoric ages, the more philosophical does the prototypic figure of the later Satan appear. The first " Adversary" in individual human form that one meets with in old Purânic literature is one of her greatest Rishis and Yogis—Nârada, surnamed the " Strife-maker."

And he is a Brahmâputra, a son of Brahmâ, the male. But of him later on. Who the great " Deceiver" really is, one can ascertain by searching for him *with open eyes* and an unprejudiced mind, in every old cosmogony and Scripture.

It is the anthropomorphised *Demiurge*, the Creator of Heaven and Earth, when separated from the collective Hosts of his fellow-Creators, whom, so to speak, he represents and synthesizes. It is *now* the God of *theologies*. " The thought is father to the wish." Once upon a time, a philosophical symbol left to perverse human fancy; afterwards fashioned into a fiendish, deceiving, cunning, and jealous God.

Dragons and other fallen angels being described in other parts of this work, a few words upon the much-slandered Satan will be sufficient. That which the student will do well to remember is that, with every people except the Christian nations, the Devil is to this day no worse an entity than the opposite aspect in the dual nature of the so-called Creator. This is only natural. One cannot claim God as the synthesis of the whole Universe, as Omnipresent and Omniscient and Infinite, and then divorce him from evil. As there is far more evil than good in the world, it follows on logical grounds that either God must include evil, or stand as the direct cause of it, or else surrender his claims to absoluteness. The ancients understood this so well that their philosophers —now followed by the Kabalists—defined evil as the lining of God or Good : *Demon est Deus inversus*, being a very old adage. Indeed, evil is but an antagonizing blind force in nature ; it is *reaction, opposition*, and *contrast*,—evil for some, good for others. There is no *malum in se :* only the shadow of light, without which light could have no existence, even in our perceptions. If evil disappeared, good would disappear along with it from Earth. The " Old Dragon " was pure spirit before he became matter, *passive* before he became *active*. In the Syro-Chaldean magic both Ophis and Ophiomorphos are joined in the Zodiac, at the sign of the Androgyne *Virgo-Scorpio*. Before its fall on earth the " Serpent " was *Ophis-Christos*, and after its fall it became Ophiomorphos-CHRESTOS. Everywhere the speculations of the Kabalists treat of Evil as a FORCE, which is antagonistic, but at the same time essential, to Good, as giving it vitality and existence, which it could never have otherwise. There would be no *life* possible (in the *Mayavic* sense) without *Death*, nor regeneration and reconstruction without destruction. Plants would perish in eternal sunlight, and so would man, who would become an automaton without the exercise of his free will and aspirations after that sunlight, which would lose its being and value for him had he nothing but light. Good is infinite and eternal only in the eternally concealed from us, and this is why we imagine it eternal. On the manifested planes, one equilibrates the other. Few are those theists and believers in a personal God, who do not make of Satan the shadow of God ; or who, confounding both, do not believe they have a right to pray to that idol asking its help and protection for the exercise and impunity of their evil and cruel deeds. " Lead us not into Temptation " is addressed daily to " our Father, which art in Heaven," and not to the Devil, by millions of human Christian hearts. They do so, repeating the very words put in the mouth of their Saviour, and do not give one thought to the fact that their meaning is contradicted point blank by James "the brother of the Lord." " Let no man say when he is tempted, I am tempted of God : for God cannot be tempted with evil, neither tempteth he any man."—(The Gen. Ep. of James, i, 13). Why, then, say that it is the Devil who tempts us, when the Church teaches us *on the authority of Christ* that it is God who does so ? Open any pious volume in which the word " temptation " is defined in its theological sense, and forthwith you find two definitions: (1) " Those afflictions and troubles *whereby God tries his people ;*" (2) Those means and enticements which the Devil makes use of to *ensnare* and allure mankind. (St. James i., 2, 12, and Mat. vi., 13.) If accepted literally, the two teachings of Christ and James contradict each other, and what dogma can reconcile the two if the occult meaning is rejected ?

Between the alternative allurements, wise will be that philosopher who will be able to decide where God disappears to make room for the Devil! Therefore when we read that " the Devil is a liar and the father of it," *i.e.*, INCARNATE LIE, and are told in the same breath that Satan—the Devil—was a son of God and the most beautiful of his archangels, rather than believe that Father and Son are a gigantic, per-sonified and eternal LIE, we prefer to turn to Pantheism and to Pagan philosophy for information.

Once that the key to Genesis is in our hands, it is the scientific and symbolical Kabala which unveils the secret. The great Serpent of the Garden of Eden and the " Lord God " are identical, and so are Jehovah and Cain ONE—that Cain who is referred to in theology as the " murderer " and the LIAR to God ! Jehovah tempts the King of Israel to number the people, and Satan tempts him to do the same in another place. Jehovah turns into the fiery serpents to bite those he is dis-pleased with ; and Jehovah informs the brazen serpent that heals them.

These short, and seemingly contradictory, statements in the Old Testament (contradictory because the two Powers are separated instead of being regarded as the two faces of one and the same thing) are the echoes—distorted out of recognition by exotericism and theology—of the universal and philosophical dogmas in nature, so well understood by the primitive Sages. We find the same groundwork in several personifications in the Purânas, only far more ample and philosophically suggestive.

Thus Pulâstya, a "Son of God"—one of the first progeny—is made the progenitor of Demons, the Râkshasas, the tempters and the Devourers of men. *Pisâcha* (female Demon) is a daughter of Daksha, a "Son of God" too, and a God, and the mother of all the Pisâchas (*Padma Purâna*). The Demons, so called in the Purânas, are very extraordinary devils when judged from the standpoint of European and orthodox views about these creatures, since all of them—Dânavas, Daityas, Pisâchas, and the Râkshasas—are represented as extremely pious, following the precepts of the Vedas, some of them even being great Yogis. But they oppose the clergy and Ritualism, sacrifices and forms—just what the full-blown Yogins do to this day in India—and are no less respected for it, though they are allowed to follow neither caste nor ritual; hence all those Purânic giants and Titans are called Devils. The Missionaries, ever on the watch to show, if they can, the Hindu traditions no better than *a reflection* of the Jewish Bible, have evolved a whole romance on the alleged identity of Pulâstya with Cain, and of the Râkshasas with the Cainites, "the accursed," the cause of the *Noachian* Deluge. (See the work of Abbé Gorresio, who "etymologises" Pulâstya's name as meaning the "rejected," hence Cain, if you please). Pulâstya dwells in *Kedara*, he says, which means a "dug-up place," a *mine*, and Cain is shown in tradition and the Bible as the first worker in metals and a miner thereof!

While it is very probable that the *Gibborim* (the giants) of the Bible are the Râkshasas of the Hindus, it is still more certain that both are Atlanteans, and belong to the submerged races. However it may be, no Satan could be more persistent in slandering his enemy, or more spiteful in his hatred, than the Christian theologians are in cursing him as the father of every evil. Compare their vituperations and opinions given about the Devil with the philosophical views of the Purânic sages and their Christ-like mansuetude. When Parâsara, whose father was devoured by a Râkshasa, was preparing himself to destroy (magically) the whole race, his grandsire, Vasishta, says a few extremely suggestive words to him. He shows the irate Sage, on his own confession, that there is Evil and *Karma*, but no "evil spirits." "Let thy wrath be appeased," he says. "The Râkshasas are not culpable; thy father's death *was the work of Karma*. Anger is the passion of fools; it becometh not a wise man. *By whom, it may be asked, is any one killed? Every man reaps the consequences of his own acts.* Anger, my son, is the destruction of all that man obtains . . . and prevents the attainment of emancipation. The sages shun wrath. Be not thou, my child, subject to its influence. Let not those *unoffending* spirits of darkness be consumed; let thy sacrifice cease. Mercy is the might of the righteous" (*Vishnu Purâna*, Book i., ch. i.). Thus, every such " sacrifice " or prayer to God for help is *no better than an act of black magic.* That which Pârasara prayed for, was the destruction of the Spirits of Darkness, for his personal revenge. He is called a *Pagan,* and the Christians have doomed him as such, to eternal hell. Yet, in what respect is the prayer of sovereigns and generals, who pray before every battle for the destruction of their enemy, any better ? Such a prayer is in every case *black magic* of the worst kind, concealed like a demon " Mr. Hyde " under a sanctimonious " Dr. Jekyll."

In human nature, evil denotes only the polarity of matter and Spirit, a struggle for life between the two manifested Principles in Space and Time, which principles are one *per se,* inasmuch they are rooted in the Absolute. In Kosmos, the equilibrium must be preserved. The operations of the two contraries produce harmony, like the centripetal and centrifugal forces, which are necessary to each other— mutually inter-dependent—"in order that both should live." If one is arrested, the action of the other will become immediately self-destructive.

Since the personification called Satan has been amply analyzed from its triple aspect—in the Old Testament, Christian theology and the ancient Gentile attitude of thought—those who would learn more of it are referred to Vol. II. of Isis UNVEILED, chap. x. See also several sections in Book II., Part II. of this work. The present subject is touched upon and fresh explanations attempted for a very good reason. Before we can approach the evolution of physical and *divine* man, we have first to master the idea of cyclic evolution, to acquaint ourselves with the philosophies and beliefs of the four races which preceded our present race, to learn what were the ideas of those Titans and giants—giants, verily, mentally as well as physically. The whole of antiquity was imbued with that philosophy which teaches the involution of spirit into matter, the progressive, downward cyclic descent, or active, self-conscious evolution. The Alexandrian Gnostics have sufficiently divulged the secret of initiations, and their records are full of " the sliding down of Æons" in their double qualification of Angelic Beings and Periods : the one the natural evolution of the other. On the other hand, Oriental traditions on both sides of the " black water"—the oceans that separate the two *Easts*—are as full of allegories about the downfall of Pleroma, of that of the gods and Devas. One and all, they allegorized and explained the FALL as *the desire to learn and acquire knowledge*—to KNOW. This is the natural sequence of mental evolution, the spiritual becoming transmuted into the material or physical. The same law of descent into materiality and re-ascent into spirituality asserted itself during the Christian era, the reaction having stopped only just now, in our own special *sub-race*.

That which, perhaps ten millenniums ago, was allegorized in *Pymander* in a triune character of interpretation, meant as a record of an astronomical, anthropological, and even alchemical fact, namely, the allegory of the seven rectors breaking through the seven circles of fire, was dwarfed into one material and anthropomorphic interpretation—the rebellion and *Fall of the Angels*. The multivocal, profoundly philosophical narrative, under its poetical form of the " Marriage of Heaven with Earth," the love of nature for Divine form and the " Heavenly man," enraptured with his own beauty mirrored in nature—*i.e.*, Spirit attracted into matter—has now become, under theological handling : " the seven Rectors disobeying Jehovah, self admiration generating Satanic Pride, followed by their FALL, Jehovah permitting no worship to be lost save upon himself." In short, the beautiful Planet-Angels, the glorious cyclic æons of the ancients, became henceforward synthesized in their most orthodox shape in Samael, the chief of the Demons in the Talmud, " That great serpent with *twelve wings* that draws down after himself, in his Fall, the solar system, or the Titans." But *Schemal*, the *alter ego* and the Sabean type of Samael, meant, in his philosophical and esoteric aspect, the " year " in its astrological evil aspect, its twelve months or wings of unavoidable evils, in nature ; and in esoteric theogony (see Chwolson in NABATHEAN AGRICULTURE, Vol. II., p. 217), both Schemal and Samael represented a particular divinity. With the Kabalists they are "the Spirit of the Earth," the personal god that governs it, identical *de facto* with Jehavoh. For the Talmudists admit themselves that SAMAEL is a god-name of one of the seven Elohim. The Kabalists, moreover, show the two, Schemal and Samael, as a symbolical form of Saturn, CHRONOS, the twelve wings standing for the 12 months, and the symbol in its collectivity representing *a racial cycle*. Jehovah and Saturn are also glyphically identical.

This leads in its turn to a very curious deduction from a Roman Catholic dogma. Many renowned writers belonging to the Latin Church admit that a difference exists, and should be made, between the Uranian Titans, the antediluvian giants (also Titans), and those post-diluvian giants in whom they (the Roman Catholics) *will* see the descendants of the mythical Ham. In clearer words, there is a difference to be made between the Cosmic, *primordial* opposing Forces—guided by cyclic law— the Atlantean human giants, and the post-diluvian great adepts, whether of the *right* or the *left* hand. At the same time they show that Michäel, "the *generalissimus* of the fighting Celestial Host, the *bodyguard of Jehovah*," as it would seem (see de Mirville) is also a Titan, only with the adjective of "divine" before the cognomen. Thus those "Uranides" who are called everywhere "divine Titans," and who, having rebelled against Kronos (Saturn), are therefore also shown to be the enemies of Samäel (an Elohim, also and synonymous with Jehovah in his collectivity), are identical with Michäel and his host. In short, the *rôles* are reversed, all the combatants are confused, and no student is able to distinguish clearly which is which. Esoteric explanation may, however, bring some order into this confusion, in which Jehovah becomes Saturn, and Michäel and his army, Satan and the rebellious angels, owing to the indiscreet endeavours of the too faithful zealots to see in every pagan god a devil. The true meaning is far more philosophical, and the legend of the first " Fall " (of the angels) assumes a scientific colouring when correctly understood.

Kronos stands for endless (hence immovable) Duration, without beginning, without an end, beyond divided Time and beyond Space. Those " Angels," genii, or Devas, who were born *to act in space and time, i.e.*, to break through the *seven circles of the superspiritual* planes into the phenomenal, or circumscribed, super-terrestrial regions, are said allegorically to *have rebelled* against Kronos and fought the (then) one living and highest God. In his turn, when Kronos is represented as mutilating Uranus, his father, the meaning of this mutilation is very simple : Absolute Time is made to become the finite and the conditioned ; a portion is robbed from the whole, thus showing that Saturn, the father of the gods, has been transformed from *Eternal Duration* into a limited Period. Chronos cuts down with his scythe even the longest and (to us) seemingly endless cycles, yet, for all that, limited in Eternity, and puts down with the same scythe the mightiest rebels. Aye, not one will escape the scythe of Time ! Praise the god or gods, or flout, one or both, and that scythe will not be made to tremble one millionth of a second in its ascending or descending course,

The Titans of Hesiod's *Theogony* were copied in Greece from the *Suras* and *Asuras* of India. These Hesiodic Titans, the *Uranides*, numbered once upon a time as only six, have been recently discovered to be *seven*—the seventh being called Phoreg—in an old fragment relating to the Greek myth. Thus their identity with the Seven rectors is fully demonstrated. The origin of the " War in Heaven " and the FALL has, in our mind, to be traced unavoidably to India, and perhaps far earlier than the Purânic accounts thereof. For TARAMAYA was in a later age, and there are three accounts, each of a distinct war, to be traced in almost every Cosmogony.

The first war happened in the night of time, between the gods the (A)-*suras*, and lasted for the period of one "divine year."* On this occasion the deities were defeated by the Daityas, under the leadership of Hrada. After that, owing to a device of Vishnu, to whom the conquered gods applied for help, the latter defeated the Asuras. In the Vishnu Purâna no interval is found between the two wars. In the Esoteric Doctrine, one war takes place before the building of the Solar system; another, on earth, at the "creation" of man; and a third "war" is mentioned as taking place at the close of the 4th Race, between its adepts and those of the 5th Race, *i.e.*, between the Initiates of the "Sacred Island" and the Sorcerers of Atlantis. We shall notice the first contest, as recounted by Parâsara, while trying to separate the two accounts, purposely blended together. It is there stated that as the Daityas and Asuras were engaged in the duties of their respective orders (*Varna*) and followed the paths prescribed by holy writ, practising also religious penance (a queer employment for *demons* if they are *identical with our devils*, as it is claimed)—it was impossible for the gods to destroy them. The prayers addressed by the gods to Vishnu are curious as showing the ideas involved in an anthropomorphic deity. Having, after their defeat, "fled to the Northern shore of the Milky Ocean (Atlantic Ocean),‡ the discomfited gods address many supplications "to the first

---

* One "Day of Brahmâ" lasting 4,320,000,000 years—multiply this by 365! The Asuras here (no-gods, but demons) are still *Suras*, gods higher in hierarchy than such secondary gods as are not even mentioned in the Vedas. The duration of the war shows its significance, and that they are only the personified Cosmic powers. It is evidently for sectarian purposes and out of *odium theologicum* that the illusive form assumed by Vishnu *Mayamoha*, was attributed in later rearrangements of old texts to Buddha and the Daityas, in the *Vishnu Purâna*, unless it was a fancy of Wilson himself. He also fancied he found an allusion to Buddhism in Bhagavatgita, whereas, as proved by K. T. Telang, he had only confused the Buddhists and the older Chârvâka materialists. The version exists nowhere in other Purânas if the inference does, as Professor Wilson claims, in the "Vishnu Purâna"; the translation of which, especially of Book iii., ch. xviii., where the reverend Orientalist arbitrarily introduces Buddha, and shows him teaching Buddhism to Daityas—led to another "great war" between himself and Col. Vans Kennedy. The latter charged him publicly with wilfully distorting Purânic texts. "I affirm," wrote the Colonel at Bombay, in 1840, "that the Purânas do not contain what Professor Wilson has stated is contained in them . . . until such passages are produced I may be allowed to repeat my former conclusions, that Professor Wilson's opinion, that the Purânas as now extant are compilations made between the eighth and seventeenth centuries (A.D.!) rests solely *on gratuitous assumptions and unfounded assertions*, and that his reasoning in support of it is either futile, fallacious, contradictory, or improbable." (See *Vishnu Purâna*, trans. by Wilson, edit. by Fitzedward Hall, Vol. V., Appendix.)

‡ This statement belongs to the *third* War, since the terrestrial continents, seas and rivers are mentioned in connection with it.

of beings, the divine Vishnu," and among others this one: "Glory to thee, who art one with the Saints, whose perfect nature is ever blessed. . . . Glory to thee, *who art one with the Serpent-race, double-tongued, impetuous, cruel, insatiate of enjoyment* and abounding with wealth. . . . Glory to thee, ... O Lord, *who hast neither colour nor extension,* nor size (*ghana*), *nor any predicable qualities,* and whose essence (*rupa*), purest of the pure is appreciable only by holy *Paramarshi* (greatest of sages or Rishis). We bow to thee, in the nature of Brahma uncreated, undecaying (*avyaya*), who *art in our bodies* and *in all other bodies, and in all living creatures,* and beside whom nothing exists. We glorify that Vasudeva, the lord of all, who is without soil, the seed of all things, exempt from dissolution, unborn, eternal; being in essence *Paramapadātmavat* (beyond the condition of spirit) and in essence and substance (*rupa*), the whole of this (Universe)." (Book III., ch. xvii., *Vish. Purāna.*)

The above is quoted as an illustration of the vast field offered by the Purânas to adverse and erroneous criticism, by every European bigot who forms an estimate of an alien religion on mere external evidence. Any man accustomed to subject what he reads to thoughtful analysis, will see at a glance the incongruity of addressing the accepted "Unknowable," the formless, and attributeless ABSOLUTE, such as the Vedantins define BRAHMA, as being "one with the serpent-race, double-tongued, cruel and insatiable," thus associating the abstract with the concrete, and bestowing adjectives on that which is freed from any limitations, and conditionless. Even Dr. Wilson, who, after living surrounded by Brahmins and Pundits in India for so many years, ought to have known better—even that scholar lost no opportunity to criticize the Hindu Scriptures on this account. Thus, he exclaims:—*

"The Purânas constantly teach incompatible doctrines! According to this passage, the Supreme being is not the inert cause of creation only, but exercises the functions of an active providence. The Commentator quotes a text of the Veda in support of this view : ' Universal Soul entering into men, governs their conduct.' Incongruities, however, are as frequent in the Vedas as in the Purânas. . . . ."

Less frequent, in sober truth, than in the Mosaic Bible. But prejudice is great in the hearts of our Orientalists—especially in those of "reverend" scholars. UNIVERSAL SOUL is *not* the inert Cause of Creation or (Para) Brahma, but simply that which we call the sixth principle of *intellectual* Kosmos, on the manifested plane of being. It is Mahat, or *Mahabuddhi,* the great Soul, the vehicle of Spirit, the first primeval reflection of the formless CAUSE, and that which is even *beyond* SPÍRIT.

---

* In Book I., chap. xvii., narrating the story of Prahlada—the Son of Hiranyaka-sipu, the Puranic *Satan,* the great enemy of Vishnu, and the King of the three worlds —into whose heart Vishnu entered.

So much for Professor Wilson's uncalled-for fling. As for the apparently incongruous appeal to Vishnu by the defeated gods, the explanation is there, in the text of Vishnu Purâna, if Orientalists would only notice it.* There is Vishnu, as Brahmâ, and Vishnu *in his two aspects*, philosophy teaches. There is but one Brahma, "essentially *prakriti* and *Spirit*," &c.

Therefore, it is not Vishnu—"the inert cause of creation"—which exercised the functions of an *active* Providence, but the Universal Soul, that which E. Lévi calls *Astral Light* in its material aspect. And this "Soul" is, in its dual aspect of spirit and matter, the true anthropomorphic God of the Theists; as this God is a *personification* of that Universal Creative Agent, pure and impure both, owing to its manifested condition and differentiation in this Mayavic World—*God* and *Devil*—truly. But Dr. Wilson failed to see how Vishnu, in this character, closely resembles the Lord God of Israel, "especially in his policy of deception, temptation, and cunning."

In the Vishnu Purana this is made as plain as can be. For it is said there, that "at the conclusion of their prayers (*stotra*) the gods beheld the Sovereign Deity Hari (Vishnu) armed with the conch, the discus, and the mace, *riding on Garuda*. ." Now "Garuda" is the manvantaric *cycle*, as will be shown in its place. Vishnu, therefore, is the deity *in space and time*; the peculiar God of the Vaishnavas (a *tribal* or *racial* God, as they are called in esoteric philosophy): *i.e.*, one of the many Dhyanis or Gods, or Elohim, one of whom was generally chosen for some special reasons by a nation or a tribe, and thus became gradually a "God *above all* Gods" (2 Chronicles ii. 5,) the "highest God" as Jehovah, Osiris, Bel, or any other of the *Seven* Regents.

"The tree is known by its fruit,"—the nature of a God by his actions. The latter, we have either to judge by the dead-letter narratives, or to accept allegorically. If we compare the two—Vishnu, as the defender and champion of the defeated gods; and Jehovah, the defender and champion of the "chosen" people, so called by antiphrasis, no doubt, as it is the Jews who had *chosen* that "jealous" God—we shall find that both use deceit and cunning. They do so on the principle of "the end justifying the means," in order to have the best of their

* This ignorance is truly and beautifully expressed in the praise of the Yogins to Brahmâ, "the upholder of the earth" (in Book I., chap. iv. of V. P.), when they say, "Those who have not practised devotion conceive erroneously of the nature of the world. The ignorant who do not perceive that this Universe is of the nature of wisdom, and judge of it as an object of perception only, are lost in the ocean of spiritual ignorance. But they who know true wisdom, and whose minds are pure, behold this whole world *as one with divine knowledge*, as one with thee, O God! Be favourable, O universal Spirit!"

respective opponents and foes—the demons. Thus while (according to the Kabalists) Jehovah assumes the shape of the tempting Serpent in the Garden of Eden ; sends Satan with a special mission to tempt Job ; and harasses and wearies Pharaoh with Saraï, Abraham's wife, and " *hardens* " his heart against Moses, lest there should be no opportunity for *plaguing* his victims "with great plagues" (*Genesis* xii., *Exodus*)— Vishnu is made in *his* Purâna to resort to a trick no less unworthy of any respectable god.

"Have compassion upon us, O Lord, and protect us, who have come to thee for succour from the Daityas (demons)!" pray the defeated Gods. "They have seized upon the three worlds, and appropriated the offerings which are our portion, *taking care not to transgress the precepts of the Veda*. Although *we, as well as they, are parts of thee.** . . . . engaged as they are in the paths prescribed by the holy writ . . . . it is impossible for us to destroy them. Do thou, whose wisdom is immeasurable *(Ameyâtman)* instruct us *in some* device by which we may be able to exterminate the enemies of the gods !"

"When the mighty Vishnu heard their request, he emitted from his body an *illusory* form (*Mâyâmoha*, " the deluder by illusion ") which he gave to the Gods and thus spake : " This *Mâyâmoha* shall *wholly beguile the Daityas*, so that being led astray from the path of the Vedas, they may be put to death. . . . Go then and fear not. Let this delusive vision precede you. It shall this day be of great service unto you, O Gods !"

"After this, the great Delusion, *Mâyâmoha*, descending to earth, beheld the Daityas engaged in ascetic penances, and approaching them, in the semblance of a *Digambara* (naked mendicant) with his head shaven . . . he thus addressed them, in gentle accents: "Ho, lords of the Daitya race, wherefore is it that you practise these acts of penances ? " etc., etc. (Book II., xviii.).

Finally the Daityas were seduced by the wily talk of *Mahâmoha*, as Eve was seduced by the advice of the Serpent. They became apostates to the Vedas. As Dr. Muir translates the passage :—

"The great Deceiver, practising illusion, next beguiled other Daityas, by means of many other sorts of heresy. In a very short time, these Asuras (-Daityas) deluded by the Deceiver (who was Vishnu) abandoned the entire system founded on the ordinances of the triple Veda. Some reviled the Vedas, others the Gods, others the ceremonial of sacrifice, and others the Brahmans. This, they exclaimed, is a doctrine which will not bear discussion. The slaughter of animals in sacrifice is not conducive to religious merit. To say that oblations of butter consumed in the fire produce any future reward, is the assertion of a child. . . . If it be a fact that a beast slain in sacrifice is exalted to heaven, why does not the worshipper slaughter his own father ? . . . . Infallible utterances do not, great Asuras, fall from the skies ; it is only assertions founded on reasoning that are accepted by me and by other intelligent persons like yourselves ! Thus by numerous methods the Daityas were unsettled by the great Deceiver (*Reason*). . . . When

---

* " There was a day when the *Sons of God* came before the Lord, and Satan came *with his brothers*, also before the Lord " (*Job* ii., Abyss., *Ethiopic* text).

they had entered on the path of error, the gods mustered all their energies and approached to battle. Then followed a combat between the gods and the Asuras; and the latter, who had abandoned the right road, were smitten by the former. In previous times they had been defended by the armour of righteousness which they bore, but when that had been destroyed they, also, perished." (*Journal of the Royal Asiat. Society*, Vol. XIX., p. 302.)

Whatever may be thought of Hindus, no enemy of theirs can regard them as fools. A people whose holy men and sages have left to the world the greatest and most sublime philosophies that ever emanated from the minds of men, must have known the difference between right and wrong. Even a savage can discern white from black, good from bad, and deceit from sincerity and truthfulness. Those who had narrated this event in the biography of their god, must have seen that in this case it was that God who was the arch-Deceiver, and the Daityas, who " never transgressed the precepts of the Vedas," who had the sunny side in the transaction, and who were the true " Gods." Thence there must have been, and *there is* a secret meaning hidden under this allegory. In no class of Society, in no nation, are deceit and craft considered as *Divine* virtues—except perhaps in the clerical classes of theologians and modern Jesuitism.

The Vishnu Purâna,* like all other works of this kind, has passed at a later period into the hands of the temple-Brahmins, and the old MSS. have, no doubt, been once more tampered with by sectarians. But there was a time when the Purânas were esoteric works, and so they are still for the Initiates who can read them with the key that is in their possession.

Whether the Brahmin Initiates will ever give out the full meaning of these allegories, is a question with which the writer is not concerned. The present object is to show that, while honouring the *creative Powers* in their multiple forms, no philosopher could, or ever has, accepted the allegory for the true Spirit, except, perhaps, some philosophers belonging to the present " superior and civilized " Christian races. For, as shown, Jehovah is not one whit the superior of Vishnu on the plane of ethics. This is why the Occultists and even some Kabalists, whether they regard or not those creative Forces *as living and conscious Entities*— and one does not see why they should not be so accepted—will never confuse the CAUSE with the effect, and accept the Spirit of the Earth for Parabrahm or Ain-Soph. At all events they know well the true nature of what was called Father-Æther by the Greeks, Jupiter-Titan, etc., etc. They know that the soul of the ASTRAL LIGHT is divine, and

---

* Wilson's opinion that the " Vishnu Purâna " is a production *of our era*, and that in its present form it is not earlier than between the VIIIth and the XVIIth (! !) century, is absurd beyond noticing.

its body (the light-waves on the lower planes) infernal. This Light is symbolized by the " Magic Head " in the *Zohar*, the double Face on the double Pyramid : the black pyramid rising against a pure white ground, with *a white head and face within its black triangle;* the white pyramid, inverted—the reflection of the first in the dark waters, showing the *black reflection of the white face.* . . . .

This is the " Astral Light," or DEMON EST DEUS INVERSUS.

§ XII.
THE THEOGONY OF THE CREATIVE GODS.

To thoroughly comprehend the idea underlying every ancient cosmology necessitates the study, in a comparative analysis, of all the great religions of antiquity; as it is only by this method that the root idea will be made plain. Exact science—could the latter soar so high, while tracing the operations of nature to their ultimate and original sources—would call this idea the hierarchy of Forces. The original, transcendental and philosophical conception was one. But as systems began to reflect with every age more and more the idiosyncrasies of nations; and as the latter, after separating, settled into distinct groups, each evolving along its own national or tribal groove, the main idea gradually became veiled with the overgrowth of human fancy. While in some countries the FORCES, or rather the intelligent Powers of nature, received divine honours they were hardly entitled to, in others—as now in Europe and the *civilized* lands—the very thought of any such Force being endowed with intelligence seems absurd, and is proclaimed *unscientific.* Therefore one finds relief in such statements as are found in the *Introduction* to "Asgard and the Gods : Tales and Traditions of our Northern Ancestors," by W. S. W. Anson. The author remarks, on p. 3 : " Although in Central Asia, or on the banks of the Indus, in the land of the Pyramids, and in the Greek and Italian peninsulas, and even in the North, whither Kelts, Teutons and Slavs wandered, the religious conceptions of the people have taken different forms, *yet their common origin* is still perceptible. We point out this connection between the stories of the gods, and the deep thought contained in them, and their importance, in order that the reader may see that *it is not a magic world of erratic fancy* which opens out before him, but that . . . *Life and nature* formed the basis of the existence and action of these divinities." And though it is impossible for any Occultist or student of Eastern Esotericism to concur in the strange idea that " the religious conceptions of the most famous nations of antiquity are connected with the beginnings of civilization amongst the Germanic races," he is yet glad to find such truths expressed as that : " These fairy tales are not senseless stories written for the amusement of the idle ; they embody the profound religion of our forefathers . . .''

Precisely so.   Not only their religion, but likewise their History. For a myth, in Greek μῦθος, means oral tradition, passed from mouth to mouth from one generation to the other; and even in the modern etymology the term stands for a *fabulous* statement conveying some important truth ; a tale of some extraordinary personage whose biography has become overgrown, owing to the veneration of successive generations, with rich popular fancy, but which is no *wholesale* fable. Like our ancestors, the primitive Aryans, we believe firmly in the personality and intelligence of more than one phenomenon-producing Force in nature.

As time rolled on, the archaic teaching grew dimmer ; and those nations more or less lost sight of the highest and One principle of all things, and began to transfer the abstract attributes of the " causeless cause" to the caused effects—become in their turn causative—the creative Powers of the Universe : the great nations, out of the fear of profaning the IDEA, the smaller, because they either failed to grasp it or lacked the power of philosophic conception needed to preserve it in all its immaculate purity.   But one and all, with the exception of the latest Aryans, now become Europeans and Christians, show this veneration in their Cosmogonies.   As Thomas Taylor,* the most intuitional of all the translators of Greek Fragments, shows, no nation has ever conceived the One principle as the immediate creator of the visible Universe, for no sane man would credit a planner and architect with having built the edifice he admires with his own hands.   On the testimony of Damascius (Περὶ 'αρχῶν) they referred to it as "the Unknown DARKNESS."   The Babylonians passed over this principle in silence : " To that god," says Porphyry, in Περὶ ἀποχῆς ἐμψυχῶν, " who is above all things, neither external speech ought to be addressed, nor yet that which is inward. . . . ." Hesiod begins his theogony with : " Chaos of all things was the first produced,"† thus allowing the inference that its cause or producer must be passed over in reverential silence.   Homer in his poems ascends no higher than *Night*, whom he represents Zeus as reverencing.   According to all the ancient theologists, and to the doctrines of Pythagoras and Plato, Zeus, or the

---

* See " Magazine " for April, 1797.

† Ἤτοι μεν πρώτιστα χάος γένετ' ; γένετο being considered in antiquity as meaning " was *generated* " and not simply *was*. (*See* " *Taylor's Introd. to the Parmenides of Plato,*" p 260.

immediate artificer of the universe, *is not the highest god;* any more than Sir Christopher Wren in his physical, human aspect is the MIND in him which produced his great works of art. Homer, therefore, is not only silent with respect to the first principle, but likewise with respect to those two principles immediately posterior to the first, the *Æther* and *Chaos* of Orpheus and Hesiod, and the *bound* and infinity of Pythagoras and Plato.* . . . . Proclus says of this highest principle that it is. . . . "the Unity of Unities, and beyond the first adyte. . . . . more ineffable than all silence, and more occult than all Essence. . . . . concealed amidst the intelligible gods." (*Ibid.*)

To what was written by Thomas Taylor in 1797--namely, that the "Jews appear to have ascended no higher. . . . than the *immediate* artificer of the universe;" as "Moses introduces a darkness on the face of the deep, without even insinuating that there was any cause of its existence,"† one might add something more. Never have the Jews in their Bible (a purely esoteric, symbolical work) degraded so profoundly their metaphorical deity as have the Christians, by accepting Jehovah as their one living yet *personal* God.

This first, or rather ONE, principle was called "the circle of Heaven," symbolized by the hierogram of a point within a circle or equilateral triangle, the point being the LOGOS. Thus, in the Rig Veda, wherein Brahmâ is not even named, Cosmogony is preluded with the *Hiranyagharba*, "the Golden Egg," and Prajâpati (Brahmâ later on), from whom emanate all the hierarchies of "Creators." The Monad, or point, is the original and is the unit from which follows the entire numeral system. This Point is the First Cause, but THAT from which it emanates, or of which, rather, it is the expression, the Logos, is passed over in silence. In its turn, the universal symbol, the *point within the circle,* was not yet the Architect, but the cause of that Architect ; and the latter stood to it in precisely the same relation as the point itself stood to the *circumference* of the Circle, which cannot be defined, according to Hermes Trismegistus. Porphyry shows that the Monad and the Duad of Pythagoras are identical with Plato's *infinite* and *finite* in "Philebus" —or what Plato calls the ἄπειρον and πέρας. It is the latter only (the mother) which is substantial, the former being the "*cause of all unity and measure of all things*" (*Vit. Pyth. p.* 47) ; the Duad (Mulaprakriti, the VEIL) being thus shown to be the mother of the Logos and, at the same time, his *daughter—i.e.,* the object of his perception—the produced

---

* It is the "*bound*" confused with the "*Infinite,*" that Kapila overwhelms with sarcasms in his disputations with the Brahman Yogis, who claim in their mystical visions to see the "Highest One."

† See T. Taylor's article in his Monthly Magazine quoted in the *Platonist,* edited by T. M. Johnson, F.T.S., Osceola, Missouri. (Feb. Number of 1887.)

producer and the secondary cause of it. With Pythagoras, the MONAD returns into silence and Darkness as soon as it has evolved the *triad*, from which emanate the remaining seven numbers of the 10 (ten) numbers which are at the base of the manifested universe.

In the Norse cosmogony it is again the same. " In the beginning was a great abyss (Chaos), neither day nor night existed ; the abyss was Ginnungagap, the yawning gulf, without beginning, without end. ALL FATHER, the Uncreated, the Unseen, dwelt in the depth of the ' Abyss' (SPACE) and *willed*, and what was willed came into being." (See "*Asgard and the Gods.*") As in the Hindu cosmogony, the evolution of the universe is divided into two acts: called in India the *Prakriti* and *Padma* Creations. Before the warm rays pouring from the " Home of Brightness " awake life in the Great Waters of Space, the Elements of the first creation come into view, and from them is formed the Giant Ymir (also Orgelmir)—primordial matter differentiated from Chaos (literally *seething clay*). Then comes the cow Audumla, the nourisher,* from whom is born Buri (the Producer) who, by Bestla, the daughter of the " Frost-Giants" (the sons of Ymir) had three sons, *Odin, Willi* and *We*, or " Spirit," " Will," and " Holiness." (*Compare the Genesis of the Primordial Races, in this work.*) This was when Darkness still reigned throughout Space, when the *Ases*, the creative Powers (Dhyan Chohans) were not yet evolved, and the Yggdrasil, the *tree* of the universe of Time and of Life, had not yet grown, and there was, as yet, no Walhalla, or Hall of Heroes. The Scandinavian legends of creation, of our earth and world, begin with *time* and human life. All that precedes it is for them " Darkness," wherein All-Father, the cause of all, dwells. As observed by the editor of " Asgard and the Gods," though these legends have in them the idea of that ALL-FATHER, the original cause of all, " he is scarcely more than mentioned in the poems," not because, as he thinks, before the preaching of the gospel, the idea " could not rise to distinct conceptions of the Eternal," but on account of its great esoteric character. Therefore, all the creative gods, or *personal* Deities, begin at the secondary stage of Cosmic evolution. Zeus is born *in*, and *out* of *Kronos*—Time. So is Brahmâ the production and emanation of *Kala*, " eternity and time," Kala being one of the names of Vishnu. Hence we find Odin, the father *of the gods and of the Ases*, as Brahmâ is the father of *the gods and of the Asuras*, and hence also the androgyne character of all the chief creative gods, from the second MONAD of the Greeks down to the Sephiroth Adam Kadmon, the Brahmâ or Prajâpati-Vâch of the Vedas, and the androgyne of Plato, which is but another version of the Indian symbol.

* Vâch—the " melodious cow, who milks sustenance and water," and yields us " nourishment and sustenance " as described in Rig-Veda.

The best metaphysical definition of primeval theogony in the spirit of the Vedantins may be found in the " Notes on the Bhagavat-Gita," by Mr. T. Subba Row. (*See "Theosophist" for February*, 1887.) Para-brahmam, the unknown and the incognisable, as the lecturer tells his audience :

" . . . . . Is not Ego, it is not non-ego, nor is it consciousness . . . . . it is not even *Atma* " . . . . . " but though not itself an object of knowledge, it is yet capable of supporting and giving rise to every kind of object and every kind of existence which becomes an object of knowledge. It is the one essence from which starts into existence a centre of energy . . . . ." which he calls *Logos.*

This Logos is the *Sabda Brahmam* of the Hindus, which he will not even call *Eswara* (the " lord " God), lest the term should create confu-sion in the people's minds. But it is the *Avalokiteswara* of the Hindus, the *Verbum* of the Christians in its real *esoteric* meaning, not in the theological disfigurement.

" It is," he says, "the *Gnatha* or the Ego in the Kosmos, and every other Ego . . . . . . is but its reflection and manifestation. . . . . . It exists in a latent condition in the bosom of Parabrahmam at the time of *Pralaya*. . . ." (During Manvantara) " it has a consciousness and an individuality of its own . . . . ." (It is a centre of energy, but) . . . . . "such centres of energy are almost innumerable in the bosom of Parabrahmam . . . . ." " It must not be supposed, that even the logos is *the* Creator, or that it is but a single centre of energy . . . . . . their number is almost infinite." " This Ego," he adds, " is the first that appears in Kosmos, and is the end of all evolution. It is the abstract Ego " . . . . . " this is the *first* manifestation (or aspect) of Parabrahmam." " When once it starts into conscious being . . . . . . from its objective standpoint, *Parabrahmam* appears to it as *Mulaprakriti*." " Please bear this in mind," observes the lecturer, " for here is the root of the whole difficulty about *Purusha* and *Prakriti* felt by the various writers on Vedantic philosophy. This *Mulaprakriti* is material to it (the Logos), as any material object is material to us. This *Mulaprakriti* is no more *Parabrahmam* than the bundle of attributes of a pillar is the pillar itself ; Parabrahmam is an uncondi-tioned and absolute reality, and Mulaprakriti is a sort of veil thrown over it. Parabrahmam by itself cannot be seen as it is. It is seen by the *Logos* with a veil thrown over it, and that veil is the mighty expanse of Cosmic matter. . . ." " Parabrahmam, after having appeared on the one hand as the Ego, and on the other as Mulaprakriti, acts as the one energy through the *Logos*."

And the lecturer explains what he means by this acting of something which is *nothing*, though it is the ALL, by a fine simile. He compares the Logos to the sun through which light and heat radiate, but whose energy, light and heat, exist in some unknown condition in Space and are diffused in Space only as *visible* light and heat, the sun being only the agent thereof. This is the first triadic hypostasis. The quaternary is made up by the *energizing light* shed by the Logos.

The Hebrew Kabalists give it in a shape which esoterically is identical with the Vedantic. Ain-Soph, they taught, could not be comprehended, could not be located, nor named, though the causeless cause of all. Hence its name—Ain-Soph—is a term of negation, "the inscrutable, the incognizable, and the unnameable." They made of it, therefore, a boundless circle, a sphere, of which human intellect, with the utmost stretch, could only perceive the vault. In the words of one who has unriddled much in the Kabalistical system, in one of its meanings thoroughly, in its numerical and geometrical esotericism :—" Close your eyes, and from your own consciousness of perception try and think outward to the extremest limits in every direction. You will find that equal lines or rays of perception extend out evenly in all directions, so that the utmost effort of perception will terminate in the *vault of a sphere*. The limitation of this sphere will, of necessity, be a great *Circle*, and the direct rays of thought in any and every direction must be *right line radii* of the circle. This, then, *must* be, humanly speaking, the extremest all-embracing conception of the Ain-Soph *manifest*, which formulates itself as a *geometrical figure*, viz., of a circle, with its elements of curved circumference and right line diameter divided into radii. Hence, a geometrical shape is the first recognisable means of connection between the Ain-Soph and the intelligence of man."*

This great circle (which Eastern Esotericism reduces to the point within the Boundless Circle) is the Avalôkitêswara, the *Logos* or *Verbum* of which Mr. Subba Row speaks. But this circle or manifested God is as unknown to us, except through its *manifested* universe, as the one, though easier, or rather more possible to our highest conceptions. This Logos which sleeps in the bosom of Parabrahmam during Pralaya, as our "*Ego* is latent (in us) at the time *of sushupti*, sleep ;" which cannot cognize Parabrahmam otherwise than as *Mulaprakriti*—the latter being a cosmic veil which is "the mighty expanse of cosmic matter" —is thus only an organ in cosmic creation, through which radiate the energy and wisdom of Parabrahmam, *unknown to the Logos, as it is to ourselves*. Moreover, as the Logos is as unknown to us as Parabrahmam is unknown in reality to the Logos, both Eastern Esotericism and the Kabala—in order to bring the Logos within the range of our conceptions —have resolved the abstract synthesis into concrete images ; viz., into the reflections or multiplied aspects of that Logos or Avalôkitêswara, Brahmâ, Ormazd, Osiris, Adam-Kadmon, call it by any of these names —which aspects or Manvantaric emanations are the Dhyan Chohans, the Elohim, the Devas, the Amshaspends, &c., &c. Metaphysicians explain the root and germ of the latter, according to Mr. Subba Row, as the first manifestation of Parabrahmam, " the highest trinity that we

---

* From the *Masonic Review* for June, 1886.

are capable of understanding," which is *Mulaprakriti* (the veil), the
Logos, and the conscious energy " of the latter," or its power and
light*; or—"matter, force and the *Ego*, or the one root of self, of which
every other kind of self is but a manifestation or a reflection." It is
then only in this " light " (of consciousness) of mental and
physical perception, that *practical* Occultism can throw this
into visibility by geometrical figures ; which, when closely studied,
will yield not only a scientific explanation of the real, objective,
existence† of the " Seven sons of the divine Sophia," which is this light
of the Logos, but show by means of other yet undiscovered keys that,
with regard to Humanity, these " Seven Sons " and their numberless
emanations, centres of energy personified, are an absolute necessity.
Make away with them, and the mystery of Being and Mankind *will never
be unriddled, not even closely approached*.

It is through *this light* that everything is created. This ROOT of mental
SELF is also the root of physical *Self*, for this light is the permutation,
in our manifested world, of Mulaprakriti, called *Aditi* in the Vedas. In
its third aspect it becomes *Vâch*,‡ the daughter and the mother of the
Logos, as Isis is the daughter and the mother of Osiris, who is Horus ;
and *Mout*, the daughter, wife, and mother of Ammon, in the Egyptian
Moon-glyph. In the Kabala, Sephira is the same as Shekinah, and is,
in another synthesis, the wife, daughter, and mother of the " Heavenly
man," Adam Kadmon, and is even identical with him, just as Vâch is
identical with Brahmâ, and is called the female Logos. In the Rig-
Veda, Vâch is " mystic speech," by whom Occult Knowledge and
Wisdom are communicated to man, and thus Vâch is said to have
" entered the Rishis." She is " generated by the gods ; " she is the
divine Vâch—the " Queen of gods " ; and she is associated—like Sephira
with the Sephiroth—with the Prajâpati in their work of creation. Moreover, she is called " the mother of the Vedas," " since it is through her
power (as mystic *speech*) that Brahmâ revealed them, and also owing to
her power that he produced the universe "—*i.e.*, through speech, and
words (synthesized by the " WORD ") and numbers.§

But Vâch being also spoken of as the daughter of Daksha—" the god
who lives in all the Kalpas "—her Mayavic character is thereby shown:

---

* Called, in the Bhagavat-Gita, *Daiviprakriti*.

† *Objective*—in the world of Maya, of course ; still as real as we are.

‡ " In the course of cosmic manifestation, this *Daiviprakriti*, instead of being the
mother of the Logos, should, strictly speaking, be called his daughter." (" *Notes on the
Bhagavat-Gita*," *p*. 305, *Theosophist*.)

§ The wise men, like Stanley Jevons amongst the moderns, who invented the scheme
which makes the incomprehensible assume a tangible form, could only do so by
resorting to numbers and geometrical figures.

during the *pralaya* she disappears, absorbed in the one, all-devouring Ray.

But there are two distinct aspects in universal Esotericism, Eastern and Western, in all those personations of the *female* Power in nature, or nature—the *noumenal* and the *phenomenal*. One is its purely metaphysical aspect, as described by the learned lecturer in his " Notes on the Bhagavat-Gita ; " the other terrestrial and physical, and at the same time *divine* from the stand-point of practical human conception and Occultism. They are all the symbols and personifications of *Chaos*, the " Great Deep " or the Primordial Waters of Space, the impenetrable VEIL between the INCOGNISABLE and the LOGOS of Creation. " Connecting himself through his mind with Vâch, Brahmâ (the Logos) created the primordial waters." In the Kathaka Upanishad it is stated still more clearly : " Prajâpati was this Universe. *Vâch was a second to him.* He associated with her . . . she produced these creatures and again re-entered Prajâpati."*

And here we may incidentally point out one of the many unjust slurs thrown by the pious and *good* missionaries in India on the religion of the land. This allegory—in the " Satapatha Brâhmana "—namely, that Brahmâ, as the father of men, performed the work of procreation by incestuous intercourse with his own daughter Vâch, also called Sandhya (twilight), and *Satarupa* (the hundred formed), is incessantly thrown into the teeth of the Brahmins, as condemning their " detestable, *false* religion." Besides the fact, conveniently forgotten by the Europeans, that the Patriarch Lot is shown guilty of the same crime under the *human form*, whereas Brahmâ, or rather Prajâpati, accomplished the incest under the form of a buck with his daughter, who had that of a hind (*rohit*), the esoteric reading of Genesis (*ch. iii.*) shows the same. Moreover, there is certainly a *cosmic*, not a physiological meaning attached to the Indian allegory, since Vâch is a permutation of Aditi and Mulaprakriti (Chaos), and Brahmâ a permutation of Narâyana, the Spirit of God entering into, and fructifying nature ; therefore, there is nothing *phallic* in the conception at all.

As already stated, Aditi-Vâch is the female *Logos*, or the " word," *Verbum ;* and Sephira in the Kabala is the same. These feminine Logoi are all correlations, in their *noumenal* aspect, of Light, and Sound, and Ether, showing how well-informed were the ancients both in

* This connects Vâch and Sephira with the goddess Kwan-Yin, the " merciful mother," the *divine* VOICE *of the soul* even in Exoteric Buddhism ; and with the female aspect of *Kwan-Shai-yin*, the Logos, the *verbum* of Creation, and at the same time with the voice that speaks audibly to the Initiate, according to Esoteric Buddhism. Bath Kol, the *filia Vocis*, the daughter of the divine voice of the Hebrews, responding from the mercy seat within the veil of the temple is—a result.

physical science (as now known to the moderns), and as to the birth of
that science in the Spiritual and Astral spheres.

"Our old writers said that *Vâch* is of four kinds . . . . *para, pasyanti, mad-*
hyama, vaikhari (a statement found in the Rig-Veda and the Upanishads) . . . .
Vaikhari Vâch is what we utter." It is sound, *speech*, that again which becomes
comprehensive and objective to one of our physical senses and may be brought
under the laws of perception. Hence : " Every kind of *Vaikhari-Vâch* exists in
its *Madhyama* . . . . *Pasyanti* and ultimately in its *Para* form. . . . . The
reason why this *Pranava* * is called Vâch is this, that these four principles of the
great Kosmos correspond to these four forms of Vâch. . . . . The whole
Kosmos in its objective form is *Vaikhari* Vâch; the light of the *Logos* is the
madhyama form; and the *Logos* itself the *pasyanti* form ; while Parabrahmam is
the *para* (beyond the *noumenon* of all *Noumena*) aspect of that Vâch." (*Notes on
the Bhagavad-Gita*).

Thus Vâch, Shekinah, or the "music of the spheres" of Pythagoras,
are one, if we take for our example instances in the three most (apparently) dissimilar religious philosophies in the world—the Hindu, the
Greek and the Chaldean Hebrew. These personations and allegories
may be viewed under *four* (chief) and three (lesser) aspects or *seven* in
all, as in Esotericism. The *para* form is the ever subjective and latent
Light and Sound, which exist eternally in the bosom of the INCOGNIS-
ABLE ; when transferred into the ideation of the Logos, or its latent
light, it is called *pasyanti*, and when it becomes that light *expressed*, it is
madhyama.

Now the Kabala gives the definition thus : " There are three kinds
of light, and that (fourth) which interpenetrates the others ; (1) the
clear and the penetrating, the *objective light*, (2) the *reflected* light, and
(3) the *abstract* light. The ten Sephiroth, the *three* and the Seven, are
called in the Kabala the 10 words, D-BRIM (Dabarim), the numbers and
the Emanations of the heavenly light, which is both Adam Kadmon
and Sephira, or (Brahmâ) Prajâpati-Vâch. Light, Sound, Number, are
the three factors of creation in the Kabala. Parabrahmam cannot be
known except through the luminous Point (the LOGOS), which knows
not *Parabrahmam* but only *Mulaprakriti*. Similarly Adam Kadmon knew
only Shekinah, though he was the *vehicle* of Ain-Soph. And, as Adam
Kadmon, he is in the esoteric interpretation the total of the number
ten, the Sephiroth (himself a trinity, or the three attributes of the

* *Pranava*, like *Om*, is a mystic term pronounced by the Yogis during meditation ; of
the terms called, according to exoteric Commentators, *Vyahritis*, or "*Om, Bhur,
Bhuva, Swar* " (Om, earth, sky, heaven)—Pranava is the most sacred, perhaps. They
are pronounced with breath suppressed. *See Manu II.* 76-81, *and Mitakshara commenting
on the Yajnavahkya-Suriti*, i. 23. But the esoteric explanation goes a great deal
further.

incognisable DEITY in One).* "When the Heavenly man (or Logos) first assumed the form of the Crown† (Kether) and identified himself with Sephira, he caused seven splendid lights to emanate from it (the Crown)," which made in their totality ten; so the Brahmâ-Prajâpati, once he became separated from, yet identical with Vâch, caused the seven Rishis, the seven Manus or Prajâpatis to issue from that crown. In Exotericism one will always find 10 and 7, of either Sephiroth or Prajâpati; in *Esoteric* rendering always 3 and 7, which yield also 10. Only when divided in the manifested sphere into 3 and 7, they form ⵔ, the androgyne, and ⊕, or the figure X manifested and differentiated.

This will help the student to understand why Pythagoras esteemed the Deity (the Logos) to be the *centre of unity* and "Source of Harmony." We say this Deity was the *Logos*, not the MONAD that dwelleth in Solitude and Silence, because Pythagoras taught that UNITY being indivisible is *no number*. And this is also why it was required of the candidate, who applied for admittance into his school, that he should have already studied as a preliminary step, the Sciences of Arithmetic, Astronomy, Geometry and *Music*, held as the four divisions of Mathematics.‡ Again, this explains why the Pythagoreans asserted that the doctrine of Numbers—the chief of all in Esotericism—had been revealed to man by the celestial deities; that the world had been called forth out of Chaos by Sound or Harmony, and constructed according to the principles of musical proportion; that the seven planets which rule the destiny of mortals have a harmonious motion "and intervals corresponding to musical diastemes, rendering various sounds, so perfectly consonant, that they produce the sweetest melody, which is inaudible to us, only by reason of the greatness of the sound, which our ears are incapable of receiving." (*Censorinus.*)

In the Pythagorean Theogony the hierarchies of the heavenly Host and Gods were numbered and expressed numerically. Pythagoras had studied Esoteric Science in India; therefore we find his pupils saying "The monad (the manifested one) is the principle of all things. From the Monad and the indeterminate duad (Chaos), numbers; from

---

* It is this *trinity* that is meant by the "three steps of Vishnu"; which means: (Vishnu being considered as the *Infinite* in exotericism)—that from the Parabrahm issued Mulaprakriti, Purusha (the Logos), and Prakriti: the four forms (with itself, the synthesis) of Vâch. And in the Kabala—Ain-Soph, Shekinah, Adam Kadmon and Sephirah, the four—or the three emanations being distinct—yet ONE.

† Chaldean *Book of Numbers*. In the current *Kabala* the name Jehovah replaces Adam Kadmon.

‡ Justin Martyr tells us that, owing to his ignorance of these four sciences, he was rejected by the Pythagoreans as a candidate for admission into their school.

numbers, *Points*; from points, *Lines*; from lines, *Superficies*; from superficies, *Solids*; from these, solid Bodies, whose elements are four—Fire,
Water, Air, Earth; of all which transmuted (correlated), and totally
changed, the world consists."—(Diogenes Laertius *in Vit. Pythag.*)

And this may also, if it does not unriddle the mystery altogether, at any
rate lift a corner of the veil off those wondrous allegories that have
been thrown upon Vâch, the most mysterious of all the Brahmanical
goddesses, she who is termed "the *melodious* cow who milked forth
sustenance and water" (the Earth with all her mystic powers); and
again she "who yields us nourishment and sustenance" (physical
Earth). *Isis* is also mystic Nature and also Earth; and her cow's
horns identify her with Vâch. The latter, after having been recognised
in her highest form as *para*, becomes at the lower or material end of
creation—*Vaikhari*. Hence she is mystic, though physical, Nature, with
all her magic ways and properties.

Again, as goddess of Speech and of Sound, and a permutation of
Aditi—she is *Chaos*, in one sense. At any rate, she is the "Mother of
the gods," and it is from Brahmâ (Iswara, or the Logos) and Vâch, as
from Adam Kadmon and Sephira, that the real *manifested* theogony has
to start. Beyond, all is darkness and abstract speculation. With the
Dhyan Chohans, or the gods, the Seers, the Prophets and the adepts in
general are on firm ground. Whether as Aditi, or the *divine* Sophia of
the Greek Gnostics, she is the mother of the seven sons: the "Angels
of the Face," of the "Deep," or the "Great Green One" of the "Book of
the Dead." Says the Book of Dzyan (Knowledge through meditation)—

"*The great mother lay with* △, *and the* |, *and the* ☐, *the second* | *and
the* ⚹* *in her bosom, ready to bring them forth, the valiant sons of the* ☐△||
(*or* 4,320,000, *the Cycle*) *whose two elders are the* ◯ *and the* · (*Point*)."

At the beginning of every cycle of 4,320,000, the *Seven* (or, as some
nations had it, eight) great gods, descended to establish the new order
of things and give the impetus to the new cycle. That *eighth* god was
the unifying *Circle* or LOGOS, separated and made distinct from its
host, in exoteric dogma, just as the three divine hypostases of the
ancient Greeks are now considered in the Churches as three distinct
personæ. "The MIGHTY ONES perform their great works, and leave
behind them everlasting monuments to commemorate their visit, every
time they penetrate within our mayavic veil (atmosphere)," says a

---

* 31415, or π. The synthesis, or the *Host unified* in the Logos and the Point
called in Roman Catholicism the "Angel of the Face," and in Hebrew םיכאל
"who is (like unto, or the same) as God"—the manifested representation.

Commentary.* Thus we are taught that the great Pyramids were built under their direct supervision, "when *Dhruva* (the then Pole-star) was at his lowest culmination, and the Krittika (Pleiades) looked over his head (were on the same meridian but above) to watch the work of the giants." Thus, as the first Pyramids were built at the beginning of a Sidereal year, under Dhruva (Alpha Polaris), it must have been over 31,000 years (31,105) ago. Bunsen was right in admitting for Egypt an antiquity of over 21,000 years, but this concession hardly exhausts truth and fact in this question. "The stories told by Egyptian priests and others of time-keeping in Egypt, are now beginning to look less like lies in the sight of all who have escaped from biblical bondage," writes the author of "*The Natural Genesis.*" "Inscriptions have lately been found at Sakkarah, making mention of two Sothiac cycles . . . registered at that time, now some 6,000 years ago. Thus when Herodotus was in Egypt, the Egyptians had—as now known—observed at least five different Sothiac cycles of 1,461 years. The priests informed the Greek inquirer that time had been reckoned by them for so long that the sun had twice risen where it then set, and twice set where it then arose. This . . . can only be realized as a fact in nature by means of two cycles of Precession, or a period of 51,736 years," (vol. ii, p. 318. But see in our Book II., "CHRONOLOGY OF THE BRAHMINS.")

Mor Isaac (*See* Kircher's *Œdipus, vol. ii., p.* 425) shows the ancient Syrians defining their world of the "Rulers" and "active gods" in the same way as the Chaldeans. The lowest world was the SUBLUNARY— our own—watched by the "Angels" of the first or lower order ; the one that came next in rank, was Mercury, ruled by the "ARCHANGELS" ; then came Venus, whose gods were the PRINCIPALITIES ; the fourth was that of the SUN, the domain and region of the highest and mightiest gods of our system, the solar gods of all nations ; the fifth was Mars, ruled by the "VIRTUES" ; the sixth—that of *Bel* or Jupiter—was governed by the DOMINIONS ; the seventh—the world of Saturn—by the THRONES. These are the worlds of form. Above come the four higher ones, making seven again, since the three *highest* are "unmentionable and un-pronounceable." The eighth, composed of 1,122 stars, is the domain of the *Cherubs ;* the ninth, belonging to the *walking* and numberless stars on account of their distance, has the seraphs ; as to the tenth— Kircher, quoting Mor Isaac, says that it is composed "of invisible stars that could be taken, they said, for clouds — so massed are they in the zone that we call *Via Straminis*, the

---

* Appearing at the beginning of Cycles, as also of every sidereal year (of 25,868 years) therefore the Kabeiri or *Kabarim* received their name in Chaldea, as it means the *measures of Heaven* from *Kob*—measure of, and Urim—heavens.

Milky Way;" and he hastens to explain that "these are the stars of Lucifer, engulfed with him in his terrible shipwreck." That which comes after and beyond the tenth world (our Quaternary, or the *Arupa* world), the Syrians could not tell. " All they knew was that it is there that begins the vast and incomprehensible ocean of the infinite, the abode of the true divinity without boundary or end."

Champollion shows the same belief among the Egyptians. Hermes having spoken of the Father-Mother and Son, whose spirit (collectively the DIVINE FIAT) shapes the Universe, says :—*Seven Agents* (mediums) were also formed, to contain the material (or manifested) worlds, within their respective *circles* and the action of these agents was named DESTINY." He further enumerates seven and ten and twelve orders, which would take too long to detail here.

As the "*Rig Vidhana*" together with the "*Brahmanda Purâna*" and all such works, whether describing the magic efficacy of the Rig-Vedic *Mantras* or the future Kalpas, are declared by Dr. Weber and others to be *modern compilations* "belonging probably only to the time of the Purânas," it is useless to refer the reader to their mystic explanations ; and one may as well quote simply from the archaic books utterly unknown to the Orientalists. These works explain that which so puzzles the scholars, namely that the *Saptarshi*, the " mind-born sons " of Brahmâ, are referred to in the *Satapatha Brâhmana* under one set of names ; in the *Mahabhârata* under another set ; and that the Vayu Purâna makes even *nine* instead of *seven* Rishis, by adding the names of Bhrigu and Daksha to the list. But the same occurs in every exoteric Scripture. The secret doctrine gives a long genealogy of Rishis, but separates them into many classes. Like the Gods of the Egyptians, who were divided into seven, and even twelve, classes, so are the Indian Rishis in their Hierarchies. The first three groups are the Divine, the Cosmical and the Sub-lunary. Then come the Solar Gods of *our* system, the Planetary, the Sub-Mundane, and the purely human—the heroes and the *Manoushi*.

At present, however, we are only concerned with the *pre*-cosmic, divine gods, the Prajâpati or the " Seven Builders." This group is found unmistakably in every Cosmogony. Owing to the loss of Egyptian archaic documents—since, according to M. Maspero, " the materials and historical data on hand to study the history of the religious evolution in Egypt are neither complete nor very often intelligible "— in order to have the statements brought forward from the Secret Doctrine corroborated partially and indirectly, the ancient hymns and inscriptions on the tombs must be appealed to. One such, at any rate, shows that Osiris was, like Brahmâ-Prajâpati, Adam Kadmon, Ormazd, and so many other Logoi, the chief and synthesis of the group of " Creators " or Builders. Before Osiris became the " One " and the *highest* god of Egypt he was worshipped at Abydos as the head or leader of the Heavenly Host of the Builders belonging to the higher of the three orders. The hymn engraved on the votive stela of a tomb from Abydos (3rd register) addresses Osiris thus : " Salutations to thee, Osiris, elder son of *Sib* ; thou the greatest over the six gods issued from the goddess *Noo* (primordial Water), thou the great favourite of thy father *Ra* ; father of fathers, King of Duration, master in the eternity . . . who, as soon as these issued from thy mother's bosom, gathered all the crowns and attached the *Uræus* (serpent or naja)* on thy head ; multiform god, *whose name is unknown* and who has many names in towns and provinces. . ." Coming out from the primordial water crowned with the *uræus*, which is the serpent emblem of Cosmic fire, and himself the *seventh* over the six primary gods issued from Father-Mother, *Nou* and *Nout* (the sky), who can Osiris be, but the chief Prajâpati, the chief Sephiroth, the chief Amshaspend-Ormazd ! That this latter solar and cosmic god stood, in the beginning of religious evolution, in the same position as the archangel "whose name was secret," is certain. This Archangel was the representative on earth of the *Hidden* Jewish God, Michael, in short : it is his " Face " that is said to have gone before the Jews like a " Pillar of Fire." Burnouf says, " The seven Amshaspends, who are most assuredly our archangels, designate also the personifications of the divine Virtues." (*Comment on the Yaçna, p.* 174.) And these archangels, therefore, are as " certainly " the *Saptarishi* of the Hindus, though it is next to impossible to class each with its pagan prototype and parallel, since, as in the case of Osiris, they have all so " many names in towns and provinces." Some of the most important, however, will be shown in their order.

One thing is thus undeniably proven. The more one studies their Hierarchies and finds out their identity, the more proofs one acquires that there is not one of the past and present *personal* gods, known to us from the earliest days of History, that does not belong to the third stage of Cosmic manifestation. In every religion we find the concealed deity forming the ground work ; then the ray therefrom, that falls into primordial Cosmic matter (first manifestation) ; then the androgyne result, the dual Male and Female abstract Force, personified (*second* stage) ; this separates itself finally, in the *third*, into seven Forces, called the creative Powers by all the ancient Religions, and the

---

* This Egyptian word *Naja* reminds one a good deal of the Indian *Naga*, the Serpent-God. Brahmâ and Siva and Vishnu are all crowned with, and connected with Nagas —a sign of their cyclic and cosmic character.

" Virtues of God " by the Christians.   The later explanation and metaphysical abstract qualifications have never prevented the Roman and Greek Churches from worshipping these "Virtues" under the personifications and distinct names of the seven Archangels.   In the Book of *Druschim* (*p.* 59, 1*st Treatise*) in the Talmud, a distinction between these groups is given which is the correct Kabalistical explanation. It says :

"There are three groups (or orders) of *Sephiroth.*   1st. The Sephiroth called "the divine attributes" (abstract).   2nd. The physical or *sidereal* Sephiroth (personal)—one group of *seven*, the other of *ten*.   3rd. The metaphysical Sephiroth, or *periphrasis of Jehovah*, who are the first three Sephiroth (Kether, Chochma and Binah), the rest of the seven being the (personal) seven spirits of the Presence " (also of the planets).

The same division has to be applied to the primary, secondary and tertiary evolution of gods in every theogony, if one wishes to translate the meaning esoterically.   We must not confuse the purely metaphysical personifications of the *abstract* attributes of Deity, with their reflection —the sidereal gods.   This reflection, however, is in reality the objective expression of the abstraction : *living* Entities and the models formed on that divine prototype.   Moreover, the three metaphysical Sephiroth or " *the periphrasis of Jehovah* " are *not* Jehovah ; it is the latter himself with the additional titles of Adonai, Elohim, Sabbaoth, and the numerous names lavished on him, who is the periphrasis of the Shaddai, שׁ דּ י, the Omnipotent.   The name is a circumlocution, indeed, a too abundant figure of Jewish rhetoric, and has always been denounced by the Occultists.   To the Jewish Kabalists, and even the Christian Alchemists and Rosicrucians, Jehovah was a convenient *screen*, unified by the folding of its many flaps, and adopted as a substitute : one name of an individual Sephiroth being as good as another name, for those who had the secret.   The Tetragrammaton, the Ineffable, the sidereal " *Sum Total*," was invented for no other purpose than to mislead the profane and to symbolize life and generation.*   The real secret and *unpronounceable* name—"the word that is no word "—has to be sought in the seven names of the first seven emanations, or the " Sons of the Fire,"

---

* Says the translator of Avicebron's " *Qabbalah* " (Mr. Isaac Myer, LL.B., of Philadelphia) of this " Sum Total ": "The letter of Kether is י (Yod), of Binah ה (Hêh), together YaH, the feminine Name ; the third letter, that of Hokhmah, is ו (Vau), making together, יהו YHV of יהוה YHVH, the Tetragrammaton, and really the complete symbols of its efficaciousness.   The last ה (Hêh) of this Ineffable Name *being always applied to the Six Lower and the last, together the Seven remaining Sephiroth.*" . . . Thus the Tetragrammaton is holy only in its abstract synthesis.   As a quaternary containing the lower Seven Sephiroth, *it is phallic.*

in the secret Scriptures of all the great nations, and even in the *Zohar*, the Kabalistic lore of that smallest of all, the Jewish. This word, composed of seven letters in each tongue, is found embodied in the architectural remains of every grand building in the world ; from the Cyclopean remains on Easter Island (part of a continent buried under the seas nearer four million years ago* than 20,000) down to the earliest Egyptian pyramids.

We shall have to enter more fully upon this subject, and bring practical illustrations to prove the statements made in the text.

For the present it is sufficient to show, by a few instances, the truth of what was asserted at the beginning of this Monograph, namely, that no Cosmogony, the world over, with the sole exception of the Christian, has ever attributed to the One Highest cause, the UNIVERSAL Deific Principle, the immediate creation of our Earth, man, or anything connected with these. This statement holds as good for the Hebrew or Chaldean Kabala as it does for *Genesis*, had the latter been ever thoroughly understood, and—what is still more important—correctly translated.† Everywhere there is either a LOGOS—a "*Light* shining

---

* The statement will, of course, be found preposterous and absurd, and simply laughed at. But if one believes in the final submersion of Atlantis 850,000 years ago, as taught in " *Esoteric Buddhism* " (the gradual first sinking having begun during the Eocene age), one has to accept the statement for the so-called Lemuria, the continent of the Third Root Race, first nearly destroyed by combustion, and then submerged. This is what the Commentary says : " The first earth having been purified by the forty-nine fires, her people, born of Fire and Water, could not die . . . etc.; the Second Earth (with its race) disappeared as vapour vanishes in the air . . . the Third Earth had everything consumed on it after the *separation*, and went down into the lower Deep (the Ocean). This was *twice* eighty-two cyclic years ago." Now a *cyclic* year is what we call a *sidereal* year, and is founded on the precession of the equinoxes, or 25,868 years each, and this is equal, therefore, in all to 4,242,352 years. More details will be found in the text of Book II. Meanwhile, this doctrine is embodied in the " Kings of Edom."

† The same reserve is found in the Talmud and in every national system of religion whether monotheistic or exoterically polytheistical. From the superb religious poem by the Kabalist Rabbi Solomon Ben Gabirol in " the Kether Malchuth," we select a few definitions given in the prayers of Kippûr. . . . " Thou art one, the beginning of all numbers, and the foundation of all edifices ; Thou art One, and in the secret of Thy unity the wisest of men are lost, because they know it not. Thou art one, and Thy Unity is never diminished, never extended, and cannot be changed. Thou art one, but *not as an element of numeration ; for Thy Unity admits not of multiplication, change or form.* Thou art existent ; but the understanding and vision of mortals cannot attain to thy existence, nor determine for thee the Where, the How, and the Why. Thou art Existent, but in thyself alone, there being none other that can exist with thee. Thou art Existent, before all time and without Place. Thou art Existent, and thy existence is so profound and secret that none can penetrate and discover thy secrecy. Thou art Living, but within no time that can be fixed or known ; Thou art Living, but not by a spirit or a soul, for *Thou art thyself,* THE SOUL OF ALL SOULS," etc., etc. There is

in DARKNESS," truly—or the Architect of the Worlds is *esoterically* a plural number. The Latin Church, paradoxical as ever, while applying the epithet of Creator to Jehovah alone, adopts a whole *Kyriel* of names for the *working* FORCES *of the latter*, those names betraying the secret. For if the said Forces had nought to do with "Creation" so-called, why call them *Elohim* (Alhim) in plural; "divine workmen" and *Energies* (Ἐνεργεία), *incandescent celestial stones* (lapides igniti cœlorum), and especially, "*supporters* of the World" (Κοσμοκράτορες), governors or RULERS of *the World* (*rectores mundi*), the "Wheels" of the World (*Rotæ*), Ophanim, Flames and POWERS, "Sons of God" (*B'ne Alhim*), "Vigilant COUNSELLORS," etc., etc.

It was often premised (and as unjustly as usual) that China, nearly as old a country as India, had no cosmogony. "It was unknown to Confucius, and the Buddhists extended their Cosmogony without introducing a personal God,"* it is complained. The *Yi-King*, "the very essence of ancient thought and the combined work of the most venerated sages, fails to show a distinct cosmogony." Nevertheless, there is one, and a very distinct one. Only as Confucius did not admit of a future life† and the Chinese Buddhists reject the idea of *One* Creator, accepting one cause and its numberless effects, they are misunderstood by the believers in a *personal* God. The "great Extreme" as the commencement "of changes" (transmigrations) is the shortest and perhaps the most suggestive of all Cosmogonies, for those who, like the Confucianists, love virtue for its own sake, and try to do good unselfishly without perpetually looking to reward and profit. The "great Extreme" of Confucius produces "two figures." These "two" produce in their turn "the four images"; these again "the eight symbols." It is complained that though the Confucianists see in them "Heaven, Earth and man in miniature," . . . we can see in them anything we like. No doubt, and so it is with regard to many symbols, especially in those of the latest religions. But they who know something of Occult numerals, see in these "figures" the symbol, however rude, of a harmonious progressive Evolution of Kosmos and its beings, both the Heavenly and the Terrestrial. And any one who has studied the numerical evolution in the primeval cosmogony of Pythagoras (a contemporary of Confucius) can never fail to find in his *Triad*, *Tetractis* and

---

a distance between this Kabalistical Deity and the Biblical Jehovah, the spiteful and revengeful God of Abram, Isaac, and Jacob, *who tempted* the former and wrestled with the last. No Vedantin but would repudiate such a Parabrahm.

* Rev. Joseph Edkins "*On Cosmogony,*" p. 320. And very wisely they have acted.

† If he rejected it, it was on the ground of what he calls the changes—in other words, rebirths—of man, and constant transformations. He denied immortality to the *personality* of man—as we do—not to MAN.

Decade emerging from the ONE and solitary Monad, the same idea. Confucius is laughed at by his Christian biographer for " talking of divination" before and after this passage, and is represented as saying: " The eight symbols determine good and ill fortune, and these lead to great deeds. There are no imitable images greater than heaven and earth. There are no changes greater than the four seasons (meaning North, South, East and West, *et seq.*). There are no suspended images brighter than the sun and moon. In preparing *things for use, there is none greater than the sage.* In determining good and ill-luck there is nothing greater than *the divining straws and the tortoise.*"*

Therefore, the " divining straws" and the " tortoise," the " symbolic sets of lines," and the great sage who looks at them as they become one and two, and two become four, and four become eight, and the other sets " three and six," are laughed to scorn, only because his wise symbols are misunderstood.

So the author and his colleagues will scoff no doubt at the *Stanzas* given in our text, for they represent *precisely the same idea.* The old archaic map of Cosmogony is full of *lines* in the Confucian style, of concentric circles and dots. Yet all these represent the most abstract and philosophical conceptions of the Cosmogony of our Universe. At all events it may answer, perhaps, better to the requirements and the scientific purposes of our age, than the cosmogonical essays of St. Augustine and the "Venerable Bede," though these were published over a millennium later than the Confucian.

Confucius, one of the greatest sages of the ancient world, believed in ancient magic, and practised it himself "if we take for granted the statements of *Kin-yu*" . . . . and "he praised it to the skies in *Yi-kin*," we are told by his reverend critic. Nevertheless, even in his age—*i.e.*, 600 B.C., Confucius and his school taught the sphericity of the Earth and even the heliocentric system ; while, at about thrice 600 years after the Chinese philosopher, the Popes of Rome threatened and even burnt " heretics" for asserting the same. He is laughed at for speaking of the " Sacred Tortoise." No unprejudiced person can see any great difference between a *tortoise* and a *lamb* as candidates for sacredness, as both are symbols and no more. The Ox, the Eagle,† the Lion, and occasionally

---

* He may be laughed at by the Protestants ; but the Roman Catholics have no right to mock him, without becoming guilty of blasphemy and sacrilege. For it is over 200 years since Confucius was canonized as a Saint in China by the Roman Catholics, who have thereby obtained many converts among the ignorant Confucianists.

† The animals regarded as *sacred* in the Bible are not few : the goat for one, the *Azaz-el*, or God of Victory. As Aben Ezra says : " If thou art capable of comprehending the mystery of *Azazel*, thou wilt learn the mystery cf His (God's) name, for it has similar associates in Scriptures. I will tell thee by allusion one portion of the mystery ;

the Dove, are " the sacred animals " of the Western Bible, the first three being found grouped round the Evangelists ; and the fourth (the human face) is a Seraph, *i.e.*, a fiery serpent, the Gnostic Agathodæmon probably.* As explained, the "sacred animals" and the Flames or " Sparks " within the " Holy Four " refer to the prototypes of all that is found in the Universe in the *Divine Thought*, in the ROOT, which is the perfect cube, or the foundation of the Kosmos collectively and individually. They have all an occult reference to primordial Cosmic forms and its first concretions, work, and evolution.

In the earliest Hindu exoteric cosmogonies, it is not even the Demiurge who creates. For it is said in one of the Purânas that : " The great Architect of the World gives the first impulse to the rotatory motion of our planetary system by stepping in turn over each planet and body." It is this action "that causes each sphere to turn around itself, and all around the Sun." After which action, " it is the *Brahmandica*, the Solar and Lunar Pitris (the Dhyani-Chohans) " who take charge of their respective spheres (earths and planets), to the end of the Kalpa." The Creators are the Rishis ; most of whom are credited with the authorship of the mantras or Hymns of the Rig Veda. They are sometimes seven, sometimes ten, when they become *prajâpati*, the "Lord of Beings " ; then they rebecome the *seven* and the *fourteen* Manus, as the representatives of the seven and fourteen *cycles* of Existence (" Days of Brahmâ ") ; thus answering to the seven Æons, when at the end of the first stage of Evolution they are transformed into the seven stellar Rishis, the Saptarishis ; while their *human* doubles appear as heroes, Kings and Sages on this earth.

when thou shalt have *thirty three years of age* thou wilt comprehend me." So with the mystery of the *tortoise*. Rejoicing over the poetry of Biblical metaphors, associating with the name of Jehovah, " incandescent stones," " sacred animals," etc., and quoting from the *Bible de Vence* (*Vol. XIX. p.* 318) a French pious writer says : " Indeed all of them are *Elohim like their God ;* for, these Angels assume, *through a holy usurpation*, the very divine name of Jehovah each time they represent him." (*Pneumatologie, Vol. II., p.* 294). No one ever doubted that *the* NAME must have been *assumed*, when under the guise of the Infinite, One Incognizable, the *Malachim* (messengers) descended to eat and drink with men. But if the Elohim (and even lower Beings), *assuming* the god-name, were and are still worshipped, why should the same Elohim be called *devils*, when appearing under the names of other Gods ?

* The choice is curious, and shows how paradoxical were the first Christians in their selections. For why should they have chosen these symbols of Egyptian paganism, when the eagle is never mentioned in the New Testament save once, when Jesus refers to it as a *carrion* eater ? (*Matt.* xxiv. 28) ; and in the Old Testament it is called *unclean* ; that the Lion is made a point of comparison with *Satan*, both roaring for men to devour ; and the oxen are driven out of the Temple. On the other hand the Serpent, brought as an exemplar of wisdom to follow, is now regarded as the symbol of the Devil. The esoteric pearl of Christ's religion degraded into Christian theology, may indeed be said to have chosen a strange and unfitting *shell* to be born in and evolved from.

The Esoteric doctrine of the East having thus furnished and struck the key-note—which is as scientific as it is philosophical and poetical, as may be seen, under its allegorical garb—every nation has followed its lead. It is from the exoteric religions that we have to dig out the root-idea before we turn to esoteric truths, lest the latter should be rejected. Furthermore, every symbol—in *every* national religion—may be read esoterically, and the proof furnished for its being correctly read by transliterating it into its corresponding numerals and geometrical forms— by the extraordinary agreement of all—however much the glyphs and symbols may vary among themselves. For in the origin those symbols were all identical. Take, for instance, the opening sentences in various cosmogonies : in every case it is either a *circle*, an *egg*, or a *head*. DARKNESS is always associated with this first symbol and surrounds it,—as shown in the Hindu, the Egyptian, the Chaldeo-Hebrew and even the Scandinavian systems—hence black ravens, black doves, black waters and even black flames ; the *seventh* tongue of Agni, the *fire-god* being called " *Kali*," " the black," as it was a black flickering flame. Two *black* doves flew from Egypt and settling on the oaks of Dodona, gave their names to the Grecian gods. Noah lets out a *black* raven after the deluge, which is a symbol for the Cosmic pralaya, after which began the real creation or evolution of our earth and humanity. Odin's black ravens fluttered around the Goddess Saga and " whispered to her of the past and of the future." What is the real meaning of all those black birds ? They are all connected with the primeval wisdom, which flows out of the pre-cosmic Source of all, symbolised by the Head, the Circle, the Egg ; and they all have an identical meaning and relate to the primordial Archetypal man (Adam Kadmon) the creative origin of all things, which is composed of the Host of Cosmic Powers—the Creative Dhyan-Chohans, beyond which all is darkness.

Let us inquire of the wisdom of the Kabala—even veiled and distorted as it now is,—to explain in its numerical language an approximate meaning, at least of the word "raven." This is its number value as given in the " Source of Measures."

" The term *Raven* is used but once, and taken as *eth-h'orebv* את־הערב, =678, or 113×6; while the Dove is mentioned five times. Its value is 71, and 71×5 = 355. Six diameters, or the *raven*, crossing, would divide the circumference of a circle of 355 into 12 parts or compartments ; and 355 subdivided for each unit by 6, would equal 213-0, or the *head* (" beginning ") in the first verse of Genesis. This divided or subdivided, after the same fashion, by 2, or the 355 by 12, would give 213-2, or the word *B'râsh*, ב־ראש, or the first word of Genesis, with its prepositional prefix, signifying the same concreted general form astronomically, with the one here intended." Now the secret reading of the first verse of Genesis being : " In Rash (B'rash) or head, developed gods, the Heavens and the Earth "—it is easy to comprehend the esoteric meaning of the *raven*, once that the like meaning of the Flood (or Noah's Deluge) is ascertained. Whatever the many other meanings of this emblematical allegory may be, its *chief* meaning is that of a new cycle and a new Round (our *Fourth* Round.)* The " Raven," or the *Eth-H'Orebv*, yields the same numerical value as the " Head," and returned not to the ark, while the dove returned, carrying the olive-branch, when Noah, the new man of the new Race (whose prototype is Vaivasvata Manu), prepared to leave the ark, the womb (or *Argha*) of terrestrial nature, is the symbol of the purely spiritual, sexless and androgyne man of the first three Races, who vanished from earth for ever. Numerically Jehovah, Adam, Noah, are one in the Kabala : at best, then, it is Deity descending on to Ararat (later on Sinai), to incarnate in man his *image*, through the natural process, henceforth : the mother's womb, whose symbols are the ark, the mount (Sinai), etc., in *Genesis*. The Jewish allegory is at once astronomical, and purely physiological rather than anthropomorphic.

And here lies the abyss between the two systems (Aryan and Semitic), though built on the same foundation. As shown by an expounder of the Kabala, " the basic idea underlying the philosophy of the Hebrews was that God contained all things within himself and that man was *his image ;* man, including woman (as Androgynes) ; " and that " geometry and numbers (and measures applicable to astronomy) are contained in the terms *man* and *woman ;* and the apparent incongruity of such a mode was eliminated by showing the connection of man and woman with a particular system of numbers and measures and geometry, by the parturient time-periods, which furnished the connecting link between the terms and the facts shown, and perfected the mode used." It is argued that, the primal cause being absolutely incognizable, " the symbol of its first *comprehensible manifestation* was the conception of a circle with its diameter line, so as at once to carry the idea of geometry, phallicism, and astronomy ; " and this was finally applied to the " signification of simply human generative organs."† Hence the whole cycle of events

---

* Bryant is right in saying "Druid Bardesin says of Noah that when he came out of the ark (the birth of a new cycle), after a stay therein of a year and a day, that 364+1 =365 days, he was congratulated by Neptune upon his birth from the waters of the Flood, who wished him a *happy New Year*." The " Year," or cycle, esoterically, was the new race of men *born from woman* after the separation of the sexes, which is *the secondary* meaning of the allegory : its primary meaning being the beginning of the Fourth Round, or the *new* Creation. † *Unpubl. MSS.* (But see " *Source of Measures*.")

from Adam and the Patriarchs down to Noah is made to apply to phallic and astronomical uses, the one regulating the other, as the lunar periods, for instance. Hence, too, their *genesis* begins after their coming out of the Ark, and the close of the flood—at the Fourth Race. With the Aryan people it is different.

Eastern Esotericism has never degraded the One Infinite Deity, the container of all things, to such uses; and this is shown by the absence of Brahmâ from the Rig Veda and the modest positions occupied therein by Rudra and Vishnu, who became the powerful and great Gods, the " Infinites" of the exoteric creeds, ages later. But even they, " Creators" as the three may be, are not the direct creators and " forefathers of men." The latter are shown occupying a still lower scale, and are called Prajâpatis, the Pitris (our lunar ancestors), etc., etc.—never the " One Infinite God." Esoteric philosophy shows only *physical* man as created *in the image* of the Deity ; but the latter is but " the *minor gods*." It is the HIGHER-SELF, the real EGO who alone is divine and GOD.

---

§ XIII.

THE SEVEN CREATIONS.

" THERE was neither day nor night, nor sky nor earth, nor darkness nor light, nor any other thing save only ONE, unapprehensible by intellect, or THAT which is Brahma and Pumis (Spirit) and Prâdhâna (crude matter)" (*Veda: " Vishnu Purâna Commentary"*)*;* or literally: " One Prâdhânika Brahma Spirit: THAT was." The " Prâdhânika Brahma Spirit " is Mulaprakriti and Parabrahmam.

In Vishnu Purâna, Parâsara says to Maitreya, his pupil:—" I have thus explained to you, excellent Muni, six creations. . . . the creation of the Arvâksrotas beings was the seventh, and was that of man." Then he proceeds to speak of two additional and very mysterious creations, variously interpreted by the commentators.

Origen, commenting upon the books written by Celsus, his opponent —books which were all destroyed by the prudent Church Fathers— evidently answers the objections of his contradictor and reveals his system at the same time. This was evidently *septenary*. But his theogony, the genesis of the stars or planets, that of sound and colour, all found as an answer satire, and no better. Celsus, you see, " desiring to exhibit his learning," speaks of a ladder of creation with *seven gates*, and on the top of it the eighth—ever closed. The mysteries of the Persian Mithras are explained and "musical reasons, moreover, are added." . . . . And to these again he strives "to add a second explanation connected also with musical considerations,"*—*i.e.*, with the seven notes of the scale, the Seven Spirits of the Stars, &c., &c.

Valentinus expatiates upon the power of the great *Seven*, who were called to bring forth this universe after *Ar(r)hetos*, or the Ineffable, whose name is composed of seven letters, had represented the first *hebdomad*. This name (Ar(r)hetos) is one to indicate the Sevenfold nature of the One (the *logos*). "The goddess Rhea," says Proclus in *Timæus* (p. 121), "is a Monad, Duad, and Heptad," comprehending in herself all the *Titanidæ*, "who are seven."

The *Seven Creations* are found in almost every Purâna. They are all preceded by what Wilson translates—"the indiscrete Principle," absolute Spirit independent of any relation with objects of sense. They are—(1) *Mahattattwa*, the Universal Soul, Infinite Intellect, or Divine Mind; (2) *Bhûta* or *Bhûtasarga*, elemental creation, the first differentiation of Universal indiscrete Substance; (3) *Indriya* or *Aindriyaka*, organic evolution. "These three were the Prâkrita creations, the *developments of indiscrete nature* preceded by indiscrete principle"; (4) *Mukhya*, the fundamental creation of perceptible things, was that of inanimate bodies †; (5) *Tairyagyonya*, or *Tiryaksrotas*, was that of animals; (6) *Urdhwasrotas*, or that of divinities‡ (?); (7) *Arvaksrotas*, was that of man. (*See Vishnu Purâna.*)

This is the order given in the *exoteric* texts. According to esoteric teaching there are seven primary, and seven secondary "creations;" the former being the Forces *self-evolving* from the one *causeless* FORCE; the latter, showing the manifested Universe emanating from the already differentiated *divine* elements.

Esoterically, as well as exoterically, all the above enumerated Creations stand for the (7) periods of Evolution, whether after an "Age" or a "Day" of Brahmâ. This is the teaching *par excellence* of Occult Philosophy, which, however, never uses the term "creation," nor even that of evolution, "with regard to *primary* 'Creation':" but calls all such *forces* "the *aspects* of the Causeless Force." In the Bible

---

* Origen *contra* Celsum, b. vi., chap. xxii.

† The text says: "And the fourth creation is *here* the primary, for *things* immovable are emphatically known as primary." (*See Fitzedward Hall's Corrections.*)

‡ How can "divinities" have been created *after* the animals? The esoteric meaning of the expression "animals" is the *germs of all animal life* including man. Man is called a *sacrificial animal*, and an animal that is the only one among animal creation who sacrifices to the gods. *Moreover*, by the "sacred animals," the 12 signs of the zodiac are often meant in the sacred texts, as already stated.

the seven periods are dwarfed into the six days of creation and the seventh *day* of rest, and the Westerns adhere to the letter. In the Hindu philosophy, when the active Creator has produced the world of gods, the *germs* of all the undifferentiated elements and the rudiments of future senses (the world of noumena, in short), the Universe remains unaltered for a "Day of Brahmâ," a period of 4,320,000,000 years. This is the *seventh* passive period or the "Sabbath day" of Eastern philosophy, that follows six periods of active evolution. In the *Satapatha Brâhmana* "Brahma" (neuter), the *absolute Cause* of all Causes, *radiates* the gods. Having radiated the gods (through its inherent nature) the work is interrupted. In the 1st Book of Manu it is said, "At the expiration of each night (pralaya) Brahmâ, having been asleep, awakes, and, *through the sole energy of the motion*, CAUSES to emanate from *itself* the spirit, which in its essence is, and yet is not."

In the *Sepher Jezirah*, the Kabalistic Book of Creation, the author has evidently repeated the words of Manu. In it the Divine Substance is represented as having alone existed from the eternity, boundless and absolute ; and as having emitted from itself the Spirit. "One is the Spirit of the living God, blessed be his Name, who liveth for ever ! Voice, Spirit, and Word, this is the Holy Spirit." (*Sepher Jezireh, chap.* 1, *Mishna IX.*) And this is the Kabalistic abstract Trinity, so unceremoniously anthropomorphized by the Fathers. From this triple ONE emanated the whole Kosmos. First from ONE emanated number TWO, or Air, the creative element; and then number THREE, *Water*, proceeded from the air ; *Ether* or *Fire* complete the mystic four, the Arba-il. (Ibid.) In the Eastern doctrine Fire is the first Element— *Ether*, synthesizing the whole (since it contains all of them).

In the *Vishnu Purâna*, the whole seven periods are given, and the progressive Evolution of "Spirit-Soul," and of the seven forms of matter (or principles) are shown. It is impossible to enumerate them in this work. The reader is asked to peruse one of the Purânas.

"R. Yehudah began, it is written : 'Elohim said : Let there be a firmament, in the midst of waters. . . . . At the time that the Holy . . . created the world, He (they) created seven heavens Above. He created seven earths Below, seven seas, seven days, seven rivers, seven weeks, seven years, seven times, and 7,000 years that the world has been. . . . . the seventh of all the millennium. So here are seven earths Below, they are all inhabited except those which are above, and those . . . . below. And . . . . between each earth, a heaven (firmament) is spread out between each other. . . . . And there are in them (these earths) creatures who look different from each other . . . . but if you object and say that all the children of the world came out from Adam, it is not so. . . . . And the lower earths, where do they come from ? They are *from the chain of the earth*, and from the heaven below," etc., etc.*

Irenæus is our witness (and a very unwilling one, too) that the Gnostics taught the same system, veiling very carefully the true esoteric meaning. This "veiling," however, is identical with that of the Vishnu Purâna and others. Thus Irenæus writes of the Marcosians: "They maintain that first of all the four elements, fire, water, earth and air, were produced after the image of the primary *tetrad* above, and that then if we add their operations, namely, heat, cold, dryness and moisture, an exact likeness of the ogdoad is presented." (B. i. ch. xvii.)

Only this "likeness" and the *ogdoad* itself is a blind, just as in the seven creations of the Vishnu Purânas, to which two more are added of which the eighth, termed Anûgraha, "possesses both the qualities of goodness and darkness," a Sankhyan more than a Purânic idea. For Irenæus says again (b. i. xxx. 6) that "they (the Gnostics) had a like eighth creation which was good and bad, divine and human. They affirm that man was formed *on the eighth day*. Sometimes they affirm that he was made on the *sixth day*, and at others on the eighth; unless, perchance, they mean that his earthly part was formed on the sixth day and his fleshly part (?) on the eighth day; these two being distinguished by them."

They were so "distinguished," but not as Irenæus gives it. The Gnostics had a superior *Hebdomad*, and an inferior one, in Heaven; and a third terrestial *Hebdomad*, on the plane of matter. IAO, the mystery god and the Regent of the Moon, as given in Origen's chart, was the chief of these superior "*Seven Heavens*,"† hence identical with the chief of the lunar Pitris, that name being given by them to the lunar Dhyan-Chohans. "They affirm that these seven heavens are intelligent, and *speak of them as being angels*," writes the same Irenæus; and adds that on this account they termed Iao Hebdomas, while his mother was called "*Ogdoas*," because, as he explains, "she preserved the number of *the first begotten and primary Ogdoad of the Pleroma*." (Ibid. b. i, v. 2).

This "first begotten *Ogdoad*" was (*a*) in theogony the *second Logos* (the manifested) because he was born of the Seven-fold *first Logos*, hence he is the eighth on this manifested plane; and (*b*) in astrolatry, it was the *Sun*, Mârttanda—the eighth son of Aditi, whom she rejects while preserving her Seven Sons, *the planets*. For the ancients have never regarded the Sun as a planet, but *as a central and fixed Star*. This, then, is the second Hebdomad born of the *Seven-rayed* one, Agni, the Sun

---

* Qabbalah, p. 415-16, by T. Myer, Philadelphia.
† Superior to the Spirits or "Heavens" of the Earth only.

and what not, only not the seven planets, which are Surya's *brothers*, not his *Sons*. These *Astral* gods, whose chief with the Gnostics was Ildabaoth* (from *Ilda* "child," and *Baoth* "the egg"), the son of Sophia Achamoth, the daughter of Sophia (Wisdom), whose region is the Pleroma, were his (Ildaboth's) sons. He produces from himself these six stellar spirits : *Jove* (Jehovah), *Sabaoth, Adonai, Eloi, Osraios, Astaphaios,*† and it is they who are the second, or inferior *Hebdomad*. As to the third, it is composed of the seven primeval men, the shadows of the lunar gods, projected by the first Hebdomad. In this the Gnostics did not, as seen, differ much from the esoteric doctrine except that they veiled it. As to the charge made by Irenæus, who was evidently ignorant of the true tenets of the "Heretics," with regard to man being created on the *sixth* day, and man being created on the *eighth*, this relates to the mysteries of the *inner* man. It will become com prehensible to the reader only after he has read Book II., and under-stood well the *Anthropogenesis* of the Esoteric doctrine.

Ildabaoth is a copy of Manu. The latter boasts, "Oh, best of twice-born men ! Know that I (Manu) am he, the creator of all this world, whom that male Virâj . . . spontaneously produced " (I., 33). He first creates the ten lords of Being, the Prajâpatis, who, as verse 36 says . . . "produce seven other Manus." (*The Ordinances of Manu.*) Ildabaoth does likewise : " I am Father and God, and there is no one above me," he exclaims. For which his mother coolly puts him down by saying, " Do not lie, Ildabaoth, for the father of all, the *first* man (*Anthropos*) *is above thee, and so is Anthropos, the Son of Anthropos*" (Irenæus, b. 1, ch. xxx., 6). This is a good proof that there were three Logoi (besides the Seven born of the First), one of these being the *Solar Logos*. And, again, who was that " Anthropos " himself, so much higher than Ildabaoth ? The Gnostic records alone can solve this riddle. In *Pistis Sophia* the four-vowelled name Iεov is in each case accompanied by the epithet of "the Primal, or First man." This shows again that the gnosis was but an echo of our archaic doctrine. The names answering to Parabrahm, to Brahm, and Manu (the first *thinking* man) are composed of one-vowelled, three-vowelled and seven-vowelled sounds. Marcus, whose philosophy was certainly more Pythagorean than anything else, speaks of a revelation to him of the seven heavens sounding each one vowel as they pronounced the seven names of the seven (angelic) hierarchies.

When spirit has permeated every minutest atom of the seven prin-ciples of Kosmos, then the *secondary* creation, after the above-mentioned period of rest, begins.

---

* See " Isis Unveiled," Vol. II., p. 183.

† See also King's *Gnostics*. Other sects regarded Jehovah as Ildabaoth himself King identifies him with Saturn.

" The creators (Elohim) outline in the *second* 'hour' the shape of man," says Rabbi Simeon (*The Nuctameron of the Hebrews*). " There are twelve hours in the day," says the *Mishna*, " and it is during these that creation is accomplished." The " twelve hours of the day " are again the dwarfed copy, the faint, yet faithful, echo of primitive Wisdom. They are like the 12,000 divine years of the gods, a cyclic blind. Every " Day of Brahmâ " has 14 Manus, which the Hebrew Kabalists, following, however, in this the Chaldeans, have disguised into 12 " Hours."* The *Nuctameron* of Apollonius of Tyana is the same thing. " The Dodecahedron lies concealed in the perfect Cube," say the Kabalists. The mystic meaning of this is, that the twelve great transformations of Spirit into matter (the 12,000 divine years) take place during the four great ages, or the first *Mahayuga*. Beginning with the metaphysical and the supra-human, it ends in the physical and purely human natures of Kosmos and man. Eastern philosophy can give the number of mortal years that run along the line of spiritual and physical evolutions of the seen and the unseen, if Western science fails to do so.

Primary Creation is called the *Creation of Light* (Spirit); and the *Secondary*—that of Darkness (matter).† Both are found in *Genesis*, chap. i., v. 2, and at the beginning of chapter ii. The first is the emanation of *self*-born gods (Elohim); the second of physical nature.

This is why it is said in the Zohar :—" Oh, companions, companions, man as emanation was both man and woman ; as well on the side of the FATHER as on the side of the MOTHER. And this is the sense of the words:—And Elohim spoke: ' Let there be Light and it was Light ! ' . . . And this is the ' two-fold man ! ' " Light, moreover, on our plane, is *darkness* in the higher spheres.

" Man and woman on the side of the FATHER " (Spirit) refers to Primary Creation ; and on the side of the *Mother* (matter) to the secondary. The two-fold man is Adam Kadmon, the male and female abstract prototype and the *differentiated* Elohim. *Man* proceeds from the Dhyan Chohan, and is a " Fallen Angel," a god in exile, as will be shown.

In India these creations were described as follows :—

(I.) Mahat-tattwa creation—so-called because it was the primordial self-evolution of that which had to become *Mahat*—the " divine MIND, conscious and intelligent "; esoterically, " the *spirit* of the Universal soul." . . . " Worthiest of ascetics, through its potency (*the potency of that cause*); every *produced* cause comes by its proper nature." (*Vishnu Purâna*.) " Seeing that the potencies of all beings are under-

---

* Elsewhere, however, the identity is revealed. *See supra*, the quotation from Ibn-Gabirol and his 7 heavens, 7 earths, etc.

† This must not be confused with *precosmic* " DARKNESS," the Divine ALL.

stood *only* through the knowledge of *That* (Brahma), which is beyond reasoning, creation, and the like, such potencies are referable to Brahma." THAT, then, precedes the manifestation. " The first was *Mahat,*" says *Linga Purâna;* for the ONE (the *That*) is neither *first* nor *last,* but ALL. Exoterically, however, this manifestation is the *work* of the " Supreme One " (a natural *effect,* rather, of an Eternal Cause) ; or, as the Commentator says, it might have been understood to mean that Brahmâ was then *created* (?), being identified with Mahat, active intelligence or the operating will of the Supreme. Esoteric philosophy renders it " the operating LAW."

It is on the right comprehension of this tenet in the Brâhmanas and Purânas that hangs, we believe, the apple of discord between the three Vedantin Sects: the Advaita, Dwaita, and the Visishtadvaitas. The first arguing rightly that Parabrahman, having no relation, as the absolute *all,* to the manifested world—the Infinite having no connection with the finite—can neither *will* nor *create;* that, therefore, Brahmâ, Mahat, Iswara, or whatever name the creative power may be known by, creative gods and all, are simply an illusive aspect of Parabrahmam in the conception of the conceivers ; while the other sects identify the impersonal Cause with the Creator, or Iswara.

Mahat (or Maha-Buddhi) is, with the Vaishnavas, however, divine mind *in active operation,* or, as Anaxagoras has it, " an ordering and disposing mind, which was the cause of all things,"—Νοῦς ὅ διακοσμῶντε καὶ πάντων ἄιτιος.

Wilson saw at a glance the suggestive connection between *Mahat* and the Phœnician Mot, or *Mut,* who was female with the Egyptians—the Goddess Mout, the " Mother "—" which, like Mahat," he says, " was the first product of the mixture (?) of Spirit and matter, and the first rudiment of Creation : " " Ex connexione autem ejus spiritus prodiit Mot . . . . . From whose seed were created all living things "—repeats Brücker (I., 240)—giving it a still more materialistic and anthropomorphic colouring.

Nevertheless, the esoteric sense of the doctrine is seen through every exoteric sentence on the very face of the old Sanscrit texts that treat of primordial Creation. " The Supreme Soul, the *all permeant* (Sarvaga) Substance of the World, having entered (*been drawn*) into matter (prakriti) and Spirit (purusha), *agitated* the *mutable and the immutable principles* the season of Creation (manvantara) having arrived."* . . .

---

* The *nous* of the Greeks, which is (spiritual or divine) mind, or *mens,* " Mahat," operates upon matter in the same way ; it " enters into " and *agitates* it:
> " Spiritus intus alit, totamque infusa per artus,
> Mens agitat molem, et magno se corpore miscet."
In the Phœnician Cosmogony, " Spirit mixing with its own principles gives rise to

Esoteric doctrine teaches that the Dhyan Chohans are the collective aggregate of divine Intelligence or primordial *mind*, and that the first Manus—the seven " mind-born" Spiritual Intelligences—are identical with the former. Hence the " Kwan-shi-yin"—" the golden Dragon in whom are the seven," of Stanza III.—is the primordial Logos, or Brahmâ, the first manifested creative Power ; and the Dhyani-Energies are the Manus, or *Manu-Swayambhûva collectively*. The direct connection, moreover, between the " Manus" and " Mahat" is easy to see. *Manu* is from the root *man*, " to think"; and thinking proceeds from the mind. It is, in Cosmogony, the pre-nebular period.

(II.) " The *second* Creation," " Bhûta," was of the rudimental principles (Tanmâtras), thence termed the elemental creation (*Bhûta-sarga*).* It is the period of the first breath of the differentiation of the *pre-Cosmic* Elements or matter. *Bhûtâdi* means literally " the origin of the Elements," and precedes *Bhûta-sarga*—the " creation" or differentiation of those Elements in primordial " Akâsa" (Chaos or Vacuity).† In the " Vishnu Purâna " it is said to proceed along, and belong to, the triple aspect of *Ahankâra*, translated Egotism, but meaning rather that untranslatable term the " I-AM-NESS," that which first issues from " Mahat," or divine mind ; the first shadowy outline of Self-hood, for " pure" Ahankâra becomes " passionate" and finally " rudimental "

creation " also ; (*Brücker*, I., 240) ; the Orphic triad shows an identical doctrine : for there *Phanes* (or Eros), *Chaos*, containing crude *undifferentiated* Cosmic matter, and *Chronos* (time), are the three co-operating principles, emanating from the Unknowable and concealed *point*, which produce the work of " Creation." And they are the Hindu *Purusha* (phanes), *Pradhâna* (chaos), and *Kâla* (Chronos) or *time*. The good Professor Wilson does not like the idea, as no Christian clergyman, however liberal, would. He remarks that " as presently explained, the *mixture* (of the *Supreme* Spirit or Soul) *is not mechanical;* it is *an influence or effect exerted upon intermediate agents* which produce effects." The sentence in *Vishnu Purâna:* " As fragrance affects the mind from its proximity merely, *and not from any immediate operation upon mind itself,* so the Supreme influenced the elements of creation," the reverend and erudite Sanscritist correctly explains . . . : " As perfumes do not delight the mind by actual contact, but by the impression they make upon the sense of smelling, which communicates it to the mind," adding : " The entrance of the *Supreme* into spirit, as well as matter, *is less intelligible* than the view elsewhere taken of it, as the *infusion* of spirit, identified with the supreme, into Prakriti or matter alone." He prefers the verse in *Padma Purâna:* " He who is called the *male* (spirit) of Prakriti . . . that same divine Vishnu entered into Prakriti." This " view " is certainly more akin to the plastic character of certain verses in the Bible concerning the Patriarchs, such as Lot (*Gen. xix.*, 34-38) and even Adam (*iv., v.* 1), and others of a still more anthropomorphic nature. But it is just that which led Humanity to *Phallicism*, Christian religion being honeycombed with it, from the first chapter of *Genesis* down to the *Revelation*.

* All these sentences are quoted from " Vishnu Purâna," Book I., ch. ii.

† Vishnu is both Bhûtesa, " Lord of the Elements, and all things," and *Viswarûpa*, " Universal Substance or Soul."

(initial) ; it is " the origin of conscious as of all *unconscious* being," though the Esoteric school rejects the idea of anything being "unconscious" —save on this (our) plane of illusion and ignorance. At this stage of the Second Creation, the second hierarchy of the Manus appear, the Dhyan Chohans or Devas, who are the origin of Form (rûpa) : the *Chitrasikhandina* (bright-crested) or the *Riksha*—those Rishis who have become the informing souls of the seven stars (of the Great Bear).* In astronomical and Cosmogonical language this Creation relates to the first stage of Cosmic-life, the *Fire-Mist* Period after its Chaotic stage,† when atoms issue from *Laya*.

(III.) The third (the *Indriya*) was the modified form of *Ahankâra*, the conception of " I," (from " *Aham*," " I ") termed the organic Creation, or creation of the senses (*Aindriyaka*). " These three were the Prâkrita creation, the (discrete) developments of indiscrete nature preceded by the indiscrete principle." " Preceded by," ought to be replaced here with " beginning by," Buddhi ; for the latter is neither a discrete nor an *indiscrete quantity*, but partakes of the nature of both, in man as in Kosmos : a unit—a human MONAD on the plane of illusion — when once freed from the three forms of Ahankâra and liberated from its terrestrial manas, *Buddhi* becomes truly a continued quantity, both in duration and extension, because eternal and immortal. Earlier it is stated, that the *third* Creation " abounding with the quality of goodness, is termed *Urdhvasrotas;* " and a page or two further the *Urdhvasrotas* creation is referred to as " the sixth creation . . . that of the divinities" (p. 75). This shows plainly that earlier as well as later manvantaras have been purposely confused, to prevent the pro-

---

* See concerning their *post-types*, the Treatise written by Trithemius (Agrippa's master, 16th cent.). "Concerning the seven secondaries, or Spiritual Intelligences, who, after God, actuate the Universe ;" giving out, besides secret cycles and several prophecies, certain facts and beliefs about the Genii, or the Elohim, which preside over and guide the septenary stages of the World's Course.

† From the first, the Orientalists have found themselves beset by great difficulties with regard to any possible order in the Purânic *Creations*. Brahma is very often confused with Brahmâ, by Wilson, for which he is criticised by his successors. The " *Original Sanscrit Texts*" are preferred by Mr. Fitzedward Hall for the translation of *Vishnu Purâna* and texts, to those used by Wilson. " Had Professor Wilson enjoyed the advantages which are now at the command of the student of Indian philosophy, unquestionably he would have expressed himself differently," as said by the editor of his works. This reminds one of the answer given by one of Thomas Taylor's admirers to those scholars who criticised his translations of Plato. " Thomas Taylor may have had less knowledge of the Greek than his critics have, but he understood Plato far better than they do," he said. Our present Orientalists disfigure the *mystic* sense of the Sanskrit texts far more than Wilson ever did, though the latter is undeniably guilty of very gross errors.

fane from perceiving the truth. This is called "incongruity" and "contradictions" by the Orientalists.*

This "creation" of the immortals, the "*Deva-Sarga*," is the last of the first series, and has a universal reference; namely, to Evolutions in general, not specifically to our *Manvantara*; but the latter begins with the same over and over again, showing that it refers to several distinct Kalpas. For it is said "at the close of the past (*Padma*) Kalpa the divine Brahmâ awoke from his night of sleep and beheld the universe void." Then Brahmâ is shown going once more over the "seven creations" in the secondary stage of evolution, repeating the first three on the objective plane.

(IV.) The *Mukhya*, the Primary as it begins the series of four. Neither the word "inanimate" bodies nor yet *immovable* things, as translated by Wilson, gives a correct idea of the Sanskrit terms used. Esoteric philosophy is not the only one to reject the idea of any atom being *inorganic*, for it is found also in orthodox Hinduism. Moreover, Wilson himself says (*in his collected Works, vol. iii., p.* 381): "All the Hindu systems consider vegetable bodies as endowed with life . . ." *Charâchara*, or the synonymous *sthâvara* and *jangama*, is, therefore, inaccurately rendered by "animate and inanimate," "sentient beings," and "unconscious," or "conscious and unconscious beings," etc., etc. "Locomotive and fixed" would be better, since trees are considered to possess souls." *Mukhya* is the "creation" or organic evolution of the vegetable kingdom. In this *secondary* Period, the three degrees of Elemental or Rudimental Kingdoms are evolved in this world, corresponding *inversely* in order to the three Prakritic creations during the Primary period of Brahmâ's activity. As in that period, in the words of "Vishnu Purâna": "The first creation was that of *Mahat* (Intellect), the second, of *Tanmâtras* (rudimental principles), and the third, that of the senses (Aindriyaka)"; in this one, the order of the Elemental Forces stands thus: (1) The *nascent* centres of Force (intellectual and physical); (2) the rudimental principles—*nerve force*, so to say; and (3) nascent *apperception*, which is the *Mahat* of the lower kingdoms, especially developed in the third order of Elementals; these are succeeded by the

---

* "The three Creations beginning with Intelligence are elemental, but the six creations which proceed from the series of which Intellect is the first are the work of Brahmâ (*Vâyu-Purâna*). Here "creations" mean everywhere *stages* of Evolution. *Mahat,* "Intellect" or *mind* (which corresponds with Manas, the former being on the Cosmic, and the latter on the human plane) stands here, too, lower than *Buddhi* or Supra-divine Intelligence. Therefore, when we read in *Linga Purâna* that "the first Creation was that of Mahat, Intellect being the first in manifestation," we must refer that (specified) creation to the first evolution of our system or even our Earth, none of the preceding ones being discussed in the *Purânas*, but only occasionally hinted at.

objective kingdom of minerals, in which latter that apperception is entirely latent, to re-develop only in the plants). The *mukhya* "Creation," then, is the middle point between the three lower and the three higher kingdoms, which represent the seven esoteric kingdoms of Kosmos, as of Earth.

(V.) The *Tiryaksrotas* (or Tairyagyonya) creation,* that of the " (*sacred*) animals," corresponding only on Earth, to the dumb animal creation. That which is meant by " animals," in *primary* Creation, is the germ of awakening consciousness or of *apperception*, that which is faintly traceable in some sensitive plants on Earth and more distinctly in the *protistic* monera.† On our globe, during the first round, animal " creation " precedes that of man, while the former (or mammal) evolves from the latter in our fourth round—on the physical plane: in Round I. the animal atoms are drawn into a cohesion of human physical form ; while in Round IV. the reverse occurs according to magnetic conditions developed during life. And this is *metempsychosis* (*See " Mineral Monad" in "Five Years of Theosophy,"*. *p.* 276). This fifth stage of evolution, called exoterically " Creation," may be viewed in both the *Primary* and *Secondary* periods, one as the Spiritual and Cosmic, the other as the material and *terrestrial*. It is *Archibiosis*, or life-origination—" origination," so far, of course, as the *manifestation* of life on all the seven planes is concerned. It is at this period of Evolution that the *absolutely eternal* universal motion, or vibration, that which is called in Esoteric language " the GREAT BREATH," differentiates in the primordial, first manifested ATOM. More and more, as chemical and physical sciences progress, does this occult axiom find its corroboration in the world of knowledge : the scientific hypothesis, that even the simplest elements of matter are identical in nature and differ from each other only owing to the variety of the distributions of *atoms* in the molecule or speck of substance, or by the modes of its *atomic vibration*, gains every day more ground.

Thus, as the differentiation of the primordial germ of life has to precede the evolution of the Dhyan Chohan of *the third* group or hierarchy of Being in Primary Creation, before those " gods " can become *rûpa* (embodied in their first ethereal form), so animal creation has to *precede*,

---

* Professor Wilson translates it, as though animals were higher on the scale of "creation " than divinities, or angels, although the truth about the devas is very plainly stated further on. This " creation," says the text, is both primary (*Prâkrita*) and secondary (*Vaikrita*). It is the latter, as regards the origin of the gods from Brahmâ (the *personal* anthropormorphic *creator* of our material universe); it is the former (*primary*) as affecting Rudra, who is the immediate production of the first principle. Rudra is not alone a title of Siva, but embraces agents of creation, angels and men, as will be shown further on.

† Neither plant nor animal, but an existence between the two.

for that same reason, *divine* MAN on earth.   And this is why we find in
the Purânas : " The fifth, the Tairyagyonya creation, was that of
animals, and—

(VI). The Urdhvasrotas creation, or that of divinities *(Vishnu Purâna
Book I. chap. i.).*   But these (divinities) are simply the prototypes of
the First Race, the fathers of their " mind-born " progeny with the *soft*
bones.*   It is these who became the *Evolvers* of the " Sweat-born "—an
expression explained in Book II.   Finally, the sixth " Creation " is
followed, and " *Creation* in general, closed by—

(VII.) The evolution of the " *Arvaksrotas* beings, which was the
seventh, and was that of man " (*Vishnu Purâna, Book I.*).

The " eighth creation " mentioned is no *Creation* at all ; it is a *blind*
again, for it refers to a purely mental process : the cognition of the
" ninth " creation, which, in its turn, is an effect, manifesting in the
secondary of that which was a " Creation " in the *Primary* (*Prâkrita*)
Creation.†   The *Eighth*, then, called *Anûgraha* (the *Pratyayasarga* or the
intellectual creation of the Sankhyas, explained in *Karika*, v. 46,
p. 146), is " that creation of which *we have a perception*"—in its
esoteric aspect — and " to which we give intellectual assent
Anûgraha) in contradistinction to *organic creation.*"   It is the
correct perception of our relations to the whole range of " gods "
and especially of those we bear to the *Kumâras*—the so-called " Ninth
Creation "—which is in reality an aspect of or reflection of the sixth in
our manvantara (the Vaivasvata).   " There is a *ninth*, the Kumâra
Creation, which is both primary and secondary," says *Vishnu Purâna,*
the oldest of such texts.‡   " The *Kumâras*," explains an *esoteric* text,

---

* " Created beings "—explains *Vishnu Purana*—" although they are destroyed (in
their individual forms) at the periods of dissolution, yet being affected by the good or
evil acts of former *existences*, are never exempted from their consequences.   And
when Brahmâ produces the world anew, they are the progeny of his will . . ."
" *Collecting his mind into itself* (*Yoga* willing), Brahmâ creates the four orders of beings,
termed gods, demons, *progenitors*, and *MEN* " . . . " progenitors " meaning the prototypes and Evolvers of the first Root Race of men.   The progenitors are the Pitris, and
are of seven classes.   They are said in *exoteric* mythology to be born of *Brahma's side,*
like Eve from the rib of Adam.

† " These notions," remarks Dr. Wilson, " the birth of Rudra and the saints, seem
to have been *borrowed* from the Saivas, and to have been awkwardly engrafted upon the
Vaishnava system."   The esoteric meaning ought to have been consulted before ven-
turing such a hypothesis.

‡ Parâsara, the Vedic Rishi, who received the Vishnu Purâna from Pulastya and
taught it to Maitreya, is placed by the Orientalists at various epochs.   As correctly
observed, in the *Hindu Class. Dict :*—" Speculations as to his era differ widely from 575
B.C. to 1391 B.C., and *cannot be trusted.*"   Quite so ; but no less, however, than any
other date as assigned by the Sanskritists, so famous in this department of arbitrary
fancy.

" are the Dhyanis, derived immediately from the supreme Principle, who reappear in the Vaivasvata Manu period, for the progress of mankind."* The commentator of the *Vishnu Purâna* corroborates it, by remarking that " these *sages* live as long as Brahmâ ; and they are only created by him in the *first* Kalpa, although their generation is very commonly and inconsistently introduced in the *Varaha*, or *Padma Kalpa* " (the secondary). Thus, the Kumâras are, exoterically, " the creation of Rudra or Nilalohita, a form of Siva, by Brahmâ, and of certain other mind-born sons of Brahmâ. But, in the esoteric teaching, they are the progenitors of the true spiritual SELF in the physical man—the higher Prajâpati, while the Pitris, or lower Prajâpati, are no more than the *fathers* of the model, or type of his physical form, made " in *their* image." Four (and occasionally *five*) are mentioned freely in the exoteric texts, three Kumâras being secret.† (Compare what is said of " The Fallen Angels " in Book II.).

The Exoteric four are : Sanât-Kumâra, Sananda, Sanaka, and Sanatana ; and the esoteric three are : Sana, Kapila, and Sanatsujâta. Special attention is once more drawn to this class of Dhyan Chohans, for herein lies the mystery of generation and heredity hinted at in Book I. (*See the four Orders of Angelic Beings ; Comment on Stanza VII.*). Book II. explains their position in the divine Hierarchy. Meanwhile, let us see what the *exoteric* texts say about them.

They do not say much ; nothing to him who fails to read between the lines. " We must have recourse, here, to other Purânas for the elucidation of this term," remarks Wilson, who does not suspect for one moment that he is in the presence of the " Angels of Darkness," the mythical " great enemy " of his Church. Therefore, he contrives to *elucidate* no more than that these (divinities) DECLINING TO CREATE PROGENY‡ (and thus rebelling against Brahmâ), remained, as the name

---

* They may indeed mark a " special" or extra *creation*, since it is they who, by incarnating themselves within the senseless human shells of the two first Root-races, and a great portion of the Third Root-race—create, so to speak, a *new race :* that of thinking, self-conscious and *divine* men.

† " The four Kumâras (are) the mind-born Sons of Brahmâ. Some *specify seven* " (*H. Class. Dict.*). All these seven Vaidhatra, the patronymic of the Kumâras, " the Maker's Sons," are mentioned and described in Iswara Krishna's " Sânkhya Kârika " with the Commentary of Gaudapâdâcharya (Sankarâchârya's *Paraguru*) attached to it. It discusses the nature of the Kumâras, though it refrains from mentioning *by name* all the seven Kumâras, but calls them instead " the seven sons of Brahmâ," which they are, as they are created by Brahmâ in Rudra. The list of names it gives us is : Sanaka, Sanandana, Sanatana, Kapila, Ribhu, and Panchasikha. But these are again all *aliases*.

‡ So untrustworthy are some translations of the Orientalists that in the French Translation of *Hari-Vamsa*, it is said " The seven Prajâpati, Rudra, Skanda (his son)

of the first implies, ever boys, Kumâras: that is, ever pure and innocent, whence their creation is also called the " Kumâra." *(Book I. chap. v., Vishnu Purâna.)* The Purânas, however, may afford a little more light. " Being ever as he was born, he is here called a youth; and hence his name is well known as Sanat-Kumâra" *(Linga purâna, prior section LXX.* 174.) In the *Saiva Purâna*, the Kumâras are always described as Yogins. The Kurma Purâna, after enumerating them, says: " These five, O Brahmans, were Yogins, who acquired entire exemption from passion." They are *five*, because two of the Kumâras *fell*.

Of all the seven great divisions of Dhyan-Chohans, or Devas, there is none with which humanity is more concerned than with the Kumâras. Imprudent are the Christian Theologians who have degraded them into *fallen* Angels, and now call them "Satan" and Demons; as among these heavenly denizens who *refuse to create*, the Archangel Michael—the greatest patron Saint of Western and Eastern Churches, under his double name of St. Michael and his supposed copy on earth, St. George conquering the DRAGON—has to be allowed one of the most prominent places. (See Book II., " The Sacred Dragons and their Slayers.")

The Kumâras, the "mind-born Sons" of *Brahmâ-Rudra* (or Siva)

---

and Sanat-Kumâra proceeded to create beings." Whereas, as Wilson shows, the original is: " These seven . . . created progeny; and so did Rudra, but Skanda and Sanat Kumâra, *restraining their power, abstained* from creation." The " four orders of beings" are referred to sometimes as " Ambhamsi," which Wilson renders: "literally Waters," and believes it "a mystic term." It is one, no doubt; but he evidently failed to catch the *real* esoteric meaning. " Waters" and " water" stand as the symbol for Akâsa, the "primordial Ocean of Space," on which Narâyana, the self-born Spirit, moves: reclining on that *which is its progeny (See Manu).* " Water is the body of Nara; thus we have heard the name of water explained. Since *Brahmâ* rests on the water, therefore he is termed *Narâyana* " *(Linga, Vayu, and Markandeya Purânas)* ". . . Pure, Purusha created the waters pure . . ." at the same time Water is the third principle in material Kosmos, and the third in the realm of the Spiritual: *Spirit* of Fire, Flame, Akâsa, Ether, Water, Air, Earth, are the cosmic, sidereal, psychic, spiritual and mystic principles, *pre-eminently occult*, in every *plane* of being. " Gods, Demons, Pitris and men," are the four orders of beings to whom the term Ambhamsi is applied (in the Vedas it is a synonym of gods): because they are all the product of WATERS (mystically), of the Akâsic Ocean, and of the Third principle in nature. Pitris and men on earth are the transformations (rebirths) of gods and demons (Spirits) on a higher plane. Water is, in another sense, the feminine principle. Venus Aphrodite is the personified Sea, and the mother of the god of love, the generator of all the gods as much as the Christian Virgin Mary is Mare (the sea), the mother of the Western God of Love, Mercy and Charity. If the student of Esoteric philosophy thinks deeply over the subject he is sure to find out all the suggestiveness of the term Ambhamsi, in its manifold relations to the Virgin in Heaven, to the Celestial Virgin of the Alchemists, and even to the " Waters of Grace " of the modern Baptist.

the howling and terrific *destroyer of human passions and physical senses*, which are ever in the way of the development of the higher spiritual perceptions and the growth of the *inner* eternal man—mystically,* are the progeny of Siva, the *Mahâyogi*, the great patron of all the Yogis and mystics of India. They themselves, being the " Virgin-Ascetics," refuse to create the *material* being MAN. Well may they be suspected of a direct connection with the Christian Archangel Michael, the " Virgin Combatant " of the Dragon *Apophis*, whose victim is every soul united too loosely to its immortal Spirit, the Angel who, as shown by the Gnostics, *refused to create* just as the Kumâras did. (*See Book II.*, "*The Mystic Dragons and their Slayers.*") . . . Does not that patron-Angel of the Jews *preside* over Saturn (Siva or Rudra), and the Sabbath, the day of Saturn ? Is he not shown of the same essence with his father (Saturn), and called the " Son of Time," *Kronos, or Kâla* (time), a form of Brahmâ (Vishnu and Siva) ? " And is not " Old Time " of the Greeks, with its scythe and sand-glass, identical with the " Ancient of Days " of the Kabalists ; the latter " Ancient " being one with the Hindu " Ancient of Days," Brahmâ (in his *triune* form), whose name is also " Sanat," the Ancient ? Every Kumâra bears the prefix of *Sanat* and *Sana ;* and Sanaischara is Saturn, the planet (Sani and Sarra), the King Saturn whose Secretary in Egypt was Thot-Hermes the first. They are thus identified both with the planet and the god (Siva), who are, in their turn, shown the prototypes of Saturn, who is the same as Bel, Baal, Siva, and Jehovah Sabbaoth, *The angel of whose face is* MIKAEL (מיכאל " who is as God "). He is the patron, and guardian Angel of the Jews, as Daniel tells us (v. 21); and, before the Kumâras were degraded, by those who were ignorant of their very name, into demons and fallen angels, the Greek Ophites, the occultly inclined predecessors and precursors of the Roman Catholic Church after its secession and separation from the primitive Greek Church, had identified Michael with their *Ophiomorphos*, the rebellious and opposing spirit. This means nothing more than the reverse aspect (symbolically) of Ophis—divine Wisdom or Christos. In the *Talmud*, *Mikael* (Michael) is " Prince of *Water* " and the chief of the seven Spirits, for the same reason that his prototype (among many others) Sanat-Sujâta,

---

* Siva-Rudra is the Destroyer, as Vishnu is the preserver ; and both are the regenerators of spiritual as well as of physical nature. To live as a plant, the *seed* must die. To live as a conscious entity in the Eternity, the passions and senses of man must first DIE before his body does. " To live is to die and to die is to live," has been too little understood in the West. Siva, the *destroyer*, is the *creator* and the Saviour of Spiritual man, as he is the good gardener of nature. He weeds out the plants, human and cosmic, and kills the passions of the physical, to call to life the perceptions of the spiritual, man.

—the chief of the Kumâras—is called Ambhamsi, "Waters,"—according to the commentary on *Vishnu Purâna*. Why? Because the " Waters " is another name of the "Great Deep," the primordial Waters of space or *Chaos*, and also means "Mother," *Amba*, meaning Aditi and Akâsa, the Celestial Virgin-Mother of the visible universe. Furthermore, the " Waters of the flood " are also called " the GREAT DRAGON," or Ophis, Ophio-Morphos.

The Rudras will be noticed in their Septenary character of " Fire-Spirits" in the "Symbolism" attached to the Stanzas in Book II. There we shall also consider the Cross (3 + 4) under its primeval and later forms, and shall use for purposes of comparison the Pythagorean numbers side by side with Hebrew Metrology. The immense importance of the number *seven* will thus become evident, as the root number of nature. We shall examine it from the standpoints of the Vedas and the Chaldean Scriptures, as it existed in Egypt thousands of years B.C., and as treated in the Gnostic records ; we shall show how its importance as a basic number has gained recognition in physical Science; and we shall endeavour to prove that the importance attached to the number *seven* throughout all antiquity was due to no fanciful imaginings of uneducated priests, but to a profound knowledge of natural law.

---

§ XIV.

THE FOUR ELEMENTS.

METAPHYSICALLY and esoterically there is but One ELEMENT in nature, and at the root of it is the Deity ; and the so-called *seven* elements, of which five have already manifested and asserted their existence, are the garment, *the veil, of that deity ;* direct from the essence whereof comes MAN, whether physically, psychically, mentally or spiritually considered. Four elements only are generally spoken of in later antiquity, five admitted only in philosophy. For the body of ether is not fully manifested yet, and its noumenon is still "the Omnipotent Father— Æther, the synthesis of the rest." But what are these " ELEMENTS " whose compound bodies have now been discovered by Chemistry and Physics to contain numberless sub-elements, even the sixty or seventy of which no longer embrace the whole number suspected. (Vide *Addenda*, §§ XI. and XII., quotations from Mr. Crookes' Lectures.) Let us follow their evolution from the *historical* beginnings, at any rate.

The four Elements were fully characterized by Plato when he said that they were *that* " which *composes* and *decomposes* the *compound bodies*."

Hence Cosmolatry was never, even in its worst aspect, the fetishism which adores or worships the passive external form and matter of any object, but looked ever to the *noumenon* therein. Fire, Air, Water, Earth, were but the visible garb, the symbols of the informing, invisible Souls or Spirits—the Cosmic gods to whom worship was offered by the ignorant, and simple, respectful recognition by the wiser. In their turn the *phenomenal* subdivisions of the noumenal Elements were informed by the Elementals, so called, the "Nature Spirits" of lower grades.

In the *Theogony* of Moschus, we find Ether first, and then the air; the two principles from which Ulom the *intelligible* (νοητός) God (the visible universe of matter) is born.*

In the Orphic hymns, the Eros-Phanes evolves from the Spiritual Egg, which the Æthereal winds impregnate, Wind being "the Spirit of God," who is said to move in Æther, "brooding over the chaos"— the Divine "Idea." In the Hindu *Katakopanisâd*, Purusha, the Divine Spirit, already stands before the original matter, from whose union springs the great Soul of the World, "Mahâ=Atma, Brahm, the Spirit of Life;"† these latter appellations being again identical with the Universal Soul, or *Anima Mundi*, the Astral Light of the Theurgists and Kabalists, being its last and lowest division."

The στοιχεῖα, (Elements) of Plato and Aristotle, were thus the *incorporeal principles* attached to the four great divisions of our Cosmic World, and it is with justice that Creuzer defines those primitive beliefs . . . *as a species of magism, a psychic paganism, and a deification of potencies*; a spiritualization which placed the believers in a close community with these potencies," (Book IX, p. 850). So close, indeed, that the hierarchies of those potencies or Forces have been classified on a graduated scale of seven from the ponderable to the imponderable. They are Septenary,—not as an artificial aid to facilitate their comprehension—but in their real *Cosmic* gradation, from their chemical (or physical) to their purely spiritual composition. *Gods*—with the ignorant masses—gods independent and supreme; dæmons with the fanatics, who, intellectual as they often may be, are unable to understand the Spirit of the philosophical sentence, *in pluribus unum*. With the hermetic philosopher they are FORCES *relatively* "*blind*," or "*intelligent*," according to which of the principles in them he deals with. It required long millenniums before they found themselves, in our cultured age, finally degraded into simple chemical elements.

At any rate, good Christians, and especially the Biblical Protestants,

---

* Movers: "Phoinizer," 282.
† Weber: "Akad. Vorles," 213, 214, etc.

ought to show more reverence for the four Elements, if they would show any for Moses. For the Bible manifests the consideration and mystic significance in which they were held by the Hebrew Lawgiver, on every page of the Pentateuch. The tent which contained the Holy of Holies "was a Cosmic Symbol, sacred, in one of its meanings, to the Elements, the four cardinal points, and ETHER. Josephus shows it built in white, the colour of Ether. And this explains also why, in the Egyptian and the Hebrew temples — according to Clemens Alex- andrinus—a gigantic curtain, supported by five pillars, separated the *sanctum sanctorum* (now represented by the altar in Christian churches) wherein the priests alone were permitted to enter, from the part accessible to the profane. By its *four* colours the curtain symbolized the four principal Elements, and signified the knowledge of the divine that the *five* senses of men can enable man to acquire with the help of the *four* Elements. (See *Stromata* I., v. § 6).

In Cory's *Ancient Fragments*, one of the " Chaldean Oracles " expresses ideas about the elements and Ether in language singularly like that of the *Unseen Universe*, written by two eminent scientists of our day.

It states that "from ether have come all things, and to it all will return; that the images of all things are indelibly impressed upon it ; and that it is the store-house of the germs or of the remains of all visible forms, and even ideas. It appears as if this case strangely corroborates our assertion that whatever discoveries may be made in our days will be found to have been anticipated by many thousand years by our ' simple-minded ancestors.' "—(*Isis Unveiled.*)

Whence came the four elements and the *malachim* of the Hebrews ? They have been made to merge, by a theological sleight-of-hand on the part of the Rabbins and the later Fathers of the Church into Jehovah, but their origin is identical with that of the Cosmic gods of all other nations. Their symbols, whether born on the shores of the Oxus, on the burning sands of Upper Egypt, or in the wild forests, weird and glacial, which cover the slopes and peaks of the sacred snowy mountains of Thessaly, or again, in the *pampas* of America, their symbols, we repeat, when traced to their source, are ever one and the same. Whether Egyptian or Pelasgian, Aryan or Semitic, the *genius loci*, the local god, embraced in its unity all nature; but not especially the four elements any more than one of their creations, such as trees, rivers, mounts or stars. The *genius loci*—a very late after-thought of the last sub-races of the Fifth Root-race, when the primitive and grandiose meaning had become nearly lost—was ever the representative in his accumulated titles of all his colleagues. It was the god of *fire*, symbolised by thunder, as Jove or Agni ; the god of *water*, symbolised by the fluvial bull or some sacred river or fountain, as Varuna, Neptune, etc. ; the god of *air*, manifesting in the hurricane and tempest, as Vayu and Indra ; and the god or spirit of the earth, who appeared in earthquakes, like Pluto, Yama, and so many others.

These were the Cosmic gods, ever synthesizing all in one, as found in every cosmogony or mythology. Thus, the Greeks had their Dodonean Jupiter, who included in himself the four elements and the four cardinal points, and who was recognized, therefore, in old Rome under the pantheistic title of *Jupiter Mundus* ; and who now, in modern Rome, has become the *Deus Mundus*, the one mundane god, who is made to swallow all others in the latest theology—by the arbitrary decision of his special ministers.

As gods of Fire, Air, Water, they were *celestial* gods; as gods of the *lower region*, they were *infernal* deities : the latter adjective applying simply *to the Earth*. They were " Spirits of the Earth " under their respective names of Yama, Pluto, Osiris, the " Lord of the lower kingdom, etc., etc.," and their tellurial character proves it sufficiently.* The ancients knew of no worse abode after death than the *Kâmaloka*, the *limbus* on this Earth. If it is argued that the Dodonean Jupiter was identified with Aidoneus, the king of the subterranean world, and *Dis*, or the Roman Pluto and the Dionysius Chthonios, the subterranean, wherein, according to Creuzer (I, vi., ch. 1), oracles were rendered, then it will become the pleasure of the Occultists to prove that both Aidoneus and Dionysius are the bases of Adonaï, or " Jurbo Adonaï," as Jehovah is called in Codex Nazaræus. " Thou shalt not worship the Sun, who is named Adonaï, whose name is also *Kadush* and El-El " (*Cod. Naz.*, 1, 47; see also Psalm lxxxix., 18), and also " Lord Bacchus." Baal-Adonis of the *Sods* or Mysteries of the pre-Babylonian Jews became the Adonaï by the Massorah, the later-vowelled Jehovah. Hence the Roman Catholics are right. All these Jupiters are of the same family ; but Jehovah has to be included therein to make it complete. Jupiter-*Aerios* or *Pan*, the Jupiter Ammon, and the Jupiter-Bel-Moloch, are all correlations and one with Yurbo-Adonaï, because they are all one cosmic nature. It is that nature and power which create the specific terrestrial symbol, and the physical and material fabric of the latter, which proves the Energy manifesting through it as *extrinsic*.

For primitive religion was something better than simple pre-occupation about physical phenomena, as remarked by Schilling ; and principles, more elevated than we modern Sadducees know of, " were hidden under the transparent veil of such merely natural divinities as thunder,

---

* The *Gehenna* of the Bible was a valley near Jerusalem, where the monotheistic Jews immolated their children to Moloch, if the prophet Jeremiah is to be believed on his word. The Scandinavian *Hel* or *Hela* was a frigid region—again Kamaloka—and the Egyptian Amenti a place of purification. (See *Isis Unveiled*, Vol. II., p. 11.)

the winds, and rain." The ancients knew and could distinguish the *corporeal* from the *spiritual* elements, in the forces of nature.

The four-fold Jupiter, as the four-faced Brahmâ—the aerial, the fulgurant, the terrestrial, and the marine god—the lord and master of the four elements, may stand as a representative for the great Cosmic gods of every nation.   While passing power over the fire to Hephaistos-Vulcan, over the sea, to Poseidon-Neptune, and over the Earth, to Pluto-Aidoneus—the AERIAL Jove was all these ; for ÆTHER, from the first, had pre-eminence over, and was the synthesis of, all the elements.

Tradition points to a grotto, a vast cave in the deserts of Central Asia, whereinto light pours through its four seemingly natural apertures or clefts placed crossways at the four cardinal points of the place. From noon till an hour before sunset that light streams in, of four different colours, as averred—red, blue, orange-gold, and white—owing to some either natural or artificially prepared conditions of vegetation and soil. The light converges in the centre around a pillar of white marble with a globe upon it, which represents our earth.   It is named the "grotto of Zaratushta."

When included under the arts and sciences of the fourth race, the Atlanteans, the phenomenal manifestation of the four elements, justly attributed by the believers in Cosmic gods to the intelligent interference of the latter, assumed a scientific character.   The *magic* of the ancient priests consisted, in those days, in addressing *their gods in their own language.* " The speech of the men of the earth cannot reach the Lords.   Each must be addressed in the language of his respective element "—is a sentence which will be shown pregnant with meaning. " *The Book of Rules* " cited adds as an explanation of the nature of that *Element*-language : " It is composed of *sounds*, not words ; of sounds, numbers and figures.   He who knows how to blend the three, will call forth the response of the superintending Power " (the regent-god of the specific element needed).

Thus this " language " is that of *incantations* or of MANTRAS, as they are called in India, sound being *the most potent and effectual magic agent, and the first of the keys which opens the door of communication between Mortals and the Immortals.*   He who believes in the words and teachings of St. Paul, has no right to pick out from the latter those sentences only that he chooses to accept, to the rejection of others ; and St. Paul teaches most undeniably the existence of cosmic gods and their presence among us.   Paganism preached a dual and simultaneous evolution : " creation "—" *spiritualem ac mundanum*," as the Roman Church has it— ages before the advent of that Roman Church.   Exoteric phraseology has changed little with respect to divine hierarchies since the most palmy days of Paganism, or " Idolatry."   Names alone have changed,

along with claims which have now become false pretences. For
when Plato put in the mouth of the Highest Principle—" Father
Æther " or Jupiter—these words, for instance : " The gods of
the gods of whom I am the *maker* (*opifex*) as I am the father of
all their works (*operumque parens*) " ; he knew the spirit of this sentence
as fully, we suspect, as St. Paul did, when saying : " For though there
be that are called gods, whether in heaven or in earth, as there be gods
many and lords many," . . . . etc. (1 Cor. viii. 5.)* Both knew the
sense and the meaning of what they put forward in such guarded terms.

Says Sir W. Grove, F.R.S., speaking of the correlation of forces,
" The ancients when they witnessed a natural phenomenon, removed
from ordinary analogies, and unexplained by any mechanical action
known to them, referred it to a soul, a spiritual or preternatural
power. . . . Air and gases were also at first deemed spiritual, but
subsequently they became invested with a more material character ; and
the same words πνεῦμα, spirit, etc., were used to signify the soul or a gas ; the
very word gas, from *geist*, a ghost or spirit, affords us an instance of the
gradual transmutation of a spiritual into a physical conception. . . . . ."
(P. 89.) This, the great man of science (in his preface to the fifth
edition of " Correlation of Physical Forces ") considers as the *only* concern
of exact science, which has no business to meddle with the CAUSES. " Cause
and effect," he explains, " are therefore, in their abstract relation to
these forces, words solely of convenience. We are totally unacquainted
with the ultimate generating power of each and all of them, and probably
shall ever remain so ; we can only ascertain the norma of their actions ;
we must humbly refer their causation to one omnipresent influence, and
content ourselves with studying their effects and developing, by experiment, their mutual relations " (p. xiv.).

This policy once accepted, and the system virtually admitted in the
above-quoted words, namely, the *spirituality* of the " ultimate generating
power," it would be more than illogical to refuse to recognise this
quality which is inherent in the *material elements*, or rather, in their com-

---

* We cannot be taken to task by the Protestants for interpreting the verse from the
Corinthians as we do ; for, if the translation in the English Bible is made ambiguous, it
is not so in the original texts, and the Roman Catholic Church accepts the words of
the Apostle in their true sense. For a proof see the *Commentaries on St. Paul's Epistles,*
by St. John Chrysostom " *directly inspired* by the Apostle," and " who wrote under his
dictation," as we are assured by the Marquis de Mirville, whose works are approved by
Rome. And St. Chrysostom says, commenting on that special verse, " And, though there
are (in fact) they who are called gods . . . .—for it seems, there are really *several gods*
—withal, and for all that, the God-*principle* and the Superior God ceasing to remain
essentially *one* and indivisible." . . . Thus spoke the old Initiates also, knowing
that the worship of minor gods could never affect the " God *Principle* " (See de Mirville,
" *Des Esprits*," vol. ii., 322).

pounds—as present in the fire, air, water or earth.   The ancients knew these powers so well, that, while concealing their true nature under various allegories, for the benefit (or to the detriment) of the uneducated rabble, they never departed from the multiple object in view, while inverting them.   They contrived to throw a thick veil over the nucleus of truth concealed by the symbol, but they ever tried to preserve the latter as a *record* for future generations, sufficiently transparent to allow their wise men to discern that truth behind the fabulous form of the glyph or allegory.   They are accused of *superstition* and *credulity*, those ancient sages; and this by those very nations, which, learned in all the modern arts and sciences, cultured and wise in their generation, accept to this day as their one living and infinite God, the anthropomorphic " Jehovah " of the Jews.

What were some of the alleged " superstitions " ?   Hesiod believed, for instance, that " the winds were the sons of the giant Typhœus," who were chained and unchained at will by Æolus, and the polytheistic Greeks accepted it along with Hesiod.   Why should not they, since the monotheistic Jews had the same beliefs, with other names for their *dramatis personæ*, and since Christians believe in the same to this day ?   The Hesiodic Æolus, Boreas, etc., etc., were named *Kadim, Tzaphon, Daren, and Ruach Hajan* by the " chosen people " of Israel.   What is, then, the fundamental difference ?   While the Hellenes were taught that Æolus tied and untied the winds, the Jews believed as fervently that their Lord God, " *with smoke coming out of his nostrils and fire out of his mouth, rode upon a cherub and did fly;* and was seen *upon the wings of the wind* " (*II. Sam., xxii.* 9 *and* 11).   The expressions of the two nations are either both figures of speech, or both *superstitions*.   We think they are neither; but only arise from a keen sense of oneness with nature, and a perception of the mysterious and the intelligent behind every natural phenomenon, which the moderns no longer possess.   Nor was it " superstitious " in the Greek pagans to listen to the oracle of Delphi, when, at the approach of the fleet of Xerxes, that oracle advised them to " sacrifice to the Winds," if the same has to be regarded as *Divine* Worship in the Israelites, who sacrificed as often to the wind and fire—especially to the latter element.   Do they not say that their " God is a consuming fire " (*Deut. iv.,* 24), who appeared generally *as* Fire and " encompassed by fire " ? and did not Elijah seek for him (the Lord) in the " great strong wind, and in the earthquake " ?   Do not the Christians repeat the same after them ?   Do not they, moreover, sacrifice to this day, to the same *God of Wind and Water* ? "   They do; because special prayers for rain, dry weather, trade-winds and the calming of storms on the seas exist to this hour in the prayer-books of the three Christian churches; and the several hundred sects of the Protestant religion offer them to their God upon every threat of calamity ? The fact that they are no more answered by Jehovah, than they were, probably, by Jupiter *Pluvius*, does not alter the fact of these prayers being addressed to the Power or Powers supposed to rule over the Elements, or of these Powers being identical in Paganism and Christianity; or have we to believe that such prayers are crass idolatry and absurd " superstition " *only* when addressed by a Pagan to his *idol,* and that the same superstition is suddenly transformed into *praiseworthy piety* and *religion* whenever the name of the celestial addressee is changed ? But the tree *is* known by its fruit. And the fruit of the Christian tree being no better than that of the tree of Paganism, why should the former command more reverence than the latter.

Thus, when we are told by the Chevalier Drach, a converted Jew, and the Marquis de Mirville, a Roman Catholic fanatic of the French aristocracy, that in Hebrew *lightning* is a synonym of *fury,* and is always handled by an *evil* Spirit ; that *Jupiter Fulgur* or *Fulgurans* is also called by the Christians *œlicius,* and denounced as the *soul of lightning,* its dæmon ; * we have either to apply the same explanation and definitions to the " Lord God of Israel," under the same circumstances, or renounce our right of abusing the gods and creeds of other nations.

The foregoing statements emanating as they do from two ardent and learned Roman Catholics, are, to say the least, *dangerous,* in the presence of the Bible and its prophets. Indeed, if Jupiter, the " chief Dæmon of the Pagan Greeks," hurled his deadly thunder-bolts and lightnings at those who excited his wrath, so did the Lord God of Abraham and Jacob. We find in II. Samuel, that " the Lord thundered from heaven, and the most High uttered *his* voice, and he sent out arrows (thunder bolts) and scattered them (Saul's armies) with lightning, and discomforted them." (*Chap. xxii.* 14, 15.)

The Athenians are accused of having sacrificed to Boreas ; and this " Demon " is charged with having submerged and wrecked 400 ships of the Persian fleet on the rocks of Mount Pelion, and of having become so furious " that all the Magi of Xerxes could hardly counteract it by offering contra-sacrifices to Tethys " [*Herodotus* " Polym." cxc]. Very fortunately, no authenticated instance is on the records of Christian wars showing a like catastrophe on the same scale happening to one Christian fleet owing to the " prayers " of its enemy—another Christian nation. But this is from no fault of theirs, for each prays as ardently to Jehovah for the destruction of the other, as the Athenians prayed to Boreas. Both resorted to a neat little piece of black magic *con amore.* Such abstinence from divine interference being hardly due to lack of

---

* Cosmolatry, p. 415.

prayers, sent to a *common* Almighty God for mutual destruction, where, then, shall we draw the line between Pagan and Christian ? And who can doubt that all Protestant England would rejoice and offer thanks to the Lord, if, during some future war, 400 ships of the hostile fleet were to be wrecked owing to such holy prayers. What is, then, the difference, we ask again, between a Jupiter, a Boreas, and a Jehovah ? No more than this : The crime of one's own next-of-kin—say of one's "father" —is always excused and often exalted, whereas the crime of our neighbour's parent is ever gladly punished by hanging. Yet the crime is the same.

So far the "blessings of Christianity" do not seem to have made any appreciable advance on the morals of the converted Pagans.

The above is not a defence of Pagan gods, nor is it an attack on the Christian deity, nor does it mean belief in either. The writer is quite impartial, and rejects the testimony in favour of either, neither praying to, believing in, nor dreading any such "personal" and anthropomorphic God. The parallels are brought forward simply as one more curious exhibition of the illogical and blind fanaticism of the civilized theologian. For, so far, there is not a very great difference between the two beliefs, and there is none in their respective effects upon *morality*, or spiritual nature. The "light of Christ" shines upon as hideous features of the animal-man now, as the "light of Lucifer" did in days of old.

"Those unfortunate heathens in their superstition regard even the Elements as something that has comprehension ! . . . . They still have faith in their idol Vayu—the god or, rather, Demon of the Wind and Air . . . they firmly believe in the efficacy of their prayers, and in the powers of their Brahmins over the winds and storms. . . . ." (The Missionary Lavoisier, of Cochin, in the *Journal des Colonies*.) In reply to this, we may quote from *Luke viii.*, 24 : "And he (Jesus) arose and *rebuked the Wind and the raging of the Water, and they ceased and there was a calm*." And here is another quotation from a prayer book : . . . "Oh, Virgin of the Sea, blessed Mother and Lady of the Waters, stay thy waves . . ." etc., etc. (prayer of the Neapolitan and Provençal sailors, copied textually from that of the Phœnician mariners to their Virgin-goddess Astarte.) The logical and irrepressible conclusion arising from the parallels brought forward, and the denunciation of the Missionary is this : The *commands* of the Brahmins to their element-gods *not remaining* "*ineffectual*," the power of the Brahmins is thus placed on a par with that of Jesus. Moreover, Astarte is shown not a whit weaker in potency than the "Virgin of the Sea" of Christian sailors. It is not enough to give a dog a bad name, and then hang him ; the dog has to be proven guilty. Boreas and Astarte may be *devils* in theological fancy, but, as just remarked, the tree has to be judged by its fruit. And once the Christians are shown as immoral and wicked as the pagans ever were, what benefit has humanity derived from its change of gods and idols?

That, however, which God and the Christian Saints are justified in doing, becomes a crime, if successful, in simple mortals. Sorcery and incantations are regarded as fables now; yet from the day of the *Institutes of Justinian* down to the laws against witchcraft of England and America —*obsolete* but not repealed to this day—such incantations, even when only suspected, were punished as criminal. Why punish a chimera? And still we read of Constantine, the Emperor, sentencing to death the philosopher Sopatrus *for unchaining the winds*, and thus preventing ships loaded with grain from arriving in time to put an end to famine. Pausanias, when affirming that he saw with his own eyes " men who by simple *prayers and incantations* " stopped a strong hail-storm, is derided. This does not prevent modern Christian writers from advising prayer during storm and danger, and believing in its efficacy. Hoppo and Stadlein— two magicians and sorcerers—were sentenced to death for throwing *charms on fruit* and transferring a harvest *by magic arts* from one field to another, hardly a century ago, if we can believe Sprenger, the famous writer, who vouches for it : " *Qui fruges excantassent segetem pellicentes incantando.*"

Let us close by reminding the reader that, without the smallest shadow of superstition, one may believe in the dual nature of every object on Earth—in the spiritual and the material, the visible and the invisible nature, and that science virtually proves this, while denying its own demonstration. For if, as Sir William Grove has it, the electricity we handle is but the *result* of ordinary matter affected by something *invisible*, the " *ultimate* generating power " of every Force, the " *one omnipresent influence*," then it only becomes natural that one should believe as the ancients did ; namely, that every Element is *dual* in its nature. " ETHEREAL fire is the emanation of the KABIR proper ; the *aerial* is but the union (correlation) of the former with *terrestrial fire*, and its guidance and application on our earthly plane belongs to a *Kabir* of a lesser dignity "—an Elemental, perhaps, as an Occultist would call it ; and the same may be said of every Cosmic Element.

No one will deny that the human being is possessed of various forces: magnetic, sympathetic, antipathetic, nervous, dynamical, occult, mechanical, mental—every kind of force ; and that the physical forces are all biological in their essence, seeing that they intermingle with, and often merge into, those forces that we have named intellectual and moral—the first being the vehicles, so to say, the *upadhi*, of the second. No one, who does not deny soul in man, would hesitate in saying that their presence and commingling are the very essence of our being; that they constitute the *Ego* in man, in fact. These potencies have their physiological, physical, mechanical, as well as their nervous, ecstatic, clairaudient, and clairvoyant phenomena, which are now regarded and recognised as perfectly natural, even by science. Why should man be the only exception in nature, and why cannot even the ELEMENTS have their *vehicles*, their "Vahans" in what we call the PHYSICAL FORCES? And why, above all, should such beliefs be called "superstition" along with the religions of old?

§ XV.

ON KWAN-SHI-YIN AND KWAN-YIN.

LIKE Avalokiteshwara, Kwan-shi-yin has passed through several transformations, but it is an error to say of him that he is a modern invention of the Northern Buddhists, for under another appellation he has been known from the earliest times. The Secret Doctrine teaches that " He who is the first to appear at Renovation will be the last to come before Re-absorption (pralaya)." Thus the logoi of all nations, from the Vedic Visvakarma of the Mysteries down to the Saviour of the present civilised nations, are the "Word" who was "in the beginning" (or the reawakening of the energising powers of Nature) with the One ABSO-LUTE. Born of Fire and Water, before these became distinct elements, IT was the "Maker" (fashioner or modeller) of all things; "without him was not anything made that was made"; "in whom was life, and the life was the light of men "; and who finally may be called, as he ever has been, the Alpha and the Omega of manifested Nature. "The great Dragon of Wisdom is born of Fire and Water, and into Fire and Water will all be re-absorbed with him" (*Fa-Hwa-King*). As this Bodhisatva is said "to assume any form he pleases" from the beginning of a Manvantara to its end, though his special birthday (memorial day) is celebrated according to the Kin-kwang-ming-King ("Luminous Sutra of Golden Light") in the second month on the nineteenth day, and that of "Maitreya Buddha" in the first month on the first day, yet the two are one. He will appear as Maitreya Buddha, the last of the Avatars and Buddhas, in the seventh Race. This belief and expectation are universal throughout the East. Only it is not in the *Kali yug*, our present terrifically materialistic age of Darkness, the "Black Age," that a new Saviour of Humanity can ever appear. The Kali yug is

" l'Age d'Or " (!) only in the *mystic* writings of some French pseudo-Occultists. (See " La Mission des Juifs.")

Hence the ritual in the exoteric worship of this deity was founded on magic. The Mantras are all taken from special books kept secret by the priests, and each is said to work a magical effect; as the reciter or reader produces, by simply chanting them, a secret causation which results in immediate effects. Kwan-Shi-Yin is Avalokiteshwara, and both are forms of the seventh Universal Principle ; while in its highest metaphysical character this deity is the synthetic aggregation of all the planetary Spirits, Dhyani Chohans. He is the " Self-manifested ; " in short, the " Son of the Father." Crowned with seven dragons, above his statue there appears the inscription Pu-Tsi-K'iun-ling, " the universal Saviour of all living beings."

Of course the name given in the archaic volume of the Stanzas is quite different, but Kwan-Yin is a perfect equivalent. In a temple of Pu'to, the sacred island of the Buddhists in China, Kwan-Shi-Yin is represented floating on a black aquatic bird (*Kâla-Hansa*), and pouring on the heads of mortals the elixir of life, which, as it flows, is transformed into one of the chief Dhyani-Buddhas—the Regent of a star called the " Star of Salvation." In his third transformation Kwan-Yin is the informing spirit or genius of Water. In China the Dalai-Lama is believed to be an incarnation of Kwan-Shi-Yin, who in his third terrestrial appearance was a Bodhisattva, while the Teshu Lama is an incarnation of Amitabha Buddha, or Gautama.

It may be remarked *en passant* that a writer must indeed have a diseased imagination to discover phallic worship everywhere, as do the authors of " China Revealed " (McClatchey) and " Phallicism." The first discovers " the old phallic gods, represented under two evident symbols —the Khan or Yang, which is the *membrum virile*, and the Kwan or Yin, the *pudendum muliebre*." (See " *Phallicism,*" p. 273.) Such a rendering seems the more strange as Kwan-Shi-Yin (Avalokiteswara) and Kwan-Yin, besides being now the patron deities of the Buddhist ascetics, the Yogis of Thibet, are the gods of chastity, and are, in their esoteric meaning, not even that which is implied in the rendering of Mr. Rhys Davids' " Buddhism," (p. 202) : " The name Avalokiteshwara . . . means ' the Lord who looks down from on high.' " Nor is Kwan-Shi-Yin " the Spirit of the Buddhas present in the Church," but, literally interpreted, it means " the Lord that is seen," and in one sense, " the divine SELF perceived by Self " (the human)—the Atman or seventh principle merged in the Universal, perceived by, or the object of perception to, Buddhi, the sixth principle or divine Soul in man. In a still higher sense, Avalokiteshwara=Kwan-Shi-Yin, referred to as the seventh Universal principle, is the Logos perceived by the Universal Buddhi—or Soul, as the synthetic aggregate of the Dhyani-Buddhas: and is not the " Spirit of Buddha present in the Church," but the omnipresent universal Spirit manifested in the temple of Kosmos or Nature. This Orientalistic etymology of Kwan and Yin is on a par with that of " Yogini," which, we are told by Mr. Hargrave Jennings, " is a Sanskrit word, in the dialects pronounced Yogi or Zogee (!), and is equivalent to Sena, and exactly the same as Duti or Duti-Ca '—*i.e.*, a sacred prostitute of the temple, worshipped as Yoni or Sakti" (p. 6o). " The books of morality," in India, "direct a faithful wife to shun the society of Yogini or females who have been adored as Sakti . . . amongst the votaries of a most licentious description." Nothing should surprise us after this. And it is, there-fore, with hardly a smile that we find another preposterous absurdity quoted about " Budh," as being a name " which signifies not only the sun as the source of generation but also the male organ (*Round Towers of Ireland;* quoted by Mr. Hargrave Jennings in " *Phallicism*," p. 264). Max Müller, in his " False Analogies," says that " the most celebrated Chinese scholar of his time, Abel Rémusat," maintains "that the three syllables I Hi Wei (in the fourteenth chapter of the *Tao-te-king*) were meant for Je-ho-vah (*Science of Religion*, p. 332) ; and again, Father Amyot, who " feels certain that the three persons of the Trinity could be recognised " in the same work. And if Abel Rémusat, why not Hargrave Jennings ? Every scholar will recognise the absurdity of ever seeing in Budh, " the enlightened " and " the awakened," a " phallic symbol."

Kwan-shi-yin, then, is " the Son identical with his Father " mys-tically, or the Logos—the word. He is called the " Dragon of Wisdom " in Stanza III., as all the Logoi of all the ancient religious systems are connected with, and symbolised by, serpents. In old Egypt, the God Nahbkoon, " he who unites the doubles, " (astral light re-uniting by its dual physiological and spiritual potency the divine human to its purely divine Monad, the prototype " in heaven " or Nature) was represented as a serpent on human legs, either with or without arms. It was the emblem of the resurrection of Nature, as also of Christ with the Ophites, and of Jehovah as the brazen serpent healing those who looked at him ; the serpent being an emblem of Christ with the Templars also, (see the Templar degree in Masonry). The symbol of Knouph (Khoum also), or the soul of the world, says Champollion (*Pantheon, text* 3), " is repre-sented among other forms under that of a huge serpent on human legs ; this reptile, being the emblem of the good genius and the veritable Agathodæmon, is sometimes bearded." The sacred animal is thus identical with the serpent of the Ophites, and is figured on a great number of engraved stones, called Gnostic or Basilidean gems. This serpent appears with various heads (human and animal), but its gems are always found inscribed with the name ΧΝΟΥΒΙΣ (Chnoubis). This symbol is identical with one which, according to Jamblichus and Champollion, was called "the first of the celestial gods"; the god Hermes, or Mercury with the Greeks, to which god Hermes Trismegistos attributes the invention of, and the first initiation of men into, magic; and Mercury is Budh, Wisdom, Enlightenment, or "Re-awakening" into the divine Science.

To close, Kwan-Shi-Yin and Kwan-Yin are the two aspects (male and female) of the same principle in Kosmos, Nature and Man, of divine wisdom and intelligence. They are the "Christos-Sophia" of the mystic Gnostics—the Logos and its Sakti. In their longing for the expression of some mysteries never to be wholly comprehended by the profane, the Ancients, knowing that nothing could be preserved in human memory without some outward symbol, have chosen the (to us) often ridiculous images of the Kwan-Yins to remind man of his origin and inner nature. To the impartial, however, the Madonnas in crinolines and the Christs in white kid gloves must appear far more absurd than the Kwan-Shi-Yin and Kwan-Yin in their dragon garb. The subjective can hardly be expressed by the objective. Therefore, since the symbolic formula attempts to characterise that which is above scientific reasoning, and as often far beyond our intellects, it must needs go beyond that intellect in some shape or other, or else it will fade out from human remembrance.

BOOK I.—PART III.

ADDENDA.

SCIENCE AND THE SECRET DOCTRINE CONTRASTED.

"The knowledge of this nether world—
Say, friend, what is it, false or true?
The false, what mortal cares to know?
The true, what mortal ever knew?"

CONTENTS.

ADDENDA TO BOOK I.

I.

REASONS FOR THESE ADDENDA.

MANY of the doctrines contained in the foregoing Seven Stanzas and Commentaries having been studied and critically examined by some Western Theosophists, certain of the occult teachings have been found wanting from the ordinary stand-point of modern scientific knowledge. They seemed to encounter insuperable difficulties in the way of their acceptance, and to require reconsideration in view of scientific criticism. Some friends have already been tempted to regret the necessity of so often calling in question the assertions of modern Science. It appeared to them—and I here repeat only their arguments—that " to run counter to the teachings of its most eminent exponents, was to court a premature discomfiture in the eyes of the Western World."

It is, therefore, desirable to define once and for all the position which the writer, who does not agree in this with her friends, intends to main tain. So far as Science remains what in the words of Prof. Huxley it is, viz., " organized common sense "; so far as its inferences are drawn from accurate premises—its generalizations resting on a purely inductive basis—every Theosophist and Occultist welcomes respectfully and with due admiration its contributions to the domain of cosmological law. There can be no possible conflict between the teachings of occult and so-called exact Science, where the conclusions of the latter are grounded on a substratum of unassailable fact. It is only when its more ardent exponents, over-stepping the limits of observed phenomena in order to penetrate into the arcana of Being, attempt to wrench the formation of Kosmos and its *living* Forces from Spirit, and attribute all to blind matter, that the Occultists claim the right to dispute and call in question their theories. Science cannot, owing to the very nature of things, unveil the mystery of the universe around us. Science can, it is true, collect, classify, and generalize upon phenomena ; but the occultist, arguing from admitted metaphysical data, declares that the daring explorer, who would probe the inmost secrets of Nature, must transcend the narrow limitations of sense, and transfer his consciousness into the region of noumena and the sphere of primal causes. To effect this, he must develop faculties which are absolutely dormant—save in a few rare and exceptional cases—in the constitution of the off-shoots of our present Fifth Root-race in Europe and America. He can in no other conceivable manner collect the facts on which to base his speculations.   Is this not apparent on the principles of Inductive Logic and Metaphysics alike ?

On the other hand, whatever the writer may do, she will never be able to satisfy both Truth and Science. To offer the reader a systematic and uninterrupted version of the Archaic Stanzas is impossible.   A gap of 43 verses or *Slokas* has to be left between the 7th (already given) and the 51st, which is the subject of Book II., though the latter are made to run from 1 *et seq.* for easier reading and reference.   The appearance of man on Earth alone occupies as many stanzas, which describe minutely his primal evolution from the human Dhyan Chohans; the state of the globe at that time, etc., etc.   A great number of names referring to chemical substances and other compounds, which have now ceased to combine together, and are therefore unknown to the later offshoots of our Fifth Race, occupy a considerable space.   As they are simply untranslateable, and would remain in every case inex-plicable, they are omitted, along with those which cannot be made public.   Nevertheless, even the little that is given will irritate any follower and defender of dogmatic materialistic Science who happens to read this.

Before proceeding to other Stanzas, it is proposed, therefore, to defend those already given.   They are not in perfect accord or harmony with modern Science—this we all know.   Had they been, however, as much in agreement with the views of modern knowledge as a lecture by Sir W. Thomson, they would have been rejected all the same.   For they teach belief in conscious Powers and Spiritual Entities ; in terrestrial, semi-intelligent, and highly intellectual Forces on other planes* ; and in Beings that dwell around us in spheres imperceptible, whether through telescope or microscope.   Hence the necessity of examining the beliefs of materialistic Science : of comparing its views about the "Elements" with the opinions of the ancients, and of analysing the physical Forces as they exist in modern perception before the Occultists admit themselves to be in the wrong.   We shall touch upon the constitution of the Sun and planets, and the occult characteristics of what are called *Devas* and *Genii*, and are now termed by Science, Force, or "modes of motion," and see whether esoteric belief is defen-sible or not (*Vide infra*, "*Gods, Monads, and Atoms*)."   Notwithstanding the efforts made to the contrary, an unprejudiced mind will discover

---

* Their intellection, of course, being of quite a different nature to any we can conceive of on Earth.

under Newton's " agent, material or immaterial " (of his third letter to Bentley), the agent which *causes gravity*, and, in his personal *working* God, one finds just as much of the metaphysical *devas* and *genii*, as in Kepler's *angelus rector* conducting each planet, and the *species immateriata* by which the celestial bodies were carried along in their courses, according to that astronomer.

We shall have, in Book II., to openly approach dangerous subjects. We must bravely face Science and declare, in the teeth of materialistic learning, of Idealism, Hylo-Idealism, Positivism and all-denying modern Psychology, that the true Occultist believes in " Lords of Light ; " that he believes in a Sun, which, far from being simply " a lamp of day " moving in accordance with physical law, and far from being merely one of those Suns, which according to Richter— " . . . . are Sun-flowers of a higher light "—is, like milliards of other Suns, the dwelling or the vehicle of a god, and a host of gods.

In this question, of course, it is the Occultists who will be worsted. They will be considered on the *primâ facie* aspect of the dispute to be ignoramuses, and labelled with more than one of the usual epithets given to those whom the superficially judging public, itself ignorant of the great underlying truths in nature, accuses of believing in mediæval superstitions. Let it be so. Submitting beforehand to every criticism in order to go on with their task, they only claim the privilege of showing that the physicists are as much at loggerheads among themselves in their speculations, as the latter are with the teachings of Occultism.

The Sun is matter, and the Sun is Spirit. Our ancestors—the " heathen,"—along with their modern successors, the Parsis—were, and are, wise enough in their generation to see in it the symbol of Divinity, and at the same time to sense within, concealed by the physical Symbol, the bright God of Spiritual and terrestial Light. Such belief is now regarded as a superstition only by rank materialism, which denies Deity, Spirit, Soul, and admits no intelligence outside the mind of man. But if too much of wrong superstition bred by " Churchianity "—as Lawrence Oliphant calls it—" renders a man a fool," too much scepticism makes him mad. We prefer the charge of folly in believing too much, to that of a madness which denies everything, as do Materialism and Idealism. Hence, the Occultists are fully prepared to receive their dues from Materialism, and to meet the adverse criticism which will be poured on this work, not for writing it, but *for believing in that which it contains*.

Therefore the discoveries, hypotheses, and unavoidable objections which will be brought forward by the scientific critics must be anticipated and disposed of. It has also to be shown how far the occult teachings depart from real science, and whether the ancient or the modern theories are the most logically and philosophically correct. The unity and mutual relations of all parts of Kosmos were known to the ancients, before they became evident to modern astronomers and philosophers. And if even the external and visible portions of the Universe and their mutual relations cannot be explained in any other terms than those used by the adherents of the mechanical theory of the Universe in physical science, it follows that no materialist, who denies that the Soul of Kosmos (which appertains to metaphysical philosophy) exists, has the right to trespass upon that metaphysical domain. That physical science is trying to, and actually does, encroach upon it, is only one more proof that "might is right," and no more.

Another good reason for these Addenda is this. Since only a certain portion of the Secret teachings can be given out in the present age, if they were published without any explanations or commentary, the doctrines would never be understood even by theosophists. Therefore they must be contrasted with the speculations of modern science. Archaic axioms must be placed side by side with modern hypotheses and comparison left to the sagacious reader.

On the question of the "Seven Governors," as Hermes calls the "Seven Builders," the Spirits which guide the operations of nature, the animated atoms of which are the shadows, in their world, of their Primaries in the astral realms—this work will, of course, besides the men of Science, have every materialist against it. But this opposition can, at most, be only temporary. People have laughed at everything and scouted every unpopular idea at first, and then ended by accepting it. Materialism and scepticism are evils that must remain in the world as long as man has not quitted his present gross form to don the one he had during the first and second races of this Round. Unless scepticism and our present natural ignorance are equilibrated by intuition and a natural spirituality, every being afflicted with such feelings will see in himself no better than a bundle of flesh, bones, and muscles, with an empty garret inside him which serves the purpose of storing his sensations and feelings. Sir Humphry Davy was a great scientist, as deeply versed in physics as any theorist of our day, yet he loathed materialism. "I heard with disgust," he says, "in the dissecting-rooms, the plan of the physiologist, of the gradual secretion of matter, and its becoming endued with irritability, ripening into sensibility, and acquiring such organs as were necessary, by its own inherent forces, and at last rising into intellectual existence." Nevertheless, physiologists are not the most to be blamed for speaking of that only which they can see and estimate on the evidence of their physical senses. Astronomers and physicists are, we consider, far more illogical in their materialistic views than even physiologists, and this has to be proved.   Milton's—

> . . . . "Light
> Ethereal, first of things, quintessence pure,"

has become with the materialists only—

> . . . . . . Prime cheerer, light,
> Of all material beings, first and best.

For the occultists it is both Spirit and Matter.   Behind the "mode of motion," now regarded as "the property of matter" and nothing more, they perceive the radiant noumenon.   It is the "Spirit of Light," the first born of the Eternal pure Element, whose energy (or emanation) is stored in the Sun, the great Life-Giver of the physical world, as the hidden Concealed Spiritual Sun is the Light- and Life-Giver of the Spiritual and Psychic Realms.   Bacon was one of the first to strike the key-note of materialism, not only by his inductive method (renovated from ill-digested Aristotle), but by the general tenor of his writings.   He inverts the order of mental Evolution when saying that "the first Creation of God was the light of the sense; the last was the light of the reason; and his Sabbath work ever since is the illumination of the Spirit."   It is just the reverse.   The light of Spirit is the eternal Sabbath of the mystic or occultist, and he pays little attention to that of mere sense.   That which is meant by the allegorical sentence, "*Fiat Lux*" is,—when esoterically rendered—"Let there be the 'Sons of Light,'" or the noumena of all phenomena.   Thus the Roman Catholics rightly interpret the passage as referring to Angels, and wrongly as meaning Powers created by an anthropomorphic God, whom they personify in the ever thundering and punishing Jehovah.

These beings are the "Sons of Light," because they emanate from, and are self-generated in, that infinite Ocean of Light, whose one pole is pure *Spirit* lost in the absoluteness of Non-Being, and the other, the *matter* in which it condenses, crystallizing into a more and more gross type as it descends into manifestation.   Therefore matter, though it is, in one sense, but the illusive dregs of that Light whose limbs are the Creative Forces, yet has in it the full presence of the Soul thereof, of that Principle, which none—not even the "Sons of Light," evolved from its ABSOLUTE DARKNESS—will ever know.   The idea is as beautifully, as it is truthfully, expressed by Milton, who hails the holy Light, which is the—

> ". . . . . Offspring of Heaven, first-born,
> And of th' Eternal co-eternal beam;
> . . . . . Since God is light,
> And never but in unapproached Light
> Dwelt from Eternity, dwelt then in thee
> Bright effluence, of bright essence increate."

II.

MODERN PHYSICISTS ARE PLAYING AT BLIND MAN'S BUFF.

AND now Occultism puts to Science the question : " Is light a body, or is it not ?" Whatever the answer of the latter, the former is prepared to show that, to this day, the most eminent physicists know neither one way nor the other. To know what is light, and whether it is an actual substance or a mere undulation of the " ethereal medium," Science has first to learn what are in reality Matter, Atom, Ether, Force. Now, the truth is, that *it knows nothing of any of these,* and admits it. It has not even agreed what to believe in, as dozens of hypotheses emanating from various and very eminent Scientists on the same subject, are antagonistic to each other and often self-contradictory. Thus their learned speculations may, with a stretch of good-will, be accepted as " working hypotheses" in a secondary sense, as Stallo puts it. But being radically inconsistent with each other, they must finally end by mutually destroying themselves. As declared by the author of " Concepts of Modern Physics " : —

" It must not be forgotten that the several departments of Science are simply *arbitrary divisions of labour.* In these several departments the same physical object may be considered under different aspects. The physicist may study its molecular relations, while the chemist determines its atomic constitution. But when they both deal with the same element or agent, it cannot have one set of properties in physics, and another set contradictory of them, in chemistry. If the physicist and chemist alike assume the existence of ultimate atoms absolutely invariable in bulk and weight, *the atom cannot be a cube or oblate spheroid for physical, and a sphere for chemical purposes. A group of constant atoms cannot be an aggregate of extended and absolutely inert and impenetrable masses in a crucible or retort, and a system of mere centres of force as part of a magnet or of a Clamond battery. The universal Ether cannot be soft and mobile to please the chemist, and rigid-elastic to satisfy the physicist ; it cannot be continuous at the command of Sir William Thomson and discontinuous on the suggestion of Couchy or Fresnel.*"[*]

The eminent physicist, G. A. Hirn, may likewise be quoted saying the same in the 43rd Volume of the *Mémoires de l'Academie Royale de Belgique,* which we translate from the French, as cited : "When one sees the assurance with which are to-day affirmed doctrines which attribute the collectivity, the universality of the phenomena to the motions alone of the atom, one has a right to expect to find likewise unanimity on the qualities described to this unique being, the foundation of all that exists. Now, from the first examination of the particular systems proposed, one feels the strangest deception ; one perceives that the atom of the chemist, the atom of the physicist, that of the metaphysician, and that of the mathematician . . . . have *absolutely nothing in common but the name!* The inevitable result is the existing

---

[*] " Concepts of Modern Physics," p. xi.-xii., Introd. to the 2nd Edit.

subdivision of our sciences, each of which, in its own little pigeon-hole, constructs an atom which satisfies the requirements of the phenomena it studies, without troubling itself in the least about the requirements proper to the phenomena of the neighbouring pigeon-hole. The metaphysician banishes the principles of attraction and repulsion as dreams; the mathematician, who analyses the laws of elasticity and those of the propagation of light, admits them implicitly, without even naming them. . . . The chemist cannot explain the grouping of the atoms, in his often complicated molecules, without attributing to his atoms specific distinguishing qualities; *for the physicist and the metaphysician, partisans of the modern doctrines, the atom is, on the contrary, always and everywhere the same.* What am I saying? THERE IS NO AGREEMENT EVEN IN ONE AND THE SAME SCIENCE AS TO THE PROPERTIES OF THE ATOM. Each constructs an atom to suit his own fancy, in order to explain some special phenomenon with which he is particularly concerned." *

The above is the photographically correct image of modern Science and physics. The "pre-requisite of that incessant play of the 'scientific imagination,'" which is so often found in Professor Tyndall's eloquent discourses, is *vivid* indeed, as shown by Stallo, and for contradictory variety leaves far behind it any "phantasies" of occultism. However it may be, if physical theories are confessedly "mere formal, explanatory, didactic devices," and if "atomism is only a symbolical graphic system,"† then the occultist can hardly be regarded as assuming too much, when he places alongside of these *devices* and "*symbolical* systems" of modern Science, the symbols and devices of Archaic teachings.

III.

"AN LUMEN SIT CORPUS, NEC NON?"

MOST decidedly Light is not a body, we are told. Physical Sciences say Light is a Force, a vibration, the undulation of ether. It is the property or quality of matter, or even an affection thereof—never *a body!*

Just so. For this discovery, the knowledge—whatever it may be worth—that light or caloric is not a motion of *material particles*, Science is chiefly indebted, if not solely, to Sir W. Grove. It was he who was the first in a lecture at the London Institution, in 1842, to show that

---

* "*Recherches expérimentales sur la relation qui existe entre la résistance de l'air et sa température*," p. 68.

† From the criticism of "Concepts of Modern Physics" in *Nature*. See Stallo's work, p. xvi. of *Introduction*.

" light, heat, etc., etc.* are *affections* of matter itself, and not a distinct
ethereal, ' imponderable,' fluid, (a state of matter *now*) permeating it."
(*See "Correlation of the Physical Forces," Preface*). Yet, perhaps, for
some physicists—as for Oersted, a very eminent Scientist—FORCE and
FORCES were tacitly "Spirit (*and hence Spirits*) *in Nature.*" What
several rather mystical Scientists taught was that light, heat, magnetism, electricity and gravity, etc., were not the final *causes* of the
visible phenomena, including planetary motion, but themselves the
Secondary *effects of other Causes*, for which Science in our day cares very
little, but in which Occultism believes, for the Occultists have exhibited
proofs of the validity of their claims in every age. And in what age
were there no *Occultists* and no ADEPTS ?

Sir Isaac Newton held to the Pythagorean corpuscular theory, and
was also inclined to admit its consequences ; which made the Count de
Maistre hope, at one time, that Newton would ultimately lead Science
back to the recognition of the fact that *Forces* and the Celestial
bodies *were propelled and guided by Intelligences* (*Soirées*, vol. ii.). But de
Maistre counted without his host. The innermost thoughts and ideas
of Newton were perverted, and of his great mathematical learning only
the mere physical husk was turned to account. Had poor Sir Isaac
foreseen to what use his successors and followers would apply his
" gravity," † that pious and religious man would surely have quietly
eaten his apple, and never breathed a word about any mechanical ideas
connected with its fall.

Great contempt is shown for metaphysics generally and for onto-

---

* Mr. Robert Ward, discussing the questions of Heat and Light in the November
Journal of Science, 1881, shows us how utterly ignorant is Science about one of the
commonest facts of nature—the heat of the sun. He says :—" The question of the
temperature of the sun has been the subject of investigation with many scientists:
Newton, one of the first investigators of this problem, tried to determine it, and after
him all the scientists who have been occupied with calorimetry have followed his
example. *All have believed themselves successful*, and have formulated their results with
great confidence. The following, in the chronological order of the publication of the
results, are the temperatures (in centigrade degrees) found by each of them : Newton,
1,699,300deg. ; Pouillet, 1,461deg. ; Tollner, 102,200deg, ; Secchi, 5,344,840deg. ;
Ericsson, 2,726,700deg. ; Fizeau, 7,500deg. ; Waterston, 9,000,000deg. ; Spoëren,
27,000deg. ; Deville, 9,500deg. ; Soret, 5,801,846deg. ; Vicaire, 1,500deg. ; Rosetti,
20,000deg. The difference is as 1,400deg. against 9,000,000deg., or no less than
8,998,600deg. !! There probably does not exist in science a more astonishing contradiction than that revealed in these figures. And yet without doubt if an *Occultist*
were to give out an estimate, each of these gentlemen would vehemently protest in the
name of ' EXACT ' Science at the rejection of his special result." (From the *Theosophist*.)

† According to one atheistic idealist—Dr. Lewins—" When Sir Isaac, in 1687 . . . .
showed mass and atom acted upon . . . . by innate activity . . . . he effectually
disposed of Spirit, Anima, or Divinity, as supererogatory."

logical metaphysics especially. But we see, whenever the Occultists are bold enough to raise their diminished heads, that materialistic, physical science is honey-combed with metaphysics; * that its most fundamental principles, while inseparably wedded to transcendentalism, are nevertheless, in order to show modern science divorced from such "dreams," tortured and often ignored in the maze of contradictory theories and hypotheses. A very good corroboration of this charge lies in the fact that Science finds itself absolutely compelled to accept the "hypothetical" Ether and to try to explain it on the materialistic grounds of atomo-mechanical laws. This attempt has led directly to the most fatal discrepancies and radical inconsistencies between the assumed nature of Ether and its physical actions. A second proof is found in the many contradictory statements about the atom—the most metaphysical object in creation.

Now, what does the modern science of physics know of Æther, the first concept of which belongs undeniably to ancient philosophers, the Greeks having borrowed it from the Aryans, and the origin of modern Æther being found in, and *disfigured* from, AKÂSA ? This disfigurement

---

* Stallo's above-cited work, "Concepts of Modern Physics," a volume which has called forth the liveliest protests and criticisms, is recommended to anyone inclined to doubt this statement. "The professed antagonism of Science to metaphysics," he writes, "has led the majority of scientific specialists to assume that the methods and results of empirical research are wholly independent of the control of the laws of thought. They either silently ignore, or openly repudiate, the simplest canons of logic, including the laws of non-contradiction and . . . resent with the utmost vehemence, every application of the rule of consistency to their hypotheses and theories . . . . and they regard an examination (of these) . . . . in the light of these laws as an impertinent intrusion of '*à priori* principles and methods' into the domains of empirical science. Persons of this cast of mind find no difficulty in holding that atoms are absolutely inert, and at the same time asserting that these atoms are perfectly elastic; or in maintaining that the physical universe, in its last analysis, resolves itself into 'dead' matter and motion, and yet denying that all physical energy is in reality kinetic ; or in proclaiming that all phenomenal differences in the objective world are ultimately due to the various motions of absolutely simple material units, and, nevertheless, repudiating the proposition that these units are equal " . . . . (p. xix.) "The blindness of eminent physicists to some of the most obvious consequences of their own theories is marvellous . . . . When Prof. Tait, in conjunction with Prof. Stewart, announces that 'matter is simply passive' (*The Unseen Universe*, sec. 104), and then, in connection with Sir W. Thomson, declares that 'matter has an innate power of resisting external influences' (*Treat. on Nat. Phil.*, Vol. I., sec. 216), it is hardly impertinent to inquire how these statements are to be reconciled. When Prof. Du Bois Reymond . . . . insists upon the necessity of reducing all the processes of nature to motions of a substantial, indifferent substratum, *wholly destitute of quality (' Ueber die Grenzen des Naturerkennens,'* p. 5), having declared shortly before in the same lecture that 'resolution of all changes in the material world into motions of atoms *caused by their constant central forces* would be the completion of natural science,' we are in a perplexity from which we have to be relieved." (Pref. xliii.)

is claimed to be a modification and refinement of the idea of Lucretius. Let us then examine the modern concept from several scientific volumes containing the admissions of the physicists themselves.

The existence of Ether is accepted by physical astronomy, in ordinary physics, and in chemistry. Astronomers, who first began by regarding it as a fluid of extreme tenuity and mobility, offering no sensible resistance to the motions of celestial bodies, never gave a thought to its continuity or discontinuity. " Its main function in modern astronomy has been to serve as a basis for hydrodynamical theories of gravitation. In physics this fluid appeared for some time in several *rôles* in connection with the 'imponderables'"—so cruelly put to death by Sir W. Grove. Some physicists have even identified the ether of space with those "imponderables." Then came their Kinetic theories; and from the date of the dynamical theory of heat, it was chosen in optics as a substratum for luminous undulations. Then, in order to explain the dispersion and polarization of light, physicists had to resort once more to their "scientific imagination" and forthwith endowed the Ether with (*a*) atomic or molecular structure, and (*b*) with an enormous elasticity, "so that its resistance to deformation far exceeded that of the most rigid elastic bodies" (*Stallo*). This necessitated the *theory of the essential discontinuity of matter*, hence of Ether. After having accepted this discontinuity, in order to account for dispersion and polarization, theoretical impossibilities were discovered with regard to such dispersions. Cauchy's " scientific imagination " saw in atoms " material points without extension," and he proposed, in order to obviate the most formidable obstacles to the undulatory theory (namely, some well-known mechanical theorems which stood in the way), to assume that the ethereal medium of propagation, instead of being continuous, should consist of particles separated by sensible distances. Fresnel rendered the same service to the phenomena of polarization. E. B. Hunt upset the theories of both (*Silliman's Journal*, vol. viii., p. 364 *et seq.*) There are now men of Science who proclaim them "materially fallacious," while others — the " atomo-mechanicalists " — cling to to them with desperate tenacity. The supposition of an *atomic* or *molecular constitution* of ether is upset, moreover, by thermo-dynamics, for Clerk Maxwell showed that such a medium would be simply *gas*.[*] The hypothesis of " finite intervals " is thus proven of no avail as a supplement to the undulatory theory. Besides, eclipses fail to reveal any such variation of colour as supposed by Cauchy (on the assumption that the chromatic rays are propagated with different velocities).

---

[*] See Clerk Maxwell's " Treatise on Electricity of Magnetism " and compare with Cauchy's " *Mémoire sur la Dispersion de la lumière.*"

Astronomy has pointed out more than one phenomenon absolutely at variance with this doctrine.

Thus, while in one department of physics the atomo-molecular constitution of the ether is accepted in order to account for one set of special phenomena, in another department such a constitution is found quite subversive of a number of well-ascertained facts, Hirn's charges being thus justified (*vide supra*). Chemistry deemed it impossible to concede enormous elasticity to the *ether* without depriving it of other properties, upon the assumption of which the construction of *its* modern theories depended. This ended in a final transformation of ether. The exigencies of the atomo-mechanical theory have led distinguished mathematicians and physicists to attempt to substitute for the traditional atoms of matter, peculiar forms of *vortical motion* in a " universal homogeneous, incompressible, and *continuous* material medium," or Æther. (*See Stallo.*)

The present writer, claiming no great scientific education, but only a tolerable acquaintance with modern theories, and a better one with Occult Sciences, picks up weapons against the detractors of the esoteric teaching in the very arsenal of modern Science. The glaring contradictions, the mutually-destructive hypotheses of world-renowned Scientists, their mutual accusations, denunciations and disputes, show plainly that, whether accepted or not, the Occult theories have as much right to a hearing as any of the so-called learned and academical hypotheses. Thus whether the followers of the Royal Society choose to accept ether as a *continuous* or a *discontinuous* fluid matters little, and is indifferent to the present purpose. It simply points to one certainty : Official Science *knows nothing to this day of the constitution of ether.* Let Science call it matter, if it likes ; only neither as *akâsa* nor as the one sacred Æther of the Greeks, is it to be found in any of the states of matter known to modern physics. It is MATTER on quite another plane of perception and being, and it can neither be analyzed by scientific apparatus, appreciated, nor even conceived by " scientific imagination," unless the possessors thereof study the Occult Sciences. That which follows proves this statement.

It is clearly demonstrated by Stallo as regards the crucial problems of modern physics (as was done by De Quatrefages and several others in those of anthropology, biology, etc., etc.) that, in their efforts to support their individual hypotheses and systems, the majority of the eminent and learned materialists very often utter the greatest fallacies. Let us take the following case. Most of them reject *actio in distans* (one of the fundamental principles in the question of Æther or Akâsa in Occultism), while, as Stallo justly observes, there is no physical action, "which, on close examination, does not resolve itself into *actio in distans*"; and he proves it.

Now, metaphysical arguments, according to Professor Lodge (*Nature, vol. xxvii., p.* 304), are "unconscious appeals to experience." And he adds that if such an experience *is not conceivable*, then it does not exist, etc. In his own words:—". . . If a highly-developed mind or set of minds, find a doctrine about some comparatively simple and fundamental matter *absolutely unthinkable*, it is an evidence . . . that *the unthinkable state of things has no existence*, etc."

And thereupon, toward the end of his lecture, Professor Lodge indicates that the explanation of cohesion, as well as of gravity, "is to be looked for in the vortex-atom theory of Sir William Thomson" (Stallo).

It is needless to stop to inquire whether it is to this vortex-theory, also, that we have to look for the dropping down on earth of the first life-germ by a passing meteor or comet (Sir W. Thomson's hypothesis). But Mr. Lodge might be reminded of the wise criticism on his lecture in the same "Concepts of Modern Physics." Noticing the above quoted declaration by the London Professor, the author asks "whether . . . the elements of the vortex-theory are *familiar*, or even possible, facts of experience? For, if they are not, *clearly that theory is obnoxious to the same criticism which is said to invalidate the assumption* of ACTIO IN DISTANS" (p. xxiv). And then the able critic shows clearly what the Ether *is not*, nor can ever be, notwithstanding all scientific claims to the contrary. And thus he opens widely, if unconsciously, the entrance door to our occult teachings. For, as he says:—

"The medium in which the vortex-movements arise is, according to Professor Lodge's own express statement (NATURE, vol. xxvii., p. 305), 'a perfectly homogeneous, incompressible, continuous body, incapable of being resolved into simple elements or atoms: it is, in fact, continuous, not molecular.' And after making this statement Professor Lodge adds: '*There is no other body of which we can say this, and hence the properties of the æther must be somewhat* DIFFERENT *from those of ordinary matter.*' It appears, then, that the whole vortex-atom theory, which is offered to us as a substitute for the 'metaphysical theory' *of actio in distans*, rests upon the hypothesis of the existence of a material medium which is utterly *unknown to experience*, and which has properties *somewhat* different* from those of ordinary matter. Hence this theory, instead of being, as is claimed, a reduction of an unfamiliar fact of *experience* to a familiar fact, is,

---

* "*Somewhat* different!" exclaims Stallo. "The real import of this 'somewhat' is, that the medium in question *is not, in any intelligible sense, material at all*, having none of the properties of matter." All the properties of matter depend upon differences and changes, and the "hypothetical" æther here defined is not only destitute of differences, but incapable of difference and change—(in the physical sense let us add). This proves that if æther is "matter" *it is so* only as something visible, tangible and existing, for *spiritual* senses alone; that it is a Being indeed—but not of our plane: Pater Æther, or Akâsa.

on the contrary, a reduction of a fact which is perfectly familiar, to a fact which is not only unfamiliar, but wholly unknown, unobserved and unobservable. Furthermore, the alleged vortical motion of, or rather in, the assumed ethereal medium is . . . impossible, because "motion in a perfectly homogeneous, incompressible, and therefore continuous fluid, is not sensible motion." . . . . It is manifest, therefore, that wherever the vortex-atom theory may lead us, it certainly *does not lead us anywhere in the region of physics*, or in the domain of *veræ causæ.** And I may add that, inasmuch as the hypothetical undifferentiated† and undifferentiable medium is clearly an involuntary re-ification of the old ontological concept *pure being*, the theory under discussion has all the attributes of an *inapprehensible metaphysical phantom."*

A "phantom" indeed, which can be made apprehensible only by Occultism. From such scientific metaphysics to Occultism there is hardly one step. Those physicists who hold the view that the atomic constitution of matter is consistent with its penetrability, need not go far out of their way to be able to account for the greatest phenomena of Occultism, now so derided by physical scientists and materialists. Cauchy's "material points without extension" are Leibnitz's monads, and at the same time the materials out of which the "Gods" and other invisible powers cloth themselves in bodies (*vide infra*, " *Gods, Monads and Atoms* "). The disintegration and reintegration of "material" particles without extension as a chief factor in phenomenal manifestations ought to suggest themselves very easily as a *clear possibility*, at any rate to those few scientific minds which accept M. Cauchy's views. For, disposing of that property of matter which they call impenetrability by simply regarding the atoms as "material points exerting on each other attractions and repulsions which vary with the distances that separate them"—the French theorist explains that : "From this it follows that, if it pleased the author of nature‡ simply to *modify* the laws according to which the atoms attract or repel each other, *we might instantly see the hardest bodies penetrating each other*, the smallest particles of matter *occupying immense spaces*, or the largest masses reducing themselves to the smallest volumes, the entire universe concentrating itself, as it were, in a single point." (*Sept leçons de physique Générale*, p. 38 *et seq.*, ed. Moigno.)

And that " point," *invisible on our plane of perception and matter*, is quite visible to the eye of the adept who can follow and see it present on other planes.

---

* *Veræ causæ* for physical science are *mayavic* or illusionary causes to the Occultist, and *vice versâ*.

† Very much " differentiated," on the contrary, since the day it left its *laya* condition.

‡ For the Occultists who say that the author of nature *is nature itself*, something indistinct and inseparable from the Deity, it follows that those who are conversant with the *occult laws* of nature, and know how to change and provoke new conditions in ether, may—*not* modify the laws, but work and do the same *in accordance with* those *immutable* laws.

IV.

IS GRAVITATION A LAW?

THE corpuscular theory has been unceremoniously put aside; but gravitation—the principle that all bodies attract each other with a force proportional directly to their masses, and inversely to the squares of the distances between them—survives to this day and reigns, supreme as ever, in the alleged ethereal waves of Space. As a hypothesis, it had been threatened with death for its inadequacy to embrace all the facts presented to it; as a *physical law*, it is the King of the late and once all-potent "Imponderables." " It is little short of blasphemy . . . . an insult to Newton's grand memory to doubt it, ... " is the exclamation of an American reviewer of "*Isis Unveiled.*" Well; what is finally that *invisible and intangible* God in whom we should believe on blind faith? Astronomers who see in gravitation an easy-going solution for many things, and an *universal* force which allows them to calculate thereby planetary motions, care little about the Cause of Attraction. They call Gravity a law, a *cause* in itself. We call the forces acting under that name *effects*, and very secondary effects, too. One day it will be found that the scientific hypothesis does not answer after all; and then it will follow the corpuscular theory of light and be consigned to rest for many scientific *æons* in the archives of all exploded speculations. Has not Newton himself expressed grave doubts about the Nature of Force and the corporeality of the "Agents," as they were then called? So has Cuvier, another scientific light shining in the night of research. He warns his readers, in the *Révolution du Globe*, about the doubtful nature of the so-called Forces, saying that " it is not so sure whether those agents were not *Spiritual Powers* after all (*des agents spirituels*). At the outset of his " Principia," Sir Isaac Newton took the greatest care to impress upon his school that he did not use the word " attraction " with regard to the mutual action of bodies in a physical sense. To him it was, he said, a purely mathematical conception involving no considera-tion of real and primary physical causes. In one of the passages of his " Principia " (*Defin.* 8, *B. I. Prop.* 69, " *Scholium* "), he tells us plainly that, physically considered, attractions are rather *impulses*. In section XI. (*Introduction*) he expresses the opinion that " there *is some subtle spirit by the force and action of which* all movements of matter are determined " (see *Mod. Mater.*, by *Rev. W. F. Wilkinson*); and in his third Letter to Bentley he says: " It is inconceivable that inanimate brute matter should, with-out the mediation of something else *which is not material*, operate upon and affect other matter, without mutual contact, as it must do if gravi-

tation, in the sense of Epicurus, be essential and inherent in it. . . .
That gravity should be innate, inherent and essential to matter, so that
one body may act upon another at a distance, through a vacuum, without
the mediation of anything else by and through which their action may
be conveyed from one to another, is to me so great an absurdity that I
believe no man, who has in philosophical matters a competent faculty
of thinking, can ever fall into it.   Gravity must be caused by an agent
acting constantly according to certain laws ; but *whether this agent* be
material or immaterial I have left to the consideration of my readers."

At this, even Newton's contemporaries got frightened—at the apparent
return of *occult* causes into the domain of physics.   Leibnitz called his
principle of attraction " an incorporeal and inexplicable power."   The
supposition of an attractive faculty and a perfect *void* was characterized
by Bernouilli as " revolting," the principle of *actio in distans* finding thus
no more favour then than it does now.   Euler, on the other hand,
thought the action of gravity was due to either a *Spirit* or some subtle
medium.   And yet Newton knew of, if he did not accept, the Ether of
the Ancients.   He regarded the intermediate space between the sidereal
bodies as *vacuum*.   Therefore he believed in " subtle spirit " and *Spirits*
as we do, guiding the so-called attraction.   The above-quoted words of
the great man have produced poor results.   The " absurdity " has now
become a dogma in the case of pure materialism, which repeats, " No
matter without force, no force without matter ; matter and force are
inseparable, eternal and indestructible (*true*) ; there can be no independent force, since all force is *an inherent and necessary property of matter*
(*false*) ; consequently, *there is no immaterial* creative power."   Oh, poor
Sir Isaac !

If, leaving aside all the other eminent men of Science who shared
in the same opinion as Euler and Leibnitz, the Occultists claim
as their authorities and supporters only Sir Isaac Newton and Cuvier,
as above cited, they need fear little from modern Science, and may
loudly and proudly proclaim their beliefs.   But, the hesitation and
doubts of the two before cited authorities, and of many others, too, whom
we could name, did not in the least prevent scientific speculation from
wool-gathering on the fields of brute matter just as before.   First it was
matter and an imponderable fluid distinct from it ; then came the *imponderable* fluid so much criticised by Grove ; and Æther, which was at
first *discontinuous* and then became continuous ; after which came the
" mechanical " Forces.   These have now settled in life as " modes of
motion " and the æther has become more mysterious and problematical
than ever.   More than one man of Science objects to such crude
materialistic views.   But then since the days of Plato, who repeatedly asks his readers not to confuse *incorporeal* Elements with

their Principles—transcendental or spiritual Elements; from those of the great Alchemists, who, like Paracelsus, made a great difference between phenomenon and its cause, or the Noumenon; and Grove, who, though he sees "no reason to divest universally diffused matter of the *functions* common to all matter," yet uses the term *Forces* where his critics, "who do not attach to the word any idea of a *specific action*," say Force—from those days to this nothing has proved competent to stem the tide of brutal materialism. Gravitation *is the sole cause*, the acting God, and matter is its prophet, said the men of science only a few years ago.

They have changed their views several times since then. But do the men of Science understand the innermost thought of Newton, one of the most spiritual-minded and religious men of his day, any better now than they did then? It is certainly to be doubted. Newton is credited with having given the death-blow to the Elemental Vortices of Descartes (the idea of Anaxagoras, resurrected, by-the-bye), though the last modern "vortical atoms" of Sir W. Thomson do not, in truth, differ much from the former. Nevertheless, when his disciple Forbes wrote in the *Preface* to the chief work of his Master a sentence declaring that "attraction was the *cause* of the System," Newton was the first to solemly protest. That which in the mind of the great mathematician assumed the shadowy, but firmly rooted image of God, as the *noumenon* of all,* was called more philosophically by the ancient (and modern) philosophers and Occultists — "Gods," or the *creative* fashioning Powers. The modes of expression may have been different, and the ideas more or less philosophically enunciated by all sacred and profane Antiquity; but the fundamental thought was the same.† For Pythagoras the Forces were Spiritual Entities, Gods inde-

---

* "*Attraction*," Le Couturier, a materialist, writes, "has now become for the public that which it was for Newton himself—a simple word, an *idea*" (*Panorama des Mondes*), since its cause is unknown. Herschell virtually says the same, when remarking, that whenever studying the motion of the heavenly bodies, and the phenomena of attraction, he feels penetrated at every moment with the idea of "the *existence of causes* that act for us under a veil, disguising *their direct* action." (*Musée des Sciences*, August, 1856.)

† If we are taken to task for believing in operating "Gods" and "Spirits" while rejecting a *personal* God, we answer to the Theists and Monotheists; "Admit that your Jehovah is *one of the Elohim*, and we are ready to recognise him. Make of him, as you do, the Infinite, the one and the *Eternal* God, and we will never accept him in this character." Of *tribal* Gods there were many; the One Universal Deity is a principle, an abstract Root-Idea which has nought to do with the unclean work of finite Form. We do not worship the Gods, we only honour Them, as beings superior to ourselves. In this we obey the Mosaic injunction, while Christians *disobey* their Bible—Missionaries foremost of all. "*Thou shalt not revile the gods*," says one of them—(Jehovah)—in *Exodus xxii.* 28); but at the same time in verse 20 it is commanded, "He that sacrificeth to *any* God, save unto the Lord, he shall be utterly destroyed." Now in the

pendent of planets and Matter as we see and know them on Earth, who are the rulers of the Sidereal Heaven. Plato represented the planets as moved by an *intrinsic* Rector, one with his dwelling, like " A boatman in his boat." As for Aristotle, he called those rulers "*immaterial* substances ; " * though as one who had never been initiated, he rejected the gods as *Entities (See Vossius, Vol. II., p.* 528). But this did not prevent him from recognising the fact that the stars and planets " were not inanimate masses but *acting* and *living* bodies indeed. . . . . . ." As if " *sidereal spirits were the divine* portion of their phenomena, τὰ θειότερα τῶν φανερῶν " (*De Caelo. I.* 9).

If we look for corroboration in more modern and Scientific times, we find Tycho Brahè recognising in the stars a triple force, *divine, spiritual and vital.* Kepler, putting together the Pythagorean sentence, "The Sun, guardian of Jupiter," and the verses of David, " He placed his throne in the Sun," and " The Lord is the Sun," etc., said that he understood perfectly how the Pythagoreans could believe that all the globes disseminated through Space were rational Intelligences, *facultates ratiocinativæ,* circulating around the Sun, "in which resides *a pure Spirit of fire ;* the source of the general harmony" (*De Motibus planetarum harmonicis, p.* 248).

When an Occultist speaks of Fohat—the energising and guiding intelligence in the Universal Electric or *Vital* Fluid,—he is laughed at. Withal, as now shown, neither the nature of electricity, nor of Life nor even of Light, are to this day understood. The Occultist sees in the manifestation of every force in Nature, the action of the quality, or the special characteristic of its noumenon ; which *noumenon* is a distinct and intelligent Individuality *on the other side of the manifested mechanical Universe.* Now the Occultist does not deny—on the contrary he will support the claim—that light, heat, electricity and so on are *affections* (not properties or qualities) of matter. To put it more clearly : matter is the condition—the necessary basis or vehicle, a *sine quâ non*—for the manifestation of these forces, or agents, on this plane.

But in order to gain the point the Occultists have to examine the credentials of the law of gravity, first of all, of " Gravitation, the King

---

original texts it is not " god " but *Elohim,*—and we challenge contradiction—and Jehovah is one of the Elohim, as proved by his own words in *Genesis iii.* 22, when " the Lord God said : Behold the Man has become *as one of us,*" etc. Hence both those who worship and sacrifice to the *Elohim,* the angels, and to Jehovah, those who *revile the gods* of their fellow-men, are far greater transgressors then the Occultists or any Theosophist. Meanwhile many of the latter prefer believing in some one " Lord " or other, and are quite welcome to do as they like.

* To liken the " immateriate species to *wooden iron,*" and laugh at Spiller referring to them as " incorporeal matter " does not solve the mystery (See " Concepts of Modern Physics," p. 165 *et infra*).

and Ruler of Matter," under every form. To do so effectually, the hypothesis in its earliest appearance has to be recalled to mind. To begin with, is it Newton who was the first to discover it? The *Athenæum* of Jan. 26, 1867, has some curious information upon this subject. It says that " positive evidence can be adduced that Newton derived all his knowledge of gravitation and its laws from Bœhme, *with whom gravitation or* ATTRACTION *is the first property of Nature.*" . . . For with him "his (Bœhme's) system, shows us the *inside* of things, while modern physical science is content with looking at the outside." Then again, " the science of electricity, which was not yet in existence when he (Boehme) wrote, is there anticipated (in his writings) ; and not only does Bœhme describe all the now known phenomena of that force, but he even gives us the origin, generation, and birth of electricity, itself, etc."

Thus Newton, whose profound mind read easily between the lines, and fathomed the spiritual thought of the great Seer in its mystic rendering, owes his great discovery to Jacob Bœhme, the nursling of the genii (Nirmânakâyas) who watched over and guided him, of whom the author of the article in question so truly remarks, that " every new scientific discovery goes to prove *his profound and intuitive insight into the most secret workings of nature.*" And having *discovered* gravity, Newton, in order to render possible the action of attraction in space, had, so to speak, to *annihilate* every physical obstacle capable of impeding its free action ; ether among others, though he had more than a presentiment of its existence. Advocating the corpuscular theory, he made an *absolute vacuum* between the heavenly bodies. . . . Whatever may have been his suspicions and *inner* convictions about Ether ; however many friends he may have unbosomed himself to—as in the case of his corre-spondence with Bentley—his teachings never showed that he had any such belief. If he *was* " persuaded that the power of attraction could not be exerted by matter across a vacuum,"* how is it that so late as 1860, French astronomers (Le Couturier, for instance), combated " the *disastrous* results of the theory of vacuum established by the great man ? "† Professor Winchell writes, " These passages (letter to Bentley) show what were his views respecting the nature of the interplanetary medium of communication. Though declaring that the heavens ' *are void of sensible matter,*' he elsewhere excepted '*perhaps*

---

* World-Life. Prof. Winchell, LL.D (pp. 49 and 50).

† " Il n'est plus possible aujourd'hui, *de soutenir comme Newton,* que les corps célestes se mouvent au milieu du VIDE immense des espaces. . . . Parmi les conséquences de la *théorie du vide établie* par ce grand homme, il ne reste plus debout *que le mot ' attraction,'* et nous verrons le jour ou ce dernier mot disparaitra du vocabulaire scientifique." *(" Panorama des mondes,"* pp. 47 *and* 53.)

some very thin vapours, streams, and effluvia, arising from the atmospheres of the earth, planets, and comets, and from such an exceedingly rare ethereal medium as we have elsewhere described." (*Newton, Optics, III., query* 28, 1704 ; *quoted in* " *World-Life.*")

This only shows that even such great men as Newton have not always the courage of their opinions. Dr. T. S. Hunt " called attention to some long-neglected passages in Newton's works, from which it appears that a belief in such universal, intercosmical medium gradually took root in his mind." (*Ibid.*) But such attention was never called to the said passages before Nov. 28, 1881, when Dr. Hunt read his " *Celestial Chemistry, from the time of Newton.*" " Till then the idea was universal, even among the men of Science, that Newton had, while advocating the corpuscular theory, preached *a void*," as Le Couturier says. The passages had been " long neglected," no doubt because they contradicted and clashed with the preconceived pet theories of the day, till finally the undulatory theory imperiously required the presence of an " ethereal medium " to explain it. This is the whole secret.

Anyhow, it is from that theory of Newton's of a universal void— *taught*, if not believed in by himself,—that dates the immense scorn now shown by modern for ancient physics. The old sages had maintained that " Nature abhorred vacuum," and the greatest mathematicians of the world (read of the Western races) had discovered the antiquated "fallacy" and exposed it. And now modern science vindicates, however ungracefully, archaic knowledge, having, moreover, to vindicate Newton's character and powers of observation at this late hour, after having neglected for one century and a half to pay any attention to such very important passages—perchance, because it was wiser not to attract any notice to them. Better late than never.

And now Father Æther is *re-welcomed* with open arms ; and wedded to gravitation ; linked to it for weal or woe, until the day when it, or both, shall be replaced by something else. Three hundred years ago it was *plenum* everywhere, then it became one dismal *vacuity ;* later still the sidereal ocean-beds, dried up by science, rolled onward once more their ethereal waves. *Recede ut procedes* must become the motto of exact Science—" exact," chiefly, in finding itself inexact every leap-year.

But we will not quarrel with the great men. They had to go back to the earliest " Gods of Pythagoras and old Kanada " for the very backbone and marrow of their correlations and "newest" discoveries, and this may well afford good hope to the Occultists, for their minor gods. For we believe in Le Couturier's prophecy about gravitation. We know the day is approaching when an *absolute reform* will be demanded in the present modes of Science by the scientists themselves—as was done by Sir W. Grove, F.R.S. Till that day there is nothing to be done. For if gravitation

were dethroned to-morrow, the day after the Scientists would discover
some other new mode of mechanical motion.* Rough and up-hill is
the path of true Science, and its days are full of vexation of Spirit.
But in the face of its "thousand" contradictory hypotheses to explain
physical phenomena, there never was yet a better one than that of
" motion "—however paradoxically interpreted by materialism. As
may be found on the first pages of Book I., Occultists have nothing
surely against *motion*† the GREAT BREATH of Mr. Herbert Spencer's
"UNKNOWN." But, believing that everything on Earth is the *shadow* of
something in *space*—they believe in *smaller* " Breaths," which, living,
intelligent and independent of all but Law, blow in every direction
during Manvantaric periods. These Science will reject. But whatever
replaces attraction, *alias* gravitation, the result will be the same.
Science will be as far from the solution of its difficulties as it is now,
unless it comes to some compromise with Occultism and even with
Alchemy—which supposition will be regarded as an impertinence, but
remains a fact, nevertheless. As Faye says : " *Il manque quelque chose aux
géologues pour faire la géologie de la Lune, c'est d'être astronomes. A la verité
il manque aussi quelquechose aux astronomes pour aborder avec fruit cette étude,
c'est d'être géologues.*" But he might have added, with still more pointed-
ness, " *Ce qui manque à tous les deux, c'est l'intuition du mystique.*"

Let us remember Sir William Grove's wise " concluding remarks,"
on the ultimate structure of matter, or the minutiæ of molecular actions,
which, he thought, man will never know.

" Much harm has already been done by attempting hypothetically to dissect
matter and to discuss the shapes, sizes, and numbers of atoms, and their
atmospheres of heat, ether, or electricity. . . . . Whether the regarding
electricity, light, magnetism, etc., as simply motions of ordinary matter, be or
be not admissible, certain it is that all past theories have resolved, and all
existing theories do resolve, the action of these forces into motion. Whether
it be that, on account of our familiarity with motion, we refer other affections
to it, as to a language which is most easily construed, and most capable of

---

* When read in a fair and unprejudiced spirit, Sir Isaac Newton's works are an ever
ready witness to show how he must have hesitated between gravitation and attraction,
impulse and some other *unknown cause* to explain the regular course of the planetary
motion. But see *Treatise on Colour* (Vol. III., question 31.) We are told by Herschell
that Newton left with his successors the duty of drawing all the scientific conclusions
from his discovery. How modern Science abused the privilege of building its newest
theories upon the law of gravitation, may be realised when one remembers how profoundly religious was that great man.

† The materialistic notion that because, in physics real or sensible motion is impossible in pure space or *vacuum*, therefore, the eternal MOTION of and in Cosmos (regarded
as infinite Space) is a *fiction*—only shows once more that such words as " pure space,"
"pure Being," "the Absolute," etc., of Eastern metaphysics have never been understood
in the West.

explaining them, or whether it be that it is in reality the only mode in which *our minds* as *contra-distinguished from our senses*, are able *to conceive material agencies*, certain it is that since the period at which the mystic notions of spiritual or preternatural powers were applied to account for physical phenomena, all hypotheses framed to explain them have resolved them into MOTION."

And then the learned gentleman states a purely occult tenet :—

" The term perpetual motion, which I have not infrequently used in these pages, is itself equivocal. If the doctrines here advanced be well founded, *all motion is, in one sense, perpetual.* In masses, whose motion is stopped by mutual concussion, heat or motion of the particles is generated; and thus the motion continues, so that if we could venture to extend such thoughts to the universe, we should assume the same amount of motion affecting the same amount of matter for ever."*

Thus, supposing attraction or gravitation should be given up in favour of the Sun being a *huge magnet*—which is a theory already accepted by some physicists—a magnet that acts on the planets as attraction is now supposed to do, whereto, or how much farther would it lead the astronomers from where they are now ? Not an inch farther. Kepler came to this " curious hypothesis " nearly 300 years ago. He had not discovered the theory of attraction and repulsion in Kosmos, for it was known from the days of Empedocles, the two opposite forces being called by him " hate " and " love "—which comes to the same thing. But Kepler gave a pretty fair description of cosmic magnetism. That such magnetism exists in nature, is as certain as that gravitation does not ; not at any rate, in the way in which it is taught by Science, which never took into consideration the different modes in which the dual Force—that Occultism calls attraction and repulsion—may act within our solar system, the earth's atmosphere, and *beyond* in the Kosmos.† This was proven by Newton himself; for there are many phenomena in our

---

* " *Correl. Phys. Forces*," p. 173. This is precisely what Occultism maintains, and on the same principle that " where force is made to oppose force, and produce static equilibrium, the balance of pre-existing equilibrium is affected, and *fresh motion is started* equivalent to that which is withdrawn into a state of abeyance." This process finds intervals in the pralaya, but is eternal and ceaseless as *the* " Breath," even when the manifested Kosmos rests.

† " Trans-solar space," writes the great Humboldt, " does not hitherto show any phenomenon analogous to our solar system. It is a peculiarity of *our* System, that matter should have condensed within it in nebulous rings, the nuclei of which condense into earths and moons. I say again, heretofore, *nothing of the kind has ever been observed beyond our planetary system*." (*See Revue Germanique of the* 31st Dec. 1860, *art.* " *Lettres et conversations d'Alexandre Humboldt*.") True, that since 1860 the nebular theory has sprung up, and being better known, a few identical phenomena were *supposed* to be observed beyond the solar system. Yet the great man is quite right ; and no *earths* or *moons* can be found—*except in appearance*—beyond, or of the same order of matter as found in our system. Such is the Occult teaching.

Solar system, which he confessed his inability to explain by the law of gravitation. " Such were the uniformity in the directions of planetary movements, the nearly circular forms of the orbits, and their remarkable conformity to one plane " (*Prof. Winchell*). And if there is one single exception, then the law of gravitation has no right to be referred to as an *universal law*. " These adjustments," we are told, " Newton, in his general Scholium, pronounces to be ' the work of an intelligent and all-powerful Being.' " Intelligent that " Being " may be; as to " all-powerful " there would be every reason to doubt the claim. A poor " God " he, who would work upon minor details and leave the most important to secondary forces ! The poverty of the argument and logic in this case, is surpassed only by that of Laplace, who, seeking very correctly to substitute motion for Newton's "all-powerful Being," and ignorant of the true nature of that eternal motion, saw in it a blind physical law. " Might not those arrangements be an effect of the laws of motion ? " he asks, forgetting, as all our modern Scientists do, that this *law* and this motion are a vicious circle, so long as the *nature of both* remains unexplained. His famous answer to Napoleon : " *Dieu est devenu une hypothèse inutile*," would be correctly stated only by one who adhered to the philosophy of the Vedantins. It becomes a pure fallacy, if we exclude the interference of operating, intelligent, powerful (never " *all-powerful* ") Beings, who are called " gods."

But we would ask the critics of the mediæval astronomers why should Kepler be denounced as *most unscientific*, for offering just the same solution as Newton did—only showing himself more sincere, more consistent and even more logical. Where may be the difference between Newton's " all-powerful Being" and Kepler's *Rectores*, his sidereal and Cosmic Forces, or Angels? Kepler is again criticised for his " curious hypothesis which made use of a vortical movement within the solar system ;" for his theories in general, for his favouring Empedocles' idea of attraction and repulsion, and " Solar magnetism " in particular. Yet several modern men of Science, as will be shown—Hunt (if Metcalfe is to be excluded), Dr. Richardson, etc.—favour the idea very seriously. He is half excused, however, on the plea that " to the time of Kepler no interaction between masses of matter had been distinctly recognized which was *generically* different from magnetism " (*World-Life*). Is it *distinctly* recognised now ? Does Prof. Winchell claim for Science any serious knowledge whatever of the natures of either electricity or magnetism—except that *both seem to be the effects of some result arising from an undetermined cause.*

The ideas of Kepler, weeded from their theological tendencies, are purely occult. He saw that:

(I.) The Sun is a great Magnet.* This is what some eminent modern scientists and also the Occultists believe in.

(II.) The Solar substance is immaterial.† (See "*Isis Unveiled*," *Vol. I. pp.* 270 *to* 271.)

(III.) He provided, for the constant motion and restoration of the Sun's energy and planetary motion, the perpetual care of a spirit, or spirits. The whole of Antiquity believed in this idea. The Occultists do not use the word Spirit, but say *Creative* Forces, which they *endow with intelligence.* But we may call them spirits also.

This theory is tabooed a great deal more on account of the " Spirit " that is given room in it, than of anything else. Herschell, the elder, believed in it likewise, and so do several modern scientists also. Nevertheless Professor Winchell declares that " a hypothesis more fanciful, and less in accord with the requirements of physical principles, has not been offered in ancient or modern times." *(World-Life, p.* 554.)

The same was said, once upon a time, of the universal Ether, and now it is not only accepted perforce but advocated *as the only possible theory* to explain away certain mysteries.

Grove's ideas, when he first enunciated them in London about 1840, were called as *unscientific* as the above ; nevertheless, *his* views on the correlation of forces are now universally accepted. It would, very likely, require one more conversant with science than is the writer, to combat with any success some of the now prevailing ideas about gravitation and other similar " solutions " of Cosmic Mysteries. But, let us recall a few objections that came from recognized men of Science; from astronomers and physicists of eminence, who rejected the theory of rotation, as well as that of gravitation. Thus one reads in the *French Encyclopædia* that " Science agrees, in the face of all its representatives, that it is *impossible* to explain the *physical* origin of the rotatory motion of the solar system."

If the question is asked, " what causes rotation ?" we are answered : " It is the centrifugal Force." " And this force, what is it that produces it ?" " The force of rotation," is the grave answer. (*Godefroy, Cosmogonie de la Révélation.*‡) It will be well, perhaps, to examine both these theories as being directly or indirectly connected.

---

* But see *Astronomie du Moyen Age*, by Delambre.

† In the sense, of course, of matter existing in states unknown to Science.

‡ We shall be taken to task for contradiction. It will be said that while we deny God, we admit Souls and *operative Spirits*, and quote from Roman Catholic bigoted writers in support of our argument. To this we reply : " We deny the *anthropomorphic* god of the Monotheists, but never the Divine Principle in nature. We combat Protestants and Roman Catholics on a number of dogmatic theological beliefs of human and sectarian origin. We agree with them in their belief in Spirits and *intelligent* operative powers, though we do not worship " Angels " as the Roman Latinists do.

V.

THE THEORIES OF ROTATION IN SCIENCE.

CONSIDERING that " final cause is pronounced a chimera, and the first Great Cause is remanded to the Sphere of the Unknown," as a reverend gentleman justly complains, the number of hypotheses put forward, a nebula in itself, is most remarkable. The profane student is perplexed, and does not know in which of the theories of *exact* science he has to believe. Here we have hypotheses enough for every taste and power of brain. They are all extracted from a number of scientific volumes.

CURRENT HYPOTHESES EXPLAINING THE ORIGIN OF ROTATION.

Rotation has originated either—

(*a*) By the collision of nebular masses wandering aimlessly in space; or by *attraction*, " in cases where no actual impact takes place."

(*b*) " By the tangential action of currents of nebulous matter (in the case of an amorphous nebula) descending from higher to lower levels,* or *simply by the action of the central gravity of the mass.*" †

" It is a fundamental principle in physics that *no rotation could be generated in such a mass by the action of its own parts.* As well attempt to change the course of a steamer by pulling at the deck railing," remarks to this Prof. Winchell in " World-Life."

HYPOTHESES OF THE ORIGIN OF THE SEVEN PLANETS AND COMETS.

(*a.*) We owe the birth of the Planets (1) to an explosion of the Sun— a parturition of its central mass; ‡ or (2) to some kind of disruption of the nebular rings.

(*b*) " The Comets are strangers to our planetary system " (*La Place*). " The Comets are undeniably generated in our Solar system " (*Faye*).

(*c*) The "*fixed* stars are motionless " says one authority. . . . " All the stars are actually in motion " answers another authority. . . " Undoubtedly every star is in motion " (*Wolf*).

(*d*) " For over 350,000,000 years, the slow and majestic movement of the Sun around its axis has never for a moment ceased " (*Panorama des Mondes, Le Couturier.*)

---

* The terms " high " and " low " being only relative to the position of the observer in Space, any use of those terms tending to convey the impression that they stand for abstract realities, is necessarily fallacious.

† *Jacob Ennis,* " The Origin of the Stars," p. 221 *et seq.*

‡ If such is the case, how does Science explain the comparatively small size of the planets nearest the Sun ? The theory of meteoric aggregation is only a step farther from truth than the nebular conception, and has not even the quality of the latter—its metaphysical element.

(*e*) And "the sun having Alcyone in the Pleiades for the centre of its orbit, consumes 180,000,000 of years in completing its revolution" (*Maedler*). And also,

(*f*) That, "*the Sun has existed no more than* 15,000,000 *of years*, and will emit heat for no longer *than* 10,000,000 *years more*" (*Sir W. Thomson's lecture on* "*the latent dynamical theory regarding the probable origin, total amount of heat, and duration of the Sun*," 1887).

A few years ago this eminent Scientist was telling the world that the time required for the earth to cool from incipient incrustation to its present state, could not exceed 80,000,000 years*; (*Thomson and Tait, Natural Philosophy*.) If the encrusted age of the world is only 40 millions, or the half of the duration once allowed, and the Sun's age only 15 millions, have we to understand that the earth was at one time independent of the Sun?

Since the ages of the Sun, planets, and the Earth, as stated in the many scientific hypotheses of the astronomers and physicists, are given elsewhere (*infra*), we have said enough to show the disagreement between the ministers of modern Science. Whether we accept the *fifteen* million years of Sir W. Thomson or the *thousand* millions of Mr. Huxley, for the rotational evolution of our solar system, it will always come to this; by accepting *self-generated* rotation for the heavenly bodies composed of *inert* matter and yet moved by *their own internal motion*, for millions of years, this teaching of Science amounts to—

(*a*) An evident denial of that fundamental physical law, which states that "a body *in motion tends constantly to inertia*, (*i.e.*, to continue in the same state of motion or rest), unless it is stimulated into further action *by a superior active* force."

(*b*.) To an original impulse, which culminates in an unalterable motion, within a *resisting* ether that NEWTON had declared *incompatible with that motion*.

(*c*.) Universal gravity, which, we are taught, always tends to a centre in *rectilinear* descent—*alone* the cause of the revolution of the whole solar system, which is performing an eternal *double* gyration, each body around its axis and orbit. Another occasional version is:—

(*d*.) A magnet in the Sun; or, the said revolution due to a magnetic force, which acts, just as gravitation does, in a straight line—varying inversely as the square of the distance. (Coulomb's Law.)

(*e*.) The whole acting under *invariable* and changeless laws, which are, nevertheless, often shown variable, as during some well-known freaks

---

* And even on these figures Bischof disagrees with Thomson, and calculates that 350 million years would be required for the earth to cool from a temperature of 20,000° to 200° centigrade. This is, also, the opinion of Helmholtz.

THE SECRET DOCTRINE.

of planets and other bodies, as also when the Comets approach to or recede from the Sun.

(*f.*) A MOTOR FORCE always *proportionate* to the mass it is acting upon; but *independent of the* specific nature of that mass, to which it is proportionate; which amounts to saying, as Le Couturier does, that, "without that Force independent from and of quite another nature than the said mass, the latter, were it as huge as Saturn, or as tiny as Ceres, would always fall with the same rapidity" (*Musée des Sciences*, 15 August, 1857). A mass, furthermore, which derives its weight from the body on which it weighs.

Thus neither Laplace's perceptions of a solar atmospheric fluid, which would extend beyond the orbits of the planets, nor Le Couturier's electricity, nor Foucault's heat (*Panorama des Mondes*, p. 55), nor this, nor the other, can ever help any of the numerous hypotheses about the origin and *permanency* of rotation to escape from this squirrel's wheel, any more than the theory of gravity itself. This mystery is the Procrustean bed of physical Science. If matter is, as now taught, passive, the simplest movement cannot be said to be an essential property of matter —if the latter is simply an inert mass. How, then, can such a complicated movement, compound and multiple, harmonious and equilibrated, lasting in the eternities for millions and millions of years, be attributed simply to its own inherent Force, unless the latter is an *intelligence?* A *physical will* is something new—a conception that the ancients would have never entertained, indeed! *

"We talk of the weight of the heavenly bodies," says an astronomer; "but since it is recognised that weight decreases in proportion to the distance from the centre, it becomes evident that, at a certain distance, that weight must be forcibly reduced to Zero? Were there any *attraction* there would be equilibrium . . . . And since the modern school recognizes neither a *beneath* nor an *above* in universal space, it is not clear what should cause the Earth to fall, were there even no gravitation, nor attraction." (*Cosmographie.*)

Methinks the Count de Maistre was right in solving the question in is own theological way. He cuts the Gordian knot by saying :—"The

---

* For over a century all distinction between body and force is made away with. "Force is but the property of a body in motion," say the physicists; and "*life*—the property of our *animal organs*—is but the result of their molecular arrangement," answer the physiologists. "In the bosom of that aggregate which is named planet," teaches Littré, "are developed all the forces immanent to matter . . . *i.e.*, that matter possesses *in itself* and *through itself* the forces that are proper to it . . . and which are *primary*, not *secondary*. Such forces are the property of weight, the property of electricity, of terrestrial magnetism, the property of life. . . . Every planet can develop life . . . as earth, for instance, which had not always mankind on it, and now bears (*produit*) men" . . . (*Revue des Deux Mondes*, *July* 15, 1860.)

planets rotate because *they are made to rotate* . . . . . and the modern physical system of the universe is a *physical impossibility."* (*Soirées.*) For did not Herschell say the same thing when he remarked that there is a *will* needed to impart a circular motion, and *another will* to restrain it ? (*Discours*, 165.) This shows and explains how a *retarded* planet is cunning enough to calculate so well its time as to hit off its arrival at the fixed minute. For, if Science sometimes succeeds with its great ingenuity in explaining some of such stoppages, retrograde motions, angles outside the orbits, &c., &c., by appearances resulting from the inequality of their progress and ours in the course of our mutual and respective orbits, we still know that there are others, and " very real and considerable deviations," according to Herschell, " which cannot be explained except by the mutual and irregular action of those planets and by the *perturbing* influence of the Sun."

We understand, however, that there are, besides those little and accidental perturbations, continuous perturbations called " secular "— because of the extreme slowness with which the irregularity increases and affects the relations of the elliptic movement—and that these perturbations *can be corrected*. From Newton, who found that this world needed *repairing* very often, down to Reynaud, all say the same. In his *Ciel et Terre* (*p.* 28), the latter speaks of—

". . . . The orbits described by the planets as being very far from immutable ; " on the contrary, subject to a perpetual mutation in their position and form,"—all prove gravitation and the peripatetic *laws* to be as negligent as they are quick to repair their mistakes. The charge as it stands seems to be that " they (the orbits) are alternately widening and narrowing, their great axis lengthens and diminishes, or oscillates at the same time from right to left around the Sun, the plane itself, in which they are situated, raising and lowering itself periodically while pivoting around itself with a kind of tremor. . . ."

To this, De Mirville, who believes in *intelligent* " workmen " ruling invisibly the solar system—as we do—observes very wittily*. . . . . " *Voilà certes*, a voyage which has little in it of mechanical *rigour ;* at the utmost, one could compare it to a steamer, pulled to and fro and tossed on the waves, retarded or accelerated, all and each of which impediments might put off its arrival indefinitely, were there not the intelligences of a pilot and engineers to catch up the time lost, and to repair the damages. . . . ."

The law of gravity, however, seems to be becoming an *obsolete* law in starry heaven. At any rate those long-haired sidereal *radicals*, called comets, appear to be very poor respecters of the majesty of that law,

---

* *Deuxième mémoire,* " *Manifestations Historiques,*" p. 272.

and to beard it quite impudently. Nevertheless, and though presenting in nearly every respect "phenomena *not yet fully understood*," comets and meteors are credited by the believers in modern Science with *obeying the same laws and consisting of the same matter*, "as the Suns, stars and nebulæ," and even "the earth and its inhabitants." (*Laing's "Modern Science and Modern Thought."*)

This is what one might call taking things on trust, aye, even to *blind faith*. But *exact* Science is not to be questioned, and he who rejects the hypotheses imagined by her students—gravitation, for instance—would be regarded as an ignorant fool for it; yet we are told by the just cited author a queer legend from the scientific annals. "The comet of 1811 had a tail 120 millions of miles in length and 25 millions of miles in diameter at the widest part, while the diameter of the nucleus was about 127,000 miles, more than ten times that of the earth." He tells us, "in order that bodies of this magnitude, passing near the earth, *should not affect its* motion or change the length of the year by even a single second, their actual substance must be inconceivably rare. . . ." It must be so indeed, yet :—

". . . . . The extreme tenuity of a comet's mass is also proved by the phenomenon of the tail, which, as the comet approaches the sun, is thrown out sometimes to a length of 90 millions of miles in a few hours. And what is remarkable, THIS TAIL IS THROWN OUT AGAINST THE FORCE OF GRAVITY *by some repulsive force*, probably electrical, so that it always points away from the Sun (! ! !) And yet, thin as the matter of comets must be, *IT OBEYS THE COMMON LAW OF GRAVITY* (*! ?*), and whether the comet revolves in an orbit within that of the outer planets, or shoots off into the abysses of Space, and returns only after hundreds of years, its path is, at each instant, regulated *by the same force as that which causes an apple to fall to the ground.*" (*Ibid*, p. 17.)

Science is like Cæsar's wife, and must not be suspected—this is evident. But it can be respectfully criticised, nevertheless. At all events, it may be reminded that "the apple" is a dangerous fruit. For the second time in the history of mankind, it may become the cause of the *FALL*—this time, of "exact" Science. A comet whose tail defies the law of gravity right in the Sun's face can hardly be credited with obeying that law.

In a series of scientific works on Astronomy and the nebular theory, written between 1865 and 1866, the present writer, a poor tyro in Science, has counted in a few hours, no less *than thirty-nine contradictory hypotheses* offered as explanations for the self-generated, primitive rotatory motion of the heavenly bodies. The writer is no astronomer, no mathematician, no scientist; but was obliged to examine these errors in defence of Occultism, in general, and what is still more important, in order to support the occult teachings concerning astronomy and Cosmology. Occultists were threatened with terrible penalties for questioning scientific truths. But now they feel braver; Science is less secure in its " impregnable " position than they were led to expect, and many of its strongholds are built on very shifting sands.

Thus, even this poor and unscientific examination of it was useful, and it was certainly very instructive. We have learned a good many things, in fact, having studied with particular care especially those astronomical data that would be the most likely to clash with our heterodox and " superstitious " beliefs.

So, for instance, we have found there, concerning gravitation, the axial and orbital motions, that synchronous movement having been once overcome, in the early stage—it was enough to originate a rotatory motion till the end of Manvantara. We have also come to know in all the aforesaid combinations of possibilities with regard to incipient rotation—most complicated in every case,—some of the causes *to which it may have been due*, as well as some others to which it *ought* and *should* have been due, but, in some way or other, was not. Among other things, we were informed that *incipient* rotation may be provoked with equal ease in a mass *in igneous fusion*, and in one that is characterised by *glacial opacity* (" *Heaven and Earth* "). That gravitation is a law which *nothing can overcome*, but which, nevertheless, is overcome in and out of season by the most ordinary celestial or terrestrial bodies—the tails of impudent comets, for instance. That we owe the universe to the holy creative Trinity, called *Inert Matter, Senseless Force* and *Blind Chance.* Of the real essence and nature of any of these three, Science knows nothing, but this is a trifling detail. *Ergo*, we are told that, when a mass of cosmic or nebular matter—whose nature *is unknown* (entirely so), and which may be in a state of fusion (Laplace), or *dark and cold* (Thomson), for " this intervention of heat is itself a *pure hypothesis* " (Faye)—decides to exhibit its mechanical energy under the form of rotation, it acts in this wise. It (the mass) either bursts into spontaneous conflagration, or it remains inert, tenebrous, and frigid, both states being equally capable of sending it, without *any adequate cause*, spinning through space for millions of years. Its movements may be retrograde and they may be direct, about a hundred various reasons being offered for both motions, in about as many hypotheses. Anyhow, joining the maze of stars, whose origin belongs to the same miraculous and spontaneous order—for " the *nebular theory does not profess to discover the origin of things*, but only a *stadium* in material history" (*Winchell: World-Life*)—those millions of suns, planets, and satellites, composed of inert matter, will whirl on in most impressive and majestic symmetry around the firmament, moved and guided only, their inertia notwithstanding, " *by their own internal motion.*"

Shall we wonder after this if learned mystics, pious Roman Catholics, and even such learned astronomers as were Chaubard and Godefroy,* have preferred the Kabala and the ancient systems to the modern dreary and contradictory exposition of the Universe ? The *Zohar* makes a distinction, at any rate, between " the *hajaschar* (" the light Forces "), the *hachoser* (" Reflected Lights "), and the simple *phenomenal exteriority* of their spiritual types." (*See Kabala Denudata*, 11, 67.)

The question of " gravity " may now be dismissed, and other hypotheses examined. That physical Science knows nothing of " Forces " is clear. We may close the argument, however, by calling to our help one more man of Science—Professor Jaumes, Member of the Academy of Medicine at Montpellier. Says this learned man, speaking of Forces :—

" A cause is that which is essentially acting in the genealogy of phenomena, in every production as in every modification. I said that activity (or Force) was invisible. . . . To suppose it corporeal and *residing in the properties of matter* would be a gratuitous hypothesis. . . To reduce all the causes to God. . . . would amount to embarrassing one-self with a hypothesis hostile to many verities. But to speak of *a plurality of forces* proceeding from the Deity and possessing inherent powers of their own, is not unreasonable. . . . and I am disposed to admit phenomena produced by intermediate agents called Forces or Secondary Agents. The *distinction* of Forces is the principle of the division of Sciences ; so many real and separate forces, so many mother-Sciences. . . . No : Forces are not suppositions and abstrac-tions, but realities, and the only acting realities whose attributes can be determined with the help of direct observation and induction." (" *Sur la distinction des Forces,*" published in the *Mémoires de l'Académie des Sciences de Montpellier*, Vol. II., fasc. I., 1854.)

VI.

THE MASKS OF SCIENCE.

PHYSICS OR METAPHYSICS ?

IF there is anything on earth like progress, Science will some day have to give up, *nolens volens*, such monstrous ideas as her physical, self-guiding *laws*—void of soul and Spirit,—and then turn to the occult teachings.

---

* *L'Univers expliqué par la Révélation*, and *Cosmogonie de la Révélation*. But see De Mirville's Deuxième Mémoire. The author, a terrible enemy of Occultism, was yet one who wrote great truths.

It has done so already, however altered are the title-page and revised editions of the Scientific Catechism. It is now over half a century since, in comparing modern with ancient thought, it has been found that, however different our philosophy may appear from that of our ancestors, it is, nevertheless, composed only *of additions* and *subtractions* taken from the old philosophy and *transmitted drop by drop through the filter of antecedents.*

This fact was well known to Faraday, and other eminent men of Science. Atoms, Ether, evolution itself—all comes to modern Science from ancient notions, all is based on the conceptions of the archaic nations. "Conceptions" for the profane, under the shape of allegories; plain truths taught during the Initiations to the elect, which truths have been partially divulged through Greek writers and have descended to us. This does not mean that Occultism has ever had the same views on matter, atoms and ether as found in the exotericism of the classical Greek writers. Yet, if we believe Mr. Tyndall, even Faraday was an Aristotelean, and an Agnostic more than a materialist. In his " Faraday, as a Discoverer " (p. 123) the author shows the great physicist *using* " old reflections of Aristotle " which are " concisely found in some of his works." Faraday, Boscovitch, and all others, however, who see, in the atoms and molecules, " centres of force," and in the corresponding *element force*, an ENTITY BY ITSELF, are far nearer the truth, perchance, than those, who, denouncing them, denounce at the same time the " old corpuscular Pythagorean theory" (one, by the way, which has never passed to posterity as the great philosopher *really* taught it), on the ground of its " delusion that the conceptual elements of matter *can be grasped* as separate and real entities."

The chief and most fatal mistake and fallacy made by Science, in the view of the Occultists, lies in the idea of the possibility of such a thing as inorganic, or *dead* matter, in nature. Is anything *dead* or *inorganic* capable of transformation or change ? Occultism asks. And is there anything under the sun which remains immutable or changeless ?

This fallacy is nowhere better illustrated than in the scientific work of a German *savant*, Professor Philip Spiller (*Der Weltæther als Kosmische Kraft*). In this cosmological treatise, the author attempts to prove that " no material constituent of a body, no atom, *is in itself originally endowed with force*, but that every such atom *is absolutely dead,** and without any power to act at a distance " (p. 4).

---

* Something *dead* implies that it had been at some time *living*. When, at what period of cosmogony ? Occultism says that in all cases when matter *appears* inert, it is the most active. A wooden or a stone block is motionless and impenetrable to all intents and purposes. Nevertheless, and *de facto*, its particles are in ceaseless eternal vibration which is so rapid that to the physical eye the body seems absolutely devoid of motion ;

This statement, however, does not prevent Spiller from enunciating an occult doctrine and principle. He asserts *the independent substantiality of force*, and shows it as an "incorporeal stuff" (*unkoerperlicher stoff*) or substance. Now *substance* is not *matter* in metaphysics, and for argument's sake it may be granted that it is a wrong expression to use. But this is due to the poverty of European languages, and especially to that of scientific terms. Then this "stuff" is identified and connected by Spiller with the æther. Expressed in occult language it might be said with more correctness that this "force-substance" is the ever-active phenomenal *positive* æther—*prakriti ;* while the omnipresent all pervading ether is the *noumenon* of the former, the substratum of all, or *Akâsa.* Nevertheless, Stallo falls foul of Spiller, as he does of the materialists. He is accused of "utter disregard of the fundamental correlation of force and matter" (of neither of which Science knows anything certain). For this "hypostasized half-concept" is, in the view of all other physicists, not only *imponderable*, but destitute of cohesive, chemical, thermal, electric, and magnetic forces—of all of which forces—according to occultism—æther is the source and *cause.*

Therefore Spiller, with all his mistakes, exhibits more intuition than any other modern Scientist, with the exception of Dr. Richardson, perhaps, the theorist on the "nerve force," or Nervous Ether, also on "Sun Force and Earth Force."* For ÆTHER, in Esotericism, is the very quintessence of all possible energy, and it is certainly to this universal agent (composed of many *agents*) that all the manifestations of energy in the material, psychic and spiritual worlds are due.

What are Electricity and Light, in fact? How can Science know that one is a fluid and the other a "mode of motion"? Why is it not made clear why a difference should be made between them, since both are considerd force-correlations. Electricity is a fluid, we are told, immaterial and non-molecular (though Helmholtz thinks otherwise), and the proof of it is that we can bottle it up, accumulate and store it away. Then, *it must* be simply matter, and no peculiar "fluid." Nor is it only "a mode of motion," for motion could hardly be stored in a Leyden jar. As for light, it is a still more extraordinary "mode of motion ;" since, "marvellous as it may appear, light (also) can *actually be stored up for use,*" as demonstrated by Professor Grove nearly half a century ago.

"Take an engraving which has been kept for some days in the dark, expose it to full sunshine—that is, insulate it for 15 minutes ; lay it on

---

and the spacial distance between those particles in their vibratory motion is—considered from another plane of being and perception—as great as that which separates snow flakes or drops of rain. But to physical science this will be an absurdity.

* See "Popular Science Review," Vol. V., pp. 329-34.

sensitive paper in a dark place, and at the end of 24 hours it will have left an impression of itself on the sensitive paper, the whites coming out as blacks. . . . There seems to be no limit for the reproduction of engravings, etc., etc. . . . ."

What is it that remains fixed, nailed, so to say, on the paper? It is a *Force* certainly, that fixed the thing, but what is *that thing*, the residue of which remains on the paper?

Our learned men will get out of this through some scientific technicality; but what is it that is intercepted, so as to imprison a certain quantity of it on glass, paper, or wood? Is it " Motion " or is it " Force"? Or shall we be told that what remains behind is the effect only of the force or Motion? Then what is this Force? Force or energy is a quality; but every quality must belong to a something, or a somebody. In Physics, Force is defined as " that which changes or tends to change any physical relation between bodies, whether mechanical, thermal, chemical, electrical, magnetic, etc." But it is not that " Force " or that " Motion " which remains behind on the paper, when the Force or Motion has ceased to act; and yet something, which our physical senses cannot perceive, has been left there to become a cause in its turn and produce effects. What is it? It is not matter, as defined by Science— *i.e.*, matter in any of its known states. An Alchemist would say it was a spiritual secretion—and would be laughed at. But yet, when the physicist said that Electricity, stored up, was a fluid, or that light fixed on paper is still Sunlight—this is Science.* In the opinion of an experienced Occultist, one who has verified the whole series of *Nidanas*, of causes and effects that finally project their last effect on to this our plane of manifestations; one who has traced matter back to its noumenon, the explanation of the physicist is like calling anger, or its effects—the exclamation provoked by it—a secretion or a fluid, and man, the cause of it—its *material* conductor. But, as Grove prophetically remarked, that day is fast approaching when it will be confessed that the " forces " *we* know of are but the phenomenal manifestations of realities we know nothing about,—but which *were known to the ancients and by them worshipped.*

He made one still more suggestive remark, however, which ought to have become the motto of Science, but has not. Sir W. Grove said that "SCIENCE SHOULD HAVE NEITHER DESIRES NOR PREJUDICES. TRUTH SHOULD BE HER SOLE AIM."

Meanwhile, in our days, Scientists are more self-opinionated and bigoted than even the clergy. For they minister to, if they do not actually worship,

* The newest Authorities have rejected these explanations as " exploded theories," and have now deified " Motion " as their sole Idol. But, surely, they and their idol will one day share the fate of their predecessors.

"Force-Matter," which is their *Unknown God.* And how unknown it is may be inferred from the many confessions of the most eminent physicists and biologists, with Faraday at their head. Not only, he said, could he never presume to pronounce whether Force was a property or function of Matter, but he actually did not know what was meant by the word *matter.*

There was a time, he added, when he believed he knew something of matter. But the more he lived, and the more carefully he studied it, the more he became convinced *of his utter ignorance of the nature of matter.** (See Buckwell's " Electric Science.")

The Occultists are often misunderstood because, for lack of better terms, they apply to the essence of Force *under certain aspects* the descriptive epithet of *substance.* Now the names for the varieties of " substance" on different planes of perception and being are *legion.* Eastern Occultism has a special appellation for each kind; but Science—like England, in the recollection of a witty Frenchman, blessed with thirty-six religions and only one fish-sauce—has but one name for all, namely, " Substance." Moreover, neither the orthodox physicists nor their critics seem to be very certain of their premises, and are as apt to confuse the effects as they do the causes. It is incorrect, for instance, to say, as Stallo does, that " matter can no more be realized or conceived as mere spacial presence than as a concretion of forces," or that " force is nothing without mass, and mass is nothing without force "—for one is the noumenon and the other the phenomenon. Again ; Schelling, when saying that " It is a mere delusion of the phantasy that something, we know not what, remains after we have denuded an object of all the predicates belonging to it "†—could never have applied the remark to the realm of transcendental metaphysics. It is true that pure force is *nothing* in the world of physics ; it is ALL in the domain of Spirit. Says Stallo: " If we reduce the mass upon which a given force, however small, acts to its limit zero—or, mathematically expressed, until it becomes infinitely small—the consequence is that the velocity of the resulting motion is infinitely great, and that the ' thing ' . . . is at any given moment neither here nor there, but everywhere—that there is no

---

* This ominous confession was made, we believe, at a Scientific Congress at Swansea. Faraday held a similar opinion, however, as stated by Tyndall : " What do we know of the atom *apart from its* force ? You imagine a nucleus which may be called *a* and surround it by forces which may be called *m ;* to my mind the *a* or nucleus vanishes and the substance consists of the powers *m.* And, indeed, what notion can we form of the nucleus independent of its powers ? What thought remains on which to hang the imagination of an *a* independent of the acknowledged forces ? "

† Schelling, " Ideen," etc., p. 18.

real presence; it is impossible, therefore, to construct matter by
a synthesis of forces " (p. 161).

This may be true in the phenomenal world, inasmuch as the illusive
reflection of the *one reality* of the supersensual world may appear true to
the dwarfed conceptions of a materialist. It is absolutely incorrect when
the argument is applied to things, in what the Kabalists call the super-
mundane spheres. Inertia, so called, " is force " according to Newton
(*Princ. Def. iii.*), and for the student of Esoteric Sciences the greatest of
the occult forces. A body may be considered divorced from its
relations with other bodies — which, according to physical and
mechanical sciences, give rise to its attributes—only *conceptually*, only
on this plane of illusion. In fact, it can never be so detached:
death itself being unable to detach it from its relation with the
Universal forces, of which the one FORCE or LIFE is the synthesis: but
simply continues such inter-relation on another plane. But what, if
Stallo is right, can Dr. James Croll mean when, in speaking " On the
Transformation of Gravity " (*Philosophical Magazine*, Vol. II., p. 252), he
brings forward the views advocated by Faraday, Waterston, and others ?
For he says very plainly that gravity—

" . . . . . is a force pervading Space *external to bodies*, and that, on
the mutual approach of the bodies, the force is not increased, as is
generally supposed, but the bodies merely pass into a place *where the
force exists with greater intensity.* . . . ."

No one will deny that a force (whether gravity, electricity, or any
other force) which exists *outside* of the bodies and in open space—be it
ether or vacuum—must be *something*, and not a pure *nothing*, when
conceived apart from a mass ? Otherwise it could hardly exist in one
place with a *greater* and in another with reduced " intensity." G. A.
Hirn declares the same in his *Théorie Mécanique de l'Univers*. He tries
to demonstrate that the atom of the chemists is not an entity of pure
convention, or simply an explicative device, but that it exists really,
that its volume is unalterable, and that consequently it is *not* elastic (! !).
Force, therefore, *is not in the atom; it is in the space* which *separates the
atoms from each other.*"

The above-cited views, expressed by two men of Science of great
eminence in their respective countries, show that it is not in the least
unscientific to speak of the substantiality of the so-called *Forces*. Subject to some future specific name, this force is *substance* of some kind,
and can be nothing else; and perhaps one day Science will be the first
to re-adopt the derided name of phlogiston. Whatever may be the
future name given to it, to maintain that force does *not* reside in the
atoms, but only in " space between them," may be scientific enough;
nevertheless it is not true. To the mind of an Occultist it is like saying

that water does not reside in the drops of which the ocean is composed, but only in the space between those drops !

The objection made that there are two distinct schools of physicists, by one of which " the force is assumed to be an *independent substantial entity*, which is NOT a property of matter nor is it essentially related to matter," * is hardly likely to help the profane to any clearer understanding. It is, on the contrary, still more calculated to throw the question into greater confusion than ever. For Force is, then, neither this nor the other. By viewing it as " an independent substantial entity," the theory extends the right hand of fellowship to Occultism, while the strange contradictory idea that it is not related to matter otherwise than by its power to act upon it," † leads physical science to the most absurd contradictory hypotheses. Whether "force" or "motion," (Occultism, seeing no difference between the two, never attempts to separate them) it cannot act for the adherents of the atomo-mechanical theory one way, and for those of the rival school in another way. Nor can the atoms be, in one case, *absolutely uniform in size and weight*, and in another, vary in their weight (Avogadro's law). For, in the words of the same able critic,

. . . " While the absolute equality of the primordial units of mass is thus an essential part of the very foundations of the mechanical theory, the whole modern Science of chemistry is based *upon a principle directly subversive of it*—a principle of which it has recently been said that ' it holds the same place in chemistry that the law of gravitation does in astronomy.'‡ This principle is known as the law of Avogadro or Ampère."§

This shows that either modern chemistry or modern physics is entirely wrong in its respective fundamental principles. For if the assumption of atoms of different specific gravities on the basis of the atomic theory in physics is deemed absurd, and chemistry meets, nevertheless, on its opposite basis (in the question of the formation and transformation of chemical compounds) with " *unfailing* experimental verification,"

---

* "Concepts of Modern Physics," xxxi., Introductory to the 2nd edition.

† *Loc. cit.*

‡ J. P. Cooke, *The New Chemistry*, p. 13.

§ " It imports that equal volumes of all substances, when in the gaseous state, and under like conditions of pressure and temperature, contain the same number of molecules—whence it follows that the weights of the molecules are proportional to the specific gravities of the gases; that therefore, these being different, the weights of the molecules are different also; and inasmuch as the molecules of certain elementary substances are *monatomic* (consist of but one atom each) while the molecules of various other substances contain the same number of atoms, that the ultimate atoms of such substances are of different weights " (*Concepts of Modern Physics*, p. 34). As shown further on in the same volume, this cardinal principle of modern theoretical chemistry *is in utter and irreconcilable conflict with the first proposition of the atomo-mechanical theory*—namely, the absolute equality of the primordial units of mass.

then it becomes apparent that it is the atomo-mechanical theory which is untenable. The explanations of the latter, that "the differences of weight are only differences of density, and differences of density are differences of distance between the particles contained in a given space," are not really valid, because, before a physicist can argue in his defence that, "as in the atom there is no multiplicity of particles and no void space: hence differences of density or weight are impossible in the case of atoms," he must first know what an atom is, in reality, and that he cannot know. He must bring it under the observation *of at least one of* his physical senses—and that *he cannot do :* for the simple reason that no one has ever *seen, smelt, heard, touched* or *tasted* an "atom." The atom belongs wholly to the domain of metaphysics. It is *an entified abstraction*—at any rate for physical Science—and has nought to do with physics, strictly speaking, as it can never be brought to the test of retort or balance. The mechanical conception, therefore, becomes a jumble of the most conflicting theories and dilemmas, in the minds of the many Scientists who disagree on this, as on other subjects ; the evolution of which the Eastern Occultist, who follows this scientific strife, beholds in the greatest bewilderment.

To conclude on the question of gravity. How can Science presume to know anything certain of it ? How can it maintain its position and its hypotheses against those of the Occultists, who see in gravity only sympathy and antipathy, or attraction and repulsion, caused by physical polarity on our terrestrial plane, and by spiritual causes outside of its influence ? How can they disagree with the Occultists before they agree among themselves ? Indeed one hears of the conservation of energy, and in the same breath of the perfect hardness and inelasticity of the atoms; of the Kinetic theory of gases being identical with "potential energy," so called ; and, at the same time, of the elementary units of mass being *absolutely hard* and *inelastic !* An Occultist opens a scientific work and reads as follows :—

"Physical atomism derives all the qualitative properties of matter from the forms of atomic motion. The *atoms themselves remain as elements utterly devoid of property.*" (Wundt, "*Die Theorie der Materie,*" *p.* 381.)

And further :

"Chemistry in its ultimate form *must be atomic mechanics.*" (Nazesmann, "*Thermochemie,*" p. 150.)

And a moment after he is told that :

"Gases consist of atoms which *behave* like solid, *perfectly elastic* spheres." (Krœnig, Clausius, Maxwell, etc., *Philosophical Magazine,* Vol. XIX., p. 18.)

Finally, to crown all, Sir W. Thomson is found declaring that :

"We are forbidden by the modern theory of the conservation of energy to assume inelasticity, or anything short *of perfect elasticity* of the ultimate molecules whether of ultra mundane or mundane matter." (! ! !) (" Philosophical Magazine," p. 321, *loc. cit.*)

But what do the men of *true* Science say to all this ? By the " men of true Science" we mean those who care too much for truth and too little for their personal vanity to dogmatise on anything, as the majority do. There are several among them—perhaps more than dare publish openly their secret conclusions for fear of the cry " Stone him to death ! "— men, whose intuitions have made them span the abyss that lies between the terrestrial aspect of matter, and the—to us, on our plane of illusion— subjective, *i.e.*, TRANSCENDENTALLY OBJECTIVE SUBSTANCE, and led them to proclaim the existence of the latter. Matter, to the Occultist, it must be remembered, is that totality of *existences* in the Kosmos, which falls within any of the planes of possible perception. We are but too well aware that the orthodox theories of sound, heat and light, are against the occult doctrines. But, it is not enough for the men of Science, or their defenders, to say that *they do not deny dynamic power to light and heat;* and urge as a proof the fact that Mr. Crookes' radiometer has unsettled no views. If they would fathom the ultimate nature of these Forces, they have first to admit their *substantial* nature, however *supersensuous.* Neither do the Occultists deny the correctness of the vibratory theory.* Only they limit its functions to our Earth— declaring its inadequacy on other planes than ours, since " Masters " in the Occult Sciences perceive the CAUSES that produce ethereal vibrations. Were all these only the fictions of the alchemists, or dreams of the Mystics, such men as Paracelsus, Philalethes, Van Helmont, and so many others, would have to be regarded as worse than visionaries : they would become impostors and deliberate mystificators.

The Occultists are taken to task for calling the *Cause* of light, heat, sound, cohesion, magnetism, etc., etc., a *substance.*† Mr. Clerk Maxwell has stated that the pressure of strong sunlight on a square mile is about $3\frac{1}{4}$ lbs. It is, they are told, " the energy of the myriad ether waves ;" and when they call it a "substance" impinging on that area, their explanation is proclaimed *unscientific.*

There is no justification for such an accusation. In no way—as stated

---

* Referring to the *Aura,* one of the Masters says in the " Occult World," " How could you make yourself understood by, command in fact, those semi-intelligent *forces,* whose means of communication with us are not through spoken words but *through sounds and colours* in correlation between the *vibrations* of the two." It is this " correlation " that is unknown to modern Science, yet was many times explained by the Alchemists.

† The " substance " of the Occultist, however, is to the most refined *substance* of the physicist, what *radiant matter* is to the leather of the Chemist's boots.

more than once before now—do the Occultists dispute the explanations of Science, as affording a solution of the *immediate* objective agencies at work. Science only errs in believing that, because it has detected in vibratory waves the *proximate* cause of these phenomena, it has, therefore, revealed ALL that lies beyond the threshold of Sense. It merely traces the sequence of phenomena on a plane of effects, illusory projections from the region that Occultism has long since penetrated. And the latter maintains that those etheric tremors, are not, as asserted by Science, set up by the vibrations of the molecules of *known* bodies — the matter of our terrestrial objective consciousness,—but that we must seek for the ultimate causes of light, heat, etc., etc., in MATTER existing in *super-sensuous* states—states, however, as fully objective to the spiritual eye of man, as a horse or a tree is to the ordinary mortal. Light and heat are the ghost or shadow of matter in motion. Such states can be perceived by the SEER or the Adept during the hours of trance, under the *Sushumna rav*—the first of the Seven *Mystic* rays of the Sun. *

Thus, we put forward the Occult teaching which maintains the reality of a supersubstantial and supersensible essence of that *Akâsa* (not ether, which is only an aspect of the latter), the nature of which cannot be inferred from its remoter manifestations—*its merely phenomenal phalanx of effects*—on this terrene plane. Science, on the contrary, informs us that heat can never be regarded as matter in any conceivable state.† We are also told that the two great obstacles to the fluid (?) theory of heat undoubtedly are :—

---

* The names of the Seven Rays—which are, Sushumna, Harikesa, Viswakarman, Viswatryarchas, Sannaddha, Sarvavasu and Swaraj—are all mystical, and each has its distinct application in a distinct state of consciousness, for occult purposes. The *Sushumna*, which, as said in the *Nirukta* (II, 6), is only to light up the moon, is the ray nevertheless cherished by the initiated Yogis. The totality of the Seven Rays spread through the Solar system constitute, so to say, the physical *Upadhi* (basis) of the *Ether of Science*; in which Upadhi, light, heat, electricity, etc., etc.,—the forces of orthodox science—correlate to produce their terrestrial effects. As psychic and spiritual effects, they emanate from, and have their origin in, the supra-solar Upadhi, in the ether of the Occultist—or Akâsa.

† To cite a most impartial critic, one whose authority no one can call in question, as a reminder to Western Dogmatists, that the question cannot be in any way considered as settled : " There is no fundamental difference between light and heat . . . each is merely a metamorphosis of the other. . . . Heat is light in complete repose. Light is heat in rapid motion. Directly light is combined with a body, it becomes heat ; but when it is thrown off from that body it again becomes light." *(Leslie's Fluid Theory of Light and Heat.)* " *Whether this is true or false we cannot tell*, and many years, perhaps many generations, will have to elapse before we shall be able to tell." *(Buckle's History o Civilization, Vol. III., p. 384.)*

(1.) The production of heat by friction—excitation of molecular motions.

(2.) The conversion of heat into mechanical motion.

The answer given is: There are fluids of various kinds. Electricity is called a fluid, and so was heat quite recently, but it was on the supposition that heat was some imponderable substance. This was during the supreme and autocratic reign of matter. When the latter was dethroned, and MOTION was proclaimed the sole sovereign ruler of the Universe, heat became "a mode of motion." We need not despair : it may become something else to-morrow. Like the Universe itself, Science is ever *becoming*, and can never say, "I am that I am." On the other hand, Occult Science has its *changeless* traditions from pre-historic times. It may err in particulars ; it can never become guilty of a mistake in questions of Universal laws, simply because that Science, justly referred to by philosophy as the "*divine*," was born on higher planes, and was brought on Earth by beings who were wiser than man will be, even in the seventh Race of his Seventh Round. And *that* Science maintains that Forces are not what modern learning would have them ; *e.g.*, Magnetism is *not* a "mode of motion" ; and, in this particular case, at least, *exact* "modern Science" is sure to come to grief some day. Nothing, at the first blush, can appear more ridiculous, more outrageously absurd than to say, for instance : "the Hindu initiated Yogi knows really *ten times more than the greatest European physicist of the ultimate nature and constitution of light*—both solar and lunar." Yet why is the Sushumna ray believed to be that ray which furnishes the moon with its borrowed light? Why is it "the ray cherished *by the initiated Yogi ?*" Why is the moon held as the *deity of the mind*, by those Yogis ? We say, because light, or rather all its occult properties, every combination and correlation of it with other forces, mental, psychic, and spiritual, were perfectly known to the old adepts.

Therefore, although, in its knowledge of the ultimate constitution of matter, or in the so-called ultimate analysis as opposed to the proximate in chemistry, occult science may be less well-informed as to the behaviour of compound elements in various cases of physical correlations : still, it is immeasurably higher in its knowledge of the ultimate occult states of matter, and of the true nature of matter, than all the physicists and chemists of our modern day put together.

Now, if we state the truth openly and in full sincerity, namely, that the ancient Initiates had a far wider knowledge of physics—as a Science of Nature—than our Academies of Science, all taken together, possess, the statement will be characterized as an impertinence and an absurdity ; for physical sciences are considered to have been carried in our age to the apex of perfection. Hence, the twitting query—"Can

the Occultists meet successfully the two points, namely (*a*) the production of heat by friction—excitation of molecular motions ; and (*b*) the
conversion of heat into mechanical force, if they hold to the old
" exploded " theory of heat being a substance or a fluid ? "

To answer the question, it must first be observed that the Occult
Sciences do not regard either electricity or any of the forces supposed
to be generated by it, as matter, *in any of the states known to physical
Science ;* to put it more clearly, none of these " forces," so-called, are
either solids, gases, or fluids. If it did not look pedantic, an Occultist
would even object to electricity being called a fluid—*as it is an effect and
not a cause.* But its *noumenon*, he would say, *is a conscious cause.* The same
in the cases of " Force" and the " Atom." Let us see what an
eminent Academician, Butlerof, the chemist, had to say about these two
abstractions.

" What is Force ? " argues this great man of Science, " what is it from
a strictly scientific stand-point, and as warranted by the law of conservation of energy ? Conceptions of Force are resumed by our conceptions
of this, that, or another mode of motion." Force is thus simply the
passage of *one state of motion into another state of the same :* of electricity,
into heat and light, of heat into sound or some mechanical function,
and so on.* The first time electric fluid was produced by man on earth
it must have been by friction ; hence, as well-known, it is heat that produces it by disturbing its *laya* state,† and electricity exists no more on earth
per se than heat or light, or any other force. They are all correlations, as
science says. " When a given quantity of heat, assisted by a steam
engine, is transformed into mechanical work, we speak of steam power
(or force). When a falling body strikes an obstacle in its way, thereby
generating heat and sound—we call it the power of collision. When
electricity decomposes water or heats a platinum wire, we speak of the
force of the electric fluid. When the rays of the sun are intercepted by
the thermometer bulb and its quicksilver expands, we speak of the
calorific energy of the sun. In short, when one state of a determined
quantity of motion ceases, another state of motion equivalent to the
preceding takes its place, and the result of such a transformation or correlation is—force. In all cases where such a transformation, or the
passage of one state of motion into another, is entirely absent, there no
force is possible. Let us admit for a moment an absolutely homogeneous
state of the Universe, and our conception of force falls down to nought."

---

* On the plane of manifestation and illusionary matter it may be so ; not that it is
nothing more, for it is vastly more.

† Neutral, or zero.

" Therefore it becomes evident that the force, which materialism considers as the cause of the diversity that surrounds us, is in sober reality only an effect, a result of that diversity.   From such point of view force is not the cause of motion, but a result, while the cause of that force, or forces, is not the substance or matter, but motion itself.   Matter thus must be laid aside, and with it the basic principle of materialism, which has become unnecessary, as force brought down to a state of motion can give no idea of the substance.   If force is the result of motion, then it becomes incomprehensible *why that motion should become witness to matter* and not to Spirit or a Spiritual essence.   True, our reason cannot conceive of a motion minus something moving (and our reason is right) ; but the nature or *esse* of that something moving remains to Science entirely unknown ; and the Spiritualist, in such case, has as much right to attribute it to a " Spirit," as a Materialist to creative and all-potential matter.   A Materialist has no special privileges in this instance, nor can he claim any.   The law of the conservation of energy, as thus seen, is shown to be illegitimate in its pretensions and claims in this case.   The " great dogma "—*no force without matter and no matter without force*—falls to the ground, and loses entirely the solemn significance with which materialism has tried to invest it. The conception of force still gives no idea of matter and compels us in no way to see in it "the origin of all origins."   (" *Scientific Letters*," *Professor Butlerof.)*

We are assured that real science is not materialistic ; and our own conviction tells us that it cannot be so, when its learning is real.   There is a good reason for it, well defined by some physicists and chemists themselves.   Natural sciences *cannot* go hand in hand with materialism.   To be at the height of their calling, men of science have to reject the very possibility of materialistic doctrines having aught to do with the *atomic* theory ; and we find that Lange, Butlerof, Du Bois Reymond,—the latter probably unconsciously—and several others, have proved it.   And it is, furthermore, demonstrated by the fact, that Kanada in India, and Leucippus, Democritus, and after them Epicurus—the earliest atomists in Europe —while propagating their doctrine of definite proportions, believed in *Gods* or supersensuous entities, at the same time.   Their ideas upon matter thus differed from those now prevalent.   We must be allowed to make our statement clearer in a short synopsis of the ancient and modern views of philosophy upon atoms, and thus prove that the atomic theory kills Materialism.

From the standpoint of Materialism, which reduces the beginnings of all to *matter*, the Universe consists, in its fullness, of atoms and vacuity. Even leaving aside the axiom—now absolutely demonstrated by telescope and microscope—taught by the ancients, that nature abhors vacuum, what is an atom? "It is, we are answered by Science," writes Professor Butlerof, " the limited division of substance, the indivisible particle of matter. To admit the divisibility of the atom, amounts to an admission of an infinite divisibility of substance, which is equivalent to reducing substance to *nihil*, a nothingness. Owing to a feeling of self-preservation alone, materialism cannot admit infinite divisibility ; otherwise, it would have to bid farewell for ever to its basic principle and thus sign its own death-warrant." Büchner, for instance, like a true dogmatist in materialism, declares that " to accept infinite divisibility is absurd, and amounts to doubting the very existence of matter." The Atom is indivisible then, saith Materialism ? Very well.

" See now what a curious contradiction this fundamental principle of the materialists is leading them into," writes Butlerof. " The atom is *indivisible*, and at the same time we know it to be *elastic*. An attempt to deprive it of elasticity is unthinkable ; it would amount to an absurdity. *Absolutely non-elastic atoms could never exhibit a single one of those numerous phenomena that are attributed to their correlations.* Without any elasticity, the atoms could not manifest their energy, and the substance of the materialists would remain weeded of every force. Therefore, if the Universe is composed of atoms, then those atoms *must be elastic*. It is here that we meet with an insuperable obstacle. For, what are the conditions requisite for the manifestation of elasticity ? An elastic ball, when striking against an obstacle, is flattened and contracts, which it would be impossible for it to do, were not that ball to consist of particles, the relative position of which experiences at the time of the blow a temporary change. This may be said of elasticity in general ; no elasticity is possible without change with respect to the position of the compound particles of an elastic body. This means that the elastic body is changeful and consists of particles, or, in other words, that elasticity can pertain *only to those bodies that are divisible.* And the atom *is* elastic."

This is sufficient to show how absurd are the simultaneous admissions of the non-divisibility and elasticity of the atom. The atom *is* elastic, *ergo*, the atom is divisible, and must consist of particles, or of *sub*-atoms. And these *sub*-atoms ? They are either non-elastic, and in such case they represent no dynamic importance, or, they are *elastic* also ; and in that case, they, too, are subject to divisibility. And thus *ad infinitum*. But infinite divisibility of atoms resolves matter into simple centres of force, *i.e.*, precludes the possibility of conceiving matter as an *objective* substance.

This vicious circle is fatal to materialism. It finds itself caught in its own nets, and no issue is possible for it out of the dilemma. If it says that the atom is indivisible, then it will have mechanics asking it the awkward question : " How does the Universe move in this case, and how do its forces correlate ? A world built on absolutely *non*-elastic atoms, is like an engine without steam, it is doomed to eternal inertia."*

---

* " Scientific Letters," Butlerof.

Accept the explanations and teachings of Occultism, and, the blind inertia of physical Science being replaced by the *intelligent active* Powers behind the veil of matter, motion and inertia become subservient to those Powers. It is on the doctrine of the illusive nature of matter, and the infinite divisibility of the atom, that the whole science of Occultism is built. It opens limitless horizons to *substance* informed by the divine breath of its soul in every possible state of tenuity, states still undreamt of by the most spiritually disposed chemists and physicists.

The above views were enunciated by an Academician, the greatest chemist in Russia, and a recognised authority even in Europe—the late Professor Butlerof. True, he was defending the phenomena of the Spiritualists, the materializations, so called, in which he believed as Professors Zöllner, and Hare did, as Mr. A. Russell Wallace, Mr. W. Crookes, and many another Fellow of the Royal Society, do still, whether openly or secretly. But his argument with regard to the nature of the essence that acts behind the physical phenomena of light, heat, electricity, etc., is no less scientific and authoritative for all that, and apply admirably to the case in hand. Science has no right to deny to the Occultists their claim to a more profound knowledge of the so-called Forces; which, they say, are only the effects of causes generated by Powers, substantial, yet supersensuous, and *beyond* any kind of matter with which they (the Scientists) have hitherto become acquainted. The most science can do is to assume the attitude of agnosticism and to maintain it. Then it can say: "Your case is no more proven than is ours; but we confess to knowing nothing in reality either about Force or matter, or that which lies at the bottom of the so-called correlations of Forces. Therefore, time alone can prove who is right and who is wrong. Let us wait patiently, and meanwhile show courtesy instead of scoffing at each other."

But to do this requires a boundless love of truth and the surrender of that prestige—however false—of *infallibility*, which the men of Science have acquired among the ignorant and flippant, though cultured, masses of the profane. To blend the two sciences, the archaic and the modern, requires first of all the abandonment of the actual materialistic lines. It necessitates a kind of religious mysticism and even the study of old magic, which our Academicians will never take up. The necessity is easily explained. Just as in old alchemical works the real meaning of the substances and elements meant are concealed under the most ridiculous metaphors, so are the physical, psychic, and spiritual natures of the Elements (say of fire) concealed in the Vedas, and especially in the Purânas, under allegories comprehensible only to the Initiates. Had they no meaning, then indeed all those long legends and allegories about the sacredness of the three types of fire, and the *forty-nine original fires*—

personified by the Sons of Daksha's daughters and the Rishis, their husbands, "who with the first son of Brahmâ and his three descendants constitute the forty-nine fires"—would be idiotic verbiage and no more. But it is not so. Every *fire* has a distinct function and meaning in the worlds of the physical and the spiritual. It has, moreover, in its *essential* nature a corresponding relation to one of the human psychic faculties, besides its well determined chemical and physical potencies when coming in contact with the *terrestrially* differentiated matter. Science has no speculations to offer upon fire *per se ;* Occultism and ancient religious science have. This is shown even in the meagre and purposely veiled phraseology of the Purânas, where (as in the *Vâyu Purâna*) many of the qualities of the *personified* fires are explained. Thus, *Pavaka* is electric, or *Vaidyuta,* fire ; Pavamâna, *the fire produced by friction,* (or *Nirmathya*) : and *Suchi* is solar (or *Saura*) fire*—all these three being the sons of Abhimânin, the Agni (fire), eldest son of Brahmâ and of Swâha. Pavaka, moreover, is made parent to Kavyavâhana, *the fire of the Pitris* : Suchi to Havyavâhana—the fire of the gods ; and Pavamâna, to Saharaksha, the fire of the Asuras. Now all this shows that the writers of the Purânas were perfectly conversant with the " Forces " of Science and their correlations ; moreover, with the various qualities of the latter in their bearing upon those psychic and physical phenomena which receive no credit and are unknown to physical science now. Very naturally, when an Orientalist,—especially one with materialistic tendencies—reads that these are only appellations of fire employed *in the invocations* and rituals, he calls this " Tantrika superstition and mystification " ; and he becomes more careful to avoid errors in spelling, than to give attention to the secret meaning attached to the personifications, or to seek their explanation in the physical correlations of forces, so far as known. So little credit, indeed, is given to the ancient Aryans for knowledge, that even such glaring passages as in *Book I. chap.* ii, *Vishnu Purâna,* are left without any notice. Nevertheless, what can this sentence mean ?—" Then Ether, air, light, water, and earth, severally united with the properties of sound and other qualities, existed as distinguishable according to their properties, ... but possessing many and various energies and being unconnected, they *could not, without combination,* create living beings, not having blended with each other. . . . Having combined . . . they assumed through mutual association, the character of one mass of entire unity ; and directed by Spirit . . . " etc. This means, of course, that the writers were perfectly acquainted with correlation and were well posted about the origin of Kosmos from the " undiscrete Principle "—*Avyaktânugraheña,* as applied

---

* Called the " drinker of waters," solar heat causing water to evaporate.

to Parabrahmam and Mulaprakriti conjointly, and not to " Avyakta, *either* First Cause, or matter," as Wilson gives it.   The old Initiates knew of no " miraculous creation," but taught the evolution of atoms (on our physical plane), and their first differentiation from *laya* into the *protyle*, as Mr. Crookes has suggestively named matter, or primordial substance *beyond* the zero-line :—there where we place *Mulaprakriti*, the " root-Principle " of the world stuff and of all in the world.

This can be easily demonstrated.   Take, for instance, the newly-published catechism of the *Visishtadwaita Vedantins*, an orthodox and exoteric system, yet fully enunciated and taught in the XIth century (its founder, Ramanujâcharya, being born in A.D. 1017), at a time when European " Science " still believed in the squareness and flatness of the Earth, of Cosmas-Indicopleustes of the VIth century.   It teaches that before evolution began, Prakriti (Nature) was in a condition of *laya* or absolute homogeneity, as " matter exists in two conditions, the *sukshma*, or latent and undifferentiated, and the *sthula* or differentiated condition." Then it became *anu*, atomic.   It teaches of *Sudda-satwa*—" a substance not subject to the qualities of matter, from which it is quite different," and adds that out of that substance the bodies of the inhabitants of Vaikuntaloka (the heaven of Vishnu), the gods, are formed.   That every particle or atom of Prakriti contains *Jiva* (divine life), and is the *sarira* (body) of that Jiva which it contains, while every Jiva is in its turn the *sarira* of the supreme spirit, as " Parabrahm pervades every Jiva, as well as every particle of matter."   Dualistic and anthropomorphic as may be the philosophy of the Visishtadwaita, when compared with that of the *Adwaita*—the non-dualists,—it is yet supremely higher in logic and philosophy than the cosmogony accepted by either Christianity, or its great opponent, modern Science.   The followers of one of the greatest minds that ever appeared on Earth, the *Adwaita* Vedantins are called *Atheists*, because they regard all save Parabrahm, the *secondless*, or Absolute Reality—as an illusion.   Yet the wisest Initiates came from their ranks, as also the greatest Yogis.   The *Upanishads* show that they most assuredly knew not only what is the *causal* substance in the *effects* of *friction*, and that their forefathers were acquainted with the *conversion of heat into mechanical force*, but that they were acquainted with the *noumena* of every spiritual as well as of every cosmic phenomenon.

Truly the young Brahmin who graduates in the universities and colleges of India with the highest honours ; who starts in life as an M.A. and an LL.B., with a tail initialed from Alpha to Omega after his name, and a contempt for his national gods proportioned to the honours received in his education in physical sciences ; truly he has but to read in the light of the latter, and with an eye to the correlation of physical Forces, certain passages in his Purânas, if he would learn how much more his ancestors knew than he will ever know—unless he becomes an occultist. Let him turn to the allegory of Purûravas and the celestial *Gandharva*,* who furnished the former with a vessel full of heavenly fire. The primeval mode of obtaining fire by friction has its scientific explanation in the Vedas, and is pregnant with meaning for him who reads between the lines. The *Tretagni* (sacred triad of fires) obtained by the attrition of sticks made of the wood of the *Aswattha* tree (the Bo-tree, of Wisdom and Knowledge)—sticks " as many finger-breaths long as there are syllables in the gayâtri " must have a secret meaning, or else the writers of the Vedas and Purânas were no sacred writers but mystificators. That it has such a meaning, the Hindu Occultists are a proof, and they alone are able to enlighten Science, as to why and how, " the fire, that was primevally *one*, was made three-fold (*treta*) in our present Manvantara, by the Son of Ila (Vâch), the primeval woman after the Deluge, the wife and daughter of Vaivasvata Manu. The allegory is suggestive, in whatever Purâna it may be read and studied.

VII.

AN ATTACK ON THE SCIENTIFIC THEORY OF FORCE BY A MAN OF SCIENCE.

THE wise words of several (English) men of Science have now to be quoted in our favour. Ostracised for " principle's sake " by the few, they are tacitly approved of by the many. That one of them preaches almost Occult doctrines, in some things identical with, and often amounting to a public recognition of our "*Fohat* and his seven Sons"—

---

* The Gandharva of the Veda is the deity who knows and reveals the secrets of heaven and divine truths to mortals. *Cosmically*—the Gandharvas are the aggregate powers of the solar-fire, and constitute its Forces ; *psychically*—the intelligence residing in the *Sushumna*, Solar ray, the highest of the *seven* rays ; *mystically*—the occult force in the Soma (the moon, or lunar plant) and the drink made of it ; *physically*—the phenomenal, and *spiritually*—the noumenal causes of *Sound* and the " Voice of Nature." Hence, they are called the 6,333 " heavenly Singers " and musicians of Indra's loka who personify (even in number) the various and manifold sounds in Nature, both above and below. In the latter allegories they are said to have mystic power over women, and *to be fond of them*. The esoteric meaning is plain. They are one of the forms, if not the prototypes, of Enoch's angels, the Sons of God, who saw that the daughters of men were fair (Gen. vi.) who married them, and taught the daughters of the Earth *the secrets of Heaven*.

the Occult *Gandharva* of the Vedas—will be recognised by every Occultist, and even by some profane readers.

If the latter open Volume V. of the *Popular Science Review* (pp. 329-334), they will find in it an article on "*Sun Force and Earth Force,*" by Dr. B. W. Richardson, F.R.S., which reads as follows :—

"At this moment, when the theory of mere motion as the origin of all varieties of force is again becoming the prevailing thought, it were almost heresy to re-open a debate, which for a period appears, by general consent, to be virtually closed; but I accept the risk, and shall state, therefore, what were the precise views of the immortal heretic, whose name I have whispered to the readers, (Samuel Metcalfe), respecting Sun Force. Starting with the argument on which nearly all physicists are agreed, that there exist in nature two agencies—matter which is ponderable, visible, and tangible, and a something which is imponderable, invisible, and appreciable only by its influence on matter—Metcalfe maintains that the imponderable and active agency which he calls '*caloric*' is *not a mere form of motion*, not a vibration amongst the particles of ponderable matter, but *itself a material substance flowing from the Sun* through Space,* filling the voids between the particles of solid bodies, and conveying by sensation the property called heat. The nature of caloric, or Sun-Force, is contended for by him on the following grounds :—

"(i.) That it may be added to, and abstracted from other bodies and measured with mathematical precision.

"(ii.) That it augments the volume of bodies, which are again reduced in size by its abstraction.

"(iii.) That it modifies the forms, properties, and conditions of all other bodies.

"(iv.) That *it passes by radiation through the most perfect vacuum*† that can be formed, in which it produces the same effects on the thermometer as in the atmosphere.

"(v.) That it exerts mechanical and chemical forces which nothing can restrain, as in volcanoes, the explosion of gunpowder, and other fulminating compounds.

"(vi.) That it operates in a sensible manner on the nervous system, producing intense pain ; and when in excess, disorganization of the tissues.

"As against the vibratory theory, Metcalfe further argues that if caloric were a *mere property or quality*, it could not augment the volume of other bodies; for this purpose it must itself have volume, it must occupy space, and it must, therefore, be a material agent. If caloric were *only the effect of vibratory motion* amongst the particles of ponderable matter, *it could not radiate from hot bodies* without the simultaneous transition of the vibrating particles ; but the fact stands out that heat can radiate from material ponderable substance without

---

* Not only "through space," but filling every point of our solar system, for it is the physical residue, so to say, of Ether, its *lining* on our plane ; Ether having to serve other cosmic and terrestrial purposes besides being the "*agent*" for transmitting light. It is the astral fluid or "Light" of the Kabalists, and the "Seven rays" of Sun-Vishnu.

† What need, then, of etheric waves for the transmission of light, heat, etc., if *this* substance cán pass through vacuum ?

loss of weight of such substance. . . . With this view as to the material nature of caloric or sun-force; with the impression firmly fixed on his mind that 'everything in Nature is composed of two descriptions of matter, the one essentially active and ethereal, the other passive and motionless,'* Metcalfe based the hypothesis that the Sun-force, or caloric, is a Self-active principle. For its own particles, he holds, it has repulsion; for the particles of all ponderable matter it has affinity; it attracts the particles of ponderable matter with forces which vary inversely as the squares of the distance. It thus acts *through* ponderable matter. If universal space were filled with caloric, sun-force, alone (without ponderable matter), caloric would also be inactive and would constitute a boundless Ocean of powerless or quiescent ether, because it would then have nothing on which to act, while ponderable matter, however inactive of itself, has 'certain properties by which it modifies and controls the actions of caloric, both of which are governed by immutable laws that have their origin in the mutual relations and specific properties of each.'

"And he lays down a law which he believes is absolute, and which is thus expressed :—

"' By the attraction of caloric for ponderable matter, it unites and holds together all things; by its self-repulsive energy it separates and expands all things.'"

This, of course, is almost the occult explanation of cohesion. Dr. Richardson continues :—

"As I have already said, *the tendency of modern teaching is to rest upon the hypothesis . . . that heat is motion*, or, as it would, perhaps, be better stated, a specific force or form of motion.†

"But this hypothesis, popular as it is, is not one that ought to be accepted to the exclusion of the simpler views of the material nature of sun-force, and of its influence in modifying the conditions of matter. *We do not yet know sufficient to be dogmatic.*"‡

. . . "The hypothesis of Metcalfe respecting sun-force and earth-force is not only very simple, but most fascinating. . . . Here are two elements in the Universe, the one is ponderable matter . . . The second element is the all-pervading Ether, solar-fire. It is *without weight, substance, form, or colour; it is matter infinitely divisible*, and its particles repel each other; its rarity

---

* And how can it be otherwise? Gross *ponderable* matter is the body, the Shell of matter or Substance, the female passive principle; and this *Fohatic* force is the second principle, *prâna*—the male and the active? On our globe this Substance is the second principle of the septenary *Element*—Earth; in the atmosphere, it is that of *air*, which is the cosmic gross body; in the Sun it becomes the *Solar body* and that of the Seven rays; in sidereal space it corresponds with another principle, and so on. The whole is a homogeneous Unity alone, the parts are all differentiations.

† Or the reverberation, and for *sound*, repercussion *on our plane* of that which is a perpetual motion of that *Substance* on higher planes. Our world and senses *are* victims of *Maya*, ceaselessly.

‡ An honest admission, that

is such that we have no word, except ether,* by which to express it. It pervades and fills space, but alone it too is quiescent — dead.† We bring together the two elements, the inert matter, the self-repulsive Ether (?) and thereupon dead (?) ponderable matter is vivified"; [*Ponderable matter may be inert but never dead — this is Occult Law.* —H.P.B.] . . . " through the particles of the ponderable substance the ether [*Ether's second principle.*—H.P.B.] penetrates, and, so penetrating, it combines with the ponderable particles and holds them in mass, holds them together in bond of union; they are dissolved in the Ether."

" This distribution of solid ponderable matter through ether extends, according to the theory before us, to everything that exists at this moment. The ether is all-pervading. The human body itself is charged with the ether [*Say astral light.*—H.P.B.]; its minute particles are held together by it; the plant is in the same condition; the most solid earth, rock, adamant, crystal, metal, all are the same. But there are differences in the capacities of different kinds of ponderable matter to receive sun-force, and upon this depends the various changing conditions of matter; the solid, the liquid, the gaseous condition. Solid bodies have attracted caloric in excess over fluid bodies, and hence their firm *cohesion;* when a portion of molten zinc is poured upon a plate of solid zinc, the molten zinc becomes as solid because there is a rush of caloric from the liquid to the solid, and in the equalization the particles, previously loose or liquid, are more closely brought together. . . . Metcalfe himself, dwelling on the above-named phenomena, and accounting for them by the unity of principle of action, which has already been explained, sums up his argument in very clear terms, in a comment on the densities of various bodies. ' Hardness and softness ' (he says), ' solidity and liquidity, are not essential conditions of bodies, but depend on the relative proportions of ethereal and ponderable matter of which they are composed. The most elastic gas may be reduced to the liquid form by the abstraction of caloric, and again converted into a firm solid, the particles of which would cling together with a force proportional to their augmented affinity for caloric. On the other hand, by adding a sufficient quantity of the same principle to the densest metals, their attraction for it is diminished when they are expanded into the gaseous state, and their cohesion is destroyed.' "

Having thus quoted at length the *heterodox* views of the great " heretic"—views that need only a little alteration of terms here and there, the same eminent scientist—an original and liberal thinker, undeniably—proceeds to sum up those views, and continues :—

_____

* Yet it is not *Ether*, but only one of the principles of Ether, the latter being itself *one of the principles of Akâsa.*

† And so does *prâna* (Jiva) pervade the whole living body of man; but alone, without having an atom to act upon, it would be *quiescent*—dead ; *i.e.*, would be in *laya*, or as Mr. Crookes has it, " locked in *protyle.*" It is the action of *Fohat* upon a compound or even a simple body that produces life. When a body dies it passes into the same polarity as its male energy and repels therefore the active agent, which, losing hold of the *whole*, fastens on the parts or molecules, this action being called chemical. Vishnu, the Preserver, transforms himself into Rudra-Siva, the Destroyer—a correlation seemingly unknown to Science.

" I shall not dwell at great length on this unity of sun-force and earth, which this theory implies.   But I may add that out of it, or out of the hypothesis of mere motion as force, and of virtue without substance, we may gather, as the nearest possible approach to the truth on this, the most complex and profound of all subjects, the following inferences :—

" (a) Space, inter-stellary, inter-planetary, inter-material, inter-organic, is not a vacuum, but is filled with a subtle fluid or gas, which for want of a better term* we may still call, as the ancients did, A ith-ur—Solar fire, ÆTHER. This fluid, unchangeable in composition, indestructible, invisible,† pervades everything and all [ponderable.—H. P. B.] matter,‡ the pebble in the running brook, the tree overhanging, the man looking on, is charged with the ether in various degree ; the pebble less than the tree, the tree less than man.   All in the planet is in like manner so charged ! A world is built up in ethereal fluid, and moving through a sea of it.

" (b) The Ether, whatever its nature is, is from the sun and from the suns§ the suns are the generators of it, the store-houses of it, the diffusers of it.‖

" (c.) Without the ether there could be no motion ; without it particles of ponderable matter could not glide over each other ; without it there could be no impulse to excite those particles into action.

" (d.) Ether determines the constitution of bodies.   Were there no ether there could be no change of constitution in substance ; water, for instance, could only exist as a substance, compact and insoluble beyond any conception we could form of it.   It could never even be ice, never flint, never vapour, except for ether.

" (e) Ether connects sun with planet, planet with planet, man with planet, man with man.   Without ether there could be no communication in the Universe ; no light, no heat, no phemomenon of motion."

Thus we find that Ether and *elastic* atoms are, in the alleged *mechanical* conception of the Universe, the Spirit and Soul of Kosmos, and that the theory—put it any way and under what-ever disguise—always leaves a more widely opened issue for men of

---

* Verily, unless the occult terms of the Kabalists are adopted !

† " Unchangeable " only during Manvantaric periods, after which it merges once more into Mulaprakriti ; "invisible" for ever, in its own essence, but seen in its reflected coruscations, called the Astral light by the modern Kabalists. Yet, conscious and grand Beings clothed in that same Essence move in it.

‡ One has to add (ponderable), to distinguish it from that *Ether* which is matter still, though a substratum.

§ The Occult Sciences reverse the statement, and say that it is the sun, and all the suns that are from *it*, which emanate at the Manvantaric dawn from the *Central Sun*.

‖ Here, we decidedly beg to differ with the learned gentleman. Let us remember that this Æther, whether *Akâsa* is meant by the term, or its lower principle, Ether—is septenary.   *Akâsa* is Aditi in the allegory, and the mother of Mârttânda (the sun), the *Deva-matri*—"Mother of the gods."   In the solar system, the sun is her Buddhi and *Vahan*, the Vehicle, hence the 6th principle ; in Kosmos all the suns are the Kama rupa of Akâsa and so is ours.   It is only when regarded as an individual Entity in his own Kingdom that Surya (the sun) is the 7th principle of the great body of *matter*.

Science to speculate beyond the line drawn by modern materialism—or call it *agnosticism* rather, to be more correct*—than the majority avails itself of. Atoms, Ether, or both, modern speculation cannot get out of the circle of ancient thought; and the latter was soaked through with archaic occultism. Undulatory or corpuscular theory—it is all one. It is speculation from the aspects of phenomena, not from the knowledge of the essential nature of the *cause* and *causes*. When modern Science has explained to its audience the late achievements of Bunsen and Kirchoff, and shown the seven colours, the "primary" of a ray which is decomposed in a fixed order on a screen; and described the respective lengths of luminous waves, what has it proved? It has justified its reputation for *exactness* in mathematical achievement by measuring even the length of a luminous wave—" varying from about seven hundred and sixty millionths of a millimètre at the red end of the spectrum to about three hundred and ninety-three millionths of a millimètre at the violet end." But when the exactness of the calculation with regard to the *effect* on the light-wave is thus vindicated, Science is forced to admit that the *force* (which is the *supposed cause*) is *believed* to produce " inconceivably minute undulations" in *some* medium—"*generally regarded as identical with the ethereal medium*"†—and that medium itself is still only—a *hypothetical* agent !"

Auguste Comte's pessimism with respect to the impossibility of knowing some day the chemical composition of the sun, has not been belied thirty years later by Kirchoff, as claimed. The spectroscope has helped us to see that the elements, with which the modern chemist is familiar, *must in all probability* be present in the sun's outward robes—*not in the sun itself;* and, taking these "robes," the solar cosmic veil, for the sun itself, the physicists have declared its luminosity to be due to *combustion* and *flame,* and have mistaken the vital principle of that luminary for a purely *material* thing, and called it " chromosphere."‡ We have hypotheses and theories only so far, not law—by any means.

---

* Brutal but frank materialism is more honest than Janus-faced agnosticism in our days. *Monism* is the Pecksniff of modern philosophy, turning a pharisaical face to psychology and idealism, and its natural face of a Roman Augur, swelling his cheek with his tongue—to Materialism. The Monists are worse than the Materialists; because, while looking at the Universe and psycho-spiritual man from the same negative stand-point, the latter put their case far less plausibly than sceptics of Mr. Tyndall's or even Mr. Huxley's stamp   Herbert Spencer, Bain and Lewes are more dangerous to universal truths than Büchner.

† "*Geology,*" by Professor A. Winchell.

‡ See *Five Years of Theosophy*—Articles : " Do the Adepts deny the nebular theory ?" and " Is the Sun merely a cooling mass ? "—for the true Occult teaching.

VIII.

LIFE, FORCE, OR GRAVITY.

THE *imponderable* fluids have had their day ; "mechanical Forces " are less talked about ; Science has put on a new face for this last quarter of a century ; but gravitation has remained, owing its life to new combinations after the old ones had nearly killed it. It may answer scientific hypotheses very well, but the question is whether it answers as well to truth, and represents a fact in nature. Attraction by itself is *not* sufficient to explain merely planetary motion ; how can it presume to explain the rotatory motion in the infinitudes of Space ? Attraction alone will never fill all the gaps, unless a special impulse is admitted for every sidereal body, and the rotation of every planet with its satellites is shown to be due to some *one cause* combined with attraction. And even then, says an astronomer ("*Philosophie Naturelle,*" *art.* 142), Science would have to name that cause.

Occultism has named it for ages, and so have all the ancient philosophers ; but then all such beliefs are now proclaimed exploded superstitions. The "extra cosmic" God has killed every possibility of belief in *intra* cosmic intelligent Forces, yet who, or what is the original *pusher* in that motion ? " When we have learned the cause, *unique et speciale*, that pushes, we will be ready to combine it with the one which attracts," says Francœur ("*Astronomie,*" *p.* 342). And again— " Attraction between the celestial bodies is only repulsion : it is *the Sun that drives them incessantly onward ;* for otherwise, their motion would stop."

If ever this theory of the Sun-Force being the primal cause of all life on earth and motion in heaven is accepted, and if that other far bolder one of Herschell—about certain organisms in the Sun—is accepted even as a provisional hypothesis, then will our teachings be vindicated, and esoteric allegory shown to have anticipated Modern Science by millions of years, probably, for these are the Archaic teachings. Mârttânda (the Sun) watches and threatens—without abandoning the central position to which his Mother, Aditi, relegated him—his seven brothers, the planets; " he pursues them, turning slowly around himself . . . and follows them from afar, moving in the same direction that they do, on the path that encircles their houses "—or the orbit. (*See Comment to Stanza IV., Book I.*) It is the Sun-fluids or Emanations that impart all motion and awaken all into life, in the Solar System. It is attraction and repulsion, but not as understood by modern physics and according to the law of gravity; but in harmony with *the laws of Manvantaric motion* designed from the early *Sandhya,* the Dawn of the rebuilding and higher *reformation* of the System. These laws are immutable; but the motion of all the bodies, which motion is diverse and alters with every *minor* Kalpa—is regulated by the *Movers,* the Intelligences within the Cosmic Soul.   Are we so very wrong in believing all this ? Well, here is a modern and a great man of Science who, speaking of vital electricity, uses language far more akin to Occultism than to modern materialistic thought.   We refer the sceptical reader to an article on " The Source of Heat in the Sun," by Robert Hunt, F.R.S., (in " *Popular Science Review*," Vol. IV., p. 148), who, speaking of the luminous envelope of the Sun and its " peculiar curdy appearance," says :—

" Arago proposed that this envelope should be called the Photosphere, a name now generally adopted. By the elder Herschell, the surface of this photo-phere was compared to mother-of-pearl. . . . . It resembles the Ocean on tranquil summer-day, when its surface is slightly crisped by a gentle breeze. . . . Mr. Nasmyth has discovered a more remarkable condition than any that had previously been suspected. . . . objects which are peculiarly lens-shaped . . . . like ' willow leaves' . . . . different in size . . . . . not arranged in any order . . . . . crossing each other in all direc-tions . . . . . with an irregular motion among themselves . . . . They are seen approaching to and receding from each other, and sometimes assuming new angular positions, so that the appearance . . . . . has been compared to a dense shoal of fish, which, indeed, they resemble in shape. . . . The size of these objects gives a grand idea of the gigantic scale upon which physical (?) operations are carried out in the Sun. They cannot be less than 1,000 miles in length, and from two to three hundred miles in breadth. *The most probable conjecture which has been offered* respecting those leaf or lens-like objects, is *that the photosphere* * is an immense ocean of gaseous matter (what kind of " matter ? ") . . . in a state of intense (apparent) incandescence, and that they are perspective projections of the sheets of flame. . . ."

Solar " flames " seen through telescopes are *reflections,* says Occultism. But see what Occultists have to say to this in Book I.

" Whatever they may be (those sheets of flame), *it is evident they are the immediate sources of solar heat and light.* Here we have a surrounding envelope of photogenic matter,† which pendulates with mighty energies, and by communicating its motion to the ethereal medium in stellar space, produces heat and light in far distant worlds. We have said that those forms have been compared to certain organisms, and Herschell says, ' Though it would be too daring to speak of such organizations as *partaking of life* [why not ?],‡ yet we do not know that vital action is competent to develop heat, light, and electricity.' . . . *Can it be that there is truth in this fine thought ? May the pulsing of vital matter*

---

* And the *central mass,* too, as will be found, or rather the centre of the reflection.

† That " matter " is just like the reflection in a mirror of the flame from a " photo-genic " *lamp-wick.*

‡ See " *Five Years of Theosophy,*" p. 258—answer to this speculation of Herschell's.

*in the central Sun of our System be the source of all that life which crowds the
earth, and without doubt overspreads the other planets, to which the Sun is the mighty
Minister ?"* . . .

Occultism answers these queries in the affirmative ; and Science will
find this to be the case, one day.

Again, on p. 156, Mr. Hunt writes :—

" But regarding Life—Vital Force—as a power far more exalted than either
light, heat, or electricity, and indeed *capable of exerting a controlling power over
them all* " (this is absolutely occult). . . . . " we are certainly disposed to
view with satisfaction that speculation which supposes the photosphere to be
the primary seat of vital power, and to regard *with a poetic pleasure that hypothesis
which refers the Solar energies to Life."*

Thus, we have an important scientific corroboration for one of our
fundamental dogmas—namely, that (*a*) the Sun is the store-house of
Vital Force, which *is* the *Noumenon* of Electricity ; and (*b*) that it is
from its mysterious, never-to-be-fathomed depths, that issue those life
currents which thrill through Space, as through the organisms of every
living thing on Earth. For see what another eminent physician says,
who calls this (our life-fluid) "nervous Ether." Change a few sentences in the article, extracts from which now follow, and you have
another *quasi-Occult treatise* on Life Force. This once, it is again Dr.
B. W. Richardson, F.R.S., who gives his views in the "*Popular Science
Review," Vol. X., p.* 380—3, on " Nervous Ether," as he has on " Sun-
Force " and " Earth-Force " :—

" The idea attempted to be conveyed by the theory is, that between the
molecules of the matter, solid or fluid, of which the nervous organisms, and,
indeed, of which all the organic parts of a body are composed, there exists a
refined subtle medium, vaporous or gaseous, which holds the molecules in a
condition for motion upon each other, and for arrangement and rearrangement
of form ; a medium by and through which all motion is conveyed ; by and
through which the one organ or part of the body is held in communion with the
other parts, by which and through which the outer living world communicates
with the living man : a medium, which, being present, enables the phenomena
of life to be demonstrated, and which, being universally absent, leaves the body
actually dead. . . . . . "

And the whole Solar System falls into *Pralaya*—the author might
have added. But let us read further :

. . . " I use the word *Ether* in its general sense as meaning a very light,
vaporous or gaseous matter ; I use it, in short, as the astronomer uses it when he
speaks of the Ether of Space, by which he means a subtle but material medium.
. . . . When I speak of a *nervous* Ether, I do not convey that the ether
is existent in nervous structure only : I believe truly that it is a special part of
the nervous organization ; but, as nerves pass into all structures that have
capacities for movement and sensibilities, so the nervous ether passes into all
such parts ; and as the nervous ether is, according to my view, a direct product
from blood, so we may look upon it as a part of the atmosphere of the blood.

. . . The evidence in favour of the existence of an elastic medium pervading the nervous matter and capable of being influenced by simple pressure is all-convincing. . . . In nervous structure there is, unquestionably, a true nervous fluid, *as our predecessors* taught.* The precise chemical (?) † composi-ion of this fluid is not yet well known; the physical characters of it have been little studied. Whether it moves in currents, we do not know; whether it circulates, we do not know; whether it is formed in the centres and passes from them to the nerves, or whether it is formed everywhere where blood enters nerve, we do not know. The exact uses of the fluid we do not consequently know. It occurs to my mind, however, that the veritable fluid of nervous matter is not of itself sufficient to act as the subtle medium that connects the outer with the inner universe of man and animal. I think—and this is the modification I suggest to the older theory—there must be another form of matter present during life; a matter which exists in the condition of vapour or gas, which pervades the whole nervous organism, *surrounds as an enveloping atmosphere*‡ each molecule of nervous structure, and is the medium of all motion, communicated to and from the nervous centres. . . . When it is once fairly presented to the mind that during life *there is in the animal body a finely diffused form of matter*, a vapour filling every part—and even stored in some parts; a matter constantly renewed by the vital chemistry; a matter as easily disposed of as the breath, after it has served its purpose—a new flood of light breaks on the Intelligence." . . . .

A new flood of light is certainly thrown on the wisdom of ancient and mediæval Occultism and its votaries. For Paracelus wrote the same thing more than three hundred years ago, namely, in the sixteenth century, as follows:—

" The whole of the Microcosm is potentially contained in the *Liquor Vitæ*, a nerve fluid . . . in which is contained the nature, quality, character, and essence of beings." . . . (*De Generatione Hominis*). . . .
" The Archæus or *Liquor Vitæ* is an essence that is equally distributed in all parts of the human body. . . . The *Spiritus Vitæ* takes it origin from the *Spiritus Mundi*. Being an *emanation of the latter*, it contains the elements of all cosmic influences, and is therefore the cause by which the action of the stars (cosmic forces) upon the invisible body of man (his *vital lingasharira*) may be explained." (*De Viribus Membrorum*. See " Life of Paracelsus " by Franz Hartmann, M.D., F.T.S.)

Had Dr. Richardson studied all the secret works of Paracelsus, he would not have been obliged to confess so often—" we do not know " . . . . " it is not known to us " . . . . etc., etc. Nor would he have ever pronounced the following sentence, recanting the best portions of his independent *rediscovery*, in which he says (*p.* 384):—

---

* Paracelsus for one, who called it *liquor vitæ*, and *Archæus*.
† Rather *alchemical*—" composition."
‡ " This vital force . . . radiates around man like a luminous sphere " . . .
says Paracelsus in *Paragranum*.

" It may be urged that in this line of thought is included no more than the theory of the existence of the ether . . . . supposed to pervade space. . . . . It may be said that this universal ether pervades all the organism of the animal body as from without, and as part of every organization. This view would be Pantheism physically discovered *if it were true* (*! !*)   It fails to be true because it would destroy the individuality of every individual sense. . . . ."

We fail to see it, and *we know* it is not so. Pantheism *may* be " physically *rediscovered.*"   It was known, seen, and felt by the whole of antiquity.   Pantheism manifests itself in the vast expanse of the starry heavens, in the breathing of the seas and oceans and the quiver of life of the smallest blade of grass.   Philosophy rejects one *finite* and *imperfect* God in the universe, as the anthropomorphic deity of the monotheist is represented by his followers. It repudiates in its name of *Philo-Theo-Sophia* the grotesque idea that Infinite, *Absolute* Deity should, or rather *could*, have any, whether direct or indirect, relation to finite illusive evolutions of matter, and therefore cannot imagine a universe *outside* that Deity, or the latter absent from the smallest speck of animate or inanimate substance.*   Why either the Ether of Space, or " nervous Ether " should " destroy the individuality of every sense " seems incomprehensible for one acquainted with the real nature of that " nervous ether " under its Sanskrit, or rather esoteric and Kabalistic name.   Dr. Richardson agrees that—

" If we did not individually produce the medium of communication between ourselves and the outer world, if it were produced from without and adapted *to one kind of vibration alone*, there were fewer senses required than we possess : for, taking two illustrations only—ether of light is not adapted for sound, and yet we hear as well as see ; while air, the medium of motion of sound, is not the medium of light, and yet we see and hear."

This is not so.   The opinion that " Pantheism *fails to be true* because it would destroy the individuality of every individual sense " shows that all the conclusions of the learned doctor are based on the modern physical theories, though he would fain reform them.   But he will find it impossible to do this unless he allows the existence of spiritual senses to replace the gradual atrophy of the physical.   " We see and hear," in accordance (of course in Dr. Richardson's mind) with the explanations of the phenomena of sight and hearing, by that same materialistic

---

* This does not mean that every bush, tree or stone is God or *a* god ; but only that every speck of the manifested material of Kosmos belongs to and is the substance of " God," however low it may have fallen in its cyclic gyration through the Eternities of the ever becoming ; and also that every such speck individually, and Kosmos collectively, is an aspect and a reminder of that universal *One Soul*—which philosophy refuses to call God, thus limiting the eternal and ever-present root and essence.

science which postulates that we cannot see and hear otherwise. The Occultists and mystics know better. The Vedic Aryans were as familiar with the mysteries of sound and colour as our physiologists are on the physical plane, but they had mastered the secrets of both on planes inaccessible to the materialist. They knew of a double set of senses; spiritual and material. In a man who is deprived of one or more senses, the remaining become the more developed : *e.g.*, the blind man will recover his sight through the senses of touch, of hearing, etc., and he who is deaf will be able to hear through sight, by *seeing audibly* the words uttered by the lips and mouth of the speaker. But these are cases that belong to the world of matter still. The spiritual senses, those that act on a higher plane of consciousness are rejected *a priori* by physiology because the latter is ignorant of the sacred science. It limits the action of ether to vibrations, and, dividing it from air—though air is simply *differentiated* and compound ether—makes it assume functions to fit in with the special theories of the physiologist. But there is more real science in the teachings of the Upanishads when these are correctly understood, than the Orientalists, who do not understand them at all, are ready to admit. *Mental as well as physical correlations of the seven senses* (seven on the physical and seven on the mental planes) are clearly explained and defined in the Vedas, and especially in the Upanishad called Anugîtâ : " The indestructible and the destructible, such is the double manifestation of the Self. Of these the indestructible is the existent (the true essence or nature of Self, the underlying principles). The manifestation as an individual (or entity) is called the destructible." Thus speaks the ASCETIC in Anugîtâ ; and also : " Every one who is twice-born (initiated) knows such is the teaching of the ancients. . . . . Space is the first entity. . . . . Now Space (*Akâsa*, or the noumenon of Ether) has one quality . . . and that is sound only . . . and the qualities of sound are Shadga, Rishabha, Gândhâra, Madhyama, Panchama, and beyond these five Nishâda and Dhaivata "; (the Hindu gamut). These seven notes of the scale are the principles of sound. (*Vide* ch. xxxvi. of *Anugîtâ*.) The qualities of every Element, as of every sense, are septenary, and to judge and dogmatize on them from their manifestation (likewise sevenfold in itself) on the material or objective plane above is quite arbitrary. For it is only by the SELF emancipating itself from these (seven) causes of illusion that one acqnires the knowledge (secret wisdom) of the qualities of objects of sense on their dual plane of manifestation—the visible and the invisible. Thus it is said :—

" State this wonderful mystery . . . . . Hear the assignment of causes exhaustively. The nose, and the tongue, and the eye, and the skin, and the ear as the fifth (organ of sense) Mind and Understanding,* these seven (senses) should be understood to be the causes of (the knowledge of their) qualities.   Smell, and taste, and colour, sound, and touch as the fifth, the object of the mental operation, and the object of the Understanding (the highest spiritual sense or perception), *these seven are causes of action.*   He who smells, he who eats, he who sees, he who speaks, and he who hears as the fifth, he who thinks, and he who understands, these seven should be regarded as the *causes of the agents.*†   These (the agents) being possessed of qualities (*sattwa, rajas, tamas*), enjoy their own qualities, agreeable and disagreeable " (*Anugîtâ*).

Then one reads in the Bhagavadgîtâ (chap. vii.) the Deity (or Krishna) saying :—

" . . . . Only some know me truly.   Earth, Water, Fire, Air, Space (or *Akâsa*, Æther), Mind, Understanding and Egoism (or the perception of all the former on the illusive plane). . . This is *a lower* form of my nature.   Know (that there is) another (form of my) nature, and higher than this, which is animate, O you of mighty arms ! and by which this Universe is upheld. . . . All this is woven upon me, like numbers of pearls upon a thread (*Mundakopanishâ*, p. 298). . . . I *am the taste* in the

---

* The division of the physical senses into five, comes to us from great antiquity. But while adopting the number, no modern philosopher has asked himself how these senses could exist, *i.e.*, be perceived and used in a self-conscious way, unless there was the *sixth* sense, mental perception to register and record them ; and (this for the Metaphysicians and Occultists) the SEVENTH to preserve the spiritual fruition and remembrance thereof, as in a Book of Life which belongs to Karma.   The ancients divided the senses into five, simply because their teachers (the Initiates) stopped at the *hearing*, as being that sense which developed in the *physical plane* (got dwarfed rather, limited to this plane) only at the beginning of the Fifth Race.   (The Fourth Race already had begun to lose the *spiritual* condition, so pre-eminently developed in the Third Race.)

† The modern commentators, failing to comprehend the subtle meaning of the ancient Scholiasts, take this sentence, " causes of the agents," to mean " that the powers of smelling, etc., when attributed to the Self, make him appear as an agent, as an active principle " (!), which is entirely fanciful.   These " seven " are understood to be the causes of the Agents, because " the objects are causes, as their enjoyment causes an impression."   It means esoterically that they, these seven senses, *are caused by the* AGENTS, which are the " deities," for what does, or can, the sentence which follows this one mean ?   " Thus," it is said, " these seven (senses) are the causes of emancipation " (*i.e.*, when these causes are made ineffectual).   " And among the learned (the wise Initiates) who understand the qualities *which are in the position* (in the nature, rather) *of the deities*, each in its place," means simply that the " learned " understand the nature of the *noumenoi* of the various phenomena " ; and that " qualities," in this instance, mean the qualities of the high planetary or Elementary gods or Intelligences, which rule the elements and their *products*, and not at all " the senses," as the modern commentator thinks.   For the " learned do not suppose their senses to have aught to do with them, any more than with their SELF."   (*Vide* pp. 278 and 279 of the VIII. Vol. of " The Sacred Books of the East."   *Anugîtâ.*)

water, O son of Kunti! I am the light of the sun and moon. I am . . . sound ('*i.e.*, the Occult essence which underlies all these and the other qualities of the various things mentioned,' *Transl.*), in space . . . the fragrant smell in the earth, refulgence in the fire . . . etc., etc."

Truly, then, one should study Occult philosophy before one begins to verify and seek the mysteries of nature on its surface alone, as he alone " who knows the truth about the qualities of nature, who understands the creation of all entities . . . is emancipated " from error. Says the " preceptor " : " Accurately understanding the great tree of which the unperceived (Occult nature, the root of all) is the sprout from the seed (Parabrahmam) which consists of the understanding (*Mahat*, or the universal intelligent Soul) as its trunk, the branches of which are the great egoism,* in the holes of which are the sprouts, namely, the senses, of which the great (Occult, or invisible) elements are the flower-bunches,† the gross elements (the gross objective matter), the smaller boughs, which are always possessed of leaves, always possessed of flowers . . . . which is eternal and the seed of which is the Brahman (the deity); and cutting it with that excellent sword—knowledge (secret wisdom)—one attains immortality and casts off birth and death."

This is the Tree of Life, the Asvattha tree, only *after* the cutting of which the slave of life and death, MAN, can be emancipated.

But the men of Science know nought, nor will they hear of the " Sword of Knowledge " used by the adepts and ascetics. Hence the one-sided remarks of the most liberal among them, based on and flow-ing from undue importance given to the arbitrary divisions and classifi-cation of physical science. Occultism heeds them very little, and nature still less. The whole range of physical phenomena proceed from the *Primary* of Ether—Akâsa, as dual-natured Akâsa proceeds from undifferentiated *Chaos*, so-called, the latter being the primary *aspect* of Mulaprakriti, the root-matter and the first abstract Idea one can form of Parabrahmam. Modern Science may divide its hypothetically con-ceived ether in as many ways as it likes ; the *real* Æther of Space will remain as it is throughout. It has its seven principles, as all the rest of nature has, and where there was no Ether *there would be no sound*, as it is the vibrating sound-board in nature in all of its seven differentiations. This is the first mystery the Initiates of old have learned. Our present normal physical senses were (from our present point of view) abnormal in those days of slow and progressive downward evolution and fall into matter. And there was a day when all that which in our modern times is regarded as phenomena, so puzzling to the

---

* *Ahamkara*, I suppose, that *Egoship* (or Ahamship) which leads to every error.

† The elements are the five tanmâtras of earth, water, fire, air and ether, the producers of the grosser elements.

physiologists now compelled to believe in them—such as thought transference, clairvoyance, clairaudience, etc. ; in short, all that which is called now " wonderful and abnormal "—all that and much more belonged to the senses and faculties common to all humanity. We are, however, cycling back and cycling forward ; *i.e.*, having lost in spirituality that which we acquired in physical development until almost the end of the Fourth Race, we (mankind) are as gradually and imperceptibly losing now in the physical all that we regain once more in the spiritual *re*-evolution. This process must go on until the period which will bring the Sixth Root-Race on a parallel line with the spirituality of the Second, long extinct mankind.

But this will hardly be understood at present. We must return to Dr. Richardson's hopeful though somewhat incorrect hypothesis about " nervous ether." Under the misleading translation of the word as " Space " (*Akâsa*), it has just been shown in the ancient Hindu system as the "first born" of the One, having but one quality, SOUND (which is septenary). In esoteric language this " One " is the " Father " Deity, and " Sound " is synonymous with *Logos* (Verbum, or the *Son*). Whether consciously or otherwise, it must be the latter ; and Dr. Richardson, while preaching an Occult doctrine—chooses the lowest form of the septenary nature of that " SOUND " and speculates upon it, adding :—

"The theory, I offer, is that the nervous Ether *is an animal product*. In different classes of animals it may differ in physical quality so as to be adapted to the special wants of the animal, but essentially it plays one part in all animals, and is produced, in all, in the same way. . . ."

Herein lies the nucleus of error leading to all the resultant mistaken views. This " Nervous Ether " is the lowest principle of the Primordial Essence which is *Life*. It is *animal vitality* diffused in all nature and acting according to the conditions it finds for its activity. It is not an " animal product," but the living animal, the living flower or plant are *its* products. The animal tissues only absorb it according to their more or less morbid or healthy state—as do *physical* materials and structures (*in their primogenial State—nota bene*)—and henceforward, from the moment of the birth of the Entity, are regulated, strengthened, and *fed* by it. It descends in a larger supply to vegetation in the *Sushumna* sun-ray which lights and feeds the moon, and it is through her beams that it pours its light upon, and penetrates man and animal, more during their sleep and rest, than when they are in full activity. Therefore Dr. Richardson errs again in stating that :—

"The nervous ether is not, according to my idea of it, in *itself active, nor an excitant of animal motion in the sense of a force;* but it is essential as supplying the conditions by which the motion is rendered possible." (It is *just the reverse*.) . . . . " It is the conductor of all vibrations of heat, of light, of sound, of electrical action, of mechanical friction.* It holds the nervous system throughout in perfect tension, during states of life (*true*). By exercise it is disposed of *(rather generated)* . . . and when demand for it is greater than the supply, its deficiency is indicated by nervous collapse or exhaustion.† It accumulates in the nervous centres during sleep, bringing them, if I may so speak, to their due tone, and therewith raising the muscles to awakening and renewed life. . . ."

Just so; this is quite correct, and as comprehensible. Therefore, " The body fully renewed by it, presents capacity for motion, fulness of form, *life*. The body bereft of it presents inertia, the configuration of shrunken death, *the evidence of having lost something physical that was in it when it lived.*"

Modern Science denies the existence of a " vital principle." This extract is a clear proof of its grand mistake. But this " physical something," that we call life-fluid—the *Liquor Vitæ* of Paracelsus—has not *deserted the body*, as Dr. Richardson thinks. It has only changed its state from activity to passivity, and become latent owing to the too morbid state of the tissues, on which it has no more hold. Once the *rigor mortis* absolute, the " *Liquor Vitæ* " will re-awaken into action, and begin its work on the atoms *chemically*. Brahmâ-Vishnu—the creator and the Preserver of Life—will have transformed himself into Siva the *Destroyer*.

Lastly he writes on p. 387 :—

" The nervous Ether may be poisoned ; it may, I mean, have diffused through it, by simple gaseous diffusion, other gases or vapours derived from without ; it may derive from within products of substances swallowed and ingested, or gases of decomposition produced during disease in the body itself."

And the learned gentleman might have added on the same Occult principle : " That the ' nervous Ether ' of one person can be poisoned by the ' nervous Ether ' of another person or his *auric emanations*. But see what Paracelsus said of ' Nervous Ether ' " :—

" The Archæus is of a magnetic nature, and *attracts or repels* other sympathetic or antipathetic forces belonging to the same plane. The less power of resistance for astral influences a person possesses, the more will he be subject to such influences. The vital force is not enclosed in man, but radiates (within) and around him like a luminous sphere (aura) and it may be made to act at a distance. . . . It *may poison the essence of life (blood) and cause diseases*, or it may purify it after

---

* The conductor in the sense of *Upadhi*—a material or physical basis ; but, as the second principle of the universal Soul and *Vital* Force in Nature, it is *intelligently* guided by the fifth principle thereof.

† And too great an exuberance of it in the nervous system leads as often to disease and death. If it were the *animal system which generated it*, such would not be the case, surely. Hence, the latter emergency shows its independence of the system, and connection with the Sun-Force, as Metcalfe and Professor Hunt explain it.

it has been made impure, and restore the health" *(Paragranum ; " Life of Paracelsus,"* by Dr. F. Hartmann.)

That the two, Archæus and " nervous Ether," are identical, is shown by the English Scientist, who says that the tension of it *generally* may be too high or too low ; that it may be so " owing to local changes in the nervous matter it invests." . . . " Under sharp excitation it may vibrate as if in a storm and plunge every muscle under cerebral or spinal control into uncontrolled motion—unconscious convulsions."

This is called nervous excitation, but no one, except Occultists, knows the reason of such nervous perturbation or explains the *primary* causes of it. The " principle of Life " may kill *when too exuberant,* as also when there is too little of it. But this principle on the manifested (or our) plane is but the effect and the result of the *intelligent action* of the " Host "—collectively, Principle—the manifesting LIFE and LIGHT. It is itself subordinate to, and emanates from the ever-invisible, eternal and Absolute ONE LIFE in a descending and a re-ascending scale of hierarchic degrees—a true septenary ladder, with SOUND (or the Logos) at the upper end and the Vidyadharas* (the inferior Pitris) at the lower.

---

* In a recent work on the Symbolism in Buddhism and Christianity (in Buddhism and Roman Catholicism, rather, many later rituals and dogmas in Northern Buddhism in its *popular exoteric form*, being identical with those of the Latin Church) some curious facts are to be found. The author of this volume, with more pretensions than erudition, has indiscriminately crammed into his work ancient and modern Buddhist teachings, and sorely confused Lamaism with Buddhism. On page 404 of this volume, called " *Buddhism in Christendom, or Jesus the Essene,*" our *pseudo-Orientalist* devotes himself to criticizing the " Seven Principles " of the Esoteric Buddhists, and attempts to ridicule them. On page 405, the closing page, he speaks enthusiastically of the *Vidyadharas,* " the seven great legions of dead men made wise." Now, these " Vidyadharas," whom some Orientalists call " demi-gods," are in fact, exoterically, a kind of Siddhas, " affluent in devotion," and, *esoterically,* they are identical with the seven classes of Pitris, one class. of which endow man in the Third Race with Self-Consciousness by incarnating in the human shells. The " Hymn to the Sun," at the end of his queer volume of mosaic, which endows Buddhism with a *personal god* (! !), is an unfortunate thrust at the very proofs so elaborately collected by the unlucky author.

Theosophists are fully aware that Mr. Rhys Davids has expressed his opinion on their beliefs likewise. He said that the theories propounded by the author of Esoteric Buddhism " were not Buddhism, and were not Esoteric." The remark is the result of (a) the unfortunate mistake of writing " Buddhism " instead of " Budhaism," or *Budhism, i.e.,* of connecting the system with Gautama's religion instead of with the Secret Wisdom taught by Krishna, Sankaracharya, and by many others, as much as by Buddha ; and (b) of the impossibility of Mr. Rhys Davids knowing anything of true esoteric teachings. But he is, at all events, the greatest Pali and Buddhist scholar of the day, and whatever he may say is entitled to respectful hearing. But when one who knows no more of exoteric Buddhism on scientific and materialistic lines, than he knows of esoteric philosophy, defames those whom he honours with his spite, and assumes with the Theosophists the airs of a profound scholar, one can only smile and —heartily laugh at him.

Of course, the Occultists are fully aware of the fact that the Vitalist "fallacy," so derided by Vogt and Huxley, is, nevertheless, still countenanced in very high scientific quarters, and, therefore, they are happy to feel that they do not stand alone.   Thus, Professor de Quatrefages writes :—

"It is very true we do not know *what* life *is;* but no more do we know *what* the force *is* that set the stars in motion. . . . . Living beings are heavy, and therefore subject to gravitation ; they are the seat of numerous and various physico-chemical phenomena which are indispensable to their existence, and which must be referred to the action of etherodynamy (electricity, heat, etc.).   But these phenomena are here manifested *under the influence of another force.* . . . . Life is not antagonistic to the inanimate forces, but it governs and rules their action by its laws."*

———

IX.

THE SOLAR THEORY.

A SHORT ANALYSIS OF THE COMPOUND AND SINGLE ELEMENTS OF SCIENCE AS AGAINST THE OCCULT TEACHINGS.   HOW FAR SCIENTIFIC IS THIS THEORY, AS GENERALLY ACCEPTED.

IN his reply to Dr. Gull's attack on the theory of vitality (connected inseparably with the Elements of the ancients in the Occult philosophy), Professor Beale, the great physiologist, has a few words as suggestive as they are beautiful :—

"There is a mystery in life—a mystery which has never been fathomed, and which appears greater, the more deeply the phenomena of life are studied and contemplated.   In living centres—far more central than the centres seen by the highest magnifying powers, in centres of living matter, where the eye cannot penetrate, but towards which the understanding may tend—proceed changes of the nature of which the most advanced physicists and chemists fail to afford us the conception : *nor is there the slightest reason to think that the nature of these changes will ever be ascertained by physical investigation,* inasmuch as they are certainly of an order or nature *totally distinct* from that to which any other phenomenon known to us can be relegated."

This "mystery," or the origin of the LIFE ESSENCE, Occultism locates in the same centre as the nucleus of *prima materia* (for they are one) of our Solar system.

———
* *"The Human Species,"* p. 11.

"*The Sun is the heart of the Solar World (System) and its brain is hidden behind the (visible) Sun. From thence, sensation is radiated into every nerve-centre of the great body, and the waves of the life-essence flow into each artery and vein. . . . The planets are its limbs and pulses. . . .*" *(Commentary.)*

It was stated elsewhere *(in the Theosophist)* that Occult philosophy denies that the Sun is a globe in combustion, but defines it simply as a world, a glowing sphere, the *real* Sun being hidden behind, and the visible being only its reflection, its *shell*. The Nasmyth willow leaves, mistaken by Sir J. Herschell for "Solar inhabitants," are the reservoirs of solar vital energy, "the vital electricity that feeds the whole system. . . . . The Sun *in abscondito* being thus the storehouse of our little Kosmos, self-generating its vital fluid, and ever receiving as much as it gives out," and the *visible* Sun only a *window cut into the real* Solar palace and presence, which reflects, however, faithfully the interior work.

Thus, there is a regular circulation of the vital fluid throughout our system, of which the Sun is the heart—the same as the circulation of the blood in the human body—during the manvantaric solar period, or life; the Sun contracting as rhythmically at every return of it, as the human heart does. Only, instead of performing the round in a second or so, it takes the solar blood ten of its years, and a whole year to pass through its *auricles* and *ventricles* before it washes the *lungs* and passes thence to the great veins and arteries of the system.

This, Science will not deny, since Astronomy knows of the fixed cycle of eleven years when the number of solar spots increases,* *which is due to the contraction* of the Solar HEART. The universe (our world in this case) breathes, just as man and every living creature, plant, and even mineral does upon the earth; and as our globe itself breathes every twenty-four hours. The dark region is *not* due "to the absorption exerted by the vapours issuing from the bosom of the sun and interposed between the observer and the photosphere," as Father Secchi would have it *("Le Soleil" II.*, 184), nor are the spots formed "by the matter (heated gaseous matter) which the irruption projects upon the solar disc" *(ibid).* It is similar to the regular and healthy pulsation of the heart, as the life fluid passes through its hollow muscles. Could the human heart be made luminous, and the living and throbbing organ be made visible, so as to have it reflected upon a screen, such as

---

* Not only does it not deny the occurrence, though attributing it to a wrong cause, as always, each theory contradicting every other, (*see the theories of Secchi, of Faye, and of Young*), the spots depending on the superficial accumulation of vapours cooler than the photosphere (?), etc., etc., but we have men of science who *astrologize* upon the spots. Professor Jevons attributes all the great periodical commercial crises to the influence of the Sun spots every eleventh cyclic year. (*See his "Investigations into Currency and Finance."*) This is worthy of praise and encouragement surely,

used by the astronomers in their lectures—say for the moon—then every one would see the Sun-spot phenomenon repeated every second —due to its contraction and the rushing of the blood.

It is said in a work on Geology that it is the *dream of Science* that "all the recognized chemical elements will one day be found *but modifications of a single material element.*" (" *World-Life,*" *p.* 48.)

Occult philosophy has taught this since the existence of human speech and languages, adding only, on the principle of the immutable law of analogy—" as it is above, so it is below "—that other axiom, that there is neither Spirit nor matter, in reality, but only numberless aspects of the One ever-hidden IS (or *Sat*). The homogeneous primordial Element is *simple* and *single only on the terrestrial plane* of consciousness and sensation, since matter, after all, is nothing else than the sequence of our own states of consciousness, and Spirit an idea of psychic intuition. Even on the next higher plane, that *single element* which is defined on our earth by current science, as the ultimate undecomposable constituent of some kind of matter, would be pronounced in the world of a higher spiritual perception as something very complex indeed. Our purest water would be found to yield, instead of its two declared *simple* elements of oxygen and hydrogen, many other constituents, undreamt of by our terrestrial modern chemistry. As in the realm of matter, so in the realm of Spirit, the shadow of that which is cognized on the plane of objectivity exists on that of pure subjectivity. The speck of the perfectly homogeneous substance, the sarcode of the Hæckelian *monera,* is now viewed as the *archebiosis* of terrestrial existence (Mr. Huxley's " protoplasm ")* ; and *Bathybius Hæckelii* has to be traced to its *pre*-terrestrial archebiosis. This is first perceived by the astrono- mers at its third stage of evolution, and in the " secondary creation," so-called. But the students of Esoteric philosophy understand too well the secret meaning of the stanza : " Brahmâ has essentially the *aspect of* prakriti, both evolved and unevolved . . . . Spirit, O twice-born, (Initiate) is the leading *aspect* of Brahmâ. The next is a two-fold aspect —of Prakriti and Purusha, both evolved and unevolved ; and *time* is the last ! *Anu* is one of the names of Brahmâ (as distinct from Brahma neuter), and it means " atom": Aníyâmsam aníyasám, " the most atomic of the atomic," the " immutable and imperishable (achyuta) Purushottama."

Surely, then, the elements now known to us—be their number what- ever it may—as they are understood and defined at present, are not,

---

* Unfortunately, as these pages are being written the " *archebiosis* of terrestial existence " has turned, under a somewhat stricter chemical analysis, into a simple pre- cipitate of sulphate of lime—hence from the scientific standpoint not even an *organic* substance ! ! ! *Sic transit gloria mundi !*

nor can they be, the *primordial* elements. Those were formed from " *the curds of the cold radiant mother* " and " the *fire-seed* of the hot Father " who " *are one*," or, to express it in the plainer language of modern science, those elements had their genesis in the depths of the primordial fire-mist —the masses of incandescent vapour of the *irresolvable* nebulæ ; for as Professor Newcomb shows (in his " *Popular Astronomy*," on pages 444), *resolvable* nebulæ are not a class of proper nebulæ.

More than half of those which were at first mistaken for nebulae—he thinks—are what he calls " starry clusters." The elements now known, have arrived at their state of permanency in this 4th Round and 5th Race. They have a short period of rest before they are propelled once more on their upward spiritual evolution ; when the "living fire of Orcus" will dissociate the most irresolvable and scatter them into the primordial ONE—again.

Meanwhile the Occultist goes further, as has been shown in the Commentaries on the Seven Stanzas. Hence he can hardly hope for any help or recognition from science, which will reject both his "ániyâmsam aníyásám (the absolutely spiritual atom) and his Manasaputras—"mind-born men." By resolving the " single material element " into one absolute *irresolvable* element—Spirit, or " Root-matter," thus placing it at once outside the reach and province of physical philosophy—he has, of course but little in common with the orthodox men of science. He maintains that Spirit and Matter are two FACETS of the unknowable UNITY, their apparently contrasted aspects depending, (*a*) on the various degrees of differentiation of the latter, and (*b*) on the grades of consciousness attained by man himself. This is, however, metaphysics, and has little to do with physics—however great in its own terrestrial limitation that physical *philosophy* may now be.

Nevertheless, once that Science admits, if not the actual existence, at any rate, the possibility of the existence, of a Universe with its number-less forms, conditions, and aspects built out of a " single substance,"* it has

---

* In his " World-Life "—page 48—in the appended foot notes, Professor Winchell says :—" It is generally admitted that at excessively high temperatures matter exists in a state of dissociation—that is, no chemical combination can exist ; " and would appeal, to prove the unity of matter, to the spectrum, which in every case of homogeneity will show a *bright* line, whereas in the case of several molecular arrangements existing—in the nebulæ say, or a star—" the spectrum should consist of two or three bright lines ! " This would be no proof either way to the physicist-Occultist, who maintains that beyond a certain limit of *visible* matter, no spectrum, no telescope and no microscope are of any use. The unity of matter, of that which is real cosmic matter to the Alchemist, or " Adam's Earth " as the Kabalists call it, can hardly be proved or disproved, by either the French *savant* Dumas, who suggests " the composite nature of the "elements " on certain relations of atomic weights," or even by Mr. Crookes's "radiant matter," though his experiments may seem

to go further.   Unless it also admits the possibility of One Element, or the ONE LIFE of the Occultists.   It will have to hang up that " single substance," especially if limited to only the solar nebulae, like the coffin of Mahomet, in mid air, though minus the attractive magnet that sustains that coffin.   Fortunately for the speculative physicists, if unable to state with any degree of precision what the nebular theory *does* imply, we have, thanks to Professor Winchell, and several disagreeing astronomers, been able to learn what *it does not* imply.* (*Vide Supra.*)

Unfortunately, this is far from clearing even the most simple of the problems that have vexed, and still do vex, the men of learning in their research after truth.   We have to proceed with our inquiries, starting with the earliest hypotheses of modern science, if we would discover *where* and *why* it sins.   Perchance it may be found that Stallo is right, after all.   That the blunders, contradictions, and fallacies made by the most eminent men of learning are simply due to their abnormal attitude.   They are, and want to remain materialistic *quand même*, and yet " the general principles of the atomo-mechanical theory—the basis of modern physics—are *substantially identical* with the cardinal doctrines of ontological metaphysics."   Thus, " the fundamental errors of ontology become apparent in proportion to the advance of physical Science." (Int. p. VI., " Concepts of Modern Physics.")   Science is honeycombed with metaphysical conceptions, but the Scientists will not admit the charge and fight desperately to put atomo-mechanical masks on purely incorporeal and spiritual laws in nature, on our plane—refusing to admit their substantiality even on other planes, the bare existence of which they reject *à priori.*

It is easy to show, however, how Scientists, wedded to their materialistic views, have endeavoured, ever since the day of Newton, to put false masks on fact and truth.   But their task is becoming with every year more difficult ; and with every year also, Chemistry, above all the other sciences, approaches nearer and nearer the realm of the Occult in nature.   It is assimilating the very truths taught by the Occult Sciences

---

" to be best understood on the hypothesis of the homogeneity of the elements of matter, and the continuity of the states of matter."   For all this does not go beyond MATERIAL matter, so to say, even in what is shown by the *spectrum*, that modern " eye of Siva " of physical experiments.   It is of this matter only, that H. St. Claire Deville could say that " when bodies, deemed to be simple, combine with one another, they vanish, they are *individually annihilated* " ; simply because he could not follow those bodies in their further transformation in the world of *spiritual* cosmic matter.   Verily modern science will never be able to dig deep enough into the cosmological formations to find the *roots* of the world-stuff or matter, unless she works on the same lines of thought as the medieval alchemist did.

* " World-Life," Ibid.

for ages, but hitherto bitterly derided. "Matter is eternal," says the Esoteric Doctrine. But the matter the Occultists conceive of in its *laya*, or *zero state*, is not the matter of modern science; not even in its most rarefied gaseous state. Mr. Crookes' "radiant matter" would appear matter of the grossest kind in the realm of the beginnings, as it becomes pure spirit before it has returned back even to its first point of differentiation. Therefore, when the adept or alchemist adds that, though matter is eternal, for it is PRADHÀNA, yet atoms *are born at every new manvantara*, or reconstruction of the universe, it is no such contradiction as a materialist, who believes in nothing beyond the atom, might think. There is a difference between *manifested* and *unmanifested* matter, between *pradhâna*, the beginningless and endless cause, and *prakriti*, or the manifested effect. Says the sloka ;—

" That which is the unevolved cause is emphatically called by the most eminent sages, *pradhâna*, *original base, which is* subtile *prakriti, viz.,* that which is eternal, and which at once is, and is not, *a mere process.*" *

That which in modern phraseology is respectively referred to as Spirit and Matter, is ONE in eternity as the perpetual cause, and it is neither Spirit nor matter, but IT—rendered in Sanskrit TAD ("that"),— all that is, was, or will be, all that the imagination of man is capable of conceiving. Even the exoteric Pantheism of Hinduism renders it as no monotheistic philosophy ever did, for in superb phraseology its cosmogony begins with the well-known words :—

" There was neither day nor night, neither heaven nor earth, neither darkness nor light. And there was not ought else apprehensible by the senses or by the mental faculties. There was then one Brahmâ, essentially *prakriti* (Nature) and Spirit. For *the two aspects* of Vishnu which are other than his supreme essential aspect are prakriti and Spirit, and Brahman. *When these two other* ASPECTS *of his no longer subsist, but are dissolved*, then that aspect whence form and the rest, *i.e., creation*, proceed *anew*, is denominated time, O twice-born."

It is that which is dissolved, or the illusionary *dual* aspect of That, the essence of which is eternally ONE, that we call eternal matter or Substance (Vide in Part II., " *Primordial Substance and Divine Thought* "), formless, sexless, inconceivable, even to our *sixth* sense or mind,† in which, therefore, we refuse to see that which Monotheists call a *personal*, anthropomorphic God.

How are these two propositions—" that matter is eternal," and " the atom periodical, and not eternal "—viewed by modern exact Science ? The materialistic physicist will criticize and laugh them to scorn. The

* Book I. ch. II. *Vishnu Purâna*, Fitzedward Hall's Translation.
† *Vide* preceding Section IX., " Life, Force, and Gravity," quotation from *Anugîtâ*.

liberal and progressive man of Science, however, the true and earnest scientific searcher after truth—*e.g.*, the eminent chemist, Mr. Crookes, will corroborate the *probability* of the two statements. For, hardly has the echo of his lecture on the " Genesis of the Elements " died away —the lecture which, delivered by him before the Chemical Section of the British Association, at the last Birmingham meeting, so startled every evolutionist who heard or read it—than there came another one in March last, 1888. Once more the President of the Chemical Society brings before the world of Science and the public the fruits of some new discoveries in the realm of atoms, and these discoveries justify the occult teachings in every way. They are more startling even than the statements made by him in the first lecture (quoted later) and deserve well the attention of every Occultist, Theosophist, and Metaphysician. This is what he says in his " Elements and *Meta*-Elements," thus justifying Stallo's charges and prevision with the fearlessness of a scientific mind which loves science for truth's sake, regardless of any consequences to his own glory and reputation. We quote his own words :

Permit me, gentlemen, now to draw your attention for a short time to a subject which concerns the fundamental principles of chemistry, a subject which may lead us to admit the possible existence of bodies which, though neither compounds nor mixtures, are not elements in the strictest sense of the word—bodies which I venture to call " meta-elements." To explain my meaning it is necessary for me to revert to our conception of an element. What is the criterion of an element ? Where are we to draw the line between distinct existence and identity ? No one doubts that oxygen, sodium, chlorine, sulphur are separate elements ; and when we come to such groups as chlorine, bromine, iodine, &c., we still feel no doubt, although were degrees of " elemen- ticity " admissible—and to that we may ultimately have to come—it might be allowed that chlorine approximates much more closely to bromine than to oxygen, sodium, or sulphur. Again, nickel and cobalt are near to each other, very near, though no one questions their claim to rank as distinct elements. Still I cannot help asking what would have been the prevalent opinion among chemists had the respective solutions of these bodies and their compounds pre- sented identical colours, instead of colours which, approximately speaking, are mutually complementary. Would their distinct nature have even now been recognised ? When we pass further and come to the so-called rare earths the ground is less secure under our feet. Perhaps we may admit scandium, ytter- bium, and others of the like sort to elemental rank ; but what are we to say in the case of praseo- and neo-dymium, between which there may be said to exist no well-marked chemical difference, their chief claim to separate individuality being slight differences in basicity and crystallizing powers, though their physical distinctions, as shown by spectrum observations, are very strongly marked ? Even here we may imagine the disposition of the majority of chemists would incline toward the side of leniency, so that they would admit these two bodies within the charmed circle. Whether in so doing they would be able to appeal to any broad principle is an open question. If we admit these candidates how in justice are we to exclude the series of elemental bodies or meta-elements made known to us by Krüss and Nilson ? Here the spectral differences are well marked, while my own researches on didymium show also a slight difference in basicity between some at least of these doubtful bodies. In the same category must be included the numerous separate bodies into which it is probable that yttrium, erbium, samarium, and other "elements"—commonly so-called— have been and are being split up. Where then are we to draw the line ? The different groupings shade off so imperceptibly the one into the other that it is impossible to erect a definite boundary between any two adjacent bodies and to say that the body on this side of the line is an element, while the one on the other side is non-elementary, or merely something which simulates or approxi- mates to an element. Wherever an apparently reasonable line might be drawn it would no doubt be easy at once to assign most bodies to their proper side, as in all cases of classification the real difficulty comes in when the border-line is approached. Slight chemical differences, of course, are admitted, and, up to a certain point, so are well-marked physical differences. What are we to say, however, when the only chemical difference is an almost imper- ceptible tendency for the one body—of a couple or of a group—to precipitate before the other ? Again, there are cases where the chemical differences reach the vanishing point, although well-marked physical differences still remain. Here we stumble on a new difficulty : in such obscurities what is chemical and what is physical ? Are we not entitled to call a slight tendency of a nascent amorphous precipitate to fall down in advance of another a " physical difference ? " And may we not call coloured reactions depending on the amount of some particular acid present and varying, according to the concentration of the solution and to the solvent employed, "chemical differences ? " I do not see how we can deny elementary character to a body which differs from another by well-marked colour, or spectrum- reactions, while we accord it to another body whose only claim is a very minute difference in basic powers. Having once opened the door wide enough to admit some spectrum differences, we have to inquire how minute a difference qualifies the candidate to pass ? I will give instances from my own experience of some of these doubtful candidates.

And here the great chemist gives several cases of the very extraordi- nary behaviour of molecules and earths, apparently the same, and which yet, when examined very closely, were found to exhibit differences which, however imperceptible, still show that none of them are *simple* bodies, and that the 6o or 7o elements accepted in chemistry, can no longer cover the ground. Their name, apparently, is legion, but as the so-called "periodic theory" stands in the way of an unlimited multipli- cation of elements, Mr. Crookes is obliged to find some means of reconciling the new discovery with the old theory. " That theory," he says :—

" Has received such abundant verification that we cannot lightly accept any interpretation of phenomena which fails to be in accordance with it. But if we suppose the elements reinforced by a vast number of bodies slightly differ- ing from each other in their properties, and forming, if I may use the expression, aggregations of nebulæ where we formerly saw, or believed we saw, separate stars, the periodic arrangement can no longer be definitely grasped. No longer, that is, if we retain our usual conception of an element. Let us, then, modify this conception. For "element" read "elementary group"—such elementary groups taking the place of the old elements in the periodic scheme —and the difficulty falls away. In defining an element, let us take not an external boundary, but an internal type. Let us say, *e.g.*, the smallest ponderable quantity of yttrium is an assemblage of ultimate atoms almost infinitely more like each other than they are to the atoms of any other approximating element. It does not necessarily follow that the atoms shall all be absolutely alike among themselves. The atomic weight which we ascribed to yttrium, therefore, merely represents a mean value around which the actual weights of the individual atoms of the " element " range within certain limits. But if my conjecture is tenable, could we separate atom from atom, we should find them varying within narrow limits on each side of the mean. The very process of fractionation implies the existence of such differences in certain bodies."

Thus fact and truth have once more forced the hand of "exact" Science, and compelled it to enlarge its views and change its terms which, masking the multitude, reduced them to one body—like the Septenary Elohim and their hosts transformed by the materialistic religionists into one Jehovah. Replace the chemical terms " Molecule," "atom," " particle," etc., by the words " Hosts," " Monads," " Devas," etc., and one might think the genesis of gods, the primeval evolution of manvantaric *intelligent* Forces, was being described. But the learned lecturer adds something still more suggestive to his descriptive remarks; whether consciously or unconsciously, who knoweth? For he says the following :—

" Until lately such bodies passed muster as elements. They had definite properties, chemical and physical; they had recognised atomic weights. If we take a pure dilute solution of such a body, yttrium for instance, and if we add to it an excess of strong ammonia, we obtain a precipitate which appears perfectly homogeneous. But if instead we add very dilute ammonia in quantity sufficient only to precipitate one-half of the base present, we obtain no immediate precipitate. If we stir up the whole thoroughly so as to insure a uniform mixture of the solution and the ammonia, and set the vessel aside for an hour, carefully excluding dust, we may still find the liquid clear and bright, without any vestige of turbidity. After three or four hours, however, an opalescence will declare itself, and the next morning a precipitate will have appeared. Now let us ask ourselves, What can be the meaning of this phenomenon? The quantity of precipitant added was insufficient to throw down more than half the yttria present, therefore a process akin to selection has been going on for several hours. The precipitation has *evidently not been effected at random*, those molecules of the base being decomposed which happened to come in contact with a corresponding molecule of ammonia, for we have taken care that the liquids should be uniformly mixed, so that one molecule of the original salt would not be more exposed to decomposition than any other. If, further, we consider the time which elapses before the appearance of a precipitate, we *cannot avoid coming to the conclusion that the action which has been going on for the first few hours is of a selective character.* The problem is not why a precipitate is produced, but what determines or directs some atoms to fall down and others to remain in solution. Out of the multitude of atoms present, *what power is it that directs each atom to choose the proper path ? We may picture to ourselves some directive force passing the atoms one by one in review, selecting one for precipitation and another for solution till all have been adjusted.*"

The italics in the above passage are ours. Well may a man of science ask himself, "What power is it that directs each atom," and what is it that its character should be *selective ?* Theists would solve the question by answering "God"; and would solve nothing philosophically. Occultism answers on its own pantheistic grounds, and refers the reader to a subsequent section, "*Gods, Monads, and Atoms.*" The learned lecturer sees in it that which is his chief concern : the finger-posts and the traces of a path which may lead to the discovery, and the full and complete demonstration of an homogeneous element in nature. He remarks :—

"In order that such a selection can be effected there evidently must be some slight differences between which it is possible to select, and this difference almost certainly must be one of basicity, so slight as to be imperceptible by any test at present known, but susceptible of being nursed and encouraged to a point when the difference can be appreciated by ordinary tests."

Occultism, which knows of the existence and presence in Nature of the One eternal element at the first differentiation of which the roots of the tree of life are periodically struck, needs no scientific proofs. It says :— Ancient Wisdom has solved the problem ages ago. Aye; earnest, as well as mocking reader, Science is slowly but as surely approaching our domains of the Occult. It is forced by its own discoveries to adopt *nolens volens* our phraseology and symbols. Chemical Science is now compelled, by the very force of things, to accept even our illustration of the evolution of the gods and atoms, so suggestively and undeniably figured in the caduceus of Mercury, the God of Wisdom, and in the allegorical language of the Archaic Sages. Says a commentary in the esoteric doctrine :—

. . . . *The trunk of the* ASVATTHA (*the tree of Life and Being, the* ROD *of the caduceus) grows from and descends at every Beginning (every new manvantara) from the two dark wings of the Swan (*HANSA*) of Life. The two Serpents, the ever-living and its illusion (Spirit and matter) whose two heads grow from the one head between the wings, descend along the trunk, interlaced in close embrace. The two tails join on earth (the manifested Universe) into one, and this is the great illusion, O Lanoo !*"

Every one knows what the caduceus is, already modified by the Greeks. The original symbol—with the triple head of the serpent—became altered into a rod with a knob, and the two lower heads were separated, thus disfiguring somewhat the original meaning. Yet it is as good an illustration as can be for our purpose, this laya rod entwined by two serpents. Verily the wonderful powers of the magic caduceus were sung by all the ancient poets, with a very good reason for those who understood the secret meaning.

Now what says the learned President of the Chemical Society of Great Britain, in that same lecture, which has any reference to, or bearing upon, our above-mentioned doctrine. Very little; only this—and nothing more :—

"In the Birmingham address already referred to I asked my audience to picture the action of two forces on the original protyle—one being time, accompanied by a lowering of temperature; the other, swinging to and fro like a mighty pendulum, having periodic cycles of ebb and swell, rest and activity, being intimately connected with the imponderable matter, essence, or source of energy we call electricity. Now, a simile like this effects its object if it fixes in the mind the particular fact it is intended to emphasize, but it must not be expected necessarily to run parallel with all the facts. Besides the lowering of temperature with the periodic ebb and flow of electricity, positive or negative, requisite to confer on the newly-born elements their particular atomicity, it is evident that a third factor must be taken into account. Nature does not act on a flat plane; she demands space for her cosmogenic operations, and if we introduce space as the third factor, all appears clear. Instead of a pendulum, which, though to a certain extent a good illustration, is impossible as a fact, let us seek some more satisfactory way of representing what I conceive may have taken place. Let us suppose the zigzag diagram not drawn upon a plane, but projected in space of three dimensions. What figure can we best select to meet all the conditions involved ? Many of the facts can be well explained by supposing the projection in space of Professor Emerson Reynolds' zigzag curve to be a spiral. This figure is, however, inadmissible, inasmuch as the curve has to pass through a point neutral as to electricity and chemical energy twice in each cycle. We must, therefore, adopt some other figure. A figure of eight (8), or lemniscate, will fore-shorten into a zigzag just as well as a spiral, and it fulfils every condition of the problem."

A *lemniscate* for the evolution downward, from Spirit into matter;

another form of a *spiral*, perhaps, in its *reinvolutionary* path onward, from matter into Spirit, and the necessary gradual and final reabsorption into the *laya* state, that which Science calls in her own way "the point neutral as to electricity" etc., or the *zero* point. Such are the Occult facts and statement. They may be left with the greatest security and confidence to Science, to be justified some day. Let us hear some more, however, about this primordial genetic type of the symbolical caduceus.

" Such a figure will result from three very simple simultaneous motions. First, a simple oscillation backwards and forwards (suppose east and west); secondly, a simple oscillation at right angles to the former (suppose north and south) of half the periodic time—*i.e.*, twice as fast; and thirdly, a motion at right angles to these two (suppose downwards), which, in its simplest form, would be with unvarying velocity. If we project this figure in space we find on examination that the points of the curves, where chlorine, bromine, and iodine are formed, come close under each other; so also will sulphur, selenium, and tellurium ; again, phosphorus, arsenic, and antimony ; and in like manner other series of analagous bodies. It may be asked whether this scheme explains how and why the elements appear in this order ? Let us imagine a cyclical trans- lation in space, each evolution witnessing the genesis of the group of elements which I previously represented as produced during one complete vibration of the pendulum. Let us suppose that one cycle has thus been completed, the centre of the unknown creative force in its mighty journey through space having scattered along its track the primitive atoms—the seeds, if I may use the expression—which presently are to coalesce and develop into the groupings now known as lithium, beryllium, boron, carbon, nitrogen, oxygen, fluorine, sodium, magnesium, aluminium, silicon, phosphorus, sulphur, and chlorine. What is most probably the form of track now pursued ? Were it strictly confined to the same plane of temperature and time, the next elementary groupings to appear would again have been those of lithium, and the original cycle would have been eternally repeated, producing again and again the same 14 elements. The conditions, however, are not quite the same. Space and electricity are as at first, but temperature has altered, and thus, instead of the atoms of lithium being supplemented with atoms in all respects analogous with themselves, the atomic groupings which come into being when the second cycle commences form, not lithium, but its lineal descendant, potassium. Suppose, therefore, the *vis generatrix* travelling to and fro in cycles along a lemniscate path, as above suggested, while simultaneously temperature is declining and time is flowing on—variations which I have endeavoured to represent by the downward sink—each coil of the lemniscate track crosses the same vertical line at lower and lower points. Projected in space, the curve shows a central line neutral as far as electricity is concerned, and neutral in chemical properties—positive electricity on the north, negative on the south. Dominant atomicities are governed by the distance east and west from the neutral centre line, monatomic elements being one remove from it, diatomic two removes, and so on. In every successive coil the same law holds good."

And, as if to prove the postulate of Occult Science and Hindu philo-

sophy, that, at the hour of the Pralaya, the two *aspects* of the unknowable deity, " the Swan in darkness "—Prakriti and Purusha, nature
or matter in all its forms and Spirit—no longer subsist but are
(*absolutely*) dissolved," we learn the conclusive scientific opinion of the
great English chemist, who caps his proofs by saying :—" We have now
traced the formation of the chemical elements from knots and voids in
a primitive, formless fluid.   We have shown the possibility, nay, the
probability that the atoms are not eternal in existence, but share with
all other created beings the attributes of decay and death."

Occultism says *amen* to this, as the Scientific " possibility" and
" probability" are for it facts demonstrated beyond the necessity of
further proof or any extraneous physical evidence.   Nevertheless, it
repeats with as much assurance as ever: " MATTER IS ETERNAL, becoming atomic (its aspect) only periodically."   This is as sure as that
the other proposition, which is almost unanimously accepted by
astronomers and physicists—namely, that the wear and tear of the body
of the Universe is steadily going on, and that it will finally lead to the
extinction of the Solar fires and the destruction of the Universe—is quite
erroneous on the lines traced by Men of Science.   There will be, as
there ever were in time and eternity, periodical dissolutions of the
manifested Universe, but (*a*) a partial *pralaya* after every " Day of
Brahmâ ; " and (*b*) an Universal pralaya—the MAHA-PRALAYA—only after
the lapse of every Brahmâ's age.   But the scientific causes for such
dissolution, as brought forward by exact Science, have nothing to do
with the true causes.   However that may be, Occultism is once more
justified by Science, for Mr. Crookes said :—

" We have shown, from arguments drawn from the chemical laboratory, that
in matter which has responded to every test of an element, there are minute
shades of difference which may admit of selection.   We have seen that the
time-honoured distinction between elements and compounds no longer keeps
pace with the developments of chemical science, but must be modified to
include a vast array of intermediate bodies—" meta-elements."   We have
shown how the objections of Clerk-Maxwell, weighty as they are, may be met;
and finally, we have adduced reasons for believing that primitive matter was
formed by the act of a generative force, throwing off at intervals of time atoms
endowed with varying quantities of primitive forms of energy.   If we may hazard
any conjectures as to the source of energy embodied in a chemical atom, we
may, I think, premise that the heat radiations propagated outwards through
the ether from the ponderable matter of the universe, by some process of
nature not yet known to us, are transformed at the confines of the universe
into the primary—the essential—motions of chemical atoms, which, the instant
they are formed, gravitate inwards, and thus restore to the universe the energy
which otherwise would be lost to it through radiant heat.   If this conjecture
be well founded, Sir William Thomson's *startling prediction of the final decrepitude
of the universe through the dissipation of its energy falls to the ground.*   In this

fashion, gentlemen, it seems to me that the question of the elements may be provisionally treated. Our slender knowledge of these first mysteries is extending steadily, surely, though slowly."

By a strong and curious coincidence even our "septenary" doctrine seems to force the hand of Science. If we understand rightly, Chemistry speaks of fourteen groupings of primitive atoms—lithium, beryllium, boron, carbon, nitrogen, oxygen, fluorine, sodium, magnesium, aluminium, silicon, phosphorus, sulphur and chlorine; and Mr. Crookes, speaking of the "dominant atomicities," enumerates seven groups of these, for he says :—

"As the mighty focus of creative energy goes round, we see it in successive cycles sowing in one tract of space seeds of lithium, potassium, rubidium, and cæsium; in another tract, chlorine, bromine, and iodine; in a third, sodium, copper, silver, and gold; in a fourth, sulphur, selenium, and tellurium; in a fifth, beryllium, calcium, strontium, and barium; in a sixth, magnesium, zinc, cadmium, and mercury; in a seventh, phosphorus, arsenic, antimony, and bismuth"—which makes seven groupings on the one hand. And after showing "in other tracts the other elements—namely, aluminium, gallium, indium, and thallium; silicon, germanium, and tin; carbon, titanium, and zirconium."

He adds: "While a natural position near the neutral axis is found for the three groups of elements relegated by Professor Mendeleeff to a sort of Hospital for Incurables—his eighth family." It might be interesting to compare these "seven of the eighth family of 'incurables' with the allegories concerning the seven primitive sons of "Mother, Infinite Space," or Aditi, and the *eighth* son rejected by her. Many a strange coincidence may thus be found between "those intermediate links . . . named ' meta-elements or elementoids and those whom occult science names their *noumenoi*,' the intelligent minds and rulers of those groupings of Monads and Atoms. But this would lead us too far. Let us be content with finding the confession of the fact that "this deviation from absolute homogeneity should mark the constitution of these molecules or aggregations of matter which we designate elements and will perhaps be clearer if we return in imagination to the earliest dawn of our material universe, and, face to face with the Great Secret, try to consider the processes of elemental evolution." Thus finally Science, in the person of its highest representatives, in order to make itself clearer to the profane, adopts the phraseology of such old adepts as Roger Bacon, and returns to the "protyle." All this is hopeful and suggestive of the "signs of the times."

Indeed these "signs" are many and multiply daily; but none are more important than those just quoted. For now the chasm between the occult "superstitious and *unscientific*" teachings and "exact" science is completely bridged, and one, at least, of the few eminent chemists of the day is in the realm of the infinite possibilities of occultism. Every new step he will take will bring him nearer and nearer to that mysterious centre, from which radiate the innumerable paths that lead down Spirit into matter, and which transform the gods and the living monads into man and sentient nature.

But we have something more to say on this subject in the following section.

X.

THE COMING FORCE.

ITS POSSIBILITIES AND IMPOSSIBILITIES.

Shall we say that Force is "moving matter," or "matter in motion," and a manifestation of energy ; or that matter and force are the phenomenal differentiated aspects of the one primary, undifferentiated Cosmic Substance ?

This query is made with regard to that Stanza which treats of FOHAT and his "Seven brothers or *Sons*," in other words, of the *cause* and the *effects* of Cosmic Electricity, the latter called, in Occult parlance, *the seven primary* forces of Electricity, whose purely phenomenal, and hence *grossest* effects are alone cognizable by physicists on the cosmic and especially on the terrestrial plane. These include, among other things, Sound, Light, Colour, etc., etc. Now what does physical Science tell us of these "Forces"? SOUND, it says, is a *sensation* produced by the impact of atmospheric molecules on the *tympanum*, which, by setting up delicate tremors in the auditory apparatus, thus communicate themselves to the brain. LIGHT is the *sensation* caused by the impact of inconceivably minute vibrations of ether on the *retina* of the eye.

So, too, we say. But this is simply the effect produced in *our* atmosphere and its immediate surroundings, all, in fact, which falls within the range of our terrestrial consciousness. *Jupiter Pluvius* sent his symbol in drops of rain, of water composed, as is believed, of two "elements," which chemistry dissociates and recombines. The compound molecules are in its power, but their atoms still elude its grasp. Occultism sees in all these Forces and manifestations a ladder, the lower rungs of which belong to *exoteric* physics, and the higher are traced to a living, intelligent, invisible Power, which is, as a rule, the unconcerned, and exceptionally, the conscious cause of the sense-born phenomenon designated as this or another natural law.

We say and maintain that SOUND, for one thing, is a tremendous Occult power ; that it is a stupendous force, of which the electricity generated by a million of Niagaras could never counteract the smallest potentiality when directed with *occult knowledge*. Sound may be produced of such a nature that the pyramid of Cheops would be raised in the air, or that a dying man, nay, one at his last breath, would be revived and filled with new energy and vigour.

For Sound generates, or rather attracts together, the elements that produce an *ozone*, the fabrication of which is beyond chemistry, but within the limits of Alchemy. It may even *resurrect* a man or an animal whose astral "vital body" has not been irreparably separated from the physical body by the severance of the magnetic or odic chord. *As one saved thrice from death* by that power, the writer ought to be credited with knowing personally something about it.

And if all this appears too *unscientific* to be even noticed, let Science explain "to what mechanical and physical laws known to it, is due the recently produced phenomena of the so-called "Keely motor ? " What is it that acts as the formidable generator of invisible but tremendous force, of that power which is not only capable of driving an engine of 25 horse-power, but has even been employed to lift the machinery bodily ? Yet this is done simply by drawing a fiddle-bow across a tuning fork, as has been repeatedly proven. For the *etheric* Force, discovered by the well-known (in America and now in Europe) John Worrell Keely, of Philadelphia, is no *hallucination*. Notwithstanding his failure to utilize it, a failure prognosticated and maintained by some Occultists from the first, the phenomena exhibited by the discoverer during the last few years have been wonderful, almost miraculous, not in the sense of the *supernatural** but of the *superhuman*. Had Keely been permitted to succeed, he might have reduced a whole army to atoms in the space of a few seconds as easily as he reduced a dead ox to the same condition.

The reader is now asked to give a serious attention to that newly-discovered potency which the discoverer has named " Inter-Etheric Force and Forces."

In the humble opinion of the Occultists, as of his immediate friends,

---

* The word "supernatural" implies *above or outside* of nature. Nature and Space are one. Now Space for the metaphysician exists outside of any act of sensation, and is a purely subjective representation ; materialism, which would connect it forcibly with one or the other datum of sensation, notwithstanding. For our senses, *it is fairly subjective* when independent of anything within it. How then can any phenomenon, or anything else, *step outside of or be performed beyond that which has no limits ?* But when spacial extension becomes simply conceptual, and is thought of in an idea connected with certain actions, as by the materialists and the physicists, then again they have hardly a right to define and claim that which can or cannot be produced by Forces generated within even limited spaces, as they have not even an approximate idea of what those forces are.

Mr. Keely, of Philadelphia, was, and still is, at the threshold of some of the greatest secrets of the Universe ; of that chiefly on which is built the whole mystery of physical Forces, and the esoteric significance of the " Mundane Egg " symbolism. Occult philosophy, viewing the manifested and the unmanifested Kosmos as a UNITY, symbolizes the ideal conception of the former by that " Golden Egg " with two poles in it. It is the positive pole that acts in the manifested world of matter, while the negative is lost in the unknowable absolute-ness of SAT—" *Be-ness.*"* Whether this agrees with the philosophy of Mr. Keely, we cannot tell, nor does it really much matter. Never-theless, his ideas about the ethero-material construction of the Universe look strangely like our own, being *in this respect* nearly identical. This is what we find him saying in an able pamphlet compiled by Mrs. Bloomfield-Moore, an American lady of wealth and position, whose incessant efforts in the pursuit of truth can never be too highly appreciated : — " Mr. Keely, in explanation of the working of his engine, says : ' In the conception of any machine heretofore constructed, the medium for inducing a neutral centre has never been found. If it had, the difficulties of perpetual-motion seekers would have ended, and this problem would have become an established and operating fact. It would only require an introductory impulse of a few pounds, on such a device, to cause it to run for centuries, In the conception of my vibratory engine, I did not seek to attain perpetual motion ; but a circuit is formed that actually has *a neutral centre*, which is in a condition to be vivified by my vibratory ether, and, while under operation by said substance, is really a machine that is virtually inde-pendent of the mass (or globe),† and it is the wonderful velocity of the vibratory circuit which makes it so. Still, with all its perfection, it requires to be fed with the vibratory ether to make it an independent motor . . . ."

" All structures require a foundation in strength according to the weight of the mass they have to carry, but the foundations of the universe rest on a vacuous point far more minute than a molecule ; in fact, to express this truth properly, on an *inter-etheric point*, which requires an infinite mind to understand it. To look down into the depths of an etheric centre is precisely the same as it would be to search into the broad space of heaven's ether to find the end, with this difference : that one is the positive field, while the other is the negative field . . . ."

<hr/>

* " It is not correct, when speaking of *idealism*, to show it based upon " the old ontological assumptions that things or entities exist independently of each other, and otherwise than as terms of relations " (Stallo). At any rate, it is incorrect to say so of idealism in Eastern philosophy and *its* cognition, for it is just the reverse.

† Independent, in a certain sense, but not *disconnected* with it.

This, as easily seen, is precisely the Eastern doctrine. His inter-etheric point is the *laya*-point of the Occultists, which, however, does not require "an infinite mind to *understand* it," but only a specific intuition and ability to trace its hiding-place in this world of matter. Of course, the *laya centre* cannot be produced, but an *inter-etheric vacuum* can—as proved in the production of bell-sounds in space. Mr. Keely speaks as an unconscious Occultist, nevertheless, when he remarks in his theory of planetary suspension :—

"As regards planetary volume, we would ask in a scientific point of view, How can the immense difference of volume in the planets exist without dis-organising the harmonious action that has always characterised them ? I can only answer this question properly by entering into a progressive analysis, starting on the rotating etheric centres that were fixed by the Creator* with their attractive or accumulative power. If you ask what power it is that gives to each etheric atom its inconceivable velocity of rotation (or introductory impulse), I must answer that no finite mind will ever be able to conceive what it is. The philosophy of accumulation is the only proof that such a power has been given. The area, if we can so speak, of such an atom, presents to the attractive or magnetic, the elective or propulsive, all the receptive force and all the antagonistic force that characterises a planet of the largest magnitude; consequently, as the accumulation goes on, the perfect equation remains the same. When this minute centre has once been fixed, the power to rend it from its position would necessarily have to be so great as to displace the most immense planet that exists. When this atomic neutral centre is displaced, the planet must go with it. The neutral centre carries the full load of any accumu-lation from the start, and remains the same, for ever balanced in the eternal space."

Mr. Keely illustrates his idea of "a neutral centre" in this way :—

"We will imagine that, after an accumulation of a planet of any diameter, say, 20,000 miles, more or less, for the size has nothing to do with the problem; there should be a displacement of all the material, with the exception of a crust 5,000 miles thick, leaving an intervening void between this crust and a centre of the size of an ordinary billiard ball, it would then require a force as great to move this small central mass as it would to move the shell of 5,000 miles thickness. Moreover, this small central mass would carry the load of this crust for ever, keeping it equidistant; and there could be no opposing power, however great, that could bring them together. The imagination stag-gers in contemplating the immense load which bears upon this point of centre, where weight ceases. . . . This is what we understand by a neutral centre."

And what Occultists understand by a "laya centre."

The above is pronounced "unscientific" by many. But so is every-thing that is not sanctioned and kept on strictly orthodox lines by physical science. Unless the explanation given by the inventor himself is accepted—and his explanations, being, as observed, quite *orthodox* from

---

* "By *Fohat*, more likely," would be an Occultist's reply.

the spiritual and the Occult stand-points, if not from that of material-istic speculative (called *exact*) Science, are therefore ours in this particular—what can science answer to *facts* already seen which it is no longer possible for anyone to deny? Occult philosophy divulges few of its most important vital mysteries. It drops them like precious pearls, one by one, far and wide apart, and only when forced to do so by the evolutionary tidal wave that carries on humanity slowly, silently, but steadily toward the dawn of the Sixth-Race mankind. For once out of the safe custody of their legitimate heirs and keepers, those mysteries cease to be occult: they fall into the public domain and have to run the risk of becoming in the hands of the selfish—of the *Cains* of the human race—curses more often than blessings. Nevertheless, whenever such individuals as the discoverer of *Etheric Force*—John Worrell Keely—men with peculiar psychic and mental capacities* are born, they are generally and more frequently helped than allowed to go unassisted; groping on their way, though, if left to their own resources, falling very soon victims to martyrdom and unscrupulous speculators. Only they are helped *on the condition that they should not become, whether consciously or unconsciously, an additional peril to their age: a danger to the poor,* now offered in daily holocaust by the less wealthy to the very wealthy.† This necessitates a short digression and an explanation.

Some twelve years back, during the Philadelphia Centennial Exhibi-tion, the writer, in answering the earnest queries of a theosophist, one of the earliest admirers of Mr. Keely, repeated to him what she had heard in quarters, information from which she could never doubt.

It had been stated that the inventor of the " Self-Motor " was what is called, in the jargon of the Kabalists, a " *natural-born* magician." That he was and would remain unconscious of the full range of his powers, and would work out merely those which he had found out and ascertained in his own nature—*firstly*, because, attribut-ing them to a wrong source, he could never give them full sway; and

---

* The reason for such psychic capacities is given farther on.

† The above was written two years ago, at a time when hopes of success for the " Keely Motor " were at their highest. What was then said by the writer proved true, in every word, and now only a few remarks are added to it with regard to the failure of his expectations, so far, which has now been admitted by the discoverer himself. Though, however, the word *failure* is here used the reader should understand it in a rela-tive sense, for as Mrs. Bloomfield-Moore explains : " What Mr. Keely does admit is that, baffled in applying vibratory force to mechanics, upon his first and second lines of experimental research, he was obliged either to confess a *commercial* failure, or to try a third departure from his base or principle ; seeking success through another channel."
    . . And this " channel " is on the *physical* plane.

secondly, because it was beyond his power to pass to others that which was *a capacity inherent in his special nature*. Hence the whole secret could not be made over permanently to anyone for practical purposes or use.*

Individuals born with such a capacity are not *very rare*. That they are not heard of more frequently is due to the fact that they live and die, in almost every case, in utter ignorance of being possessed of *abnormal* powers at all. Mr. Keely possesses powers which are called "abnormal" just because they happen in our day to be as little known as blood circulation was before Harvey's time. Blood existed, and it behaved as it does at present in the first man born from woman; and so does that *principle* in man which can control and guide etheric vibratory force. At any rate it exists in all those mortals whose *inner selves* are *primordially connected, by reason of their direct descent, with that group of Dhyan-Chohans* who are called "*the first-born of Ether.*" Mankind, psychically considered, is divided into various groups, each of which is connected with one of the Dhyanic groups that first formed *psychic* man; (*see paragraphs* 1, 2, 3, 4, 5 *in the Commentary to Stanza VII.*) Mr. Keely being greatly favoured in this respect, and moreover, besides his psychic temperament, being intellectually a genius in mechanics, may thus achieve most wonderful results. He has achieved some already—more than any mortal man, *not initiated into the final mysteries*, has achieved in this age up to the present day. What he has done is certainly quite sufficient "to demolish with the hammer of Science the idols of Science"—the idols of matter with the feet of clay—as his friends justly predict and say of him. Nor would the writer for a moment think of contradicting Mrs. Bloomfield-Moore, when in her paper on "Psychic Force and Etheric Force," she states that Mr. Keely, as a philosopher, "is great enough in soul, wise enough in mind, and sublime enough in courage to overcome all difficulties, and to stand at last before the world as the greatest discoverer and inventor in the world."

And again she writes:—"Should Keely do no more than lead scientists from the dreary realms where they are groping into the open field of elemental force, where gravity and cohesion are disturbed in their haunts and diverted to use; where, from unity of origin, emanates infinite energy in diversified forms, he will achieve immortal fame. Should he demonstrate, to the destruction of materialism, that the universe is animated by a mysterious principle to which matter, however perfectly organized, is absolutely subservient, he will be a greater spiritual benefactor to our race than the modern world has yet found in any man. Should he be able to substitute, in the treatment of disease,

---

* We learn that these remarks are not applicable to Mr. Keely's latest discovery; time alone can show the exact limit of his achievements.

the finer forces of nature for the grossly material agencies which have sent more human beings to their graves than war, pestilence and famine combined, he will merit and receive the gratitude of mankind. All this and more will he do, if he and those who have watched his progress, day by day for years, are not too sanguine in their expectations."

Writing in the T. P. S. ("Theosophical Publication Society") series (No. 9), the same lady, in her pamphlet, "Keely's Secrets," brings forward a passage from an article, written a few years ago by the writer of the present volume, in her journal, the *Theosophist*, in these words :—

"The author of No. 5 of the pamphlets issued by the Theosophical Publication Society, 'What is Matter and What is Force,' says therein, 'The men of science have just found out "a fourth state of matter," whereas the Occultists have penetrated years ago beyond the sixth, and therefore do not infer, but know of, the existence of the seventh, the last.' This knowledge comprises one of the secrets of Keely's so-called 'compound secret.' It is already known to many that his secret includes 'the augmentation of energy,' the insulation of the ether, and the adaptation of dynaspheric force to machinery."

It is just because Keely's discovery would lead to a knowledge of one of the most occult secrets, a secret which can never be allowed to fall into the hands of the masses, that his failure to push his discoveries to their logical end seems certain to Occultists. But of this more presently. Even in its limitations this discovery may prove of the greatest benefit. For :—

"Step by step, with a patient perseverance which some day the world will honour, this man of genius has made his researches, overcoming the colossal difficulties which again and again raised up in his path what seemed to be (to all but himself) insurmountable barriers to further progress : but never has the world's index finger so pointed to an hour when all is making ready for the advent of the new form of force that mankind is waiting for. Nature, always reluctant to yield her secrets, is listening to the demands made upon her by her master, necessity, The coal mines of the world cannot long afford the increasing drain made upon them. Steam has reached its utmost limits of power, and does not fulfil the requirements of the age. It knows that its days are numbered. Electricity holds back, with bated breath, dependent upon the approach of her sister colleague. Air ships are riding at anchor, as it were, waiting for the force which is to make aërial navigation something more than a dream. As easily as men communicate with their offices from their homes by means of the telephone, so will the inhabitants of separate continents talk across the ocean. Imagination is palsied when seeking to foresee the grand results of this marvellous discovery, when once it is applied to art and mechanics. In taking the throne which it will force steam to abdicate, dynaspheric force will rule the world with a power so mighty in the interests of civilization, that no finite mind can conjecture the results. Laurence Oliphant, in his preface to 'Scientific Religion,' says : 'A new moral future is dawning upon the human race—one, certainly, of which it stands much in need." In no way could this new moral future be so widely, so universally, commenced as by the utilizing of dynaspheric force to beneficial purposes in life. . . . ."

The Occultists are ready to admit all this with the eloquent writer. Molecular vibration is, undeniably, " Keely's legitimate field of research," and the discoveries made by him will prove wonderful —yet *only in his hands* and *through himself.* The world so far will get but that with which it can be safely entrusted. The truth of this assertion has, perhaps, not yet quite dawned upon the discoverer himself, since he writes that he is absolutely certain that he will accomplish all that he has promised, and will then give it out to the world ; but it must dawn upon him, and at no very far distant date. And what he says in reference to his work is a good proof it :—

" In considering the operation of my engine, the visitor, in order to have even an approximate conception of its *modus operandi*, must discard *all thought of engines that are operated upon the principle of pressure and exhaustion, by the expansion of steam or other analogous gas which impinges upon an abutment, such as the piston of a steam-engine.* My engine has neither piston nor eccentrics, nor is there one grain of pressure exerted in the engine, whatever may be the size or capacity of it.

" My system, in every part and detail, both in the developing of my power and in every branch of its utilization, *is based and founded on sympathetic vibration.* In no other way would it be possible to awaken or develop my force, and equally impossible would it be to operate my engine upon any other principle. . . . . . This, however, is the true system ; and henceforth all my operations will be conducted in this manner—that is to say, my power will be generated, my engines run, my cannon operated, *through a wire.*

" It has been only after years of incessant labour, and the making of almost innumerable experiments, involving not only the construction of a great many most peculiar mechanical structures, and the closest investigation and study of the phenomenal properties of the substance ' ether,' *per se*, produced, that I have been able to dispense with complicated mechanism, and to obtain, as I claim, *mastery over the subtle and strange force with which I am dealing.*"

The passages underlined by us, are those which bear directly on the occult side of the application of the vibratory force, or what Mr. Keely calls " sympathetic vibration." The " wire " is already a step below, or downward from the pure etheric plane into the terrestrial. The discoverer has produced marvels—the word " miracle " is not too strong—when acting through the inter-etheric Force alone, the fifth and sixth principles of Akâsa. From a " generator " six feet long, he has come down to one " no larger than an old-fashioned silver watch ; " and this by itself is a miracle of *mechanical* (but not spiritual) genius. But, as well expressed by his great patroness and defender, Mrs. Bloomfield-Moore, " the two forms of force which he has been experimenting with, and the phenomena attending them, are the very antithesis of each other." One was generated and acted upon by and through himself. No one, who should have repeated the thing done by himself, *could have produced the same results.* It was " Keely's ether " that acted truly, while "Smith's or Brown's " ether would have remained for ever barren of results. For Keely's difficulty has hitherto been to produce a machine which would develop and regulate the " force " without the intervention of any " will power" or personal influence, whether conscious or unconscious of the operator. In this he has failed, so far as others were concerned, for *no one but himself* could operate on his " machines." Occultly this was a far more advanced achievement than the " success " which he anticipates from his " wire," but the results obtained from the *fifth and sixth planes* of the etheric (or Astral) Force, *will never be permitted to serve for purposes of commerce and traffic.* That Keely's organism is directly connected with the production of the marvellous results is proven by the following statement emanating from one who knows the great discoverer intimately.

At one time the shareholders of the " Keely Motor Co. " put a man in his workshop for the express purpose of discovering his secret. After six months of close watching, he said to J. W. Keely one day : " I know how it is done, now." They had been setting up a machine together, and Keely was manipulating the stop-cock which turned the force on and off. " Try it, then," was the answer. The man turned the cock, and nothing came. " Let me see you do it again," the man said to Keely. The latter complied, and the machinery operated at once. Again the other tried, but without success. Then Keely put his hand on his shoulder and told him to try once more. He did so, with the result of an instantaneous production of the current. This fact, if true, settles the question.

We are told that Mr. Keely defines electricity "as a certain form of atomic vibration." In this he is quite right ; but this is electricity on the terrestrial plane, and through terrestrial correlations. He estimates—

Molecular vibrations at	100,000,000 per second.
Inter-molecular ,, ,,	300,000,000 ,, ,,
Atomic ,, ,,	900,000,000 ,, ,,
Inter-atomic ,, ,,	2,700,000,000 ,, ,,
Ætheric ,, ,,	8,100,000,000 ,, ,,
Inter-Ætheric ,, ,,	24,300,000,000 ,, ,,

This proves our point. There are no vibrations that could be counted or even estimated at an *approximate* rate beyond " the realm of the *fourth son of Fohat*," using an occult phraseology, or that motion which corresponds to the formation of Mr. Crookes' radiant matter, or lightly called some years ago the " fourth state of matter "—*on this our plane.*

If the question is asked why Mr. Keely was not allowed to pass a certain limit, the answer is easy; because that which he has unconsciously discovered, is the terrible sidereal Force, known to, and named by the Atlanteans MASH-MAK, and by the Aryan Rishis in their *Ashtar Vidya* by a name that we do not like to give. It is the *vril* of Bulwer Lytton's " Coming Race," and of the coming races of our mankind. The name vril may be a fiction; the Force itself is a fact doubted as little in India as the existence itself of their Rishis, since it is mentioned in all the secret works.

It is this vibratory Force, which, when aimed at an army from an *Agni Rath* fixed on a flying vessel, a balloon, according to the instructions found in *Ashtar Vidya*, reduced to ashes 100,000 men and elephants, as easily as it would a dead rat. It is allegorised in the *Vishnu Purâna*, in the Râmâyana and other works, in the fable about the sage Kapila whose *glance* made a mountain of ashes of King Sagara's 60,000 sons," and which is explained in the esoteric works, and referred to as the *Kapilaksha*—" Kapila's Eye."

And is it this Satanic Force that our generations were to be allowed to add to their stock of Anarchist's baby-toys, known as melenite, dynamite clock-works, explosive oranges, " flower baskets," and such other innocent names? Is it this destructive agency, which, once in the hands of some modern Attila, *e.g.*, a blood-thirsty anarchist, would reduce Europe in a few days to its primitive chaotic state with no man left alive to tell the tale—is this force to become the common property of all men alike?

What Mr. Keely has already done is grand and wonderful in the extreme; there is enough work before him in the demonstration of his new system to " humble the pride of those scientists who are materialistic, by revealing those mysteries which lie behind the world of matter," without revealing it *nolens volens* to all. For surely Psychists and Spiritualists—of whom there are a good number in the European armies—would be the first to experience personally the fruits of such mysteries revealed. Thousands of them would find themselves (and perhaps with the populations of whole countries to keep them company) in blue Ether very soon, were such a Force to be even entirely discovered, let alone made publicly known. The discovery in its completeness is by several thousand—or shall we say hundred thousand?—years *too premature*. It will be at its appointed place and time only when the great roaring flood of starvation, misery, and underpaid labour ebbs back again—as it will when happily at last the just demands of the many are attended to; when the proletariat exists but in name, and the pitiful cry for bread, that rings throughout the world unheeded, has died away. This may be hastened by the spread of learning, and by new openings for work and emigration, with better prospects than exist now, *and on some new continent that may appear.* Then only will " Keely's Motor and Force," as *originally contemplated* by himself and friends, be in demand, because *it will be more needed by the poor than by the wealthy.*

Meanwhile the force discovered by him will work through *wires,* and this, if he succeeds, will be quite sufficient in the present generation to make of him the greatest discoverer of this age.

What Mr. Keely says of *Sound and Colour* is also correct from the Occult stand-point. Hear him talk as though he were the nursling of the " Gods-revealers," and had gazed all his life into the depths of Father-Mother Æther.

In comparing the tenuity of the atmosphere with that of the etheric flows, obtained by him from his invention for breaking up the molecules of air by vibration, Keely says that :—

. . . " It is as platina to hydrogen gas. Molecular separation of air brings us to the first sub-division only ; inter-molecular, to the second ; atomic, to the third ; inter-atomic, to the fourth ; etheric, to the fifth ; and inter-etheric, to the sixth sub-division, or positive association with luminiferous ether.* In my introductory argument I have contended that this is the vibratory envelope of all atoms. In my definition of atom I do not confine myself to the *sixth* sub-division where this luminiferous ether is developed in its crude form as far as my researches prove.† I think this idea will be pronounced by the physicists of the present day, a wild freak of the imagination. Possibly, in time, a light may fall upon this theory that will bring its simplicity forward for scientific research. At present I can only compare it to some planet in a dark space, where the light of the sun of science has not yet reached it. . ."

" I assume that sound, like odour, is a real substance of unknown and wonderful tenuity, emanating from a body where it has been induced by percussion and throwing out absolute corpuscles of matter, inter-atomic particles, with velocity of 1,120 feet per second ; in vacuo 20,000. The substance which is thus disseminated is a part and parcel of the mass agitated, and, if kept under this agitation continuously, would, in the course of a certain cycle of time, become thoroughly absorbed by the atmosphere ; or, more truly, would pass through the atmosphere to an elevated point of tenuity corresponding to the condition of sub-division that governs its liberation from its parent body." . . .

" The sounds from vibratory forks, set so as to produce etheric chords, while disseminating their tones (compound), permeate most thoroughly all substances that come under the range of their atomic bombardment. The clapping of a bell *in vacuo* liberates these atoms with the same velocity and volume as one in the open air ; and were the agitation of the bell kept up continuously for a few millions of centuries it would

* This also is the division, made by the Occultists, under other names.

† Quite so, since there is the *seventh* beyond, which begins the same enumeration rom the first to the last, on another and higher plane.

thoroughly return to its primitive element; and, if the chamber were hermetically sealed, and strong enough, the vacuous volume surrounding the bell
would be brought to a pressure of many thousands of pounds to the square
inch, by the tenuous substance evolved. In my estimation, sound truly
defined is the disturbance of atomic equilibrium, rupturing actual atomic
corpuscles; and the substance thus liberated must certainly be a certain
order of etheric flow. Under these conditions, is it unreasonable to suppose
that, if this flow were kept up, and the body thus robbed of its element, it
would in time disappear entirely? All bodies are formed primitively from this
highly tenuous ether, animal, vegetable, and mineral, and they are only returned
to their high gaseous condition when brought under a state of differential
equilibrium." . . .

"As regards odour, we can only get some definite idea of its extreme and
wondrous tenuity by taking into consideration that a large area of atmosphere
can be impregnated for a long series of years from a single grain of musk;
which, if weighed after that long interval, will be found to be not appreciably
diminished. The great paradox attending the flow of odorous particles is that
they can be held under confinement in a glass vessel! Here is a substance of much
higher tenuity than the glass that holds it, and yet it cannot escape. It is as a
sieve with its meshes large enough to pass marbles, and yet holding fine sand
which cannot pass through; in fact, a molecular vessel holding an atomic substance. This is a problem that would confound those who stop to recognize it.
But infinitely tenuous as odour is, it holds a very crude relation to the substance of
sub-division that governs a magnetic flow (a flow of sympathy, if you please
to call it so). This sub-division comes next to sound, but is above sound. The
action of the flow of a magnet coincides somewhat to the receiving and distri-
buting portion of the human brain, giving off at all times a depreciating ratio
of the amount received. It is a grand illustration of the control of mind over
matter, which gradually depreciates the physical till dissolution takes place.
The magnet on the same ratio gradually loses its power and becomes inert. If
the relations that exist between mind and matter could be equated and so held,
we would live on in our physical state eternally, as there would be no physical
depreciation. But this physical depreciation leads, at its terminus, to the
source of a much higher development—viz., the liberation of the pure ether
from the crude molecular; which, in my estimation, is to be much desired."
—(From Mrs. Bloomfield-Moore's paper, "*The New Philosophy*.")

It may be remarked that, save a few small divergencies, no Adept
nor Alchemist could have explained the above *any better, in the light of
modern Science*, however much the latter may protest against the novel
views. This is, in all its fundamental principles, if not details, *Occultism
pure and simple*, yet withal, modern *natural philosophy* as well.

This "New Force," or whatever Science may call it, the effects of
which are undeniable—admitted by more than one naturalist and
physicist who has visited Mr. Keely's laboratory and witnessed
personally its tremendous effects—what is it? Is it a "mode of
motion," also, "*in Vacuo*," since there is no matter to generate it except
Sound—another "mode of motion," no doubt, a *sensation* caused like

colour by vibrations? Fully as we believe in these vibrations as the proximate—the immediate—cause of such sensations, we as absolutely reject the one-sided scientific theory that there is *no factor* to be considered as external to us, other than etheric or atmospheric vibrations.*

There *is* a *transcendental* set of causes put in motion—so to speak—in the occurrence of these phenomena, which, *not being in relation to our narrow range of cognition*, can only be traced to their source and their nature, and understood by the Spiritual faculties of the Adept. They are, as Asclepios puts it to the King, "incorporeal corporealities"—such as "appear in the mirror," and "abstract forms" that *we see, hear, and smell*, in our dreams, and visions. What have the "modes of motion," light, and ether to do with these? Yet we see, hear, and smell, and touch them, *ergo* they are as much *realities* to us in our dreams, as any other thing on this plane of Maya.

XI.

ON THE ELEMENTS AND ATOMS,

FROM THE STAND-POINT OF SCIENCE AND THAT OF OCCULTISM.

WHEN the Occultist speaks of "Elements," and of human Beings who lived during those geological ages, the duration of which it is found as impossible to determine, according to the opinion of one of the best

---

* In this case the American "Substantialists" are not wrong (though too anthropomorphic and material in their views to be accepted by the Occultists) when arguing through Mrs. M. S. Organ, M.D., that "there must be positive entitative properties in objects which have a constitutional relation to the nerves of animal sensations, or there can be no perception. No impression *of any kind can be made* upon brain, nerve, or mind—no stimulus to action—unless there is an actual and direct communication of a substantial force." ("Substantial" as far as it appears in the usual sense of the word in this universe of *illusion* and MAYA, of course; not so *in reality*.) "That force may be the most refined and sublimated immaterial Entity (?). Yet it must exist; for no sense, element, or faculty of the human being can have a perception, or be stimulated into action, without some substantial force coming in contact with it. This is the fundamental law pervading the whole organic and mental world. In the true philosophical sense there is no such thing as independent action: for every force or substance is correlated to some other force or substance. We can with just as much truth and reason assert that no substance possesses any inherent gustatory property or any olfactory property—that taste and odour are simply sensations caused by vibrations; and hence mere illusions of animal perceptions. . . ."

English geologists*, as the nature of matter, it is because he knows
what he is talking about. When he says " Man " and Elements, he
neither means "man" in his present physiological and anthropological
form, nor the elemental atoms, those hypothetical conceptions, the
entitative abstractions of matter in its highly attenuated state, as existing at present in scientific minds; nor, again, the compound Elements
of antiquity. In Occultism the word *Element* means " rudiment " in
every case. When we say " Elementary Man," we mean either the
proëmial, incipient sketch of man, in its unfinished and undeveloped
condition, hence in that form which now lies latent in physical man
during his life-time, and takes shape only occasionally and under certain
conditions; or that form which for a time survives the material body,
and which is better known as an " Elementary."† With regard to
" Element," when the term is used metaphysically, it means, in distinction to the mortal, the incipient *divine* man; and, in its physical usage,
inchoate matter in its first undifferentiated condition, or in the *laya*
state, which is the eternal and the *normal* condition of substance, differentiating only periodically, and is during that differentiation in an
abnormal state—in other words, a transitory illusion of the senses.

As to the " elemental atoms," so called, the Occultists refer to them
by that name with a meaning analogous to that which is given by
the Hindu to Brahmâ when he calls him Anu, the " Atom." Every
elemental *atom*, in search of which more than one Chemist has followed
the path indicated by the Alchemists, is, in their firm belief (when not
knowledge), a soul; not necessarily a disembodied soul, but a *jiva*, as the
Hindus call it, a centre of POTENTIAL VITALITY, with latent intelligence
in it, and, in the case of compound Souls—an intelligent active EXIST-
ENCE, from the highest to the lowest order, a form composed of more or
less differentiations. It requires a metaphysician—and an Eastern
metaphysician—to understand our meaning. All those atom-Souls are
differentiations from the ONE, and in the same relation to it as the
divine Soul—the Buddhi—to its informing and inseparable Spirit, or
Atman.

Modern physics, while borrowing from the ancients their atomic
theory, forgot one point, the most important of the doctrine; hence they
got only the husks and will never be able to get at the kernel. They
left behind, in the adoption of physical atoms, the suggestive fact that

---

* In answer to a friend, that eminent geologist writes: .... " I can only say, in reply
to your letter, that it is at present, and perhaps always will be, IMPOSSIBLE to reduce,
even approximately, geological time into years, or even into millenniums." (Signed
William Pengelly, F.R.S.

† Plato speaking of the irrational, turbulent Elements " composed of fire, air, water,
and earth," means Elementary Dæmons. (See *Timæus*.)

from Anaxagoras down to Epicurus, the Roman Lucretius, and finally
even to Galileo, all those Philosophers believed more or less in ANIMATED
atoms, not in invisible specks of so-called "brute" matter. Rotatory
motion was generated in their views, by larger (read, more divine and
pure) atoms forcing downwards other atoms; the lighter ones being
thrust simultaneously upward. The esoteric meaning of this is the ever
cyclic curve downward and upward of differentiated elements through
intercyclic phases of existence, until each reaches again its starting
point or birthplace. The idea was metaphysical as well as physical;
the hidden interpretation embracing "gods" or souls, in the shape of
atoms, as the *causes* of all the *effects* produced on Earth by the *secretions*
from the divine bodies.* No ancient philosopher, not even the Jewish
Kabalists, ever dissociated Spirit from matter or *vice versâ*. Everything
originated in the ONE, and, proceeding from the one, must finally return
to the One. "Light becomes heat, and consolidates into fiery particles;
which, from being ignited, become cold, hard particles, round and smooth.
And this is called *Soul*, imprisoned in its robe of matter;" † *Atoms* and
Souls having been synonymous in the language of the Initiates. The
"whirling Souls," *Gilgoolem*, a doctrine in which so many learned Jews
have believed *(See Mackenzie's Royal Masonic Cyclopædia)*, had no other
meaning esoterically. The learned Jewish Initiates never meant by the
"Promised land" Palestine alone, but the same *Nirvana* as the learned
Buddhist and Brahmin do—the bosom of the ETERNAL ONE, symbolized
by that of Abraham, and by Palestine as its substitute on Earth.‡ The
passage of the SOUL-ATOM "through the Seven Planetary Chambers"
had the same metaphysical and also physical meaning. It had the
latter when it was said to *dissolve into Ether (See Isis Unveiled*, Vol. I., p.
297.) Even Epicurus, the *model Atheist* and materialist, knew and
believed so much in the ancient Wisdom, that he taught that the

---

* Plato uses the words "*secretions*" of turbulent Elements *(Timæus)*.

† Valentinus' *Esoteric Treatise on the Doctrine of Gilgul*.

‡ Surely no *educated* Jew ever believed the *literal* sense of this allegory—namely, that
"the bodies of Jews deposited in foreign lands contain within them a principle of Soul
which cannot rest, until by a process called the "whirling of the Soul" the immortal
particle reaches once more the sacred Soil of the "Promised land." The meaning is
evident to an occultist. The process was supposed to be accomplished by a kind of
metempsychosis, the psychic spark being conveyed through bird, beast, fish, and the
most minute insect. *(See Royal Masonic Cyclo. Mackenzie.)* The Allegory relates *to the
atoms of the body*, which have each to pass through every form before all reach the *final*
state, which is the first starting point of the departure of every atom—its primitive
aya State. But the primitive meaning of *Gilgoolem*, or "Revolution of Souls," was the
idea of the re-incarnating Souls or *Egos*. "All the Souls go into the *gilgoolah*," into a
cyclic or revolving process; *i.e.*, they all proceed on the cyclic path of re-births. Some
Kabalists interpret this doctrine to mean only a kind of purgatory for the souls of the
wicked. But this is not so.

Soul (entirely distinct from immortal Spirit when the former is enshrined *latent* in it, as it is in every atomic speck), was composed of a fine, tender essence, formed from the *smoothest, roundest, and finest atoms.*

And this shows that the ancient Initiates, who were followed more or less closely by all profane antiquity, meant by the term "ATOM," a Soul, a Genius or Angel, the first-born of the ever-concealed CAUSE of all causes; and in this sense their teachings become comprehensible. They claimed, as do their successors, the existence of Gods and Genii, angels or "demons," not outside, or independent of, the Universal *Plenum*, but within it. Only this *Plenum*, during the life-cycles, is infinite. They admitted and taught a good deal of that which modern Science teaches now—namely, the existence of a primordial " World-stuff or Cosmic Substance," from which worlds are formed, ever and eternally homogeneous, except during its periodic existence, when it differentiates its universal diffusion throughout infinite space; and the gradual formation of sidereal bodies from it. They taught the revolution of the Heavens, the Earth's rotation, the Heliocentric System, and the Atomic Vortices—Atoms—in reality Souls and intelligences. But those "Atomists" were spiritual, most trancendental, and philosophical Pantheists. It is not they who would have ever conceived, or dreamt that monstrous contrasted progeny, the nightmare of our modern civilized Race; namely—*inanimate* material, self-guiding atoms, on the one hand, and an extra-Cosmic God on the other.

It may be useful to show what, in the teachings of the old Initiates, the Monad was, and what its origin.

Modern exact Science, as soon as it began to grow out of its teens, perceived the great, and, to it, hitherto *esoteric* axiom, that nothing—whether in the spiritual, psychic, or physical realm of being—could come into existence out of nothing. There is no cause in the manifested universe without its adequate effects, whether in space or time; nor can there be an effect without its primal cause, which itself owes its existence to a still higher one—the final and absolute cause having to remain to man for ever an incomprehensible CAUSELESS CAUSE. But even this is no solution, and must be viewed, if at all, from the highest philo-sophical and metaphysical standpoints, otherwise the problem had better be left unapproached. It is an abstraction, on the verge of which human reason—however trained to metaphysical subtleties—trembles, threatening to collapse. This may be demonstrated to any European who would undertake to solve the problem of existence by the articles of faith of the true Vedantin, for instance. Let him read and study the sublime teachings on the subject of Soul and Spirit, of

Sankarâchârya (*Viveka Chudâmani*)*, and the reader will realize what is now said.

While the Christian is taught that the human soul is a breath of God—being created by him for sempiternal existence, *i.e.*, having a beginning, *but no end* (and therefore never to be called eternal)—the Occult teaching says, "*Nothing is created, but is only transformed.* Nothing can manifest itself in this universe—from a globe down to a vague, rapid thought—that was not in the universe already; everything on the subjective plane is an eternal IS; as everything on the objective plane is an *ever becoming*—because transitory."

The monad—a truly "indivisible thing," as defined by Good, who did not give it the sense we now do—is here rendered as the *Atma* in conjunction with *Buddhi* and the higher Manas. This trinity is one and eternal, the latter being absorbed in the former at the termination of all conditioned and *illusive* life. The monad, then, can be traced through the course of its pilgrimage and its changes of transitory vehicles only from the incipient stage of the manifested Universe. In Pralaya, or the intermediate period between two manvantaras, it loses its name, as it loses it when the real ONE self of man merges *into Brahm* in cases of high Samadhi (the *Turiya* state) or final Nirvana; "when the disciple" in the words of Sankara, "having attained that primeval consciousness, absolute bliss, of which the nature is truth, which is without form and action, abandons this illusive body that has been assumed by the *atma* just as an actor (abandons) the dress (put on)." For Buddhi (the *Anandamaya sheath*) is but a mirror which *reflects* absolute bliss; and, moreover, *that reflection* itself is yet not free from ignorance, and is *not* the Supreme Spirit, being subject to conditions, being a spiritual modification of Prakriti, and an effect; *Atma* alone is the one real and eternal substratum of all—the essence and absolute knowledge—the *Kshetragna*.† It is called in the Esoteric philosophy "the One Witness,"

---

* Translated for the *Theosophist*, by Mohini M. Chatterji as "Crest Jewel of Wisdom," 1886. (See *Theosophist*, July and August numbers).

† Now that the revised version of the gospels has been published and the most glaring mistranslations of the old versions are corrected, one will understand better the words in St. John v., vi., and vii. : " It is the Spirit that beareth *witness* because the Spirit is the truth." The words that follow in the mistranslated version about the " three witnesses,"—hitherto supposed to stand for " the Father, the Word, and the Holy Ghost "—show the real meaning of the writer (St. John) very clearly, thus still more forcibly identifying his teaching in this respect with that of Sankarâchârya. For what can the sentence, " there are three who bear witness : the Spirit and the *Water* and the *Blood* "—mean, if they bear no relation to, or connection with, the more philosophical statement of the great Vedanta teacher, who, speaking of the *sheaths* (the *principles* in man) *Jiva*, *Vignanamaya*, etc., which *are*, in their physical manifestation, " *water* and *blood* " or life, adds that atma (spirit) alone is what remains after the

and, while it rests in Devachan, is referred to as "the Three Witnesses to Karma."

Atma (our seventh principle) being identical with the universal Spirit, and man being one with it in his essence, what is then the Monad proper? It is that homogeneous spark which radiates in millions of rays from the primeval "Seven;"—of which seven further on. It is *the* EMANATING *spark from the* UNCREATED *Ray*—a mystery. In the esoteric, and even exoteric Buddhism of the North, Adi Buddha (*Chogi dangpoi sangye*), the One unknown, without beginning or end, identical with Parabrahm and Ain-Soph, emits a bright ray from its darkness.

This is the *Logos* (the first), or Vajradhara, the Supreme Buddha (also called *Dorjechang*). As the Lord of all Mysteries he cannot manifest, but sends into the world of manifestation his heart—the "diamond heart," Vajrasattva (*Dorjesempa*). This is the second *logos* of creation, from whom emanate the seven (in the exoteric blind the five) Dhyani Buddhas, called the Anupadaka, "the parentless." These Buddhas are the primeval monads from the world of *incorporeal being*, the *Arupa* world, wherein the Intelligences (on that plane only) have neither shape nor name, in the exoteric system, but have their distinct seven names in esoteric philosophy. These Dhyani Buddhas emanate, or create from themselves, by virtue of Dhyana, celestial Selves—the *super*-human Bodhisattvas. These incarnating at the beginning of every human cycle on earth as mortal men, become occasionally, owing to their personal merit, Bodhisattvas among the Sons of Humanity, after which they may re-appear as *Manushi* (human) Buddhas. The Anupadaka (or Dhyani-Buddhas) are thus identical with the Brahminical *Manasaputra*, "mind-born sons"—whether of Brahmâ or either of the other two Trimurtian Hypostases, hence identical also with the Rishis and Prajâpatis. Thus, a passage is found in *Anugîtâ*, which, read esoterically, shows plainly, though under another imagery, the same idea and system. It says: "Whatever entities there are in this world, moveable or immoveable, they are the very first to be dissolved (at *pralaya*); and next the developments produced from the elements (from which the visible Universe is fashioned); and, after these developments (evolved entities), all the elements. Such is the upperward gradation among entities. Gods, Men, Gandharvas, Pisâchas, Asuras, Râkshasas, all have been created by Svabhâva (Prakriti, or plastic nature), not by actions, nor by a cause"—*i.e.*, not by any physical cause.

"These Brâhmanas (the Rishi Prajâpati?), the creators of the world, are born here (on earth) again and again. Whatever is produced from

---

subtraction of the sheaths and that it is the ONLY *witness*, or synthesized unity. The less spiritual and philosophical school, solely with an eye to a trinity made three witnesses out of "one," thus connecting it more with earth than with heaven.

them is dissolved in due time in those very five great elements (the five, or rather seven, Dhyani Buddhas, also called " Elements " of Mankind), like billows in the ocean. These great elements are in every way beyond the elements that make up the world (the gross elements). And he who is released even from these five elements (the tanmâtras)* goes to the highest goal." " The Lord Prajâpati (Brahmâ) created all this by the mind only," *i.e.*, by *Dhyana*, or abstract meditation and mystic powers like the Dhyani Buddhas (*vide supra*). Evidently then, these " Brâhmanas" are identical with the Bodhisattvas (the terrestrial) of the heavenly Dhyani Buddhas. Both, as primordial, intelligent " Elements," become the *creators* or the *emanators* of the monads destined to become human in that cycle; after which they evolve themselves, or, so to say, expand into their own *selves* as Bodhisattvas or Brâhmanas, in heaven and earth, to become at last simple men—" the creators of the world *are born here, on earth again and again* "—truly. In the Northern Buddhist system, or the popular exoteric religion, it is taught that every Buddha, while preaching the good law on earth, manifests himself simultaneously in three worlds: in the formless, as Dhyani Buddha, in the World of forms, as a Bodhisattva, and in the world of desire, the lowest (or our world) as a man. Esoterically the teaching differs: The divine, purely Adi-Buddhic *monad* manifests as the universal Buddhi (the *Mahâbuddhi* or Mahat in Hindu philosophies) the spiritual, omniscient and omnipotent root of divine intelligence, the highest *anima mundi* or the Logos. *This* descends " like a flame spreading from the eternal Fire, immoveable, without increase or decrease, ever the same to the end " of the cycle of existence, and becomes universal life on the Mundane Plane. From this Plane of *conscious* Life shoot out, like seven fiery tongues, the Sons of Light (the *logoi* of Life); then the Dhyani-Buddhas of contemplation: the concrete forms of their formless Fathers — the Seven Sons of Light, *still themselves*, to whom may be applied the Brahmanical mystic phrase: " Thou art ' THAT'—*Brahm.*" It is from these Dhyani-Buddhas that emanate their *chhayas* (Shadows) the Bodhisattvas of the celestial realms, the prototypes of the *super*-terrestrial Bodhisattvas, and of the terrestrial Buddhas, and finally of men. The " Seven Sons of Light " are also called " Stars."

The star under which a human Entity is born, says the Occult teaching, will remain for ever its star, throughout the whole cycle of its incarnations in one Manvantara. But *this is not his astrological star*. The latter is concerned and connected with the *personality*, the former with

* The Tanmâtras are literally the type or rudiment of an element devoid of qualities; but esoterically, they are the primeval *noumenoi* of that which becomes in the progress of evolution a Cosmic element in the sense given to the term in antiquity, not in that of physics. They are the logoi, the seven emanations or rays of the logos.

the INDIVIDUALITY. The " Angel " of that Star, or the Dhyani-Buddha will be either the guiding or simply the presiding " Angel," so to say, in every new rebirth of the monad, *which is part of his own essence*, through his vehicle, man, may remain for ever ignorant of this fact. The adepts have each their Dhyani-Buddha, their elder " twin Soul," and they know it, calling it " Father-Soul," and " Father-Fire." It is only at the last and supreme initiation, however, that they learn it when placed face to face with the bright " Image." How much has Bulwer Lytton known of this mystic fact when describing, in one of his highest inspirational moods, Zanoni face to face with his *Augoeides* ?

The *Logos*, or both the unmanifested and the manifested WORD, is called by the Hindus, Iswara, "the Lord," though the Occultists give it another name. Iswara, say the Vedantins, is the highest consciousness in nature. "This highest consciousness," answer the Occultists, "is only a *synthetic unit* in the world of the manifested Logos —or on the *plane of illusion;* for it is the sum total of Dhyan-Chohanic *consciousnesses.*" " Oh, wise man, remove the conception *that not-Spirit is Spirit*," says Sankaráchárya. Atma is *not-Spirit* in its final Parabrahmic state, *Iswara* or *Logos* is Spirit ; or, as Occultism explains, it is a compound unity of manifested living Spirits, the parent-source and nursery of all the mundane and terrestrial monads, *plus* their *divine* reflection, which emanate from, and return into, the Logos, each in the culmination of its time. There are seven chief groups of such Dhyan Chohans, which groups will be found and recognised in every religion, for they are the primeval SEVEN Rays. Humanity, occultism teaches us, is divided into seven distinct groups and their sub-divisions, mental, spiritual, and physical.* The monad, then, viewed as ONE, is above the seventh principle (in Kosmos and man), and as a triad, it is the direct radiant progeny of the said *compound* UNIT, not the breath (and special *creation* out of *nihil*) of " God," as that unit is called ; for such an idea is quite unphilosophical, and degrades Deity, dragging it down to a finite, attributive condition. As well expressed by the translator of the " Crest-Jewel of Wisdom "—though *Iswara* is " God " " unchanged in the profoundest depths of *pralayas* and in the intensest activity of the *manvantaras* " . . ., still " *beyond* (him) is

---

* Hence the seven chief planets, the *spheres* of the indwelling seven spirits, under each of which is born one of the human groups which is guided and influenced thereby. There are only seven planets (*specially* connected with earth), and twelve houses, but the possible combinations of their aspects are countless. As each planet can stand to each of the others in twelve different aspects, their combinations must, therefore, be almost infinite; as infinite, in fact, as the spiritual, psychic, mental, and physical capacities in the numberless varieties of the *genus homo*, each of which varieties is born under one of the seven planets and one of the said countless planetary combinations. See *Theosophist*, for August, 1886.

' ATMA,' round whose pavilion is the darkness of eternal MAYA."* The "triads" born under the same Parent-planet, or rather the *radiations* of one and the same Planetary Spirit (Dhyani Buddha) are, in all their after lives and rebirths, sister, or " *twin*-souls," on this Earth.†

This was known to every high Initiate in every age and in every country : " I and my Father are one," said Jesus (John x. 30).‡ When He is made to say, elsewhere (xx. 17) : " I ascend to *my* Father and your Father," it meant that which has just been stated. It was simply to show that the group of his disciples and followers attracted to Him belonged to the same Dhyani Buddha, " Star," or " Father," again of the same planetary realm and division as He did. It is the *knowledge* of this occult doctrine that found expression in the review of " The Idyll of the White Lotus," when Mr. T. Subba Row wrote : " Every Buddha meets at his last initiation all the great adepts who reached Buddhahood during the preceding ages . . . every class of adepts has its own bond of spiritual communion which knits them together. . . . . The only possible and effectual way of entering into such brotherhood . . . . is by bringing oneself within the influence of the Spiritual light which radiates *from one's own Logos.* I may further point out here . . . . that such communion is only possible *between persons whose souls derive their life and sustenance from the same divine* RAY, and that, as seven distinct rays radiate from the ' Central Spiritual Sun,' *all adepts and Dhyan Chohans are divisible into seven classes,* each of which is guided, controlled, and overshadowed *by one of the seven forms* or manifestations of the divine Wisdom." *(" Theosophist,"* Aug., 1886.)

---

* The now universal error of attributing to the ancients the knowledge of only seven planets, simply because they mentioned no others, is based on the same general ignorance of their occult doctrines. The question is not whether they were, or were not, aware of the existence of the later discovered planets ; but whether the reverence paid by them to the four exoteric and three secret great gods—the star-angels, had not some special reason. The writer ventures to say there was such a reason, and it is this. Had they known of as many planets as we do now (and this question can hardly be decided at present, either way), "they would have still connected with their religious worship only the seven, because these seven are directly and specially connected with our earth, or, using esoteric phraseology, with our septenary ring of spheres. (See *supra.*)

† It is the same, only still more metaphysical idea, as that of the Christian Trinity— " Three in One "—*i.e.*, the Universal " over-Spirit," manifesting on the two higher planes, those of Buddhi and Mahat ; and these are the three hypostases, metaphysical, but *never personal.*

‡ The identity, and at the same time the illusive differentiation of the *Angel*-Monad and the *Human*-Monad is shown by the following sentences : " My Father is *greater* than I " (John xiv. 26) ; " Glorify *your* Father *who is in Heaven* " (Matt. v. 16) ; " The righteous will *shine* in the kingdom of *their* Father " (not *our* Father) (Matt. xiii. 43) " Know ye not ye are a *temple* of God, and that the *Spirit of God dwelleth* in you ? (1 Cor. iii. 16) ; " I *ascend* to my Father," etc., etc.

It is then the " Seven Sons of Light "—called after their planets and (by the rabble) often identified with them—namely Saturn, Jupiter, Mercury, Mars, Venus, and—*presumably* for the modern critic, who goes no deeper than the surface of old religions *—the Sun and Moon, which are, according to the Occult teachings, our heavenly Parents, or " Father," synthetically. Hence, as already remarked, polytheism is really more philosophical and correct, as to fact and nature, than anthropomorphic monotheism. Saturn, Jupiter, Mercury, and Venus, the four exoteric planets, and the three others, which must remain un-named, were the heavenly bodies in direct astral and psychic com-munication with the Earth, its Guides, and Watchers—morally and physically ; the visible orbs furnishing our Humanity with its outward and inward characteristics, and their " Regents " or *Rectors* with our Monads and spiritual faculties. In order to avoid creating new mis-conceptions, let it be stated that among the three *secret* orbs (or star-angels) neither Uranus nor Neptune entered ; not only because they were unknown under these names to the ancient Sages, but because they, as all other planets, however many there may be, are the *gods* and guardians of other septenary chains of globes within our systems.

Nor do the two last discovered great planets depend entirely on the Sun like the rest of the planets. Otherwise, how explain the fact that Neptune receives 900 times less light than our Earth, and Uranus 390 times less, and that their satellites show a peculiarity of inverse rotation found in no other planets of the Solar System. At any rate, what we say applies to Uranus, though recently the fact begins again to be disputed.

This subject will, of course, be considered mere vagary by all those who confuse the universal order of being with their own systems of classification. Here, however, simple facts from Occult teachings are stated, to be either accepted or rejected, as the case may be. There are details which, on account of their great metaphysical abstractions, *cannot* be entered upon. Hence, we merely state that only seven of our planets are as intimately related to our globe, as the Sun is to all

---

* These are planets accepted for purposes of judicial astrology only. The astro-theogonical division differed from this one. The Sun, being a central *star* and no planet, stands in more occult and mysterious relations with *its* seven planets of *our* globe than is generally known. The Sun was, therefore, considered the great Father of all the Seven " Fathers," which accounts for the variations found between *seven* and *eight* great gods of the Chaldean and other countries. Neither the earth nor the moon —its satellite—nor yet stars, for another reason—were anything else than *substitutes for esoteric purposes*. Yet, even with the Sun and the Moon thrown out of the calcula-tion, the ancients seem to have known of *seven* planets. How many more are known to us, so far, if we throw out the Earth and Moon ? *Seven*, and no more : Seven primary or principal planets, the rest *planetoids* rather than planets.

the bodies subject to him in his system. Of these bodies the poor little number of *primary* and *secondary* planets known to astronomy, looks wretched enough, in truth.* Therefore, it stands to reason that there are a great number of planets, small and large, that have not been discovered yet, but of the existence of which ancient astronomers—al of them initiated adepts—must have certainly been aware. But, as their relation to the gods was sacred, it had to remain arcane, as also the names of various other planets and stars.

Besides which, even the Roman Catholic theology speaks of " *seventy* planets that preside over the destinies of the nations of this globe ;" and, save the erroneous application, there is more truth in this tradition than in exact modern astronomy. The seventy planets are connected with the *seventy* elders of the people of Israel *(Numb.* 11, 16) because the *regents* of these planets are meant, not the orbs themselves ; and the word seventy is a play and a *blind* upon the 7 × 7 of the subdivisions. Each people and nation, as said already, has its *direct* Watcher, Guardian and Father in Heaven—a Planetary Spirit. We are willing to leave their own national God, Jehovah, to the descendants of Israel, the worshippers of *Sabaoth* or SATURN ; for, indeed, the *monads* of the people chosen by him are his own, and the Bible has never made a secret of it. Only the text of the English (Protestant) Bible is, in dis- agreement, as usual, with those of the Septuagint and the Vulgate. Thus, while in the former one reads *(in Deuter.* xxxii., 8 *and* 9) "When the MOST HIGH (not Jehovah) divided to the nations their inheritance . . . he set the bounds of the people according to the number of the children of Israel," in the *Septuagint* the text reads " according *to the number of the Angels* " (Planet-Angels), which is more concordant with truth and fact. Moreover, all the texts agree that " the Lord's (Jehovah) *portion* is his people ; Jacob *is* the lot of *his* inheritance " (Deut. xxxii. 9) ; and this settles the question. The " Lord " Jehovah took *for his portion* Israel—what have other nations to do with that particular *national* Deity ? Let then, the " angel Gabriel " watch over Iran and " Mikael-Jehovah " over the Hebrews. These are not the gods of other nations, and it is difficult to see why Christians

---

* When one remembers that under the powerful telescope of Sir W. Herschell, that eminent astronomer, gauging merely that portion of heaven in the equatorial plane, the approximate centre of which is occupied by our Earth—saw pass in one quarter of an hour, 16,000 stars ; and applying this calculation to the totality of the " Milky Way " he found in it no less than 18 (eighteen) millions of SUNS—one wonders no longer that Laplace, in conversation with Napoleon I. should have called God a HYPOTHESIS—perfectly useless to speculate upon for *exact* physical Science, at any rate. Occult metaphysics and transcendental philosophy will alone be able to lift the smallest corner of the impenetrable veil in this direction.

should have selected a god against whose commandments Jesus was the first one to rise in rebellion.

The Planetary origin of the Monad (Soul) and of its faculties was taught by the Gnostics. On its way to the Earth, as on its way back from the Earth, each soul born in, and from, the " Boundless Light,"* had to pass through the seven planetary regions both ways. The pure Dhyani and Devas of the oldest religions had become, in course of time, with the Zoroastrians, the Seven Devs, the ministers of Ahriman, " each chained to his planet " (see *Origen's Copy of the Chart*); with the Brahmins, the Asuras and some of its Rishis—good, bad and indifferent; and among the Egyptian Gnostics it was *Thoth* or (Hermes) who was the chief of the seven whose names are given by Origen as *Adonai*, genius of the Sun; *Tao*, of the Moon; *Eloi*, of Jupiter; *Sabao*, of Mars; *Orai*, of Venus; *Astaphai*, of Mercury; and *Ildabaoth* (Jehovah), of Saturn. Finally, the *Pistis-Sophia*, which the greatest modern authority on *exoteric* Gnostic beliefs, the late Mr. C. W. King, refers to as "that precious monument of Gnosticism,"—this old document echoes, while distorting it to sectarian purposes, the archaic belief of the ages. The Astral Rulers of the Spheres (the planets) create the monads (the Souls) from their own substance out of the tears of their eyes, and the sweat of their torments," endowing the monads with a spark of the Divine Light, which is their substance. It will be shown in Book II. why these " Lords of the Zodiac and Spheres " have been transformed by sectarian theology into the rebellious angels of the Christians, who took them from the Seven Devs of the Magi, without understanding the significance of the allegory. (*Vide Part II.*, " On the Seven Souls," and Section xv. *in this Part*, "GODS, MONADS AND ATOMS ").

As usual, that which *is* and *was* from its beginning divine, pure, and spiritual in its earliest unity, became, by reason of its differentiation by the distorted prism of man's conceptions, human and impure, as reflecting man's own sinful nature. Thus, in time, the planet Saturn became reviled by the worshippers of other " gods." The nations born under Saturn—the Jewish, for instance—with whom he had become Jehovah, after having been held as a son of Saturn, or Ilda-Baoth, by the Ophites, and in the book of Jasher—were eternally fighting with those born under Jupiter, Mercury, or any other planet, except Saturn-Jehovah; genealogies and prophecies notwithstanding, Jesus *the initiate* (or Jehoshua) — the type from whom the " historical " Jesus was

* C. W. King, identifies it with " that *summum bonum* of Oriental aspiration, the Buddhist Nirvana," perfect repose, the Epicurean *Indolentia*, which looks flippant enough in its expression, though not quite untrue.

copied—was not of pure Jewish blood, and thus recognised no Jehovah; nor did he worship any planetary god beside his own " Father," whom he knew, and with whom he communed as every high initiate does, " Spirit to Spirit and Soul to Soul." This can hardly be taken exception to, unless the critic explains to every one's satisfaction the strange sentences put in the mouth of Jesus by the author of the Fourth Gospel (*chapter* viii.) during his disputes with the Pharisees.

" I know ye are Abraham's seed* . . . I speak the things which I have seen with *my* Father; and ye do the things which ye heard from *your* Father. . . . . Ye do the works of *your* Father. . . . . Ye are of your Father, the Devil. . . . . He was a murderer from the beginning, and stood not in the truth, because there is no truth in him. When one speaketh a lie he speaketh of his own; for his father also is a liar and the father thereof," etc., etc.

That " Father " of the Pharisees was Jehovah, because identical with Cain, Saturn, Vulcan, etc.—the planet under which they were born, and the God whom they worshipped. Evidently there must be an occult meaning sought in these words and admonitions, however mistranslated, since they are pronounced by one who threatened with hell-fire anyone who says simply *raca* (fool) to his brother (*Matthew* v., 22). And evidently, again, the planets are not merely spheres, twinkling in Space, and made to shine for no purpose, but the domains of various beings with whom the profane are so far unacquainted; nevertheless, having a mysterious, unbroken, and powerful connection with men and globes. Every heavenly body is the temple of *a* god, and these gods themselves are the temples of GOD, the Unknown "*Not* Spirit." There is nothing profane in the Universe. All Nature is a consecrated place, as Young says :—

" Each of these Stars is a religious house." . . . .

Thus can all exoteric religions be shown the falsified copies of the esoteric teaching. It is the priesthood which has to be held responsible for the reaction in favour of materialism of our day. It is by worshiping and enforcing on the the masses the worship of the shells— personified for purposes of allegory—of pagan ideals, that the latest exoteric religion has made of Western lands a Pandemonium, in which the higher classes worship the golden calf, and the lower and ignorant masses are made to worship an idol with feet of clay.

* Abraham and Saturn are identical in astro-symbology, and he is the forefather of the Jehovistic Jews.

XII.

ANCIENT THOUGHT IN MODERN DRESS.

MODERN SCIENCE IS ANCIENT THOUGHT DISTORTED, and no more. We have seen, however, WHAT INTUITIONAL SCIENTISTS THINK, and are busy about ; and now the reader may be given a few more proofs of the fact that more than one F.R.S. is unconsciously approaching the derided Secret Sciences.

With regard to cosmogony and primeval matter, modern speculations are undeniably ancient thought, *improved* by contradictory theories of recent origin. But the whole foundation belongs to Grecian and Indian Archaic astronomy and physics, in those days always called philosophy. In all the Aryan and Greek speculations, one meets with the conception of an all-pervading, unorganized, and homogeneous matter, or *Chaos*, re-named by modern scientists " Nebular condition of the world-stuff." What Anaxagoras called "Chaos" in his *Homoiomeria* is now called " primitive fluid " by Sir W. Thomson. The Hindu and Greek Atomists—Kanada, Leucippus, Democritus, Epicurus, Lucretius, etc., etc., are now reflected as in a clear mirror, in the supporters of the atomic theory of our modern days, beginning with Leibnitz's *Monads*, and ending with the " Vortical Atoms " of Sir W. Thomson.* True, the corpuscular theory of old is rejected, and the undulatory theory has taken its place. But the question is, *whether the latter is so firmly established as not to be liable to be dethroned as was its predecessor ?* Light from its metaphysical aspect was fully treated of in "*Isis Unveiled*" :—

" Light is the first begotten, and the first emanation of the Supreme, and Light is Life, says the Evangelist and the Kabalist. Both are electricity —the life principle, the *anima mundi*, pervading the universe, the electric vivifier of all things. Light is the great Protean magician, and under the divine will of the architect,† or rather the *architects*, the " Builders " (called *One* collectively), its multifarious, omnipotent waves gave birth to every form as well as to every living being. From its swelling electric bosom, spring *matter* and *spirit*. Within its beams lie the beginnings of all physical and chemical action, and of all cosmic and spiritual phenomena ; it vitalizes and disorganizes ; it gives life and produces death, and from its primordial point gradually emerged into existence the myriads of worlds, visible and invisible celestial bodies. It was at the ray of this *First* mother, one in three, that " God," according to

---

* The Elemental Vortices inaugurated by the *Mind* have not been improved by their modern transformation.

† I have been often taken to task for using expressions in *Isis* denoting belief in a *personal* and anthropomorphic God. This is *not* my idea. Kabalistically speaking, the " Architect " is the generic name for the *Sephiroth*, the Builders of the Universe, as the " Universal Mind " represents the collectivity of the Dhyan Chohanic Minds.

Plato, lighted a fire which we now call the sun,"* and which is *not* the cause of either light or heat, but merely the focus, or, as we might say, the lens, by which the rays of the primordial light become materialised, are concentrated upon our Solar System, and produce all the correlations of forces."

This is the *Ether*, as just explained in the views of Metcalfe, repeated by Dr. Richardson, save the submission of the former to some details of the modern undulatory theory. We do not say that we deny the theory, but assert only that it needs completion and re-arrangement. But the Occultists are by no means the only *heretics* in this respect; for Mr. Robert Hunt, F.R.S., remarks, in his *Researches on Light in its Chemical Relations*, that :—

. . . . "the undulatory theory does not account for the results of his experiments. Sir David Brewster, in his *Treatise on Optics*, showing 'that the colours of vegetable life arise . . . . from a specific attraction which the particles of these bodies exercise over the differently-coloured rays of light,' and that 'it is by the light of the sun that the coloured juices of plants are elaborated, that the colours of bodies are changed, etc. . . . . .' remarks that it is not easy to allow 'that such effects can be produced by the mere vibration of an ethereal medium.' And he is *forced*, he says, 'by this class of facts, to reason as if light was *material* (?).' Professor Josiah P. Cooke, of Harvard University, says that he 'cannot agree . . . . with those who regard the wave-theory of light as an established principle of science.'† Herschell's doctrine, that the intensity of light, in effect of each undulation, 'is inversely as the square of the distance from the luminous body,' if correct, damages a good deal, if it does not kill the undulatory theory. That he is right, was proved repeatedly by experiments with photometers; and though it begins to be much doubted, the undulatory theory is still alive." (" *Isis Unveiled*.")

To this remark of Sir W. Brewster—" forced to reason as if light was material"—there is a good deal to reply. Light, in one sense, is certainly as material as electricity itself is. And if electricity is *not* material, if it is only " a mode of motion," how is it that it can be *stored up* in Faure's accumulators? Helmholtz says that electricity must be as atomic as matter; and Mr. W. Crookes, F.R.S., supported the view in his address to the Chemical Section of the British Association, of which he was President (at Birmingham, 1886). This is what Helmholtz says (*in his Faraday Lectures*, 1881) :—

" If we accept the hypothesis that the elementary substances are composed of atoms, we cannot avoid concluding that electricity also, positive as well as negative, is divided into definite elementary portions, which behave like atoms of electricity."

Here we have to repeat that which was already said in Section IX. there is but one science that can henceforth direct modern research into the one path which will lead to the discovery of the whole, hitherto

---

* " Timæus."   † *Modern Chemistry*.

occult, truth, and it is the youngest of all—*chemistry*, as it now stands reformed. There is no other, not excluding astronomy, that can so unerringly guide scientific intuition, as chemistry can. Two proofs of it are to be found in the world of Science—two great chemists, each among the greatest in his own country, and these are Mr. Crookes and the late Professor Butlerof: one, a thorough believer in abnormal phenomena ; the other, as fervid a Spiritualist as he was great in natural Sciences. It becomes evident that while pondering over the ultimate divisibility of matter, and in the hitherto *fruitless* chase after the element of negative atomic weight, the scientifically trained mind of the chemist must feel irresistibly drawn towards those ever-shrouded worlds, to the mysterious beyond, whose measureless depths seem to close against the approach of the too materialistic hand that would fain draw aside its veil. " It is the unknown and the *ever unknowable*," warns the Monist-Agnostic. Not so ; answers the persevering chemist :—" We are on the track and are not daunted, and fain would we enter the mysterious region which *ignorance tickets unknown*."*

A few lines at the very close of his lecture on the *Genesis of the Elements*—two or three sentences—showed the eminent Scientist to be on the royal road to the greatest discoveries. He has been overshadowing for some time " the original *protyle*," and came to the conclusion that " he who grasps the Key will be permitted to unlock some of the deepest mysteries of creation." The *protyle*, as that great chemist explains :—

" . . . is a word analogous to protoplasm, to express the idea of the original primal matter existing before the evolution of the chemical elements. The word I have ventured to use for this purpose is compounded of πρὸ (earlier than) and ὕλη (the stuff of which things are made). The word is scarcely a new coinage, for 600 years ago Roger Bacon wrote in his *Arte Chymiae*, " The elements are made out of ὕλη and every element is converted into the nature of another element."

The *Knowledge* of Roger Bacon did not come to this wonderful old magician† by inspiration, but because he studied ancient works on

---

* Mr. Crookes' " Presidential Address " at Birmingham. " There is but one unknown—*the ultimate substratum of Spirit* (Space). That which is not the *Absolute* and the *One* is, in virtue of that very differentiation, however far removed from the physical senses, always accessible to the spiritual human mind, which is a coruscation of the undifferentiable Integral."—(*Practical Lessons on the Occult.*)

† Thus, what the writer of the present work said ten years ago in " *Isis Unveiled* ' (*Vol. I.*) was prophetic, it seems. These are the words : " Many of these mystics, by following what they were taught by some treatises, secretly preserved from one genera-tion to another, *achieved discoveries which would not be despised even in our modern days of exact sciences*. Roger Bacon, the friar, was laughed at as a quack, and is now generally numbered among ' pretenders ' to magic art ; but his discoveries were nevertheless accepted, and are now used by those who ridicule him the most. Roger Bacon belonged by right, if not by fact, to that Brotherhood which includes all those who

magic and alchemy, having a key to the real meaning of words. But see what Mr. Crookes says of *protyle*, next neighbour to the unconscious *Mulaprakriti* of the Occultists :—

..... "Let us start at the moment when the first element came into existence. Before this time, matter, as we know it, was not. It is equally impossible to conceive of matter without energy, as of energy without matter ; from one point of view both are convertible terms. Before the birth of atoms, all those forms of energy, which become evident when matter acts upon matter, could not have existed*—they were locked up in the *protyle* as latent potentialities only. Coincident with the creation of atoms, all those attributes and properties, which form the means of discriminating one chemical element from another, start into existence fully endowed with energy." (*Presidential Address*, p. 16.)

With every respect due to the great knowledge of the lecturer, the Occultist would put it otherwise. They would say that no atom is ever "created," for the atoms are eternal within the bosom of the *One Atom*,—"the atom of atoms"—viewed during Manvantara as the *Jagad-Yoni* the *material* causative womb of the world. *Pradhâna* (unmodified matter), that which is the first form of *Prakriti*, or material visible, as *well as invisible* nature, and *Purusha*, spirit, are eternally one ; and they are *Nirupadhi*, (without adventitious qualities or attributes) only during *Pralaya*, and when *beyond* any of the planes of consciousness of existence. The atom, as known to modern science, is inseparable from *Purusha*, which is spirit, but is now called "Energy" in Science. The *protyle* atom has not been comminuted or subtilized : it has simply passed into that plane, which is no plane, but the eternal state of everything beyond the planes of illusion. Both *Purusha* and *Pradhâna* are immutable and unconsumable, or *Aparinâmin* and *Avyaya*, in eternity ; and both during the Mayavic periods may be referred to as *Vyaya* and *Parinâmin*, or that which can expand, pass away and disappear, and is "modifiable." In this sense *Purusha*, must of course, be held distinct in our conceptions from *Parabrahmam*. Nevertheless that, which is called "energy" or "force" in Science and has been explained as a *dual* Force by Metcalfe, is never, in fact, and cannot be *energy* alone; for it is the substance of the world, its soul, the *all-permeant* "Sarvaga," in conjunction with *Kâla* "time." The three are the trinity in one, during Manvantara, the all-potential Unity, which acts on the plane of illusion (Maya) as three distinct things. In Orphic

---

study the occult sciences. Living in the thirteenth century, almost a contemporary, therefore, of Albertus Magnus and Thomas Aquinas, his discoveries—such as gunpowder and optical glasses, and his mechanical achievements—were considered by everyone as so many miracles. He was accused of having made a compact with the Evil One."

* Just so ; "those forms of energy . . . *which become evident* . . ." in the laboratory of the chemist and physicist ; but *there are other forms of energy* wedded to *other forms* of matter, *which are supersensuous*, yet known to the adepts.

philosophy in Greece they were called *Phanes*, *Chaos*, and *Chronos*—the triad of the Occult philosophers of that period.

But see how closely Mr. Crookes brushes by the " Unknowable," and what " potentialities " there are for the acceptance of Occult truths in his discoveries. He continues, speaking of the evolution of atoms :—

". . . . Let us pause at the end of the first complete vibration and examine the result. We have already found the elements of water, ammonia, carbonic acid, the atmosphere, plant and animal life, phosphorus for the brain, salt for the seas, clay for the solid earth . . . phosphates and silicates sufficient for a world and inhabitants not so very different from what we enjoy at the present day. True the human inhabitants would have to live in a state of more than Arcadian simplicity, and the absence of calcic phosphate would be awkward as far as the bone is concerned* . . . At the lower end of our curve . . . we see a great hiatus . . . This oasis, and the blanks which precede and follow it, may be referred with much probability to the particular way in which our Earth developed into a member of our solar system. If this be so, it may be that on our Earth only these blanks occur, and not generally throughout the universe."

This justifies several assertions in the Occult works.

Firstly, " that neither stars nor the sun can be said to be constituted of those terrestrial elements with which the chemist is familiar, though they are all present in the sun's outward robes—and a host more of elements so far unknown to science."

Secondly, that our globe has its own special laboratory on the far-away outskirts of its atmosphere, crossing which, every atom and molecule change and differentiate from their primordial nature.

And *Thirdly*, that though no element present on our earth could ever be possibly found wanting in the sun, there are many others which have either not reached, or not as yet been discovered on, our globe. " Some may be missing in certain stars and heavenly bodies in the process of formation ; or, though present in them, these elements, on account of their present state, may not respond as yet to the usual scientific tests." † Mr. Crookes speaks of an element of still lower atomic weight than hydrogen, an *element purely hypothetical* as far as our earth is concerned . . . though existing in abundance in the chromosphere of the Sun—the *helium*. Occult Science adds that not one of the *elements* regarded by chemistry as such really deserves the name.

Again we find Mr. Crookes speaking with approbation of " Dr. Carnelly's weighty argument in favour of *the compound nature of the so-called elements*, from their analogy to the compound radicles !" Hitherto,

---

* It is just the existence of such worlds in other planes of consciousness that is claimed by the Occultist. The secret science teaches that the primitive race was *boneless*. (See Book II.) ; and that there are (to us) invisible worlds, peopled as our own, besides the *populations* of Dhyan Chohans.

† " *Five Years of Theosophy*," *p.* 258 *et seq.*

alchemy alone succeeded within the historical periods, and in the so-called civilized countries, in obtaining a real *element*, or a particle of homogeneous matter, the *Mysterium Magnum* of Paracelsus. But then it was before Lord Bacon's day.*

" . . . Let us now turn to the upper portion of the scheme. With hydrogen of atomic weight =1, there is little room for other elements, save, perhaps, for hypothetical *Helium*. But what if we get 'through the looking-glass,' and cross the zero line in search of new principles—what shall we find on the other side of zero ? Dr. Carnelly asks for an element of negative atomic weight; here is ample room and verge enough for a shadow series of such unsubstantialities. Helmholtz says that electricity is probably as atomic as matter; is electricity one of the negative elements, and the luminiferous ether another ? Matter, as we now know it, does not here exist; the forms of energy which are apparent in the motions of matter are as yet only latent possibilities. *A substance of negative weight is not inconceivable.*† But can we form a clear conception of a body which combines with other bodies in proportions expressible by negative qualities ? "‡

" A genesis of the elements such as is here sketched out would not be confined to our little solar system, but would probably follow the same general sequence of events in every centre of energy now visible as a star."

" Before the birth of atoms to gravitate towards one another, no pressure could be exercised ; but at the outskirts of the fire-mist sphere, within which all is protyle—at the shell on which the tremendous forces involved in the birth a chemical element exert full sway—the fierce heat would be accompanied by gravitation sufficient to keep the newly-born elements from flying off into space. As temperature increases, expansion and molecular motion increase, molecules tend to fly asunder, and their chemical affinities become deadened ; but the enormous pressure of the gravitation of the mass of atomic matter, outside what I may for brevity call the birth-shell, would counteract the action of heat."

" Beyond the birth-shell would be a space in which no chemical action could take place, owing to the temperature there being above what is called the dissociation-point for compounds. In this space the lion and the lamb would lie down together ; phosphorus and oxygen would mix without union ; hydrogen and chlorine would show no tendency to closer bonds ; and even fluorine, that

---

* Says Mr. Crookes in the same address : " The first riddle which we encounter in chemistry is : ' What are the elements ?' Of the attempts hitherto made to define or explain an element, none satisfy the demands of the human intellect. The text books tell us that an element is ' a body which has not been decomposed ;' that it is ' a something to which we can add, but from which we can take nothing,' or ' a body which increases in weight with every chemical change.' Such definitions are doubly unsatisfactory : they are provisional, and may cease to-morrow to be applicable in any given case. They take their stand, not on any attribute of the things to be defined, but on the limitations of human power : they are confessions of intellectual impotence."

† And the lecturer quotes Sir George Airy, who says *(in Faraday's Life and Letters Vol. II., p. 354)*, " I can easily conceive that there are plenty of bodies about us no subject to this intermutual action, and *therefore not subject to the law of gravitation.*"

‡ The Vedantic philosophy conceives of such ; but then it is not physics, but metaphysics, called by Mr. Tyndall " poetry " and " fiction."

energetic gas which chemlsts have only isolated within the last month or two, would float about free and uncombined."

" Outside this space of free atomic matter would be another shell, in which the formed chemical elements would have cooled down to the combination point, and the sequence of events so graphically described by Mr. Mattieu Williams in " *The Fuel of the Sun*" would now take place, culminating in the solid earth and the commencement of geological time " (p. 19).

This is, *in a strictly scientific*, but beautiful language, the description of the evolution of the differentiated Universe in the sccret teachings. The learned gentleman closes his address in words, every sentence of which is like a flash of light from beyond the dark veil of materiality, hitherto thrown upon the exact sciences, and a step forward towards the *Sanctum Sanctorum* of the Occult. (*Vide* § *XV.*, "*Gods, Monads, and Atoms.*") Thus he says:—

" We have glanced at the difficulty of defining an element; we have noticed, too, the revolt of many leading physicists and chemists against the ordinary acceptation of the term element; we have weighed the improbability of their eternal existence,* or *their origination by chance*. As a remaining alternative, we have suggested their origin by a process of evolution like that of the heavenly bodies according to Laplace, and the plants and animals of our globe according to Lamarck, Darwin, and Wallace.† In the general array of the elements, as known to us, we have seen a striking approximation to that of the organic world.‡ In lack of direct evidence of the decomposition of any element, we have sought and found indirect evidence . . . . We have next glanced at the view of the genesis of the elements; and lastly we have reviewed a scheme of their origin suggested by Professor Reynold's method of illustrating the periodic classification § . . . Summing up all the above considerations we cannot,

---

* In the form they are now, we conceive ?

† And to Kapila and Manu—especially and originally.

‡ Here is a scientific corroboration of the eternal law of correspondences and analogy.

§ This method of illustrating the periodic law in the classification of elements is, in the words of Mr. Crookes, proposed by Professor Emerson Reynolds, of Dublin University, who . . . . "points out that in each period, the general properties of the elements vary from one to another, with approximate regularity until we reach the *seventh member*, which is in more or less striking contrast with the first element of the same period, as well as with the first of the next. Thus chlorine, the seventh member of Mendeleef's third period, contrasts sharply with both sodium, the first member of the same series, and with potassium, the first member of the next series; whilst on the other hand, sodium and potassium are closely analogous. The six elements, whose atomic weights intervene between sodium and potassium, vary in properties, step by step, until chlorine, the contrast to sodium, is reached. But from chlorine to potassium, the analogue of sodium, there is a change in properties *per saltum*. . . . . If we thus recognise a contrast in properties—more or less decided—between the first and the last members of each series, we can scarcely help admitting the existence of a point of mean variation within each system. In general the *fourth* element of each series possesses the property we might expect a transition-element to exhibit. . . . . Thus for the purpose of graphic translation, Professor Reynolds considers that the fourth member of a period—silicon, for example—may be placed at the apex of a symmetrical

indeed, venture to assert positively *that our so-called elements have been evolved from one primordial matter ; but we may contend that the balance of evidence, I think, fairly weighs in favour of this speculation.*"

Thus inductive Science, in its Branches of Astronomy, Physics, and Chemistry, while advancing timidly towards the conquest of Nature's secrets in her final effects on our terrestial plane, recedes to the days of Anaxagoras and the Chaldees in its discoveries of (a) the origin of our phenomenal world, and (b) the modes of formation of the bodies that compose the universe. And having to turn back for their cosmogonical hypotheses to the beliefs of the earliest philosophers, and the systems of the latter—systems that were all based on the teachings of a universal secret doctrine with regard to the primeval matter with its properties, functions, and laws,—have we not the right to hope that the day is not far off when Science will show a better appreciation of the wisdom of the ancients than it has hitherto done ?

No doubt Occult philosophy could learn a good deal from exact modern science ; but the latter, on the other hand, might profit by ancient learning in more than one way, and chiefly in Cosmogony. For

---

curve, which shall represent for that particular period, the direction in which the properties of the series of elements vary with rising atomatic weights.

Now, the writer humbly confesses complete ignorance of modern chemistry and its mysteries. But she is pretty well acquainted with the Occult doctrine with regard to *correspondences of types and antitypes* in nature, and perfect analogy as a fundamental law in Occultism. Hence she ventures a remark which will strike every Occultist, however it may be derided by orthodox Science. This method of illustrating the periodic law in the behaviour of elements, whether or not still a hypothesis in chemistry, *is a law in Occult Sciences.* Every well-read Occultist knows that the *seventh* and *fourth* members— whether in a septenary chain of worlds, the septenary hierarchy of angels, or in the constitution of man, animal, plant, or mineral atom—that the *seventh* and *fourth* members, we say, in the geometrically and mathematically uniform workings of the immutable laws of Nature, always play a distinct and specific part in the septenary system. From the stars twinkling high in heaven, to the sparks flying asunder from the rude fire built by the savage in his forest ; from the hierarchies and the essential constitution of the Dhyan Chohans—organized for diviner apprehensions and a loftier range of perception than the greatest Western psychologist ever dreamed of, down to Nature's *classification* of species among the humblest insects ; finally from worlds to atoms, everything in the universe, from great to small, proceeds in its spiritual and physical evolution, cyclically and septennially, showing its seventh and fourth number (the latter the turning point) behaving in the same way as shown in that periodic law of atoms. Nature never proceeds *per saltum*. Therefore, when Mr. Crookes remarks to this that he does not " wish to infer that the gaps in Mendeleef's table, and in this graphic representation of it (the diagram showing the evolution of atoms) necessarily mean that there are elements actually existing to fill up the gaps ; these gaps may only mean that at the birth of the elements there was an easy potentiality of the formation of an element which would fit into the place "—an Occultist would respectfully remark to him that the latter hypothesis can only hold good, if the septenary arrangement of atoms is not interfered with. This is *the one law*, and an infallible method that must always lead to success, one who follows it.

instance, the mystical signification, alchemical and transcendental, of the many *imponderable* substances that fill interplanetary space, and which, interpenetrating each, are the direct cause, at the lower end, of the production of natural phenomena manifesting through *vibration* (so-called). The knowledge of the *real* (not the hypothetical) nature of Ether, or rather of the *Akâsa*, and other mysteries, in short, can alone lead to the knowledge of Forces. It is that substance against which the materialistic school of the physicists rebels with such fury, especially in France,* and which exact Science has to advocate notwithstanding. They cannot make away with it without incurring the risk, like a modern Samson, of pulling down the pillars of the Temple of Science, and getting buried under its roof.

The theories built upon the rejection of Force *outside* and independent of *Matter pure and simple*, have been all shown fallacious. They do not, and cannot, cover the ground, and many of the scientific data are thus proved *unscientific*. "Ether produced Sound" is said in the Purânas, and the statement is laughed at. It is the vibrations in *the air*, we are corrected. And what is air? Could it exist if there were no etheric medium in Space to buoy up its molecules? The case stands simply thus. Materialism cannot admit the existence of anything *outside* matter, because with the acceptance of an imponderable *Force*—the source and head of all the physical physical Forces—other *intelligent* Forces would have to be admitted virtually, and that would lead Science very far. For it would have to accept as a sequel the presence in Man of a still more spiritual power— entirely independent, for once, of any kind of matter physicists know anything about. Hence, apart from an hypothetical ether of Space and gross physical bodies, the whole Sidereal and unseen Space is, in the sight of the materialists, one boundless *void* in nature—blind, unintelligent, useless.

And now the next question is: What is that Cosmic Substance, and how far can one go to suspect its nature or to wrench from it its secrets, and thus feel justified in giving it a NAME? How far, especially, has modern Science gone in the direction of those secrets, and what it is doing to solve them. The latest hobby of Science, the "Nebular Theory," may afford us some answer to this question. Let us then examine the credentials of the NEBULAR THEORY.

---

* A group of electricians has just protested against the new theory of Clausius, the famous professor of the University of Bonn. The character of the protest is shown in the signature, which has "Jules Bourdin, in the name of the group of Electricians, which had the honour of being introduced to Professor Clausius in 1881, and whose war-cry (cri de ralliement) is *A bas l'Ether*"—down with ether, even; they want Universal *Void*, you see!

XIII.

SCIENTIFIC AND ESOTERIC EVIDENCE FOR, AND OBJECTIONS TO, THE MODERN NEBULAR THEORY.

OF late Esoteric Cosmogony has been frequently opposed by the phantom of this theory and its ensuing hypotheses. " Can this most scientific teaching be denied by your adepts?" it is asked. " Not entirely," is the reply, " but the admissions of the men of Science themselves *kill* it ; and there remains nothing for the adepts to deny."

To make of Science an integral *whole* necessitates, indeed, the study of spiritual and psychic, as well as physical Nature. Otherwise it will ever be like the anatomy of man, discussed of old by the profane from the point of view of his shell-side and in ignorance of the interior work. Even Plato, the greatest philosopher of his country, became guilty, before his initiation, of such statements as that liquids pass into the stomach through the lungs. Without metaphysics, as Mr. H. J. Slack says, *real* science is inadmissible.

The nebulæ exist ; yet the nebular theory is wrong. A nebula exists in a state of entire elemental dissociation. It *is* gaseous and—something else besides, which can hardly be connected with gases, as known to physical science ; and it *is* self-luminous. But that is all. The sixty-two " coincidences " enumerated by Professor Stephen Alexander,* confirming the nebular theory, may all be explained by esoteric science ; though, as this is not an astronomical work, the refutations are not attempted at present. Laplace and Faye come nearer to the correct theory than any ; but of the speculations of Laplace there remains little in the present theory except its general features. Nevertheless, "there is in Laplace's theory," says John Stuart Mill, "*nothing hypothetical* ; it is an example of legitimate reasoning from present effect to its past cause ; it assumes nothing more than that objects which really exist, obey the laws which are known to be obeyed by all terrestrial objects resembling them." *(System of Logic, p. 229).*

This from such an eminent logician as Mill was, would be valuable, if it could only be proved that " terrestrial objects *resembling* . . ." celestial objects at such a distance as the nebulæ are—*resemble those objects in reality, not alone in appearance.*

Another of the fallacies from the Occult stand-point, which are embodied in the modern theory as it now stands, is the hypothesis that the planets were all detached from the Sun ; that they are bone of

---

* " *Smithsonian Contributions,*" xxi., Art. i, pp. 79-97.

his bone, and flesh of his flesh ; whereas, the Sun and planets are only co-uterine brothers, having had the same nebular origin, only in a different mode from that postulated by modern astronomy.

The many objections raised against the homogeneity of original diffuse matter, on the ground of the uniformity in the composition of the fixed stars, by some opponents of the modern nebular theory, do not affect the question of that homogeneity at all, but only the said theory. Our solar nebula may not be completely homogeneous, or, rather, it may fail to reveal itself as such to the astronomers, and yet be *de facto* homogeneous. The stars do differ in their constituent materials and even exhibit elements quite unknown on earth ; nevertheless, this does not affect the point that primeval matter—*i.e.*, as it *appeared even in its first* differentiation from its *laya* condition*—is yet to this day homogeneous, at immense distances, in the depths of infinitude, and likewise at points not far removed from the outskirts of our solar system.

Finally, there does not exist one single fact brought forward by the learned objectors against the " nebular theory," (false as it is, and hence, *illogically enough*, fatal to the hypothesis of the homogeneity of matter,) that can withstand criticism. One error leads into another. A false premise will naturally lead to a false conclusion, although an inadmissible inference does not *necessarily* affect the validity of the major proposition of the syllogism. Thus, one may leave every side-issue and inference from the evidence of spectra, and lines, as simply provisional for the present, and abandon all matters of detail to physical science. The duty of the Occultist lies with the *Soul and Spirit* of Cosmic Space, not merely with its illusive appearance and behaviour. That of official physical science is to analyze and study its *shell*—the *Ultima Thule* of the Universe and man, in the opinion of Materialism.

With the latter, Occultism has nought to do. It is only with the theories of such men of learning as Kepler, Kant, Oersted, and Sir W. Herschell, who believed in a Spiritual world, that Occult Cosmogony might treat, and attempt a satisfactory compromise. But the views of those physicists differed vastly from the latest modern speculations. Kant and Herschell had in their mind's eye speculations upon the origin and *the final destiny*, as well as the present aspect, of the Universe, from a far more philosophical and psychic standpoint ; whereas modern Cosmology and Astronomy now repudiate anything like research into the mysteries of being. The result is what might be expected: complete failure and inextricable contradictions in the thousand and one varieties of so-called scientific theories, and in this theory as in all others.

The nebular hypothesis, involving the theory of the existence of a

---

* Beyond the zero-line of action.

primeval matter, diffused in a nebulous condition, is of no modern date in astronomy as everyone knows. Anaximenes, of the Ionian school, had already taught that the sidereal bodies were formed through the progressive condensation of a primordial *pregenetic* matter, which had almost a negative weight, and was spread out through Space in an extremely sublimated condition.

Tycho Brahè, who viewed the Milky Way as an ethereal substance, thought the new star that appeared in Cassiopœia, in 1572, had been formed out of that matter. (" *Progymnasmata* " p. 795.) Kepler believed the star of 1606 had been likewise formed out of the ethereal substance that fills the universe (" *De stellâ novâ in pede Serpentarii*," p. 115). He attributed to that same ether the apparition of a luminous ring around the moon, during the total eclipse of the sun observed at Naples in 1605." (" *Hypothèses Cosmogoniques*," *C. Wolf.)* Still later, in 1714,— the existence of a self-luminous matter was recognised by Halley (" *Philosophical Transactions* "). Finally, the journal of this name published in 1811 the famous hypothesis on the transformation of the nebulæ into stars, by the eminent astronomer, Sir W. Herschell (*See* " *Philosophical Transactions*," *of* 1811, p. 269, *et seq.*), after which the nebular theory was accepted by the Royal Academies.

In " Five years of Theosophy," on p. 245, an article headed " *Do the Adepts deny the Nebular Theory?*" may be read. The answer there given is " No ; they do not deny *its general propositions, nor the approximative truth of the scientific* hypotheses. They only deny the *completeness* of the present, as well as the entire error of the many so-called "exploded" old theories, which, during the last century, have followed each other in such rapid succession."

This was proclaimed at the time "an evasive answer." Such disrespect to official science, it was argued, must be justified by the presentation, to replace the *orthodox* speculation, of another theory more complete than theirs, and having a firmer ground to stand upon. To this there is but one reply ; it is useless to give out isolated theories with regard to things embodied in a whole and consecutive system, which, when separated from the main body of the teaching, would necessarily lose their vital coherence and thus do no good when studied independently. To be able to appreciate and accept the occult views on the nebular theory, one has to study the whole esoteric cosmogonical system. And the time has hardly arrived for the astronomers to be asked to accept *Fohat* and the divine Builders. Even the undeniably correct surmises of Sir W. Herschell, that had nothing " supernatural " in them, about the sun being called " *globe of fire* " (perhaps) *metaphorically*, and his early speculations about the nature of that which is now called the Nasmyth willow-leaf theory—caused that most eminent of all astronomers to be smiled at by other, far less eminent colleagues, who saw and now see in his ideas only "imaginative and fanciful theories." Before the whole esoteric system could be given out and appreciated by the astronomers, they would have to return to some of those "antiquated ideas," not only to those of Herschell, but to the dreams of the oldest Hindu astronomers, and to abandon their own theories, none the less "fanciful" because they have appeared in one case nearly 80 years and in the other many thousands of years later. Foremost of all they would have to repudiate the ideas on the Sun's *solidity* and *incandescence* ; the sun "glowing" most undeniably, but not "burning." Then it is stated, with regard to Sir W. Herschell's view that those "objects," as he called the "willow leaves," are the immediate *sources of the solar light and heat.* And though the esoteric teaching does not regard these as he did—namely, *organisms* as partaking of the nature of life," for the Solar "Beings" will hardly place themselves within telescopic focus—yet it asserts that the whole Universe is full of such "organisms," conscious and active accord-ing to the proximity or distance of their planes to, or from, our plane of consciousness ; and that finally the great astronomer was right in saying that "we do not know that vital action is competent to develop at once heat, light, and electricity" while speculating on those supposed "organisms." For, at the risk of being laughed at by the whole world of physicists, the Occultists maintain that all the "Forces" of the Scientists have their origin in the *Vital Principle*, the ONE LIFE collectively of our Solar system—that "*life*" being a portion, or rather one of the *aspects* of the One Universal LIFE.

We may, therefore, as in the article under consideration, wherein, on the authority of the Adepts, it was maintained that it is "sufficient to make a *résumé* of what the solar physicists *do not know*,"—we may, we maintain, define our position with regard to the modern nebular theory and its evident incorrectness, by simply pointing out facts diametrically opposed to it in its present form. And to begin with, what does it teach ?

Summarizing the aforesaid hypotheses, it becomes plain that Laplace's theory—now made quite unrecognisable, moreover—was an unfortunate one. He postulates in the first place Cosmic matter, existing in a state of diffuse nebulosity "so fine that its presence could hardly have been suspected." No attempt is made by him to penetrate into the arcana of being, except as regards the immediate evolution of our small solar system.

Consequently, whether one accepts or rejects his theory in its bearing upon the immediate cosmological problems presented for solution, he can only be said to have thrown back the mystery a little further. To the eternal query—"Whence matter itself; whence the evolutionary impetus

592   THE SECRET DOCTRINE.

determining its cyclic aggregations and dissolutions ; whence the exquisite symmetry and order into which the primeval atoms arrange and group themselves?"—no answer is attempted by Laplace. All we are confronted with, is a sketch of the *probable* broad principles on which the actual process is assumed to be based. Well, and what is this now celebrated note on the said process ? What has he given so wonderfully new and original, that its ground-work, at any rate, should have served as a basis for the modern nebular theory ? This is what one gathers from various astronomical works.

Laplace thought that, consequent on the condensation of the atoms of the primeval nebula, according to the " Law " of gravity, the now gaseous, or perhaps, partially liquid mass, acquired a rotatory motion. As the velocity of this rotation increased, it assumed the form of a thin disc ; finally, the centrifugal force overpowering that of cohesion, huge rings were detached from the edge of the whirling incandescent masses, contracting necessarily by gravitation (as accepted) into spheroidal bodies, which would necessarily still continue to preserve the same orbit occupied previously by the outer zone from which they were separated. (" Laplace conceived that the external and internal zones of the ring would rotate with the same angular velocity, which would be the case with a solid ring ; but the principle of equal areas requires the inner zones to rotate more rapidly than the outer.")* The velocity of the outer edge of each nascent planet, he said, exceeding that of the inner, there results a rotation on its axis. The more dense bodies would be thrown off last ; and finally, during the preliminary state of their formation, the newly-segregated orbs in their turn throw off one or more satellites . . . In formulating the history of the rupture and planetation of rings, Laplace says :

" Almost always each ring of vapours must have broken up into numerous masses, which, moving with a nearly uniform velocity, must have continued to circulate at the same distance around the Sun. These masses must have taken a spheroidal form with a motion of rotation in the same direction as their revolution, since the inner molecules (those nearer to the Sun) would have less actual velocity than the exterior ones. They must then have formed as many planets in a state of vapour. But, if one of them was sufficiently powerful to unite successively, by its attraction, all the others around its centre, the ring of vapours must have been thus transformed into a single spheroidal mass of vapours circulating around the Sun with a rotation in the same direction as its revolution. The latter case has been the more common, but the solar system presents us the first case, in the four small planets which move between Jupiter and Mars."

While few will be found to deny " the magnificent audacity of this

* " World-Life." Prof. Winchell points to a good many mistakes of Laplace in his work ; but as a *geologist* he is not infallible himself in his " astronomical speculations."

hypothesis," it is impossible not to recognise the insurmountable diffi-culties with which it is attended. Why, for instance, do we find that the satellites of Neptune and Uranus display a retrograde motion ; that, in spite of its closer proximity to the Sun, Venus is less dense than the Earth ? Similarly, the more distant Uranus is more dense than Saturn ? How is it that so many variations in the inclination of their axes and orbits are present in the supposed progeny of the central orb ; that such startling variations in the size of the planets is noticeable; that the Satellites of Jupiter are more dense by ·288 than their primary ; that the phenomena of meteoric and cometic systems still remain unaccounted for ? To quote the words of a Master : " They (the Occultists) find that the centrifugal theory of Western birth is unable to cover *all* the ground. That, unaided, it can neither account for every oblate spheroid, nor explain away such evident difficulties as are presented by the relative density of some planets. How, indeed, can any calculation of centrifugal force explain to us, for instance, why Mercury, whose rotation is, we are told, only about one-third that of the Earth, and its density only about one-fourth greater than the Earth, should have a polar compression *more than ten times as great as the latter ?* And again, why Jupiter, whose equatorial rotation is said to be ' twenty-seven times greater, and its density only about one-fifth that of the earth ' should have its polar compression seventeen times greater than that of the earth ? Or why Saturn, with an equatorial velocity fifty-five times greater than Mercury for centripetal force to contend with, should have its polar compression *only three times* greater than Mercury's ? To crown the above contradictions, we are asked to believe in the Central Forces, as taught by Modern Science, even when told that the equatorial matter of the Sun, with more than four times the centrifugal velocity of the Earth's equatorial surface, and only about one-fourth part of the gravita-tion of the equatorial matter, has not manifested any tendency to bulge at the Solar equator, nor shown the least flattening of the poles of the Solar axis. In other and clearer words, the Sun, with only one fourth of our Earth's density for the centrifugal force to work upon, has no polar compression at all ! We find this objection made by more than one astronomer, yet never explained away satisfactorily so far as the ' Adepts ' are aware."

" Therefore, do they (the Adepts) say, that the great men of science of the West, knowing . . . . . next to nothing either about cometary matter, centrifugal and centripetal forces, the nature of the nebulæ, or the physical constitution of the Sun, the Stars, or even the Moon, are imprudent to speak as confidently as they do about the ' central mass of the Sun ' whirling out into space planets, comets, and what not . . . ."

" We maintain that it (the Sun) evolves out only the *life*-principle, the

Soul of those bodies, *giving and receiving* it back, in our solar system, as the 'Universal Life-Giver' . . . . in infinitude and Eternity; that the solar system is as much the *microcosm* of the ONE Macrocosm as man is the former when compared with his own little Solar Cosmos."*

The essential faculty possessed by all the cosmic and terrestrial elements, of generating within themselves a regular and harmonious series of results, a concatenation of causes and effects, is an irrefutable proof that they are either animated by an *extra* or *intra* INTELLIGENCE, or conceal such within or behind the *manifested veil.* Occultism does not deny the certainty of the mechanical origin of the Universe; it only claims the absolute necessity of mechanicians of some sort behind those Elements (or *within*)—a dogma with us. It is not the fortuitous assistance of the atoms of Lucretius, who himself knew better, that built the Kosmos and all in it. Nature herself contradicts such a theory. Celestial space, containing matter so attenuated as is Ether, cannot be called on, with or without attraction, to explain the common motion of the sidereal hosts. Although the perfect accord of their mutual revolution indicates clearly the presence of a mechanical cause in Nature, Newton, who of all men had best right to trust to his deductions and views, was nevertheless forced to abandon the idea of ever explaining, by the laws of *known* Nature and its Material forces, the original impulse given to the millions of orbs. He recognised fully the limits that separate the action of natural Forces from that of the INTELLIGENCES that set the immutable laws into order and action. And if a NEWTON had to renounce such hope, which of the modern materialistic pigmies has the right of saying : " I know better "?

To become complete and comprehensible, a cosmogonical theory has to start with a primordial Substance diffused throughout boundless Space, *of an intellectual and divine Nature.* That substance must be the Soul and Spirit, the Synthesis and *Seventh Principle* of the manifested Kosmos, and, to serve as a spiritual *Upadhi* to this, there must be the sixth, its vehicle—*primordial physical matter*, so to speak, though its nature must escape for ever our limited *normal* senses. It is easy for an astronomer, if endowed with an imaginative faculty, to build a theory of the emergence of the universe out of chaos, by simply applying to it the principles of mechanics. But such a universe will always prove, with respect to its scientific human creator, a Frankenstein's monster ; it will lead him into endless perplexities. The application of the mechanical laws only can never carry the speculator beyond the objective world ; nor will it unveil to men the origin and final destiny of Kosmos. This is

---

* "*Five Years of Theosophy,*" *pp.* 249-50. *Art.* "*Do the Adepts deny the Nebular Theory ?*"

whither the nebular theory has led Science. In sober fact and truth this theory is twin sister to that of Ether, and both are the offsprings of necessity; one as indispensable to account for the transmission of light, as the other to explain the problem of the origin of the solar systems. The question with them is, how the same homogeneous matter* could, obeying the laws of Newton, give birth to bodies—sun, planets, and their satellites—subject to conditions of identity of motion and formed of such heterogeneous elements.

Has the nebular theory helped to solve the problem, even if applied solely to bodies considered as inanimate and material ? We say most decidedly not. What progress has it made since 1811, when Sir W. Herschell's paper, first presenting facts based on observation and showing the existence of nebular matter, made the " Sons" of the Royal Society " shout for joy " ? Since then a still greater discovery has permitted, through spectrum analysis, the verification and corroboration of Sir W. Herschell'a conjecture. Laplace demanded some kind of primitive " world stuff " to prove the idea of progressive world-evolution and growth. Here it is, as offered two millenniums ago.

The " world stuff," now *nebulæ*, was known from the highest antiquity. Anaxagoras taught that, having differentiated, the subsequent commixture of heterogeneous substances remained motionless and unorganized, until finally " the Mind"—the collective body of Dhyan Chohans, we say—began to work upon and communicated to it motion and order (*Aristotle's " Physica," viii*, 1.) The theory is now taken up in its first portion, that of *any* " Mind " interfering with it being rejected. Spectrum analysis reveals the existence of nebulæ formed entirely of gases and luminous vapours. Is this the primitive nebular matter ? The spectra reveal, it is said, the physical conditions of the matter which emits cosmic light. The spectra of the resolvable and the irresolvable nebulæ are shown to be entirely different, the spectra of the latter showing their physical state to be that of glowing gas or vapour. The bright lines of one nebula reveal the existence of hydrogen in it, and of other material substances known and unknown. The same in the atmospheres of the Sun and stars. This leads to the direct inference that a star is formed by the condensation of a nebula; hence that even the metals themselves on earth are

---

* Had astronomers held simply, in their present state of knowledge, to the hypothesis of Laplace, which was simply the formation of the planetary system, it might in time have resulted in something like an approximate truth. But the two parts of the general problem, that of the formation of the universe, or the formation of the suns and stars from the primitive matter, and then the development of the planets around their sun, rest on quite different facts in nature and are even so viewed by Science itself. They are at the opposite poles of being.

formed owing to the condensation of hydrogen or some other primitive matter, some ancestral cousin to " helium," perhaps, or some yet unknown stuff? *This does not clash with the occult teachings.* And this is the problem that chemistry is trying to solve ; and it must succeed sooner or later in the task, accepting *nolens volens*, when it does, the esoteric teaching. But when this does happen, it will kill the nebular theory as it now stands.

Meanwhile Astronomy cannot accept in any way, if it is to be regarded as *an exact* science, the present theory of the filiation of stars—even if occultism does so in its own way, as it explains this filiation differently —because astronomy has *not one single physical datum* to show for it. Astronomy could anticipate Chemistry in proving the existence of the fact, if it could show a planetary nebula exhibiting a spectrum of three or four bright lines, gradually condensing and transforming into a star, with a spectrum all covered with a number of dark lines. But " the question of the variability of the nebula, even as to their form, is yet one of the mysteries of Astronomy. The data of observation possessed so far are of too recent an origin, too uncertain to permit us to affirm anything." (*Cosmogonical Hypotheses of Wolf.*)

Since the discovery of the spectroscope, its magic power has revealed to its adepts only one single transformation of a star of this kind ; and even that one showed directly the reverse of what is needed as proof in favour of the nebular theory ; namely—*a star transforming itself into a planetary nebula.* As told in *The Observatory (Vol. I., p.* 185), the temporary star which appeared in the constellation Cygnus, in November, 1876, discovered by J. F. J. Schmidt, exhibited a spectrum broken by very brilliant lines. Gradually, the continuous spectrum and most of the lines disappeared, leaving finally one single brilliant line, which appeared to coincide with the green line of the nebula.

Though this metamorphosis is not irreconcileable with the hypothesis of the nebular origin of the stars, nevertheless this single solitary case rests on no observation whatever, least of all on direct observation. The occurrence may have been due to several other causes. Since astronomers are inclined to think our planets are tending toward precipitation on the Sun, why should not that star have blazed out owing to a collision of such precipitated planets, or, as many suggest, the appulse of a comet ? Anyhow, the only known instance of a star transformation since 1811 is not favourable to the nebular theory. Moreover, on the question of this theory, as in all others, astronomers disagree.

In our own age, it was Buffon, before Laplace ever thought of it, who, very much struck by the identity of motion in the planets, was the first to propose the hypothesis of the planets and their satellites originating in the bosom of the Sun. Forthwith, and for the purpose, he invented a special comet, supposed to have torn out, by a powerful oblique blow, the quantity of matter necessary to their formation. Laplace gave its dues to the "comet" in his "*Exposition du Système du Monde.*" (Note VII.) But the idea was seized and even improved upon by a conception of the alternate evolution from the Sun's central mass of planets *apparently* without weight or influence on the motion of the visible planets—and as evidently without any more existence than the likeness of Moses in the moon.

But the modern theory is also a variation on the systems elaborated by Kant and Laplace. The idea of both was that, at the origin of things, all that matter which now enters into the composition of the planetary bodies was spread over all the space comprised in the solar system—and even beyond. It was a nebula of extremely small density, whose condensation gradually gave birth, by a mechanism that has hitherto never been explained, to the various bodies of our systems. This is the original nebular theory, an *incomplete* yet faithful repetition—a short chapter out of the large volume of universal *esoteric* cosmogony—of the teachings in the Secret Doctrine. And both systems, Kant's and Laplace's, differ greatly from the modern theory, redundant with conflicting *sub*-theories and fanciful hypotheses.

" *The essence of cometary matter and of that which composes the stars is totally different from any of the chemical or physical characteristics with which Western Science is now acquainted.* While the spectroscope has shown the probable similarity (owing *to the chemical action of terrestial light* upon the intercepted rays) of earthly and sidereal substance, the chemical actions, peculiar to the variously progressed orbs of space, have not been detected, nor proven to be identical with those observed on our own planet"—say the Teachers *(op. cit.).* Mr. Crookes says almost the same in the fragment quoted from his lecture, "*Elements and Meta-Elements.*"

" At the utmost," observes C. Wolf,[*] " could the nebular hypothesis show in its favour, with W. Herschell, the existence of planetary nebulæ in various degrees of condensation, and of spiral nebulæ, with nuclei of condensation on the branches and centre.[†] But, in fact, the knowledge of the bond that unites the nebulæ to the stars is yet denied to us; and lacking as we do direct observation, we are even debarred from establishing it even on the analogy of chemical composition."

It is evident that, even if the men of science, leaving aside the

---

[*] Member of the Institute, Astronomer of the Observatory, Paris, "Cosmogonical Hypotheses."

[†] But the spectra of these nebulæ have never yet been ascertained. When they *are* found with bright lines, then only may they be cited.

difficulty arising for them out of such undeniable variety and heterogeneity of matter in the constitution of nebulæ, did admit, with the
ancients, that the origin of all the visible and invisible heavenly bodies
must be sought for in one primordial homogeneous world-stuff, in a kind
of PRE-*protyle*,*—it is evident that this would not put an end to their
perplexities. Unless they admit also that our actual visible Universe
is merely the *Sthula-Sharira*, the gross body, of the sevenfold Kosmos,
they will have to face another problem ; especially if they risk maintaining that its now visible bodies are the result of the condensation of that
one and single primordial matter. For mere observation shows them
that the actions which produced the actual Universe are far more
complex than could ever be embraced in that theory.

First of all, there are two distinct classes of *irresolvable* nebulæ,—as
Science itself teaches.

The telescope is unable to distinguish between the two, but the
spectroscope can, and notices, therefore, an essential difference between
their physical constitutions.†

"Some of these," Wolf tells us, "have a spectrum of three or four
bright lines, others a continuous spectrum. The first are gaseous,
the others formed of a pulverulent matter. The former must constitute
a veritable atmosphere: it is among these that the solar nebula of Laplace
has to be placed. The latter form an *ensemble* of particles that may be
considered as independent, and the rotation of which obeys the laws of

---

* Mr. Crookes' " Protyle " must not be regarded as the *primary* stuff, out of which
the Dhyan Chohans, in accordance with the immutable laws of nature, wove our solar
system. This *protyle* cannot even be the first *prima-materia* of Kant, which that great
mind saw used up in the formation of the worlds, and thus existing no longer in a
diffused state. It is a MEDIATE phase in the progressive differentiation of cosmic
substance from its normal undifferentiated state. *Protyle* is then the aspect assumed by
matter in its middle passage into full objectivity.

† " The question of the resolvability of the nebulæ has been often presented in too
affirmative a manner and quite contrary to the ideas expressed by the illustrious
experimenter with the spectra of these constellations—Mr. Huggins. Every nebula
whose spectrum contains only bright lines is gaseous, it is said, and hence is irresolvable ;
every nebula with a continuous spectrum must end by resolving into stars with an
instrument of sufficient power. This assumption is contrary at once to the results
obtained, and to spectroscopic theory. The *Lyra* nebula, the *Dumb-bell* nebula, the
central region of the nebula of Orion, appear resolvable, and show a spectrum of bright
lines ; the nebula of *Canis Venatici* is not resolvable, and gives a continuous spectrum.
Because, indeed, the spectroscope informs us of the physical state of the constituent
matter of the stars, but affords us no notions of their modes of aggregation. A nebula
formed of gaseous globes (or even of nuclei, faintly luminous) surrounded by a powerful
atmosphere) would give a spectrum of lines and be still resolvable ; such seems to be
the state of Huggins' region in the Orion nebula. A nebula formed of solid or fluidic
particles in a state of incandescence, a true cloud, will give a continuous spectrum but
will be *irresolvable*." (*C. Wolf, Cosmogonical Hypotheses.*)

internal weight : such are the nebulæ adopted by Kant and Faye. Observation allows us to place the one as the other at the very origin of the planetary world. But when we try to go beyond and ascend to the primitive chaos which has produced the totality of the heavenly bodies, we have first to account for the actual existence of these two classes of nebulæ. If the primitive chaos were *a cold luminous gas,*[*] one could understand how the contraction resulting from attraction could have heated it and made it luminous. We have to explain the condensation of this gas to the state of incandescent particles, the presence of which is revealed to us in certain nebulæ by the spectroscope. If the original chaos was composed of such particles, how did certain of their portions pass into the gaseous state, while others have preserved their primitive condition ? . . . ."

Such is the synopsis of the objections and difficulties to the acceptance of the nebular theory brought forward by the French *savant,* who concludes his interesting chapter by declaring that :—

" The first part of the Cosmogonical problem,—what is the primitive matter of chaos ; and how did that matter give birth to the sun and stars ?—thus remains to this day in THE DOMAIN OF ROMANCE AND OF MERE IMAGINATION." [†]

If this is the last word of Science upon that subject, whither then should one turn in order to learn what the nebular theory is supposed to teach ? What, in fact, is this theory ? What it *is*, no one seems to know for a certainty. What it *is not*—we learn from the erudite author of the " World-Life." He tells us that :—

(I.) It " *is not a theory of the evolution* of the Universe . . . but only and primarily a genetic explanation of the phenomena of the solar system, and accessorily a co-ordination of the principal phenomena in the stellar and nebular firmament, *as far as human vision has been able to penetrate.*"

(II.) " That it does not regard the Comets as involved in that particular evolution which has produced the solar system." (*Esoteric doctrine does.*)

(It does, because it, too, recognises the comets as forms of cosmic existence *co-ordinated with earlier stages of nebular evolution ;* and it actually assigns *to them chiefly* the formation of all worlds.)

(III.) " *That it does not deny an antecedent history of the luminous fire mist* " —(the *secondary* stage of evolution in the Secret Doctrine) . . . . " and makes no claim to having reached an absolute beginning." And even

---

* See Stanza III. about " Light, or the *cold* Flame," and Commentary Number 8, where it is explained that the " mother" (Chaos) is a cold Fire, a cool Radiance, colourless, formless, devoid of every quality. " Motion is the One Eternal *is*, and contains the potentialities of every quality in the Manvantaric Worlds," it is said.

† *Hypothèses Cosmogoniques,* C. Wolf, 1886.

it allows that this " fire mist may have previously existed in a cold, non-luminous and *invisible* condition " . . . .

(IV.) " And that finally : it does not profess to discover the ORIGIN of things, *but only a stadium in material history* " . . . . leaving " the philosopher and theologian as free as they ever were to seek for the origin of the modes of being."*

But this is not all. Even the greatest philosopher of England—Mr. Herbert Spencer—arrayed himself against the fantastic theory by saying that (*a*) " The problem of existence is not resolved " by it; (*b*) the nebular hypothesis " throws no light upon the origin of diffused matter," and (*c*) that " the nebular hypothesis (as it now stands) implies a First Cause."†

The latter, we are afraid, is more than our modern physicists have bargained for. Thus, it seems that the poor " hypothesis " can hardly expect to find help or corroboration even in the world of the meta-physicians.

Considering all this, the Occultists believe they have a right to present *their* philosophy, however misunderstood and ostracised it may be at present. And they maintain that this failure of the scientists to discover the truth is entirely due to their materialism and contempt for transcendental sciences. Yet although the scientific minds in our century are as far from the true and correct doctrine of Evolution as ever, there may be still some hope left for the future, as we find another great scientist giving us a faint glimmer of it.

In an article in *Popular Science Review* (Vol. XIV., p. 252) on " Recent Researches in Minute Life," we find Mr. H. J. Slack, F.C.S., Sec. R.M.S., saying : " There is an evident convergence of all sciences, from physics to chemistry and physiology, toward *some* doctrine of evolution and development, of which the facts of Darwinism *will form part*, but what ultimate aspect this doctrine will take, there is little, if any, evidence to show, and *perhaps it will not be shaped by the human mind until metaphysical as well as physical inquiries are much more advanced.*"

This is a happy forecast indeed. The day *may* come, then, when the " Natural Selection," as taught by Mr. Darwin and Mr. Herbert Spencer, will form only *a part*, in its ultimate modification, of our Eastern doctrine of Evolution, which will be Manu and Kapila *esoterically explained.*

---

* " World-Life," p. 196.
† *Westminster Review, XX.*, July 27, 1868.

XIV.

FORCES—MODES OF MOTION OR INTELLIGENCES?

THIS is, then, the last word of physical science up to the present year, 1888. Mechanical laws will never be able to prove the homogeneity of primeval matter, except inferentially and as a desperate necessity, when there will remain no other issue—as in the case of Ether. Modern Science is secure only in its own domain and region; within the physical boundaries of our solar system, beyond which everything, every particle of matter, is different from the matter it knows: which matter exists in states of which Science can form no idea. *That* matter, which is truly homogeneous, is beyond human perceptions, if perception is tied down merely to the five senses. We feel its effects through those INTELLIGENCES which are the results of its primeval differentiation, whom we name Dhyan-Chohans; called in the Hermetic works the " Seven Governors," those to whom Pymander, the " Thought Divine," refers as the Building Powers, and whom Asklepios calls the " Supernal Gods." That matter—the real primordial substance, the noumenon of all the " matter " we know of,—even some of the astronomers have been led to believe in, and to despair of the possibility of ever accounting for rotation, gravitation, and the origin of any mechanical physical laws—unless these *Intelligences* be admitted by Science. In the above-quoted work upon astronomy, by Wolf,* the author endorses fully the theory of Kant, and the latter, if not in its general aspect, at any rate in some of its features, reminds one strongly of certain esoteric teachings. Here we have the world's system *reborn from its ashes*, through a nebula ; the emanation from the bodies, dead and dissolved in Space— resultant of the *incandescence* of the solar centre reanimated by the combustible matter of the planets. In this theory, generated and developed in the brain of a young man hardly twenty-five years of age, who had never left his native place, a small town of Northern Prussia (Königsberg) one can hardly fail to recognise either an inspiring external power, or the *reincarnation* which the Occultists see in it. It fills a gap which Newton, with all his genius, failed to bridge. And surely it is our primeval matter, Akâsa, that Kant had in view, when proposing to solve Newton's difficulty and his failure to explain, by the natural forces, the primitive impulse imparted to the planets, by the postulation of a universally pervading primordial substance. For, as he remarks in chapter viii., if it is once admitted that the perfect harmony of the stars and planets and

---

* " LES HYPOTHESES COSMOGONIQUES. *Examen des Théories Scientifiques modernes su 'Origine des Mondes, suivi de la Traduction de la Théorie du Ciel de Kant.*"

the coincidence of their orbital planes prove the existence of a natural cause, which would thus be the primal cause, " that cause *cannot really be the matter which fills to-day the heavenly spaces*." It must be that which filled space—was space—originally, whose motion in differentiated matter was the origin of the actual movements of the sidereal bodies ; and which, "*in condensing itself in those very bodies*, thus abandoned the space that is found void to-day." In other words, it is that same matter of which are now composed the planets, comets, and the Sun himself, which, having in the origin formed itself into those bodies, has preserved its inherent quality of motion ; which quality, now centred in their nuclei, directs all motion. A very slight alteration of words is needed, and a few additions, to make of this our Esoteric Doctrine.

The latter teaches that it is this original, primordial *prima materia*, divine and intelligent, the direct emanation of the Universal Mind—the *Daiviprakriti* (the divine light emanating from the *Logos**)—which formed the nuclei of all the "self-moving" orbs in Kosmos. It is the informing, ever-present moving-power and life-principle, the vital soul of the suns, moons, planets, and even of our Earth. The former latent : the last one active—the invisible Ruler and guide of the gross body attached to, and connected with, its Soul, which is the spiritual emanation, after all, of these respective planetary Spirits.

Another quite occult doctrine is the theory of Kant, that the matter of which the inhabitants and the animals of other planets are formed is of *a lighter and more subtle nature and of a more perfect conformation in proportion to their distance from the Sun*. The latter is too full of Vital Electricity, of the physical, life-giving principle. Therefore, the men on Mars are more ethereal than we are, while those of Venus are more gross, though far more intelligent, if less spiritual.

The last doctrine is not quite ours—yet those Kantian theories are as metaphysical, and as transcendental as any occult doctrines ; and more than one man of Science would, if he but *dared* speak his mind, accept them as Wolf does. From this Kantian mind and soul of the Suns and Stars to the MAHAT (mind) and Prakriti of the Purânas, there is but a step. After all, the admission of this by Science would be only the admission of a natural cause, whether it would or would not stretch its belief to such metaphysical heights. But then *Mahat*, the MIND, is a " God," and physiology admits " mind " only as a temporary function of the material brain, and no more.

The Satan of Materialism now laughs at all alike, and denies the visible as well as the invisible. Seeing in light, heat, electricity, and even in the *phenomenon of life*, only properties inherent in matter, it

---

* Which " Light " we call *Fohat*.

laughs whenever life is called VITAL PRINCIPLE, and derides the idea of its being independent of and distinct from the organism.

But here again scientific opinions differ as in everything else, and there are several men of science who accept views very similar to ours. Consider, for instance, what Dr. Richardson, F.R.S. (elsewhere quoted at length) says of that " Vital principle," which he calls " nervous ether " ("*Popular Science Review*," Vol. 10) :—

"I speak only of a veritable *material agent*, refined, it may be, to the world at large, but *actual and substantial* : an agent having quality of weight and of volume, an agent susceptible of chemical combination, and thereby of change of physical state and condition, an agent passive in its action, moved always, that is to say, by influences apart from itself,* obeying other influences, an agent possessing no initiative power, no *vis or energia naturæ*,† but still playing a most important, if not a primary part in the production of the phenomena resulting from the action of the *energeia* upon visible matter " (*p.* 379).

As Biology and Physiology now deny, *in toto*, the existence of a " vital principle," this extract, together with de Quatrefages' admission, is a clear confirmation that there are men of science who take the same views about "things occult " as theosophists and occultists do. These recognise a distinct vital principle independent of the organism— material, of course, *as physical force cannot be divorced from matter*, but of a substance existing in a state unknown to Science. *Life for them is something more than the mere interaction of molecules and atoms.* There is a vital principle without which no molecular combinations could ever have resulted in a living organism, least of all in the so-called " inorganic " matter of our plane of consciousness.

By "molecular combinations" is meant, of course, those of the matter of our present illusive perceptions, which matter energises only on this, our plane. And this is the chief point at issue.‡

---

* This is a mistake, which implies a material agent, distinct from the influences which move it, *i.e.* blind matter and perhaps " God " again, whereas this ONE Life is the very God and Gods " Itself."

† The same error.

‡ "Is the *Jîva* a myth, as science says, or is it not? " ask some Theosophists, wavering between materialistic and idealistic Science. The difficulty of really grasping esoteric problems concerning the " ultimate state of matter " is again the old crux of the *objective* and the *subjective*. What is matter? Is the matter of our present objective consciousness anything but our SENSATIONS ? True, the sensations we receive come *from without*, but can we really (except in terms of phenomena) speak of the " gross matter " of this plane as an entity apart from and independent of us? To all such arguments Occultism answers : True, in *reality* matter is not independent of, or existent outside, our perceptions. Man is an *illusion* : granted. But the existence and actuality of other, still more illusive, but not less *actual*, entities than we are, is not a claim which is lessened, but rather strengthened by this doctrine of Vedantic and even Kantian Idealism.

Thus the Occultists are not alone in their beliefs. Nor are they so foolish, after all, in rejecting even the "gravity" of modern Science along with other *physical* laws, and in accepting instead *attraction* and *repulsion*. They see, moreover, in these two opposite Forces only the two *aspects* of the universal unit, called " MANIFESTING MIND"; in which aspects, Occultism, through its great Seers, perceives an innumerable Host of operative Beings: Cosmic Dhyan-Chohans, Entities, whose essence, in its *dual* nature, is the Cause of all terrestial phenomena. For that essence is co-substantial with the universal Electric Ocean, which is LIFE; and being dual, as said—positive and negative—it is the emanations of that duality that act now on earth under the name of "modes of motion"; even *Force* having now become objectionable as a word, for fear it should lead someone, even in thought, to separate it from matter ! It is, as Occultism says, the dual *effects* of that dual essence, which have now been called centripetal and centrifugal forces, negative and positive poles, or ·polarity, heat and cold, light and darkness, etc., etc.

And it is maintained that even the Greek and Roman Catholic Christians, are wiser in believing, as they do—even if blindly connecting and tracing them all to an anthropomorphic god—in Angels, Arch- angels, Archons, Seraphs, and Morning Stars : in all those theological *Deliciæ humani generis*, in short, that rule the cosmic elements, than Science is, in disbelieving in them altogether, and advocating its mechanical Forces. For these act very often with more than human intelligence and pertinency. Nevertheless, that intelligence is denied and attributed to blind chance. But, as De Maîstre was right in calling the law of gravitation merely a *word* which replaced "the thing unknown" (*Soirées*), so are we right in applying the same remark to all the other *Forces* of Science. And if it is objected that the Count was an ardent Roman Catholic, then we may cite Le Couturier, as ardent a materialist, who said the same thing, as also did Herschell and many others. (*Vide Musée des Sciences, August,* 1856.)

From *Gods* to *men*, from Worlds to atoms, from a star to a rush-light, from the Sun to the vital heat of the meanest organic being—the world of Form and Existence is an immense chain, whose links are all connected. The law of Analogy is the first key to the world-problem, and these links have to be studied co-ordinately in their occult relations to each other.

When, therefore, the Secret Doctrine—postulating that conditioned or limited space (location) has no real being except in this world of illusion, or, in other words, in our perceptive faculties—teaches that every one of the higher, as of the lower worlds, is interblended with our own objective world ; that millions of things and beings are, in point of localization, around and *in* us, as we are around, with, and in them; it is no metaphysical figure of speech, but a sober fact in Nature, however incomprehensible to our senses.

But one has to understand the phraseology of Occultism before criticising what it asserts. For example, the Doctrine refuses (as Science does, in one sense) to use the words "above" and "below," "higher" and "lower," in reference to *invisible* spheres, as being without meaning. Even the terms "East" and "West" are merely conventional, necessary only to aid our human perceptions. For, though the Earth has its two fixed points in the poles, North and South, yet both East and West are variable relatively to our own position on the Earth's surface, and in consequence of its rotation from West to East. Hence, when "*other* worlds" are mentioned—whether better or worse, more spiritual or still more material, though both invisible—the Occultist does not locate *these spheres* either *outside* or *inside* our Earth, as the theologians and the poets do; for their location is nowhere in the space *known* to, and conceived by, the profane. They are, as it were, blended with our world—interpenetrating it and inter-penetrated by it. There are millions and millions of worlds and firmaments visible to us; there still greater numbers beyond those visible to the telescopes, and many of the latter kind do not belong to our *objective* sphere of existence. Although as invisible as if they were millions of miles beyond our solar system, they are yet with us, near us, *within* our own world, as objective and material to their respective inhabitants as ours is to us. But, again, the relation of these worlds to ours is not that of a series of egg-shaped boxes enclosed one within the other, like the toys called Chinese nests; each is entirely under its own special laws and conditions, having no direct relation to our sphere. The inhabitants of these, as already said, may be, for all we know, or feel, passing *through* and *around* us as if through empty space, their very habitations and countries being interblended with ours, though not disturbing our vision, because we have not yet the faculties necessary for discerning them. Yet by their spiritual sight the Adepts, and even some seers and sensitives, are always able to discern, whether in a greater or smaller degree, the presence and close proximity to us of Beings pertaining to other spheres of life. Those of the (spiritually) higher worlds, communicate only with those terrestrial mortals who ascend to them, through individual efforts, on to the higher plane they are occupying. . . .

"THE SONS OF *Bhumi* (EARTH) REGARD THE SONS OF *Deva-lokas* (ANGEL-SPHERES) AS THEIR GODS; AND THE SONS OF LOWER KINGDOMS LOOK UP TO THE MEN OF *Bhumi*, AS TO THEIR *devas* (GODS); MEN REMAINING UNAWARE OF IT IN THEIR BLINDNESS. . . . THEY (*men*) TREMBLE

BEFORE THEM WHILE USING THEM (*for magical purposes*). . . . THE
FIRST RACE OF MEN WERE THE "*Mind-born sons*" OF THE FORMER.
THEY (*the pitris and devas*) ARE OUR PROGENITORS. . . . (*Book II. of
Commentary on the Book of DZYAN.*)

"Educated people," so-called, deride the idea of Sylphs, Salamanders,
Undines, and Gnomes; the men of science regard as an insult any
mention of such superstitions; and with a contempt of logic and
common good sense, that is often the prerogative of " accepted
authority," they allow those, whom it is their duty to instruct, to
labour under the absurd impression that in the whole Kosmos, or at
any rate in our own atmosphere, there are no other conscious,
intelligent beings, save ourselves.* Any other humanity (composed of
distinct *human* beings) than a mankind with two legs, two arms, and a
head with man's features on it, would not be called human ; though the
etymology of the word would seem to have little to do with the general
appearance of a creature. Thus, while Science sternly rejects even the
possibility of there being such (to us, generally) invisible creatures,
Society, while believing in it all *secretly*, is made to deride the idea
openly. It hails with mirth such works as the *Count de Gabalis*, and fails
to understand that *open satire is the securest mask.*

Nevertheless, such invisible worlds do exist. Inhabited as thickly as
our own is, they are scattered throughout apparent Space in immense
number ; some far more material than our own world, others gradually
etherealizing until they become formless and are as "*Breaths.*" That
our physical eye does not see them, is no reason to disbelieve in them ;
physicists can see neither their ether, atoms, nor " modes of motion," or
Forces. Yet they accept and teach them.

If we find, even in the natural world with which we are acquainted,
matter affording a partial analogy in the difficult conception of such
invisible worlds, there seems little difficulty in recognizing the possibility
of such a presence. The tail of a comet, which, though attracting
our attention by virtue of its luminosity, yet does not disturb
or impede our vision of objects, which we perceive through and
beyond it, affords the first stepping-stone toward a proof of the
same. The tail of a comet passes rapidly across our horizon, and
we should neither feel it, nor be cognizant of its passage, but for the
brilliant coruscation, often perceived only by a few interested in the
phenomenon, while everyone else remains ignorant of its presence and
passage *through*, or across, a portion of our globe. This tail may, or may
not, be an integral portion of the being of the comet, but its tenuity sub-

---

* Even the question of the plurality of worlds inhabited by sentient creatures is
rejected or approached with the greatest caution! And yet see what the great
astronomer, Camille Flammarion, says in his " *Pluralité des Mondes.*"

serves our purpose as an illustration. Indeed, it is no question of superstition, but simply a result of transcendental science, and of logic still more, to admit the existence of worlds formed of even far more attenuated matter than the tail of a comet. By denying such a possibility, Science has played for the last century into the hands of neither philosophy nor true religion, but simply into those of theology. To be able to dispute the better the plurality of even material worlds, a belief thought by many churchmen incompatible with the teachings and doctrines of the Bible,* Maxwell had to calumniate the memory of Newton, and try to convince his public that the principles contained in the Newtonian philosophy are those "which lie at the foundation of all atheistical systems." (*Vide* Vol. II., "*Plurality of Worlds.*")

"Dr. Whewell disputed the plurality of worlds by appeal to scientific evidence," writes Professor Winchell.† And if even the habitability of physical worlds, of planets, and distant stars which shine in myriads over our heads is so disputed, how little chance is there for the acceptance of invisible worlds within the apparently transparent space of our own!

But, if we can conceive of a world composed (for *our* senses) of matter still more attenuated than the tail of a comet, hence of inhabitants in it who are as ethereal, in proportion to *their* globe, as we are in comparison with *our* rocky, hard-crusted earth, no wonder if we do not perceive them, nor sense their presence or even existence. Only, in what is the idea contrary to science? Cannot men and animals, plants and rocks, be supposed to be endowed with quite a different set of senses from those we possess? Cannot their organisms be born, developed, and exist, under other laws of being than those that rule our little world? Is it absolutely necessary that every corporeal being should be clothed in "coats of skin" like those that Adam and Eve were provided with in the legend of Genesis? Corporeality, we are told, however, by more than one man of science, "may exist under very divergent conditions."‡ Do not we know through the

---

* Nevertheless, it will be shown on the testimony of the Bible itself, and of such good Christian theologians as Cardinal Wiseman, that this plurality is taught in both the *Old* and the *New* Testaments.

† See "The Plurality of the Worlds," wherein the list of many men of Science, who wrote to prove the theory, is given.

‡ Professor A. Winchell—arguing upon the plurality of the worlds—makes the following remarks: "It is not at all improbable that substances of a refractory nature might be so mixed with other substances, known or unknown to us, as to be capable of enduring vastly greater vicissitudes of heat and cold than is possible with terrestrial organisms. The tissues of terrestrial animals are simply suited to terrestrial conditions. Yet even here we find different types and species of animals adapted to the trials of extremely dissimilar situations. . . . . . That an animal should be a quadruped or a

discoveries of that very all-denying science that we are surrounded by myriads of invisible lives ? If these microbes, bacteria and the *tutti quanti* of the infinitesimally small, are invisible to us by virtue of their minuteness, cannot there be, at the other pole of it, beings as invisible owing to the quality of their texture or matter—to its tenuity, in fact ? Conversely, as to the effects of cometary matter, have we not another example of a half visible form of life and matter? The ray of sunlight entering our apartment, reveals in its passage myriads of tiny beings living their little life and ceasing to be, independent and heedless of whether they are perceived or not by our grosser materiality. And so again, of the microbes and bacteria and such-like unseen beings in other elements. We passed them by, during those long centuries of dreary ignorance, after the lamp of knowledge in the heathen and highly philosophical systems had ceased to throw its bright light on the ages of intolerance and bigotry during early Christianity ; and we would fain pass them by again now.

And yet these *lives* surrounded us *then* as they do now. They have worked on, obedient to their own laws, and it is only as they were gradually revealed by Science that we have begun to take cognisance of them, as of the effects produced by them.

---

biped is something not depending on the necessities of organization, or instinct, or intelligence. That an animal should possess just five senses is not a necessity of per-cipient existence. There may be animals on the earth with neither smell nor taste. There may be beings on other worlds, and *even on this*, who possess more numerous senses than we. The possibility of this is apparent when we consider the high proba-bility that other properties and other modes of existence lie among the resources of the Kosmos, and even of terrestrial matter. There are animals which subsist where rational man would perish—in the soil, in the river, and the sea " . . . (and why not *human* beings of different organizations, in such case ?) . . . " Nor is incorporated rational existence conditioned on warm blood, nor on any temperature which does not change the forms of matter of which the organism may be composed. *There may be intelligences corporealized* after some concept not involving the processes of injection, assimilation, and reproduction. Such bodies would not require daily food and warmth. They might be lost in the abysses of the ocean, or laid up on a stormy cliff through the tem-pests of an Arctic winter, or plunged in a volcano for a hundred years, and yet retain consciousness and thought. It is conceivable. Why might not psychic natures be enshrined in indestructible flint and platinum ? These substances are no further from the nature of intelligence than carbon, hydrogen, oxygen, and lime. But, not to carry the thought to such an extreme (?), might not high intelligences be embodied in frames as indifferent to external conditions as the sage of the western plains, or the lichens of Labrador, the rotifers that remain dried for years, or the spores of bacteria which pass living through boiling water. . . . These suggestions are made simply to remind the reader how little can be argued respecting the necessary conditions of intelligent, organized existence, from the standard of corporeal existence found upon the earth. Intelligence is, from its nature, as universal and as uniform as the laws of the Universe. Bodies are merely the local fitting of intelligence to particular modifications of universal matter or Force." (*World-Life, or Comparative Geology*, pp. 496-498 *et seq.*)

How long has it taken the world, as it is now, to become what it is ? If it can be said of cosmic dust that some of it comes to the present day "*which had never belonged to the earth before*" ("*World-Life*"), how much more logical to believe—as the Occultists do—that through the countless ages and millions of years that have rolled away, since that dust aggregated and formed the globe we live in around its *nucleus* of *intelligent* primeval substance—many humanities, differing from our present mankind, as greatly as the one which will evolve millions of years hence will differ from our races, appeared but to disappear from the face of the earth, as our own will. Those primitive and far-distant humanities, having, as geologists think, left no tangible relics of themselves, are denied. All trace of them is swept sway, and therefore they have never existed. Yet their relics—a very few of them, truly —are to be found, and they have to be discovered by geological research. Though, even if they were never to be met with, there is no reason to say that no men could have ever lived in those geological times, to which the period of their presence on earth is assigned. For their organisms needed no warm blood, no atmosphere, no feeding ; the author of " World-Life " is right, and it is no such *great extreme* to believe even as we do, that as there may be, on scientific hypotheses, " psychic natures enshrined in indestructible flint and platinum " to this day, so there were psychic natures enshrined in forms of equal *indestructible* primeval matter—the real forefathers of our fifth race.

When we speak, therefore, as in Book II., of men who inhabited this globe 18,000,000 years back, we have in the mind neither the men of our present races, nor the present atmospheric laws, thermal conditions, etc. The Earth and mankind, like the Sun, Moon, and planets, have all their growth, changes, developments, and gradual evolution in their life-periods ; they are born, become infants, then children, adolescents, grown-up bodies, grow old, and finally die. Why should not *Mankind* be also under this universal law ? Says Uriel to Enoch : " Behold, I have showed thee all things. Thou seest the Sun, Moon, and those which conduct the stars of heaven, *which cause all their operations*, seasons, and arrivals to return. . . . *In the days of sinners* the years shall be shortened . . . everything done on Earth shall be subverted . . . the moon shall change its laws " . . . etc. Ch. *lxxix*.)

The " days of Sinners " meant the days when matter would be in its full sway on Earth, and man would have reached the apex of physical development in stature and animality. That came to pass during the period of the Atlanteans, about the middle point of their Race (the 4th), which was drowned as prophesied by Uriel. Since then man began decreasing in physical stature, strength, and years, as will be shown in

Book II. But as we are in the mid-point of our *sub-race* of the Fifth Root Race—the acme of materiality in each—therefore the animal propensities, though more refined, are not the less developed for that : and they are so chiefly in civilized countries.

---

§ XV.

GODS, MONADS, AND ATOMS.

SOME years ago we remarked[*] that "the Esoteric Doctrine may well be called the 'thread-doctrine,' since, like *Sutrâtman*, in the Vedanta philosophy,[†] it passes through and strings together all the ancient philosophical religious systems, and reconciles and explains them all." We say now it does more. It not only reconciles the various and apparently conflicting systems, but it checks the discoveries of modern exact science, and shows some of them to be necessarily correct, since they are found corroborated in the ancient records. All this will, no doubt, be regarded as terribly impertinent and disrespectful, a veritable crime of *lèse-Science ;* nevertheless, it is a fact.

Science is, undeniably, ultra-materialistic in our days ; but it finds, in one sense, its justification. Nature behaving *in actu* ever esoterically, and being, as the Kabalists say, *in abscondito*, can only be judged by the profane through her appearance, and that appearance is always deceitful on the physical plane. On the other hand, the naturalists refuse to blend physics with metaphysics, the body with its informing soul and spirit, which they prefer ignoring. This is a matter of choice with some, while the minority strive very sensibly to enlarge the domain of physical science by trespassing on the forbidden grounds of metaphysics, so distasteful to some materialists. These scientists are wise in their generation. For all their wonderful discoveries would go for nothing, and remain for ever *headless* bodies, unless they lift the veil of matter and strain their eyes to see *beyond*. Now that they have studied nature in the length, breadth, and thickness of her physical frame, it is time to remove the skeleton to the second plane and search within the unknown depths for the living and real entity, for its SUB-*stance*—the noumenon of evanescent matter.

It is only by acting on such lines that some of the truths, now called "exploded superstitions," will be discovered to be facts and the relics of ancient knowledge and wisdom.

One of such " degrading" beliefs—in the opinion of the all-denying sceptic—is found in the idea that Kosmos, besides its objective planetary inhabitants, its humanities in other inhabited worlds, is full of invisible, intelligent *Existences*. The so-called Arch-Angels, Angels and Spirits, of the West, copies of their prototypes, the Dhyan-Chohans, the Devas and Pitris, of the East, are no real Beings but fictions. On this point Materialistic Science is inexorable. To support its position, it upsets its own axiomatic law of uniformity in the laws of nature, that of continuity, and all the logical sequence of analogies in the evolution of being. The masses of the profane are asked, and made, to believe that the accumulated testimony of History, which shows even the Atheists of old—such as Epicurus and Democritus—believing in *gods*, was false ; and that philosophers like Socrates and Plato, asserting their existence, were mistaken enthusiasts and fools. If we hold our opinions merely on historical grounds, on the authority of legions of the most eminent Sages, Neo-Platonists, Mystics of all the ages, from Pythagoras down to the eminent Scientists and Professors of the present century, who, if they reject "gods," believe in "spirits," shall we consider such authorities as weak-minded and foolish as any Roman Catholic peasant, who believes in and prays to his once human Saint, or the Archangel, St. Michael ? But is there no difference between the belief of the peasant and that of the Western heirs to the Rosicrucians and Alchemists of the Middle Ages ? Is it the Van Helmonts, the Khunraths, the Paracelsuses and Agrippas, from Roger Bacon down to St. Germain, who were all blind enthusiasts, hysteriacs or cheats, or is it the handful of modern sceptics—the " leaders of thought "—who are struck with the cecity of negation ? The latter, we opine. It would be a *miracle* indeed, quite an abnormal fact in the realm of probabilities and logic, were that handful of negators to be the sole custodians of *truth*, while the million-strong hosts of believers in gods, angels, and spirits—in Europe and America alone—namely, Greek and Latin Christians, Theosophists, Spiritualists, Mystics, etc., etc., should be no better than deluded fanatics and hallucinated mediums, and often no higher than the victims of deceivers and impostors ! However varying in their external presentations and dogmas, beliefs in the Hosts of invisible Intelligences of various grades have all the same foundation. Truth and error are mixed in all. The exact extent, depth, breadth, and length of the mysteries of Nature are to be found only in Eastern esoteric sciences. So vast and so profound are these that hardly a few, a very few of the highest Initiates—those *whose very existence is known but to a small number of*

Adepts—are capable of assimilating the knowledge. Yet it is all there, and one by one facts and processes in Nature's workshops are permitted to find their way into the exact Sciences, while mysterious help is given to rare individuals in unravelling its arcana. It is at the close of great Cycles, in connection with racial development, that such events generally take place. We are at the very close of the cycle of 5,000 years of the present Aryan Kaliyuga ; and between this time and 1897 there will be a large rent made in the Veil of Nature, and materialistic science will receive a death-blow.

Without throwing any discredit upon time-honoured beliefs, in whatever direction, we are forced to draw a marked line between blind faith, evolved by theologies, and knowledge due to the independent researches of long generations of adepts ; between, in short, faith and philosophy. There have been—in all ages—undeniably learned and good men who, having been reared in sectarian beliefs, died in their crystallized convictions. For Protestants, the garden of Eden is the primeval point of departure in the drama of Humanity, and the solemn tragedy on the summit of Calvary, the prelude to the hoped-for Millennium. For Roman Catholics, Satan is at the foundation of Kosmos, Christ in its centre, and Antichrist at its apex. For both, the Hierarchy of Being begins and ends within the narrow frames of their respective theologies : one self-created *personal* God and an Empyrean ringing with the Hallelujas of *created* angels ; the rest, *false* gods, Satan and fiends.

Theophilosophy proceeds on broader lines. From the very beginning of Æons—in time and space in our Round and Globe—the Mysteries of Nature (at any rate, those which it is lawful for our races to know) were recorded by the pupils of those same now invisible "heavenly men," in geometrical figures and symbols. The keys thereto passed from one generation of "wise men" to the other. Some of the symbols, thus passed from the east to the west, were brought therefrom by Pythagoras, who was not the inventor of his famous "Triangle." The latter figure, along with the plane cube and circle, are more eloquent and scientific descriptions of the order of the evolution of the Universe, spiritual and psychic, as well as physical, than volumes of descriptive Cosmogonies and revealed "*Geneses*." The *ten points* inscribed within that "Pythagorean *triangle*" are worth all the theogonies and angelologies ever emanated from the theological brain. For he who interprets them—on their very face, and in the order given—will find in these seventeen points (the seven Mathematical Points hidden) the uninterrupted series of the genealogies from the first *Heavenly* to *terrestrial* man. And, as they give the order of Beings, so they reveal the order in which were evolved the Kosmos, our earth, and the primordial elements by which the latter was generated. Begotten in the invisible *Depths*, and in the womb of the same "Mother" as its fellow-globes—he who will master the mysteries of our Earth, will have mastered those of all others.

Whatever ignorance, pride or fanaticism may suggest to the contrary, Esoteric Cosmology can be shown inseparably connected with both philosophy and modern science. The gods of the ancients, the monads —from Pythagoras down to Leibnitz—and the atoms of the present materialistic schools (as borrowed by them from the theories of the old Greek Atomists) are only a compound unit, or a graduated unity like the human frame, which begins with body and ends with spirit. In the occult sciences they can be studied separately, but never mastered unless viewed in their mutual correlations during their life-cycle, and as a Universal Unity during *Pralayas*.

La Pluche shows sincerity, but gives a poor idea of his philosophical capacities when declaring his personal views on the Monad or the Mathematical Point. "A point," he says, "is enough to put all the schools in the world in a combustion. But what need has man to know that point, since the creation of such a small being is beyond his power? *A fortiori*, philosophy acts against probability when, from that point which absorbs and disconcerts all her meditations, she presumes to pass on to the generation of the world. . . ."

Philosophy, however, could never have formed its conception of a logical, universal, and absolute Deity if it had no Mathematical Point within the Circle to base its speculations upon. It is only the manifested Point, lost to our senses after its pregenetic appearance in the infinitude and *incognizability* of the Circle, that made a reconciliation between philosophy and theology possible—on condition that the latter should abandon its crude materialistic dogmas. And it is because it has so unwisely rejected the Pythagorean Monad and geometrical figures, that Christian theology has evolved its self-created human and personal God, the monstrous Head from whence flow in two streams the dogmas of Salvation and Damnation. This is so true that even those clergymen who would be philosophers and who were masons, have, in their arbitrary interpretations, fathered upon the ancient sages the queer idea that "the Monad represented (with them) *the throne* of the Omnipotent Deity, placed in the centre of the Empyrean to indicate T.G.A.O.T.U."*—read "the Great Architect of the Universe." A curious explanation this, more Masonic than strictly Pythagorean.

Nor did the "hierogram within a Circle, or equilateral Triangle,"

---

* "Science of Numbers," by the Rev. G. Oliver (p. 36).

ever mean "the exemplification of the unity of the divine Essence ";
for this was exemplified by the plane of the boundless Circle. What it
really meant was the triune co-equal Nature of the first differentiated
Substance, or the *con-substantiality* of the (manifested) Spirit, matter and
the Universe—their "Son," who proceeds from the Point (the real,
esoteric LOGOS) or the Pythagorean MONAD. For the Greek *Monas*
signifies " Unity " in its primary sense. Those unable to seize the
difference between the monad—the Universal Unit—and the *Monads* or
the manifested Unity, as also between the ever-hidden and the revealed
LOGOS or the *Word*, ought never to meddle in philosophy, let alone the
Esoteric Sciences. It is needless to remind the educated reader of Kant's
Thesis to demonstrate his second *Antinomy.** Those who have read and
understood it will see clearly the line we draw between the *absolutely
Ideal* Universe and the invisible though manifested Kosmos. Our Gods
and Monads are not the Elements of *extension* itself, but only those of the
invisible reality which is the basis of the manifested Kosmos. Neither
esoteric philosophy, nor Kant, nor Leibnitz would ever admit that
extension can be composed of simple or unextended parts. But
theologian-philosophers will not grasp this. The Circle and the Point,
which latter retires into and merges with the former, after having emanated the first three points and connected them with lines, thus forming
the first *noumenal* basis of the Second Triangle in the Manifested World,
have ever been an insuperable obstacle to theological flights into
dogmatic Empyreans. On the authority of this Archaic Symbol, a male,
personal god, the *Creator* and *Father* of all, becomes a third-rate emanation, the Sephiroth standing *fourth* in descent, and on the left hand of
En-Soph (see the *Kabalistic Tree of Life*). Hence, the Monad is degraded
into a Vehicle—a " throne " !

The Monad—only the emanation and reflection of the Point (Logos)
in the phenomenal World—becomes, as the *apex* of the manifested
equilateral triangle, the " Father." The left side or line is the *Duad,*
the " Mother," regarded as the evil, counteracting principle (Plutarch,
De Placitis Placitorum); the right side represents the Son (" his Mother's
husband " in *every* Cosmogony, as one with the *apex*) ; at the basic line
is the Universal plane of productive Nature, unifying on the phenomenal
plane Father-Mother-Son, as these were unified in the *apex*, in the
supersensuous World. † By mystic transmutation they became the
Quaternary—the triangle became the TETRAKTIS.

* See Kant's *Critique de la Raison pure* (Barni's transl., Vol. II., p. 54).
† In the Greek and Latin churches—which regard marriage as one of the sacraments
—the officiating priest during the marriage ceremony represents the apex of the *triangle :*
the bride its left feminine side and the bridegroom the right one, while the horizontal
line is symbolised by the row of witness, the bridesmaids and best-men. But behind

This transcendental application of geometry to Cosmic and divine theogony—the Alpha and the Omega of mystical conception—became dwarfed after Pythagoras by Aristotle. By omitting the Point and the Circle, and taking no account of the apex, he reduced the metaphysical value of the idea, and thus limited the doctrine of magnitude to a simple TRIAD—the *line*, the *surface*, and the *body*. His modern heirs, who play at Idealism, have interpreted these three geometrical figures as Space, Force, and Matter—"the potencies of an interacting Unity."* Materialistic Science, perceiving but the basic line of the *manifested* "triangle"— the plane of matter—translates it practically as (Father)-MATTER, (Mother)-MATTER, and (Son)-MATTER, and theoretically as Matter, Force, and Correlation.

But to the average physicist, as remarked by a Kabalist, "Space, Force, Matter, are, what signs in algebra are to the mathematician, merely conventional symbols;" or "Force as force, and Matter as matter, are as absolutely unknowable as is the assumed empty space in which they are held to interact." As symbols representing abstractions, "the physicist bases reasoned hypotheses of the origin of things . . . . and sees three needs in what he terms creation : (*a*) a place wherein to create ; (*b*) a medium by which to create ; (*c*) a material from which to create. And in giving a logical expression to this hypothesis through the terms space, force, matter, he believes he has proved the existence of that which each of these represents *as he conceives it to be*."†

The physicist who regards Space merely as a representation of our mind, or extension unrelated to things in it, which Locke defined as capable of neither resistance nor motion ; the paradoxical materialist, who would have a *void* there, where he can see no matter, would reject with the utmost contempt the proposition that "Space is a substantial though (apparently) absolutely unknowable living Entity." *(New Aspects*, p. 9.) Such is, nevertheless, the Kabalistic teaching, and it is that of Archaic philosophy. Space is the real world, while our world is an artificial one. It is the One Unity throughout its infinitude : in its bottomless depths as on its illusive surface ; a surface studded with countless phenomenal Universes, systems and mirage-like worlds. Nevertheless, to the Eastern Occultist, who is an objective Idealist at the bottom, in the *real* world, which is a Unity of Forces, there is "a connection of all matter in the *plenum*," as Leibnitz would say. This is symbolized in the Pythagorean Triangle.

the priest there is the altar with its mysterious containments and symbolic meaning, inside of which no one but the consecrated priests ought to enter. In the early days of Christianity the marriage ceremony was a mystery and a true symbol. Now, however, even the churches have lost the true meaning of this symbolism.

* See Von Hartmann's and Herbert Spencer's works.
† "New Aspects of Life," by Henry Pratt, M.D.

It consists of *ten points* inscribed pyramid-like (from one to the last four) within its three lines, and it symbolizes the Universe in the famous Pythagorean Decad. The upper single dot is a Monad, and represents a Unit-Point, which is *the* Unity from whence all proceeds, and all is of the same essence with it. While the ten dots within the triangle represent the phenomenal world, the three sides of the equilateral triangle which enclose the pyramid of dots are the barriers of *noumenal* Matter, or Substance, that separate it from the world of Thought. "Pythagoras considered a *point* to correspond in proportion to unity; a *line* to 2; a *superficies* to 3; a *solid* to 4; and he defined a point as a Monad having position, and the beginning of all things; a line was thought to correspond with duality, because it was produced by the first motion from indivisible nature, and formed the junction of two points. A superficies was compared to the number three because it is the first of all causes that are found in figures; for a circle, which is the principal of all round figures, comprises a triad, in centre—space— circumference. But a triangle, which is the first of all rectilineal figures, is included in a ternary, and receives its form according to that number; and was considered by the Pythagoreans to be the creator of all sublunary things. The four points at the base of the Pythagorean triangle correspond with a solid or cube, which combines the principles of length, breadth, and thickness, for no solid can have less than four extreme boundary points." *(Pythag. Triangle,* p. 19.)

It is argued that "the human mind cannot conceive an indivisible unit short of the annihilation of the idea with its subject." This is an error, as the Pythagoreans have proved, and a number of Seers before them, although there is a special training for it, and although the profane mind can hardly grasp it. But there are such things as *metamathematics* and *metageometry*. Even mathematics pure and simple proceed from the Universal to the particular, from the mathematical, hence *indivisible* Point, to solid figures. The teaching originated in India, and was taught in Europe by Pythagoras, who, throwing a veil over the Circle and the Point—which no living man can define except as incomprehensible abstractions—laid the origin of the differentiated Cosmic matter in the basic or horizontal line of the Triangle. Thus the latter became the earliest of geometrical figures. The author of "New Aspects of Life" and of the Kabalistic Mysteries—objects to the objectivization, so to speak, of the Pythagorean conception and use of the equilateral triangle, and calls it a *misnomer.* His argument that a solid equilateral body—"one whose base, and each of its sides, form equal triangles —must have four co-equal sides or surfaces, while a triangular plane will as necessarily possess five," demonstrates on the contrary the grandeur of the conception in all its esoteric application to the idea of the *pregenesis,* and the genesis of Kosmos. Granted, that an ideal triangle, depicted by mathematical, imaginary lines " can have no sides at all, being simply *a phantom of the mind* (if sides be imputed to which, they must be the sides of the object it constructively represents)." But in such case most of the scientific hypotheses are no better than " phantoms of the mind "; they are unverifiable, except on inference, and have been adopted merely to answer scientific necessities. Furthermore, the ideal triangle—" as the abstract idea of a triangular body, and, therefore, as the type of an abstract idea "—accomplished and carried out to perfection the double symbolism intended. As an emblem applicable to the objective idea, the simple triangle became a solid. When repeated in stone on the four cardinal points, it assumed the shape of the Pyramid—the symbol of the phenomenal merging into the noumenal Universe of thought—at the apex of the four triangles; and, as an " imaginary figure constructed of three mathematical lines," it symbolized the subjective spheres—those lines " enclosing a mathematical space—which is equal to nothing enclosing nothing." Because, to the senses and the untrained consciousness of profane and scientist, everything beyond the line of differentiated matter—*i.e.,* outside of, and beyond the realm of even the most spiritual *substance*—has to remain for ever *equal to nothing.* It is the AIN-SOPH—the *No-*THING.

Yet these " phantoms of the mind" are in truth no greater abstractions than the abstract ideas in general upon evolution and physical development—*e.g.,* Gravity, Matter, Force, etc.—on which the exact sciences are based. Our most eminent chemists and physicists are earnestly pursuing the not hopeless attempt of finally tracing to its hiding-place the *protyle,* or the basic line of the Pythagorean triangle. The latter is, as said, the grandest conception imaginable, as it symbolizes both the ideal and the visible universes.* For if " *the possible unit is only a possibility as an actuality of nature, as an individual of any kind,*" and as every individual natural object is capable of division, and by division loses its unity, *or ceases to be a unit,*† it is so only in the realm of exact sciences in a world as deceptive as it is illusive. In the realm of the Esoteric sciences the unit divided *ad infinitum,* instead of losing its unity, approaches with every division the planes of the only eternal REALITY. The eye of the SEER can follow and behold it in all its pregenetic glory. This same idea of the reality of the subjective, and the unreality of the objective universes, is found at the bottom of the Pythagorean and Platonic teachings—limited to the *Elect* alone ; for

---

* In the world of Form, having found its expression in the Pyramids, Symbolism has in them both a triangle and a square, with their four co-equal triangles or surfaces, the four basic points, and the fifth—the *apex.*

† " New Aspects of Life."

Porphyry, speaking of the *Monad* and the *Duad*, says that the former only was considered substantial and real, "*that most simple Being, the cause of all unity and the measure of all things.*"

But the Duad, although the origin of Evil, or Matter—thence *unreal* in philosophy—is still Substance during Manvantara, and is often called the *third* monad, in Occultism, and the connecting line as between two Points, . . . or Numbers which proceeded from THAT, "which was before all Numbers," as expressed by Rabbi Barahiel. And from this Duad proceeded all the *Scintillas* of the three upper and the four lower worlds or planes—which are in constant interaction and correspondence. This is a teaching which the Kabala has in common with Eastern Occultism. For in the occult philosophy there are the "ONE Cause" and the "*Primal* Cause," which latter thus becomes, paradoxically, the second, as clearly expressed by the author of the "*Qabbalah, from the philosophical writings of Ibn Gabirol*,"—"in the treatment of the Primal cause, two things must be considered, the Primal Cause *per se*, and the relation and connection of the Primal Cause with the visible and unseen universe.' Thus he shows the early Hebrews following in the steps of the Oriental philosophy—Chaldean, Persian, Hindu, Arabic, etc. Their Primal Cause was designated at first "by the triadic Shaddaï, the (triune) Almighty, subsequently by the Tetragrammaton, YHVH, symbol of the Past, Present, and Future," and, let us add, of the eternal Is, or the I AM. Moreover, in the Kabala the name YHVH (or Jehovah) expresses a He and a She, male and female, two in one, or Hokhmah and Binah, and his, or rather their *Shekinah* or synthesizing spirit (grace), which makes again of the Duad a Triad. This is demonstrated in the Jewish Liturgy for Pentecost, and the prayer, "In the name of Unity, of the Holy and Blessed Hû (He), and His Shekinah, the Hidden and Concealed Hû, blessed be YHVH (the Quaternary) for ever." "Hû is said to be masculine and YAH feminine, together they make the יהוה אחד *i.e.*, one YHVH. One, but of a male-female nature. The Shekinah is always considered in the Qabbalah as feminine" (p. 175). And so it is considered in the *exoteric* Purânas, for Shekinah is no more than *Sakti*—the female double or lining of any god, in such case. And so it was with the early Christians whose Holy Spirit was feminine, as Sophia was with the Gnostics. But in the transcendental Chaldean Kabala or "Book of Numbers," "Shekinah" is sexless, and the purest abstraction, a State, like Nirvana, not subject or object or anything except an absolute PRESENCE.

Thus it is only in the anthromorphised systems (such as the Kabala has now greatly become) that Shekinah-Sakti is feminine. As such she becomes the *Duad* of Pythagoras, the two straight lines of the symbol that can never meet, which therefore form no geometrical figure and are the symbol of matter. Out of this Duad, when united in one basic line of the triangle on the lower plane (the upper Triangle of the Sephirothal Tree), emerge the Elohim, or Deity in *Cosmic* Nature, with the true Kabalists the *lowest* designation, translated in the Bible "God" (see the same work and page).* Out of these issue the *Scintillas*.

The *Scintillas* are the "Souls," and these Souls appear in the three-fold form of Monads (units), atoms and gods—according to our teaching. "Every atom becomes a visible complex unit (a molecule), and once attracted into the sphere of terrestial activity, the Monadic Essence, passing through the mineral, vegetable, and animal kingdoms, becomes man." (Esot. Catechism.) Again, "God, Monad, and Atom are the correspondences of Spirit, Mind, and Body *(Atma, Manas, and Sthula Sarira)* in man." In their septenary aggregation they are the "Heavenly Man" (see *Kabala* for the latter term); thus, terrestrial man is the provisional reflection of the Heavenly. . . . . "The Monads *(Jivas)* are the Souls of the Atoms, both are the fabric in which the Chohans (Dhyanis, *gods*) cloth themselves when a form is needed." *(Esot. Cat.)*

This relates to Cosmic and sub-planetary Monads, not to the Super-Cosmic *Monas* (the Pythagorean Monad) as called, in its synthetic character, by the Pantheistical Peripatetics. The Monads of the present dissertation are treated from the standpoint of their individuality, as *atomic Souls*, before these atoms descend into pure terrestrial form. For this descent into *concrete* matter marks the medial point of their own individual pilgrimage. Here, losing in the mineral kingdom their individuality, they begin to ascend through the seven states of terrestrial evolution to that point where a correspondence is firmly established between the human and *Deva* (divine) consciousness. At present, however, we are not concerned with their terrestrial metamorphoses and tribulations, but with their life and behaviour in Space, on planes wherein the eye of the most intuitional chemist and physicist cannot reach them—unless, indeed, he develops in himself highly clairvoyant faculties.

It is well known that Leibnitz came several times very near the truth, but defined monadic evolution incorrectly, which is not to be wondered at, since he was not an INITIATE, nor even a Mystic, only a

---

* Such recent works as the Qabbalah of Mr. Isaac Myer and of Mr. S. L. MacGregor Mathers, fully justify our attitude towards the Jehovistic Deity. It is not the transcendental, philosophical, and highly metaphysical abstraction of the original Kabalistic thought—Ain-Soph-Shekinah-Adam-Kadmon, and all that follows—that we oppose, but the crystallization of all these into the highly unphilosophical, repulsive, and anthropomorphic Jehovah, the androgynous and *finite* deity for which eternity, omnipotence, and omniscience are claimed. We do not war against the IDEAL REALITY, but the hideous theological *Shadow*.

very intuitional philosopher. Yet no psycho-physicist ever came nearer than he has to the esoteric general outline of evolution. This evolution —viewed from its several standpoints—*i.e.*, as the *universal* and the *individualized* Monad; and the chief aspects of the Evolving Energy, after differentiation—the purely Spiritual, the Intellectual, the Psychic and the Physical—may be thus formulated as an invariable law; a descent of Spirit into Matter, equivalent to an ascent in physical evolution ; a re-ascent from the depths of materiality towards its *status quo ante*, with a corresponding dissipation of concrete form and substance up to the LAYA state, or what Science calls " the zero-point," and beyond.

These states—once the spirit of Esoteric philosophy is grasped— become absolutely necessary from simple logical and analogical consider- ations. Physical Science having now ascertained, through its depart- ment of Chemistry, the invariable law of this evolution of atoms—from their "*protylean*" state down to that of a physical and then a chemical particle (or molecule)—cannot well reject the same as a general law. And once it is forced by its enemies—Metaphysics and Psychology *— out of its alleged impregnable strongholds, it will find it more difficult than it now appears to refuse room *in the Spaces* of SPACE to Planetary Spirits (gods), Elementals, and even the *Elementary* Spooks or Ghosts, and others. Already Figuier and Paul D'Assier, two Positivists and Materialists, have succumbed before this logical necessity. Other and still greater Scientists will follow in that "intellectual FALL." They will be driven out of their position not by spiritual, theosophical, or any other physical or even mental phenomena, but simply by the enormous *gaps* and *chasms* that open daily and will still be opening before them, as one discovery follows the other, until they are finally knocked off their feet by the ninth wave of simple common sense.

Here is an example : Prof. W. Crookes' latest discovery of what he has named *protyle*. In the " Notes on the Bhagavat Gita," by one of the best metaphysicians and Vedantic scholars in India,† the lecturer, referring cautiously to " things occult " in that great Indian esoteric work, makes a remark as suggestive as it is strictly correct. " . . . Into the details of the evolution of the solar system itself," he says, "*it is not necessary for me to enter*. You may gather some idea *as to the way* in which the various elements start into existence from these THREE *principles into which* MULAPRAKRITI *is differentiated* (the Pythagorean triangle), by

---

* Let not the word " psychology " cause the reader to carry his thought by an association of ideas to modern " Psychologists," so-called, whose *idealism* is another name for uncompromising materialism, and whose pretended Monism is no better than a mask to conceal the void of final annihilation—even of consciousness. Here *Spiritual* psychology is meant.

† T. Subba Row, see *Theosophist* for Feb., 1887.

examining the lecture delivered by Professor Crookes a short time ago upon the so-called elements of modern chemistry. This lecture will give you some idea of the way in which these Elements spring from *Vishwanara,** the most objective of these three principles, which seems to stand in the place of the *protyle* mentioned in that lecture. *Except in a few particulars*, this lecture seems to give the outlines of the theory of physical evolution on the plane of *Vishwanara*, and is, so far as I know, *the nearest approach made by modern investigators* TO THE REAL OCCULT THEORY *on the subject.*"

These words will be re-echoed and approved by every Eastern Occultist. Much from the lectures by Prof. Crookes has already been quoted in § XII. of these Addenda. Since then, there has been another lecture delivered, as remarkable as the first one, on the " Genesis of the Elements,"† and also a third one. Here we have almost a corroboration of the teachings of Esoteric philosophy concerning the mode of primeval evolution. It is, indeed, as *near an approach*, made by a great scholar and specialist in chemistry,‡ to the Secret Doctrine, as could be made apart from the application of the monads and atoms to the dogmas of pure transcendental metaphysics, and their connection and correlation with " Gods and intelligent Conscious Monads." But Chemistry is now on its ascending plane, thanks to one of its highest European representatives. It is impossible for it to go back to that day when materialism regarded its *sub*-elements as absolutely simple and homogeneous bodies, which it had raised, in its blindness, to the rank of elements. The mask has been snatched off by too clever a hand for there to be any fear of a new disguise. And after years of pseudology, of bastard molecules parading under the name of elements, behind and beyond which there could be nought but void, a great professor of chemistry asks once more : " What are these elements, whence do they come, what is their signification ? . . . . These elements perplex us in our researches, baffle us in our speculations, and haunt us in our very dreams. They stretch like an unknown sea before us— mocking, mystifying, and murmuring strange revelations and possibilities." (*Gen. of Elem.*, p. 1.)

---

* " *Vishwanara* is not merely the manifested objective world, but the one physical basis (the horizontal line of the triangle) from which the whole objective world starts into existence." And this is the Cosmic *Duad*, the androgynous Substance. Beyond only, is the true *Protyle*.

† By W. Crookes, F.R.S., V.P.C.S., delivered at the Royal Institution, London, on Friday, February 18th, 1887.

‡ How true it is will be fully demonstrated only on that day when his discovery of radiant matter will have resulted in a further elucidation with regard to the true source of light, and revolutionized all the present speculations. Further familiarity with the northern streamers of the *aurora borealis* may help the recognition of this truth.

Those who are heirs to primeval revelations have taught these "possibilities" in every century, but have never found a fair hearing. The truths inspired to Kepler, Leibnitz, Gassendi, Swedenborg, etc., were ever alloyed with their own speculations in one or another predetermined direction—hence distorted. But now one of the great truths has dawned upon an eminent professor of modern exact science, and he fearlessly proclaims as a fundamental axiom that Science has not made itself acquainted, so far, with *real* simple elements. For Prof. Crookes tells his audience :

"If I venture to say *that our commonly received elements are* NOT *simple and primordial*, that they have *not* arisen by chance or have *not* been created in a desultory and mechanical manner, but have been evolved from simpler matters—or perhaps, indeed, from one sole kind of matter—I do but give formal utterance to an idea which has been, so to speak, for some time 'in the air' of science. Chemists, physicists, philosophers of the highest merit, declare explicitly their belief that the seventy (or thereabouts) elements of our text-books are not the pillars of Hercules which we must never hope to pass." . . . "Philosophers in the present as in the past—men who certainly have not worked in the laboratory—have reached the same view from another side." Thus Mr. Herbert Spencer records his conviction that 'the chemical atoms are produced from the true or physical atoms by processes of evolution under conditions which chemistry has not yet been able to produce.' . . . "And the poet has forestalled the philosopher. Milton ('Paradise Lost,' Book V.) makes the Archangel Raphael say to Adam, instinct with the evolutionary idea, that the Almighty had created

> . . . 'One first matter, all
> Indued with various forms, various degrees
> Of substance.'"

Nevertheless, the idea would have remained crystallized "in the air of Science," and never have descended into the thick atmosphere of materialism and profane mortals for years to come, perhaps, had not Professor Crookes bravely and fearlessly reduced it to its simple elements, and thus publicly forced it on Scientific notice. "An idea," says Plutarch, "is a *being* incorporeal, which has no subsistence by itself, but gives figure and form unto shapeless matter, and *becomes the cause of the manifestation*." (*De Placit. Philos.*) The revolution produced in old chemistry by Avogadro was the first page in the Volume of *New Chemistry*. Mr. Crookes has now turned the second page, and is boldly pointing *to what may be the last*. For once *protyle* accepted and recognized—*as invisible Ether was, both being logical and scientific necessities*—Chemistry will have virtually ceased to live : it will reappear in its reincarnation as *New Alchemy*, or METACHEMISTRY. The discoverer of radiant matter will have vindicated in time the Archaic Aryan works on Occultism and even the Vedas and Purânas. For what are the manifested " Mother," the " Father-Son-Husband " (Aditi and Daksha, a form of Brahmâ, as Creators) and the " Son,"—the three " First-born " —*but simply Hydrogen, Oxygen*, and that which in its terrestrial manifestation is called *nitrogen*. Even the exoteric descriptions of the " First Born " triad give all the characteristics of these three *gases*. Priestley, the " discoverer " of Oxygen, or that which was known in the highest antiquity !

Yet all the ancient, mediæval, and modern poets and philosophers have been anticipated even in the exoteric Hindu books. Descartes' *plenum* of matter differentiated into particles ; Leibnitz's *Ethereal Fluid* and Kant's " primitive fluid " dissolved into its elements ; Kepler's Solar Vortex and Systemic Vortices ; in short, from the Elemental Vortices inaugurated by the universal mind—through Anaxagoras, down to Galileo, Torricelli, and Swedenborg, and after them to the latest speculations by European mystics—all this is found in the Hindu hymns and Mantras to the " Gods, Monads, and Atoms," in their fulness, for they are inseparable. In esoteric teachings, the most transcendental conceptions of the universe and its mysteries, as the most (seemingly) materialistic speculations are found reconciled, because those sciences embrace the whole scope of evolution from Spirit to matter. As declared by an American Theosophist, " The Monads (of Leibnitz) may from one point of view be called *force*, from another *matter*. To occult Science, *force* and *matter* are *only two sides of the same* SUBSTANCE." (" Path," No. 10, p. 297.)

Let the reader remember these " Monads " of Leibnitz, every one of which is a living mirror of the universe, every monad reflecting every other, and compare this view and definition with certain Sanskrit stanzas (*Slokas*) translated by Sir William Jones, in which it is said that the creative source of the Divine Mind, . . . " Hidden in a veil of thick darkness, formed *mirrors of the atoms* of the world, and *cast reflection from its own face on every atom*. . . . ."

When, therefore, Professor Crookes declares that " If we can show how the so-called chemical elements might have been generated we shall be able to fill up a formidable gap in our knowledge of the universe, . . ." the answer is ready. The theoretical knowledge is contained in the esoteric meaning of every Hindu cosmogony in the *Purânas ;* the practical demonstration thereof—is in the hands of those who will not be recognised *in this* century, save by the very few. The scientific possibilities of various discoveries, that must inexorably lead exact Science into the acceptation of Eastern Occult views, which contain all the requisite material for the filling of those " gaps," are, so far, at the mercy of modern materialism. It is only by working in the direction

taken by Professor Crookes that there is any hope for the recognition
of a few, hitherto Occult, truths.

Meanwhile, one thirsting to have a glimpse at a practical diagram of
the evolution of primordial matter, which, separating and differentiating
under the impulse of cyclic law, divides itself into a septenary
gradation of SUBSTANCE (from a general view), can do no better than
examine the plates attached to Mr. Crookes' lecture: " Genesis of the
Elements," and ponder well over some passages of the text.   In one
place (p. 11) he says:—

". . . . Our notions of a chemical element have expanded.   Hitherto
the molecule has been regarded as an aggregate of two or more atoms,
and no account has been taken of the architectural design on which
these atoms have been joined.   We may consider that the structure of
a chemical element is more complicated than has hitherto been supposed.
Between the molecules we are accustomed to deal with in chemical
reactions and ultimate atoms as first created, come smaller molecules
or aggregates of physical atoms ; then sub-molecules differ one from the
other, according to the position they occupied in the yttrium edifice."

" Perhaps this hypothesis can be simplified if we imagine yttrium to
be represented by a five-shilling piece.   By chemical fractionation I
have divided it into five separate shillings, and find that these shillings
are not counterparts, but like the carbon atoms in the benzol ring, have
the impress of their position, 1, 2, 3, 4, 5, stamped on them. . . . If I
throw my shillings into the melting-pot or dissolve them chemically,
the mint stamp disappears and they all turn out to be silver." . . .

This will be the case with all the atoms and molecules when they
have separated from their compound forms and bodies—when *pralaya*
sets in.   Reverse the case, and imagine the dawn of a new manvantara.
The pure " silver " of the absorbed material will once more separate
into SUBSTANCE, which will generate " Divine Essences " whose " principles "* are the primary elements, the sub-elements, the physical
energies and subjective and objective matter ; or, as these are epitom-
ised—GODS, MONADS, and ATOMS.   If leaving for one moment the
metaphysical or transcendental side of the question,—dropping
out of the present consideration the supersensuous and intelligent
beings and entities believed in by the Kabalists and Christians—we
turn to the atomical theory of evolution, the occult teachings are
still found corroborated by exact Science and its confessions, as far, at
least, as regards the supposed " simple " elements, now suddenly

---

* Corresponding on the cosmic scale with the Spirit, Soul-mind, Life, and the three
Vehicles—the astral, the *Mayavic* and the physical bodies (of mankind) whatever division
is made.

degraded into poor and distant relatives—not even second cousins to the latter. For we are told by Prof. Crookes that :

" Hitherto, it has been considered that if the atomic weight of a metal, determined by different observers, setting out from different compounds, was always found to be constant . . . then such metal must rightly take rank among the simple or elementary bodies. We learn . . . that this is no longer the case. Again, we have here wheels within wheels. Gadolinium is not an element but a compound. . . We have shown that yttrium is a complex of five or more new constituents. And who shall venture to gainsay that each of these constituents, if attacked in some different manner, and if the result were submitted to a test more delicate and searching than the radiant-matter test, might not be still further divisible ? Where, then, is the actual ultimate element ? As we advance it recedes like the tantalizing mirage lakes and groves seen by the tired and thirsty traveller in the desert. Are we in our quest for truth to be thus deluded and baulked ? The very idea of an element, as something absolutely primary and ultimate, seems to be growing less and less distinct. . ." (p. 16).

On page 429 of *Isis Unveiled*, Vol. I., we said that " the mystery of first creation, which was ever the despair of Science, is unfathomable unless they (the Scientists) accept the doctrine of Hermes. *They will have to follow in the footsteps of the Hermetists.*" Our prophecy begins to assert itself.

But between Hermes and Huxley there is a middle course and point. Let the men of Science only throw a bridge half-way, and think seriously over the theories of Leibnitz. We have shown *our* theories with regard to atomic evolution—their last formation into compound chemical molecules being produced within our terrestrial workshops in the earth's atmosphere and not elsewhere—as strangely agreeing with the evolution of atoms shown on Mr. Crookes' plates. Several times already it was stated in this volume that *Mârttânda* (the Sun) had evolved and aggregated, together with his smaller seven Brothers, from his Mother's (Aditi's) bosom, that bosom being *prima* MATER-ia—the lecturer's primordial *protyle*. Esoteric doctrines teach the existence of " an antecedent form of energy having periodic cycles of ebb and swell, rest and activity " (p. 21)—and behold a great scholar in Science now asking the world to accept this as one of the postulates. We have shown the " Mother," fiery and hot, becoming gradually cool and radiant, and that same Scientist claims as his second postulate, a *scientific necessity*, it would seem—" an internal action akin to cooling, operating slowly in the protyle." Occult Science teaches that " Mother " lies stretched in infinity (during *Pralaya*) as the great Deep, the " *dry* Waters of Space," according to the quaint expression in the *Catechism*, and becomes *wet* only after the separation and the moving over its face of *Narayana*, the " Spirit which is invisible Flame, which never burns, but sets on fire all that it touches, and gives it life and generation."* And now Science tells us that " the first-born element . . . most nearly allied to protyle " . . . would be " *hydrogen* . . . which for some time would be the only existing form of matter " in the Universe. What says *Old* Science ? It answers : Just so ; but we would call hydrogen and oxygen (which instils the fire of life into the " Mother " by incubation) in the *pregenetic* and even pre-geological ages—the *Spirit*, the *noumenon* of that which becomes in its grossest form oxygen and hydrogen and nitrogen on Earth—nitrogen being of no divine origin, but merely an earth-born cement to unite other gases and fluids, and serve as a sponge to carry in itself the breath of LIFE — pure air.† Before these *gases* and fluids become what they are in *our* atmosphere, they are interstellar Ether; still earlier and on a *deeper* plane—something else, and so on *in infinitum*. The eminent and learned gentleman must pardon an Occultist for quoting him at such length ; but such is the penalty of a Fellow of the Royal Society who approaches so near the precincts of the Sacred Adytum of Occult mysteries as virtually to overstep the forbidden boundaries.

But it is time to leave modern *physical* science and turn to the psychological and metaphysical side of the question. We would only remark that to the " two very reasonable postulates " required by the eminent lecturer, " to get a glimpse of some few of the secrets so darkly hidden " behind " the door of the Unknown "—a third should be added‡—lest no battering at it should avail ; the postulate that Leibnitz, in his speculations, stood on a firm groundwork of fact and truth. The admirable and thoughtful synopsis of these speculations—as given by John Theodore Merz in his " Leibnitz "—shows how nearly he has brushed the hidden secrets of esoteric Theogony in his *Monadologie*. And yet that philosopher has hardly risen in his speculations above the first planes, the lower principles of the Cosmic Great Body. His theory soars to no loftier heights than those of the *manifested* life, self-consciousness and intelligence, leaving the regions of the earlier post-genetic mysteries untouched, as his ethereal fluid is post-planetary.

But this third postulate will hardly be accepted by the modern men

---

* " The Lord is a consuming *fire*." . . . " In him was *life*, and the life was the light of men."

† Which if separated ALCHEMICALLY would yield the Spirit of Life, and its Elixir.

‡ Foremost of all, the postulate that there is no such thing in Nature as *inorganic* substances or bodies. Stones, minerals, rocks, and even chemical "atoms" are simply organic units in profound lethargy. Their coma has an end and their inertia becomes activity.

of Science; and, like Descartes, they will prefer keeping to the properties of external things, which, like extension, are incapable of explaining the phenomenon of motion, rather than accept the latter as an independent Force. They will never become anti-Cartesian in this generation; nor will they admit that "this property of inertia is not a purely geometrical property, that it points to the existence of something in external bodies which is not extension merely." This is Leibnitz's idea as analyzed by Mertz, who adds that he called this *something* Force, and maintained that external things were endowed with Force, and that in order to be the bearers of this force they must have a substance, for they are not lifeless and inert masses, but the centres and bearers of form, a purely esoteric claim, since *force* was with Leibnitz an *active* principle, the division between mind and matter disappearing by this conclusion. But—

" The mathematical and dynamical inquiries of Leibnitz would not have led to the same result in the mind of a purely scientific inquirer. But Leibnitz was not a scientific man in the modern sense of the word. Had he been so, he might have worked out the conception of energy, defined mathematically the ideas of force and mechanical work, and arrived at the conclusion that even for purely scientific purposes it is desirable to look upon force, not as a primary quantity, but as a quantity derived from some other value."

But, luckily for truth—

" Leibnitz was a philosopher; and as such he had certain primary principles, which biassed him in favour of certain conclusions, and his discovery that external things were substances endowed with force was at once used for the purpose of applying these principles. One of these principles was the law of continuity, the conviction that all the world was connected, that there were no gaps and chasms which could not be bridged over. The contrast of extended thinking substances was unbearable to him. The definition of the extended substances had already become untenable: it was natural that a similar inquiry was made into the definition of mind, the thinking substance. . . "

The divisions made by Leibnitz, however incomplete and faulty from the standpoint of Occultism, show a spirit of metaphysical intuition to which no man of science, not Descartes—not even Kant—has ever reached. With him there existed ever an infinite gradation of thought. Only a small portion of the contents of our thoughts, he said, rises into the clearness of apperception, "into the light of perfect consciousness." Many remain in a confused or obscure state, in the state of "perceptions;" but they are there; . . . Descartes denied soul to the animal, Leibnitz endowed, as the Occultists do, " the whole creation with mental life, this being, according to him, capable of infinite gradations." And this, as Mertz justly observes, "at once widened the realm of mental life, destroying the contrast of *animate and inanimate matter;* it did yet more—it reacted on the conception of matter, of the extended substance. For it became evident that external or material things presented the property of extension to our senses only, not to our thinking faculties. The mathematician, in order to calculate geometrical figures, had been obliged to divide them into an infinite number of infinitely small parts, and the physicist saw no limit to the divisibility of matter into atoms. The bulk through which external things seemed to fill space was a property which they acquired only through the coarseness of our senses. . . . Leibnitz followed these arguments to some extent, but he could not rest content in assuming that matter was composed of a finite number of very small parts. His mathematical mind forced him to carry out the argument *in infinitum.* And what became of the atoms then? They lost their extension and they retained only their property of resistance; they were the centres of force. They were reduced to mathematical points . . . but if their extension in space was nothing, *so much fuller was their inner life.* Assuming that inner existence, such as that of the human mind, is a new dimension, not a geometrical but a metaphysical dimension . . . having reduced the geometrical extension of the atoms to nothing, Leibnitz endowed them with an infinite extension in the direction of their metaphysical dimension. After having lost sight of them in the world of space, the mind has, as it were, to dive into a metaphysical world to find and grasp the real essence of what appears in space merely as a mathematical point. . . . As a cone stands on its point, or a perpendicular straight line cuts a horizontal plane only in one mathematical point, but may extend infinitely in height and depth, so the essences *of things real* have only a punctual existence in this physical world of space; but have an infinite depth of inner life in the metaphysical world of thought . . ." (p. 144).

This is the spirit, the very root of occult doctrine and thought. The "Spirit-Matter" and "Matter-Spirit" extend infinitely *in depth,* and like "the essence of things" of Leibnitz, our essence of things *real* is *at the seventh depth;* while the *unreal* and gross matter of Science and the external world, is at the lowest end of our perceptive senses. The Occultist knows the worth or worthlessness of the latter.

The student must now be shown the fundamental distinction between the system of Leibnitz* and that of occult philosophy, on the question of the Monads, and this may be done with his *Monadology* before us. It may be correctly stated that were Leibnitz' and Spinoza's systems

---

* The real spelling of the name—as spelt by himself—is Leibniz. He was of Slavonian descent though a German by birth.

reconciled, the essence and Spirit of esoteric philosophy would be made
to appear. From the shock of the two—as opposed to the Cartesian
system—emerge the truths of the Archaic doctrine. Both opposed the
metaphysics of Descartes. His idea of the contrast of two substances—
Extension and Thought—radically differing from each other and
mutually irreducible, was too arbitrary and too unphilosophical for them.
Thus Leibnitz made of the two Cartesian substances two attributes of
one universal unity, in which he saw God. Spinoza recognised but one
universal indivisible substance and absolute ALL, like Parabrahmam.
Leibnitz, on the contrary perceived the existence of a plurality of
substances. There was but ONE for Spinoza ; for Leibnitz an infinitude
of Beings, *from*, and *in*, the One. Hence, though both admitted but
one real Entity, while Spinoza made it impersonal and indivisible, Leibnitz
divided his *personal* Diety into a number of divine and semi-divine
Beings. Spinoza was a *subjective*, Leibnitz an *objective* Pantheist, yet
both were great philosophers in their intuitive perceptions.

Now, if these two teachings were blended together and each corrected
by the other,—and foremost of all the One Reality weeded of its
personality—there would remain as sum total a true spirit of esoteric
philosophy in them ; the impersonal, attributeless, absolute divine
essence which is *no* " Being," but the root of all being. Draw a deep
line in your thought between that ever-incognizable essence, and the,
as invisible, yet comprehensible Presence (*Mulaprakriti*), or Schekinah,
from *beyond and through which* vibrates the Sound of the *Verbum*, and from
which evolve the numberless hierarchies of intelligent *Egos*, of conscious
as of semi-conscious, *perceptive* and *apperceptive* Beings, whose essence
is spiritual Force, whose Substance is the Elements and whose Bodies
(when needed) are the *atoms*—and our doctrine is there. For, says
Leibnitz, "the primitive Element of every material body being
Force, which has none of the characteristics of (*objective*) matter—it can
be conceived but can never be the object of any imaginative
representation." That which was for him the primordial and ultimate
element in every body and object was thus not the material atoms, or
molecules, necessarily more or less extended, as those of Epicurus and
Gassendi, but, as Mertz shows, immaterial and metaphysical atoms,
' mathematical points ' ; or *real souls*,—as explained by Henri Lachelier
(*Professeur agrégé de Philosophie*), his French biographer. " That which
exists outside of us in an absolute manner, are Souls whose essence is
force," (*Monadologie, Introd.*).

Thus, *reality* in the manifested world is composed of a *unity of units*,
so to say, immaterial (from our stand-point) and infinite. This
Leibnitz calls " Monads, " Eastern philosophy " *Jivas* "—and Occultism
gives it, with the Kabalists and all the Christians, a variety of names.

They are with us, as with Leibnitz—" the expression of the universe," *
and every physical point is but the phenomenal expression of the
noumenal, metaphysical point. His distinction between *perception* and
apperception, is the philosophical though dim expression of the Esoteric
teachings. His "reduced universes," of which "there are as many as
there are Monads"—is the chaotic representation of our Septenary
System with its divisions and sub-divisions.

As to the relation his Monads bear to our Dhyan-Chohans, Cosmic
Spirits, Devas and Elementals, we may reproduce briefly the opinion
of a learned and thoughtful theosophist, Mr. H. A. Bjerregaard, on the
subject. In an excellent paper "On the Elementals, the Elementary
Spirits, and the relationship between them and Human Beings," read
by him before the "Aryan Theosophical Society of New York" (see
PATH, Nos. 10 and 11, of Jan. and Feb. 1887), Mr. Bjerregaard formulates distinctly his opinion. . . . . "To Spinoza, substance is dead and
inactive, but to Leibnitz's penetrating mind everything is living
activity and active energy. In holding this view, *he comes infinitely nearer
the Orient than any other thinker of his day, or after him.* His discovery
that *an active energy forms the essence of Substance* is a principle that *places
him in direct relationship to the Seers of the East.*"

And the lecturer proceeds to show that to Leibnitz atoms and elements
are *centres of force*, or rather "spiritual beings whose very nature is to
act," for the elementary particles are not acting mechanically, but from
an *internal* principle. They are incorporeal spiritual units ("substantial,"
however, but not *immaterial* in our sense) inaccessible to all changes
from without, and indestructible by any external force. Leibnitz's
monads, adds the lecturer, "differ from atoms in the following
particulars, which are very important for us to remember, otherwise we
shall not be able to see the difference between elementals and mere
matter." . . . . "Atoms are not distinguished from each other, they
are qualitatively alike; but one monad differs from every other monad
qualitatively; and every one is a peculiar world to itself. Not so with
atoms; they are absolutely alike quantitatively and qualitatively, and
possess no individuality of their own.† Again, the atoms (molecules,

---

* "Leibnitz's Dynamism," says Professor Lachelier, "would offer but little difficulty
if, with him, the Monad had remained a simple atom of *blind force*. But . . . ." One
perfectly understands the perplexity of modern materialism!

† Leibnitz was an *absolute* Idealist in maintaining that "material atoms are contrary
to reason" (*Système nouveau*, Erdmann, p. 126. col. 2). For him *matter* was a simple
representation of the monad, whether human or atomic. Monads, he thought (as we do),
are everywhere. Thus the human soul is a monad, and every cell in the human body
has its monad, as every cell in animal, vegetable, and even in the (so-called) *inorganic*
bodies. His *atoms* are the molecules of modern Science, and his monads those *simple*

rather) of materialistic philosophy can be considered as extended and divisible, while the monads are mere mathematical points and indivisible. Finally, and this is a point where these monads of Leibnitz closely resemble the elementals of mystic philosophy—these monads are representative Beings. Every monad reflects every other. Every monad is a living mirror of the Universe within its own sphere. And mark this, for upon it depends the power possessed by these monads, and upon this depends the work they can do for us; in mirroring the world, the monads are not mere passive reflective agents, but *spontaneously self-active;* they produce the images spontaneously, as the soul does a dream. In every monad, therefore, the adept may read everything, even the future. Every monad or *Elemental* is a looking-glass that can speak. . ."

It is at this point that Leibnitz's philosophy breaks down. There is no provision made, nor any distinction established, between the "Elemental" monad and that of a high Planetary Spirit, or even the human monad or Soul. He even goes so far as to sometimes doubt whether "God has ever made anything but Monads or substances without extension." (*Examen des Principes du P. Malebranche.*) He draws a distinction between Monads and Atoms,* because, as he repeatedly states, "bodies with all their qualities are only phenomenal, like the rainbow. . . . *Corpora omnia cum omnibus qualitatibus suis non sunt aliud quam phenomena bene fundata, ut Iris*" (Letter to Father Desbosses, *Correspondence*, letter xviii.)—but soon after he finds a provision for this in a substantial correspondence, a certain metaphysical bond between the monads—*vinculum substantiale.* Esoteric philosophy, teaching an *objective* Idealism—though it regards the objective Universe and all in it as *Maya*, temporary illusion—draws a practical distinction between collective illusion, *Mahamaya*, from the purely metaphysical stand-point, and the objective relations in it between various conscious *Egos* so long as this illusion lasts. The adept, therefore, *may* read the future in an Elemental Monad, but he has to draw for this object a great number of them, as each monad represents only a portion of the Kingdom it belongs to. "It is not in the object, but in the modification of the cognition of the object that the Monads are limited. They all go confusedly to the infinite, to the all, but they are all limited and distinguished by the

---

atoms that materialistic Science takes on faith, though it will never succeed in *interviewing* them—except in imagination. But Leibnitz is rather contradictory in his views about Monads. He speaks of his *Metaphysical Points* and *Formal Atoms*, at one time as *realities*, occupying space; at another as pure Spiritual *ideas*; then again endows them with objectivity and aggregates and positions in their co-relations.

* The *atoms* of Leibnitz have, in truth, nothing but the name in common with the atoms of the Greek Materialists, or even the *molecules* of modern Science. He calls them *formal* atoms, and compares them to the substantial forms of Aristotle. (See *Système Nouveau*, § 3.)

degrees of distinct perceptions." (§ 60, *Monadologie.*)* And as Leibnitz
explains, " All the portions of the Universe are distinctly represented
in the Monads, *but some are reflected in one monad, some in another ;*" but a
number of monads could represent simultaneously the thoughts of the
two millions of inhabitants of Paris.

But what say the Occult Sciences to this, and what do they add ?

They say that what is called collectively *Monads* by Leibnitz—
roughly viewed, and leaving every subdivision out of calculation, for
the present†—may be separated into three distinct Hosts, which,
counted from the highest planes, are, firstly, "gods," or conscious, spiritual
Egos ; the intelligent architects, who work after the plan in the *Divine
Mind.* Then come the Elementals, or *Monads,* who form collectively
and unconsciously the grand Universal Mirrors of everything connected
with their respective realms. Lastly, the atoms, or material molecules,
which are informed in their turn by their *apperceptive* monads, just as
every cell in a human body is so informed. (See the closing pages of
Book I.) There are shoals of such *informed* atoms which, in their turn,
inform the molecules ; an infinitude of monads, or Elementals proper,
and countless spiritual Forces—*Monadless,* for they are pure incorpo-
realities,‡ except under certain laws, when they assume a form—not
necessarily human. Whence the substance that clothes them—the
apparent organism they evolve around their centres ? The *Formless*
(" Arupa ") Radiations, existing in the harmony of Universal Will,
and being what we term the collective or the aggregate of Cosmic Will
on the plane of the subjective Universe, unite together an infinitude of
monads—each the mirror of its own Universe—and thus individualize

---

* Leibnitz, like Aristotle, calls the created or *emanated* monads (the Elementals issued
from Cosmic Spirits or Gods)—*Entelechies,* 'Εντελέχεια—and " incorporeal *automata.*"
(§ 18, *Monadologie.*)

† These three " rough divisions " correspond to *spirit, mind* (or soul), and *body,* in
the human constitution.

‡ Brother C. H. A. Bjerregaard, in his lecture (already mentioned), warns his audience not to regard the *Sephiroth* too much as *individualities,* but to avoid at the same
time seeing in them *abstractions.* "We shall never arrive at the truth," he says, "much
less the power of *associating with those celestials,* until we return to the simplicity and
fearlessness of the primitive ages, when men mixed freely with the gods, and the gods
descended among men and guided them in truth and holiness " (No. 10, *Path*). . . .
"There are several designations for 'angels' in the Bible which clearly show tha
beings like the Elementals of the Kabala and the monads of Leibnitz, must be understood by that term rather than that which is commonly understood. They are called
'morning stars,' 'flaming fires,' 'the mighty ones,' and St. Paul sees them in his
cosmogonic vision as 'Principalities and Powers.' Such names as these preclude the
idea of personality, and we find ourselves compelled to think of them as impersonal
Existences . . . as an *influence,* a spiritual substance, or *conscious Force.*" (*Path,*
No. 11, p. 322.)

for the time being an independent mind, omniscient and universal; and by the same process of magnetic aggregation they create for themselves objective, visible bodies, out of the interstellar atoms. For atoms and Monads, associated or dissociated, simple or complex, are, from the moment of the first differentiation, but the *principles*, corporeal, psychic and Spiritual, of the "Gods,"—themselves the Radiations of primordial nature. Thus, to the eye of the Seer, the higher Planetary Powers appear under two aspects: the subjective—as *influences*, and the objective—as mystic FORMS, which, under Karmic law, become a *Presence*, Spirit and Matter being One, as repeatedly stated. Spirit is matter *on the seventh plane;* matter is Spirit—on the lowest point of its cyclic activity ; and both—are MAYA.

Atoms are called "Vibrations" in Occultism; also "Sound"— collectively. This does not interfere with Mr. Tyndall's scientific discovery. He traced, on the lower rung of the ladder of monadic being, the whole course of the *atmospheric vibrations*—and this constitutes the *objective* part of the process in nature. He has traced and recorded the rapidity of their motion and transmission ; the force of their impact ; their setting up vibrations in the tympanum and their transmission of these to the stolithes, etc., etc., till the vibration of the auditory nerve commences—and a new phenomenon now takes place: the *subjective side* of the process or *the sensation of Sound*. Does he perceive or see it ? No; for his speciality is to discover the behaviour of matter. But why should not a psychic see it, a spiritual seer, whose inner Eye is opened, and who can see through the veil of matter ? The waves and undulations of Science are all produced by atoms propelling their molecules into activity *from within*. Atoms fill the immensity of Space, and by their continuous vibration *are* that MOTION which keeps the wheels of Life perpetually going. It is that inner work that produces the natural phenomena called the correlation of Forces. Only, at the origin of every such "force," there stands the *conscious* guiding noumenon thereof—Angel or God, Spirit or Demon—ruling powers, yet the same.

As described by Seers—those who can see the motion of the interstellar shoals, and follow them in their evolution clairvoyantly— they are dazzling, like specks of virgin snow in radiant sunlight. Their velocity is swifter than thought, quicker than any mortal physical eye could follow, and, as well as can be judged from the tremendous rapidity of their course, the motion is circular. . . . . Standing on an open plain, on a mountain summit especially, and gazing into the vast vault above and the spacial infinitudes around, the whole atmosphere seems ablaze with them, the air soaked through with these dazzling coruscations. At times, the intensity of their motion produces flashes like the Northern lights during the *Aurora Borealis*. The sight is so marvellous, that, as the Seer gazes into this inner world, and feels the scintillating points shoot past him, he is filled with awe at the thought of other, still greater mysteries, that lie beyond, and within, this radiant ocean. . . . .

However imperfect and incomplete this explanation on " Gods, Monads and Atoms," it is hoped that some students and theosophists, at least, will feel that there may be indeed a close relation between materialistic Science, and Occultism, which is the complement and missing soul of the former.

XVI.

CYCLIC EVOLUTION AND KARMA.

It is the Spiritual evolution of the *inner*, immortal man that forms the fundamental tenet in the Occult Sciences. To realize even distantly such a process, the student has to believe (*a*) in the ONE Universal Life, independent of matter (or what Science regards as matter); and (*b*) in the individual intelligences that animate the various manifestations of this Principle. Mr. Huxley does not believe in " Vital Force," others do. Dr. J. H. Hutchinson Sterling's work " Concerning Protoplasm " has made no small havoc of this dogmatic negation. Professor Beale's decision is also in favour of a Vital Principle; and Dr. B. W. Richardson's lectures on the " Nervous Ether," have been sufficiently quoted from. Thus, opinions are divided.

The ONE LIFE is closely related to *the one* law which governs the World of Being—KARMA. Exoterically, this is simply and literally " action," or rather an " effect-producing cause." Esoterically it is quite a different thing in its far-fetching moral effects. It is the unerring LAW OF RETRIBUTION. To say to those ignorant of the real significance, characteristics and awful importance of this eternal immutable law, that no theological definition of a personal deity can give an idea of this impersonal, yet ever present and active Principle, is to speak in vain. Nor can it be called Providence. For Providence, with the Theists (the Christian Protestants, at any rate), rejoices in a personal male gender, while with the Roman Catholics it is a female potency, " Divine Providence tempers His blessings to secure their better effects," Wogan tells us. Indeed " He " tempers them, which Karma —a sexless principle—does not.

Throughout the first two Parts, it was shown that, at the first flutter of renascent life, Svâbhâvat, "the mutable radiance of the Immutable Darkness unconscious in Eternity," passes, at every new rebirth of Kosmos, from an inactive state into one of intense activity ; that it differentiates, and then begins its work through that differentiation. This work is KARMA.

The Cycles are also subservient to the effects produced by this activity. " The one Cosmic atom becomes seven atoms on the plane of matter, and each is transformed into a centre of energy ; that same atom becomes seven rays on the plane of spirit, and the seven creative forces of nature, radiating from the root-essence . . . . follow, one the right, the other the left path, separate till the end of the Kalpa, and yet are in close embrace. What unites them ? KARMA." The atoms emanated from the Central Point emanate in their turn new centres of energy, which, under the potential breath of *Fohat*, begin their work from within without, and multiply other minor centres. These, in the course of evolution and involution, form in their turn the roots or developing causes of new effects, from worlds and " man-bearing " globes, down to the genera, species, and classes of all the *seven* kingdoms* (of which *we know only four*). For " the blessed workers have received the *Thyan-kam*, in the eternity " (Book of " The Aphorisms of *Tson-ka-pa* ").

" Thyan-kam " is the power or knowledge of guiding the impulses of cosmic energy in the right direction.

The true Buddhist, recognising no " personal god," nor any " Father " and " *Creator* of Heaven and Earth," still believes in an *absolute conscious-ness*, " Adi-Buddhi " ; and the Buddhist philosopher *knows* that there are Planetary Spirits, the " Dhyan Chohans." But though he admits of " spiritual lives," yet, as they are temporary in eternity, even they, ac-cording to his philosophy, are " the *maya* of the *day*," the *illusion* of a "day of Brahmâ," a short manvantara of 4,320,000,000 years. The " Yin-Sin " is not for the speculations of men, for the Lord Buddha has strongly pro-hibited all such inquiry. If the Dhyan Chohans and all the invisible Beings the *Seven* Centres and their direct Emanations, the *minor* centres of Energy—are the direct reflex of the ONE Light, yet men are far removed from these, since the whole of the *visible* Kosmos consists of " *self-produced* beings, the creatures of *Karma*." Thus regarding a personal God " as only a gigantic shadow thrown upon the void of space by the imagination of ignorant men,"† they teach that only " two things are (objectively) eternal, namely *Akâsa* and *Nirvana* "; and that these are ONE in reality, and but a *maya* when divided. " Buddhists deny creation and cannot conceive of a *Creator*." " Everything has come out of Akâsa (or Svâbhâvat

---

* Vide Stanza VI. (Book I.) and Commentary.
† *Buddhist Catechism*, by H. S. Olcott, President of the Theosophical Society.

on our earth) in obedience to a law of motion inherent in it, and after a certain existence passes away. Nothing ever came out of nothing." (*Buddhist Catechism.*)

If a Vedantic Brahmin of the Adwaita Sect, when asked whether he believes in the existence of God, is always likely to answer, as Jacolliot was answered—" I am myself 'God'; " a Buddhist (a Sinhalese especially) would simply laugh, and say in reply, " There is no God; no Creation." Yet the root philosophy of both Adwaita and Buddhist scholars is *identical*, and both have the same respect for animal life, for both believe that every creature on earth, however small and humble, " is an immortal portion of the immortal matter "—for matter with them has quite another significance than it has with either Christian or materialist—and that every creature is subject to Karma.

The answer of the Brahmin is one which would suggest itself to every ancient philosopher, Kabalist, and Gnostic of the early days. It contains the very spirit of the Delphic and Kabalistic commandments, for esoteric philosophy solved, ages ago, the problem of what man *was*, *is*, and *will be ;* of man's origin, life-cycle—interminable in its duration of successive incarnations or rebirths—and finally of his absorption into the source from which he started.

But it is not physical Science that we can ever ask to read man for us, as the riddle of the Past, or that of the Future; since no philosopher is able to tell us even what man is, as he is known both to physiology and psychology. In doubt whether man was " a god or beast," he is now connected with the latter and derived from an animal. No doubt that the care of analyzing and classifying the human being as a *terrestrial animal* may be left to Science, which occultists—of all men— regard with veneration and respect. They recognize its ground and the wonderful work done by it, the progress achieved in physiology, and even—to a degree—in biology. But man's *inner*, spiritual, psychic, or even moral, nature cannot be left to the tender mercies of an ingrained materialism; for not even the higher psychological philosophy of the West is able, in its present incompleteness and tendency towards a decided agnosticism, to do justice to the inner; especially to his higher capacities and perceptions, and those states of consciousness, across the road to which such authorities as Mill draw a strong line, saying " So far, and no farther shalt thou go."

No Occultist would deny that man—no less than the elephant and the microbe, the crocodile and the lizard, the blade of grass or the crystal— is, in his physical formation, the simple product of the evolutionary forces of nature through a numberless series of transformations ; but he puts the case differently.

It is not against zoological and anthropological discoveries, based on the fossils of man and animal, that every mystic and believer in a divine soul inwardly revolts, but only against the uncalled-for conclusions built on preconceived theories and made to fit in with certain prejudices. Their premises may or may not be always true; and as some of these theories live but a short life, the deductions therefrom must ever be one-sided with materialistic evolutionists. Yet it is on the strength of such very ephemeral authority, that most of the men of science frequently receive undue honours where they deserve them the least.*

To make the working of Karma, in the periodical renovations of the Universe, more evident and intelligible to the student when he arrives at the origin and evolution of man, he has now to examine with us the esoteric bearing of the Karmic Cycles upon Universal Ethics. The question is, do those mysterious divisions of time, called Yugas and Kalpas by the Hindus, and so very graphically—Κύκλος—"cycle," ring or circle, by the Greeks, have any bearing upon, or any direct connection with, human life? Even exoteric philosophy explains that these perpetual circles of time are ever returning on themselves, periodically, and

---

* We refer those who would regard the statement as an impertinence or *irreverence* against accepted Science, to Mr. James Hutchinson Stirling's work concerning "Protoplasm," which is a defence of a *vital* Principle *versus* the Molecularists— Huxley, Tyndall, Vogt, and Co.—and request them to examine whether it is true or not to say that the scientific premises may not be always correct, but that they are accepted, nevertheless, to fill up a gap or a hole in some beloved materialistic hobby. Speaking of protoplasm and the organs of man, as " viewed by Mr. Huxley," the author says : " Probably then, in regard to any continuity in protoplasm of power, of form, or of substance, we have seen *lacunæ* enow. Nay, Mr. Huxley himself can be adduced in evidence on the same side. *Not rarely do we find in his essay admissions* of PROBABILITY, *where it is* CERTAINTY *that is alone in place.* He says, for example : ' It is more than probable that *when* the vegetable world is thoroughly explored we *shall* find all plants in possession of the same powers.' *When a conclusion is decidedly announced*, it is rather disappointing to be told, as here, that *the premises are still to collect* ' (!!) . . . . . Again, here is a passage in which he is seen to cut his own ' basis ' from beneath his own feet. After telling us that all forms of protoplasm consist of carbon, hydrogen, oxygen and nitrogen ' in very complex union,' he continues : ' To this complex combination, *the nature of which has never been determined with exactness (! !)*, the name of *protein* has been applied.' This, plainly, is an identification, on Mr. Huxley's own part, of protoplasm and protein ; and what is said of one, being necessarily true of the other, it follows that he admits the nature of protoplasm never to have been determined with exactness, and that even in his eyes the *lis* is still *sub judice*. This admission is strengthened by the words, too, ' If we use this term—*protein*—with such *caution* as may properly arise out of our *comparative ignorance* of the things for which it stands ' " . . . etc., etc. (p. 33 and 34, in reply to Mr. Huxley in " Yeast ").

This is the eminent Huxley, the king of physiology and biology, who is proven playing at blind man's buff with *premisses* and *facts*. What may not the " smaller fry " of science do after this !

intelligently in Space and Eternity. There are " Cycles of matter " *
and there are " Cycles of Spiritual evolution." Racial, national, and
individual cycles. May not esoteric speculation allow us a still deeper
insight into the workings of these ?

This idea is beautifully expressed in a very clever scientific work :—

" The possibility of rising to a comprehension of a system of co-ordination
so far outreaching in time and space all reach of human observations, is a
circumstance which signalizes the power of man to transcend the limitations
of changing and inconsistent matter, and assert his superiority over all unstable
and perishable forms of being. *There is a method in the succession of events*, and
in the relation of co-existent things, which the mind of man seizes hold of ; and
by means of this as a clue, he runs back or forward over æons of material
history of which human experience can never testify. Events germinate and
unfold. They have a past which is connected with their present, and we feel
a well-justified confidence that a future is appointed which will be similarly
connected with the present and the past. This continuity and unity of history
repeat themselves before our eyes in all conceivable stages of progress. The
phenomena furnish us the grounds for the generalization of two laws which
are truly *principles of scientific divination*, by which alone the human mind penetrates the sealed records of the past and the unopened pages of the future.
The first of these is the law of evolution, or, to phrase it for our purpose, *the
law of correlated successiveness or organized history in the individual*, illustrated in
the changing phrases of every single maturing system of results. . . . These
thoughts summon into our immediate presence the measureless past and the
measureless future of material history. They seem almost to open vistas
through infinity, and to endow the human intellect with an existence and a
vision exempt from the limitations of time and space and finite causation, and
lift it up toward a sublime apprehension of the Supreme Intelligence whose
dwelling place is Eternity." (" World-Life," p. 535 and 548.)

According to the teachings, Maya, or the illusive appearance of the
marshalling of events and actions on this earth, changes, varying with
nations and places. But the chief features of one's life are always in
accordance with the " Constellation " one is born under, or, we should
say, with the characteristics of its animating principle or the deity that
presides over it, whether we call it a *Dhvan Chohan*, as in Asia, or an
Archangel, as with the Greek and Latin churches. In ancient Symbolism it was always the SUN (though the Spiritual, not the visible, Sun was
meant), that was supposed to send forth the chief Saviours and Avatars.
Hence the connecting link between the Buddhas, the Avatars, and so many
other incarnations of the highest SEVEN. The closer the approach to
one's *Prototype*, " in Heaven," the better for the mortal whose personality
was chosen, by his own *personal* deity (the seventh principle), as its terrestrial abode. For, with every effort of will toward purification and unity

---

* " The Cycles of Matter," a name given by Professor Winchell to an Essay of his
written in 1860.

with that "Self-god," one of the lower rays breaks and the spiritual entity of man is drawn higher and ever higher to the ray that supersedes the first, until, from ray to ray, the inner man is drawn into the one and highest beam of the Parent-SUN. Thus, "the events of humanity *do* run co-ordinately with the number forms," since the single units of that humanity proceed one and all from the same source—the *central* and its *shadow*, the visible SUN. For the equinoxes and solstices, the periods and various phases of the Solar course, astronomically and numerically expressed, are only the concrete symbols of the eternally living verity, though they do seem *abstract ideas* to uninitiated mortals. And this explains the extraordinary numerical coincidences with geometrical relations, as shown by several authors.

Yes; "our destiny *is* written in the stars !" Only, the closer the union between the mortal reflection MAN and his celestial PROTOTYPE, the less dangerous the external conditions and subsequent reincarnations—which neither Buddhas nor Christs can escape. This is not superstition, least of all is it *Fatalism*. The latter implies a blind course of some still blinder power, and man is a free agent during his stay on earth. He cannot escape his *ruling* Destiny, but he has the choice of two paths that lead him in that direction, and he can reach the goal of misery— if such is decreed to him, either in the snowy white robes of the Martyr, or in the soiled garments of a volunteer in the iniquitous course ; for, there are *external and internal conditions* which affect the determination of our will upon our actions, and it is in our power to follow either of the two. Those who believe in *Karma* have to believe in *destiny*, which, from birth to death, every man is weaving thread by thread around himself, as a spider does his cobweb ; and this destiny is guided either by the heavenly voice of the invisible *prototype* outside of us, or by our more intimate *astral*, or inner man, who is but too often the evil genius of the embodied entity called man. Both these lead on the outward man, but one of them must prevail ; and from the very beginning of the invisible affray the stern and implacable *law of compensation* steps in and takes its course, faithfully following the fluctuations. When the last strand is woven, and man is seemingly enwrapped in the net-work of his own doing, then he finds himself completely under the empire of this *self-made* destiny. It then either fixes him like the inert shell against the immovable rock, or carries him away like a feather in a whirlwind raised by his own actions, and this is—KARMA.

A materialist, treating upon the periodical creations of our globe, has expressed it in one sentence. "The whole *past* of the Earth is nothing but an unfolded *present*." This was Büchner, who little suspected that he was repeating an axiom of the Occultists. It is quite true also, as Burmeister (quoted in "*Force and matter*") remarks, that

" the historical investigation of the development of the Earth has proved that *now and then* rest upon the same base; that the past has been developed in the same manner as the present rolls on; and that the Forces which were in action ever remained the same."

The " Forces "—their *noumena* rather—are the same, of course; therefore, the phenomenal Forces must be the same also. But how can any one feel so sure that the attributes of matter have not altered under the hand of Protean Evolution ? How can any materialist assert with such confidence, as is done by Rossmassler, that " this eternal conformity in the essence of phenomena renders it certain that fire and water possessed *at all times* the same powers and ever will possess them ? " Who are they " that darken counsel with words without knowledge," and where were the Huxleys and Büchners when the foundations of the earth were laid by the great Law ? It is a fundamental principle of the Occult philosophy, this same homogeneity of matter and immutability of natural laws, which are so much insisted upon by materialism; but that unity rests upon the inseparability of Spirit from matter, and, if the two are once divorced, the whole Kosmos would fall back into chaos and non-being. Therefore, it is absolutely *false*, and but an additional demonstration of the great conceit of our age, to assert (as men of science do) that all the great geological changes and terrible convulsions have been produced *by ordinary and known physical forces*. For these forces were but the tools and final means for the accomplishment of certain purposes, acting periodically, and apparently mechanically, through an inward impulse mixed up with, but beyond their material nature. There is a purpose in every important act of Nature, whose acts are all cyclic and periodical. But spiritual Forces having been usually confused with the purely physical, the former are denied by, and therefore, have to remain unknown to Science, because left unexamined.*

" The history of the World begins with its general aim," says Hegel; " the realization of the Idea of Spirit—only in an *implicit* form (*an sich*), that is, as Nature; a hidden, most profoundly hidden unconscious instinct, and the whole process of History . . . is directed to rendering this unconscious impulse a conscious one. Thus appearing in the form of merely natural existence, natural will—that which has been called the subjective side—physical craving, instinct, passion, private interest, as also opinion and subjective conception—spontaneously present themselves at the very commencement. *This vast congeries of volitions, interests and activities constitute the instruments and means of the* WORLD

---

* Men of science will say : We deny, because nothing of the kind has ever come within the scope of our experience. But, as argued by Charles Richet, the physiologist : " So be it, but have you at least demonstrated the contrary ? . . . Do not, at any rate, deny *a priori*. Actual Science *is not sufficiently advanced to give you such right*." (" La suggestion mentale et le calcul des probabilités.")

SPIRIT *for attaining its object;* bringing it to consciousness and realising it. And this aim is none other than finding itself—coming to itself—and contemplating itself in concrete actuality. But that those manifestations of vitality on the part of individuals and peoples, in which they seek and satisfy their own purposes, are at the same time *the means and instruments of a higher power, of a higher and broader purpose of which they know nothing*—which they realise unconsciously —might be made a matter of question ; rather has been questioned . . . on this point I announced my view at the very outset, and asserted our hypothesis . . . and our belief *that Reason governs the World and has consequently governed its history.* In relation to this independently universal and substantial existence— all else is subordinate, subservient to it, and the means for its development."[*]

No metaphysician or theosophist could demur to these truths, which are all embodied in esoteric teachings. There *is* a predestination in the geological life of our globe, as in the history, past and future, of races and nations. This is closely connected with what we call *Karma* and Western Pantheists, " Nemesis " and " Cycles." The law of evolution is now carrying us along the ascending arc of *our* cycle, *when the effects will be once more re-merged into,* and re-become the (now neutralized) causes, and all things affected by the former will have regained their original harmony. This will be the cycle of our special " Round," a moment in the duration of the great cycle, or the *Mahayuga.*

The fine philosophical remarks of Hegel are found to have their application in the teachings of Occult science, which shows nature ever acting with a given purpose, whose results are always dual. This was stated in our first Occult volumes, in *Isis Unveiled,* p. 268, Vol. II., in the following words :—

As our planet revolves once every year around the sun, and at the same time turns once in every twenty-four hours upon its own axis, thus traversing minor circles within a larger one, so is the work of the smaller cyclic periods accomplished and recommenced, within the Great Saros.

The revolution of the physical world, according to the ancient doctrine, is attended by a like revolution in the world of intellect—the spiritual evolution of the world proceeding in cycles, like the physical one.

Thus we see in history a regular alternation of ebb and flow in the tide of human progress. The great kingdoms and empires of the world, after reaching the culmination of their greatness, descend again, in accordance with the same law by which they ascended ; till, having reached the lowest point, humanity reasserts itself and mounts up once more, the height of its attainment being, by this law of ascending progression by cycles, somewhat higher than the point from which it had before descended.

But these cycles—wheels within wheels, so comprehensively and ingeniously symbolized by the various Manus and Rishis in India, and by the Kabiri in the West[†]—*do not affect all mankind at one and the same*

* " On World History " in " Philosophy of History," p. 26. (Sibree's Eng. Transl.).
† This symbolism does not prevent these now seemingly mythic personages from

time—as explained in the *Racial division of Cycles* (*See sub-section* 6.)
Hence, as we see, the difficulty of comprehending, and discriminating
between them, with regard to their physical and spiritual effects,
without having thoroughly mastered their relations with, and action
upon the respective positions of nations and races, in their destiny and
evolution. This system cannot be comprehended if the spiritual action
of these periods—*pre-ordained*, so to say, by Karmic law—is separated
from their physical course. The calculations of the best astrologers
would fail, or at any rate remain imperfect, unless this dual action is
thoroughly taken into consideration and dealt with upon these lines.
And this mastery can be achieved only through INITIATION.

The Grand Cycle includes the progress of mankind from the appearance
of primordial man of ethereal form. It runs through the inner cycles of
his (man's) progressive evolution from the ethereal down to the semi-
ethereal and purely physical : down to the redemption of man from his *coat
of skin* and matter, after which it continues running its course downward
and then upward again, to meet at the culmination of a Round, when
the manvantaric "Serpent swallows its tail" and seven minor cycles
are passed. These are the great Racial Cycles which affect equally all the
nations and tribes included in that special Race ; but there are mino^r
and national as well as tribal cycles within those, which run independently of each other. They are called in the Eastern esotericism the
Karmic cycles. In the West, since Pagan Wisdom has been
repudiated as having grown from and been developed by the dark
powers supposed to be at constant war and in opposition to the
little tribal Jehovah—the full and awful significance of the Greek
NEMESIS (or Karma) has been entirely forgotten. Otherwise Christians
would have better realized the profound truth that Nemesis is without
attributes ; that while the dreaded goddess is absolute and immutable
as a Principle, it is we ourselves—nations and individuals—who propel
her to action and give the impulse to its direction. KARMA-NEMESIS is
the creator of nations and mortals, but once created, it is they who
make of her either a fury or a rewarding Angel. Yea—

"Wise are they who worship Nemesis "*

---

having ruled the earth once upon a time under the human form of actual living, though
truly divine and god-like man. The opinion of Colonel Vallancey (and also of Count
de Gobelin) that the *names of the Kabiri appear to be all allegorical*, and to have signified no
more (?) than an almanac of the vicissitudes of the seasons—calculated for the operations
of agriculture " (*Collect. de Reb. Hibern.*, No. 13, *Præf.* Sect. 5) is as absurd as his assertion
that Œon, Kronos, Saturn and Dagon are all one, namely, the "patriarch Adam." The
Kabiri were the instructors of mankind in agriculture, because they were the *regents*
over the seasons and Cosmic cycles. Hence it was they who regulated, as planetary
Spirits or "Angels" (messengers), the *mysteries* of the *art* of agriculture.

* Who *dread* Karma-Nemesis would be better.

—as the *chorus* tells Prometheus.   And as unwise they, who believe that the goddess may be propitiated by whatever sacrifices and prayers, or have her wheel diverted from the path it has once taken.   " The triform Fates and ever mindful Furies" are her attributes only on earth, and begotten by ourselves.   There is no return from the paths she cycles over ; yet those paths are of our own making, for it is we, collectively or individually, who prepare them.   Karma-Nemesis is the synonym of PROVIDENCE, minus *design*, goodness, and every other *finite* attribute and qualification, so unphilosophically attributed to the latter. An Occultist or a philosopher will not speak of the goodness or cruelty of Providence ; but, identifying it with Karma-Nemesis, he will teach that nevertheless it guards the good and watches over them in this, as in future lives ; and that it punishes the evil-doer—aye, even to his seventh rebirth.   So long, in short, as the effect of his having thrown into perturbation even the smallest atom in the Infinite World of harmony, has not been finally readjusted.   For the only decree of Karma—an eternal and immutable decree—is absolute Harmony in the world of matter as it is in the world of Spirit.   It is not, therefore, Karma that rewards or punishes, but it is we, who reward or punish ourselves according to whether we work with, through and along with nature, abiding by the laws on which that Harmony depends, or—break them.

Nor would the ways of Karma be inscrutable were men to work in union and harmony, instead of disunion and strife.   For our ignorance of those ways—which one portion of mankind calls the ways of Providence, dark and intricate ; while another sees in them the action of blind Fatalism ; and a third, simple chance, with neither gods nor devils to guide them—would surely disappear, if we would but attribute all these to their correct cause.   With right knowledge, or at any rate with a confident conviction that our neighbours will no more work to hurt us than we would think of harming them, the two-thirds of the World's evil would vanish into thin air.   Were no man to hurt his brother, Karma-Nemesis would have neither cause to work for, nor weapons to act through.   It is the constant presence in our midst of every element of strife and opposition, and the division of races, nations, tribes, societies and individuals into Cains and Abels, wolves and lambs, that is the chief cause of the " ways of Providence."   We cut these numerous windings in our destinies daily with our own hands, while we imagine that we are pursuing a track on the royal high road of respectability and duty, and then complain of those ways being so intricate and so dark.   We stand bewildered before the mystery of our own making, and the riddles of life that *we will not* solve, and then accuse the great Sphinx of devouring us.   But verily there is not an accident in our lives, not a misshapen day, or a misfortune, that could not be traced back to our own doings in this or in another life. If one breaks the laws of Harmony, or, as a theosophical writer expresses it, " the laws of life," one must be prepared to fall into the chaos one has oneself produced. For, according to the same writer, " the only conclusion one can come to is that these laws of life are their own avengers ; and consequently that every avenging Angel is only a typified representation of their re-action."

Therefore, if any one is helpless before these immutable laws, it is not ourselves, the artificers of our destinies, but rather those angels, the guardians of harmony.   Karma-Nemesis is no more than the (spiritual) dynamical effect of causes produced and forces awakened into activity by our own actions.   It is a law of occult dynamics that " a given amount of energy expended on the spiritual or astral plane is productive of far greater results than the same amount expended on the physical objective plane of existence."

This state will last till man's spiritual intuitions are fully opened, which will not happen before we fairly cast off our thick coats of matter ; until we begin acting from *within*, instead of ever following impulses from *without ;* namely, those produced by our physical senses and gross selfish body.   Until then the only palliative to the evils of life is union and harmony—a Brotherhood IN ACTU, and *altruism* not simply in name.   The suppression of one single bad *cause* will suppress not one, but a variety of bad effects.   And if a Brotherhood or even a number of Brotherhoods may not be able to prevent nations from occasionally cutting each other's throats—still unity in thought and action, and philosophical research into the mysteries of being, will always prevent some, while trying to comprehend that which has hitherto remained to them a riddle, from creating additional causes in a world already so full of woe and evil.   Knowledge of Karma gives the conviction that if—

> " . . . . virtue in distress, and vice in triumph
> Make atheists of mankind,"*

it is only because that mankind has ever shut its eyes to the great truth that man is himself his own saviour as his own destroyer.   That he need not accuse Heaven and the gods, Fates and Providence, of the apparent injustice that reigns in the midst of humanity.   But let him rather remember and repeat this bit of Grecian wisdom, which warns man to forbear accusing *That* which—

> .   .   .   .
> " Just, though mysterious, leads us on unerring
> Through ways unmark'd from guilt to punishment . . . "

—which are now the ways and the high road on which move onward the great European nations.   The Western Aryans had, every nation

---

* Dryden.

and tribe, like their Eastern brethren of the Fifth Race, their Golden and their Iron ages, their period of comparative irresponsibility, or the Satya age of purity, while now, several of them have reached their Iron Age, the *Kali-Yuga*, an age BLACK WITH HORRORS. . . . .

It is true, on the other hand, that the exoteric cycles of every nation have been correctly made to be derived from, and depend on, sidereal motions. The latter are inseparably blended with the destinies of nations and men. But in their purely physical sense, Europe knows of no other cycles than the astronomical, and makes its computations accordingly. Nor will it hear of any other than *imaginary* circles or circuits in the starry heavens that gird them—

> " With centric and eccentric scribbled o'er
> Cycle and epicycle, orb in orb . . . "

But with the pagans, with whom, as Coleridge has it—". . . . . Time, cyclical time, was their abstraction of the Deity . ." that "Deity" manifesting co-ordinately with, and only through Karma, and being that KARMA-NEMESIS itself, the cycles meant something more than a mere succession of events, or a periodical space of time of more or less prolonged duration. For they were generally marked with recurrences of a more varied and intellectual character than are exhibited in the periodical return of seasons or of certain constellations. Modern wisdom is satisfied with astronomical computations and prophecies based on unerring mathematical laws. Ancient Wisdom added to the cold shell of astronomy the vivifying elements of its soul and spirit —ASTROLOGY. And, as the sidereal motions *do* regulate and determine other events on Earth—besides potatoes and the periodical disease of that useful vegetable—(a statement which, not being amenable to scientific explanation, is merely derided, while accepted)—those events have to be allowed to find themselves predetermined by even simple astronomical computations. Believers in astrology will understand our meaning, sceptics will laugh at the belief and mock the idea. Thus they shut their eyes, ostrich-like, to their own fate. . . . . . .*

---

* Not all, however, for there are men of Science awakening to truth. This is what we read : " Whatever way we turn our eyes we encounter a mystery . . . . all in Nature for us is *the unknown.* . . Yet they are numerous, those superficial minds for whom nothing can be produced by natural forces outside of facts observed long ago, consecrated in books and grouped more or less skilfully with the help of theories whose ephemeral duration ought, by this time, to have demonstrated their insufficiency, ... I do not pretend *to contest the possibility of invisible Beings, of a nature different from ours and susceptible of moving matter to action.* Profound philosophers have admitted it in all epochs as a consequence of the great law of continuity which rules the Universe. That intellectual life, which we see starting in some way from non-being (*néant*) and gradually reaching man, can it stop abruptly at man to reappear only in the infinite, in the sovereign regulator of the world ? This is little probable." Therefore . . " I

This because their little *historical* period, so called, allows them no margin for comparison. Sidereal heaven is before them; and though their spiritual vision is still unopened and the atmospheric dust of terrestrial origin seals their sight and chains it to the limits of physical systems, still they do not fail to perceive the movements and note the behaviour of meteors and comets. They record the periodical advents of those wanderers and "flaming messengers," and prophesy, in consequence, earthquakes, meteoric showers, the apparition of certain stars, comets, etc., etc. Are they soothsayers for all that? No, they are learned astronomers.

Why, then, should occultists and astrologers, as learned, be disbelieved, when they prophesy the return of some cyclic event on the same mathematical principle? Why should the claim that they *know it* be ridiculed? Their forefathers and predecessors, having recorded the recurrence of such events in their time and day, throughout a period embracing hundreds of thousands of years, the conjunction of the same constellations must necessarily produce, if not quite the same, at any rate, similar effects. Are the prophecies derided, because of the claim of the hundreds of thousands of years of observation, and the millions of years of the human races? In its turn modern Science is laughed at for its far more modest geological and anthropological figures, by those who hold to Biblical chronology. Thus Karma adjusts even human laughter at the mutual expense of sects, learned societies, and individuals. Yet in the prognostication of *such* future events, at any rate, all foretold on the authority of cyclic recurrences, there is no psychic phenomenon involved. It is neither *prevision, nor prophecy;* no more than is the signalling of a comet or star, several years before its appearance. It is simply knowledge and mathematically correct computations which enable the WISE MEN OF THE EAST to foretell, for instance, that England is on the eve of such or another catastrophe; France, nearing such a point of her cycle, and Europe in general threatened with, or rather, on the eve of, a cataclysm, which her own cycle of racial *Karma has led her* to. The reliability of the information depends, of course, on the acceptation or rejection of the claim for a tremendous period of historical observation. Eastern Initiates maintain that they have preserved records of the racial development and of events of universal import ever since the beginning of the Fourth Race—that which preceded being traditional. Moreover, those who believe in Seership and Occult powers will have no difficulty in crediting the general character, at least, of the information given, even if traditional, once the latter is checked and corrected by the corroboration of clairvoyance and esoteric knowledge. But in the present case no such metaphysical belief is claimed as our chief dependence, but a proof is given on what, to every Occultist, is quite scientific evidence—the records preserved through the *Zodiac* for incalculable ages.

It is now amply proved that even horoscopes and judiciary astrology are not quite based on a fiction, and that stars and constellations, consequently, have an occult and mysterious influence on, and connection with, individuals. And if with the latter, why not with nations, races, and mankind in bulk? This, again, is a claim made on the authority of the Zodiacal records. We shall examine then, if you please, how far the Zodiac was known to the ancients, and how far it is forgotten by the moderns.

XVII.

"THE ZODIAC AND ITS ANTIQUITY."

" ALL men are apt to have a high conceit of their own understanding, and to be tenacious of the opinions they profess," said Jordan, justly adding to this—" and yet almost all men *are guided by the understandings of others, not by their own ;* and may be said more truly to adopt, than to beget, their opinions."

This becomes doubly true in the matter of scientific opinions upon hypotheses offered for consideration—the prejudice and preconceptions of " authorities," so called, often deciding upon questions of the most vital importance for history. There are several such predetermined opinions among our learned Orientalists, yet few are more unjust or *illogical* than the general error with regard to the antiquity of the Zodiac. Thanks to the hobby of some German Orientalists, English and American Sanskritists have accepted Professor Weber's opinion that the peoples of India had no idea or knowledge of the Zodiac prior to the Macedonian invasion, and that it is from the Greeks that the ancient Hindus imported it into their country. We are further told, by several other " authorities," that no Eastern nation knew of the Zodiac before the Hellenes kindly acquainted their neighbours with their invention. *This,* in the face of the *Book of Job,* declared, even by themselves, to be the oldest in the Hebrew canon, certainly prior to Moses, and which speaks of the *making* " of Arcturus, Orion, and Pleiades (*Ash, Kesil,* and

Cimah) and the chambers of the South" (ix. 9); of Scorpio and the *Mazzaroths*—the TWELVE SIGNS (xxxviii., 31,32), which words, if they mean anything, imply knowledge of the Zodiac even among the nomadic Arabic tribes. The *Book of Job*, they say, precedes Homer and Hesiod by at least one thousand years—the two Greek poets having themselves flourished some eight centuries before the Christian era (!!). One who prefers, by the bye, to believe Plato, who shows Homer flourishing far earlier, could point to a number of Zodiacal signs mentioned in the *Iliad* and the *Odyssey*, in the Orphic poems, and elsewhere. But since the cock-and-bull hypothesis of some modern critics to the effect that neither Orpheus, nor yet Homer and Hesiod, ever existed, it would seem time lost to mention these Archaic authors at all. The Arabian *Job* will suffice; unless, indeed, his volume of lamentations, along with the poems of the two Greeks, adding to them those of Linus, should now be also declared to be the patriotic forgery of the Jew Aristobulus. But if the Zodiac was known in the days of Job, how could the civilized and philosophical Hindus have remained ignorant of it?

Risking the arrows of modern criticism—rather blunted by misuse—the reader may be made acquainted with Bailly's learned opinion upon the subject. Inferred speculations may be shown to be erroneous. Mathematical calculations stand on more secure grounds. Taking as a starting point several astronomical references in *Job*, Bailly devised a very ingenious means of proving that the earliest founders of the science of the Zodiac belonged to an antediluvian, primitive people. The fact that he seems willing to see in Thoth, Seth, and in *Fohi* (of China), some of the Biblical patriarchs, does not interfere with the validity of his proof as to the antiquity of the Zodiac.* Even accepting, for argument's sake, his cautious 3700 years B.C. as the correct age of the science, this date proves in the most irrefutable way that it was not the Greeks who invented the Zodiac, for the simple reason that they did not yet exist as a nation thirty-seven centuries B.C.—not as an *historical* race admitted by the critics, at any rate. Bailly then calculated the period at which the constellations manifested the atmospheric influence called by Job "sweet influences of the Pleiades"† (in Hebrew, *Chimah*, see *Job xxxviii.* 31); of the *Cesil* (Orion); and that of the *desert* rains with reference to *Scorpio*, the eighth constellation; and found that in presence the eternal conformity of those divisions of the zodiac and names of the planets applied in the same order everywhere and always; and in presence of the impossibility of attributing it all to chance and *coincidence,*

---

* *Astronomie Antique.*

† The *Pleiades*, as all know, are the seven stars beyond the Bull, which appear at the beginning of spring. They have a very occult meaning in the Hindu esoteric philosophy, and are connected with *sound* and other mystic principles in Nature.

" which never creates such similarities," there must be allowed for the zodiac a great antiquity indeed. (See *Astronomie Antique*, pp. 63 to 74.)

Again, if the Bible is supposed to be an authority on any matter (and there are some who still believe so, whether from Christian or Kabalistical considerations), then the zodiac is clearly mentioned in II Kings, xxiii. 5. Before the " book of the law " was " found " by Hilkiah, the high priest (xxii.), the signs of the zodiac were known and worshipped. They were held in the same adoration as the sun and moon, since the " priests, whom the kings of Judah had ordained to burn incense . . . unto Baal, to the sun, moon, and to the planets, and to all the host of heaven," or the *twelve signs* or *constellations*, as the marginal note in the English Bible explains (see II. Kings xxiii. 5), had followed the injunction for centuries. They were stopped in their idolatry only by King Josiah, 624 years B.C.

The Old Testament is full of allusions to the twelve zodiacal signs, and the whole scheme is built upon it—heroes, personages, and events. Thus in the dream of Joseph, who saw eleven " stars " bowing to the *twelfth*, which was *his* " star," the zodiac is meant. The Roman Catholics have discovered in it, moreover, a prophecy of Christ, who is that twelfth star, they say, and the *eleven* apostles ; the absence of the twelfth being also regarded as a prophetic allusion to the treachery of Judas. The twelve sons of Jacob are again a reference to the same, as justly pointed out by Villapandus (*Temple de Jerusalem*, Vol. II., p. 2nd part, chap. xxx.). Sir James Malcolm, in his *History of Persia* (ch. vii.), shows the *Dabistan* echoing all such traditions about the Zodiac. He traces the invention of it to the palmy days of the golden age of Iran, remarking that one of the said traditions maintains that the genii of the planets are represented under the same shapes and figures they had assumed, when *they showed themselves to several holy prophets*, and have thus led to the establishment of the rites based on the Zodiac.

Pythagoras, and after him Philo Judæus, held the number 12 as very sacred. " The dodecahedron is a PERFECT number." It is the one among the signs of the Zodiac, Philo adds, that the suns visits in twelve months, and it is to honour that sign that Moses divided his nation into twelve tribes, established the twelve cakes (Levit. xxiv., 5) of the *shewbread*, and placed twelve precious stones around the *ephod* of the pontiffs. (See *De Profugis*.)

According to Seneca, Berosus taught prophecy of every future event and cataclysm by the Zodiac ; and the time fixed by him for the conflagration of the world (*pralaya*), and another for a deluge, is found to answer to the time given in an ancient Egyptian papyrus. It comes at every renewal of the cycle of the sidereal year of 25,868 years. The names of the Akkadian months were called by, and derived from, the names of the signs of the Zodiac, and the Akkadians themselves are far earlier than the Chaldæans. Mr. Proctor shows, in his *Myths and Marvels of Astronomy*, that the ancient astronomers had acquired a system of the most accurate astronomy 2,400 years B.C.; the Hindus date their Kali Yug from a great periodical conjunction of the planets thirty-one centuries B.C.; and, withal, it is the Greeks belonging to the expedition of Alexander the Great, who were the instructors of the Aryan Hindus in astronomy!

Whether the origin of the Zodiac is Aryan or Egyptian, it is still of an immense antiquity. Simplicius (VIth cent. A.D.) writes that he had always heard that the Egyptians had kept astronomical observations and records for the last 630,000 years. This statement appears to frighten Mr. G. Massey, who remarks on this in his *Natural Genesis* (318) that " if we read this number of years by the month which Euxodus said the Egyptians termed a year, *that* would still yield the length of two cycles of precession (or 51,736 years). Diogenes Laertius carried back the astronomical calculations of the Egyptians to 48,863 years before Alexander the Great (*Proem*, 2). Martianus Capella corroborates the same by telling posterity that the Egyptians had secretly studied astronomy for over 40,000 years, before they imparted their knowledge to the world (*Astronomy of the Ancients*, Lewis, p. 264).

Several valuable quotations are made in the *Natural Genesis* with the view of supporting the author's theories, but they justify the teaching of the *Secret Doctrine* far more. For instance, Plutarch is quoted from his *Life of Sulla*, saying: " One day when the sky was serene . . . a sound was heard in it . . . of a trumpet, so loud, shrill and mournful, that it affrighted . . . the world. The Tuscan sages said that it *portended a new race of men, and a renovation of the world; for they affirmed that there were eight several kinds of men*, all being different in life and manners, and that *Heaven had allotted each its time, which was limited by the circuit of the great year*" (25,868 years).

This reminds one strongly of our seven races of men, and of the eighth—the " animal man "—descended from the later Third Race; as also of the successive submersions and destruction of the continents which finally disposed of almost the entire bulk of that race.

" The Assyrians," says Iamblichus, " have not only preserved the memorials of seven and twenty myriads of years (270,000 years) as Hipparchus says they have, but likewise of the whole apocatastases and periods of the seven rulers of the world." (Proclus, in *Timæus*, b. I.) This is the calculation of the *Esoteric Doctrine*, as approximately as it can be. For 1,000,000 of years are allowed for our present Root-race (the Fifth), and about 850,000 years since the submersion of the last large island (part of the Continent), the Ruta of the Fourth Race, or the Atlanteans;

THE JEWISH PATRIARCHS ZODIACAL SIGNS.

while Daitya, a small island inhabited by a mixed race, was destroyed about 270,000 years ago, during the glacial period or thereabouts (*vide* Book II.). But the Seven Rulers, or the seven great Dynasties of the *divine* kings belong to the traditions of every great people of antiquity. Wherever twelve are mentioned, these are invariably the 12 signs of the zodiac.

So patent is the fact, that the Roman Catholic writers—especially among the French Ultramontanes—have tacitly agreed to connect the twelve Jewish Patriarchs with the *signs* of the Zodiac. This is done in a kind of prophetico-mystic way, which would sound to pious and ignorant ears like a portentous sign, a tacit divine recognition of the "chosen people of God," whose finger has purposely traced in heaven, from the beginning of creation, the numbers of these patriarchs. For instance, these writers (De Mirville among others) recognise curiously enough all the characteristics of the 12 signs of the Zodiac, in the words addressed by the dying Jacob to his Sons, and in his definitions of the future of each Tribe. *(Vide Genesis, ch. xlix.)* Moreover, the respective banners of the same tribes are claimed to have exhibited the same symbols and the same names as the signs, repeated in the 12 stones of the *Urim* and *Thummim*, and on the 12 wings of the cherub. Leaving the proof of exactitude in the alleged correspondence to the said mystics, it is as follows : Man, or the *Aquarius*, is in the sphere of Reuben, who is declared as " unstable as water " (the *Vulgate* has it, to be " *rushing* like water,"; *Gemini*, in the strong fraternal association of Simeon and Levi ; *Leo*, in that of Judah, "the strong Lion " of his tribe, "the lion's whelp"; the *Pisces*, in Zabulon, who "shall dwell at the haven of the sea "; *Taurus*, in Issachar, because he is "a strong ass couching down," etc., and therefore associated with the stables ; Virgo-*Scorpio*, in Dan, who in described as " a serpent, an adder in the path that biteth," etc. ; *Capricornus* in Naphtali, who is " a hind (a deer) let loose ;" *Cancer*, in Benjamin, for he is "*ravenous*" ; *Libra*, the " Balance," in Asher, whose "bread shall be fat " ; *Saggitarius* in Joseph, because " his bow abode in strength." To make up for the *twelvth* sign, *Virgo*, made independent of *Scorpio*, is Dina, the only daughter of Jacob. (See *Genesis xlix.*) Tradition shows the *alleged* tribes carrying the 12 signs on their banners. But the Bible is, besides these, full of theo-cosmological and astronomical symbols and personifications.

It remains to wonder, and query—if the actual, living Patriarch's destiny was so indissolubly wound up with the Zodiac—how it is that after the loss of the ten tribes, ten signs out of the twelve have not also miraculously disappeared from the sidereal fields ? But this is of no great concern. Let us rather busy ourselves with the history of the Zodiac itself.

Now the reader may be reminded of some opinions expressed on the subject by several of the highest authorities in Science.

Newton believed the invention of the Zodiac could be traced as far back as the expedition of the Argonauts ; and Dulaure fixed its origin at 6,500 years B.C., just 2,496 years before the creation of the World according to the Bible chronology.

Creuzer believes it very easy to show that most of the theogonies are intimately connected with religious calendars, and point to the Zodiac as their prime origin—if not identical with the Zodiac known to us now, then something very analogous to it. He feels certain that the Zodiac and its mystic relations are at the bottom of all the mythologies, under one form or the other. and that it had existed in the old form for ages before ; owing to some singular co-ordination of events, it was brought out in the present defined astronomical garb. (*Creuzer*, Book III., page 930.)

Whether " the genii of the planets " (our Dhyan Chohans of supramundane spheres) showed themselves to "holy prophets" or not, as claimed in the *Dabistan*, it would seem that great laymen and warriors were favoured in the same way in days of old, when astrological *magic* and *theophania* went hand in hand in Chaldea. For Xenophon, no ordinary man, narrates of Cyrus, that at the moment of his death that king was giving ardent thanks to gods and heroes, for having *so often* instructed him *themselves* about the *signs* in heaven, ἐν οὐρανίοις σημείοις (*Cyropédie*, " Ant. du Zodiaque.")

Unless the science of the zodiac is supposed to be of the highest antiquity and universality, how account for its signs being traced in the oldest theogonies ? Laplace is said to have felt struck with amazement at the idea of the days of Mercury (Wednesday), Venus (Friday), Jupiter (Thursday), Saturn (Saturday), and others being related to the days of the week in the same order and with the same names in India as in Northern Europe. " Try, if you can, with the present system of *autochthonous* civilizations, so much in fashion in our day, to explain how nations with no ancestry, no traditions or birthplace in common, could have succeeded in inventing a kind of celestial phantasmagoria, a veritable *imbroglio* of sidereal denominations, without sequence or object, having no figurative relation with the constellations they represent, and still less, *apparently*, with the phases of our terrestrial life they are made to signify," had there not been a *general* intention and a *universal* cause and belief, at the root of all this ? (*Pneumatologie*, Vol. IV., p. 61.) Most truly has Dupuis asserted the same : " Il est impossible de découvrir le moindre trait de ressemblance entre les parties du ciel et les figures que les astronomes y ont *arbitrairement* tracées, et de l'autre côté ; *le hazard est impossible*," he says. (*Origine des Cultes*, " Zodiaque.")

Most certainly chance is "*impossible*." There is no "chance" in Nature, wherein everything is mathematically co-ordinate and mutually related in its units. "Chance," says Coleridge, "is but the pseudonym of God (or Nature), for those particular cases which He does not choose to subscribe openly with His sign manual." Replace the word "God" by that of *Karma* and it will become an Eastern axiom. Therefore, the *sidereal* "prophecies" of the zodiac, as they are called by Christian mystics, never point to any one particular event, however solemn and sacred it may be for some one portion of humanity, but to ever-recurrent, periodical laws in nature, understood but by the Initiates of the sidereal *gods* themselves.

No occultist, no astrologer of Eastern birth, will ever agree with Christian mystics, or even with Kepler's mystical astronomy, his great science and erudition notwithstanding; simply because, if his premises are quite correct, his deductions therefrom are one-sided and biassed by Christian preconceptions. Where the latter finds a prophecy directly pointing at the Saviour, other nations see a symbol of an eternal law decreed for the actual manvantara. Why see in the *Pisces* a direct reference to Christ—one of the several world-reformers, a Saviour but for his direct followers, but only a great and glorious Initiate for all the rest—when that constellation shines as a symbol of all the past, present, and future Spiritual Saviours who dispense light and dispel mental darkness? Christian symbologists have tried to prove that it was that of Ephraim (Joseph's son), the *elect* of Jacob, that therefore, it was at the moment of the Sun entering into the sign of the Fish (*Pisces*) that "the Elect Messiah, the Ἰχθὺς of the first Christians, had to be born. But, if Jesus of Nazareth was that Messiah—was he really born at that "moment," or was he made to be so born by the adaptation of theologians, who sought only to make their preconceived ideas fit in with sidereal *facts* and popular belief? Everyone knows that the real time and year of the birth of Jesus are totally unknown. And it is the Jews, whose forefathers have made the word *Dag* signify both "fish" and "Messiah," who, during the forced development of their rabbinical language, are the first to deny this Christian claim. And what of the further facts that Brahmins also connect *their* "Messiah," the eternal Avatar Vishnu, with a *fish* and the Deluge, and that the Babylonians made of their *Dag-On*, equally a fish and a Messiah, the Man-Fish and Prophet?

There are those learned iconoclasts among Egyptologists, who say that "when the Pharisees sought a '*sign from heaven*' Jesus said, '*there shall no sign be given but the sign of Jonas*' (Mat. xvi. 4). . . . . The sign of Jonas is that of the Oan or fishman of Nineveh. . . . . Assuredly there was no other sign than that of the Sun reborn in *Pisces*. The voice of the Secret Wisdom says those who are looking for signs can have no other than that of the returning fish-man Ichthys, Oannes, or Jonas—who could not be made flesh."

It would appear that Kepler maintained it as a positive *fact* that, at the moment of the "incarnation," all the planets were in conjunction in the sign of *Pisces*, called by the Jews (the Kabalists) the " constellation of the Messiah." "It is this constellation," he averred, "that was placed the *star of the Magi.*" This statement, quoted by Dr. Sepp (*Vie de nôtre Seigneur Jésus Christ*, Vol. I. p. 9), emboldened him to remark that " all the Jewish traditions while announcing that *star*, that *many nations* have seen," (!)* added that "it would absorb the *seventy planets* that preside over the destinies of various nations on this globe." † "In virtue of those natural prophecies," explains Dr. Sepp, "it was written in the stars of the firmament that the Messiah would be born in the lunar year of the world 4320, in that memorable year when the entire choir of the planets would be feasting its jubilee."

There was indeed a rage, at the beginning of the present century, for claiming from the Hindus restoration of an alleged robbery from the Jews of their "gods," patriarchs, and chronology. It was Wilford who had recognized Noah in Prithee and in Satyavrata, Enos in Dhruva, and even Assur in Iswara. Yet, after being residents for so many years in India, some Orientalists, at least, ought to have known that it was not the Hindus alone who had these figures, or who had divided their great age into four minor ages. Nevertheless writers in the *Asiatic Researches* indulged in the most extravagant speculations.

" Christian theologians think it their duty to write against the long periods of Hindu chronology," argues very pertinently S. A. Mackey, the Norwich " philosopher, astronomer, and shoemaker." " But when a man of learning crucifies the names and numbers of the ancients, and wrings and twists them into a form which means something quite foreign to the intention of the ancient authors; but which, so mutilated, fits in with the birth of some maggot pre-existing in his own brain with so much exactness that he pretends *to be amazed* at the discovery, I cannot think him quite so pardonable " (*Key of Urania*).

This is intended to apply to Captain (later Colonel) Wilford, but the

---

* Whether many nations have seen that identical star, or not, we all know that the sepulchres of "the three Magi," who rejoice in the quite *Teutonic* names of Kaspar and Melchior, Balthazar being the only exception, and the two having little of the Chaldean ring in them—are shown by the priests in the famous cathedral of Cologne, where the Magian bodies are not only supposed, but firmly believed to have been buried,

† This tradition about the *seventy planets* that preside over the destinies of nations, is based on the occult cosmogonical teaching that besides our own septenary chain of world-planets, there are many more in the solar system.

words may fit more than one of our modern Orientalists. The former was the first to crown his unlucky speculations in Hindu chronology and the Purânas by connecting the 4,320,000 years with biblical chronology, simply dwarfing the figures to 4,320 years (the supposed lunar year of the Nativity), and Dr. Sepp has simply plagiarized the idea from this gallant officer. Moreover, he persisted in seeing in them Jewish property, as well as a Christian prophecy, thus accusing the Aryans of having helped themselves to Semitic revelation, whereas it was the reverse. The Jews, moreover, need not be accused of despoiling the Hindus, of whose figures Ezra probably knew nothing. They had evidently and undeniably borrowed them from the Chaldeans, along with their gods. Of the 432,000 years of the Chaldean divine Dynasties* they made 4,320 lunar years from the world's creation to the Christian era ; as to the Babylonian and Egyptian Gods, they transformed them as quietly and modestly into Patriarchs. Every nation was more or less guilty of such refashioning and adaptation of a Pantheon (common once to all) of universal, into national, tribal gods and Heroes. It was their property in its new Pentateuchal garb, and no one of the Israelites has ever forced it upon any other nation—least of all upon Europeans.

Without stopping to notice this very unscientific chronology more than is necessary, we may make a few remarks that may be found to the point. These figures of 4,320 *lunar* years of the world (in the Bible the *solar* years are used) are not fanciful, as such, even if their application is quite erroneous ; for they are only the distorted echo of the primitive esoteric, and later on Brahminical doctrine concerning the Yugas. A " Day " of Brahmâ equals 4,320,000,000 years, as also a " Night " of Brahmâ, or the duration of Pralaya, after which a *new* SUN rises trium-

---

* Every scholar is aware, of course, that the Chaldeans claimed the same figures (432) or (432,000) for their divine dynasties as the Hindus do for their Mahayuga, namely, 4,320,000. Therefore has Dr. Sepp, of Munich, undertaken to support Kepler and Wilford in their charge that the Hindus had borrowed them from the Christians, and the Chaldeans from the Jews, who, as claimed, expected their Messiah in the luna year of the world 4,320 !!! As those figures, according to ancient writers, were based by Berosus on the 120 Saroses—each of the divisions meaning six neroses of 600 years each, making a sum total of 432,000 years—they do not thus appear peremptory. But the pious professor of Munich undertook to explain them in *the correct way*. He claims to have solved the riddle by showing that " the saros being composed according to Pliny of 222 synodial months, to wit, 18 years 6/10," the calculator naturally fell back into the figures " given by Suidas," who affirmed that the 120 saroses made 2,222 sacerdotal and cyclic years, which equalled 1,656 solar years." *(Vie de Nôtre Seigneur Jésus Christ, Vol. II., p. 417.)*

Suidas said nothing of the kind, and, if he had, he would prove little, if anything, by it. The *neroses and saroses* were the same thorn in the side of *uninitiated* ancient writers, as the apocalyptic 666 of the "great Beast " is in that of the modern, and they have found their unlucky Newtons as the latter figures have.

phantly over a *new manvantara*, for the septenary chain it illuminates. The teaching had penetrated into Palestine and Europe centuries before the Christian era (see *Isis Unveiled* II. 132), and was present in the minds of the Mosaic Jews, who based upon it their small cycle, though it received full expression only through the Christian chronologers of the Bible, who adopted it, as also the 25th of December, the day on which all the *solar* gods were said to have been incarnated. What wonder, then, that the Messiah was *made* to be born " the *lunar* year of the world 4,320 ? " The " Son of Righteousness and *Salvation* " had once more arisen and had dispelled *pralayic* darkness of chaos and *non-being* on the plane of our objective little globe and chain. Once the subject of the adoration was settled upon, it was easy to make the supposed events of his birth, life, and death, fit in with the Zodiacal exigencies and old traditions, though they had to be somewhat remodelled for the occasion.

Thus what Kepler said, as a great astronomer, becomes comprehensible. He recognised the grand and universal importance of all such planetary conjunctions, " each of which "—as he has well said—" is a *climacteric* year of Humanity."* The rare conjunction of Saturn, Jupiter, and Mars has its significance and importance on account of its *certain great results*—in India and China as much as it has in Europe for the respective mystics of all those countries. And it is certainly no better now than a mere assumption to maintain that nature had only Christ in view, when building her (to the profane) fantastic and meaningless constellations. If it is claimed that it was no hazard that could lead the archaic architects of the Zodiac, thousands of years ago, to mark with the asterisk (*a*) the figure of *Taurus*, with no better or more valid proof of it being *prophetic* of the *Verbum* or Christ than that the *aleph* of *Taurus* means " the ONE " and the FIRST, and that Christ was also the *alpha* or the ONE, then this " proof " may be shown strangely invalidated in more than one way. To begin with, the Zodiac existed before the Christian era, at all events ; further, all the Sun-gods had been mystically connected with that constellation (Taurus)—Osiris, for instance—and were all called by their respective votaries "the First." Then the compilers of the mystical epithets given to the Christian Saviour, were all more or less acquainted with

* The reader has to bear in mind that the phrase "climacteric year " has more than the usual significance, when used by Occultists and Mystics. It is not only a critical period, during which some great change is periodically expected, whether in human or cosmic constitution, but it likewise pertains to spiritual universal changes. The Europeans called every 63rd year " the grand climacteric," and perhaps justly supposed those years to be the years produced by multiplying 7 into the odd numbers 3, 5, 7 and 9. But *seven* is the real scale of nature, in Occultism, and 7 has to be multiplied in quite a different way and method, unknown as yet to European nations.

the significance of the Zodiacal signs; and it is easier to suppose that they should have arranged their claims so as to answer the mystic signs, than that the latter should have shone as a prophecy for one portion of humanity, for millions of years, taking no heed of the numberless generations that had gone before, and those to be born hereafter.

" It is not simple chance," we are told, "that has placed in certain spheres, on a throne, the head of that bull (*Taurus*), trying to push away with the *ansated cross* on its horns, a *Dragon*; the more so, since this constellation of *Taurus* was called ' *the great city of God* and *the mother of revelations*,' and also ' *the interpreter of the divine voice*,' the *Apis pacis* of Hermoutis, in Egypt, which (as the *patristic* fathers would assure the world) preferred oracles that related to the birth of the Saviour" (*Pneumatologie*, iv., 71).

To this theological assumption there are several answers. *Firstly*, the ansated Egyptian cross, or *tau*, the Jaina cross, or Swastica, and the Christian cross have all the same meaning. *Secondly*, no peoples or nations except the Christians gave the significance to the Dragon that is given to it now. The serpent was the symbol of WISDOM; and the Bull (*Taurus*) the symbol of physical or terrestrial *generation*. Thus the latter, pushing off the Dragon, or *spiritual*, Divine Wisdom, with the *Tau*, or Cross—which is esoterically "the foundation and frame-work of all construction "—would have an entirely *phallic*, physiological meaning, had it not still another significance unknown to our Biblical scholars and symbologists. At any rate, it shows no special reference to the *Verbum* of St. John, except, perhaps, in a general sense. The *taurus* (which, by the way, is no *lamb*, but a bull) was sacred in every Cosmogony, with the Hindus as with the Zoroastrians, with the Chaldees as with the Egyptians. So much, every schoolboy knows.

It may perhaps help to refresh the memory of our Theosophists by referring them to what was said of the Virgin and the Dragon, and the universality of periodical births and re-births of World-Saviours—solar gods—in *Isis*, II., 490, with reference to certain passages in Revelations.

In 1853, the *savant* known as Erard-Mollien read before the Institute of France a paper tending to prove the antiquity of the Indian Zodiac, in the signs of which were found the root and philosophy of all the most important religious festivals of that country, the origin of which religious ceremonies goes back into the night of time at least 3,000 B.C., as the lecturer tried to demonstrate. The Zodiac of the Hindus, he thought, was far anterior to the Zodiac of the Greeks, and differed from it in some particulars vastly. In it one sees the *Dragon* on a tree, at the foot of which the " Virgin," *Kanya-Durga*, one of the most ancient goddesses, is placed on a *lion* dragging after him the *solar* car. " This is the reason why," he added, " this Virgin *Durga* is not the simple *memento* of an astronomical fact, but verily the most ancient divinity of the Indian Olympus. She is evidently the same of whom all the Sibylline books spoke, those works that have been the source of the inspiration of Virgil ; the virgin whose return was prophesied as a sign of universal renovation. . . . . And why," he added, " when we see to this day, the months named after the deity-names of this solar Zodiac by the Malayalim-speaking people of southern India—why should that people have abandoned their ancestral Zodiac to burden themselves with that of the Greeks ? Everything proves, on the contrary, that these zodiacal figures have been transmitted to the Greeks by the Chaldees, who got them from the Brahmans." (*See Recueil de l'Académie des Inscriptions*, 1853.)

But all this is very poor testimony. Let us remember, however, also that which was said and accepted by the contemporaries of Volney, who, in his " Ruins of Empires," p. 360, remarks that as *Aries* was in its fifteenth degree 1447 B.C., it follows that the first degree of " Libra " could not have coincided with the Vernal equinox more lately than 15,194 years B.C., to which, if you add 1,790 years since Christ, it appears that 16,984 years have elapsed since the origin of the *Zodiac*.

Dr. Schlegel, moreover, in his *Uranographie Chinoise* assigns to the Chinese Astronomical Sphere an antiquity of 18,000 years. (*Vide* pp. 54, 196, *et seq.*)

Nevertheless, as opinions quoted without adequate proofs are of little avail, it may be more useful to turn to scientific evidence. M. Bailly, the famous French astronomer of the last century, Member of the Academy, etc., etc., asserts that the Hindu systems of astronomy are by far the oldest, and that from them the Egyptians, Greeks, Romans, and even the Jews derived their knowledge. In support of these views he says—

" The astronomers who preceded the epoch 1,491 are, first, the Alexandrian Greeks ; Hipparchus, who flourished 125 years before our era, and Ptolemy, 260 years after Hipparchus. Following these were the Arabs, who revived the study of astronomy in the ninth century. These were succeeded by the Persians and the Tartars, to whom we owe the tables of Massireddin in 1269, and those of Ulug-beg in 1437. Such is the succession of events in Asia as known prior to the Indian epoch 1491. What, then, is an epoch ? It is the observation of the longitude of a star at a given moment, the place in the sky where it was *seen*, and which serves as a point of reference, a starting-point from which to calculate both the past and future positions of the star from its observed motion. But an epoch is useless unless the motion of the star has been determined. A people, new to science and obliged to borrow a foreign astronomy, finds no difficulty in fixing an epoch, since the only observation needed is one which can be made at any moment. But what it needs above all, what it is obliged to borrow, are those elements which depend on accurate determination, and which require continuous observation ; above all, those motions which depend on time, and which can only be accurately determined by centuries of observation. These motions, then, must be borrowed from a nation which has made such observations, and has behind it the labours of centuries. We conclude, therefore, that a new people will not borrow the epochs of an ancient one, without also borrowing from them the 'average motions.' Starting from this principle we shall find that the Hindu epochs 1491 and 3102 could not have been derived from those of either Ptolemy or Ulug-beg."

There remains the supposition that the Hindus, comparing their observations in 1491 with those previously made by Ulug-beg and Ptolemy, used the intervals between these observations to determine the " average motions." The date of Ulug-beg is too recent for such a determination ; while those of Ptolemy and Hipparchus were barely remote enough. But if the Hindu motions had been determined from these comparisons, the epochs would be connected together. Starting from the epochs of Ulug-beg and Ptolemy we should arrive at all those of the Hindus. But this is not the case. Hence foreign epochs were either unknown or useless to the Hindus.*

We may add to this another important consideration. When a nation is obliged to borrow from its neighbours the methods or the average motions of its astronomical tables, it has even greater need to borrow, besides these, the knowledge of the inequalities of the motions of the heavenly bodies, the motions of the apogee, of the nodes, and of the inclination of the ecliptic ; in short, all those elements the determination of which requires the art of observing, some instrumental appliances, and great industry. All these astronomical elements, differing more or less with the Greeks of Alexandria, the Arabs, the Persians and the Tartars, exhibit no resemblance whatever with those of the Hindus. The latter, therefore, borrowed nothing from their neighbours.

Condensing Bailly's remarks, he comes to the following conclusions:—

If the Hindus did not borrow their epoch, they must have possessed a real one of their own, based on their own observations ; and this must be either the epoch of the year 1491 after, or that of the year 3102 before our era, the latter preceding by 4592 years the epoch 1491. We have to choose between these two epochs and to decide which of them is based on observation. But before stating the arguments which can and must

---

* For a detailed scientific proof of this conclusion, see page 121 of Mr. Bailly's work, where the subject is discussed technically.

decide the question, we may be permitted to make a few remarks to those who may be inclined to believe that it is modern observations and calculations which have enabled the Hindus to determine the past positions of the heavenly bodies. It is far from easy to determine the celestial movements with sufficient accuracy to ascend the stream of time for 4592 years, and to describe the phenomena which must have occurred at that period.

We possess to-day excellent instruments; exact observations have been made for some two or three centuries, which already permit us to calculate with considerable accuracy the average motions of the planets; we have the observations of the Chaldeans, of Hipparchus and of Ptolemy, which, owing to their remoteness from the present time, permit us to fix these motions with greater certainty. Still we cannot undertake to represent with invariable accuracy the observations throughout the long period intervening between the Chaldeans and ourselves; and still less can we undertake to determine with exactitude events occurring 4592 years before our day. Cassini and Maier have each determined the secular motion of the moon, and they differ by 3m. 43s. This difference would give rise in forty-six centuries to an uncertainty of nearly three degrees in the moon's place. Doubtless one of these determinations is more accurate than the other; and it is for observations of very great antiquity to decide between them. But in very remote periods, where observations are lacking, it follows that we are uncertain as to the phenomena. How, then, could the Hindus have calculated back from the year 1491 A.D. to the year 3102 before our era, if they were only recent students of astronomy?

The Orientals have never been what we are. However high an opinion of their knowledge we may form from the examination of their Astronomy, we cannot suppose them ever to have possessed that great array of instruments which distinguishes our modern observatories, and which is the product of simultaneous progress in various arts, nor could they have possessed that genius for discovery, which has hitherto seemed to belong exclusively to Europe, and which, supplying the place of time, causes the rapid progress of science and of human intelligence. If the Asiatics have been powerful, learned and wise, it is power and time which have produced their merit and success of all kinds. Power has founded or destroyed their empires; now it has erected edifices imposing by their bulk, now it has reduced them to venerable ruins; and while these vicissitudes alternated with each other, patience accumulated knowledge; and prolonged experience produced wisdom. It is the antiquity of the nations of the East which has erected their scientific fame.

If the Hindus possessed in 1491 a knowledge of the heavenly motions sufficiently accurate to enable them to calculate backwards for 4,592 years, it follows that they could only have obtained this knowledge from very ancient observations. To grant them such knowledge, while refusing them the observations from which it is derived, is to suppose an impossibility; it would be equivalent to assuming that at the outset of their career they had already reaped the harvest of time and experience. While on the other hand, if their epoch of 3102 is assumed to be real, it would follow that the Hindus had simply kept pace with successive centuries down to the year 1491 of our era. Thus, time itself was their teacher; they knew the motions of the heavenly bodies during these periods, because they had seen them; and the duration of the Hindu people on earth is the cause of the fidelity of its records and the accuracy of its calculations.

It would seem that the problem as to which of the two epochs of 3102 and 1491 is the real one ought to be solved by one consideration, viz., that the ancients in general, and particularly the Hindus, calculated, and therefore observed, eclipses only. Says Bailly:—

Now, there was no eclipse of the sun at the moment of the epoch 1492; and no eclipse of the moon either 14 days before or after that moment. Therefore the epoch 1491 is not based on an observation. As regards the epoch 3102, the Brahmins of Tirvalour place it at sunrise on February 18th. The sun was then in the first point of the Zodiac according to its true longitude. The other tables show that at the preceding midnight the moon was in the same place, but according to its average longitude. The Brahmins tell us also that this first point, the origin of their Zodiac, was, in the year 3102, 54 degrees behind the equinox. It follows that the origin—the first point of their Zodiac— was therefore in the sixth degree of Libra.

There occurred, therefore, about this time and place an average conjunction; "and indeed this conjunction is given in our best tables: La Caille's for the sun and Maier's for the moon." There was no eclipse of the sun, the moon being too distant from her node; but fourteen days later, the moon having approached the node, must have been eclipsed. Maier's tables, used without correction for acceleration, give this eclipse; but they place it during the day when it could not have been observed in India. Cassini's tables give it as occurring at night, which shows that Maier's motions are too rapid for distant centuries, when the acceleration is not allowed for; and which also proves that in spite of the improvement of our knowledge we can still be uncertain as to the actual aspect of the heavens in past times.

Therefore we believe that as between the two Hindu epochs, the real one is the year 3102, because it was accompanied by an eclipse which could be observed, and which must have served to determine it. This is a first proof of the truth of the longitude assigned by the Hindus to the sun and the moon at this instant; and this proof would perhaps be sufficient, were it not that this ancient determination becomes of the greatest importance for the verification of the motions of these bodies, and must therefore be borne out by every possible proof of its authenticity.

We notice, first, that the Hindus seem to have combined two epochs together into the year 3102. The Tirvalour Brahmins reckon primarily from the first moment of the Kali-Yug; but they have a second epoch placed 2d. 3h. 32m. 30s. later. The latter is the true astronomical epoch, while the former seems to be a civil era. But if this epoch of the Kali-Yug had no reality, and was the mere result of a calculation, why should it be thus divided? Their calculated astronomical epoch would have become that of the Kali-Yug, which would have been placed at the conjunction of the sun and the moon, as is the case with the epochs of the three other tables. They must have had some reason for distinguishing between the two; and this reason can only be due to the circumstances and the time of the epoch; which therefore could not be the result of calculation. This is not all; starting from the solar epoch determined by the rising of the sun on February 18th, 3102, and tracing back events 2d. 3h. 32m. 30s., we come to 2h. 27m. 30s. a.m. of February 16th, which is the instant of the beginning of Kali-Yuga. It is curious that this age has not been made to commence at one of the four great divisions of the day. It might be suspected that the epoch should be midnight, and that the 2h. 27m. 30s. are a meridian correction. But whatever may have been the reason for fixing on this moment, it is plain that were this epoch the result of calculation, it would have been just as easy to carry it back to midnight, so as to make the epoch correspond to one of the chief divisions of the day, instead of placing it at a moment fixed by the fraction of a day.

2nd. The Hindus assert that at the first moment of Kali-Yug there was a conjunction of all the planets; and their tables show this conjunction while ours indicate that it might actually have occurred. Jupiter and Mercury were in exactly the same degree of the ecliptic; Mars being 8° and Saturn 17° distant from it. It follows that about this time, or some fourteen days after the commencement of Kali-Yug, the Hindus saw four planets emerge successively from the Sun's rays; first Saturn, then Mars, then Jupiter and Mercury, and these planets appeared united in a somewhat small space. Although Venus was not among them, the taste for the marvellous caused it to be called a general conjunction of all the planets. The testimony of the Brahmins here coincides with that of our tables; and this evidence, the result of a tradition, must be founded on actual observation.

3rd. We may remark that this phenomenon was visible about a fort-night after the epoch, and exactly at the time when the eclipse of the moon must have been observed, which served to fix the epoch. The two observations mutually confirm each other ; and whoever made the one must have made the other also.

4th. We may believe also that the Hindus made at the same time a determination of the place of the moon's node; this seems indicated by their calculation. They give the longitude of this point of the lunar orbit for the time of their epoch, and to this they add as a constant 40m., which is the node's motion in 12d. 14h. It is as if they stated that this determination was made 13 days after their epoch, and that to make it correspond to that epoch, we must add the 40m. through which the node has retrograded in the interval.

This observation is, therefore, of the same date as that of the lunar eclipse ; thus giving three observations, which are mutually confir-matory.

5th. It appears from the description of the Hindu Zodiac given by M. C. Gentil, that on it the places of the stars named " The Eye of Taurus" and the "Wheat-ear of Virgo," can be determined for the commencement of the Kali-Yug.

Now, comparing these places with the actual positions, reduced by *our* precession of the equinoxes to the moment in question, we see that the point of origin of the Hindu Zodiac must lie between the fifth and sixth degree of Libra. The Brahmins, therefore, were right in placing it in the sixth degree of that sign, the more so since this small difference may be due to the proper motion of the stars which is unknown.

Thus it was yet another observation which guided the Hindus in this fairly accurate determination of the first point of their movable zodiac.

It does not seem possible to doubt the existence in antiquity of obser-vations of this date. The Persians say that four beautiful stars were placed as guardians at the four corners of the world. Now it so happens that at the commencement of Kali Yug, 3000 or 3100 years before our era, the " Eye of the Bull " and the " Heart of the Scorpion " were exactly at the equinoctial points, while the " Heart of the Lion " and the " Southern Fish " were pretty near the solstitial points. An obser-vation of the rising of the Pleiades in the evening, seven days before the autumnal equinox, also belongs to the year 3000 before our era. This and similar observations collected in Ptolemy's calendars, though he does not give their authors, these observations, which are older than those of the Chaldeans, may well be the work of the Hindus. They are well acquainted with the constellation of the Pleiades, and while we call it vulgarly the " Poussinière " we name it : *Pillaloo-codi*—the " Hen and chickens." This name has therefore, passed from people to people, and comes to us from the most ancient nations of Asia. We see that the Hindus must have observed the rising of the Pleiades, and have made use of it to regulate their years and their months; for this constellation is also called Krittika. Now they have a month of the same name, and this coincidence can only be due to the fact that this month was announced by the rising or setting of the consellation in question. But what is even more decisive as showing that the Hindus observed the stars, and in the same way that we do, marking their position by their longitude, is a fact mentioned by Augustinus Riccius that, according to observations attributed to Hermes, and made 1,985 years before Ptolemy, the brilliant star in the Lyre and that in the Heart of the Hydra were each seven degrees in advance of their respective positions as determined by Ptolemy.

This determination seems very extraordinary. The stars advance regularly with respect to the equinox; and Ptolemy ought to have found the longitudes 28 degrees in excess of what they were 1985 years before his time. Besides, there is a remarkable peculiarity about this fact; the same error or difference being found in the positions of both stars; therefore the error was due to some cause affecting both stars equally. It was to explain this peculiarity that the Arab Thebith imagined the stars to have an oscillatory movement, causing them to advance and recede alternately.

This hypothesis was easily disproved; but the observations attributed to Hermes remained unexplained. Their explanation, however, is found in Hindu Astronomy. At the date fixed for these observations, 1985 years before Ptolemy, the first point of the Hindu Zodiac was 35 degrees in advance of the equinox; therefore the longitudes reckoned for this point are 35 degrees in excess of those reckoned from the equinox. But after the lapse of 1985 years the stars would have advanced 28 degrees, and there would remain a difference of only 7 degrees between the longitudes of Hermes and those of Ptolemy, and the difference would be the same for the two stars, since it is due to the difference between the starting-points of the Hindu Zodiac and that of Ptolemy, which reckons from the equinox. This explanation is so simple and natural that it must be true. We do not know whether Hermes, so celebrated in antiquity, was a Hindu, but we see that the observations attributed to him are reckoned in the Hindu manner, and we conclude that they were made by the Hindus, who, therefore, were able to make all the observations we have enumerated, and which we find noted in their tables.

6th. The observation of the year 3102, which seems to have fixed their epoch, was not a difficult one. We see that the Hindus, having once determined the moon's daily motion of 13deg. 10m. 35sec., made use of it to divide the Zodiac into 27 constellations, related to the period of the moon, which takes about 27 days to describe it.

It was by this method that they determined the positions of the stars in this Zodiac ; it was thus they found that a certain star of the Lyre was in 8h. 24m., the Heart of the Hydra in 4d. 7h., longitudes which are ascribed to Hermes, but which are calculated on the Hindu Zodiac. Similarily, they discovered that the " Wheatear of Virgo " forms the commencement of their fifteenth constellation, and the " Eye of Taurus " the end of the fourth ; these stars being the one in 6d. 6h. 40m., the other in 1d. 23h. 20min. of the Hindu Zodiac. This being so, the eclipse of Moon which occurred 14 days after the Kali Yug epoch, took place at a point between the " Wheat Ear " of Virgo and the star θ of the same constellation. These stars are very approximately a constellation apart, the one beginning the fifteenth, the other the sixteenth. Thus it would not be difficult to determine the moon's place by measuring her distance from one of these stars ; from this they deduced the position of the sun, which is opposite to the moon, and then, knowing their average motions, they calculated that the moon was at the first point of the Zodiac according to her average longitude at midnight on the 17th-18th February of the year 3,102 before our era, and that the sun occupied the same place six hours later according to his true longitude ; an event which fixes the commencement of the Hindu year.

7th. The Hindus state that 20,400 years before the age of Kali Yug, the first point of their Zodiac coincided with the vernal equinox, and that the sun and moon were in conjunction there. This epoch is obviously fictitious ;* but we may inquire from what point, from what epoch, the Hindus set out in establishing it. Taking the Hindu values for the revolution of the sun and moon, viz., 365d. 6h. 12m. 30s., and 27d. 7h. 43m. 13s., we have—

20,400 revolutions of the sun = 7,451,277d. 2h.

272,724   ,,   ,,   moon = 7,451,277d. 7h.

Such is the result obtained by starting from the Kali Yuga epoch ; and the assertion of the Hindus, that there was a conjunction at the time stated, is founded on their tables ; but if, using the same elements, we start from the era of the year 1491, or from another placed in the year 1282, of which we shall speak later, there will always be a difference of almost one or two days. It is both just and natural, in verifying the Hindu calculations, to take those among their elements which give the same result as they had themselves arrived at, and to set out from that one among their epochs which enables us to arrive at

---

* Why it should be " fictitious " can *never* be made plain by European scientists.

the fictitious epoch in question. Hence, since to make this calculation they must have set out from their real epoch, the one which was founded on an observation and not from any of those which were derived by this very calculation from the former, it follows that their real epoch was that of the year 3102 before our era.

8th. The Tiravalore Brahmins give the Moon's motion as 7d. 2h. 8m. on the movable Zodiac, and as 9d. 7h. 45m. 1s. as referred to the equinox in a great period of 1,600,984 days, or 4,386 years and 94 days. We believe this motion to have been determined by observation; and we must state at the outset that this period is of an extent which renders it but ill suited to the calculation of the mean motions.

In their astronomical calculations the Hindus make use of periods of 248, 3,031, and 12,372 days; but, apart from the fact that these periods, though much too short, do not present the inconvenience of the former, they contain an exact number of revolutions of the moon referred to its apogee. They are in reality mean motions. The great period of 1,600,984 is not a sum of accumulated revolutions; there is no reason why it should contain 1,600,984 rather than 1,600,985 days. It would seem that observation alone must have fixed the number of days and marked the beginning and end of the period. This period ends on the 21st of May, 1282, of our era at 5h. 15m. 30s. at Benares. The moon was then in apogee, according to the Hindus, and her longitude was ... 7d. 13h. 45m. 1s.
Maier gives the longitude as ... 7d. 13h. 53m. 48s.
And places the apogee at ... ... 7d. 14h. 6m. 54s.

The determination of the moon's place by the Brahmins thus differs only by nine minutes from ours, and that of the apogee by twenty-two minutes, and it is very evident that they could only have obtained this agreement with our best tables and this exactitude in the celestial positions by observation. If then, observation fixed the end of this period, there is every reason to believe that it determined its commencement. But then this motion, determined directly, and from nature, would of necessity be in close agreement with the true motions of the heavenly bodies.

And in fact the Hindu motion during this long period of 4,883 years, does not differ by a minute from that of Cassini, and agrees equally with that of Maier. Thus two peoples, the Hindus and the Europeans, placed at the two extremities of the world, and perhaps as distant by their institutions, have obtained precisely the same results as regards the moon's motions; and an agreement which would be inconceivable, if it were not based on the observation and mutual imitation of nature. We must remark that the four tables of the Hindus are all copies of the same Astronomy. It cannot be denied that the Siamese tables existed in 1687, when they were brought from India by M. de la Loubère. At that time the tables of Cassini and Maier were not in existence, and thus the Hindus were already in possession of the exact motion contained in these tables, while we did not yet possess it.* It must, therefore, be admitted that the accuracy of this Hindu motion is the point of observation. It is exact throughout this period of 4,383 years, because it was taken from the sky itself; and if observation determined its close, it fixed its commencement also. It is the longest period which has been observed and of which the recollection is preserved in the annals of Astronomy. It has its origin in the epoch of the year 3102, B.C., and it is a demonstrative proof of the reality of that epoch.

Bailly is referred to at such length, as he is one of the few scientific men who have tried to do full justice to the Astronomy of the Aryans. From John Bentley down to Burgess' "Sûrya-Siddhânta," not one astronomer has been fair enough to the most learned people of Antiquity. However distorted and misunderstood the Hindu Symbology, no Occultist can fail to do it justice once that he knows something of the Secret Sciences; nor will he turn away from their metaphysical and mystical

---

* The following is an answer to those men of science who might suspect that our Astronomy was carried to India and communicated to the Hindus by our Missionaries. 1st. Hindu astronomy has its own peculiar forms, characterized by their originality; if it had been our astronomy translated, great skill and knowledge would have been needed to disguise the theft. 2nd. When adopting the mean movement of the moon, they would have adopted also the inclination of the ecliptic, the equation of the sun's centre, the length of the year; these elements differ completely from ours, and are remarkably accurate as applying to the epoch of 3102; while they would be exceedingly erroneous if they had been calculated for last century. 3rd, finally, our missionaries could not have communicated to the Hindus in 1687 the tables of Cassini, which were not then in existence; they could have known only the mean motions of Tycho, Riccioli, Copernicus, Bouilland, Kepler, Longomontanus, and those of the tables of Alphonso. I will now give a tabular view of these mean motions for 4383 years and 94 days:—

Table.	Mean Motion.				Difference from Hindu.		
	D.	H.	M.	S.	H.	M.	S.
Alphonso	9	7	2	47	— 0	42	14
Copernicus	9	6	2	13	— 1	42	48
Tycho	9	7	54	40	+ 0	9	39
Kepler	9	6	57	35	— 0	47	26
Longomontanus..........	9	7	2	13	— 0	42	48
Bouilland	9	6	48	8	— 0	58	53
Riccioli	9	7	53	57	+ 0	8	56
Cassini..................	9	7	44	11	— 0	0	50
Indian	9	7	45	1			

None of these mean motions, except Cassini's, agrees with that of the Hindus, who therefore, did not borrow their mean motions, since their figures agree only with those of Cassini, whose tables were not in existence in 1687. This mean motion of the moon belongs, therefore, to the Hindus, who could only have obtained it by observation."—Bailly's " Traité de l'Astronomie Indienne et Orientale."

interpretation of the Zodiac, even though the whole Pleiades of Royal Astronomical Societies rise in arms against their mathematical rendering of it. The descent and re-ascent of the Monad or Soul cannot be disconnected from the Zodiacal signs, and it looks more natural, in the sense of the fitness of things, to believe in a mysterious sympathy between the metaphysical soul and the bright constellations, and in the influence of the latter on the former, than in the absurd notion that the creators of Heaven and Earth have placed in heaven the types of twelve vicious Jews. And if, as the author of *The Gnostics* asserts, the aim of all the Gnostic schools and the later Platonists " was to accommodate the old faith to the influence of Buddhistic theosophy, *the very essence of which was that the innumerable gods of the Hindu mythology were but names for the* ENERGIES *of the First Triad in its successive* AVATARS *or manifestations unto man,*" whither can we turn to trace these theosophic ideas to their very root—better than to old Indian wisdom? We say it again : archaic Occultism would remain incomprehensible to all, if it were rendered otherwise than through the more familiar channels of Buddhism and Hinduism. For the former is the emanation of the latter ; and both are children of one mother— ancient *Lemuro-Atlantean Wisdom.*

XVIII.

SUMMARY OF THE MUTUAL POSITION.

THE reader has had the whole case presented to him from both sides, and it remains with him to decide whether its summary stands in our favour or not. If there were such a thing as void, a *vacuum* in Nature, one would find it produced, according to a physical law, in the minds of helpless admirers of the "lights" of science, who pass their time in mutually destroying their teachings. If ever the theory that "two lights make darkness" found its application it is in this case, when one half of the "lights" imposes its Forces and "modes of motion" on the belief of the faithful, and the other half opposes the very existence of the same. "Ether, Matter, Energy"—the sacred hypostatical trinity, the three principles of the truly *unknown* God of Science, called by them PHYSICAL NATURE !

Theology is taken to task and ridiculed for believing in the union of three persons in one Godhead—one God as to substance, three persons as to individuality ; and we are laughed at for our belief in unproved and unprovable doctrines, in Angels and Devils, Gods and Spirits. And, indeed, that which made the Scientists win the day over Theology in the Great "Conflict between Religion and Science," was precisely the argument that neither the identity of that substance, nor the triple individuality claimed, after having been conceived, invented, and worked out in the depths of Theological Consciousness, could be proved by any Scientific inductive process of reasoning, least of all on the evidence of our senses.   Religion must perish, it is said, because it teaches *mysteries*.   *Mystery is the negation of Common Sense*, and Science repels it.   According to Mr. Tyndall, metaphysics is *fiction*, like poetry.   The man of Science *takes nothing on trust;* rejects everything *that is not proven to him*, while the Theologian accepts *everything on blind faith*.   The Theosophist and the Occultist, who take nothing on trust, not even *exact* Science, the Spiritualist who denies dogma but believes in Spirits and in *invisible but potential influences*, all share in the same contempt.   Very well, then ; what we have to do now, is to examine for the last time whether *exact* Science does not act precisely in the same way as Theosophy, Spiritualism, and Theology do.

In a work by Mr. S. Laing, considered a standard book on Science, "Modern Science and Modern Thought," the author of which, according to the laudatory review of the *Times*, "exhibits with much power and effect the immense discoveries of Science, and its numerous victories over old opinions, whenever THEY HAVE THE RASHNESS TO CHALLENGE CONCLUSIONS WITH IT," one reads in chapter III., "On Matter," as follows :

"WHAT IS THE MATERIAL UNIVERSE COMPOSED OF ?   ETHER MATTER, ENERGY" . . . . . is the answer.

We stop to ask, "What is Ether ? "   And Mr. Laing answers in the name of Science :—

"*Ether is not actually known to us* BY ANY TEST OF WHICH THE SENSES CAN TAKE COGNIZANCE, *but is a sort of mathematical substance which* WE ARE COMPELLED TO ASSUME *in order to account for the phenomena of light and heat*."

Aud what is matter ?   Do you know more about it than you do about the "hypothetical" agent, Ether?

"*In perfect strictness, it is true that chemical investigations can tell us* . . . . NOTHING DIRECTLY *of the composition of living matter, and* . . . . *it is also in strictness true*, THAT WE KNOW NOTHING *about the compositions of* ANY (*material*) BODY WHATEVER AS IT IS."   (*Lecture on Plotoplasm by Mr. Huxley.*)

And Energy ?   Surely you can define the third person of the Trinity of your Material universe ?

"THE EI'ERGY IS THAT WHICH IS ONLY KNOWN TO US BY ITS EFFECTS."   (*Books on Physics*.)

Pray explain, for this is rather hazy.

"IN MECHANICS THERE IS ACTUAL AND POTENTIAL ENERGY: WORK

ACTUALLY PERFORMED, AND THE CAPACITY FOR PERFORMING IT. AS TO THE
NATURE OF MOLECULAR ENERGY OR FORCES, THE VARIOUS PHENOMENA
WHICH BODIES PRESENT SHOW THAT THEIR MOLECULES ARE UNDER THE
INFLUENCE OF TWO CONTRARY FORCES—ONE WHICH TENDS TO BRING THEM
TOGETHER, THE OTHER TO SEPARATE THEM. . . . . THE FIRST IS MOLE-
CULAR ATTRACTION, THE SECOND FORCE IS DUE TO *vis viva*, OR MOVING
FORCE." . . . . (*Ganot's Physics.*)

Just so : it is the nature of this *moving force*, the *vis viva* that we want
to know. What is it ? . . . . .

" WE DO NOT KNOW ! ' IS THE INVARIABLE ANSWER. " IT IS AN
EMPTY SHADOW OF MY IMAGINATION," explains Mr. Huxley in his
Physical Basis of Life.

Thus the whole structure of Modern Science is built on a kind of
" mathematical abstraction," on a Protean " Substance which eludes
the senses," (Dubois Reymond,) and on *effects*, the shadowy and illusive
will-o'-the-wisps of a *something* entirely unknown to and beyond the reach
of Science, " *Self-moving* " atoms ! *Self-moving* Suns, planets, and stars !
But who, then, or *what* are they all, if they are self-endowed with
motion ?   Why then should you, physicists, laugh and deride our " Self-
moving *ARCHÆUS* " ?   Mystery is rejected and scorned by Science,
and " *MYSTERY is the fatality of Science*," as Father Felix has truly
said. . . . . " Science *cannot* escape it ! "   The language of the French
preacher is *ours*, and we quote it in " *Isis Unveiled* " (*Vide* Vol. I. 338-9).
Who—he asks—who of you, men of Science :

" . . . . has been able to penetrate the secret of the formation of a body, the
generation of a single atom ?   What is there, I will not say at the centre of a
sun, but at the centre of an atom ?   Who has sounded to the bottom the abyss
in a grain of sand ?   The grain of sand, gentlemen, has been studied four
thousand years by science, she has turned and returned it ; she divides it and
subdivides it ; she torments it with her experiments ; she vexes it with her
questions to snatch from it the final word as to its secret constitution ; she asks
it, with an insatiable curiosity : ' Shall I divide thee infinitesimally ? '   Then
suspended over this abyss, science hesitates, she stumbles, she feels dazzled,
she becomes dizzy, and in despair says : *I DO NOT KNOW.*"

" But if you are so fatally ignorant of the genesis and hidden nature of a
grain of sand, how should you have an intuition as to the generation of a single
living being ?   Whence in the living being does life come ?   Where does it
commence ?   What is the life principle ? "*

Do the men of science deny all these charges ?   Not at all, for here
is a confession of Tyndall, which shows how powerless is science, even
over the world of matter.

" The first marshalling of the atoms, on which all subsequent action depends,

----

* " Le Mystère et la Science," Conférences, *Père Félix de Nôtre Dame ;* des Mousseaux :
" *Hauts Phen. Magiques.*"

baffles a keener power than that of the microscope." "Through pure excess of complexity, and long before observation can have any voice in the matter, the most highly trained intellect, the most refined and disciplined imagination, *retires in bewilderment from the contemplation of the problem.* We are struck dumb by an astonishment which no microscope can relieve, doubting not only the power of our instrument, but even whether we ourselves possess the intellectual elements which will ever enable us to grapple with the ultimate structural energies of nature."

How little is known of the material universe, indeed, has now been suspected for years, on the very admissions of these men of science themselves. And now there are some materialists who would even make away with Ether—or whatever Science calls the infinite Substance, the noumenon of which the Buddhists call Swâbhâvat—as well as with atoms, too dangerous both on account of their ancient philosophical and their present Christian and theological associations. From the earliest philosophers whose records passed to posterity, down to our present age, which, if it denies "invisible Beings" in Space, can never be so insane as to deny a *plenum* of some sort—the *fulness* of the universe was an accepted belief. And what it was said to contain, one learns from Hermes Trismegistus (in Mrs. Kingsford's able rendering)—who is made to say:—

"Concerning the void . . . my judgment is that it does not exist, that it never existed, and that it never will exist, for all the various parts of the universe are filled, as the earth also is complete and full of bodies, differing in quality and in form, having their species and their magnitude, one larger, one smaller, one solid, one tenuous. The larger . . . are easily perceived; the smaller . . . are difficult to apprehend, or altogether invisible. We know only of their existence by the sensation of feeling, wherefore *many persons deny such entities to be bodies, and regard them as simply spaces,** but it is impossible there should be such spaces. For if indeed there should be anything outside the universe . . . then it would be a space occupied by intelligent beings analogous to its (the universe's) divinity . . . . . . I speak of the genii, for I hold they dwell with us, and of the heroes who dwell above us, between the earth and the highest airs; wherein are neither clouds nor any tempest " (p. 84).

And we "hold" it too. Only, as already remarked, no Eastern Initiate would speak of spheres "*above* us, between the earth and the

---

* Behold the work of Cycles and their periodical return ! Those who denied such " Entities " (Forces) to be bodies, and called them " Spaces," were the prototypes of our modern " Science-struck " public, and their official teachers, who speak of the Forces of nature as the imponderable energy of matter and modes of motion, and yet hold electricity (for one) as being as *atomic as matter* itself--(Helmholtz). Inconsistency and contradiction reign as much in official as in heterodox Science.

airs," even the highest, as there is no such division or measurement in
occult speech, no "*above*" as no "*below*," but an eternal "within,"
within two other withins, or the planes of subjectivity merging gradually
into that of terrestrial objectivity—this being for *man* the last one, his
own plane.   This necessary explanation may be closed here by giving,
in the words of Hermes, the belief on this particular point of the whole
world of mystics :—

    " There are many orders of the gods ; and in all there is an intelligent part. It
is not to be supposed they do not come within the range of our senses; on the
contrary, we perceive them, better even than those which are called visible. . .
There are then gods, superior to all appearances ; after them come the gods
whose principle is spiritual; these gods being sensible, in conformity with their
double origin, *manifest all things* by a sensible nature, each of them illuminating
his works one by another.*   The Supreme Being of Heaven, or of all that is
comprehended under this name, is Zeus, for it is by Heaven that Zeus gives
life to all things.   The Supreme Being of *the Sun is Light*, for it is by the disk
of the Sun that we receive the benefit of the light.   The thirty-six horoscopes
of the fixed stars have for supreme Being or Prince, him whose name is *Panto-
morphos*, or having all forms, because he gives divine forms to divers types. The
seven planets, or wandering spheres, have for Supreme Spirits Fortune and
Destiny, who uphold the eternal stability of the laws of nature throughout
incessant transformation and perpetual agitation.   The ether is the instrument
or medium by which all is produced."

    This is quite philosophical and in accordance with the spirit of
Eastern esotericism : for all the Forces, such as Light, Heat, Electricity,
etc., etc., are called the " Gods "—esoterically.

    It must be so, since the esoteric teachings in Egypt and India were
identical.   And, therefore, the personification of *Fohat* synthesizing all
the manifesting forces in nature is a legitimate result.   Moreover, as
will be shown in the division that follows this one, the real and *Occult*
forces in nature only now begin to be known—and even in this case,
by heterodox, not orthodox, Science (*See also* § X., THE COMING
FORCE), though their existence, in one instance at any rate, is corroborated, and certified to by an immense number of educated people and
even by some official men of science.

    This sentence, moreover, in Stanza VI., " Fohat sets in motion the
primordial World-germs, or the aggregation of Cosmic atoms and
matter, some one way, some another, in the opposite direction "—looks
orthodox and Scientific enough.   For there is, at all events, one fact in
support of this position fully recognized by Science, and it is this.
The meteoric showers (periodical in November and August) belong to

---

    * " Hermes here includes as gods the *sensible Forces* of nature, the elements and the
phenomena of the Universe," remarks Mrs. A. Kingsford in a foot-note explaining it
very correctly.   So does Eastern philosophy.

a system moving in an elliptical orbit around the Sun. The aphelion of this ring is 1,732 millions of miles beyond the orbit of Neptune, its plane is inclined to the Earth's orbit at an angle of 64° 3′, and the direction of the meteoric swarm moving round this orbit *is contrary to that of the Earth's revolution.*

This fact, recognized only in 1833, shows it to be the modern rediscovery of what was very anciently known. *Fohat* turns with his two hands in contrary directions the "seed" and "the curds," or Cosmic matter; is turning, in clearer language, particles in a highly attenuated condition, and nebulæ.

Outside the boundaries of the solar system, it is other Suns, and especially the mysterious "central Sun" (the "Abode of the invisible deity" as some reverend gentlemen have called it) that determines the motion of bodies and their direction. That motion serves also to differentiate the homogeneous matter, round and between the several bodies, into elements and sub-elements unknown to our earth, which are regarded by modern Science as distinct individual elements, whereas they are merely temporary appearances, changing with every small cycle within the Manvantara, some Esoteric works calling them "Kalpic Masks."

Fohat is the key in Occultism which opens and unriddles the multiform symbols and respective allegories in the so-called mythology of every nation; demonstrating the wonderful philosophy and the deep insight into the mysteries of nature, in the Egyptian and Chaldean as well as in the Aryan religions. Fohat, shown in his true character, proves how deeply versed were all those prehistoric nations in every science of nature, now called physical and chemical branches of natural philosophy. In India, Fohat is the scientific aspect of both Vishnu and Indra, the latter older and more important in the Rig Veda than his sectarian successor; while in Egypt Fohat was known as Toum issued of Noot,* or Osiris in his character of a primordial god, creator of heaven and of beings (see chapter xvii., "*Book of the Dead*"). For *Toum* is spoken of as the *Protean* god who *generates other gods* and gives himself the form he likes; the "master of life" "giving their vigour to the gods" (chapter lxxix.) He is the *overseer* of the gods, and he "who creates spirits and gives them shape and life"; he is "the *north wind* and the *spirit of the west;*" and finally the "Setting Sun of Life," or the vital electric force that leaves the body at death, wherefore the *defunct* begs that Toum should give him the breath from his *right* nostril (positive elec-

---

* "Oh Toum, Toum! issued from the great (female) which is in the bosom of the waters" (the great Deep or *Space*) . . . "Thou, luminous through the *two Lions*" (the dual Force or power of the two *solar eyes*, or the electro-positive and the electro-negative forces. (See *Book of the Dead, III.*, and *Egyptian Pantheon*, chapter ii.)

tricity) that he might live in his *second* form. Both the hieroglyph, and the text of chapter lxii. in the "*Book of the Dead*," show the identity of Toum with Fohat. The former represents a man standing erect with the hieroglyph *of the breaths* in his hands. The latter says :—

"I open to the chief of An (Heliopolis), I am Toum. I cross the water spilt by Thot-Hapi, the lord of the horizon, and am the *divider of the earth*" (Fohat divides Space and, with his *Sons*, the earth into seven zones) . . . .

. . . . "I cross the heavens, and am the two Lions. I am *Ra*, I am *Aam*, I ate my heir. * . . . . I glide on the soil of the field of *Aanroo*,† given me by the master of limitless eternity. I am the germ of eternity. I am Toum, to whom eternity is accorded. . . ."

The very words used by Fohat in the XIth Book, and the very titles given him. In the Egyptian Papyri the whole Cosmogony of the Secret Doctrine is found scattered about in isolated sentences, even in the " Book of Dead." Number seven is quite as much insisted upon and emphasized therein as in the *Book of Dzyan*. "The Great Water (the Deep or Chaos) is said to be *seven* cubits deep "--" cubits " standing here of course for divisions, zones, and principles. Therein, " in the great mother, all the Gods, and the *seven great ones* are born." (See chapter cviii., 4, *Book of the Dead* and *Egyptian Pantheon*). Both Fohat and Toum are addressed as the "Great ones of the Seven Magic Forces," who, "conquer the Serpent *Apap*" or Matter.

No student of occultism, however, ought to be betrayed, by the usual phraseology used in the translations of Hermetic Works, into believing that the ancient Egyptians or Greeks spoke of, and referred, monk-like, at every moment in conversation, to a Supreme Being, God, the "One Father and Creator of all," etc., as found on every page of such translations. No such thing indeed; and those texts *are not the original Egyptian* texts. They are Greek compilations, the earliest of which does not go beyond the early period of Neo-Platonism. No Hermetic

---

* An image expressing the succession of divine functions, the substitution from one form into another, or the *correlation of forces. Aam* is the electro-positive force, devouring all others as Saturn devoured his progeny.

† *Aanroo* is in the domain of Osiris, a field divided into *fourteen* sections "surrounded with an *iron* enclosure, within which grows the *corn of life seven* cubits high," the *Kama-loka* of the Egyptians. Those only of the dead, who know the names of the janitors of the " seven halls," will be admitted into Amenti *for ever; i.e.,* those who have passed through the seven races of each *round*—otherwise they will rest in the *lower fields;* "and it represents also the seven successive Devachans, or *lokas.* In Amenti, one becomes pure spirit for the eternity (xxx. 4.) ; while in *Aanroo* "the soul of the spirit," or the defunct, is *devoured* each time by *Uræus*—the Serpent, Son of the earth (in another sense the primordial vital principles in the Sun), *i.e.,* the Astral body of the deceased or the "Elementary" fades out and disappears in the "Son of the earth," *limited* time. The soul quits the fields of Aanroo and goes on earth under any shape it likes to assume. (See chapter xcix., *Book of the Dead.*)

work written by Egyptians (*vide* "Book of the Dead") would speak of the one universal God of the Monotheistic systems ; the one *Absolute* cause of all, was as unnameable and unpronounceable in the mind of the ancient philosopher of Egypt, as it is for ever *Unknowable* in the conception of Mr. Herbert Spencer. As for the Egyptian in general, as M. Maspero well remarks, whenever he "arrived at the notion of divine Unity, the God One was never 'God,' simply." And Lepage Renouf very justly observed that the word *Nouter, nouti,* "god" had never ceased *being a generic name* with the Egyptians, nor has it ever become a personal pronoun. Every God was the "one living and unique God" with them. Their "monotheism was purely geographical. If the Egyptian of Memphis proclaimed the unity of Phtah to the exclusion of Ammon, the Thebeian Egyptian proclaimed the unity of Ammon to the exclusion of Phtah," as we now see done in India in the case of the Saivas and the Vaishnavas. "*Ra,* the 'One God' at Heliopolis is not the same as Osiris, the 'One God' at Abydos, and can be worshipped side by side with him, without being absorbed by his neighbour. The one god is but the god of the *nome* or the city, *noutir, noutti,* and does not exclude the existence of the one god of that town or of the neighbouring nome. In short, whenever speaking of Egpytian Monotheism, one ought to speak of the Gods 'One' of Egypt, and not of the one god" (Maspero, in the *Guide au Musée de Boulak.* It is by this feature, pre-eminently Egyptian, that the authenticity of the various so-called *Hermetic Books,* ought to be tested ; and it is totally absent from the Greek fragments known as such. This proves that a Greek Neo-Platonic, or even a Christian hand, had no small share in the editing of such works. Of course the fundamental philosophy is there, and in many a place—intact. But the style has been altered and smoothed in a monotheistic direction, as much, if not more than that of the Hebrew Genesis in its Greek and Latin translations. They *may* be *Hermetic* works, but not works written by either of the two Hermes—or rather, by Thot (Hermes) the directing intelligence of the Universe (*See ch. xciv., Book of the Dead*), or by Thot, his terrestial incarnation called Trismegistus, of the Rosetta stone.

But all is doubt, negation, iconoclasm and brutal indifference, in our age of the hundred "isms" and no religion. Every idol is broken save the Golden Calf.

Unfortunately, no nation or nations can escape their Karmic fate any more than units and individuals do. History itself is dealt with by the so-called historians as unscrupulously as legendary lore. For this, Augustin Thierry has made the *amende honorable,* if one may believe his biographers. He deplored the erroneous principle that made them all (the *would-be* historiographers) lose their way, and each presume to correct tradition, "that *vox populi* which nine times out of ten is *vox Dei*"; and he finally admitted that *in legend alone rests real history; for* "legend," he adds, "is *living* tradition, and three times out of four it is truer than what we call History." *

While Materialists deny everything in the universe, save matter, Archæologists are trying to dwarf antiquity, and seek to destroy every claim to ancient Wisdom by tampering with Chronology. Our present-day Orientalists and Historical writers are to ancient History that which the white ants are to the buildings in India. More dangerous even than those Termites, the modern Archæologists—the "authorities" of the future in the matter of Universal History—are preparing for the History of past nations the fate of certain edifices in tropical countries: "History will tumble down and break into atoms in the lap of the twentieth century, devoured to its foundations by her annalists," said Michelet. Very soon, indeed, under their combined efforts, it will share the fate of those ruined cities in both Americas, which lie deeply buried under impassable virgin forests. Historical facts will remain as concealed from view by the inextricable jungles of modern hypotheses, denials and scepticism. But very happily *actual* History repeats herself, for she proceeds, like everything else, in cycles; and dead facts and events deliberately drowned in the sea of modern scepticism will ascend once more and reappear on the surface. . . .

In our Book II. the very fact that a work with pretensions to philosophy, and which is an exposition of the most abstruse problems, has to be commenced by tracing the evolution of mankind from what *are* regarded as supernatural beings—*Spirits*—will arouse the most malevolent criticism. Believers in, and the defenders of, the Secret Doctrine, however, will have to bear the accusation of madness *and worse*, as philosophically as for long years already the writer has done. Whenever a Theosophist is taxed with insanity, he ought to reply by quoting from Montesquieu's "*Lettres Persanes*." "By opening so freely their lunatic asylums to their supposed madmen, men only seek to assure each other that they are not themselves mad."

---

* *Revue des Deux Mondes*, 1865, *pp*. 157 *and* 158.

END OF VOL. I.